COMPREHENSIVE
WORLD
REFERENCE
GUIDE

Publisher
Instructional Fair, Inc.
Grand Rapids, Michigan

CREDITS

AUTHORS: Mollie Brittenum
Lisa Hancock
Christine Jensen
Lisa Molengraft
Ruth Ostrowski
Caroline Venza

GRAPHIC DESIGNERS: Victoria Lane
Ruth Ostrowski

COVER GRAPHICS: Julie Foster

PROJECT DIRECTOR: Ruth Ostrowski

PROJECT ASSISTANT: Sara Geasler

EDITORS: Rhonda DeWaard
Lisa Hancock
Jill Kaufman
Alyson Kieda
Sharon Kirkwood
Mina McMullin
Ruth Ostrowski
Sue Sutton
Linda Triemstra
Jean Wolff
Kathy Zaun

PRODUCTION: Pat Geasler
Ruth Ostrowski

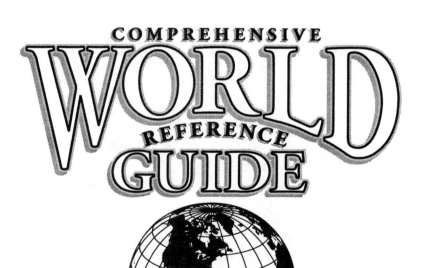

Comprehensive World Reference Guide
ISBN 1-56822-242-4
©1995 Instructional Fair, Inc.
Grand Rapids, Michigan

Printed in the USA

TABLE OF CONTENTS

COMPREHENSIVE
WORLD
REFERENCE
GUIDE

AFGHANISTAN

OFFICIAL NAME: Da Afghanistan Jamhouriat (Pashto)
Jamhury Afghanistan (Dari)
(Republic of Afghanistan)
LOCATION: Southwestern Asia
AREA: 251,773 sq. mi. (652,090 sq. km)
POPULATION (Est. 1993): 20,102,000
CAPITAL: Kabul
LARGEST CITIES: Kabul, Qandahar, Herat, Mazar-e Sharif, Jalalabad, Qonduz, Baghlan
GOVERNMENT: Transitional government consisting of a 51-member council headed by a president.
FLAG: Adopted in 1980. Three horizontal stripes of black, red, and green with the coat of arms in the upper, hoist-side corner.
ETHNIC GROUPS: Pushtuns (or Pathans), Tajiks, other (about 20 total)
LANGUAGES: Pashto (or Pushtu), Dari, others
RELIGION: Islam
BASIC MONETARY UNIT: Afghani

GEOGRAPHY

At its greatest distances, Afghanistan, a landlocked country, measures 630 mi. (1,012 km) from north to south and 820 mi. (1,320 km) from east to west.

Afghanistan has three main land regions: 1) the Northern Plains, 2) the Central Highlands, and 3) the Southwestern Lowlands. The Northern Plains feature mountain plateaus, rolling hills, and vast grasslands. Its fertile soils can only be used for agriculture if water is readily available. The Central Highlands account for two-thirds of the country's area and are home to the Hindu Kush mountain range, which consists of rolling plains in the southwest and towering heights in the east. The Southwestern Lowlands consist mainly of deserts and semideserts. Fruits and grains are grown in the Helmand River Valley. The Rigestan Desert lies in the south.

CLIMATE

Afghanistan's climate varies by region. The Northern Plains have an average annual temperature of 38°F (3°C) in January and 90°F (32°C) in July, with average precipitation levels of 7 in. (18 cm) per year. The Central Highlands have an average annual temperature of 25°F (-4°C) in January and 75°F (24°C) in July, with average precipitation levels of 15 in. (38 cm) per year. The Southwestern Lowlands have an average annual temperature of 35°F (2°C) in January and 85°F (29°C) in July, with average precipitation levels of 2-9 in. (5-23 cm) per year.

ECONOMY

Afghanistan's economy—one of the world's least developed—is based mainly on agriculture. Natural gas production is on the rise. Afghanistan is the leading producer of lapis lazuli, a semiprecious gemstone.

Agriculture - barley, corn, cotton, fruits, karakul sheep skins, mutton, nuts, rice, vegetables, wheat, and wool

Manufacturing - cement, handcrafted items, matches, processed foods, rugs, shoes, and textiles

Mining - coal, lapis lazuli, and natural gas

Exports - cotton, fruits, karakul sheep skins, natural gas, nuts, and rugs

Imports - machinery, motor vehicles, petroleum products, and textiles

LIFE-STYLE

Most Afghans live in the valleys of the Hindu Kush mountain range. Over 80 percent of all Afghans make a living in agriculture. Most Afghans live in sun-dried, mud brick homes, but a few urban Afghans live in modern homes or apartments. Some seminomadic Afghans roam the grasslands with their livestock during the summer and farm the rest of the year. Most of these Afghans live in goat-hair tents.

Most Afghans wear traditional clothing of brightly colored robes in the summer, covered by coats of sheepskin, quilted fabric, or felt in the winter. Most rural men wear a turban, which, when tied a certain way, indicates their ethnic group. Rural women cover their heads with a shawl; some urban women wear a *chadri* (full-length, hooded garment covering all but the eyes).

Staples of the diet include cheese, mutton, and rice. Flat loaves of bread are eaten at every meal, and dessert is usually fruit and nuts. Tea is the favorite drink.

Almost all Afghans share the same religion: Islam. Religious leaders, called *mullahs*, are found in most villages or seminomadic groups. Mullahs influence their communities by interpreting Islamic law and educating the young.

Children ages seven to ten are required to attend school. Because of a shortage of schools and teachers, however, not all attend. Only about one-fifth of all Afghans—ages 15 and over—can read and write. As a result, folklore, folk songs, and folk dances play an important part in Afghan life.

Afghanistan has a shortage of medical facilities. Because of this, as many as half of all infants living in some parts of the country will die before they are one year old.

Popular recreational activities include hunting and *buzkashi* (game played by men of the Northern Plains in which dozens of horsemen try to grab a headless calf and carry it across a goal).

IT'S A FACT!

Nowshak - the country's highest point, rises 24,557 ft. (7,485 m) above sea level.

 DID YOU KNOW...
- It wasn't until 1964 that the law granted Afghan women equal status with men?

ALBANIA

OFFICIAL NAME: Shqipëria (The Land of the Eagle)
Republika e Shqipërisë (Republic of Albania)
LOCATION: Southeastern Europe
AREA: 11,100 sq. mi. (28,748 sq. km)
POPULATION (Est. 1993): 3,395,000
CAPITAL: Tiranë
LARGEST CITIES: Tiranë, Durrës, Shkodër, Elbasan, Vlorë, Korcë
GOVERNMENT: Multiparty parliament headed by a president and a prime minister.
FLAG: Red field with a two-headed black eagle in the center.
ETHNIC GROUPS: Albanian (Ghegs and Tosks), Greek
LANGUAGES: Albanian (Gheg and Tosk dialects), Greek
RELIGIONS: Islam, Christianity (mainly Greek Orthodox and Roman Catholic)
BASIC MONETARY UNIT: Lek

GEOGRAPHY

Albania is the smallest country in the Balkan Peninsula. At its greatest distances, Albania measures 215 mi. (346 km) from north to south and 90 mi. (145 km) from east to west. It has 175 mi. (282 km) of coastline along thè Adriatic Sea.

Albania is about 70 percent mountainous with about one-third of its land covered by scrub forests. The North Albanian Alps rise about 8,500 ft. (2,590 m) above sea level, tapering off to a coastal plain that lies along the Adriatic Sea. Because the country lies on an active geologic zone, it is subject to destructive earthquakes throughout and tsunami along the southwestern coast.

Albania's major rivers empty into the Adriatic Sea, but only the Buenë River can be used for shipping purposes. The country's three large lakes are shared with other countries.

CLIMATE

Albania's coastal plain enjoys a mild climate with warm, dry summers and rainy winters. Its mountain region has hot, rainy summers and harsh, cold winters. The average July temperature is 75° to 81°F (24° to 27°C). The average annual rainfall is 40-60 in. (100-150 cm).

ECONOMY

Albania is one of the least developed countries in Europe, with most of its people making a living through agriculture. Mining ranks as the country's leading industrial activity.

Agriculture - cattle, corn, fruits, goats, grapes, olives, potatoes, poultry, sheep, sugar beets, and wheat

Manufacturing - cement, chemicals, fertilizers, food products, lumber, oil, and textiles

Mining - chromite, coal, copper, iron ore, lignite, nickel, natural gas, and petroleum

Exports - asphalt, chromite, copper ore, crude oil, fruits, vegetables, metals and metallic ores, nickel, petroleum, and tobacco

Imports - consumer goods, farm and industrial machinery, grains, and mining equipment

LIFE-STYLE

Two major groups of people form the populace of Albania: the Ghegs and the Tosks. These two groups are divided according to the dialect they speak, but are also culturally divided by the natural boundary formed by the Shkumbin River. Most Ghegs live north of it, while most Tosks live south of it.

About two-thirds of the population live on farms or in rural villages. Until 1991, most farmers worked on large, state-owned collective farms. Now most own small farms where they raise crops and some livestock. Some people along the coastline make a living by fishing. While the average Albanian income is generally small, the people pay no income tax and health care, social services, and education are free. Children ages seven to 15 are required to attend school. Higher education is offered at the government-operated university of Tiranë and seven other institutions.

The Albanian diet is very simple, and includes bread, cheese, milk, and vegetables.

Buses, bicycles, and trains are the country's most common means of transportation. A railroad network connects the cities of Tiranë and Durrës, the country's chief port, to other major industrial centers. The country has one airport used only for international flights. Prior to 1991, Albanian law forbade the private ownership of automobiles. Although it is now legal to privately own a car, most Albanians don't have the economic means to afford one.

Films are very popular in Albania, and film studios produce documentaries, newsreels, and feature films. Folk traditions are preserved and expressed through dance, music, and popular literature.

IT'S A FACT!

Drin River - the country's longest river, originates in Yugoslavia and has 175 mi. (282 km) in Albania.

Mount Korabit - the country's highest point, rises 9,026 ft. (2,751 m) above sea level.

National Library - located in Tiranë, is the country's major cultural institution.

 DID YOU KNOW...

- In 1967, Albania's Communist government outlawed religion, and it wasn't until 1990 that religion was again allowed to be practiced in public?
- Polygamy and the prearranged marriage of children were once practiced, and sometimes still are, but have been officially abolished?

ALGERIA

OFFICIAL NAME: Al-Jumhuriyah al-Jaza'iriyah ad-Dimuqratiyah wa ash-Sha'biyah (Democratic and Popular Republic of Algeria)
LOCATION: Northwestern Africa
AREA: 919,595 sq. mi. (2,381,741 sq. km)
POPULATION (Est. 1993): 27,108,000
CAPITAL: Algiers (Alger)
LARGEST CITIES: Algiers (Alger), Oran, Constantine, Annaba (Bone)
GOVERNMENT: In transition. Republic governed by a president.
FLAG: Adopted in 1962 when Algeria gained independence from France. A red star and a red crescent are centered on a background of green and white.
ETHNIC GROUPS: Arab, Berber
LANGUAGES: Arabic, French, Berber dialects
RELIGION: Islam (mainly Sunni Muslim)
BASIC MONETARY UNIT: Algerian Dinar

GEOGRAPHY

Algeria is the second largest country in Africa. At its greatest distances, Algeria measures 1,300 mi. (2,100 km) from north to south and 1,500 mi. (2,400 km) from east to west. It has 750 mi. (1,200 km) of coastline on the Mediterranean Sea.

Algeria has three main land regions: 1) the Tell, 2) the High Plateaus, and 3) the Sahara. The *Tell* (Arabic for "hill") stretches along the coast and ranges from 80-200 mi. (130-320 km) wide. It is bordered on the south by the Tell Atlas Mountains. South of the mountains are the grass- and shrub-covered High Plateaus. *Chotts* (shallow salt lakes) form on the plateaus during rainy periods. The Sahara covers 80 percent of Algeria's land area and consists of sand dunes and stone. It is dotted by oases watered by underground springs. The Sahara is bordered by the Saharan Atlas Mountains in the north and by the Ahaggar Mountains in the southeast.

CLIMATE

The Tell has a Mediterranean climate with hot, dry summers and cool, rainy winters. The average annual temperature ranges from 77°F (25°C) in summer to 52°F (11°C) in winter. The average annual rainfall ranges from 27 in. (69 cm) in the east to 16 in. (41 cm) in the west. The High Plateaus are generally dry, with hot summers and cold winters. The average annual temperature ranges from 81°F (27°C) in summer to 41°F (5°C) in winter. The average yearly rainfall is usually less than 16 in. (41 cm). The Sahara may experience daytime temperatures over 120°F (49°C). A *sirocco* (hot, dusty wind) blows northward through the Sahara in the summer, parching both the High Plateaus and the Tell for short periods.

ECONOMY

Algeria has a developing economy based mainly on its deposits of natural gas and petroleum in the Sahara. Algeria is Africa's only producer of mercury, and accounts for one-tenth of the world's supply.

Agriculture - barley, cattle, citrus fruits, dates, goats, grapes, milk, olives, potatoes, sheep, and wheat

Forestry - cork oak

Manufacturing - construction materials, iron and steel, liquid natural gas, refined petroleum products, textiles, and transport vehicles

Mining - iron ore, lead, mercury, natural gas, petroleum, phosphate rock, and zinc

Exports - citrus fruits, dates, iron ore, mercury, natural gas, petroleum, refined petroleum products, phosphate rock, and wine

Imports - food, machinery, and raw materials

LIFE-STYLE

Algeria's population is about half urban and half rural, with over 90 percent of Algerians living in the Tell. Small numbers of herders and nomads live in the High Plateaus and the Sahara.

Rural Algerians typically have large, extended families and live in mud, straw, or stone homes with flat tile or tin roofs. Most make a living by raising livestock or farming small plots. Many rural Algerians wear traditional clothing such as a *haik* (worn by women, it is a long, white, outer garment that covers all but the eyes) or a *burnoose* (worn by men, it is a long, hooded cloak).

Urban Algerians typically live in nuclear family units, wear Western-style clothing, and eat Western-style dishes. Many men hold factory or office jobs.

The staple of the diet is grains (such as wheat and barley). Popular foods include chicken, lamb, pasta, and stew. *Couscous* (steamed wheat with meat, vegetables, and a soup-like sauce) is the national dish.

Children ages six to 15 are required to attend school. While education is free, only about 90 percent of children attend elementary school, and only about a third of them pursue a secondary education. Only 45 percent of Algerians over age 15 are literate.

Recreational activities include sports (soccer is the most popular) and going to the movies.

IT'S A FACT!

Chott Melrhir (Lake) - the country's lowest point of elevation, is located 102 ft. (31 m) below sea level.

Mount Tahat - the country's highest point, is located in the Ahaggar Mountains and rises 9,573 ft. (2,918 m) above sea level.

 DID YOU KNOW...
- People have lived in the area of Algeria for at least 40,000 years?
- Algeria's official name is the second longest of all the countries in the world?

AMERICAN SAMOA
Territory of the United States

OFFICIAL NAME: American Samoa
LOCATION: South Pacific Ocean
AREA: 77 sq. mi. (199 sq. km)
POPULATION (Est. 1993): 53,139
CAPITAL/LARGEST CITY: Pago Pago
GOVERNMENT: Unorganized and unincorporated territory administered by the U.S. Department of the Interior and headed by a governor.
FLAG: Blue field with a white triangle edged in red that is based on the fly side and extends to the hoist side. A brown and white American bald eagle is flying toward the hoist side carrying two traditional Samoan symbols: a staff and a war club.
ETHNIC GROUP: Polynesian
LANGUAGES: Samoan (a Polynesian dialect), English
RELIGIONS: Christian Congregationalist, Roman Catholic, other Protestant groups
BASIC MONETARY UNIT: United States Dollar

AMERICAN SAMOA

South Pacific Ocean

Swains Island

Pago Pago

Olosega Island
Ofu Island
Tau Island
Aunuu Island
Tutuila Island
Rose Island

GEOGRAPHY

American Samoa is a United States territory located about 2,300 mi. (3,700 km) southwest of Hawaii. The territory consists of seven islands—six of which lie in the Samoan chain—divided among three groups: Tutuila and Aunuu; Ofu, Olosega, and Tau (the Manua Islands); and Rose. The seventh, Swains Island, lies 200 mi. (320 km) north. Together, the islands have 72 mi. (116 km) of coastline along the South Pacific Ocean.

Tutuila is the largest and most important of the seven islands. It accounts for two-thirds of the territory's total land area and is home to Pago Pago, the territory's only port and urban center. About 95 percent of the territory's population resides on Tutuila.

Two of the islands—Rose and Swains—consist of coral. Rose Island is uninhabited, and Swains Island—which has been privately owned by the Jennings family since 1856—rises only 20 ft. (6 m) above sea level. The other five islands are the rocky remains of extinct volcanoes. Tutuila and Tau Islands have tropical rainforests.

CLIMATE

The islands of American Samoa have a wet, tropical climate with high humidity levels. The average annual temperature ranges from 70° to 90°F (21° to 32°C). The average annual rainfall is 200 in. (510 cm), with a majority of the rain falling during the months of November to April. Typhoons are fairly common during the months of December to March.

ECONOMY

American Samoa has few natural resources and only one-third of the land has soil suitable for cultivation. In the 1960s, a jet airport and a luxury hotel were built, leading to an increase in tourism. The territory's prosperous economy is based on large amounts of money provided by the United States.

Agriculture - bananas, breadfruit, coconuts, dairy farming, papayas, pineapples, taro, vegetables, and yams
Manufacturing - tuna canning
Exports - fish products and handicrafts
Imports - cannery materials, clothing, food products, machinery and parts, and petroleum products

LIFE-STYLE

American Samoans are nationals—not citizens—of the United States. This means they may freely enter the United States at any time. Most of them live as family groups in villages. A chief heads each family group, controlling the family's property, taking care of sick or aged family members, and representing the family in the village council.

After the United States implemented a program for economic development in 1961, many villagers went to work in industries around Pago Pago. Their thatch-roofed homes, called *fale*, were replaced by hurricane-proof concrete buildings, and new schools were built.

Children ages six to 18 are required to attend school; some of them are taught by television. Vocational training is offered at the American Samoan Community College. The territory's principal hospital is the Lyndon B. Johnson Tropical Medical Centre. Various clinics operate throughout the islands.

IT'S A FACT!

Lata Mountain - the territory's highest point, is located on Tau Island and rises more than 3,000 ft. (9,100 m) above sea level.

Mount Pioa - the territory's most noted peak, rises 1,842 ft. (563 m) above sea level and is known as the "Rainmaker" because of its frequent cloud cover.

National Park of American Samoa - established in 1988 to protect the territory's tropical rainforests, a white sand beach and a coral reef on Ofu Island, and the traditional Samoan way of life.

 DID YOU KNOW...
- The United States had a naval base on Tutuila Island until 1951?
- In 1787—after 11 members of a French expedition were massacred—and for 40 years thereafter, the islands were avoided by European explorers and became a haven for runaway sailors and escaped convicts?

ANDORRA

OFFICIAL NAME: Valls d'Andorra (Valleys of Andorra)
LOCATION: Western Europe
AREA: 175 sq. mi. (453 sq. km)
POPULATION (Est. 1993): 56,000
CAPITAL/LARGEST CITY: Andorra or Andorra-la-Vella
GOVERNMENT: Parliamentary co-principality jointly ruled by the bishop of Urgel, Spain, and the president of France.
FLAG: Three vertical stripes of blue, yellow, and red. The state flag—used by the government—has a coat of arms in the center of the yellow stripe. The national flag—used by the people—does not.
ETHNIC GROUPS: Spanish, Andorran, French
LANGUAGES: Catalan, French, Spanish
RELIGION: Roman Catholic
BASIC MONETARY UNITS: French Franc and Spanish Peseta

GEOGRAPHY

One of the smallest countries in the world in area, Andorra is a landlocked cluster of mountain valleys lying between France and Spain in the Pyrenees Mountains. At its greatest distances, Andorra measures 16 mi. (26 km) from north to south and 19 mi. (31 km) from east to west.

Two rivers—the Valira del Norte (Northern Valira) and the Valira del Orient (Eastern Valira)—meet near the town of Andorra, forming the Valira River. The country's two main roads follow the Valira del Norte and the Valira River toward France and Spain, respectively.

CLIMATE

Andorra has warm, dry summers and cold winters with heavy snowfall. While even snowplows cannot keep the mountain road between Andorra and France open all winter, the snow that falls in southern Andorra usually melts in a few days. Temperatures range from 70° to 80°F (21° to 27°C) in the summer, and from 20° to 30°F (-7° to -1°C) in the winter.

ECONOMY

Tourism is Andorra's main source of income. Tourists are attracted to its ancient buildings, beautiful mountains, and the ski slopes of Pas de la Casa, Soldeu, and other resorts. Because of low import duties, Andorra is able to sell imported goods from Europe and Asia—like Swiss watches, Japanese cameras and French wines—at low prices to tourists.

Agriculture - barley, buckwheat, cattle, corn, oats, potatoes, rye, sheep, and tobacco

Manufacturing - cigarettes and other tobacco products, and furniture

Natural Resources - iron ore, lead, mineral water, timber, and water power

Exports - electricity, furniture, and tobacco products

Imports - consumer goods and food

LIFE-STYLE

Because of Andorra's remote location in the Pyrenees, the life-style of its people remained relatively unchanged between the 1100s and 1930s. During this time, Andorrans worked as farmers and shepherds. Farmers often passed three-fourths of their inheritance to one of their children—usually the oldest son—to prevent the dividing of their land into small plots. Since this left other children with nothing, they often emigrated from Andorra.

In the 1800s, farmers began growing tobacco, and up until the early 1900s, made a living by smuggling it into France and Spain. In the 1930s, roads leading to France and Spain opened, paving the way for tourism. This changed the Andorrans' way of life. Many became storekeepers and hotel owners. However, some Andorrans still farm and raise tobacco.

Other things have changed little. Family clans still decide political issues. Many Andorrans continue to live in three-story farmhouses constructed with stone walls and slate roofs. The first floor serves as a tool shed or a barn, the second floor features the kitchen and living area, and the third floor contains bedrooms opening onto balconies.

Because Andorra is jointly ruled, the country has two basic monetary units, two postal systems, and two school systems. The legal system is based on ancient laws and common law that date back to the Roman Empire.

IT'S A FACT!

Coma Pedrosa - the country's highest point, rises 9,665 ft. (2,946 m) above sea level.

DID YOU KNOW...

- Only Roman Catholics can get married in Andorra?
- Up until the 1930s, only male citizens who were the heads of households could vote in Andorra? In 1933, all male citizens over the age of 25 could vote. It wasn't until 1970—when the voting age was reduced to age 21—that female citizens were allowed to vote.
- Andorra has no railway system?

ANGOLA

OFFICIAL NAME: República Popular de Angola (People's Republic of Angola)
LOCATION: Southwest Africa
AREA: 481,354 sq. mi. (1,246,700 sq. km)
POPULATION (Est. 1993): 10,889,000
CAPITAL: Luanda
LARGEST CITIES: Benguela, Cabinda, Huambo, Lobito, Luanda, Namibe
GOVERNMENT: Headed by a president. A 220-member legislature called the National Assembly chooses a prime minister to help run daily governmental affairs.
FLAG: Adopted in 1975. Two horizontal stripes of red and black, with a yellow emblem in the center. The emblem features a five-pointed star, a half cogwheel, and a machete, representing socialism, industry, and agriculture, accordingly.
ETHNIC GROUPS: Black (including Ovimbundu, Mbundu, Kongo, and Luanda-Chokwe), European, Mestizo
LANGUAGES: Bantu dialects, Portuguese
RELIGIONS: Roman Catholic, Protestant, Traditional African Religions
BASIC MONETARY UNIT: Kwanza

GEOGRAPHY

At its greatest distances, Angola measures 850 mi. (1,368 km) from north to south and 800 mi. (1,287 km) from east to west. It has 928 mi. (1,493 km) of coastline on the South Atlantic Ocean. One of Angola's districts, Cabinda, is separated from the rest of the country by Zaire and the Congo River.

Angola is part of southern Africa's inland plateau. Its elevation is high, except where it drops sharply in the west to form a narrow coastal plain. The land is mainly hilly grassland, but has tropical forests in the north, a rocky desert in the south, and little natural vegetation on the coastal plain. Many rivers run through the country, some of which flow to the interior and serve as waterways.

CLIMATE

Temperatures vary little by season and by elevation level. Coastal plain temperatures range from 60° to 70°F (16° to 21°C). Inland temperatures range from 60° to 79°F (16° to 26°C). Approximately 40-60 in. (100-150 cm) of rain falls annually on the northern coast and the interior, while only about 2 in. (5 cm) falls in the desert.

ECONOMY

Angola's economy is based primarily on agriculture and the mining of petroleum and minerals.

Agriculture - bananas, cassava, coffee, corn, cotton, honey, livestock (cattle, goats, pigs, and sheep), plantains, sisal, sugar cane, sweet potatoes, tobacco, and vegetables

Fishing - mackerel and sardines

Manufacturing - brewing, cement, chemicals, processed foods, refined petroleum, steel, sugar, textiles, and tobacco

Mining - bauxite, copper, diamonds, feldspar, gold, iron ore, petroleum, phosphates, and uranium

Exports - coffee, cotton, diamonds, fish and fish products, oil, petroleum and petroleum products, sisal, and timber

Imports - clothing, electrical equipment, food, machinery, medicines, metals, textiles, and vehicles and spare parts

LIFE-STYLE

Two-thirds of Angola's people live in rural areas and work as farmers and herders, usually raising only enough food for their own use. Most rural Angolans live in traditional houses of wattle and clay, or timber, with separate buildings for the kitchen and for food storage. Urban Angolans mainly own small businesses or have technical or managerial jobs, and live in modern villas or apartment buildings. Those located on the outskirts of town live in *musseques* (cities of sand) or shanty towns.

Popular leisure activities include football, volleyball, basketball, swimming, gymnastics, athletics, and judo. Angolans are known for their baskets, carved furniture, pottery, and woven textiles. In some remote areas, region, tribe, and social and economic status are indicated by the wearing of shell bracelets and necklaces, tattooing, and elaborately dressed hairstyles.

All Angolan citizens are guaranteed a free education, but only primary schoolchildren are required to attend school. Although medical care is free, Angolan health and medical facilities are very poor. Disease in both rural and urban areas is primarily caused by widespread malnutrition and lack of sanitary education.

Most of Angola's roads are unpaved, but an extensive railroad system serves many Angolan cities. The country has only one daily newspaper.

IT'S A FACT!

Cambambe Dam - located southeast of Luanda on the Kwanza River, provides much of the country's hydroelectric power.

Luanda - the country's capital and largest city, it has many modern buildings and serves as a major African seaport.

Môco - the country's highest point, rises 8,596 ft. (2,620 m) above sea level.

 DID YOU KNOW...
- As early as 50,000 B.C., prehistoric people lived in what is now Angola?
- Under Portuguese rule, Angola was sometimes called Portuguese West Africa?

ANGUILLA
Dependent Territory of the United Kingdom

OFFICIAL NAME: Anguilla
LOCATION: Eastern Caribbean Sea
AREA: 37 sq. mi. (96 sq. km)
POPULATION (Est. 1993): 7,006
CAPITAL/LARGEST CITY: The Valley
GOVERNMENT: Self-governed by a governor, who is appointed by the monarch of the United Kingdom.
FLAG: Two horizontal stripes of white and light blue, with three orange, interlocking, circular-designed dolphins in the center of the white stripe. (A new flag may have been in use since May 30, 1990.)
ETHNIC GROUPS: Black, Mulatto, White
LANGUAGE: English
RELIGIONS: Anglican, Methodist, others
BASIC MONETARY UNIT: East Caribbean Dollar

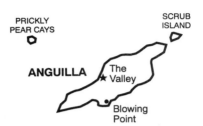

SOMBRERO ISLAND

Caribbean Sea

PRICKLY PEAR CAYS

SCRUB ISLAND

ANGUILLA
The Valley
Blowing Point

GEOGRAPHY

Anguilla is a long, narrow-shaped coral and limestone island located approximately 168 mi. (270 km) east of Puerto Rico. It is the most northerly of the Leeward Islands in the Lesser Antilles and its territory includes Prickly Pear Cays and Scrub, Seal, Dog, and Sombrero Islands, all of which are uninhabited.

At its greatest distances, Anguilla measures about 16 mi. (26 km) from north to south and about 3.5 mi. (6 km) from east to west. It has about 38 mi. (61 km) of coastline along the Caribbean Sea. The land has very little fertile soil, a few salt ponds, and no rivers.

CLIMATE

Anguilla has a hot, dry tropical climate throughout most of the year with an average annual temperature of 80°F (27°C). The average annual rainfall is 35 in. (90 cm), with most rain falling between September and January. Hurricane season in Anguilla can be devastating and usually occurs between July and October.

ECONOMY

Fishing and salt processing were once Anguilla's major economic contributors, but they have recently been surpassed by an increasing surge in tourism. Since the island has a dry climate and only a small amount of decent soil, agriculture plays a very small role in the economy.

Agriculture - cattle, corn, goats, pigeon peas, pigs, poultry, sheep, and sweet potatoes
Fishing - lobster, others
Manufacturing - salt processing
Exports - livestock, lobster, and salt

LIFE-STYLE

Because of the economy, Anguillans experience unsteady employment and poor living conditions. Most of the houses are relatively spacious and built of concrete. The people are provided limited health services by the island's cottage hospital. If specialized health service is required, it must be sought from another Caribbean island.

Elementary and secondary education is free, and children ages five to 14 are required to attend. Advanced training and higher education must be sought at other Caribbean islands.

In 1650, Anguilla became a British colony, and in 1883, joined with the islands of St. Kitts and Nevis to form a larger colony. In 1967, Anguilla became an associated British state, and in 1980, separated from St. Kitts and Nevis to become a separate British dependency.

IT'S A FACT!

Blowing Point and Road Bay - the island's two seaports.
Crocus Hill - the island's highest point, rises 213 ft. (65 m) above sea level.

 DID YOU KNOW...

- Anguilla (Latin for *eel*) received its name because of its long, narrow shape?
- Only about half of Anguilla's roads are paved?

ANTIGUA & BARBUDA

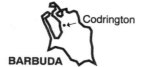

OFFICIAL NAME: Antigua and Barbuda
LOCATION: Caribbean Sea
AREA: 171 sq. mi. (442 sq. km)
POPULATION (Est. 1993): 77,000
CAPITAL: St. John's
LARGEST CITIES: St. John's, Codrington
GOVERNMENT: Constitutional monarchy headed by a prime minister.
FLAG: Red background with an inverted triangle of three horizontal stripes: black, blue, and white. A yellow sun rises on the black stripe.
ETHNIC GROUPS: Black, British, Lebanese, Portuguese, Syrian
LANGUAGES: English, Local dialects
RELIGION: Christianity (mainly Anglican and Roman Catholic)
BASIC MONETARY UNIT: East Caribbean Dollar

GEOGRAPHY

The country of Antigua and Barbuda consists of three islands—Antigua, Barbuda, and Redonda—that were formed by eroded volcanoes. Antigua, the largest of the three islands, covers 108 sq. mi. (280 sq. km) and is home to about 98 percent of the population. It is sparsely covered with vegetation and has a number of bays, inlets, and white sand beaches. Barbuda, located about 25 mi. (40 km) north of Antigua, covers 62 sq. mi. (161 sq. km). The wooded, flat, coral island has one settlement and serves as a game reserve. Redonda, located about 25 mi. (40 km) southwest of Antigua, is basically an uninhabited rock, measuring 0.5 sq. mi. (1.3 sq. km). Together, the islands have 95 mi. (153 km) of coastline.

CLIMATE

Antigua and Barbuda enjoy a tropical climate with little seasonal temperature variation. The average temperature is 80°F (27°C), and the average annual rainfall is 45 in. (114 cm). The islands often experience long periods of drought and, during the months of July to October, are subject to hurricanes and other tropical storms.

ECONOMY

More than half of the country's economy is based on tourism. This is supplemented by manufacturing.
Agriculture - bananas, coconuts, cotton, cucumbers, eggplants, livestock, mangoes, pineapples, and sugar cane
Fishing - lobster
Manufacturing - appliances, chemicals, clothing, concrete blocks, optical lenses, paint, paper products, processed foods and beverages, sugar, and textiles
Exports - electronic components, food, livestock, machinery, manufactures, petroleum products, and transport equipment
Imports - chemicals, food, fuel, livestock, machinery and transport equipment, manufactures, and oil

LIFE-STYLE

Almost half of the country's population is urban and lives in St. John's. The remainder are rural dwellers. Most are employed by tourism, while others are employed in farming or manufacturing. Shelters are mainly single-story houses constructed of wood or concrete blocks. Clothing is generally Western-style. Antiguans' and Barbudans' dressiest clothes are worn to church, funerals, weddings, and other special events.

Staples of the diet include beans, beef, chicken, fish, goat, lobster, pork, rice, sweet potatoes, and seasonal fruits and vegetables. Popular dishes include *doucana* (coconut, seasoned rice, sweet potatoes, flour, sugar, and spices) served with *saltfish* (dried cod), *fungee* (spoon bread made with corn meal and okra), *Johnny Cakes* (sweet fried dumplings), *pepperpot* (spicy vegetable stew), *souse* (pickled pigs' feet), and *rice* or *black pudding* (blood sausage).

Antiguans and Barbudans enjoy music and dancing. Cricket is the most popular sport, followed by soccer and basketball. A game called *netball*, which is similar to basketball, is common among girls. Other leisure activities include dominoes, *draughts* (a form of checkers), and *Warri* (a strategic game in which a team tries to capture its opponent's 24 seeds, four each in six cups).

Children ages five to 11 are required to attend school. Both public and private education are offered, but only the former is free.

About half of the country's roads are paved, and motor vehicles provide most of the transportation. Buses do not follow a schedule, but rather leave when full and stop upon request.

IT'S A FACT!

Boggy Peak - the country's highest point, is located on Antigua and rises 1,319 ft. (402 m) above sea level.
The Court House - built in 1748-50, is located in St. John's and is where parliament meets.
St. John's Cathedral - built in 1847, is located in St. John's and is the country's largest cathedral.

 DID YOU KNOW...
- Antigua was named by Christopher Columbus in 1493 for the Church of Santa Maria de la Antigua in Seville, Spain?
- Barbuda was formerly called Dulcina?
- Most of the country's population are descendants of African slaves who were brought to the islands to work on the sugar plantations?
- The country's Midsummer Carnival—which is second in size only to Trinidad's—is a festive time of celebrations that includes calypso contests and processions?

ARGENTINA

OFFICIAL NAME: República Argentina (Argentine Republic)
LOCATION: Eastern South America
AREA: 1,073,400 sq. mi. (2,780,092 sq. km)
POPULATION (Est. 1995): 34,883,000
CAPITAL: Buenos Aires
LARGEST CITIES: Buenos Aires, Córdoba, Rosario, Mendoza, La Plata, Tucumán, Mar del Plata,
GOVERNMENT: Republic governed by an elected president and Congress.
FLAG: Three equal horizontal stripes of light blue (top and bottom) with white in the middle. In the center of the white stripe is a yellow sun with a human face on it.
ETHNIC GROUPS: Spanish, Italian, White, Mestizo, Indian
LANGUAGES: Spanish, English, Italian, German, French
RELIGION: Roman Catholic
BASIC MONETARY UNIT: Peso

GEOGRAPHY

Argentina is the second largest country in South America in area and population, and the eighth largest country in the world in area. It measures 2,300 mi. (3,700 km) from north to south and 980 mi. (1,577 km) from east to west at its greatest distances. It has 2,940 mi. (4,731 km) of coastline on the South Atlantic Ocean. The country's southernmost tip lies only about 600 mi. (970 km) from Antarctica.

Argentina can be divided into four main land regions: 1) Northern Argentina, 2) the Pampa, 3) the Andine, and 4) Patagonia.

Northern Argentina, a lowland plain, lies east of the Andes Mountains and north of the Córdoba Mountains. It is made up of two subregions: the Gran Chaco and Mesopotamia. The Gran Chaco (also called Chaco) is mainly covered by forests and is home to few Argentines. It is plagued with drought most of the year, but heavy summer rains cause riverbeds to overflow, allowing farmers to plant corn, wheat, cotton and other crops. Mesopotamia, a fertile region between two rivers, has a humid climate with many rolling, grass-covered plains and hot, swampy forests in the northeast.

The Pampa is a fertile, grassy plain that extends from the Atlantic Ocean to the Andes Mountains. It covers about a fifth of Argentina and has some of the world's richest topsoil.

The Andine is a mountainous region in western Argentina. It is made up of two subregions: the Andes Mountains and the Piedmont. The Andes Mountains are located in western Argentina, separating the country from Chile. The Piedmont is located east of the Andes Mountains and consists of low mountains and desert valleys.

Patagonia is a dry, windswept plateau that extends through southern Argentina. It accounts for more than a quarter of Argentina's land, but is home to less than three percent of the country's population. Poor soil and little rainfall make it inadequate for raising crops.

CLIMATE

Argentina's climate is generally temperate, though the north has the highest temperatures and the south the lowest. Since the country is located south of the equator, its seasons are opposite those of the Northern Hemisphere. Summer lasts from late December to late March, and winter from late June to late September. Average January temperatures range from about 80°F (27°C) in the north to about 60°F (16°C) in the south. Average July temperatures range from about 60°F (16°C) in the north to about 32°F (0°C) in the south.

Northeastern Argentina receives more rain than other parts of the country. Mesopotamia averages 60 in. (150 cm) or more per year, while the Piedmont and most of Patagonia may receive less than 10 in. (25 cm) of rain per year.

Wind also has an effect on Argentina's climate. Moist air off the Atlantic makes summers unbearably humid in Mesopotamia and the Pampa. Winds off the Pacific lose their moisture as they pass over the Andes Mountains, leaving the Piedmont and Patagonia dry. Winds blow over Patagonia from both oceans, warming it in winter and cooling it in summer. Occasionally, winds from Antarctica move northward in the winter, bringing cold weather and light snow to Patagonia and the Pampa.

ECONOMY

Argentina is rich in natural resources and was one of the world's wealthiest nations during the 1920s. It is no longer an economic giant; however, manufacturing is becoming very important in Argentina's economy.

Agriculture - alfalfa, cattle, citrus fruits, corn, cotton, flaxseed, grapes, hogs, horses, milk, potatoes, rice, sheep, sorghum, soybeans, sugar cane, sunflower seeds, tea, wheat, and wool

Forestry - Quebracho trees

Manufacturing - chemicals, electrical equipment, food processing, leather-making, meat-packing, metal products, motor vehicles, printed materials, and textiles

Mining - iron ore, lead, natural gas, petroleum, uranium, and zinc

Exports - beef, corn, flaxseed, hides and skins, vegetable oils, wheat, and wool

Imports - chemicals, iron, machinery, and steel

LIFE-STYLE

Approximately 88 percent of Argentina's population live in cities and towns, with about one-third living in Buenos Aires and another one-fourth living in the Pampa. Many of the middle class work in industry, own small businesses, or have professional jobs. They live in modern apartment buildings or small single-family homes. The upper class live in mansions or luxury apartments in the cities or suburbs.

The other 12 percent of Argentina's population live in rural areas. They work on *estancias* (large ranches) or own their own farms. Many rural houses are made of adobe, with poorer people living in huts made of adobe walls, dirt floors, with roofs of straw and mud.

Argentines in urban areas tend to wear more modern clothing, while rural people may wear the traditional *gaucho* (cowboy) costume. The costume consists of a wide-brimmed hat, a *poncho* (blanket with a slit in its center for the head), and loose trousers tucked into low boots. The Indians of northwestern Argentina wear ponchos, colorful shirts, and derbies.

Beef is the staple of the Argentine diet. They enjoy *asado con cuero* (beef roasted in its hide over an open fire), *pucheros* (stews with chicken, or other meat, and vegetables), and *empanadas* (pastries stuffed with meat or seafood, eggs, vegetables, and fruit). Argentines also enjoy spaghetti and other pastas—introduced by Italian settlers—and tea time—introduced by English settlers. The national beverage, *maté* (tea brewed from the dried leaves of the native holly tree), is traditionally sipped from a gourd through a straw. Many fine, locally made wines are enjoyed by Argentines. Soft drinks are coming into popularity as well.

Soccer is the most popular national sport. *Pato* is a favorite. Pato is played with two teams riding on horseback. The object of the game is to grab a six-handled ball and toss it into the opposing team's basket at the end of a field. Other popular sports include boating, horse racing, rugby, polo, automobile racing, and basketball. Skiing, hunting, and hiking in the Andes Mountains and vacationing on the South Atlantic coast are also popular recreational activities.

The Colón Theater, located in Buenos Aires, offers concerts, ballets, and operas. Plays and motion pictures are also enjoyed by Argentines. Religious festivals are celebrated with colorful processions and fireworks. For example, during the pre-Lenten festival of *carnival*, costumed Argentines dance in the streets.

Public elementary and high school education is provided free by the Argentine government. Children ages six to 14 are required to attend school, although only a small percentage actually finish high school.

IT'S A FACT!

Aconcagua - the country's highest point, rises 22,831 ft. (6,959 m) above sea level.

The Andes Mountains - stretching along the western border, separate Argentina from Chile. Their highest peaks include the tallest mountain in the Western Hemisphere, Aconcagua.

Buenos Aires - Spanish for "fair winds," is the name of Argentina's capital, largest city, chief port, and leading industrial center.

Casa Rosado (Pink House) - houses the office of the Argentine president and other government offices.

Greater Buenos Aires - home to about 10 million residents, is the fifth largest metropolitan area in the world.

Iguaçu Falls - formed by 275 waterfalls that meet at the junction of the Paraná and Iguaçu Rivers, is one of the most spectacular waterfalls in South America. It measures about 2 mi. (3 km) in width and falls 237 ft. (72 m).

Plaza de Mayo - a square located in the heart of Buenos Aires, resembles the plazas of other Spanish cities.

Tierra del Fuego - an island that lies at the southern tip of South America, is shared by Argentina and Chile.

The University of Buenos Aires - the largest university in South America, has more than 140,000 students.

Ushuaia - located on Argentina's half of Tierra del Fuego, is one of the southernmost towns in the world.

Valdés Peninsula - the country's lowest point of elevation, is located 131 ft. (40 m) below sea level.

 DID YOU KNOW...

- Argentina's name comes from *argentum*, the Latin word for silver?
- Over 45 percent of the Argentine population is under age 15?
- The *Tango*, a popular dance, originated in Argentina?
- *Avenida 9 de Julio*, located in Buenos Aires, is the widest street in the world at 425 ft. (130 m)?
- It is considered improper for a man and a woman to show affection in public?
- Up until 1987, divorce was illegal in Argentina?
- When eating, hands (but not elbows) should always be above the table, not in the lap?
- Punctuality is not important in Argentina, and a person may be as much as 30 minutes late without offending anyone?
- It is considered bad manners to use a toothpick in public, eat in the street or on public transportation, and blow one's nose or clear one's throat at the table?

ARMENIA

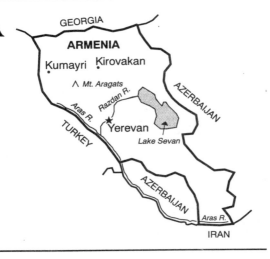

OFFICIAL NAME: Haikakan Hanrapetoutioun
(Republic of Armenia)
LOCATION: Southeastern Europe
AREA: 11,500 sq. mi. (29,800 sq. km)
POPULATION (Est. 1993): 3,373,000
CAPITAL: Yerevan
LARGEST CITIES: Yerevan, Kirovakan, Kumayri
GOVERNMENT: Independent nation governed by a president.
FLAG: Three horizontal stripes of red, blue, and orange.
ETHNIC GROUPS: Armenian, Kurd, Russian, Azerbaijani
LANGUAGES: Armenian, Russian
RELIGION: Christianity
BASIC MONETARY UNIT: Russian Ruble

GEOGRAPHY

Armenia, a landlocked country, is located in the Caucasus Mountain region and lies on the Armenian Plateau. At its greatest distances, Armenia measures 170 mi. (275 km) from north to south and 130 mi. (210 km) from east to west.

Armenia is mostly covered with volcanic stones, which formed the Armenian Plateau from volcanic activity millions of years ago. Grasses and shrubs make up most of the country's vegetation, with some forests found in the northeast and southeast.

Besides its many mountains and gorges, Armenia has about 100 mountain lakes and a number of small, fast-flowing rivers and streams. The rivers and streams serve as a source for irrigation and energy for the country.

CLIMATE

Armenia has a dry climate with long, cold winters and short, hot summers. The average January temperature can range from 10° to 23°F (-12° to -5°C) and may fall below -22°F (-30°C). Average July temperatures range from about 50°F (10°C) in the mountains and about 77°F (25°C) in other parts of the country. The average annual rainfall is about 8-31 in. (20-80 cm), which increases with elevation. The country's highest peaks are snow-covered all year.

ECONOMY

Manufacturing and mining make up two-thirds of Armenia's economic activity, service industries account for about one-fourth, and the remainder is accounted for by agriculture.

While under Soviet control, most of Armenia's businesses, factories, and farmland were owned by the government. It wasn't until January of 1991 that the country began to enjoy a free-enterprise system.

Agriculture - apricots, barley, cattle, peaches, potatoes, quinces, sheep, walnuts, wheat, and wine grapes

Manufacturing - chemicals, cognac, electronic products, machinery, processed foods, synthetic rubber, and textiles

Mining - copper, gold, lead, and zinc

LIFE-STYLE

About 70 percent of Armenians live in cities while the remaining 30 percent live in rural areas. Apartment buildings are the most common form of shelter, with single-family houses common in smaller cities and villages.

Because family is important to Armenians, it is not uncommon to find more than two generations of a family living together. Many urban women hold jobs outside the home, along with doing most of the housework and shopping.

Armenians enjoy foods such as barbecued shish kebab, bean salads, *lavash* (a thin bread), and *dolma* (cabbage or grape leaves stuffed with rice and meat). Popular beverages include cognac, fruit juices, *tan* (a mixture of water, yogurt, and salt), and wine.

Education is free and required of all children between the ages of six and 16. Higher education is available at one of Armenia's 14 universities or specialized institutes. Health care is also free.

Armenians enjoy such sports as basketball, tennis, and soccer. Other popular recreational activities include chess and backgammon. During the summer, Lake Sevan serves as a popular resort area for vacationers.

Armenia has many cultural institutions, including the State Academic Theatre of Opera and Ballet, drama theatres, children's theatres, symphony orchestras, and the Yerevan Film Studio. The country also has an artistic tradition rich in the crafts of rug weaving, metalwork, and the making of *khatchkars* (decorative carved stone monuments).

IT'S A FACT!

Aras River - the country's longest river, separates Armenia from the bordering countries of Iran and Turkey. It is also the country's lowest point of elevation (near the southeastern border) at 1,475 ft. (450 m) above sea level.

Lake Sevan - the country's largest mountain lake, covers approximately five percent of Armenia.

Mount Aragats - the country's highest point, rises 13,419 ft. (4,090 m) above sea level.

Razdan River - located between Lake Sevan and the city of Yerevan, is home to a chain of hydroelectric power stations.

 DID YOU KNOW...

- Armenia was the first country in the world to make Christianity its official religion?
- Armenia was under Soviet control until 1991—about 70 years—after which time it gained independence?

ARUBA

OFFICIAL NAME: Aruba
LOCATION: Southern Caribbean Sea
AREA: 75 sq. mi. (193 sq. km)
POPULATION (Est. 1993): 65,117
CAPITAL/LARGEST CITY: Oranjestad
GOVERNMENT: Governor, appointed by the Dutch crown, is the chief of state, but is dependent on the Netherlands in matters of defense and foreign affairs.
FLAG: Blue field with two narrow horizontal yellow stripes near the bottom and a red, four-pointed star, outlined in white, in the upper hoist-side corner.
ETHNIC GROUPS: American or Caribbean Indian, Black, White, other
LANGUAGES: Dutch, English, Papiamento (dialect of Spanish, Portuguese, Dutch, and English), Spanish
RELIGIONS: Roman Catholic, Protestant
BASIC MONETARY UNIT: Aruban Florin

GEOGRAPHY

Aruba is a West Indies island that belongs to the Netherlands. It is located approximately 17 mi. (28 km) north of Venezuela and 78 mi. (125 km) east of Colombia.

Aruba is a flat, rocky island with some hills that supports very little vegetation. However, its white sand beaches, warm climate, and coral reefs make it a popular tourist attraction.

CLIMATE

Aruba has a warm, dry tropical climate with very little temperature variation throughout the year. The average annual temperature is 81°F (27°C) and rainfall averages 19 in. (48 cm) per year.

ECONOMY

The Aruban economy is based mainly on tourism and oil refining.

Agriculture - aloes and some livestock
Exports - petroleum products and refined crude oil
Imports - consumer goods, crude oil, food, manufactures, and petroleum products

LIFE-STYLE

Aruba's first inhabitants were Arawak Indians, who have intermarried with Europeans and make up a large portion of the country's population. Most Arubans work in one of three areas: government, oil refinement, or tourism.

The Netherlands overtook Aruba in 1634 and made it part of the Netherlands Antilles. Aruba gained partial independence from the Netherlands in 1986.

IT'S A FACT!

Mount Jamanota - the country's highest point, rises 620 ft (180 m) above sea level.

 DID YOU KNOW...
- Most of Aruba's drinking water comes from desalinated seawater?
- Aruba became a center of piracy and smuggling after 1499 when it was claimed by Spain?

AUSTRALIA

OFFICIAL NAME: Commonwealth of Australia
LOCATION: Between the South Pacific and Indian Oceans
AREA: 2,978,147 sq. mi.
(7,713,364 sq. km)
POPULATION (Est. 1995): 17,820,000
CAPITAL: Canberra
LARGEST CITIES: Sydney, Melbourne, Brisbane
GOVERNMENT: Constitutional monarchy.
FLAG: Blue field with the United Kingdom's flag in the upper hoist-side quadrant, below which is centered a large seven-pointed white star representing the country's states and territories. Five white stars, representing the constellation *Southern Cross*, are centered on the flag's outer half.

ETHNIC GROUPS: European, Asian, Aboriginal
LANGUAGE: English
RELIGION: Christianity
BASIC MONETARY UNIT: Australian Dollar

GEOGRAPHY

Australia, including the island of Tasmania, lies well south of the equator in both the Indian and Pacific Oceans. It is the only country that also makes up an entire continent. It ranks as the sixth largest country in the world in terms of square miles. Australia was given the nickname "Land Down Under" because of its location entirely within the Southern Hemisphere. Australia is similar in area to the United States, but it has about 18 million inhabitants compared to over 250 million in the United States. It is noted for its bright sunshine, vast expanses of land, and huge numbers of sheep, cattle, and unique wildlife.

Australia's rivers are a vital resource because they provide drinking water for towns and cities and supply farmers with water for irrigation. Because most of Australia's rivers are dry—except during the rainy season—dams and reservoirs have been built on all the largest rivers.

Australia is made up of six states—New South Wales, Queensland, South Australia, Tasmania, Victoria, and Western Australia—and two territories—Australian Capital and Northern. The country has three main land regions: 1) the Eastern Highlands, 2) the Central Lowlands, and 3) the Western Plateau.

The Eastern Highlands contain the highest elevations in Australia, beginning with the Cape York Peninsula in far northeastern Australia and ending with the south coast of Tasmania. The area includes a low plain edged by sandy beaches and rocky cliffs. The term "Great Dividing Range" has often been applied to this region because the terrain divides the flow of rivers in the region.

The Central Lowlands have the lowest elevations in the country. The area is quite flat with many rivers appearing after heavy rains. Inland river beds remain dry much of the year.

The Western Plateau, covering the western two-thirds of the country, is primarily flat with three deserts—Great Sandy, Gibson, and Great Victoria—in the central part of the plateau.

CLIMATE

The northern third of Australia is warm to hot due to its location in the tropics. Because the rest of the country lies south of the tropics, it experiences warm summers and mild to cool winters. Since Australia is in the Southern Hemisphere, the winter season lasts from June to August and the summer season lasts from December to February. Most of Australia's precipitation falls in the form of rain. Snow occurs only in the interior of Tasmania, a large island off Australia's southeastern tip, and in the Australian Alps. The desert areas get less than 10 in. (25 cm) of rain per year. The remaining two-thirds of Australia gets less than 20 in. (51 cm) of rain per year. The wettest part of the continent is on the northeastern coast. Tasmania and the southeast coast receive the most consistent rainfall throughout the year. In the rest of Australia, rainfall is very seasonal.

ECONOMY

Much of Australia's wealth comes from farming and mining. Its livelihood contrasts with that of other developed countries whose wealth is attributed to producing and exporting manufactured goods. Australia depends on its mines and farms to produce the goods necessary for export. The country has been handicapped by the lack of Australian capital/money to finance business and industry. Therefore, many businesses are owned by American, British, and Japanese investors.

Agriculture - apples, barley, cattle, chickens, dairy products, oats, oranges, potatoes, rice, sheep, sugar cane, wheat, and wool

Fishing - lobsters, oysters, and shrimp

Forestry - eucalyptus and pine timber, and wood pulp

Manufacturing - chemicals, clothing and shoes, iron and steel, other metals, paper, processed foods, textiles, and transportation equipment

Mining - bauxite, coal, copper, diamonds, gold, iron ore, lead, manganese, natural gas, nickel, opals, tin, zinc, and zircon

Exports - farm products, minerals, and wool

Imports - construction equipment and factory machinery

LIFE-STYLE

The vast majority of Australians live in the cities along the southeastern coast of the country. Australia is considered one of the most urbanized countries in the world. The majority of the people live in the *suburbs*. For the most part, families live in single-story houses with lawns and gardens; there are few apartment buildings. However, like any large city, Australia's cities fight air pollution and rush-hour traffic.

Living in rural areas can be very lonely due to the widely scattered farms and settlements. Some *stations* (sheep or cattle ranches) cover as much as 1,000 sq. mi. (2,600 sq. km) and can be over 100 miles (160 km) from the nearest town. Although most farm families own their own farms and make a decent living, poverty can be found as well, due to a lack of other kinds of employment.

Because meat is in abundant supply, it plays an important part in the Australian diet. A typical dinner consists of meat, potatoes, and a second vegetable. Due to an influx of immigrants over recent years, Chinese, Greek, Indian, Italian, and Thai dishes have become popular as well.

Australian family life is very similar to that of the American family. And since much of the population originally came from Great Britain, one sees the British influence manifested in much of the culture. It is particularly evident in the language in which many British terms have been retained.

Education varies, depending on state or territory. Tasmania requires children to attend school from ages six to 16. In the other areas, children attend from the age of five or six to age 15. Most children attend free public schools.

Australians enjoy outdoor sports such as swimming, Australian rules football, skin diving, surfing, boating, golf, tennis, cricket, rugby, and soccer. Other leisure time activities include frequenting the arts and the opera, symphony, ballet, theater, and motion pictures.

The *outback* (rural interior of the country) has primarily dirt roads so travel by automobile can be difficult. Financially well-off families often own a light airplane for transportation.

IT'S A FACT!

Ayers Rock - a rock formation located in central Australia that contains numerous small caves. The cave walls are covered with rock paintings by Aboriginal artists of long ago.

Great Artesian Basin - an underground rock formation that serves as Australia's chief source of artesian water.

The Great Barrier Reef - a chain of more than 2,500 coral reefs, including many small islands, that extends about 1,250 mi. (2,010 km) along Australia's northeast coast.

Lakes Argyle and *Gordon* - artificially created, are the country's only large, permanent lakes.

Mount Kosciusko - the country's highest point, rises 7,310 ft. (2,228 m) above sea level. It attracts many skiers.

Nullarbor Plain - an immense, dry, treeless plateau found along the southern edge of the Western Plateau.

Snowy Mountains Scheme - the world's largest water conservation project, which consists of an extensive system of dams, aqueducts, and tunnels.

 DID YOU KNOW...

- Australia was one of the first countries to develop a motion-picture industry?
- Koala bears still live in the forests of eastern Australia?
- Many children in the Australian "outback" study at home and are instructed by a teacher who talks to them via a two-way radio?
- The Sydney Opera House, a world-famous landmark, is a white, shell-like structure, located on the banks of Sydney Harbour?
- The Aborigines, the native inhabitants of Australia, lived in Australia for at least 40,000 years before the arrival of the first white settlers?

AUSTRIA

OFFICIAL NAME: Republik Österreich (Republic of Austria)
LOCATION: Central Europe
AREA: 32,376 sq. mi. (83,853 sq. km)
POPULATION (Est. 1995): 7,861,000
CAPITAL: Vienna
LARGEST CITIES: Vienna, Graz, Linz, Salzburg, Innsbruck
GOVERNMENT: Parliamentary democracy governed by a president.
FLAG: Three horizontal stripes of red, white, and red. The state flag features the coat of arms, while the national flag does not.
ETHNIC GROUP: German
LANGUAGE: German
RELIGION: Roman Catholic
BASIC MONETARY UNIT: Austrian Schilling

GEOGRAPHY

Austria is a landlocked country famous for its scenic mountains. It measures 180 mi. (290 km) from north to south and 355 mi. (571 km) from east to west at its greatest distances.

Austria has six main land areas: 1) the Granite Plateau, 2) the Eastern Forelands, 3) the Alpine Forelands, 4) the Northern Limestone Alps, 5) the Central Alps, and 6) the Southern Limestone Alps. Mountains cover three-fourths of the country. The Alps cover the western, central, and southern parts of the country. The Granite Plateau lies in the north. The Eastern Forelands is Austria's primary agricultural area.

CLIMATE

There are four distinct seasons in Austria partially determined by the winds. Eastern and western winds affect the climate. The warm, moist winds from the Atlantic bring precipitation and moderate temperatures. The dry winds from the Asian plains bring hot temperatures in the summer and cold in the winter.

The temperature averages about 27°F (-3°C) in January and about 67°F (19°C) in July. An average of 25 in. (64 cm) of precipitation falls yearly.

ECONOMY

Austria is a prosperous country with a very low unemployment rate. Tourism adds about $1 billion to Austria's annual national income.

Agriculture - barley, cattle, corn, grapes, hogs, milk, potatoes, sugar beets, and wheat

Manufacturing - cement, chemical products, clothing and textiles, electrical equipment, furniture, glass, iron and steel, leather goods, lumber, machines and tools, motor vehicles, optical instruments, paper and pulp, and processed foods and beverages

Mining - coal, copper, graphite, iron ore, lead, magnesite, natural gas, petroleum, salt, and zinc

Exports - forest products (including paper and pulp), iron and steel, manufactured goods, and magnesite

Imports - food, machinery, petroleum, and vehicles

LIFE-STYLE

More than half of all Austrians live in towns and cities. Most of these city dwellers live in four- or five-story apartment buildings. Some live in single-family homes or high-rise apartments.

Many rural dwellers live in one-family homes that vary from region to region.

Austrians usually wear clothing similar to that worn in the United States. On special occasions, many wear traditional clothing. Men wear a gray, wool suit that includes a coat and *knickers* (short, loose-fitting pants gathered below the knees). Women wear a *dirndl*, a peasant costume that includes a blouse with a wide girdle laced over it and a colorful skirt and apron.

Virtually all Austrian adults are literate. Children ages six to 15 are required to attend school. Most attend free public schools.

Austrians enjoy good food. Popular meats are beef, chicken, pork, sausage, and veal. Most meals include one or more side dishes, such as dumplings, noodles, or potatoes. Popular dishes include *Weiner schnitzel* (breaded veal cutlet), *Sachertorte* (chocolate cake with apricot jam and chocolate icing), and *Knödel* (moist potato dumplings). Austrian bakers are noted for their world famous cakes and pastries.

Austrians love being outdoors, especially to go for walks. Favorite sports include mountain climbing, skiing, ice skating, swimming, hiking, and soccer. Large crowds attend the ballet, concerts, operas, movie theaters, and plays.

Austria is one of the great cultural centers of Europe. It is particularly famous for its music. Austria's many great composers include Haydn, Mozart, Schubert, and Strauss. Many people consider *Don Giovanni*—written by Austrian composer, Mozart—the world's greatest opera. Today, the Vienna Boys' Choir (among other groups) are internationally renowned.

IT'S A FACT!

Danube River - the country's longest river, flows 217 mi. (350 km) from east to west.

Grossglockner - the country's highest point, rises 12,457 ft. (3,797 m) above sea level.

Neusiedler Lake - located on the Hungarian border, is the country's largest lake. The Austrian part of the lake has an area of 51 sq. mi. (132 sq. km).

 DID YOU KNOW...
- Austria does not have public drinking fountains because it is customary for the people to drink bottled water?

AZERBAIJAN

OFFICIAL NAME: Azerbaijan Respublikasi (Azerbaijani Republic)
LOCATION: Western Asia/Europe
FORMERLY: Part of the Soviet Union
AREA: 33,436 sq. mi. (86,600 sq. km)
POPULATION (Est. 1993): 7,222,000
CAPITAL/LARGEST CITY: Baku
GOVERNMENT: Republic governed by a president.
FLAG: Three horizontal stripes of light blue, red, and green with a white crescent and an eight-pointed, white star in the center.
ETHNIC GROUPS: Azerbaijani (Azeri), Armenian, Russian
LANGUAGES: Azerbaijani (Azeri), Armenian, Russian
RELIGIONS: Islam, Christianity (Eastern Orthodox, Russian Orthodox)
BASIC MONETARY UNIT: Manat

GEOGRAPHY

Azerbaijan is located in Asia's Caucasus Mountain region along the western coast of the Caspian Sea. It measures 240 mi. (385 km) from north to south and 295 mi. (475 km) from east to west at its greatest distances. Although a majority of the country lies in Asia, the portion located north of the Caucasus Mountains is considered part of Europe. Unlike other countries, Azerbaijan is dissected by another country. Western Azerbaijan—called the Nakhichevan Autonomous Republic—is separated from eastern Azerbaijan by Armenia.

More than 40 percent of the land consists of lowlands at elevations of 1,300 to 4,900 ft. (400 to 1,500 m) above sea level. Mountain slopes are covered with beech, oak, and pine trees.

CLIMATE

Azerbaijan's climate is quite varied from the lowlands to the Caucasus Mountains. The lowlands have long, hot summers and cool winters. The average temperature is 79°F (26°C) in August and 39°F (4°C) in January. The average temperature in parts of the Caucasus Mountains is 56°F (13°C) in August and 21°F (6°C) in January. Precipitation levels average 5-15 in. (13-38 cm) in most of the lowland areas and 40-55 in. (100-140 cm) in the highlands and in the southeast region on the Caspian Sea.

ECONOMY

Azerbaijan's economic production is composed of industries and agriculture, but petroleum mining is the country's major source of wealth. Although little of the country's land is arable, its agricultural output accounted for one-tenth of the Soviet Union's total output.

Under Soviet control, the government owned most of the country's farms, factories, and businesses. It was not until 1992 that the government began passing laws encouraging a free enterprise system.

Agriculture - cattle, cotton, fruit, goats, grain, grapes, pigs, rice, sheep, silkworms, tea, tobacco, and vegetables

Manufacturing - chemical processing, fuels, herbicides, industrial oils, machine building, petroleum refining, plastics, synthetic rubber, textile production, and wine

Mining - aluminum, building materials, copper, iron, lead, natural gas, petroleum, salt, and zinc

Exports - chemicals, cotton, oil and gas, oilfield equipment, and textiles

Imports - food, machinery and parts, and textiles

LIFE-STYLE

Azerbaijan is approximately half urban and half rural. Most urban Azerbaijanis live in multistory apartment buildings while most rural Azerbaijanis live in one- or two-story houses. Most Azerbaijanis wear Western-style clothing, but clothing type varies with location, religious background, and special occasions. Some rural women wear wide skirts and blouses with long, wide sleeves, while some urban women wear black shawls with brightly colored designs. Rural Muslim women often wear a black shawl that covers the head and shoulders and may be pulled over the face. During holidays, men may dress traditionally in a costume of pants, a long shirt, boots, and a long jacket.

Azerbaijani fare consists of *pilaf* (a rice dish) and grilled or boiled meats, including beef, goat, and lamb. Two traditional dishes are *bozartma* (mutton stew) and *dovga* (soup made of yogurt, meat, and herbs). Popular drinks include tea and wine.

Children ages six to 17 are required by the government to attend school. The country has 17 schools of higher education.

Azerbaijanis enjoy walking and swimming for exercise, and soccer is the most popular sport. Teahouses are great meeting places, and many men spend much of their leisure time in them.

Azerbaijanis are known for their handwoven rugs and brightly-patterned shawls.

IT'S A FACT!

Mount Bazar Dyuzi - the country's highest point, rises 14,652 ft. (4,466 m) above sea level.

Coast of Caspian Sea - the country's lowest point, lies 92 ft (28 m) below sea level.

 DID YOU KNOW...

- Azerbaijan did not gain its independence until 1991, after nearly 70 years as a part of the Soviet Union?
- Up until 1990, Azerbaijan's Communist government restricted the practice of religion by closing down almost all of the mosques and religious schools?
- Azerbaijanis enjoy over 300 days of sunshine each year?

AZORES
Dependency of Portugal

OFFICIAL NAME: Azores
LOCATION: North Atlantic Ocean
AREA: 868 sq. mi. (2,247 sq. km)
POPULATION (Est. 1993): 254,000
MOST IMPORTANT CITY: Ponta Delgada
LARGEST CITIES: Angra do Heroísmo (Terceira), Lajes (Pico), Horta (Faial), Ponta Delgada (São Miguel), Santa Cruz (Flores)
GOVERNMENT: Autonomous (self-governing) region of Portugal.
ETHNIC GROUPS: Azorean, others

GEOGRAPHY

The Azores are an archipelago composed of nine islands in the North Atlantic Ocean. They are located about 800 mi. (1,300 km) west of Portugal and have a total of 320 mi. (515 km) of coastline. The Azores were formed from the peaks of a vast underwater volcanic mountain chain called the Gibraltar-Azores Ridge. Much of the land is hilly and wooded. Earthquakes are fairly common.

The nine islands that make up the Azores are Flores, Corvo, Faial, Pico, São Jorge, Graciosa, Terceira, São Miguel, and Santa Maria.

ECONOMY

Agriculture - cattle, citrus fruits, corn, grapes, and pineapples

Manufacturing - beet-sugar processing (Ponta Delgada, São Miguel Island) and dairying (Flores Island)

Exports - canned fish, hand embroideries, pineapples, and wine

Imports - automobiles, coal, machinery, mineral oils, petroleum products, and textiles

IT'S A FACT!

Ponta do Pico - the islands' highest point, is located on Pico Island and rises 7,713 ft. (2,351 m) above sea level.

 DID YOU KNOW...

- Prior to the development of weather satellites, European weather forecasting relied on meteorological data from the Azores?
- During World War II, Great Britain used the Azores as a naval base in the warfare against Nazi submarines? The United States and Europe also established important air bases on these islands and used them as centers of communication.
- The Azores are farther from mainland Europe than any other eastern Atlantic islands?

BAHAMAS

BAHAMAS

OFFICIAL NAME: The Commonwealth of the Bahamas
LOCATION: Northwestern Atlantic Ocean
AREA: 5,385 sq. mi. (13,878 sq. km)
POPULATION (Est. 1993): 265,000
CAPITAL: Nassau
LARGEST CITIES: Nassau, Freeport
GOVERNMENT: Independent commonwealth governed by a governor-general representing Queen Elizabeth II of Great Britain.
FLAG: Adopted in 1973. Three horizontal stripes of blue, gold, and blue overlapped by a black triangle that is based on the hoist side. Blue, gold, and black represent the sea, the land, and the Bahamian people, accordingly.
ETHNIC GROUPS: Black, White, Mulatto
LANGUAGE: English
RELIGIONS: Anglican, Baptist, Methodist, Roman Catholic
BASIC MONETARY UNIT: Bahamian Dollar

GEOGRAPHY

The Bahamas are composed of a chain of about 3,000 coral islands and reefs, with a combined coastline of about 1,580 mi. (2,543 km). The islands—referred to as an archipelago—extend from about 50 mi. (80 km) off Florida's eastern coast to Cuba's northeastern tip, a distance of more than 500 mi. (800 km). The major islands are Acklins, Andros, Cat, Eleuthera, Grand Bahama, Great Abaco, Great Exuma, Great Inagua, Little Abaco, New Providence, and San Salvador (or Watling's Island). Most of the islands are long, narrow strips of limestone covered by a thin layer of soil. Many of the islands are partially covered by pine forests. The islands are mostly flat and have no freshwater streams. People inhabit about 20 of the islands.

CLIMATE

The Bahamas have a subtropical climate. The average temperature ranges from 72°F (22°C) in the winter to 85°F (29°C) in the summer. The average annual rainfall is 45 in. (114 cm). Hurricanes are frequent between June and November.

ECONOMY

The leading economic activity is tourism, with more than 1.25 million tourists visiting the islands annually. Investment management and international banking have also become major industries.

Agriculture - bananas, citrus fruit, cucumbers, pineapples, poultry, and tomatoes

Fishing - crawfish and other seafood

Manufacturing - cement, petroleum products, pharmaceuticals, rum, and food products

Natural Resources - aragonite, salt, and timber

Exports - pharmaceuticals, cement, rum, and crawfish and other seafood

Imports - crude oil, foodstuffs, manufactured goods, and mineral fuels

LIFE-STYLE

Approximately three-fourths of the Bahamian population lives on two of the islands: New Providence and Grand Bahama. Many of the people work in hotels and other businesses related to tourism. Some Bahamians make crafts, such as colorful straw items, to sell to tourists. But life-styles vary. In Nassau, some residents live in attractive, pastel-colored houses. Other residents live in run-down houses, some of which lack running water. Less than two percent of the country's people are farmers.

About four-fifths of the Bahamian people are black. Many are descendents of slaves brought to the area by British Loyalists after the American Revolution.

People travel to the Bahamas for the warm climate, beautiful sandy beaches, and clear water. Many cruise ships dock at Nassau's busy harbor. Tourists are attracted to Nassau's casinos, restaurants, and shops.

Children ages five to 14 are required to attend school. Over 90 percent of the Bahamian people can read and write. The country has one college, the College of the Bahamas, which is located in Nassau.

DID YOU KNOW...

- On his trip to the Americas in 1492, Christopher Columbus landed first on San Salvador Island in the Bahamas?
- Pirates used the Bahamas as a base for their expeditions in the 17th and 18th centuries?
- During the American Civil War, the Bahamas became prosperous as a base for ships breaking the Union blockade of Confederate ports?
- Only about 2 percent of the country's people are farmers?
- The Bahamas were ruled by Britain from 1717 to 1973, when the country gained its independence?
- San Salvador features a monument dedicated to Christopher Columbus?

BAHRAIN

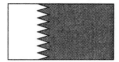

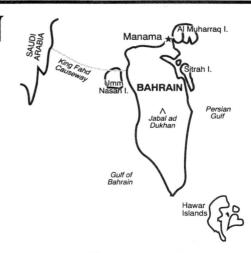

OFFICIAL NAME: The State of Bahrain
LOCATION: Persian Gulf; Southwest Asia
AREA: 262 sq. mi. (678 sq. km)
POPULATION (Est. 1993): 565,000
CAPITAL/LARGEST CITY: Manama
GOVERNMENT: Monarchy headed by an emir who appoints a cabinet; the cabinet runs the government.
FLAG: Red field adjacent to a white, eight-pointed, serrated-edge band on the hoist side.
ETHNIC GROUPS: Arab, Asian Indian, Iranian, Pakistani
LANGUAGES: Arabic, English, Farsi, Urdu
RELIGIONS: Islam (Sunni and Shi´a Muslim)
BASIC MONETARY UNIT: Bahraini Dinar

GEOGRAPHY

Bahrain is an archipelago consisting of more than 30 islands. It measures 50 mi. (80 km) from north to south and 26 mi. (42 km) from east to west at its greatest distances. It has 78 mi. (126 km) of coastline.

The largest of Bahrain's islands is Bahrain Island. It accounts for 225 sq. mi. (584 sq. km) of the country's total land area. It consists of freshwater springs in the north—which provide water for drinking and irrigation—and a sandy plain and salt marshes in the south. It is linked to Al Muharraq, Sitrah, and Umm Nasan Islands by bridges. These islands, along with others, make up one of Bahrain's two island groups. The country's other island group consists of the Hawar Islands—located about 12 mi. (19 km) southeast of Bahrain Island—which are small, rocky, and mainly uninhabited. Some of these small islands actually lie underwater at high tide.

CLIMATE

Bahrain is known for its high humidity and warm temperatures year-round. During the summer months (June through September), there is very little, if any, rainfall and temperatures often rise above 100°F (38°C). During the winter months, there is an average of 3 in. (8 cm) of rainfall and temperatures range from 50° to 80°F (10° to 27°C).

ECONOMY

The Bahraini economy is based primarily on the petroleum industry. Although the country does not have a large petroleum supply, its oil refinery on Sitrah Island ranks as one of the world's largest and most modern. The country also has valuable reserves of natural gas. Banking and financial services, construction, manufacturing, and transportation are also important.

Agriculture - bananas, cattle, citrus fruits, cucumbers, dates, goats, mangoes, pomegranates, poultry, sheep, and tomatoes

Fishing - fish and shrimp

Manufacturing - aluminum and aluminum products, ammonia, iron, asphalt, liquid natural gas, methanol, paper products, petroleum products, plastics, ship repairing, soft drinks, tile and cement blocks, and wheat flour

Mining - natural gas and petroleum

Exports - aluminum and aluminum products, machinery, petroleum products, and transport services

Imports - chemicals, clothing, crude petroleum, food, industrial machinery, manufactured goods, and motor vehicles

LIFE-STYLE

Most Bahrainis live in northern Bahrain Island. Approximately four-fifths live in urban areas. Most Bahrainis live in apartments or concrete houses. The houses are very private, as they have few windows and surround an open-air courtyard. Many homes have air conditioners and refrigerators. Some rural Bahrain villagers live in thatched huts.

Western-style clothing is sometimes worn, especially by young Bahrainis. Traditional clothing for men consists of a *thobe* (light, long robe) that is generally white in summer and colored in winter. They also wear a *gutra* (light cloth headdress) held in place by an *ocal* (heavy cloth ring). Traditional clothing for women consists of an *ubaiya* (full-length, black robe), usually worn over a colorful dress that cannot be seen in public. Some women cover their hair with a *hijab* (scarf) and wear a *burqa* (a veil which covers all but the eyes). Sandals are worn by both men and women.

Bahraini dishes include *beryani* (rice with meat) or *machbous* (rice, meat, tomatoes, and lentils), *halwa* (starch pudding mixed with crushed cardamom seeds, saffron, sugar, and fat), and *qahwa* (unsweetened coffee). *Rottab* (dates) are served at every meal and tea is the most common beverage.

Education is free and compulsory through the secondary level. Medical care for all and benefit programs for the old and disabled are free or at low cost.

Soccer is the most popular sport. Other popular sports include basketball, volleyball, field hockey, and cricket. Popular recreational activities include sailing, water skiing, fishing, softball, ice skating, horseback riding, and tennis. Wealthier Bahrainis also take part in falconry, gazelle and hare coursing, and horse and camel racing.

IT'S A FACT!

Jabal ad Dukhan - the country's highest point, is located on Bahrain Island and rises 443 ft. (135 m) above sea level.

King Fahd Causeway - measuring 15.5 mi. (25 km) long, links Bahrain Island to the Saudi Arabian mainland.

 DID YOU KNOW...

- There are several thousand burial mounds in northern Bahrain Island, some of which are 3,000 years old?
- Bahraini males are still allowed to have four wives, as long as they provide for each wife equally? Few among the younger generation continue this practice.

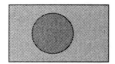

BANGLADESH

OFFICIAL NAME: People's Republic of Bangladesh
FORMERLY: East Pakistan (until 1971)
LOCATION: South Asia
AREA: 55,598 sq. mi. (143,998 sq. km)
POPULATION (Est. 1993): 125,175,000
CAPITAL: Dhaka
LARGEST CITIES: Dhaka, Chittagong, Khulna
GOVERNMENT: Republic governed by a president.
FLAG: Green field with a red circle shifted slightly to the hoist side. Green and red represent scenic beauty and the sun, accordingly. Green is also a traditional Islamic color.
ETHNIC GROUP: Bengali
LANGUAGES: Bengali, Chakma, Magh
RELIGIONS: Islam, Hinduism
BASIC MONETARY UNIT: Taka

GEOGRAPHY

Bangladesh measures 464 mi. (747 km) from north to south and 288 mi. (463 km) from east to west at its greatest distances. It has 357 mi. (575 km) of coastline along the Bay of Bengal.

Most of Bangladesh is a flat, low-lying plain, except for the extreme northeast and southeast corners which have hills. Three major rivers—the Brahmaputra, the Ganges, and the Meghna—flow over the plain. The fertile soil deposited at the mouths of these rivers has formed the large Ganges Delta where rice and jute, the country's most important crops, thrive.

CLIMATE

Bangladesh is warm and humid throughout the year, with little variation in temperature from one area to another. Temperatures average 82°F (28°C) in April, the hottest month. During January, the coldest month, the temperature averages 64°F (18°C).

In the east, the country has an average rainfall of 100 in. (250 cm). The western part of Bangladesh receives an average of 65 in. (165 cm) yearly. During the monsoon season, from May to October, the rivers flood the country. At the end of the monsoon season, Bangladesh is frequently hit with violent cyclones, often accompanied by *tsunamis* (huge destructive waves) originating in the Bay of Bengal. Thousands of Bangladeshis have been killed by cyclones and tsunamis.

ECONOMY

Bangladesh is one of the poorest and most-populated countries in the world. The average per capita income is about $150 a year. The economy is dependent on agriculture. About 80 percent of the people farm for a living using outdated tools and methods.

Agriculture - jute, rice, sugar cane, tea, tobacco, and wheat
Manufacturing - jute products, leather, paper and paper products, and textiles
Mining - natural gas
Exports - jute, fish, leather, and tea
Imports - building materials, chemicals, coal, electric appliances, food and food products, machinery, petroleum, textiles, and transportation equipment

LIFE-STYLE

About 84 percent of Bangladesh's people live in rural areas. Most rural villagers have one- or two-room homes made of bamboo. Most urban dwellers live in small wooden houses. In urban slum areas, the homes are built of cardboard, wood scraps, or sticks.

In Bangladesh, most women wear *saris*, a long cloth wrapped around the waist and draped over a shoulder, with a short blouse underneath. Many Muslim men wear a *lungi* (a tight, skirtlike garment), while Hindu men wear a *dhoti* (a cloth wrapped around the waist and between the legs). Rural dwellers usually go barefoot.

Most Bangladeshis do not have enough food to eat. Rice is the main staple of the diet. Most vegetables are fried in oil. The people prefer spicy dishes, and common spices are cumin, ginger, coriander, tumeric, and pepper. *Shu'ra*, a sauce made from chopped onions and spices, is often used to marinate food. The most popular beverage is tea sweetened with sugar.

Children are not required to attend school, and only about 30 percent of all adult Bangladeshis are literate.

Due to food shortages and unsanitary conditions, diseases such as cholera, leprosy, and tuberculosis are common.

The most popular sports are soccer, field hockey, cricket, ping pong, and badminton.

IT'S A FACT!

Mount Keokradong - the country's highest point, rises 4,034 ft. (1,230 m) above sea level.

 DID YOU KNOW...
- Bangladesh has the eighth highest population in the world?
- Farms in Bangladesh average only 3.5 acres (1.4 hectares)?
- The main forms of transportation are buses, rickshaws, and *babi-taxis* (three-wheeled motor scooters)?
- Muslims do not drink alcohol or eat pork, while Hindus do not eat beef?

BARBADOS

North Atlantic
Ocean

Mt. Hillaby Λ

BARBADOS

Caribbean
Sea

★ Bridgetown

OFFICIAL NAME: Barbados
LOCATION: West Indies
AREA: 166 sq. mi. (430 sq. km)
POPULATION (Est. 1993): 259,000
CAPITAL/LARGEST CITY: Bridgetown
GOVERNMENT: Constitutional monarchy governed by the prime minister and the Cabinet, though a governor general represents the British Crown as head of state.
FLAG: Three vertical stripes of blue, gold, and blue. Blue and gold represent the sea and sky, and the sand of the beaches, accordingly. A black trident head with a broken shaft—which stands for Neptune, the sea god, and for the move from dependence to independence—is centered on the yellow stripe.
ETHNIC GROUPS: Black, Mulatto, European
LANGUAGE: English
RELIGIONS: Anglican, Roman Catholic, Methodist, Moravian
BASIC MONETARY UNIT: Barbados Dollar

GEOGRAPHY

Barbados lies about 250 mi. (402 km) northeast of Venezuela and is the easternmost of the West Indian islands. At its greatest distances, Barbados measures 21 mi. (34 km) from north to south and 14 mi. (23 km) from east to west. It has 56 mi. (90 km) of coastline on the North Atlantic Ocean and the Caribbean Sea.

Although Barbados is almost totally covered with coral rock, about 85 percent of the land is still arable. The land is mostly flat with higher elevations in the northeastern coastal region. There are fine, sandy beaches in the west and southwest.

CLIMATE

Barbados has a tropical climate and a rainy season that lasts from June to October. The average annual temperature ranges from 70° to 87°F (21° to 31°C) and rainfall ranges from 80 in. (200 cm) in the north to 40-60 in. (100-150 cm) in the south. Hurricanes sometimes strike, causing extensive damage.

ECONOMY

Sugar has played an important part in Barbados's economy for over 300 years. The economy is also based on manufacturing and tourism.

Agriculture - carrots, corn, milk, pigs, sugar cane, sweet potatoes, and yams

Fishing - flying fish and others

Manufacturing - chemicals, clothing, edible oils, electronic products, lard, margarine, molasses, rum, and sugar

Exports - chemicals, clothing, electrical parts, machinery and transport equipment, molasses, rum, and sugar

Imports - chemicals, construction materials, crude oil, food, fuels, machinery, manufactured goods, and raw materials

LIFE-STYLE

Just over half of the population are rural dwellers. Many rural Barbadians make a living by farming or working on sugar plantations. Other Barbadians work in construction, factories, government, processing plants, tourism, or other service industries. Many families live in traditional *chattel houses* (wooden homes), which are easily assembled/disassembled and are set on coral stone about 3-4 ft. (0.9-1.2 m) above the ground. Other houses are constructed of cement and painted pastel colors.

The country's national dish is the flying fish and *cou cou* (made of okra and cornmeal). Popular foods include Crane Chubb fish, dorado, king fish, lobster, pork, shrimp, red snapper, turtle, and tuna, along with a wide variety of tropical fruits and vegetables. Some popular local dishes include *conkies* (cornmeal, coconut, pumpkin, raisins, sweet potatoes, and spice steamed in a banana leaf), *jug-jug* (Guinea corn and green peas), and *pepperpot* (a spicy stew). Cow and goat milk are commonly consumed.

The national sport is cricket, and the national table game is dominoes. Other popular sports and leisure activities include basketball, bridge, chess, cycling, golf, horseracing, polo, rugby, sailing, scuba diving, skin diving, soccer, squash, surfing, swimming, tennis, volleyball, waterskiing, and windsurfing. Music—including calypso and folk songs—and dancing are also popular.

Primary and secondary education is free, and children are required to attend school up to the age of 16. About 98 percent of all Barbadian adults are literate.

IT'S A FACT!

Mount Hillaby - the country's highest point, rises 1,115 ft. (340 m) above sea level.

 DID YOU KNOW...

- Barbados was a British colony from the 1600s until 1966, when the country gained its independence?
- Barbadians' way of life is quite similar to that found in England: traffic moves on the left and cricket is the favorite sport?
- About 80 percent of the population is descended from slaves brought to Barbados between 1636 and 1833?
- Bridgetown—founded by the Englishman Charles Wolverstone in 1628—was originally called Indian Bridge or Indian-Bridge Town because of an Indian-built bridge that existed on the city's site?
- Barbados is one of the world's most densely populated countries, with an average of 1,566 persons per sq. mi. (602 per sq. km)?

BELARUS

OFFICIAL NAME: Respublika Byelarus (Republic of Belarus)
FORMERLY: Byelorussian Soviet Socialist Republic; Byelorussia
LOCATION: Eastern Europe
AREA: 80,155 sq. mi. (207,600 sq. km)
POPULATION (Est. 1993): 10,480,000
CAPITAL/LARGEST CITY: Minsk
GOVERNMENT: Parliamentary government headed by a chairman.
FLAG: Three horizontal stripes of white, red, and white.
ETHNIC GROUPS: Belarusian, Russian, Polish, Ukrainian
LANGUAGES: Russian, Belarusian
RELIGIONS: Belarusian Catholic, Eastern Orthodox
BASIC MONETARY UNIT: Ruble

GEOGRAPHY

At its greatest distances, Belarus, a landlocked country, measures 340 mi. (545 km) from north to south and 385 mi. (620 km) from east to west.

Belarus consists mainly of flat lowlands alternating with hills and plains. It has four main rivers—the Bug, the Dnepr, the Neman, and the Western Dvina—and more than 10,000 lakes. Northern Belarus is covered by forests, central Belarus is formed by a ridge, and southern Belarus consists of marshes, swamps, and forests. The Pripyat Marshes, a forested swamp, lie in the south.

CLIMATE

The Belarusian climate includes cold winters and warm summers. The average annual temperature ranges from about 22°F (-6°C) in January to about 65°F (18°C) in July, with average precipitation levels of 20-26 in. (50-66 cm) per year.

ECONOMY

As part of the Soviet Union, Belarus's economy was controlled by the Communist government. Independence, however, is expected to promote the growth of private business, creating a free enterprise system. Belarus's economy is currently well-developed. More than half of the country's income economic output comes from manufacturing.

Agriculture - barley, cattle, eggs, flax, fur farming, hogs, milk, potatoes, rye, and sugar beets

Forestry - timber

Manufacturing - bicycles, clocks and watches, computers, engineering equipment, furniture, trucks and tractors, matches, metal-cutting tools, motorcycles, paper and plywood, potassium fertilizer, radios, refrigerators, television sets, and textiles

Mining - coal, dolomite, limestone, marl, peat, petroleum, potash, potassium, quartz sand, and rock salts

Exports - chemicals, foodstuffs, machinery and transport equipment, and tractors

Imports - chemicals, machinery, and textiles

LIFE-STYLE

Belarus's population is approximately two-thirds urban and one-third rural. Urban Belarusians generally live in apartments. Rural Belarusians generally live in small, wooden houses or community housing blocks and work on government-operated collective or state farms. The average Belarusian family is small, with only one or two children.

Belarusian fare includes stews, vegetable soups (such as *turnip borsch*), and rye and oat bread. Especially popular are dishes containing potatoes and mushrooms. The most frequently consumed beverages include tea and coffee.

Primary and secondary education is free and compulsory for all Belarusians, many of whom finish high school and continue their education at one of the country's three universities or 30 technical institutes.

Belarusians usually wear Western-style clothing. Traditional clothing—usually white with colorful embroidery—is worn on special occasions. For recreation, Belarusians enjoy soccer, volleyball, track and field, swimming, camping, and chess.

Belarusians are known for their hand-crafted items—such as elaborately patterned, woven textiles and straw-inlaid boxes—and for performing arts—such as dancing and puppetry. The country has a State Theatre of Opera and Ballet (located in Minsk), two other state theaters, a conservatory of music, and a number of folk-music companies. Belarus has architecture and literature that dates back to the 11th century.

Most Belarusians use the country's railway system to travel long distances and buses for transportation within its cities.

IT'S A FACT!

Belovezha Forest - located on the border of Belarus and Poland, is the oldest nature preserve on the continent. It is a remnant of the forest that, in prehistoric times, covered much of Europe. Majestic trees and rare animals (such as a herd of European bison) are found here.

Cathedral of St. Sophia - located in the city of Polotsk, has architecture that dates back to the 11th century.

Dzerzhinskaya Gora - the country's highest point, rises 1,135 ft. (346 m) above sea level.

 DID YOU KNOW...
- Belarus was a republic of the Soviet Union and did not gain independence until 1991, when the Soviet Union broke up?
- Belarus's capital was almost totally destroyed during World War II?

BELGIUM

OFFICIAL NAME: Koninkrijk België (Dutch), Royaume de Belgique (French) (Kingdom of Belgium)
LOCATION: Northwestern Europe
AREA: 11,783 sq. mi. (30,519 sq. km)
POPULATION (Est. 1993): 9,845,000
CAPITAL: Brussels
LARGEST CITIES: Brussels, Antwerp, Ghent
GOVERNMENT: Constitutional monarchy.
FLAG: Adopted as the national flag in 1830 but first used in 1789 during the revolt against Austrian rule. Three vertical stripes of black, yellow, and red.
ETHNIC GROUPS: Fleming, Walloon
LANGUAGES: Dutch, French
RELIGION: Roman Catholic
BASIC MONETARY UNIT: Belgian Franc

GEOGRAPHY

Belgium is a small, densely populated country in northwestern Europe. It measures 140 mi. (225 km) from north to south and 170 mi. (274 km) from east to west at its greatest distances. It has 39 mi. (63 km) of coastline along the North Sea.

Belgium's terrain varies greatly for such a small area, though it contains no mountains. The Schelde, Sambre, and Meuse Rivers serve as transportation routes.

Belgium has four main land regions: 1) the Coastal and Interior Lowlands, 2) the Kempenland, 3) the Central Low Plateaus, and 4) the Ardennes. Most of Northern Belgium is covered by the Coastal and Interior Lowlands. Sandy beaches lie along the coast. Lowlands, called *polders*, extend from the coast and form a humid, treeless plain. The northeastern region, the Kempenland, is a major mining and industrial center. The Central Low Plateaus region has the best soil. Southeastern Belgium is covered by the Ardennes. This area has sandstone ridges, limestone valleys, and forest-covered hills. The Famenne is an area in the Ardennes where, over the years, rivers have carved caves in the soft limestone.

CLIMATE

Belgium has cool summers and mild winters. West winds from the sea bring moderate temperatures. As in the Netherlands, Belgium has a system of dikes and seawalls to prevent tidal flooding in the polders. Summer temperatures range from 54° to 72°F (12° to 22°C). In the winter, temperatures rarely fall below freezing. With its close proximity to the sea, fog and rain are common. Average precipitation near the coast is 28 in. (71 cm) yearly. The Ardennes receives a yearly average of 40 in. (100 cm) of precipitation.

ECONOMY

Belgium has a highly developed economy based on free enterprise. Fortunately, the climate benefits both industry and agriculture.

Agriculture - barley, cattle, flax, hops, milk, potatoes, sugar beets, and wheat

Manufacturing - cement, chemicals and chemical products, glass, leather goods, paper, processed foods, steel, and textiles

Mining - coal, limestone, marble, sandstone, and slate

Exports - chemicals, diamonds, engineering goods, glass products, machines, processed foods, steel, and textiles

Imports - chemicals, cotton, diamonds, engineering goods, grains, machines, and petroleum

LIFE-STYLE

About 95 percent of all Belgians live in urban areas. Many Belgians who live in rural areas commute to jobs in the cities. Only a small minority live in isolated communities.

The Belgian diet includes pork, beef, game birds, fish, cheese, fruit, vegetables, bread, and soup. The country is famous for mussels, chocolates, 300 varieties of beer, waffles, and French fries. Two famous Belgian dishes are *carbonades* (beef stewed in beer) and *waterzooi* (chowder made with chicken or fish). It is customary to shop daily for fresh food in open-air markets. Almost every neighborhood has sidewalk cafes and open-air markets.

Most adult Belgians are literate. Children ages six to 18 are required to attend school. Most also attend preschool and kindergarten.

Bicycle racing and soccer are popular sports. In rural areas, hunting, fishing, and pigeon racing are enjoyed. Pigeon races begin when the males are released far from their mates. Owners place bets on which will reach its mate first.

Family activities include attending picnics, the theater, and movies. Many families take a month-long vacation each year.

IT'S A FACT!

Botrange Mountain - the country's highest point, rises 2,277 ft. (694 m) above sea level.

 DID YOU KNOW...

- All citizens aged 18 or older must vote or risk a fine?
- A Belgian named Minuit purchased Manhattan Island from American Indians for $24 worth of goods?
- Belgians claim to be the inventors of French fries, which they serve with mayonnaise, mustard, or vinegar rather than ketchup?
- Belgium is famous for its beautiful handmade lace?

BELIZE

OFFICIAL NAME: Belize
FORMERLY: British Honduras (until 1973)
LOCATION: Central America
AREA: 8,867 sq. mi. (22,965 sq. km)
POPULATION (Est. 1993): 199,000
CAPITAL: Belmopan
LARGEST CITIES: Belize City, Belmopan
GOVERNMENT: Parliamentary democracy.
FLAG: Blue field with narrow red horizontal stripes at the top and bottom. On a white circle in the flag's center is the coat of arms, which features a shield flanked by two workers in front of a mahogany tree in the center, a scroll with the motto *Sub Umbra Floreo* (I Flourish in the Shade) at the bottom, and a green garland on the outer edge.
ETHNIC GROUPS: Creole, Mestizo, Indian (Carib and Maya)
LANGUAGES: English, Spanish, native Indian dialects
RELIGIONS: Roman Catholic, Protestant
BASIC MONETARY UNIT: Belizean Dollar

GEOGRAPHY

Belize is Central America's most thinly populated country. It lies on the southeast coast of the Yucatán Peninsula. At its greatest distances, Belize measures 180 mi. (230 km) from north to south and 85 mi. (137 km) from east to west. It has 220 mi. (354 km) of coastline along the Caribbean Sea. Most of the coastal area is swampy lowland. Offshore are small islands and the second-longest barrier reef in the world. In the south, the land rises to the low peaks of the Maya Mountains. Northern Belize is flat. The country has a large amount of forest land throughout.

CLIMATE

Belize's climate is hot and humid. Temperatures range from 60° to 90°F (15.6° to 32°C) on the coast, with inland temperatures usually climbing higher. Average annual rainfall ranges from 50 in. (130 cm) in the north to over 150 in. (380 cm) in the south.

ECONOMY

Belize is a developing country with an economy based on agriculture. Sugar cane is the country's main crop. The country is working to develop its tourist industry.

Agriculture - bananas, corn, grapefruit, oranges, and sugar cane

Fishing - conch, lobster, and shrimp

Forestry - pines and tropical hardwoods

Manufacturing - bricks, cement, clothing, processing foods and wood, and sugar refining

Exports - bananas, citrus fruits, clothing, fish products, molasses, and sugar

Imports - chemicals and pharmaceuticals, food, fuels, machinery and transportation equipment, and manufactured goods

LIFE-STYLE

Belize's population is divided equally between rural and urban areas. Unemployment is high and farm production is low, which accounts for many poor Belizeans.

Thatched huts are common in the rural areas. Along the coast, houses of cement or wood are built on stilts because of the threat of hurricanes.

Many men, especially professionals, wear *guaya beras*, which are untucked embroidered cotton shirts.

Indian women generally wear the traditional long, bright-colored skirts and white blouses, and the men wear work clothes and straw hats.

White rice and kidney beans form the staples of the diet. Stewed chicken, beef, or fish often accompany the rice and beans. Corn is a staple for Mayans. Fruits are often a part of the daily diet.

Children ages six to 14 are required to attend school. About 91 percent of those aged 15 and over have attended school, but the literacy rate is estimated to be between 50 and 60 percent.

Soccer and basketball are the most popular sports. Cycling is also very popular. A cross-country bicycle race is held every year on Easter weekend.

IT'S A FACT!

Belize River - the chief waterway of Belize, is 180 mi. (290 km) long and travels from west to east across the country.

Fort George - built by the English in 1803 in present-day Belize City, is still standing.

Victoria Peak - the country's highest point, rises 3,680 ft. (1,122 m) above sea level.

 DID YOU KNOW...
- Between 1500 B.C. and A.D. 300 the Maya Indian civilization spread into what is now Belize?
- Fresh coconut is often offered to guests in areas where refrigeration is not available?

BENIN

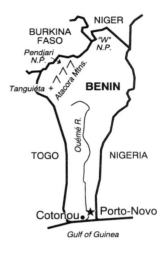

OFFICIAL NAME: République Populaire du Bénin (People's Republic of Benin)
FORMERLY: Dahomey
LOCATION: Western Africa
AREA: 43,484 sq. mi. (112,622 sq. km)
POPULATION (Est. 1993): 5,081,000
CAPITAL: Porto-Novo (official); Cotonou (de facto)
LARGEST CITIES: Cotonou, Porto-Novo
GOVERNMENT: Republic headed by a president.
FLAG: Two horizontal stripes of yellow and red that edge a vertical green stripe on the hoist side.
ETHNIC GROUPS: Fon, Adja, Yoruba, Bariba, European, other
LANGUAGES: French, Adja, Fon, Yoruba, Bariba, other
RELIGIONS: Traditional African Religions, Christianity, Islam
BASIC MONETARY UNIT: CFA Franc

GEOGRAPHY

At its greatest distances, Benin measures 415 mi. (668 km) from north to south and 202 mi. (325 km) from east to west. It has 77 mi. (124 km) of coastline along the Gulf of Guinea.

Benin's coastal region is a long sandbar backed by tidal marshes and lagoons. Directly behind this region is the *barre* (clay) region, which is home to a vast swampy area called the Lama Marsh. South-central Benin is composed of a group of plateaus while the Atacora Mountains—a continuation of the Togo Mountains—lie in the northwest. The Niger plains lie in the northeast.

Southern Benin was originally home to a rainforest, which was cleared for agricultural purposes. Central and northern Benin are covered by forests and savannas. "W" and Pendjari National Parks lie in the north and northwest, respectively.

CLIMATE

Southern Benin has a hot, humid climate year-round. It has four seasons: two rainy seasons (April to July and September to November) separated by two dry seasons. The average annual temperature ranges from 72° to 93°F (22° to 34°C) and the average annual rainfall ranges from 32-50 in. (80-127 cm).

Northern Benin has one rainy season (April to October) and one dry season. Most of this region's rain falls in August, and a *harmattan* (hot, dry wind) blows from the northeast during the months of December to March. The average annual temperature is 80°F (27°C), which varies from day to day and may reach as high as 110°F (43°C) during the month of March. The average annual rainfall ranges from 53 in. (135 cm) in the Atacora Mountains to 38 in. (97 cm) in the north.

ECONOMY

Benin's economy is based largely on agriculture and the country is relatively self-sufficient in staple foods.

Agriculture - beans, cassava, cattle, corn, cotton, goats, millet, palm oil, peanuts, pigs, rice, sheep, sorghum, tobacco, and yams

Forestry - timber

Manufacturing - cigarettes, construction materials, cotton mills, food production, industrial bakeries, palm oil refineries, petroleum, and textiles

Mining - limestone, marble

Exports - cacao, coffee, cotton, crude oil, palm kernels, palm oil, palm products, peanuts, shea nuts, and tobacco

Imports - beverages, consumer goods, food, fuels, machinery, petroleum products, and tobacco

LIFE-STYLE

The Beninese population is composed of approximately 60 ethnic groups, most of whom live in southern Benin. Beninese shelters vary by region. Most people live in simple, handmade houses while some live in concrete homes, the latter being more common in urban areas. Those in lagoon areas live in bamboo huts built on stilts and those in the Atacora Mountains live in round houses constructed with mud walls and thatched roofs.

Each ethnic group has its own language and style of dress. Mainly, though, Beninese women wear brightly colored dresses while men wear an outfit called an *agbade* (trousers, a short jacket, and a full robe). Many Beninese, especially in the south, wear Western-style clothing.

Children ages five to 11 are required to attend school. However, only about 60 percent of the children attend primary school, and only about 20 percent attend secondary school. Most of the children attending school are male.

Overall, the country's health conditions are poor. Serious diseases suffered by the Beninese include meningitis, leprosy, malaria, and sleeping sickness.

Beninese art is reflective of the various cultures. Carved wooden masks are used during ceremonies to represent spirits, and appliquéd tapestries depict history. Other art forms include plastic art, pottery, and bronze statuettes. Traditional music and dance are featured at ceremonies. The national sport is football (soccer).

IT'S A FACT!

Ouémé River - the country's longest river, flows 280 mi. (451 km) into the Gulf of Guinea.

Tanguiéta - the country's highest point, is located in the Atacora Mountains and rises 2,083 ft. (635 m) above sea level.

 DID YOU KNOW...
- From the 17th through the mid-19th centuries, the country's main export was slaves, gaining it the title of "Slave Coast" among Europeans?

BERMUDA
Dependency of the United Kingdom

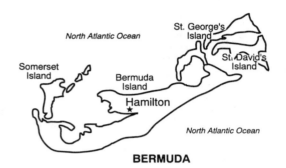

BERMUDA

OFFICIAL NAME: Bermuda
LOCATION: North Atlantic Ocean
AREA: 21 sq. mi. (54 sq. km)
POPULATION (Est. 1993): 58,000
CAPITAL/LARGEST CITY: Hamilton
GOVERNMENT: Self-governing British dependency.
FLAG: Red field with the flag of the United Kingdom in the upper hoist-side quadrant. Centered on the outer half of the flag is the Bermudian coat of arms.
ETHNIC GROUPS: African, European
LANGUAGE: English
RELIGION: Christianity
BASIC MONETARY UNIT: Bermudian Dollar

GEOGRAPHY

Bermuda consists of over 300 islands that lie approximately 600 mi. (965 km) east of North Carolina. People live on only 20 of the islands, many of which are connected by bridges. The name "Bermuda" usually refers to the seven main islands, which form the shape of a fishhook. Some of the largest islands are Bermuda, St. George's, St. David's, and Somerset.

Located the farthest north of any group of coral islands, Bermuda emerged from the sea when coral slowly accumulated on the peaks of an extinct, underwater volcanic mountain range. Hills and ridges rising to heights of 260 ft. (80 m) cover the island, which is known for its pleasant climate, beautiful flowers, palm trees, and inviting beaches and seas. The islands contain no rivers or lakes.

CLIMATE

Although numerous palms and brilliantly colored flowers may fool people into thinking otherwise, Bermuda's climate is not considered tropical. Temperatures throughout the year average 70°F (21°C). In the fall, hurricanes sometimes strike.

Bermuda receives about 58 in. (147 cm) of rainfall per year. Rainwater is an important source of fresh water and is caught on the whitewashed roofs of houses and stored in tanks.

ECONOMY

Bermuda's major source of income is tourism, with over 500,000 tourists visiting per year. About 7,000 foreign companies operate out of Bermuda, benefiting from the dependency's tax exemption policies.

Agriculture - bananas, citrus fruits, milk, vegetables
Manufacturing - paint, pharmaceuticals, and printed material
Exports - fruits and vegetables, light manufactured goods, and medical and pharmaceutical products
Imports - food, fuel, machinery, and textiles

LIFE-STYLE

Almost all of Bermuda's people enjoy a relatively high standard of living. Most workers are involved directly or indirectly with tourism. Primary and secondary schools are free, and children ages five to 16 must attend. Almost the entire population is literate. About 15,000 British and U.S. military personnel live in Bermuda (not included in the population figures above).

The conservative influence of British colonialism is very much in evidence: Bermudians enjoy late-afternoon tea, pubs, cricket, and fish and chips. Other lively influences have brought the area calypso singers, steel bands, and Bermudian Gombey dancers. The magnificently attired Gombey dancers perform for large crowds on major holidays.

IT'S A FACT!

Horseshoe Bay Beach - the most famous of Bermuda's beautiful beaches, is one-quarter mile of gleaming sand tinted pink by billions of tiny bits of coral.

The Railway Trail - an 18-mi. (29-km) track, stretches the length of the main island. It provides a quiet trail for hikers and bicyclists to enjoy Bermuda.

 DID YOU KNOW...

- Police officers (called *bobbies*) and businessmen wear shorts hemmed just above the knees as part of their "very proper" dress? These long shorts are called "Bermudas."
- Bermuda's tourist industry blossomed during America's Prohibition (1920-33) when vacationing mainlanders sought a place to legally drink alcoholic beverages?
- The Warwick Academy, established in 1626, is considered the oldest secondary school in the Western Hemisphere?
- In Bermuda's flag, the shield that is part of the coat of arms shows the shipwreck of the *Sea Venture*? Two of the survivors from this wreck in 1609 were the first settlers on the uninhabited island.

BHUTAN

OFFICIAL NAME: Druk-Yul (Kingdom of Bhutan)
LOCATION: South-central Asia
AREA: 18,147 sq. mi. (47,000 sq. km)
POPULATION (Est. 1993): 1,621,000
CAPITAL: Thimphu
GOVERNMENT: Monarchy headed by a king.
FLAG: Divided diagonally into orange (upper hoist side) and yellow (lower fly side) areas. A white dragon with jeweled claws lies in the center.
ETHNIC GROUPS: Ngalop and Sharchop (sometimes known together as Bhote or Bhutia), Nepalese, Assamese, Gurung
LANGUAGES: Dzongkha (Tibetan dialect), various other Tibetan and Nepalese dialects
RELIGIONS: Buddhism, Hinduism, Islam
BASIC MONETARY UNIT: Ngultrum

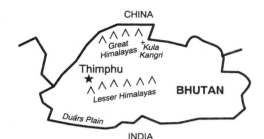

GEOGRAPHY

At its greatest distances, Bhutan, a landlocked country, measures 110 mi. (177 km) from north to south and 200 mi. (322 km) from east to west.

Bhutan has three main land regions: 1) the Great Himalayas, 2) the Lesser Himalayas, and 3) the Duārs Plain. Northern Bhutan lies in the Great Himalayas. It is a region of mountains and high valleys averaging 12,000-18,000 ft. (3,700-5,500 m) above sea level and covered by snow and glaciers.

Central Bhutan lies in the Lesser Himalayas. This region is home to the Black Mountain Range, forests, fertile valleys, and the country's principal rivers. Its average elevation lies 5,000-9,000 ft. (1,500-2,700 m) above sea level.

Southern Bhutan lies in Duārs Plain, which is an area measuring 8-10 mi. (13-16 km) wide. This region is home to foothills, plains, river valleys, savannas, and a dense semitropical forest.

CLIMATE

Bhutan's climate varies by region. The country's average monthly temperature is 39°F (4°C) in January and 63°F (17°C) in July. The Great Himalayas region is typically very cold and extremely dry. The Lesser Himalayas region has a moderate climate with an average annual rainfall of 40-50 in. (102-127 cm). The Duārs Plain region is extremely hot and receives an average of 200-300 in. (508-762 cm) of rain per year.

ECONOMY

Bhutan's economy, which is one of the world's least developed, is based mainly on agriculture and the raising of livestock.

Agriculture - bananas, barley, buckwheat, cattle, citrus fruit, corn, dairy products, eggs, goats, pigs, ponies, potatoes, rice, root crops, sheep, wheat, and yaks

Handicrafts - blankets, leatherwork, metalwork, pottery, weaving, and wood carving

Manufacturing - alcoholic beverages, calcium carbide, cement, fruit preservation, textiles, and wood products

Mining - coal, gypsum

Natural Resources - hydroelectric power and timber

Exports - cardamon, cement, coal, fruit, gypsum, handicrafts, rice, and timber

Imports - fabrics, gasoline, grain, kerosene, machinery, sugar, and vehicles

LIFE-STYLE

Almost all of Bhutan's population live in rural areas, with most Bhutanese living in mountain valley villages and working as farmers and livestock raisers. The type of shelter occupied by the Bhutanese is dependent upon region and/or religion.

Bhutanese in the Upper Himalayas region live in small villages surrounded by stone walls. Those in the Lesser Himalayas region live in two-story oblong homes constructed of stone blocks and pine-shingle roofs. Typically, the upper level houses the family and the lower level serves as a barn. Those in the Duārs Plain region live in rectangular homes built on high ground and constructed of stones and mud blocks, protecting their inhabitants from floods, snakes, and wild animals.

Bhutan's Buddhist population has approximately 4,500 *lamas* (monks who teach doctrine, perform rituals, and treat illnesses) who live in *dzongs* (fortified monasteries). The dzongs serve as centers of art and culture. Bhutanese cultural arts include music and dance, in which the symbolic movements depict stories.

About one-fourth of the children ages seven to 12 attend school. As a result, about 90 percent of those aged 15 and older are illiterate.

IT'S A FACT!

Kula Kangri - the country's highest point, rises 24,783 ft. (7,554 m) above sea level.

 DID YOU KNOW...

- Bhutan was practically isolated from the rest of the world until the late 1950s?
- Until 1960, Bhutan had no technical sources of communication and power?
- Bhutan's government sells collectors postage stamps to make money?
- Himalayan storms gave the country its name, which translates into "Land of the Thunder Dragon"?

BOLIVIA

OFFICIAL NAME: República de Bolivia (Republic of Bolivia)
LOCATION: Central South America
AREA: 424,165 sq. mi. (1,098,581 sq. km)
POPULATION (Est. 1993): 7,950,000
CAPITAL: La Paz (actual), Sucre (official)
LARGEST CITIES: La Paz, Santa Cruz, Cochabamba
GOVERNMENT: Republic governed by a president.
FLAG: Three horizontal stripes of red, yellow, and green. The coat of arms is centered on the yellow stripe.
ETHNIC GROUPS: Indian, Mestizo
LANGUAGES: Spanish, Quechua, Aymara
RELIGION: Roman Catholic
BASIC MONETARY UNIT: Peso Boliviano

GEOGRAPHY

Bolivia is one of two landlocked South American countries. At its greatest distances, Bolivia measures 900 mi. (1,448 km) from north to south and 800 mi. (1, 287 km) from east to west.

Bolivia has four main land regions: 1) the Andean Highlands, 2) the Yungas, 3) the Valles, and 4) the Oriente. The Andes Mountains cover much of western Bolivia. The Altiplano, a high plateau, lies between a western range that runs along Bolivia's western border and an eastern range that separates the Altiplano from the rest of Bolivia. About 40 percent of the population live on the Altiplano. The Yungas, a small region of steep hills covered with subtropical forests, lies northeast of the Andean Highlands. The Valles, in south-central Bolivia, are covered by grasslands and many farms. The Oriente, a large, lowland plain that covers northern and eastern Bolivia, has tropical rainforests in the north and grasslands, shrubby forests, and swamps over the remainder of the region.

CLIMATE

Bolivia's climate varies by region. The country is south of the equator, so its seasons are opposite those of the Northern Hemisphere. In the Andes Mountains, snow covers high mountain peaks all year. The Altiplano has a dry, cool climate with temperatures averaging 55°F (13.1°C) in January and 40°F (4.4°C) in July.

The Yungas have a warm, humid climate. The climate in the Valles is similar, but less humid. In both regions, temperatures average 72°F (22°C) in January and 52°F (10.9°C) in July. The majority of the Oriente has a hot, humid climate with year-round temperature averages of 75°F (24°C).

ECONOMY

Although Bolivia is considered a developing country, it has a wealth of natural resources that are not being utilized. It has one of the lowest standards of living in the Western Hemisphere.

Agriculture - coca, coffee, corn, cotton, potatoes, rice, sugar, and wheat

Forestry - rubber and timber

Manufacturing - processed foods, refined tin, and textiles

Mining - antimony, copper, gold, lead, natural gas, petroleum, silver, tin, tungsten, and zinc

Exports - antimony, coca (illegally), coffee, gold, lumber, natural gas, rubber, silver, sugar, tin, and tungsten

Imports - heavy machinery, transportation equipment, clothing, food, and household items

LIFE-STYLE

A class system is prevalent in Bolivia. The *elite* class is mainly made up of Bolivians who have had money in their families for years. This is the smallest class. The middle class lives much like the elite, although not as lavishly. Doctors, lawyers, and other professionals fall into this category. Next, are the *cholos*, the working class. They are farmers, factory workers, and peddlers. In rural areas, they live in adobe homes with tile roofs. In cities, most live in crowded *barrios* (neighborhooods).

The largest social class is the *campesinos*, poor farmers, who barely raise enough food to live on. Most live in small adobe homes with thatched roofs. Most wealthy and middle-class Bolivians wear Western-style clothes. The *cholos* and *campesinos* often wear traditional clothing which includes striped ponchos for men and colorful shawls, full skirts, and derby hats for the women.

Traditional foods include potatoes, corn, and a grain called *quinoa*. Meat pies called *saltenas* are very popular.

Soccer is the Bolivian's favorite sport. Colorful festivals, including parades, feasts, and elaborate dances, are an important part of life in Bolivia.

Children ages six to 14 are required to attend school; however, the country has one of the highest illiteracy rates in South America. Almost one-third of Bolivians aged 15 and older cannot read or write.

IT'S A FACT!

Lake Titicaca - located on the Peruvian border, is the world's highest navigable lake at 12,507 ft. (3,812 m) above sea level. Bolivians use *totoras*, boats made of reeds, on the lake.

Mount Illimani - located south of La Paz, is one of the most beautiful peaks found in the Andes Mountains.

Nevado Sajama - the country's highest point, rises 21,463 ft. (6,542 m) above sea level.

 DID YOU KNOW...

- Over half of Bolivia's original territory has been lost in wars or treaties with Argentina, Chile, Brazil, Peru, and Paraguay?
- Bolivia is often called "The Capital of Folklore"?
- On Christmas Eve, children place old shoes in a window for Santa Claus to exchange for new gifts?

BOSNIA-HERZEGOVINA

OFFICIAL NAME: Socijalisticka Republika Bosna I Herzegovina
(Socialist Republic of Bosnia and Herzegovina)
FORMERLY: Part of Yugoslavia
LOCATION: Southeastern Europe
AREA: 19,741 sq. mi. (51,129 sq. km)
POPULATION (Est. 1993): 4,548,000
CAPITAL: Sarajevo
LARGEST CITIES: Sarajevo, Banja Luka, Mostar, Tuzla, Travnik
GOVERNMENT: Republic headed by a president, who is elected by a seven-member collective presidency.
FLAG: White field with a blue shield in the center. Six yellow fleurs-de-lis on the shield are bisected by a white diagonal stripe.
ETHNIC GROUPS: Bosnian Muslim, Serb, Croat, Albanian, Gypsy, Ukrainian
LANGUAGE: Serbo-Croatian (Cyrillic and Roman alphabets used in writing)
RELIGIONS: Islam, Serbian Orthodox, Roman Catholic, Protestant
BASIC MONETARY UNIT: Dinar

GEOGRAPHY

Bosnia-Herzegovina—sometimes simply referred to as Bosnia—is located on the Balkan Peninsula. At its greatest distances, Bosnia measures 195 mi. (315 km) from north to south and 195 mi. (315 km) from east to west. It has 13 mi. (20 km) of coastline along the Adriatic Sea.

The country has two regions: Bosnia and Herzegovina. Bosnia, in the north, is a forest-covered, mountainous area. Its main rivers include the Bosna, Drina, Neretva, Sava, Una, and Vrbas. Herzegovina, in the south, consists of rocky hills and flat farmland. An area in the southeast consists of *karst* (irregular limestone area with fissures, sinkholes, underground streams, and caverns).

CLIMATE

The country's climate varies greatly. Winters are generally cold in mountain valleys and very severe and snowy at higher elevations. Summers are generally warm in mountain valleys and cool with heavy rains at higher elevations. In Sarajevo, the average annual temperature is 30°F (-1°C) in January and 68°F (20°C) in July. The *karst* area receives heavy rainfall in winter. Bosnia experiences frequent, destructive earthquakes.

ECONOMY

Prior to its civil war, the country's economy was dependent on agriculture, manufacturing, and mining.

Agriculture - cattle, cherries, corn, figs, grapes, hogs, lemons, melons, mulberries, oranges, peaches, pears, plums, pomegranates, potatoes, rape seed, rice, sheep, soybeans, tobacco, walnuts, and wheat

Manufacturing - electric appliances, oil refining, steel production, textiles, tobacco products, vehicle assembly, and wood furniture

Mining - bauxite, chromium, coal, copper, iron ore, lead, manganese, and zinc

Natural Resources - coal, hydroelectric power, iron ore, and timber

Exports - chemicals, food and live animals, fuel and lubricants, machinery and transport equipment, manufactured goods, raw materials

Imports - beverages, chemicals, food and live animals, fuel and lubricants, machinery and transport equipment, raw materials, and tobacco

LIFE-STYLE

The Bosnian population is approximately 36 percent urban and 64 percent rural.

Bosnian cuisine is highly influenced by its Turkish and Muslim ties. Popular dishes include *musaka* (roasted meat and eggplant) and *kapama* (mutton with spinach and green onions). The city of Mostar produces an exceptional white wine.

Eight years of elementary-level education is required of Bosnian children, with further education available at universities in the cities of Banja Luka, Mostar, Sarajevo, and Tuzla.

Prior to the outbreak of civil war, popular leisure activities included skiing, fishing, kayaking, hiking, and hunting.

IT'S A FACT!

Mount Maglić - the country's highest point, rises 7,828 ft. (2,386 m) above sea level.

Sarajevo - the country's capital, is famous for the crafts of its carpet weavers and silversmiths, and for its *mosques* (Muslim houses of worship) that were built by the Turks who ruled the city from the mid-1400s to 1878.

 DID YOU KNOW...
- Prior to being called Herzegovina, that area of the country was called *Hum* while under Hungarian rule?
- The June 1914 assassination in Sarajevo of Archduke Francis Ferdinand of Austria-Hungary by Bosnian Gavrilo Princip led to the outbreak of World War I?
- Bosnia-Herzegovina declared its independence in March 1992, after which civil war erupted?
- Sarajevo was home to the 1984 Winter Olympics?
- Bosnian writer, Ivo Andrić, won the Nobel Prize for literature in 1961?

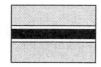

BOTSWANA

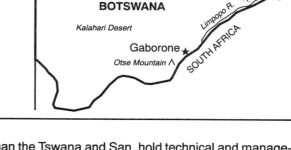

OFFICIAL NAME: Republic of Botswana
FORMERLY: Bechuanaland Protectorate
LOCATION: South-central Africa
AREA: 224,607 sq. mi. (581,730 sq. km)
POPULATION (Est. 1993): 1,325,920
CAPITAL/LARGEST CITY: Gaborone
GOVERNMENT: Republic headed by a president.
FLAG: Three horizontal stripes of blue, black, and blue separated by bands of white.
ETHNIC GROUPS: Tswana (black Africans made up of eight ethnic groups, the largest of which is the Bamangwato), San or Bushmen (yellowish-brown skinned), White
LANGUAGES: Setswana, English
RELIGIONS: Traditional African Religions, Christianity
BASIC MONETARY UNIT: Pula

GEOGRAPHY

Botswana, a landlocked country, lies on part of the African Plateau in central southern Africa. At its greatest distances, Botswana measures 625 mi. (1,006 km) from north to south and 590 mi. (950 km) from east to west. Northern Botswana is partially covered with forests and has a marshland in the northwest, the Okavango Swamps, which is formed by streams off the Okavango River. Central and southwest Botswana is almost totally covered by the Kalahari Desert, whose plantlife consists of dry grassland and scrubby acacias. Eastern Botswana is hilly and has the most fertile land. It is home to 80 percent of the country's population.

CLIMATE

Botswana's climate is dry and subtropical, and the country is often plagued by droughts. During the summer—October through April—daytime temperatures may reach 100°F (38°C). During the winter—May through September—days are warm with nighttime temperatures often dropping below freezing. Eastern Botswana receives an average of 22 in. (56 cm) of rain per year, while the west receives an average of 12 in. (30 cm) of rain per year.

ECONOMY

Botswana is a poor, but rapidly developing, country whose economy is based on mining and livestock.

Agriculture - beef, corn, cottonseed, hides and skins, milk, millet, onions, oranges, peanuts, sorghum, and wheat

Mining - coal, cobalt, copper, diamonds, and nickel

Exports - beef, diamonds and other mineral products, hides and skins, and textiles

Imports - chemicals, food, fuel, machinery, and transportation equipment

LIFE-STYLE

Approximately three-fourths of Botswana's people live in rural areas, but more are moving to cities each year. Many of the Tswana who live in rural villages make a living by farming or raising livestock. Those San who have not been forced onto permanent settlements either live by traditional means of hunting and gathering food in the Kalahari Desert, or work on cattle farms. The white population, which generally enjoys a better life-style than the Tswana and San, hold technical and managerial positions in industry, business, or government. Some even own ranches.

Because Botswana is a poor country and unemployment is a major problem, about 50,000 Botswanans travel to South Africa and work for several months out of the year.

Approximately 80 percent of the country's children attend elementary school, with only about 15 percent going on to high school. The country has a university, located in Gaborone, and several teacher-training colleges.

IT'S A FACT!

Diamond Pipe at Orapa - a huge funnel of volcanic origin, measures 1 mi. (1.6 km) wide at its surface and is one of the biggest diamond finds in the world.

Kalahari Desert - measuring approximately 190,000 sq. mi. (500,000 sq. km), covers most of Botswana and parts of its neighboring countries Namibia and South Africa.

Makgadikgadi Game Reserve & Nxai Pan National Park - located in northern Botswana near *pans* (lakes that have dried up but fill with water when it rains, attracting a variety of wildlife).

Otse Mountain - the country's highest point, rises 4,886 ft. (1,489 m) above sea level.

 DID YOU KNOW...

- Botswana is one of the most thinly populated countries in Africa, with an average population density of 6 persons per sq. mi. (2 persons per sq. km)?
- Botswana had no written language until recent times?
- About 60,000 elephants live in Botswana?

BRAZIL

OFFICIAL NAME: República Federativa do Brasil (Federative Republic of Brazil)
LOCATION: South America
AREA: 3,286,502 sq. mi. (8,511,999 sq. km)
POPULATION (Est. 1995): 161,382,000
CAPITAL: Brasília
LARGEST CITIES: São Paulo, Rio de Janeiro, Salvador, Belo Horizonte, Recife, Pôrto Alegre
GOVERNMENT: Federal republic governed by a president.
FLAG: Bears the motto "Order and Progress." The green background and golden-yellow diamond colors represent forests and minerals. The blue and white of the circle are Portugal's historic colors.
ETHNIC GROUPS: White, Black, Mixed, Asian, Indian
LANGUAGE: Portuguese
RELIGION: Roman Catholic
BASIC MONETARY UNIT: Real

GEOGRAPHY

Brazil is the fifth largest nation in the world in population and area and occupies almost half of the total area of South America. It shares borders with all other South American countries except Chile and Ecuador. Two-thirds of Brazil consist of low mountains and broad plateaus. Lowlands covered with forests spread over the rest of the country. Brazil has over 1,000 rivers, the largest of which include the Amazon, the Paraná, and the São Francisco.

Brazil has three main land regions, each with its own distinctive qualities: 1) the Amazon Region, 2) the Northeast Region, and 3) the Central and Southern Plateaus.

The Amazon Region covers most of northern Brazil and consists of jungle-covered lowlands as well as tropical rainforests called *selva*. This area also has two mountain areas.

The Northeast Region is the area that juts into the Atlantic Ocean. The land in this region covers less than a fifth of Brazil. The coastal plain in this region has areas of red, fertile soil. The *sertão* (interior backlands), which is the region's interior, has poor soil and often experiences droughts. The sertão has hilly parts of what are called the Brazilian Highlands as well as plateaus.

The Central and Southern Plateaus lie south of both the Amazon and Northeast Regions. This area includes the majority of the Brazilian Highlands and spans over about one-fourth of Brazil. The highlands reach up to 1,000 to 3,000 ft. (300 and 900 m), with the highest elevations being near the coast. The *Great Escarpment*, a steep slope, is located along the coast on the southeastern edge of the highlands.

CLIMATE

Because all but the southernmost part of Brazil lies in the tropics, the climate is warm to hot year-round. The hottest month is January, and the coolest is July. In the Amazon Region, rainfall is especially heavy from December to May. The western part of this area receives over 160 in. (400 cm) of rain per year and the eastern part averages 40-80 in. (102-203 cm). A large city in this area, Manaus, has an average annual temperature of 81°F (27°C).

The Northeast Region has an annual average rainfall of about 65 in. (169 cm) in some coastal areas with only about 10 in. (26 cm) in parts of the interior. Temperatures in the interior vary from 53° to 107°F (12° to 42°C) during the year. Coastal temperatures are about 80°F (27°C) year-round.

The Central and Southern Plateaus have a somewhat cooler climate. For example, the average temperature in São Paulo is about 73°F (23°C) in January and 60°F (16°C) in July. Rainfall is about 50 in. (130 cm) a year. Frost or light snow occasionally covers the ground here.

ECONOMY

Though Brazil's economy is based on private enterprise, the government controls many basic industries such as the oil, petrochemical, and steel industries. Service industries have become increasingly important—they account for about 55 percent of the employment in Brazil.

Agriculture - bananas, cacao beans, cashews, cassava, coffee, corn, cotton, lemons, livestock, oranges, papaya, pineapples, rice, soybeans, sugar cane, and tobacco

Forestry - Brazil nuts, carnauba wax, latex, and timber

Manufacturing - automobiles, cement, chemicals, electrical equipment, food products, machinery, nickel, paper, petrochemicals, rubber, steel, textiles, and trucks

Mining - amethysts, bauxite, beryllium, chrome, diamonds, gold, graphite, iron ore, magnesite, magnesium, mica, natural gas, petroleum, quartz crystals, and tin

Exports - automobiles, cocoa, coffee, food products, foot wear, iron, orange juice, soybeans, steel, and sugar

Imports - capital goods, coal, crude oil, chemical products, and wheat

LIFE-STYLE

About three-fourths of Brazil's people live in urban areas. (Nearly all of Brazil's big cities are located near the coast.) Many urban people work in banks, factories, offices, stores, and hotels. Others have professional or government jobs. Middle-class Brazilians live in small houses or modern apartments, while the upper classes live in luxury. Most poor city dwellers live in *favelas*, or slums. Living conditions are primitive. The favelas do not have sewers or running water.

Rural people usually work on ranches or large plantations, though some own their own small farms. Rural families have a hard time earning enough to feed themselves. Most live in one- or two-room stone or adobe houses with clay tile roofs. Houses are made of wood or wild cane plants in the Amazon Region, with palm leaves forming the roofs. Houses near rivers are built on stilts. Many rural people sleep in hammocks.

In poor sections of cities and in rural areas, the chief foods are beans, rice, and *manioc* (a starchy root). People who live in the city might enjoy eating hamburgers, wheat bread, and a variety of meats. A favorite meal in Brazil is *feijoada*, a stew made with black beans and chunks of pork. Coffee is the most popular drink. *Maté*, an herbal tea, is also served.

Soccer is Brazil's most popular sport. Other popular sports are automobile racing, horse racing, and basketball. People enjoy relaxing at the many beautiful beaches.

A number of colorful festivals take place in Brazil, the most famous of which is *Carnival*. This festival is held four days before Lent. Parades, dancing, and singing make this an exciting celebration.

Brazil has free public elementary education, and children ages seven to 14 are required to attend school. About 80 percent of the adults can read and write.

IT'S A FACT!

Amazon Rainforest - the world's largest tropical rainforest, has growth in several distinct layers.

Amazon River - the world's second longest river, is 4,000 mi. (6,436 km) long.

Iguaçu Falls - located in the southern part of the country, these falls drop about 250 feet (76 m) in a semicircle, creating white foam as well as a rainbow.

Pico da Neblina - Brazil's highest mountain, rises 9,888 ft. (3,014 m) above sea level.

The Seven Enchanted Cities - refers to an unusual rock formation in the northeast region that looks like it is man-made. When viewed from above, the formation looks like small cities, arranged in streets and squares, with castles, monuments, and tunnels.

Trans-Amazon Highway - links Brazil's easternmost and westernmost points on the southern edge of the Amazon Basin, opening up the area to settlement which might adversely affect the rainforest.

 DID YOU KNOW...
- In some Brazilian cities, up to 30 percent of the people live in *favelas*, or slums?
- In Brasília, the country's capital, government buildings are known for their modern architecture? For example, Brazil's Chamber of Deputies meets in a bowl-shaped building.
- The Amazon region is home to about 1,500 varieties of birds?
- Brazil has the largest military force in Latin America?
- Brazil got its name from a native tree called *pau-brasil*?
- Brazil's rainforests contain over 40,000 kinds of plants?

BRITISH VIRGIN ISLANDS
Dependency of the United Kingdom

OFFICIAL NAME: Colony of the Virgin Islands
LOCATION: Eastern Caribbean Sea/North Atlantic Ocean
AREA: 59 sq. mi. (153 sq. km)
POPULATION (Est. 1993): 13,000
CAPITAL/LARGEST CITY: Road Town
GOVERNMENT: Dependency of the United Kingdom headed by the chief executive officer who acts as governor.
FLAG: Blue field with the United Kingdom's flag in the upper hoist-side quadrant. The Virgin Islander coat of arms is centered in the outer half of the flag. It features a woman flanked on either side by a vertical column of six oil lamps above a scroll that says *Vigilate*, meaning "be watchful."
ETHNIC GROUPS: Black African, Mulatto, European, Asian
LANGUAGE: English (spoken in a Calypso dialect)
RELIGION: Protestant
BASIC MONETARY UNIT: United States Dollar

GEOGRAPHY

The British Virgin Islands are the easternmost portion of the Virgin Islands, which are located approximately 50 mi. (80 km) west of Puerto Rico. They are separated from the United States Virgin Islands by a channel called *the Narrows*.

The British Virgin Islands consist of four large islands and 32 smaller islands and islets. The large islands include Anegada, Jost van Dyke, Tortola (Turtle Dove), and Virgin Gorda (Fat Virgin). A few of the smaller islands include Beef, Cooper, Great Thatch, Great Tobago, Guana, Little Thatch, Marina Cay, Norman, Peter, and Salt Islands. Of the 36 islands, only 16 are inhabited.

Tortola is the largest of the islands, with an area of 21 sq. mi. (56 sq. km). It is followed in size by Anegada, Virgin Gorda, and Jost van Dyke, respectively.

Almost all of the islands are rocky and hilly and of volcanic origin. Anegada Island is a relatively flat coral island surrounded by reefs. None of the islands have rivers. The islands have 50 mi. (80 km) of coastline.

CLIMATE

The British Virgin Islands enjoy a warm, subtropical climate throughout the year. Average annual temperatures range from 71° to 88°F (22° to 31°C). The average annual rainfall is 50 in. (130 cm), most of which falls during the months of September to December. The islands are subject to tropical storms and hurricanes during the months of July to October.

ECONOMY

Agriculture was once the main economic activity of the islands. It has been replaced by tourism, which accounts for 50 percent of the economy. Some fruits and vegetables are still exported, but most crops are only grown for local consumption.

Agriculture - bananas, citrus fruits, coconuts, livestock (beef cattle and chickens), mangoes, root crops, rum, sugar cane, and vegetables

   Fishing - bonito, clam, crab, lobster, shark, and tuna
   Manufacturing - building materials, paint, and rum
   Mining - gravel and sand
   Exports - fresh fish, gravel, livestock, rum, and sand

Imports - automobiles, beverages, building and raw materials, food, machinery, petroleum products, and water

LIFE-STYLE

The country's population is approximately 40 percent rural and 60 percent urban. The rural population mainly consists of farmers who live in one- or two-room thatch-roofed huts. The urban population primarily makes a living in the tourism industry, or working in factories, shops, or government offices. Urban housing ranges from wood shacks in slum areas to modern apartments and small suburban homes. The country's wealthy population generally lives in beautiful hillside homes looking out on the sea.

Clothing is generally Western in style, following the warm-weather clothing trends of Canada and the United States.

The people's diet consists mainly of fish, those foods grown on the islands, and imported foods. The freshwater supply is a problem, so water is frequently imported.

Education is free and compulsory up to the age of 15. Although there are no institutions of higher education on the islands, some students attend the University of the West Indies and other overseas institutions. Health is generally good.

IT'S A FACT!

Mount Sage - the country's highest point, and the highest point of all the Virgin Islands, is located on Tortola Island and rises 1,780 ft. (543 m) above sea level.

 DID YOU KNOW...

- Christopher Columbus discovered the islands in 1493 on his second voyage to America and named them *Santa Ursula y las Once Mil Virgenes* or "St. Ursula and the 11,000 Virgins"?
- A bridge connects Tortola Island to Beef Island, which is home to the country's main airport?
- The Virgin Islands at one time served as a pirate hangout?

BRUNEI

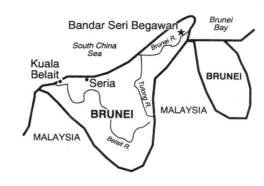

OFFICIAL NAME: Brunei Darussalam (Brunei, Abode of Peace)
LOCATION: Southeast Asia
AREA: 2,226 sq. mi. (5,765 sq. km)
POPULATION (Est. 1993): 276,984
CAPITAL: Bandar Seri Begawan (formerly the city of Brunei)
LARGEST CITIES: Bandar Seri Begawan, Seria, Kuala Belait
GOVERNMENT: Independent sultanate headed by a monarch called a sultan who is chosen for life by a council of succession.
FLAG: Yellow with two diagonal stripes of white and black starting at the upper hoist side. Brunei's national emblem (in red) is centered on the stripes.
ETHNIC GROUPS: Malay, Chinese
LANGUAGES: Malay, English, Chinese (Mandarin)
RELIGIONS: Islam, Buddhism, Christianity
BASIC MONETARY UNIT: Bruneian Dollar

GEOGRAPHY

Brunei occupies the northwestern coast of the island of Borneo and is divided by Malaysian states. At its greatest distances, Brunei measures 56 mi. (90 km) from north to southwest and 71 mi. (114 km) from east to northwest. It has 100 mi. (161 km) of coastline along the South China Sea.

Brunei is made up of a flat coastal plain, hilly lowlands in the west, and mountains in the east. Its major rivers include Belait, Brunei, and Tutong. Three-fourths of its area is covered by a dense tropical rainforest.

CLIMATE

Brunei has a tropical climate with high humidity and an average annual temperature range of 76° to 86°F (24° to 30°C). Its average yearly rainfall is about 100 in. (250 cm) along the coast and about 150 in. (320 cm) in the interior. The northeast monsoon provides rain during the months of November to March and the southwest monsoon brings rain from June to August.

ECONOMY

Brunei's economy is based mainly on its offshore petroleum and natural gas deposits. The country enjoys very little unemployment.

Agriculture - bananas, buffaloes, cassava, pigs, and rice
Natural Resources - natural gas, petroleum, and timber
Exports - crude petroleum, liquefied natural gas, and petroleum products.
Imports - chemicals, food, machinery and transport equipment, and manufactured goods

LIFE-STYLE

Brunei is about 58 percent urban and 42 percent rural. Urban Bruneians live in modern houses or apartment buildings constructed of brick or stone and wear clothing similar to that worn in Western countries. Many Muslim women wear long skirts and long-sleeved blouses. Rural Bruneians live in houses constructed of wood with thatched roofs and mainly wear loose shirts and *sarongs* (long pieces of cloth tied at the waist and worn as a skirt).

While Brunei's economy is based mainly on offshore petroleum and natural gas deposits, only about ten percent of its people are employed in those industries. About half of the population is actually employed by the government.

Education and health care are provided by the government free of charge. Most Bruneian children complete elementary school and continue on to high school. The country's first university, the University of Brunei Darussalam, opened in 1985. Should Bruneians choose to study at foreign universities, many of whom do, this education is also paid for by the government.

IT'S A FACT!

Bandar Seri Begawan - the country's capital, is home to the biggest palace in the world. The palace contains 1,788 rooms covering 50 acres (20 hectares) and cost $400 million to build.

DID YOU KNOW...

- The country's road system is poorly developed, so its rivers remain the main means of transportation in much of the interior?
- Brunei became an independent nation on January 1, 1984?

BULGARIA

OFFICIAL NAME: Republika Bulgariya (Republic of Bulgaria)
LOCATION: Southeastern Europe/Balkan Peninsula
AREA: 42,823 sq. mi. (110,912 sq. km)
POPULATION (Est. 1993): 9,026,000
CAPITAL: Sofia
LARGEST CITIES: Sofia, Plovdiv, Varna
GOVERNMENT: Emerging democracy. A prime minister is head of government and a president is chief of state.
FLAG: Three horizontal stripes of white, green, and red.
ETHNIC GROUPS: Bulgarian, Turk
LANGUAGES: Bulgarian, Turkish
RELIGIONS: Bulgarian Orthodox, Islam
BASIC MONETARY UNIT: Lev

GEOGRAPHY

At its greatest distances, Bulgaria measures 170 mi. (274 km) from north to south and 306 mi. (492 km) from east to west. It has 175 mi. (282 km) of coastline along the Black Sea. Mountains stretch over most of Bulgaria and are divided by fertile plains and valleys.

Bulgaria has four main land regions: 1) the Danubian Plateau, 2) the Balkan Mountains, 3) the Transitional Mountains and Lowlands, and 4) the Rhodope Mountains. The Danubian Plateau covers Bulgaria from the Danube River, which forms the country's northern border, to the Balkan Mountains, which run from east to west in the central region. The Danubian Plateau is home to the country's most fertile farmland. The Transitional Mountains and Lowlands region is located between the Black Sea in the east and the Rhodope Mountains region, which lies in the south and the west.

CLIMATE

Bulgaria's climate varies by region due to differing terrains. Summers range from humid in the north to dry in the south, and winters are generally cold and damp throughout. The average January temperature ranges from 35°F (2°C) near the Black Sea to 0°F (-17°C) in the central region. The average temperature in July is 75°F (24°C). The average yearly precipitation ranges from 25 in. (63 cm) throughout most of the country to over 40 in. (100 cm) in some mountain areas. Except in the mountain regions, snowfall is generally light.

ECONOMY

Despite its developing economy, Bulgaria has one of the lowest standards of living in Europe.

Agriculture - barley, corn, grapes, livestock, milk, oats, rice, roses, rye, sugar beets, tobacco, vegetables, and wheat

Manufacturing - building materials, chemicals, machinery, metal products, processed foods, rose oil, and textiles

Mining - coal, copper, kaolin, lead, pyrite, salt, sulfur, and zinc

Exports - agricultural products, cigarettes and tobacco, grapes, machinery and equipment, manufactured consumer goods, metals, minerals, raw materials, rose oil, and wine

Imports - agricultural products, fuel, industrial equipment, machinery and equipment, manufactured consumer goods, metals, minerals, and raw materials (iron ore and coke)

LIFE-STYLE

Prior to Communist rule beginning in 1946, poverty was widespread and most of Bulgaria's population was rural. The government industrialized the country and made improvements such as paving roads and providing telephone service and electricity in many rural areas. Today, the population is approximately one-third rural and two-thirds urban. Most women work outside the home. The rural population largely makes a living by working on large government-owned or state-run cooperative farms. The people live in simple houses, many of which lack central heating and plumbing. Urban dwellers usually work in government-owned factories and businesses and live in apartment buildings that lack many comforts. Jobs are lacking and wages tend to be low.

Commonly eaten foods include cheese, yogurt, and simple stews and other dishes containing beef, fish, lamb, and pork. Popular dishes include *moussaka* (casserole made with pork or lamb, potatoes, tomatoes, and yogurt), *sarmi* (pepper or cabbage stuffed with pork and rice), *shopska* (salad made with cucumbers, tomatoes, and Bulgarian cheese), and *tarator* (cold soup made with cucumbers, yogurt, garlic, dill, walnuts, and oil). Popular desserts include *baklava* (thin, leafy pastry with a syrup and nut filling) and *banitsa* (layered pastry) made with cheese or pumpkin. Preferred drinks include coffee (either espresso or Turkish style), and soft drinks.

Popular sports include basketball, skiing, and soccer. Popular leisure activities include dancing and listening to music, reading books, socializing, and walking and hiking. The country is known for its performing arts, particularly music. Festivals take place throughout the year.

Children ages seven to 15 are required to attend elementary school, and nearly all continue on to high school. Approximately 98 percent of all Bulgarians aged 15 and above are literate.

IT'S A FACT!

Alexander Nevsky Cathedral - located in Sofia, the country's capital, was built in the late 1800s commemorating Bulgaria's liberation from Turkish rule.

Musala Peak - the country's highest point, rises 9,596 ft. (2,925 m) above sea level.

 DID YOU KNOW...
- Bulgaria is the world's fourth-largest tobacco exporter?
- Sofia, the country's capital, was originally founded in the early A.D. 100s by the Roman Emperor Trajan, and destroyed in 447 by Attila and the Huns?

BURKINA FASO

OFFICIAL NAME: Burkina Faso
FORMERLY: Republic of Upper Volta
LOCATION: Western Africa
AREA: 105,869 sq. mi. (274,200 sq. km)
POPULATION (Est. 1993): 9,799,000
CAPITAL: Ouagadougou
LARGEST CITIES: Ouagadougou, Bobo Dioulasso
GOVERNMENT: Parliamentary type of government headed by a president, who is a military leader.
FLAG: Two horizontal stripes of red and green with a yellow star in the center.
ETHNIC GROUPS: Black (Voltaic and Mande groups), Fulani, Tuareg
LANGUAGES: French (official), Voltaic, Mande, other tribal languages
RELIGIONS: Traditional African Religions, Islam, Christianity
BASIC MONETARY UNIT: CFA Franc

GEOGRAPHY

At its greatest distances, Burkina Faso, a landlocked country, measures 400 mi. (644 km) from north to south and 525 mi. (845 km) from east to west.

The country contains a dry, rocky plateau of poor soil that is either a semidesert or savanna in the north (depending on the season), shrub and scattered forests in the south, wooded hills in the west and a swampy region in the southeast. It has many valleys that have been cut by rivers, such as the Black Volta, Red Volta, and White Volta. These valleys are home to most of the country's farmland.

CLIMATE

Burkina Faso's climate ranges from semiarid in the north to tropical in the south. Overall, it is generally hot and dry during the months of March and April, hot and wet during the months of May to October, and cool and dry during the months of November to February. The average annual temperature ranges from 68° to 95°F (20° to 35°C) and the average annual rainfall ranges from 10 in. (25 cm) in the north to 40 in. (100 cm) in the south.

ECONOMY

Burkina Faso is one of the poorest countries in the world. The main economic activity is cattle raising.

Agriculture - beans, cassava, cattle, corn, cotton, *fonio*, goats, millet, peanuts, rice, shea nuts, sheep, sorghum, sugar cane, and sweet potatoes

Manufacturing - beverage bottling, food processing, soap, and textiles

Mining - bauxite, copper, gold, manganese, marble, and uranium

Exports - animal products, cotton, gold, livestock (cattle, goats, sheep), oilseeds, and shea nuts

Imports - agricultural equipment, consumer goods, dairy products, food, fuel, and machinery

LIFE-STYLE

Burkina Faso is approximately nine-tenths rural. It has two main cultural groups: the Voltaic and the Mande. The Voltaic group consists of the Mossi, the Bobo, the Gurunsi, and the Lobi peoples. The Mande group consists of the Boussance, the Marka, the Samo, and the Senufo peoples. The Mossi peoples make up about half of the country's population. They work as farmers and live in groups of mud-brick huts, called *yiris*, which surround small courts. The courts are used to pen goats and sheep. The Bobo peoples live in castlelike houses constructed of clay brick walls with straw roofs. The Lobi peoples are good hunters and farmers, and many of them now work as migrant laborers in urban areas. The country is also home to Fulani and Tuareg nomads, who travel the northern grazing areas with their livestock.

Many of Burkina Faso's young men make a living working on cocoa and coffee plantations in the neighboring countries of Ghana and Ivory Coast. They usually stay for two to three years, and send money home to their families.

Education in Burkina Faso is officially mandatory, but only about 15 percent of the children attend elementary school and only about two percent continue on to high school. Therefore, only about one-tenth of the country's population is literate.

The country has very poor health conditions due to improper sanitation and living conditions. Pests, such as the tsetse fly and the simulium fly, spread sleeping sickness and *onchocerciasis* (river blindness). The population, especially children, suffer from malnutrition. Other illnesses include leprosy, meningitis, trachoma, and schistosomiasis. Due to the fact that the country has few medical doctors, the people receive little or no medical care.

IT'S A FACT!

Aiguille de Sindou - the country's highest point, rises 2,352 ft. (717 m) above sea level.

Ouagadougou - the country's capital, is home to a number of *mosques* (Islamic houses of worship); the University of Ouagadougou, which is the country's only university; and, the palace of the *Moro Naba* (the traditional leader of the country's Mossi people).

 DID YOU KNOW...

- *Burkina Faso* means "land of the honest people"?
- Burkina Faso was once part of French West Africa until it gained its independence in 1960?
- Up until 1984, Burkina Faso was known as Upper Volta?
- Almost one-half of the country's population is under the age of 15?

BURUNDI

OFFICIAL NAME: République Du Burundi
FORMERLY: Urundi, the southern half of what was once Ruanda-Urundi (until 1962)
LOCATION: East-central Africa
AREA: 10,747 sq. mi. (27,834 sq. km)
POPULATION (Est. 1993): 5,981,000
CAPITAL/LARGEST CITY: Bujumbura
GOVERNMENT: One-party republic headed by a president who is advised by a group of military officers called the Military Committee for National Redemption.
FLAG: Two white diagonal lines that meet in the middle to form a circle, in which are three red stars. Above and below the center, the areas are red. To the left and right of the center, the areas are green.
ETHNIC GROUPS: Hutu (Bahutu), Tutsi (Watusi), Twa Pygmy
LANGUAGES: Kirundi, French, Swahili
RELIGIONS: Roman Catholic, Traditional African Religions, Protestant
BASIC MONETARY UNIT: Burundi Franc

GEOGRAPHY

Burundi, a landlocked country, measures 150 mi. (241 km) from north to south and 135 mi. (217 km) from east to west at its greatest distances.

Northwestern Burundi rises from a valley to over 8,800 ft. (2,680 m) above sea level; western Burundi borders the Great Rift Valley, Lake Tanganyika, and the Rusizi River; central and eastern Burundi are bordered by steep slopes and swamps; and southern Burundi is covered by a highland region. Because of heavy rainfall, erosion, and poor farming methods, the country's soil is very poor.

CLIMATE

Although located just south of the equator, Burundi's high elevations give it a cool, pleasant climate. The Great Rift Valley region has an average annual temperature of 73°F (23°C) and an average annual rainfall of 30 in. (76 cm). The western region has an average annual temperature of 63°F (17°C) and an average annual rainfall of 58 in. (147 cm). The plateaus have an average annual temperature of 68°F (20°C) and an average annual rainfall of 47 in. (119 cm). The country's rainy season generally occurs during the months of February through May.

ECONOMY

Burundi has a poor economy due to few minerals and little industry.

Agriculture - bananas, beans, cassava, cattle, coffee, corn, cotton, dry beans and peas, goats, millet, sheep, sweet potatoes, sorghum, and tea

Fishing - freshwater fish

Manufacturing - bananas, beer, cement, cigarettes, cotton textiles, cosmetics, insecticides, paint, palm oil, pottery, processed coffee and tea, shoes, and soap

Mining - gold, kaolin clay, lime, nickel, and peat

Exports - cattle, coffee, cotton, hides, and tea

Imports - food and petroleum products

LIFE-STYLE

Burundi, one of the smallest and most crowded African countries, is almost entirely rural. The Hutu are mainly farmers, raising only enough food to feed their families. Many Tutsi raise cattle and other livestock. They also control the country's government, military, and most of the country's wealth. The Twa Pygmy, once hunters and berry collectors, now raise crops and make pottery.

Education is free, but only about one-fourth of primary school-aged children attend school.

Burundi has few doctors and poor health conditions with widespread diseases such as dysentery, malaria, measles, and pulmonary tuberculosis.

Burundi's culture is passed on through oral literature that includes fables, legends, poetry, songs, and stories. Their musical instruments include the *dingidi* (single-stringed fiddle), the *ikimbe* (linguaphone), and the *inanga* (harp). The country's folk dancing—especially that of the Tutsi people—is internationally famous.

IT'S A FACT!

Ruvubu River Basin - located on Burundi's plateau, contains the southernmost extension of the Nile Basin.

 DID YOU KNOW...
- Most of Burundi's roads are unpaved and the country has no railroads?
- Burundi is one of Africa's most densely populated countries, with approximately 557 persons per sq. mi. (215 persons per sq. km)?

CAMBODIA

OFFICIAL NAME: Roat Kampuchea (State of Cambodia)
LOCATION: Southeast Asia
AREA: 69,898 sq. mi. (181,035 sq. km)
POPULATION (Est. 1993): 8,802,000
CAPITAL/LARGEST CITY: Phnom Penh
GOVERNMENT: Constitutional monarchy with king as head of state. In practice, two prime ministers share powers as head of government.
FLAG: A white map of the country on a background of dark blue. The country's name is written in blue Khmer script in the center of the map.
ETHNIC GROUPS: Cambodian (Khmer), Vietnamese, Chinese
LANGUAGES: Khmer, French
RELIGIONS: Buddhism, Islam
BASIC MONETARY UNIT: Riel

GEOGRAPHY

Cambodia is a circular-shaped country with 220 mi. (354 km) of coastline on the Gulf of Thailand. It measures 280 mi. (451 km) from north to south and 350 mi. (563 km) from east to west at its greatest distances. Mountains border the country in the north and southwest. The center of the country is a fertile plain formed by the Mekong River basin and Tonle Sap Lake. Forests cover about two-thirds of the land.

CLIMATE

Cambodia has a tropical climate with a rainy, monsoon season (May to October) and a dry season (December to March). Temperatures range from 80° to 100°F (26° to 38°C). The coast receives almost 200 in. (510 cm) of rain yearly. The area around Phnom Penh gets less than 60 in. (150 cm) of rain annually.

ECONOMY

Two decades of war have virtually destroyed Cambodia's economy. Today, the economy is based chiefly on agriculture, although food shortages are common.
Agriculture - cattle, corn, rice, rubber, and soybeans
Manufacturing - cement, paper, plywood, processed rice and fish, rubber tires, and textiles
Natural Resources - gemstones, iron ore, manganese, phosphate, and timber
Exports - fish, pepper, rice, rubber, and wood
Imports - consumer goods, food, fuel, and machinery

LIFE-STYLE

Most Cambodians live in small rural villages of only 100 to 400 people and work on nearby rice paddies. Farmers have few modern tools with which to work their small farms. The country has few factories and must import most of its needed manufactured goods.

Because so many men died during the wars, there are a large number of orphans, widows, and single-parent families. The average two-parent family has four children, but the family often adopts orphans or cares for foster children. Many generations may live together under one roof. The family (or group or community) is considered more important than the individual. Many houses in Cambodian villages are built on stilts to provide protection during the rainy season.

Western-style clothing is quite common in Cambodia, particularly in Phnom Penh, though it is not up-to-date. Women may wear the traditional *sampot* and *sarong*, and men the *sarong soet*. (Each one is a long, rectangular, colored cloth wrapped around like a skirt or kilt.) Young women may also wear small, colored hats.

Eating utensils used—chopsticks, spoons, or fingers—depend on the type of food served. Rice is the staple of the diet. Most meals include both rice and soup. Soup may include fish, eggs, vegetables, meat, and a spicy broth. Vegetables and a wide variety of fruits are common throughout the year, as are seafood and fish.

Only about half of the population aged 15 and older is literate. Adequate schools, books, and other materials are not available in many parts of Cambodia. But literacy is rising as many schools reopen.

Cambodians lack proper medical care. Sanitation is poor and running water is available only in some hotels. Diseases from mosquitoes and water, such as malaria, hepatitis, and internal parasites, are common. Many people still suffer from wounds received by stepping on long-forgotten mines.

After years of war, few theaters and sports facilities are in existence. The people enjoy soccer, ping pong, volleyball, and badminton. Leisure activities include singing, dancing, picnics, playing cards, and bicycling or motorcycling.

IT'S A FACT!

Angkor Wat - the largest religious building in the world, was built in the 12th century and today is the national symbol of Cambodia.

 DID YOU KNOW...
- Buddhist places of worship and religious education in Cambodia are called *pagodas*?
- The average life expectancy in Cambodia is 50 years?

CAMEROON

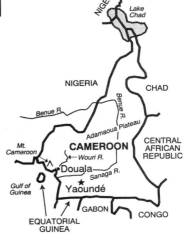

OFFICIAL NAME: République du Cameroun (Republic of Cameroon)
FORMERLY: French Cameroun (until 1960)
LOCATION: West-central Africa
AREA: 183,569 sq. mi. (475,442 sq. km)
POPULATION (Est. 1993): 13,089,000
CAPITAL: Yaoundé
LARGEST CITIES: Douala, Yaoundé
GOVERNMENT: Unitary republic, multiparty presidential regime.
FLAG: Three vertical stripes of green, red, and yellow with a five-pointed, yellow star centered on the red stripe.
ETHNIC GROUPS: Bamiléké, Fulani, Douala, Ewondo, Fang, others (about 200 total)
LANGUAGES: African languages (about 54 total), English, French
RELIGIONS: Traditional African Religions, Christianity, Islam
BASIC MONETARY UNIT: CFA Franc

GEOGRAPHY

At its greatest distances, Cameroon measures 770 mi. (1,239 km) from north to south and 450 mi. (724 km) from east to west. It has 250 mi. (400 km) of coastline along the Gulf of Guinea.

Cameroon has tropical lowlands along the coast in the south. In the central region is the forested Adamaoua Plateau, north of which is a savanna. The western border is comprised of hills and mountains and Lake Chad lies on the northern border. The country has three main rivers: the Benue, the Sanaga, and the Wouri.

CLIMATE

Cameroon's climate ranges from tropical along the coast to hot and dry in the north. The coast has an average annual temperature of 80°F (27°C), and some portions of the region may receive as much as 200 in. (500 cm) of rainfall per year. The savanna region has an average temperature of 82°F (28°C), but daytime temperatures may reach 120°F (49°C). The Adamaoua Plateau has an average temperature of about 75°F (24°C).

ECONOMY

Cameroon has a developing economy based primarily on agriculture, which employs about three-fourths of the population.

Agriculture - bananas, cacao beans, cassava, coffee, corn, cotton, millet, peanuts, and root crops

Forestry - palm oil, rubber, and timber

Manufacturing - agricultural raw materials, aluminum products, beer, cigarettes, cocoa, petroleum products, shoes, soap, and soft drinks

Mining - bauxite and petroleum

Exports - aluminum, cocoa, coffee, cotton, petroleum, and timber

Imports - food, consumer goods, machinery, and transportation equipment

LIFE-STYLE

Cameroon's population is about three-fifths rural, with most residents living in villages or small towns and employed in farming or herding. Those in the mountain region usually live in square, brick shelters, while those in the south live in rectangular shelters constructed of clay, palm leaves, and wood. Along the coastal region, people live in wooden dwellings covered with metal sheets or tree bark, while northern village dwellers live in round clay huts or rectangular brick shelters. Some herders live in light shelters of poles and woven mats. Each year, many rural dwellers move to urban areas in search of jobs. The urban population is employed mainly in manufacturing and service industries. Urban homes range from slums to modern houses and apartments. Of the country's main ethnic groups, the Bamiléké live in the mountain region, the Fulani live in the north, and the Douala, the Ewondo, and the Fang live in the central and southern regions.

Staples of the diet include cassava, corn, millet, peanuts, plantains, and yams. Two common dishes are *fufu* (a stiff paste made of boiled cassava, corn, or millet), and *garri* (grated cassava dried over a fire until light and flaky). Beer is a popular beverage and is sometimes consumed in place of water.

Soccer is the most popular sport. In schools and cities, team sports include basketball, handball, and volleyball. Leisure activities include dancing, listening to music, and playing traditional board games that use pebbles or seeds. Cameroonian artists are known for their woodcarving, which includes building decorations, ceremonial masks, and small statues.

Public education is free, but many children do not attend because of a shortage of schools and teachers. Only around 40 percent of the adults are literate.

IT'S A FACT!

Mount Cameroon - the country's highest point, rises 13,353 ft. (4,070 m) above sea level.

 DID YOU KNOW...

- For special occasions, such as weddings, some Cameroonian women use henna to draw intricate designs on their arms and legs?

- Large families are common in Cameroon, and rural families may have as many as ten children?

- Rock carvings and stone tools have been found in the area, giving Cameroon a history that dates back to prehistoric times?

- Though many free-roaming, wild animals of southern Cameroon have been killed, many animals, such as antelope, elephants, giraffes, and monkeys can now be found at Waza National Park, a wildlife reserve in the north?

CANADA

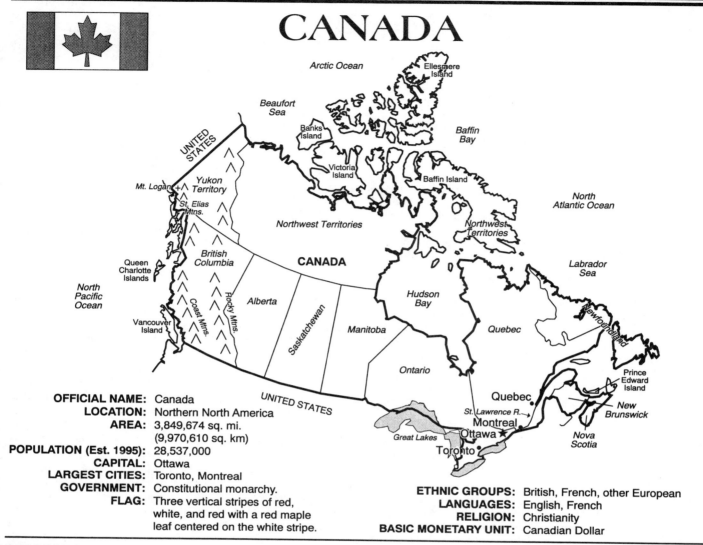

OFFICIAL NAME: Canada
LOCATION: Northern North America
AREA: 3,849,674 sq. mi.
(9,970,610 sq. km)
POPULATION (Est. 1995): 28,537,000
CAPITAL: Ottawa
LARGEST CITIES: Toronto, Montreal
GOVERNMENT: Constitutional monarchy.
FLAG: Three vertical stripes of red,
white, and red with a red maple
leaf centered on the white stripe.

ETHNIC GROUPS: British, French, other European
LANGUAGES: English, French
RELIGION: Christianity
BASIC MONETARY UNIT: Canadian Dollar

GEOGRAPHY

Stretching from the North Atlantic Ocean on the east to the North Pacific Ocean on the west, Canada is the second largest country in the world, after Russia. Because much of the terrain in Canada is very rugged and the climate is severe, about 75 percent of the people live on or near its southern border. The far west region of Canada contains lush green forests and towering mountains. Inland, crops of wheat and other grains cover Canada's vast prairies. The northern part of Canada consists of frozen land called tundra. The southern central portion of Canada around the Great Lakes and the St. Lawrence River is where the largest concentrations of the population and industrial centers are located. Fishing villages and sandy beaches are found in the east, along the Atlantic coast.

Canada is divided into provinces and territories. They are the provinces of Newfoundland, New Brunswick, Prince Edward Island, Nova Scotia, Quebec, Ontario, Alberta, Saskatchewan, Manitoba, British Columbia; and the Yukon Territory and the Northwest Territories.

Canada has eight major land regions: 1) the Pacific Ranges and Lowlands, 2) the Rocky Mountains, 3) the Arctic Islands, 4) the Interior Plains, 5) the Canadian Shield, 6) the Hudson Bay Lowlands, 7) the St. Lawrence Lowlands, and 8) the Appalachian Region.

The Pacific Ranges and Lowlands make up Canada's westernmost land region. They comprise most of British Columbia and the southwestern part of the Yukon Territory. The region includes the Coast Mountains and the St. Elias Mountains. East of the Coast Mountains lies the Interior Plateau, an area of smaller mountains, plus plains, rivers, valleys, and forests. Many farms and orchards as well as grasslands for cattle grazing are found here.

The Rocky Mountains are found east of the Pacific Ranges and Lowlands. Juniper and pine forests grow on the lower elevations, while firs and spruces can be found higher up the mountains.

The Arctic Islands, found almost exclusively within the Arctic Circle, are a dozen, large barren islands and hundreds of smaller ones, most of which are unexplored. These islands are *tundras*—places too cold and dry for trees to grow. Baffin Island and Ellesmere Island, two of the largest islands, have many glaciers.

The Interior Plains take in the northeastern corner of British Columbia, large portions of Alberta and Saskatchewan, as well as the southwestern part of Manitoba. Grasslands, forests, and tundras cover the land.

The Canadian Shield is a large region that envelops the Hudson Bay from the Arctic coast of the Northwest Territories to the mainland of Newfoundland. About half of Canada makes up this region of low hills and thousands of lakes.

Between the Canadian Shield and the southwestern coast of the Hudson Bay lies the flat, swampy region of the Hudson Bay Lowlands. Forests of poor quality and deposits of decayed vegetable matter called *peat* cover much of the region.

The smallest of the land regions—the St. Lawrence Lowlands—is inhabited by about 55 percent of the people. The region consists of farmland, deciduous forests, and a section of wilderness. Because of easy access to U.S. markets and excellent transportation facilities, this region has become the manufacturing center of Canada.

The Appalachian Region encompasses southeastern Quebec and all of the Atlantic Provinces region except Labrador. The terrain is mostly hilly. Evergreen and deciduous forests cover the majority of this region. The area also has farmland.

CLIMATE

Canada's northern location gives it a cold climate overall, but with much variation from region to region. Most of Canada experiences long, cold winters. January temperatures average below 0°F (-18°C) in over two-thirds of the country, while the coastal areas around British Columbia average January temperatures above 32°F (0°C). Northern Canada has short, cool summers with July temperatures averaging about 40°F (4°C). Southern Canada has summers that are warm enough and long enough to grow crops, with average July temperatures of 70°F (21°C) or more. Rainfall in Canada varies widely from region to region. The coastal areas along the Pacific receive more than 80 in. (200 cm) of rain per year, while the Canadian prairies average about 10-20 in. (25-50 cm) of rain per year.

ECONOMY

Canada is rich in natural resources. It leads in producing the most newsprint and it ranks as a leader in the production of hydroelectric power. Service industries and manufacturing are its main economic activities. Foreign investment and ownership have also had a great influence on Canada's economy.

Agriculture - beef cattle, canola, chickens, eggs, hogs, milk, and wheat

Fishing - cod, lobster, and salmon

Forestry - fir, pine, and spruce

Manufacturing - aluminum, chemicals, electrical equipment, fabricated metal products, food products, motor vehicles and parts, paper products, petroleum products, steel, and wood products

Mining - coal, copper, gold, iron ore, natural gas, petroleum, uranium, and zinc

Exports - fish, metals, natural gas, newsprint, petroleum, wheat and other crops, wood and wood products

Imports - chemicals, computers, durable consumer goods, motor vehicles and parts, petroleum, and telecommunications equipment

LIFE-STYLE

Canadians have a life-style very similar to that of their southern neighbors in the United States. About 77 percent of the population reside in urban areas, nearly half of them living in rented apartments. People who live in rural areas work in industries such as fishing, mining, lumbering, or farming. Farms are primarily family owned and, with the help of modern machinery, most of the work is done by family members.

Education is available to all, provided free by each province and territory. Each school system requires at least eight years of schooling, beginning at age six or seven.

Because of the long winters, Canadians take part in a number of snow-related sports such as skiing, skating, sledding, tobogganing, and snowshoeing. Summer sports include golf, tennis, swimming, hiking, and so on. The most popular professional sport in Canada is ice hockey. Canada also has professional football, baseball, and soccer teams. Canadians also enjoy attending concerts and plays and visiting museums and parks.

A typical meal for Canadians includes beef, bread, potatoes, and vegetables. Soup is often served with lunch and dinner.

Canada has two official languages, English and French. About one-fourth of the people speak mainly French, and most of these people live in Quebec.

IT'S A FACT!

Mount Logan - Canada's highest point, rises 19,524 ft. (5,951 m) above sea level.

Quetico Provincial Park - a wilderness park in southwestern Ontario, has canoe routes that connect with routes in Minnesota.

St. Lawrence River - is referred to as the "Mother of Canada" because it was the primary route of the original European explorers, fur traders, and colonists who came to Canada. It flows about 800 mi. (1,300 km) from Lake Ontario to the Gulf of St. Lawrence. As part of the St. Lawrence Seaway, it moves more freight than any other Canadian river.

DID YOU KNOW...

- Amherstburg, located in Ontario, is an old Loyalist settlement where British settlers made their homes in 1796?
- Old Fort Henry is a living museum of British and Canadian military history?
- The name *Canada* probably comes from an Iroquois Indian word meaning "to the village" or "to the small house"?
- Serpent Mounds Provincial Park, located on the shore of Rice Lake, contains a burial mound that measures 200 ft. (60 m) long?
- Bowmanville Museum displays toys that children played with over 100 years ago?
- Quebec is Canada's oldest city?
- Toronto is considered the commercial center of Canada?

CANARY ISLANDS
Province of Spain

North Atlantic Ocean

CANARY ISLANDS

OFFICIAL NAME:	Islas Canarias (Canary Islands)
LOCATION:	North Atlantic Ocean
AREA:	2,796 sq. mi. (7,242 sq. km)
POPULATION (Est. 1993):	1,445,000
CAPITALS:	Santa Cruz de Tenerife (Western Province); Las Palmas de Gran Canaria (Eastern Province)
LARGEST CITY:	Las Palmas
ETHNIC GROUP:	Spanish/Guanches
LANGUAGE:	Castilian
RELIGION:	Roman Catholic
BASIC MONETARY UNIT:	Peseta

GEOGRAPHY

The Canary Islands form an archipelago approximately 60 mi. (97 km) off mainland Africa's northwest coast. They have 626 mi. (1,007 km) of coastline along the North Atlantic Ocean.

The Canary Islands are made up of 13 islands—seven of which are inhabited—forming two provinces. The western province is called Province of Santa Cruz de Tenerife and includes the inhabited islands of Gomera, Hierro, La Palma, and Tenerife. The eastern province is called Province of Las Palmas and includes the inhabited islands of Fuerteventura, Gran Canaria, and Lanzarote. The largest of the islands is Tenerife. The islands have fertile soil and mountainous terrain. Many of the mountains are volcanic.

CLIMATE

The Canary Islands have a subtropical climate. Average annual temperatures range from 64°F (18°C) in January to 75°F (24°C) in July. The average annual rainfall is 8 in. (19.6 cm) per year. Sunshine is abundant in all seasons.

ECONOMY

The Canary Islands' economy includes agriculture, fishing, and tourism.

Agriculture - bananas, flowers and plants, fruit, grain, tomatoes, and other vegetables

Forestry - timber

Manufacturing - canning, chemical products, cork, footwear, leatherwork, metal products, petroleum refining, and textiles

Exports - tomatoes

Imports - cereals

LIFE-STYLE

Canarios are hardly distinguishable from the people of Spain, and they follow the same customs.

Fish and grains are the staples of the diet of the poorer people. Fish is often served with potatoes and *mojo picón* (a piquant sauce). Anchovy, cuttlefish, mackerel, and sardines are caught locally. Grains are often served in the form of *go fio* (barley, corn, or wheat roasted, salted, ground, and kneaded with milk or water).

Education has progressed rapidly since 1900, when 80 percent of the Canarios could neither read nor write. Now, good schools are numerous and there is a university at La Laguna, Tenerife.

IT'S A FACT!

Pico de Teide - the country's highest point, is located on Tenerife Island and rises 12,198 ft. (3,718 m) above sea level.

 DID YOU KNOW...

- The original inhabitants of the Canary Islands were a people called the Gaunches, who no longer exist as a separate race?
- The Canary Islands are used as a refueling point for ships traveling down West Africa's coast?
- The islands were named from the Latin word *canis*, meaning "dog," because ancients who discovered the islands found them inhabited by large, fierce dogs?
- Canary birds were so named because they were first discovered on the Canary Islands?
- Camels are used as draft animals on the Canary Islands?
- Up until 1927, the Canary Islands formed one province, with the current separation into two provinces caused by disputes between the two ports, Santa Cruz de Tenerife and Las Palmas de Gran Canaria?

CAPE VERDE

OFFICIAL NAME: República de Cabo Verde (Republic of Cape Verde)
LOCATION: Atlantic Ocean
AREA: 1,577 sq. mi. (4,033 sq. km)
POPULATION (Est. 1993): 409,000
CAPITAL: Praia
LARGEST CITIES: Praia, Mindelo
GOVERNMENT: Republic governed by a president.
FLAG: A black star and a yellow seashell, framed by two curved cornstalks, lie on a red vertical stripe on the hoist side. Two horizontal stripes of yellow and green are on the fly side.
ETHNIC GROUPS: Creole, African, European
LANGUAGES: Portuguese, Crioulo
RELIGIONS: Roman Catholic, Animism
BASIC MONETARY UNIT: Escudo

CAPE VERDE

North Atlantic Ocean

GEOGRAPHY

Cape Verde is a crescent-shaped archipelago of 15 islands (10 main islands, 5 islets) in the Atlantic Ocean. It lies approximately 400 mi. (640 km) west of Senegal on the African mainland.

The largest island, Saõ Tiago, covers 383 sq. mi. (992 sq. km). The islands were formed by volcanic eruptions 2.5 to 65 million years ago. Most of the islands are mountainous with tall cliffs along the coast and little, if any, plant life. In the interior valleys, some large areas of tropical vegetation exists. The five islets and one main island, Santa Luzia, are uninhabited.

CLIMATE

The country has a warm, dry climate. Temperatures average 75°F (24°C) throughout the year. The rainy season is from July to November, but there are many years with no rainfall.

ECONOMY

Cape Verde has an underdeveloped economy. Fishing and farming, the primary occupations, offer only a bare income.

Agriculture - bananas, beans, cassava, cattle, coffee beans, corn, goats, pigs, potatoes, sheep, sugar cane, sweet potatoes, and tomatoes

Fishing - lobsters and tuna

Manufacturing - fish processing and salt refining

Mining - pozzuolana and salt

Exports - bananas, fish, and salt

Imports - foodstuffs, machinery and transport equipment, and petroleum products

LIFE-STYLE

Almost three-fourths of all Cape Verdeans have mixed black African and Portuguese ancestry. The remainder are mainly black Africans. The country has an extremely low standard of living because there is not enough available work. Since the mid-1900s, as many as 700,000 Cape Verdeans have emigrated to the United States, Europe, Brazil, Portugal, and other countries. The money they send home continues to help the economy.

The majority of those who remain on Cape Verde are subsistence farmers, although most of the land is too dry for farming. Since the late 1960s, agricultural production has dropped about 90 percent and most livestock have died due to droughts. Today, the country receives food aid from the United Nations and financial aid from a variety of countries.

Cape Verde has approximately 500 elementary schools and several high school and technical schools. About half of those aged 14 or older are literate.

The country has about 920 mi. (1,480 km) of roads, no railroads, and one airport. Boats operate among the islands only occasionally. There are three radio stations and two newspapers in Cape Verde.

IT'S A FACT!

Pico do Fogo - the country's highest point and only active volcano, rises 9,281 ft. (2,829 m) above sea level. It last erupted in 1951.

 DID YOU KNOW...

- *Pozzuolana* is a volcanic rock used by the cement industry?
- While most of the people of Cape Verde are Roman Catholics, many practice *animism*, the belief that everything in nature has a soul?
- Animal life on the islands is limited to farm animals?
- The waters around the archipelago are clear, have fish of all species, and are great for underwater fishing?
- In 1460, Portuguese explorers discovered the Cape Verde islands? They soon began to settle there and brought in slaves from Africa to work the fields.

CAYMAN ISLANDS
Dependency of the United Kingdom

OFFICIAL NAME: Cayman Islands
LOCATION: Northwestern Caribbean Sea
AREA: 100 sq. mi. (259 sq. km)
POPULATION (Est. 1993): 30,440
CAPITAL/LARGEST CITY: George Town
GOVERNMENT: British dependency; a governor represents the British monarch.
FLAG: Blue field with the flag of the United Kingdom in the upper hoist-side quadrant. The Caymanian coat of arms on a white disk is centered on the flag's outer half. The coat of arms bears a pineapple, a turtle, a shield with three stars—representing the three islands—and a scroll bearing the motto, "He Hath Founded It upon the Seas."
ETHNIC GROUPS: Mixed, Black, European
LANGUAGE: English
RELIGIONS: United Church (Presbyterian and Congregational), Anglican, Baptist, Roman Catholic, Church of God
BASIC MONETARY UNIT: Cayman Islands Dollar

Caribbean Sea

CAYMAN ISLANDS

Cayman Brac

Little Cayman

George Town

Grand Cayman

Caribbean Sea

GEOGRAPHY

The Cayman Islands consists of three islands—Grand Cayman, Little Cayman, and Cayman Brac—which lie 200 mi. (320 km) northwest of Jamaica, and have a combined coastline of 99 mi. (160 km) along the Caribbean Sea. The largest of the islands is Grand Cayman with an area of 76 sq. mi. (197 sq. km). It is home to the country's capital. Cayman Brac is the second largest in area and has the highest elevation, which is located on the island's plateau and reaches 138 ft. (42 m) above sea level. The islands are generally low-lying and the coasts are reefed and rocky. Cayman Brac contains a central limestone bluff. About 30 percent of the Cayman Islands' area is covered by mangrove swamps.

CLIMATE

The Cayman Islands have a tropical climate with a warm, rainy summer season—May to October—and a cool, relatively dry winter season—November to April. Average summer temperatures range from 75° to 90°F (24° to 32°C). Average winter temperatures range from 61° to 75°F (16° to 24°C). The average annual rainfall is 56 in. (142 cm). Hurricane season generally lasts from July to November.

ECONOMY

The Cayman Islands' main export is turtle products. Because of extremely low taxes, many foreign companies conduct business on the Cayman Islands. These businesses, along with tourism and off-shore banking, are the basis for the country's economy.

Agriculture - bananas, coconuts, livestock, mangoes, plantains, sweet potatoes, tomatoes, turtle farming, and yams

Manufacturing - turtle products (mainly food, leather, and shell)

Exports - honey, jewelry, manufactured consumer goods, shrimp, and turtle products

Imports - food, fuel, machinery, manufactured goods, and transport equipment

LIFE-STYLE

Most of the country's population lives on Grand Cayman in the capital city. Only a small percentage of Caymanians are occupied by agriculture. Most work in clerical or service jobs or in construction. Children between the ages of four years, nine months and 16 are required to attend school. Primary education is provided free. The islands contain a middle school and two high schools. Further education is available at the Community College and at the International College of the Cayman Islands.

For leisure, community organizations hold art exhibits and theater performances. Craftwork is popular, including the making of jewelry from black coral.

The Cayman Islands were first sighted by Columbus in 1503, at which time they had no inhabitants. The islands were originally named *Las Tortugas* because of the large number of turtles in the surrounding waters. Sometime between 1527 and 1530, the islands' name changed to Cayman, from the Spanish *caimán* meaning "alligator," possibly a mistaken references to the islands' iguanas.

 DID YOU KNOW...

- The Cayman Islands were once a favorite hideaway for pirates and buccaneers?
- The Cayman Islands were a dependency of Jamaica until 1959 and became a British dependency in 1962?
- The Cayman Islands' white sand beaches are composed mainly of coral, thus making them cool to the touch even on the hottest days?
- The islands' only indigenous mammal is the *agouti* (a burrowing rodent)?

CENTRAL AFRICAN REPUBLIC

OFFICIAL NAME: République Centrafricaine
(Central African Republic)
FORMERLY: French Equatorial Africa
LOCATION: Central Africa
AREA: 240,535 sq. mi. (622,984 sq. km)
POPULATION (Est. 1993): 3,310,000
CAPITAL: Bangui
LARGEST CITIES: Bangui, Berbérati, Bouar, Bambari
GOVERNMENT: Republic under military rule.
FLAG: Four horizontal stripes of blue, white, green, and yellow bisected by a vertical red stripe. Red, white, and blue recall the French flag; green, yellow, and red represent the people and their unity; and a yellow star represents the guiding light of the future.
ETHNIC GROUPS: Baya, Banda, Bwaka, Mandjia, Sara
LANGUAGES: French, Sango, local dialects
RELIGIONS: Christianity, Islam, Traditional African Religions
BASIC MONETARY UNIT: CFA Franc

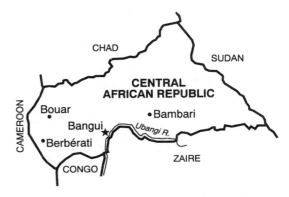

GEOGRAPHY

The Central African Republic is a thinly populated, land-locked country. Much of the land is a huge, rolling plateau broken by deep river valleys. The average elevation of the plateau is 2,000-3,000 ft. (600-900 m). Most of the land is covered by a savanna, but in the southwest there are areas of tropical rainforests.

CLIMATE

Central African Republic has a tropical climate. The average temperature is 80°F (27°C). In the north, the average rainfall is 31.5 in. (80 cm) per year. The south receives an average of 63 in. (160 cm) of rainfall annually. There are two seasons: rainy (March to October) and dry (November to February).

ECONOMY

Central African Republic is one of the most underdeveloped countries in Africa. Most of the people farm for a living.

Agriculture - bananas, coffee, cotton, goats, guavas, mangoes, manioc, palm kernels, papayas, peanuts, pigs, poultry, rubber, sesame, sheep, and yams

Forestry - timber

Manufacturing/Industries - hides and skins tanning, raw cotton, sawmills, soap, textiles, and vegetable oils

Mining - diamonds, gold, and uranium

Exports - coffee, cotton, diamonds, oil, palm kernels, timber, and tobacco

Imports - cotton textiles, machinery, and motor vehicles

LIFE-STYLE

About half of the country's people live in rural areas in villages. Traditional housing is a mostly round hut with walls of mud and sticks topped by a conical thatched roof. Today, larger rectangular huts are being built. They have walls of dried mud, grass mats, or planks. Roofs may be constructed of thatch or sheets of corrugated iron.

The staple of the diet is a porridge made from manioc flour. Manioc porridge is eaten with a vegetable sauce called *gombo* and with meat or fish bits. Chickens and pigs are the main source of meat. Fish is eaten dried or smoked. Tropical fruits, such as mangoes, papayas, and guavas are available throughout the year. Beverages include beer, brewed from millet, and palm wine, which is made for special feasts. Some rural Central Africans also gather insects and caterpillars for food.

Most men wear Western-style clothes. Women wear *wraparounds* (colorful garments) with head kerchiefs. Ornaments of copper and iron wire worn around the neck, wrists, or ankles can be seen in the interior of the country.

Wildlife is abundant in the Central African Republic. Buffalo, elephants, giraffes, hyenas, jackals, and lions roam the open spaces. Chimpanzees, baboons, and some gorillas inhabit the rainforest in the southern part of the country. Crocodiles, hippotomuses, colorful birds, reptiles, and insects also are seen.

Most older people cannot read or write and only about 40 percent of the children receive an elementary education. The country also has secondary schools and one university.

There are no railroads and the country's waters are only infrequently navigable. Air transport, however, is well-developed.

 DID YOU KNOW...
- Huge termite mounds of red and yellow earth are seen throughout the countryside?
- There are few cattle in the country because of the tsetse fly, which spreads the African sleeping sickness?

CHAD

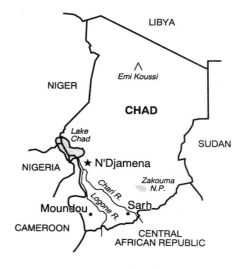

OFFICIAL NAME: République du Tchad
(Republic of Chad)
LOCATION: North-Central Africa
AREA: 496,000 sq. mi. (1,284,000 sq. km)
POPULATION (Est. 1995): 6,361,000
CAPITAL: N'Djamena
LARGEST CITIES: N'Djamena, Sarh, Moundou
GOVERNMENT: Republic governed by a president.
FLAG: Three vertical stripes of blue, yellow, and red representing sky and hope, the sun, and fire and unity, respectively.
ETHNIC GROUPS: Arab, African Toubou, Sara
LANGUAGES: French, Arabic, Sara, Sango, other local languages
RELIGIONS: Islam, Christianity, Traditional African Religions
BASIC MONETARY UNIT: CFA Franc

GEOGRAPHY

Chad, a landlocked country, measures 1,097 mi. (1,765 km) from north to south and 640 mi. (1,030 km) from east to west at its greatest distances. Northern Chad—home to the Tibesti mountain range—consists of desert and rocky plateaus; central Chad is a savanna; and southern Chad contains the country's richest farmland. Chad has several rivers, most of which are found in the southern portion of the country. The largest of these are the Chari and the Logone Rivers, which flow from the south, meet in N'Djamena, and flow into Lake Chad to the northwest.

CLIMATE

Chad's climate ranges from desertlike in the north to tropical in the south. The northern region has an average annual temperature often reaching 120°F (49°C) and receives less than 5 in. (13 cm) of rain per year. Central and southern Chad have an average annual temperature of 82°F (28°C) with an average annual rainfall of 25 in. (64 cm) and 40 in. (100 cm), respectively.

ECONOMY

Chad is one of the world's most underdeveloped countries due to poor economic resources and its almost constant state of civil war since the mid-1960s.

Agriculture - cattle, cotton, millet, peanuts, rice, and sorghum

Manufacturing - beer, cigarettes, cotton and cotton oil processing, natron (sodium carbonate), peanut processing, soap, and textiles

Mining - natron (sodium carbonate) and uranium

Exports - cattle, cotton, and textiles

Imports - food, industrial goods, machinery and transportation equipment, and petroleum products

LIFE-STYLE

Chad's population is approximately two-thirds rural and one-third urban. Rural Chadians are primarily farmers and wandering herders. Some urban Chadians also work on nearby farms.

The country's northern population consists mainly of Arabic and Toubou cattle traders. Their tentlike homes are constructed of sticks and woven mats. Their clothing usually consists of loose gowns and turbans or small skullcaps for the men

and one-piece, black or light blue robes for the women. For protection against sandstorms, northern Chadian men may wrap long, white scarves around their heads and faces. They eat mostly meat and milk from their herds, but sometimes eat dates and vegetables found in their travels.

Most southern Chadians are farmers. They live in circular adobe, mud, or straw houses with straw roofs. Their clothing commonly consists of cotton shorts or trousers and loose shirts for the men and brightly colored blouses and skirts for the women. The people only occasionally eat meat or vegetables. Instead, their diet consists mostly of millet, sorghum, and rice.

IT'S A FACT!

Emi Koussi - the country's highest point, rises 11,204 ft. (3,415 m) above sea level.

Lake Chad - the country's lowest point, is 922 ft. (281 m) above sea level. Its size changes with the rainy and dry seasons, and it is home to crocodiles, hippopotamuses, and cranes.

Zakouma National Park - a tropical forest region, is located in the southeast and is home to antelope, elephants, lions, and giraffes.

 DID YOU KNOW...
- Chad was ruled by France between 1920 and 1960, after which time the country gained its independence?
- More than 100 different languages and dialects are spoken in Chad?
- Only one-sixth of the adults know how to read and write?
- Chad has no railroads, almost no paved roads, and less than one percent of the population own an automobile?
- Chad has limited communication services and averages only one radio for every four persons and only about one television set for every 850 persons?

IF8201 Comprehensive World Reference Guide

CHANNEL ISLANDS
British Crown Dependencies

OFFICIAL NAME: Îles Normandes; Anglo-Normandes (Channel Islands)
LOCATION: English Channel
AREA: 75 sq. mi. (195 sq. km)
POPULATION: 143,000
LARGEST CITIES: St. Peter Port (Guernsey), St. Helier (Jersey)
GOVERNMENT: Local laws; the chief executive is a lieutenant governor appointed by the British crown (one on Jersey, another on Guernsey).
ETHNIC GROUP: English
LANGUAGE: English
RELIGION: Anglican
BASIC MONETARY UNIT: Guernsey Pound, Jersey Pound

GEOGRAPHY

The Channel Islands form an archipelago in the English Channel, near the Gulf of St.-Malo and about 10-30 mi. (16-48 km) west of France's Cotentin Peninsula. They consist of four main islands, several smaller islands, and some tiny, rocky islets. The four main islands are Alderney, Guernsey, Jersey, and Sark.

Alderney is the northernmost of the Channel Islands and has an area of 3 sq. mi. (7.8 sq. km).

Guernsey is the westernmost of the Channel Islands and has an area of 24 sq. mi. (63 sq. km). Its dependencies include Alderney, Sark, and several smaller islands.

Jersey is the southernmost of the Channel Islands and the largest, with an area of 45 sq. mi. (117 sq. km). It has two dependencies: Les Minquiers and Ecrehous rocks. It has good farmland and many beaches.

Sark has an area of 2 sq. mi. (5.2 sq. km) with cliffs rising on all of its sides.

CLIMATE

The Channel Islands enjoy a mild maritime climate.

ECONOMY

The Channel Islands' economy is based primarily on tourism but also on banking and financial services, and farming.

Agriculture - dairy cattle, flowers, fruit, early potatoes, tomatoes, and other vegetables

Manufacturing - knitted textiles

Exports - flowers, fruit, and vegetables

LIFE-STYLE

Guernsey has a population of about 56,000. It is covered with small farms and fields used in raising the famous tan-and-white Guernsey cattle, which produce rich milk. Greenhouses are used in the growing of tomatoes and several varieties of flowers.

Jersey has a population of about 80,000 and is a popular vacation resort because of its fine, sandy beaches. Farmers raise Jersey cattle and grow early potatoes, tomatoes, and other vegetables.

On the island of Sark, the only motorized vehicles are island tractors. Other forms of transportation include bicycles and horse-drawn carriages.

The islands have been tied to England since the Conquest of 1066 when they became part of the Duchy of Normandy. Loyal to the British Crown, the islands are largely self-governing. Law is based on the different constitutions used by the bailiwicks of Guernsey and Jersey, which have been influenced by Norman laws and local customs. British laws have no influence on the islands unless the law specifically mentions the Channel Islands.

 DID YOU KNOW...

- Sark is the smallest self-governing unit in the United Kingdom?
- The Channel Islands were the only British soil occupied by German troops during World War II?
- The islands of Alderney, Guernsey, and Jersey are famous for their breeds of dairy cattle?

CHILE

OFFICIAL NAME: República de Chile (Republic of Chile)
LOCATION: Southwestern South America
AREA: 292,258 sq. mi. (756,945 sq. km)
POPULATION (Est. 1995): 14,237,000
CAPITAL: Santiago
LARGEST CITIES: Santiago, Valparaíso, Viña del Mar, Concepción
GOVERNMENT: Republic governed by a president.
FLAG: Two horizontal stripes of white and red with a blue square in the upper, hoist-side corner. A white star—representing honor and progress—is centered on the blue square.
ETHNIC GROUPS: Mestizo, Spanish or British, Indian
LANGUAGE: Spanish
RELIGION: Christianity
BASIC MONETARY UNIT: Peso

GEOGRAPHY

Chile is a long, narrow country. It is more than ten times longer than it is wide. At its greatest distances, Chile stretches 2,650 ft. (4,265 km) from north to south, and only 265 mi. (427 km) from east to west. Chile's western border is along the South Pacific Ocean. It is frequently hit by huge waves called *tsunamis*. Chile often has earthquakes since it lies along an earthquake belt. The eastern border is formed by the lofty Andes Mountains.

Chile is made up of a wide variety of landforms. One of the driest places on earth, the Atacama Desert, lies in the north, and one of the rainiest areas is in the south. In the center of Chile lies a series of fertile river basins. Southern Chile has spectacular snow-capped volcanoes, glaciers, and dense forests. Many rocky, windswept islands line the shore of the Archipelago.

CLIMATE

Since Chile lies south of the equator, its seasons are opposite those in North America. Summer lasts from December to late March, and winter from late June to late September. The Northern Desert region may not receive rain for years, but the area is not unusually hot. Along the coast, temperatures average 69°F (20°C) in January and 57°F (14°C) in July. The Central Valley has a mild climate with dry summers and rainy winters. Temperatures average 69°F (20°C) in January and 48°F (9°C) in July. The Archipelago is battered with cold rains, piercing winds, and frequent storms. Temperatures average 59°F (15°C) in January and 46°F (8°C) in July. Parts of the region receive up to 200 in. (508 cm) of rain per year.

ECONOMY

Chile's economy is based on the export of copper and other minerals.

Agriculture - apples, barley, beans, beef cattle, beets, citrus fruits, corn, grapes, nuts, oats, peaches, potatoes, poultry, rice, sheep, sugar, and wheat

Fishing - anchovettas, jack mackerel, and sardines

Manufacturing - beverages, cement, chemicals, clothing, food products, iron and steel, metal products, paper products, textiles, transportation equipment, and wood products

Mining - coal, copper, gold, iron ore, lithium, lead, manganese, molybdenum, petroleum, silver, and sodium nitrate

Exports - copper, chemical products, fish meal, fruits, iron ore, molybdenum, and metal and wood products

Imports - electronic equipment, machinery, manufactured goods, petroleum, vehicles, and wheat

LIFE-STYLE

The majority of Chileans are urban dwellers. The cities have modern skyscrapers, as well as many Spanish-style buildings. They are also known for their *plazas* (public squares), parks, and gardens. Unfortunately, slums called *callampas* (mushrooms) sprawl around the edges of the cities. These slums received their name by the way they seem to sprout up overnight. Many of the slum dwellers are people who have left rural areas in search of employment.

Many rural dwellers own their own small farms. Others work as laborers or sharecroppers on large farms

For the most part, Chileans dress in the Western style. Cowboys called *huasos* dress up for special occasions by wearing ponchos, colorful sashes, big, flat-topped hats, leather leggings with fringe, boots, and spurs.

Staples of the diet are bread, beans and potatoes. Meat and fish are eaten quite regularly by most. A traditional dish is *cazuela de ave*, a soup made with chicken, rice, and vegetables.

Soccer is the favorite sport. Skiing is enjoyed by the wealthy. In cities, attending movies, concerts, plays and other performances are popular forms of recreation. In rural areas, people enjoy family outings and visits with neighbors and friends. Two popular resort areas are Viña del Mar, located on the Pacific Coast near Valparaíso, and The Lake Country, an area of snow-capped volcanoes on the western slope of the Andes.

More than 90 percent of Chile's adult population are literate. Education is free and children must attend at least eight years of elementary school.

 DID YOU KNOW...

- Because of its beauty, Chile is often called the Switzerland of South America?
- Chile's name probably came from *chilli*, an Indian word meaning "where the land ends"?
- Some rural areas feature river markets, where merchants bring boatloads of goods to sell?

CHINA

OFFICIAL NAME: Zhonghua Renmin Gongheguo
(People's Republic of China)
CONTINENT: Asia
AREA: 3,696,032 sq. mi. (9,572,678 sq. km)
POPULATION (Est. 1995): 1,238,319,000
CAPITAL: Beijing
LARGEST CITIES: Shanghai, Beijing, Tianjin, Shenyang,
Wuhan, Guangzhou (Canton)
GOVERNMENT: Controlled by Communist Party
FLAG: Five yellow stars on a red background.
The large star represents the leadership
of the Communist Party. The four small
stars stand for groups of workers.

ETHNIC GROUPS: Han Chinese, over 50 minorities
LANGUAGES: Northern Chinese
(Mandarin or *Putonghua*)
RELIGIONS: Confucianism, Taoism, Buddhism
BASIC MONETARY UNIT: Renminbi

GEOGRAPHY

China is the world's third largest country in size and the most populated country on earth. Its terrain varies greatly. China has subarctic regions in the north and tropical lowlands in the south. It has fertile plains in the east and deserts in the west.

China can be divided into eight land regions: 1) the Tibetan Highlands, which lie in southwestern China, consist of a vast plateau bordered by high mountains; 2) the Xinjiang-Mongolian Uplands, which occupy the huge desert areas of northwestern China; 3) the Mongolian Border Uplands, which lie between the Gobi Desert and the Eastern Lowlands, have mountains in the north and fertile, yellowish soil in the south; 4) the Eastern Highlands, which consist of Shandong Peninsula—a hilly region with sea harbors and good deposits of coal—and eastern Manchuria—a region containing China's best forests; 5) the Eastern Lowlands, which lie between the Mongolian Border Uplands and the Eastern Highlands and extend south to the Southern Uplands, contain China's best farmland; 6) the Central Uplands, located between the Eastern Lowlands and the Tibetan Highlands, consist of hills and mountains; 7) the Sichuan Basin lies south of the Central Uplands and consists of hills and valleys surrounded by high mountains; and 8) the Southern Uplands, which cover southeastern China and include the island of Hainan, are a region of green hills and mountains and contains the Xi Jiang (West River) which, with its tributaries, forms the main transportation route for southern China.

CLIMATE

Because China is so large and its landscape so diverse, it has a broad range of contrasting climates. The most extreme weather conditions occur in the Taklimakan and Gobi Deserts, which can have daytime temperatures of more than 100°F (38°C) and nighttime temperatures of -30°F (-34°C). Northern portions of the country may have bitterly cold winters, while southern coastal areas have tropical climates. Monsoons—seasonal winds—greatly affect the weather in China. Winter monsoons send cold, dry air over China from central Asia. These same winds create dust storms in the north, and in late spring to early fall, spread moist, wet air inland from the sea. Summers tend to be hot and humid throughout southern China, with average temperatures of about 80°F (27°C), while winters tend to be very frigid, especially in the north. Average January temperatures in Manchuria and Tibet are below 0°F (-18°C), while the south coast of China averages temperatures over 60°F (16°C). Average July temperatures are above 75°F (24°C) throughout southeastern China and in southern Manchuria. The amount of precipitation varies throughout the country. The deserts of Xinjiang and Inner Mongolia have less than 4 in. (10 cm) of rain yearly. The southeastern part of China receives from 40-80 in. (100-200 cm) of rain yearly. The northern section of China may receive snowfall, although very infrequently and lightly. The amount of precipitation this section receives varies greatly from year to year, though most areas receive less than 40 in. (100 cm).

ECONOMY

China has one of the world's biggest economies, determined by its total economic production, not by economic output per person. It is considered a developing economy, which is controlled by the national government. Economic reforms of the early 1980s which encouraged privately run businesses have led to tremendous economic growth.

Agriculture - barley, cabbages, corn, cotton, eggs, fruit, hogs, millet, peanuts, potatoes, rice, sorghum, soybeans, sweet potatoes, tea, tobacco, tomatoes, and wheat

Manufacturing - cement, chemicals, clothing and textiles, consumer goods, machinery, processed foods, steel, and vehicles

Mining - antimony, coal, gold, iron ore, lead, petroleum, salt, tin, and tungsten

Exports - clothing, fruit, minerals, petroleum, tea, textiles, pork, recording and telecommunications equipment, and vegetables

Imports - chemicals, fertilizers, grain, machinery, manufactured goods, metals, and textile yarn

LIFE-STYLE

About a fifth of all the world's population lives in China. Most of the people live in crowded conditions in the eastern third of the country since this area contains most major cities and nearly all the good farmlands. Rural villages are home to 74 percent of the people. Approximately 60 percent of all Chinese workers are farmers.

Most rural families have adequate food and clothing and also own a radio, a bicycle, and a sewing machine. Most live in three- or four-room houses made of mud or clay bricks or stone and have a straw or tile roof. Most have electricity. Though rural people work many hours a day, they attend political meetings and classes at night. Each family is a part of a larger group, called a *collective*, which decides what to grow and how a set amount of the crops should be distributed. The family chooses how to use what is left over.

Though China has some of the largest cities in the world, only about one-fourth of the population is urban. Many city dwellers live in old neighborhoods which are similar to rural villages. Many others live in large apartment complexes. Families are told where to live by their employers. Most apartments are very small but have plumbing and heating. Sometimes two families share an apartment. The living standard is higher in urban areas than in rural areas. Each city apartment complex or neighborhood elects a residents' committee, which supervises buildings and organizes programs such as evening classes, day-care centers, and after-school activities.

Grains are the main foods in China, with vegetables—especially cabbage and tofu—ranking second. People in the south favor rice while those in the north prefer wheat made into bread or noodles. Pork and poultry are favorite meats, but people also enjoy eggs, fish, fruits, and shellfish. A typical meal might consist of vegetables with little pieces of meat or seafood, soup, and rice or noodles. Tea is the most popular drink.

Many of the Chinese make their own clothing out of cotton or synthetic materials. They dress simply, emphasizing comfort and utility rather than style.

The Chinese enjoy a variety of sports, such as baseball, basketball, soccer, table tennis, and volleyball.

Ancient Chinese exercises, called *tai ji quan*, are done every morning by many Chinese. Tai ji quan emphasizes relaxation, balance, and proper breathing. It is also a kind of self-defense.

The Communist government discourages religion; however, since the 1970s its attitude has softened.

The Chinese heavily stress education and even adults may go to school to learn to read and write. The literacy rate for age 15 and older is about 70 percent. Children must attend school for nine years, beginning at age six or seven. Rural schools, however, are often small and poorly equipped.

China is famous for its ceremonial art objects, and many Chinese also enjoy various forms of music and drama as a way to relax.

IT'S A FACT!

"Children's Palaces" - recreation centers that children frequently go to after school. Children enjoy activities such as drawing, clay modeling, and dancing. Children who are extra good at one activity, such as gymnastics, get extra training.

Great Wall of China - at 4,000 mi. (6,400 km) long, is the longest structure ever built. It was built completely by hand.

Mount Everest - the country's and world's highest point, is located in the Himalaya Mountains on the border with Nepal and rises 29,028 ft. (8,848 m) above sea level.

Turpan Depression - the country's lowest point of elevation, is located 505 ft. (154 m) below sea level.

Yangtze River - the world's third longest river and the longest, most important river in China.

 DID YOU KNOW...
- English is the most widely studied foreign language in China?
- Chinese men and women are encouraged to postpone marriage until they are in their late 20s and to limit their families to one or two children?
- Beijing Opera is the most popular form of drama in China and is based on Chinese history and folklore?
- The Great Wall of China is the only human-made structure in the world that can be seen from space?
- China has borders with sixteen other countries?

COLOMBIA

OFFICIAL NAME: República de Colombia (Republic of Colombia)
LOCATION: Northwestern South America
AREA: 439,737 sq. mi. (1,138,914 sq. km)
POPULATION (Est. 1993): 34,842,000
CAPITAL: Bogotá
LARGEST CITIES: Bogotá, Medellín, Cali
GOVERNMENT: Republic governed by a president.
FLAG: Three horizontal stripes of yellow, blue, and red representing the golden New World, the blood shed for independence, and the Atlantic Ocean, accordingly.
ETHNIC GROUPS: Mestizo, European, Mulatto, others
LANGUAGE: Spanish
RELIGION: Roman Catholic
BASIC MONETARY UNIT: Colombian Peso

GEOGRAPHY

Colombia is the only South American country with a coast along both the Atlantic and Pacific Oceans. The landscape offers striking contrasts, from the snow-covered peaks of the Andes Mountains to the hot, lowland plains.

Colombia can be divided into three main land regions: 1) the Coastal Lowlands, 2) the Andes Mountains, and 3) the Eastern Plains. The Coastal Lowlands include the Caribbean Lowlands and the Pacific Lowlands. The Caribbean Lowlands feature many busy ports, and plantations, cattle ranches, and small farms. In the Caribbean Lowlands, the Guajira Peninsula, home of many Guajiro Indians and excellent coal deposits, forms the northernmost tip of Colombia. The Pacific Lowlands are largely swamps and thick forests. The Andes Mountains have three ranges that cover about a third of the country. This is Colombia's most productive area and includes fertile farms, rich mines, and large factories. Coffee trees thrive on the mountain slopes. The Eastern Plains cover nearly 60 percent of Colombia yet only two percent of the population live here.

CLIMATE

The climate varies with elevation even though the southern part of Colombia is crossed by the equator. The highest temperatures occur in the Coastal Lowlands and Eastern Plains. Temperatures are much cooler in the mountains. Temperatures within a region vary little between seasons. For example, the capital city of Bogotá, which lies about 8,660 ft. (2,640 m) above sea level, has an average temperature of 58°F (14°C) in January and 57°F (14°C) in July. Most of the country experiences one or two wet seasons and one or two dry seasons per year.

ECONOMY

Colombia is a developing country that has depended heavily on agriculture. Now manufacturing is gaining in importance.

Agriculture - bananas, cassava, cattle, coffee, corn, cotton, milk, potatoes, rice, and sugar cane

Manufacturing - beverages, cement, chemicals, clothing, metal products, processed foods, and textiles

Mining - coal, emeralds, gold, iron ore, natural gas, petroleum, and salt deposits

Exports - coal, cocaine and marijuana (illegally), coffee, emeralds, and petroleum

Imports - chemicals, machinery, and transportation equipment

LIFE-STYLE

Most of the country's people live in western Colombia, mainly in basins and valleys of the Andes Mountains. Urban dwellers generally live better than rural dwellers. Cities contain most of the country's schools, medical facilities, and cultural activities. Tall office and apartment buildings are replacing traditional Spanish-style architecture (adobe structures). In rural areas, homes are built from any available materials. In warm, wet coastal areas, bamboo poles and palm leaves are used. In cooler mountainous areas, homes have thick adobe walls. The middle class and working class are growing in Colombia's cities, yet crowded squatter settlements with no running water, electricity, or sewers sprawl on the edges of these cities.

Children ages seven to 11 are required to attend school. An estimated 80 percent of all Chilean adults can read and write.

Colombians eat a lot of starchy food, such as potatoes, rice, and noodles. *Ajiaco*, a favorite soup, contains potatoes, chicken, corn, and cassava. Adults and children drink a beverage made of brown sugar dissolved in water called *agua de panela*.

Soccer, bullfights, and auto races are popular spectator sports. Swimming and skiing are popular recreational activities.

IT'S A FACT!

Cristóbal Colón - the country's highest point, rises 18,947 ft. (5,775 m) above sea level.

Gold Museum - located in Bogotá, displays jewelry, small figures, and other objects crafted hundreds of years ago by Indian goldsmiths.

Nevado del Ruiz - is an active volcano west of Bogotá. It last erupted in 1985 (twice) causing 25,000 deaths.

 DID YOU KNOW...
- Yawning in front of strangers is considered impolite because it is a sign of hunger?
- Colombia was named after Christopher Columbus?
- Gigantic stone statues of Indian gods still stand high in the Andes Mountains in southern Colombia? These were created by advanced Indian civilizations hundreds of years ago.

COMOROS

OFFICIAL NAME: Federal and Islamic Republic of the Comoros
LOCATION: Indian Ocean
AREA: 863 sq. mi. (2,235 sq. km)
POPULATION (Est. 1992): 552,000
CAPITAL: Moroni
LARGEST CITIES: Moroni, Dzaoudzi
GOVERNMENT: Republic governed by a president.
FLAG: A crescent moon and four five-pointed stars are centered on a green background. The color green and the crescent symbolize Islam. The four stars represent the four islands.
ETHNIC GROUPS: Arab, African, East Indian
LANGUAGES: Comorian (Swahili and Arabic blend), French
RELIGIONS: Islam (mainly Sunni Muslim), Roman Catholic
BASIC MONETARY UNIT: CFA Franc

GEOGRAPHY

Comoros is an archipelago in the Indian Ocean, located between the mainland of Africa and the country of Madagascar. Comoros has four main islands—Anjouan, Grande Comore, Mayotte, and Moheli—and several smaller islands.

Most of the country's islands were formed by volcanic activity. Mangrove swamps and beaches are found along the coastlines. In the interior, there are mountain peaks with deep valleys, plateaus, and ravines along the base of the mountains. In places, the islands have thick forests and lush green vegetation, though much of its forests have been cleared for farming.

CLIMATE

Comoros has two seasons: a cool, dry season that lasts from May to October, and a hot, rainy season that lasts from November to April. Heavy rains during the rainy season provide the people with the only natural source for drinking water. The people store the rainwater for use during the dry season.

ECONOMY

Comoros is one of the world's poorest countries. The economy depends upon agriculture.

Agriculture - bananas, cassava, cloves, coffee, coconuts, corn, perfume oil, rice, sisal, spices, sugar cane, sweet potatoes, and vanilla

Manufacturing - perfume

Exports - cloves, copra, perfume oils, and vanilla

Imports - cement, consumer goods, food, and petroleum products

LIFE-STYLE

The majority of Comorans live in rural villages. About 85 percent of the people have jobs related to farming. However, good farmland is lacking.

The staple of the Comorans diet is rice. Other popular foods are bananas, cassava, coconuts, corn, fish, and sweet potatoes. Much of the country's food must be imported.

Although the official languages are Comorian and French, few Comorans speak or write French.

Only about 15 percent of the population are literate and less than 20 percent attend secondary schools.

Comoros has many serious problems, such as poverty, disease, and hunger. Malnutrition occurs frequently among the people because the country has a shortage of doctors and hospitals. The death rate, especially among children, is very high.

The country has several radio stations, and it has an international airport on Grande Comore.

IT'S A FACT!

Mont Kartala - the country's highest point and an active volcano, rises 7,746 ft. (2,361 m) above sea level. Its crater is one of the world's largest, with a diameter of 2 mi. (3 km).

DID YOU KNOW...

- Comoros became an independent nation in 1975, but the people of one island, Mayotte, voted to remain under French rule? Despite this, the Comoran government considers Mayotte part of the country and the island's area and population are included.
- Perfume oil exported by Comoros comes from such plants as *ylang ylang* trees?

CONGO

OFFICIAL NAME: République du Congo (Republic of Congo)
FORMERLY: Territory in French Equatorial Africa called Middle Congo
LOCATION: West-central Africa
AREA: 132,047 sq. mi. (342,000 sq. km)
POPULATION (Est. 1993): 2,503,000
CAPITAL/LARGEST CITY: Brazzaville
GOVERNMENT: Republic headed by a president.
FLAG: Adopted in 1991. Green triangle in the upper, hoist-side corner and a red triangle in the lower, fly-side corner, separated by a yellow diagonal stripe.
ETHNIC GROUPS: Kongo, Batéké, M'Bochi, Sangha, European (mostly French)
LANGUAGES: French, local African languages (Lingala and Kikongo most common)
RELIGIONS: Christianity, Animism, Islam
BASIC MONETARY UNIT: CFA Franc

GEOGRAPHY

At its greatest distances, Congo measures 590 mi. (950 km) from north to south and 515 mi. (829 km) from east to west. It has 100 mi. (160 km) of coastline along the South Atlantic Ocean. The equator runs through the country.

Congo is divided into six regions: 1) Coastal Plain, 2) Mayombé Escarpment, 3) Niari Valley, 4) Stanley Pool Region, 5) Batéké Plateau, and 6) Congo River Basin.

The Coastal Plain region—generally a dry, treeless region with lagoons near the coast—extends approximately 40 mi. (64 km) inland from the Atlantic Ocean. Behind this is the Mayombé Escarpment, which consists of plateaus and river valleys. The Niari Valley lies beyond the Mayombé Escarpment and is home to rich farmland, forests, and savannas. East of the Niari Valley is the Stanley Pool Region, a lake formed by the widening of the Congo River. The Stanley Pool is covered with a series of bare hills which have been cleared for farming. The Batéké Plateau is a region of plains and deep, forested valleys, which were formed by the Congo River's tributaries. The Congo River Basin is a large swampy area and home to the Ubangi, the Congo's main tributary, which forms the country's northeastern border.

CLIMATE

Congo has a tropical climate. Average annual temperatures range from 70° to 80°F (21° to 27°C) in the Batéké Plateau region and from 75° to 78°F (24° to 26°C) in the Congo River Basin region. The average rainfall ranges from less than 60 in. (150 cm) in the Batéké Plateau region to about 100 in. (250 cm) in the Congo River Basin region. The Coastal Plain region is the country's coolest and driest region, because the cold Benguela ocean current flows near its coast.

ECONOMY

Congo's economy is based on a mixture of village agriculture, forestry, and mineral resources. The country has a high unemployment rate. Of the labor force, about three-fourths work in agriculture.

Agriculture - bananas, cassava, cocoa, coffee, corn, palm kernels and oil, peanuts, plantains, rice, rubber, sugar cane, sweet potatoes, and yams

Forestry - limba, mahogany, and okoumé

Manufacturing - beverages, cement, cigarettes, lumbering, palm oil, petroleum refining, soap, and sugar milling

Mining - lead, natural gas, petroleum, potash, and zinc

Exports - cocoa, coffee, crude oil, diamonds, lumber, plywood, and sugar

Imports - capital equipment, consumer goods, food, and intermediate manufactures

LIFE-STYLE

Congo's population is three-fifths rural and two-fifths urban. Much of the population lives either on the southern border near Brazzaville or on the coast near the city of Pointe-Noire. The Kongo mainly live west and southwest of Brazzaville and make a living by farming. The Batéké mainly live north of Brazzaville and make a living by fishing and hunting. The M'Bochi used to make a living by fishing and now mainly work as clerks and technicians. The Sangha live in the thick, northern forests which are mainly inhabited by wild animals and travel by means of dugout canoes.

Most older Congolese cannot read or write, but today about 75 percent of Congolese children receive some elementary education. The literacy rate is a little over 55 percent.

IT'S A FACT!

Congo River - the world's fifth longest river, flows 2,900 mi. (4,667 km), is Congo's most important waterway, and carries more water than all but the Amazon River.

Mont de la Lékéti - the country's highest point, rises 3,412 ft. (1,040 m) above sea level.

 DID YOU KNOW...

- Congo has one of Africa's longest transportation systems, with its Congo-Ocean railroad measuring 320 mi. (515 km)?
- Congo became an independent country in 1960?

COOK ISLANDS
Dependency of New Zealand

OFFICIAL NAME: Cook Islands
LOCATION: South Pacific Ocean
AREA: 93 sq. mi. (240 sq. km)
POPULATION (Est. 1993): 18,903
CAPITAL/LARGEST CITY: Avarua
GOVERNMENT: Self-governing parliamentary democracy in free association with New Zealand. New Zealand takes care of defense and foreign affairs.
FLAG: Blue field with the United Kingdom's *Union Jack* in the upper hoist-side quadrant. Fifteen white, five-pointed stars—one for each island—form a circle on the flag's outer half.
ETHNIC GROUPS: Polynesian, Polynesian-European
LANGUAGES: English, Maori
RELIGION: Christianity
BASIC MONETARY UNIT: New Zealand Dollar

● Penrhyn
Rakahanga ●
Pukapuka ●   ● Manihiki
Nassau ●
Suwarrow ●   *South Pacific Ocean*
Palmerston ● Aitutaki ●
● Manuae
Takutea ● ● Mitiaro
● Mauke
★Avarua → ● Rarotonga
● Mangaia

COOK ISLANDS

GEOGRAPHY

The Cook Islands are located about 1,800 mi. (2,900 km) northeast of New Zealand. The 15 islands in the group are spread out over 850,000 sq. mi. (2.2 million sq. km). They have a combined coastline of 90 mi. (145 km) on the South Pacific Ocean.

The islands form two groups: six Northern Islands and nine Southern Islands. The Northern Islands—Manihiki, Nassau, Palmerston, Penrhyn, Pukapuka (Danger), Rakahanga, and Suwarrow (Suvarov)—and two Southern Islands—Manuae and Takutea—are mainly low-lying coral atolls. The other southern islands—Aitutaki, Atiu, Mangaia, Mauke, Mitiaro, and Rarotonga—were formed by volcanoes and have fertile soil. The largest of the Cook Islands is Rarotonga, with an area of 27 sq. mi. (70 sq. km). Small lakes can be found on Mangaia and Mitiaro Islands.

CLIMATE

The Cook Islands have a tropical climate that is subject to typhoons during the rainy season—November or December through March. The average daily temperature ranges from 58° to 92°F (15° to 33°C) in the southern group and 70° to 92°F (21° to 33°C) in the northern group. The average annual rainfall ranges from 80 in. (200 cm) on Rarotonga to as much as 128 in. (325 cm) on the Northern Islands.

ECONOMY

Due in part to the great distances between the country's islands, economic development has been slow. Currently, the economy is based on tourism, light industry, and its fish and fruit exports, with an important part of the revenue coming from coins and stamps.

Agriculture - bananas, citrus fruit, coconuts, coffee, cotton, pineapples, and tomatoes
Manufacturing - clothing, fruit processing, and handicrafts
Exports - clothing, copra, fish, fruit, and tomatoes
Imports - food, fuel, textiles, and timber

LIFE-STYLE

About 90 percent of the country's population lives in the southern group of islands. About half of the population lives on Rarotonga Island, mainly along its shoreline. Most Cook Islanders are employed in traditional or cash crop agriculture, fishing, government service, or industries on Rarotonga. Many emigrate to New Zealand or migrate to Rarotonga Island from other islands for work.

Staples of the diet include breadfruit, sweet potatoes, taro, and yams. Chickens, goats, and pigs are raised and fish are caught mainly for the islanders' consumption. Some delicacies of the Cook Islands include *itiki* (Mitiaro eel caught in that island's lake), *paua* (clam from Manihiki atoll's lagoon), and *piere* (dried banana wrapped in banana leaf). Because the soil is porous on the Northern Islands, water catchments are necessary in order to provide an adequate water supply.

The islands have strong Maori traditions, and dancing and *umukai* (feasts) are common. Some of the islands are known for the woven work produced by their residents.

Education is free, and children ages six to 15 are required to attend school. Higher education is available in Fiji and New Zealand. Health care is free to all and dental care is free for school-aged children.

IT'S A FACT!

Ara Metua - located on Rarotonga Island, is a stone road that was probably built in the 11th century by chief Toi and is still in use.

Te Manga - the islands' highest point, is located on Rarotonga Island and rises 2,142 ft. (653 m) above sea level.

 DID YOU KNOW...
- The Cook Islands are named for Captain James Cook, who in 1773 became the first known European to explore the islands?
- Suwarrow atoll is a bird sanctuary?
- Pukapuka Island was first discovered in 1595 by the Spanish navigator Alvaro de Mendaña de Neira?
- Cook Islanders from the northern group—especially Manihiki and Penrhyn—suffered from Peruvian slave raids in the 1860s?
- Some of the islands in the northern group are so near sea level that waves wash over them during hurricanes?
- European missionaries began to convert Cook Islanders to Christianity during the 1820s?

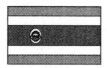

COSTA RICA

OFFICIAL NAME: República de Costa Rica
(Republic of Costa Rica)
LOCATION: Central America
AREA: 19,730 sq. mi. (51,100 sq. km)
POPULATION (Est. 1993): 3,223,000
CAPITAL/LARGEST CITY: San José
GOVERNMENT: Democratic republic governed by a president.
FLAG: Five horizontal stripes of blue, white, red, white, and blue. A white oval featuring the coat of arms is located left of center on the red stripe.
ETHNIC GROUP: Mestizo
LANGUAGE: Spanish
RELIGION: Roman Catholic
BASIC MONETARY UNIT: Costa Rican Colón

GEOGRAPHY

Costa Rica is a small, mountainous country. It measures 220 mi. (354 km) from north to south and 237 mi. (381 km) from east to west at its greatest distances. Costa Rica has 380 mi. (612 km) of coastline along the Pacific Ocean and 133 mi. (214 km) of coastline along the Caribbean Sea. A chain of high mountain ranges, called *cordilleras*, runs down the center of Costa Rica and divides the country into three land regions: 1) the Central Highlands, 2) the Caribbean Lowlands, and 3) the Pacific Coastal Strip. The Central Highlands consist of two areas of fertile farmland: the *Meseta Central* (Central Plateau) and the *Valle del General* (Valley of the General). These areas are surrounded by steep cordilleras. The Caribbean Lowlands, along part of the eastern border of Costa Rica, are comprised of tropical jungles. The Pacific Coastal Strip to the west is made up of low mountains that line the coast.

CLIMATE

Temperatures vary within the two areas of the Central Highlands. In the *Meseta Central*, daytime temperatures average 75° to 80°F (24° to 27°C) year-round. The area averages 70 in. (180 cm) of rainfall annually. The average daytime temperature in the *Valle del General* ranges from 80° to 90°F (27° to 32°C). Yearly rainfall averages 110 in. (279 cm).

The daily high temperature in the Caribbean Lowlands averages 100°F (38°C). The region receives 150-200 in. (381-510 cm) of rain yearly.

Daytime temperatures in the Pacific Coastal Strip average from 77° to 100°F (25° to 38°C). The average rainfall is 130 in. (330 cm).

ECONOMY

Costa Rica's most valuable resource is its fertile volcanic soil. Its economy greatly depends on foreign trade.

Agriculture - bananas, beef cattle, cacao, coffee, corn, rice, and sugar cane

Manufacturing - cement, clothing, furniture, machinery, processed foods, and textiles

Exports - bananas, beef, coffee, and sugar

Imports - chemicals, petroleum, and manufactured goods

LIFE-STYLE

Costa Rica's population is divided almost equally between rural and urban areas. Many Costa Ricans live on farms or in rural towns. Their homes are adobe cottages with thick, white stucco walls and red- or pink-tiled roofs. Most city dwellers live in row houses. The wealthy own ranch- or Spanish-style homes surrounded by gardens.

Most Costa Ricans' diet is comprised of corn, beans, eggs, rice, coffee, and tropical fruits. They often have tamales and tortillas. A popular dish in Costa Rica is *olla de carne*, a beef stew with potatoes, onions, and a variety of vegetables.

About 93 percent of Costa Rica's population can read and write. This is the highest percentage of literacy in all of Central America.

The national sport, soccer, is the most popular sport in Costa Rica. Basketball, baseball, swimming, and tennis are also popular. At various times during the year, Costa Ricans enjoy festivals and bullfights. National parks are enjoyed by locals and tourists alike.

IT'S A FACT!

Chirripó Grande - the country's highest point, rises 12,530 ft. (3,819 m) above sea level.

Irazú - is a volcano that spewed ash over San José and surrounding areas from 1963-1965.

 DID YOU KNOW...

- Over 45 percent of the population is under age 20?
- Indians were the first people to live in what is now Costa Rica? The Spanish began arriving after 1502 when Columbus first came to the area.
- San José, the capital city, features bullfights, festivals, and masked parades as part of its annual Christmas festivities?

CROATIA

OFFICIAL NAME: Republika Hrvatska (Republic of Croatia)
FORMERLY: A republic of Yugoslavia
LOCATION: Southeastern Europe
AREA: 21,829 sq. mi. (56,538 sq. km)
POPULATION (Est. 1993): 4,793,000
CAPITAL: Zagreb
LARGEST CITIES: Zagreb, Split, Rijeka, Osijek, Dubrovnik
GOVERNMENT: Parliamentary democracy governed by a president.
FLAG: Three horizontal stripes of red, white, and blue. The coat of arms is centered on the white stripe.
ETHNIC GROUPS: Croat, Serb
LANGUAGES: Croatian, Serbian
RELIGIONS: Roman Catholic, Serbian Orthodox
BASIC MONETARY UNIT: Croatian Dinar

GEOGRAPHY

At its greatest distances, Croatia measures 290 mi. (465 km) both from north to south and from east to west. Its area includes many islands, giving the country a combined coastline of 3,596 mi (5,790 km) along the Adriatic Sea.

Croatia has two main land regions: 1) Dalmatia and 2) the Pannonian Plains. Dalmatia is a coastal region of rocky cliffs and very little fertile soil. The Pannonian Plains is a region of very fertile soil in the north. The Dinaric Alps—a rocky, barren area—lies behind Dalmatia in the southeast. The country has two main rivers—the Drava and the Sava—which flow into the Danube River in the northeast. More than one-third of Croatia's area is forest-covered.

CLIMATE

Croatia's climate is Mediterranean in Dalmatia and continental elsewhere. The average annual temperature along the coast ranges from about 43°F (6°C) in January to about 75°F (24°C) in July. The average annual temperature in the plains region ranges from about 30°F (-1°C) in January to about 66°F (19°C) in July. The average annual rainfall is 30 in. (75 cm). The country is subject to frequent and destructive earthquakes. In spring and autumn, heavy rains often cause the Danube River and its tributaries to flood.

ECONOMY

Croatia's economy is based mainly on agriculture, cattle breeding, shipbuilding, and tourism. In 1990, the country began to establish a free-enterprise system.

Agriculture - alfalfa, apples, cherries, citrus fruits, clover, corn, grapes, livestock (cattle, pigs, poultry, and sheep), olives, pears, plums, potatoes, soybeans, sugar beets, sunflowers, tobacco, and wheat

Manufacturing - cement, chemicals, electronics, paper, petroleum, processed foods and beverages, shipbuilding, steel, textiles, and wood products (including furniture)

Mining - bauxite and coal

Exports - chemicals, food, fuel, furniture, livestock, machinery and transport equipment, raw materials, ships, and textiles

Imports - chemicals, food, fuel, livestock, machinery and transport equipment, manufactured goods, and raw materials

LIFE-STYLE

Croatia's rural families tend to be extended with several generations living in wooden shelters with steep roofs. Suburban Croats live mainly in modern high-rise apartment buildings, while urban Croats live in older apartment buildings or houses.

Croatian dishes commonly consist of beef, chicken, corn, fish, lamb, pork, potatoes, and rice. Popular traditional dishes include *gibanica* (layered cheese pastry eaten either alone or with a meat dish), *strukli* (boiled or casseroled salt cottage cheese strudel), and *Zagreb veal cutlet* (breaded veal slices). Wine is the most popular beverage. Other commonly consumed beverages include beer, fruit drinks, and mineral water.

Popular sports include archery, basketball, bowling, boxing, chess, fishing, handball, hockey, hunting, rowing, sailing, skiing, soccer, swimming, tennis, volleyball, and water polo. Croats in northern villages enjoy painting on glass. Socializing is a popular leisure activity, as well as watching movies and television. Summer vacations of one to four weeks are often taken by families.

Music and dance are important to Croatian culture. Folk music, jazz festivals, and rock music are popular. A popular traditional dance is the *kolo* (fast-paced dance performed in a circle).

Children ages six to 14 are required to attend school.

IT'S A FACT!

Dubrovnik - a historic walled city on the southern coast of the Adriatic Sea, draws many sightseers.

Mount Troglav - the country's highest point, rises 6,276 ft. (1,913 m) above sea level.

DID YOU KNOW...

- Croatia was a Yugoslavian republic from 1918 to 1991, after which time the country gained its independence?
- Croatian and Serbian are often referred to as Serbo-Croatian because they are so similar that language experts consider them to be two forms of a single language?
- Slavic tribes settled what is now known as Croatia during the A.D. 600s?
- Croats consider yawning in public to be inconsiderate?

The map labels: Drava R., Sava R., SLOVENIA, HUNGARY, Danube R., Zagreb, Pannonian Plains, CROATIA, Rijeka, Osijek, YUGOSLAVIA, BOSNIA-HERZEGOVINA, Mt. Troglav, Dinaric Alps, Dalmatia, Adriatic Sea, Split, Dubrovnik

CUBA

OFFICIAL NAME: República de Cuba (Republic of Cuba)
LOCATION: West Indies
AREA: 42,804 sq. mi. (110,861 sq. km)
POPULATION (Est. 1995): 11,091,000
CAPITAL: Havana
LARGEST CITIES: Havana, Santiago de Cuba, Camagüey
GOVERNMENT: Socialist state and a republic governed by a dictator.
FLAG: Adopted in 1902. Five horizontal blue and white stripes overlapped by a red triangle based on the hoist side. A white star—representing independence—is centered on the triangle.
ETHNIC GROUPS: Spanish, Black, Mulatto
LANGUAGE: Spanish
RELIGION: Christianity
BASIC MONETARY UNIT: Cuban Peso

GEOGRAPHY

Cuba is an island country in the West Indies located about 90 mi. (140 km) south of Key West, Florida. It is an archipelago that includes the island of Cuba, Isla de la Juventud (Island of Youth), and over 1,600 other islands. At its greatest distances, Cuba measures 759 mi. (1,221 km) from northwest to southeast and 135 mi. (217 km) from north to south. Its narrowest point is 19 mi. (31 km) wide. A fourth of the island is covered with towering mountains and rolling hills. The majority of its land is covered by gentle slopes, fertile valleys, and rolling grasslands. Cuba's 2,100 mi. (3,380 km) of coastline includes deep bays and sandy beaches fringed with coral islands and reefs. The country has over 200 streams and rivers.

CLIMATE

Cuba has a semitropical climate. Ocean breezes give the island a mild climate year-round. It has a rainy season and a dry season. The dry, winter season begins in mid-November and ends in April. During the rainy summer season (May through October), it rains almost every day. The average annual rainfall is 54 in. (137 cm). The average temperature ranges from about 70°F (21°C) in winter to about 80°F (27°C) in summer. Cuba is often struck by hurricanes, especially on the island's western half.

ECONOMY

The government controls the Cuban economy and owns all industries, banks, and small businesses. It also owns over 70 percent of the farmland. The Cuban economy is developing slowly. Sugar is the country's leading crop.

Agriculture - citrus fruit, coffee, milk, sugar cane, tobacco, and vegetables
Manufacturing - cement, cigars, fertilizers, refined petroleum, refined sugar, rum, and textiles
Mining - chromium, iron, and nickel
Exports - cigars, citrus fruit, fish, refined nickel ore, rum, and sugar
Imports - grains, machinery, and petroleum

LIFE-STYLE

Approximately one-fourth of all Cubans live in rural areas. Many of these rural dwellers are poor and live in thatch-roofed huts with cement floors. The government is now devoting much money to the education, housing, and feeding of its rural people.

The cities lack adequate housing. Many city dwellers live in crowded apartment buildings that are in disrepair. An apartment is sometimes shared by two or more families. New housing built by the government cannot keep up with the demand.

Rice and beans are staple foods for most Cubans. Cuban cooking is based on the cooking traditions inherited from Spain, on the influence of African cooking, and on the fruits and vegetables grown there. Cuban food is highly seasoned, but not hot. A favorite meal is *arroz con pollo* (rice with chicken). Since many foods are scarce, the Cuban government has instituted a type of food rationing. Moreover, schoolchildren and some workers are daily given one or two free meals.

Education is free, and children are required to attend school for six years. Over 95 percent of the adult population is literate.

Cubans participate in baseball, basketball, swimming, and track and field. Most Cubans also enjoy singing and dancing to such dances as the cha-cha-cha, the mambo, and the rumba. Young people enjoy rock music. The Cuban government sponsors many free ballets, plays, and other cultural events.

IT'S A FACT!

Bay of Pigs - site of the 1961 invasion led by Cuban exiles that was approved by late President John F. Kennedy. Castro defeated the exiles and later released many to the United States in exchange for non-military supplies.

Pico Turquino - the country's highest point, rises 6,542 ft. (1,994 m) above sea level and is located in the Sierra Maestra Mountains.

Río Cauto - the country's longest river, flows approximately 150 mi. (241 km) through the southeast.

Sierra de los Órganos - a mountain range in northwestern Cuba, got its name from Spanish conquerors who thought that the range's long, parallel formation looked like organ pipes.

 DID YOU KNOW...
- Cuba is called the "Pearl of the Antilles" because it is so beautiful?
- A normal after-school snack is *pan con timba*, a bread roll that contains guava jelly and cheese?
- Cuba is world famous for its Havana cigars, which are traditionally rolled by hand?

CYPRUS

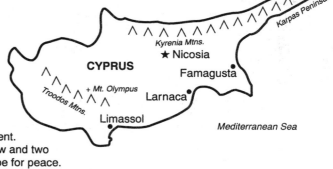

Mediterranean Sea

Kyrenia Mtns.

Karpas Peninsula

★ Nicosia

CYPRUS

Famagusta

Troodos Mtns.

+ Mt. Olympus

Larnaca

Limassol

Mediterranean Sea

OFFICIAL NAME:	Kypriakí Dimokratía (in Greek)
	Kibris Cumhuriyeti (in Turkish)
	(Republic of Cyprus)
LOCATION:	Northeast Mediterranean Sea
AREA:	3,572 sq. mi. (9,251 sq. km)
POPULATION (Est. 1993):	723,371
CAPITAL:	Nicosia
LARGEST CITIES:	Famagusta, Larnaca, Limassol, Nicosia
GOVERNMENT:	Republic governed by a Greek Cypriot president and a Turkish Cypriot vice-president.
FLAG:	White with a map of Cyprus in copper-yellow and two crossed olive branches symbolizing the hope for peace.
ETHNIC GROUPS:	Greek, Turkish
LANGUAGES:	Greek, Turkish, English
RELIGIONS:	Eastern Orthodox (Greek pop.), Sunnite Muslim (Turkish pop.)
BASIC MONETARY UNITS:	Cypriot Pound, Turkish Lira

GEOGRAPHY

Cyprus is located about 40 mi. (64 km) south of Turkey and 60 mi. (97 km) west of Syria. It measures 75 mi. (121 km) from north to south and 128 mi. (206 km) from east to west at its greatest distances. It has 402 mi. (648 km) of coastline on the Mediterranean Sea.

The country is made up of four regions: 1) the Kyrenia Mountains, 2) the Mesaoria Plain, 3) the Troodos Mountains, and 4) a high plateau area. The Kyrenia Mountain region which spans 100 mi. (160 km) along the country's northern coast and the Karpas Peninsula, a narrow limestone range in the northeast. The wide, fertile Mesaoria Plain lies in central Cyprus and divides the Kyrenia Mountains from the Troodos Mountains in the southwest. The southeastern part of the island has a high plateau that meets with the fertile coastal plains.

CLIMATE

Cyprus has a Mediterranean climate with cool, wet winters and hot, dry summers. The average annual temperature at Nicosia, the country's capital, is about 67°F (19°C). Temperatures in the Mesaoria Plain may exceed 100°F (38°C) during the summer months. Most of the country receives an average of 12-16 in. (30-41 cm) of rain per year. The inadequate water supply inhibits agricultural productivity. Parts of the Troodos Mountains receive more than 40 in. (100 cm) of rain per year. Most of the country's precipitation falls during the winter months.

ECONOMY

Cyprus's economy relies heavily on tourism, attracting tourists with its beaches, castles, churches, and mountains.

Agriculture - barley, goats, grapefruit, grapes, lemons, olives, oranges, pigs, potatoes, sheep, vegetables, and wheat

Manufacturing - asbestos pipe, beer, bricks, cement, cigarettes, clothing, footwear, mosaic tile, olive oil, petroleum refinement, shoes, textiles, and wine

Mining - asbestos and chromium

Exports - carob, cement, citrus fruits, clothing, grapes, potatoes, shoes, tobacco, and wine

Imports - feed grains, food, machinery, and petroleum

LIFE-STYLE

The country's two ethnic groups live in separate areas, with most Turkish Cypriots living in the northeast and most Greek Cypriots living in the southwest. Roughly four-fifths of Cyprus's people are of Greek origin, and most of the rest are of Turkish origin.

Many urban Cypriots live in large Western-style apartment buildings, while villagers live in simple houses constructed of stone or brick around a courtyard.

Clothing for older, rural men may consist of decorated vests and *vrakas* (baggy black trousers). Clothing for rural women may consist of long skirts and *sarkas* (short blouses).

Primary education is free and required of children between the ages of six and 12. The first three years of secondary education are also free.

IT'S A FACT!

Mount Olympus - the country's highest point, is located in the Troodos Mountains and rises 6,403 ft. (1,952 m) above sea level.

 DID YOU KNOW...

- Cyprus was ruled by Great Britain between 1878 and 1960, after which time the country gained its independence?
- Cyprus is the third largest island in the Mediterranean, following Sicily and Sardinia?
- All of Cyprus's rivers are dry at least part of the year?

CZECH REPUBLIC

OFFICIAL NAME: Ceská Republika (Czech Republic)
FORMERLY: Part of Czechoslovakia (until 1993)
LOCATION: Central Europe
AREA: 30,450 sq. mi. (78,864 sq. km)
POPULATION (Est. 1994): 10,470,000
CAPITAL: Prague
LARGEST CITIES: Prague, Brno, Ostrava, Plzeň
GOVERNMENT: Parliamentary democracy headed by a president.
FLAG: Two horizontal stripes of white and red, with a blue isosceles triangle based on the hoist side.
ETHNIC GROUPS: Czech, Moravian, Slovak
LANGUAGES: Czech, Slovak
RELIGIONS: Roman Catholic, Orthodox, Protestant
BASIC MONETARY UNIT: Koruna

GEOGRAPHY

At its greatest distances, Czech Republic, a landlocked country, measures 175 mi. (282 km) from north to south and 305 mi. (491 km) from east to west. The country has five main geographic regions: 1) the Bohemian Mountains, 2) the Sudeten Mountains, 3) the Bohemian Basin, 4) the Bohemian-Moravian Highlands, and 5) the Moravian Lowlands.

The Bohemian Mountains lie in the west and include the Ore Mountains in the northwest and the Bohemian Forest in the west and southwest. The Sudeten Mountains lie in the north and include the Krkonose (Giant) Mountains, which are home to one of the country's largest nature preserves. The Bohemian Basin lies in north-central Czech Republic and consists of fertile farmland, rolling hills, and low plains. Several major rivers flow through this region, including the Elbe, Ohre, and Vltava. The Bohemian-Moravian Highlands, which are mainly an agricultural region, lie in central Czech Republic and consist of low hills, high plains, and plateaus. The Moravian Lowlands lie in the southeast and include a fertile valley near the Morava River.

CLIMATE

Czech Republic generally has a temperate climate with warm summers and cold, cloudy, often humid winters. Average temperatures range from 23°F (-5°C) in the winter to 68°F (20°C) in the summer. Precipitation levels range from 18-41 in. (45-103 cm) annually.

ECONOMY

Under Communist rule, all factories and farms were state-controlled and the economy thrived until the1960s. After the Communist government resigned, a free-enterprise system was created.

Agriculture - barley, cattle, corn, fruits, hogs, hops, oats, potatoes, poultry, rapeseed, rye, sheep, sugar beets, other vegetables, and wheat

Forestry - lumber

Manufacturing - automaking, beer brewing, footwear, glass, iron and steel, textiles, and wood products

Mining - coal and uranium

Exports - automobiles, chemicals, coal, footwear, fuel, glass, iron and steel, machinery and transport equipment, manufactured goods, metals, minerals, and textiles

Imports - agricultural products, automobiles, chemicals, fuels, iron ore, natural gas, machinery and transport equipment, manufactured goods, and raw materials

LIFE-STYLE

Czech Republic's population is mainly urban. Though the country still has one of the highest living standards of post-Communist central and eastern Europe, urban areas suffer a severe housing shortage and many Czechs live in poorly-built apartment buildings from the Communist era. Some urban families also have country cottages. Rural Czechs often live in single-family homes and make a living by farming or commuting to nearby factories or cities for work.

A common Czech dish is *vepro-knedlo-zelo* (pork roast, dumplings, and sauerkraut). A traditional Christmas meal is carp with potato salad. Apple strudel is a favorite dessert, and beer, juice, and soda are the most common beverages.

Popular recreational activities include attending concerts, dancing, participating in outdoor activities (especially camping, gardening, hiking, skating, skiing, and swimming), playing sports (especially ice hockey, soccer, and tennis), socializing, and watching movies and television.

Public education is free, and children are required to attend school beginning at age six. At age 11, children begin their eight-year, specialized secondary education in one of three areas: academic, teaching, or technical.

IT'S A FACT!

Charles University - located in Prague, was founded in 1348 and is one of the oldest European universities.

Sněžka - the country's highest point, rises 5,256 ft. (1,602 m) above sea level.

 DID YOU KNOW...

- Franz Kafka, a renowned author, was from the former Czechoslovakia?
- Prague, one of the most beautiful cities in central Europe, is the home of the Charles Bridge, a major tourist attraction?

DENMARK

OFFICIAL NAME: Kongeriget Danmark (Kingdom of Denmark)
LOCATION: Northern Europe
AREA: 16,632 sq. mi. (43,077 sq. km)
POPULATION (Est. 1995): 5,192,000
CAPITAL: Copenhagen
LARGEST CITIES: Copenhagen, Århus, Ålborg, Odense
GOVERNMENT: Constitutional monarchy.
FLAG: Red field with a white cross shifted slightly to the hoist side.
ETHNIC GROUP: Scandinavian
LANGUAGES: Danish, German, English
RELIGION: Evangelical Lutheran
BASIC MONETARY UNIT: Krone

GEOGRAPHY

Denmark consists of a peninsula called Jutland and 482 nearby islands. The peninsula measures 225 mi. (362 km) from north to south and 250 mi. (402 km) from east to west at its greatest distances. Greenland is a province of Denmark although it lies 1,300 mi. (2,090 km) away, just northeast of Canada. The Faeroe Islands are a self-governing part of the Danish kingdom.

Denmark may be divided into five regions: 1) the Western Dune Coast, 2) the Western Sand Plains, 3) the East-Central Hills, 4) the Northern Flat Plains, and 5) Bornholm. The majority of Denmark is covered by *moraine*, earth and stone left by the melting of glaciers thousands of years ago.

CLIMATE

Denmark has a mild, damp climate because it is almost surrounded by water. The North Atlantic Current of the Gulf Stream brings warm, west winds. Temperatures average about 15° to 32°F (9° to 0°C) in the winter and 63° to 82°F (17° to 28°C) in summer. The country receives a yearly average of 24 in. (61 cm) of precipitation. Fog and mist often occur, especially on the west coast in winter.

ECONOMY

Despite its lack of natural resources, Denmark has a strong economy and one of the highest standards of living in the world. It is known for its shipping and fishing.

Agriculture - barley, beef and dairy cattle, eggs, hogs, milk, potatoes, poultry, sugar beets, and wheat

Fishing - cod, sand lances, and trout

Manufacturing - diesel engines, electrical and electronic equipment, furniture, machinery, porcelain, processed foods (bacon, butter, cheese, ham), ships, and silverware

Exports - beer, dairy products, fish, furniture, machinery, meat, and medical goods

Imports - chemicals, coal, grain, iron, paper, petroleum, textiles, and transportation equipment

LIFE-STYLE

Most of the Danish population live in urban areas. The cities are an interesting mixture of castles, cobblestone streets, and modern office buildings. Most city dwellers live in apartments. Cities are virtually free of slums.

Roofs of houses throughout the countryside are made of colorful red or blue tile, or are thatched. Storks sometimes build nests on rooftops and are thought to bring good luck. Though only one-fifth of all Danes live in these rural areas, three-fourths of the country is covered with farmland.

A traditional Danish dinner consists of roast duckling stuffed with apples and prunes, served with red cabbage and boiled potatoes. The *smørrebrød* (open-faced sandwich) is very popular in Denmark.

Soccer is the most popular sport. Other recreational activities include bicycling, gymnastics, rowing, sailing, swimming, and tennis.

IT'S A FACT!

Christiansborg Palace - is the home of the parliament, Supreme Court, and the Queen's Audience Chambers.

Copenhagen's Nyhavn Canal - is the location of many beautiful, old buildings and fashionable cafes.

Lake Arresø - the country's largest lake, covers 16 sq. mi. (41 sq. km).

Lim Fiord - Denmark's largest inlet, winds across the northern portion of the Jutland peninsula for 112 mi. (180 km).

Tivoli Gardens - a world-famous amusement park in Copenhagen, offers ballet, pantomime, rides, shooting galleries, restaurants, circus acts, concerts, and fireworks.

Yding Skovhøj - the country's highest point, rises 568 ft. (173 m) above sea level.

 DID YOU KNOW...
- Hans Christian Andersen, Denmark's best-known writer, is famous for his fairy tales?
- Denmark is famous for rich, flaky sweet rolls known as *Danish pastries?*

DJIBOUTI

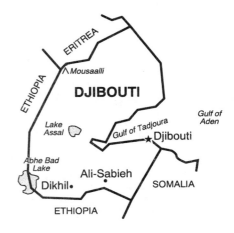

OFFICIAL NAME: Jumhouriyya Djibouti (Republic of Djibouti)
FORMERLY: French Somaliland; French Territory of the Afars and Issas
LOCATION: Northeastern Africa
AREA: 8,958 sq. mi. (23,200 sq. km)
POPULATION (Est. 1993): 448,000
CAPITAL: Djibouti
LARGEST CITIES: Djibouti, Dikhil, Ali-Sabieh
GOVERNMENT: Republic governed by a president.
FLAG: Two horizontal stripes of light blue and light green. A white triangle, based on the hoist side, features a red star.
ETHNIC GROUPS: Afars, Issas, French, Arab
LANGUAGES: French, Arabic, Afar, Somali
RELIGION: Islam (mainly Sunni Muslim)
BASIC MONETARY UNIT: Djiboutian Franc

GEOGRAPHY

At its greatest distances, Djibouti measures 125 mi. (201 km) from north to south and 110 mi. (177 km) from east to west. Djibouti has 152 mi. (245 km) of coastline along the Gulf of Aden.

Most of the country is desert, especially in the lowland interior. It has three fairly distinct landforms: 1) low coastal plain, 2) mountain ranges, and 3) high plateaus and sunken plains. There is little grass and few shrubs on the plains and plateaus. Small forest areas are found on the mountain slopes.

CLIMATE

Djibouti has one of the hottest and driest climates in the world. The average temperature throughout the year is 85°F (29°C). The average yearly rainfall for the entire country is less than 5 in. (13 cm), but some highland areas receive more than 20 in. (51 cm) annually.

ECONOMY

Djibouti is a very poor, underdeveloped country with little arable land and virtually no natural resources. Its sole industry is two small soft-drink plants.

Agriculture - dates, garden vegetables, and livestock
Manufacturing - bottled mineral water, construction plants, hides and skins, meat packing, milk products, ships' supplies, and transit trade
Exports - hides and skins
Imports - chemicals, cotton goods, flour, machinery and electrical equipment, and sugar

LIFE-STYLE

More than half of the country's people live in the city of Djibouti. The Afars and Issas have traditionally been nomads, so it is difficult to determine exact population figures. Many wander over the countryside with herds of goats, sheep, camels, and cattle. Life is difficult for the nomads because of the country's terrible heat, scarcity of water, and shortage of vegetation for grazing. As a result, almost 250,000 Issas and Afars now live in the capital city of Djibouti. However, life in the city is not much better because of poverty and an unemployment rate of almost 80 percent. Some workers in Djibouti are employed on the docks or in ship-repair yards. Some find work with the railroad, which links the country of Ethiopia to the port at Djibouti. A French military garrison also provides limited employment.

An additional problem for the country and its workers is the addiction of many people to *khat*. Khat is a leaf that, when chewed, produces a feeling of well-being. Vast numbers of workers spend up to 50 percent of their pay on this leaf.

IT'S A FACT!

Mousaalli - the country's highest point, rises 6,768 ft. (2,063 m) above sea level.

Lake Assal - the country's lowest point of elevation and the lowest point in Africa, is located 509 ft. (155 m) below sea level.

DID YOU KNOW...

- Djibouti's importance as a port city is due to its location on the waters leading to the Suez Canal? Djibouti is a free port where no custom duties are paid.
- In ancient times, the country of Djibouti exported frankincense and myrrh, and at one time, salt was traded for its weight in gold?

DOMINICA

North
Atlantic
Ocean

∧ Morne Diablotin

DOMINICA

★ Roseau

Caribbean
Sea

OFFICIAL NAME: Commonwealth of Dominica
LOCATION: Caribbean Sea/North Atlantic Ocean
AREA: 290 sq. mi. (751 sq. km)
POPULATION (Est. 1993): 86,000
CAPITAL/LARGEST CITY: Roseau
GOVERNMENT: Republic governed by a president.
FLAG: Narrow vertical and horizontal stripes of yellow, black, and white divide the green background into four rectangles. A red circle in the center of the flag features a parrot surrounded by ten five-pointed, green stars edged in yellow.
ETHNIC GROUPS: African, Mulatto, Carib Indians
LANGUAGES: English, French Creole (French *patois*)
RELIGIONS: Roman Catholic, Protestant
BASIC MONETARY UNIT: East Caribbean Dollar

GEOGRAPHY

Dominica is one of the Windward Islands of the Lesser Antilles in the Caribbean Sea. It lies approximately 320 mi. (515 km) north of the coast of Venezuela. It has 92 mi. (148 km) of coastline along the Caribbean Sea.

Dominica is a mountainous island that was formed by volcanic eruptions. Most of the island is covered by dense tropical forests. There is flat land along some of the coast. The country boasts many rivers, but most are too rough for use other than by canoes.

CLIMATE

Dominica has a tropical climate moderated by northeast trade winds. From December to March, the climate is mild, but it becomes very hot in July. Temperatures rarely rise above 90°F (32°C) or fall below 65°F (18°C). The mountain areas receive an average of 400 in. (1,000 cm) of rainfall annually. The average rainfall along the coast is 79 in. (201 cm) annually. Dominica occasionally suffers from hurricanes. Because of the heavy rainfall, flash floods are a constant hazard.

ECONOMY

Dominica's economy is based on agriculture. Over 60 percent of the people work on farms. The other 40 percent are employed in processing agricultural products.

Agriculture - bananas, citrus fruits, coconuts, and spices
Manufacturing - clothing, copra, lime juice, straw handicrafts, vanilla, and wines
Mining - pumice
Natural Resource - forests
Exports - bananas, bay oil, coconuts and coconut by-products, grapefruit, oranges, and vegetables
Imports - chemicals, food, machinery and equipment, and manufactured goods

LIFE-STYLE

Most Dominicans have African or mixed African, British, and French ancestry. A small percentage have Carib Indian ancestry.

About four-fifths of the people live in rural villages. They farm small plots of land and raise only enough food for their own use. Houses tend to be Western-style or thatch-roofed huts. Clothing is Western-style.

The Dominicans' main foods include bananas, crabs, crayfish, frog legs, lobsters, and sweet potatoes.

The population of Dominica has a literacy rate of about 90 percent. It has about 55 elementary schools and seven high schools.

IT'S A FACT!

Morne Diablotin - the country's highest point, rises 4,747 ft. (1,447 m) above sea level.

DID YOU KNOW...

• The first inhabitants of Dominica were the Arawak Indians, who settled there about 2,000 years ago?
• In 1493, Christopher Columbus was the first European to sight the island? He named it *Dominica*, the Latin word for "Sunday," because he saw the island on Sunday.
• Dominica is the site of the only remaining settlement of Carib Indians—who took over the island 1,000 years ago—in the Americas?
• In 1980, Dominica elected the first woman prime minister in the Caribbean region, Mary Eugenia Charles?

DOMINICAN REPUBLIC

OFFICIAL NAME: República Dominicana (Dominican Republic)
LOCATION: Northern Caribbean Sea
AREA: 18,816 sq. mi. (48,734 sq. km)
POPULATION (Est. 1993): 7,604,000
CAPITAL: Santo Domingo
LARGEST CITIES: Santo Domingo, Santiago de los Caballeros
GOVERNMENT: Republic headed by a president.
FLAG: The national flag has a white cross in the center with blue and red quadrants at the top and red and blue quadrants at the bottom. White represents salvation, blue represents liberty, and red represents the blood of heroes.
ETHNIC GROUPS: Black/White mix, Black, White, Jewish
LANGUAGES: Spanish, English
RELIGIONS: Roman Catholic, voodoo
BASIC MONETARY UNIT: Dominican Peso

GEOGRAPHY

Dominican Republic is a country which makes up the eastern two-thirds of Hispaniola Island, which it shares with the country of Haiti. At its greatest distances, Dominican Republic measures 170 mi. (274 km) from north to south and 240 mi. (388 km) from east to west. It has 604 mi. (972 km) of coastline along the North Atlantic Ocean and the Caribbean Sea.

Dominican Republic has mountainous terrain. The *Cordillera Central* (Central Mountain Range) crosses the country from the northwest to the southeast. The land west of this is dry and desertlike, and includes the Sierra de Neiba and the Sierra de Bahoruco mountain ranges. North of the Cordillera Central is an area of pine-covered slopes known as the *Cibao* and a fertile plain known as the *Vega Real* (Royal Plain). The latter is where most of the country's crops are grown. To the far north is the *Cordillera Septentrional* (Northerly Range).

CLIMATE

Dominican Republic has a warm, tropical climate all year long. There are two rainy seasons—a northern one which lasts from December to April and a southern one which lasts from May to November. Average daily temperatures range from 60° to 90°F (16° to 32°C), and the average rainfall is about 60 in. (150 cm) per year. Hurricanes sometimes strike between the months of July and October.

ECONOMY

Dominican Republic's economy is based on agriculture.
Agriculture - avocados, bananas, beans, cacao beans, cattle, coffee, corn, cotton, dairy products, hogs, mangoes, oranges, potatoes, rice, sugar cane, and tobacco
Manufacturing - cement, molasses, sugar processing, textiles, and tobacco
Mining - clay, gold, gypsum, limestone, nickel, and salt.
Exports - cocoa, coffee, gold, nickel, and sugar
Imports - chemicals, cotton and fabrics, food, petroleum, and pharmaceuticals

LIFE-STYLE

Dominican Republic's population is about half urban and half rural. The rural population lives mainly in small, two-room shacks with dirt floors and thatched roofs or in small, government-built houses and makes a living by working on small farms or large plantations. The urban population mainly lives in crowded, Spanish-style apartments and makes a living by fishing, working in factories, or working for the government. Most Dominicans wear modern clothing.

Staples of the Dominican diet include beans, rice, and *yuca* (cassava), the latter of which is commonly served boiled, as fritters, or as *casabe* (baked into crisp cracker bread rounds). Tropical fruits are eaten when in season and chicken, beef, goat, and pork are eaten in small quantities. Fresh fish is generally eaten only in coastal areas. *Sancocho* (stew of meats and vegetables) is served on special occasions and *habichuelas con dulce* (a sweetened drink made from beans) is served at Easter. Commonly consumed beverages include beer, coffee (usually served strong and sweet), rum, soft drinks, and sweetened fruit juices.

Baseball is the most popular sport. Other recreational activities include attending concerts and the theater, socializing, and watching television. Cockfights and dominoes are both national pastimes. The *merengue* is the national dance; the *salsa* and other Latino styles are also popular. Dominican music mixes African drums, Spanish *maracas* (dried gourd shells filled with seeds and lead), and North American jazz and pop. Most Dominicans speak Spanish and follow Spanish customs.

Children ages seven to 14 are required to attend school. Health care is free, but public institutions are generally understaffed and lack adequate facilities. Rural Dominicans often have to travel in order to receive adequate care. *Curanderos* (native healers) are still consulted by many. Dominicans commonly suffer from malaria and intestinal parasites.

IT'S A FACT!

Duarte Peak - the country's highest point, rises 10,417 ft. (3,175 m) above sea level.

Lake Enriquillo - the country's lowest point, is located 150 ft. (46 m) below sea level.

 DID YOU KNOW...

- Only about one in every 15 Dominicans owns a television set, and less than two percent own an automobile?
- Many Dominicans have become famous American and Canadian major league baseball players?

EASTER ISLAND
Dependency of Chile

EASTER ISLAND

★Hanga Roa

•Orongo   *South Pacific Ocean*

OFFICIAL NAME: Easter Island
LOCATION: South Pacific Ocean
AREA: 47 sq. mi. (122 sq. km)
POPULATION (Est. 1993): 2,000
CAPITAL/LARGEST CITY: Hanga Roa
GOVERNMENT: Dependency of Chile.
ETHNIC GROUP: Polynesian, Chilean
LANGUAGES: Spanish, Rapanui (a Polynesian language)
RELIGION: Roman Catholic

GEOGRAPHY

Easter Island is at the easternmost end of a group of Pacific Islands referred to as Polynesia. The island is located about 2,300 mi. (3,700 km) west of Chile. At its greatest distances, Easter Island measures 15 mi. (24 km) from north to south and 11 mi. (17 km) from east to west. The soil is stony, a result of the island's three extinct volcanoes.

ECONOMY

Easter Island's economy is based mainly on tourism and wool production for export.

LIFE-STYLE

The family is the most important social unit in the country. Traditionally, the people have lived on what they could produce or take from the land. They hunted birds and wild animals and also gathered fruit and grew crops. The island's source of fresh water comes from crater lakes (formed in the island's three extinct volcanoes), tanks (pools), and wells.

Control over the land or exclusive ownership by an individual is not part of the islanders' tradition. Labor for the sole purpose of earning money seems unusual for them. Work is done in groups and involves only those activities necessary for sustaining life. Among these chores are building houses, defending the group, growing food, hunting, and making tools and weapons.

IT'S A FACT!

Orongo - an ancient sacred village.
Stone Statues - carved hundreds of years ago, there are more than 600 are scattered throughout the island.

 DID YOU KNOW...

- The country's name was selected by a Dutch explorer, Jacob Roggeveen, who landed there on Easter Sunday in 1722?
- Some of the island's stone statues stand 40 ft. (12 m) high and weigh as much as 90 short tons (82 metric tons)?
- The island's stone statues are called *moai* and were placed on raised temple platforms called *ahu*?
- In 1877, after years of slave raids and exposure to deadly diseases, only 110 natives remained on the island? Since then the native population has grown.
- In Spanish, the country's name is *Isla de Pascua* ; in Rapanui, the country's name is *Rapa Nui* ?

- Because of vast distances from the mainland, the South Pacific (of which Easter Island is a part) was the last major area of the world to be explored, populated, and colonized? This isolation did not end until 1960.
- Easter Island has been governed by Chile since 1888?

ECUADOR

OFFICIAL NAME: República del Ecuador (Republic of Ecuador)
LOCATION: South America
AREA: 109,484 sq. mi. (283,561 sq. km)
POPULATION (Est. 1995): 11,822,000
CAPITAL: Quito
LARGEST CITIES: Guayaquil, Quito
GOVERNMENT: Republic governed by a president.
FLAG: Three horizontal stripes of yellow, blue, and red with the coat of arms in the center.
ETHNIC GROUPS: Mestizo, Indian, Black, White
LANGUAGES: Spanish, Quechua
RELIGION: Roman Catholic
BASIC MONETARY UNIT: Sucre

GEOGRAPHY

Ecuador is one of the smallest countries in South America. The Galapagos Islands, which lie 600 mi. (970 km) off the Pacific coast, belong to Ecuador. At its greatest distances, Ecuador measures 450 mi. (724 km) from north to south and 395 mi. (636 km) from east to west. It has 1,278 mi. (2,057 km) of coastline—including that of the Galapagos Islands—along the Pacific Ocean. The mainland has three regions: 1) the Coastal Lowland, 2) the Andes Highland, and 3) the Eastern Lowland.

The Coastal Lowland is a flat plain formed by mud and sand deposits. It covers about one-fourth of Ecuador. In the north, it is swampy, while in the south, near Peru, it is a desert. Tropical forests are found in between. The Andes Highland, often called the Sierra, covers another fourth of the country and includes some active volcanoes. The Eastern Lowland, frequently called the *Oriente*, covers about half of Ecuador. It is a region of thick tropical forests.

CLIMATE

Ecuador's climate varies with the altitude. The Coastal and Eastern Lowlands are hot and humid. The temperature averages about 75°F (24°C). In the Andes, the plateaus have springlike weather year-round. The average temperature is 57°F (14°C). However, the higher the altitude the lower the temperature. Snow covers the Andes from heights of 16,000 ft. (4,880 m) and above. Ecuador's rainfall averages 55 in. (140 cm) per year.

ECONOMY

Service industries make up 45 percent of Ecuador's gross domestic product. These industries include communication and transportation, as well as finance, insurance, and real estate.

Agriculture - bananas, beef, cacao, coffee, corn, milk, oranges, potatoes, rice, sugar cane, and wheat

Fishing - herring, mackerel, and shrimp

Forestry - balsa wood

Manufacturing - cement, drugs, processed food, straw hats, and textiles

Mining - petroleum

Exports - bananas, cocoa, coffee, petroleum, and shrimp

Imports - cars, chemicals, machinery, and trucks

LIFE-STYLE

About 45 percent of Ecuador's population live in rural areas. The small wealthy class (mostly of European descent) live in cities. Some are absentee landowners who employ managers to run their *haciendas* (large farms or estates). Others own large plantations.

Many mestizos live along the coast in wooden homes with thatched roofs. They work primarily on large banana or cacao plantations. Most of the Indians live in adobe homes in Andean villages. Some work on haciendas and instead of monetary payment are given small plots of land to grow food on for their families.

Approximately 20 percent of Ecuadorians over age 14 cannot read or write. This is due partly to the fact that most of the schools are in urban areas.

Some favorite dishes are *arroz con pollo* (fried chicken with rice), *llapingachos* (cheese and potato cakes), and *empanada* (pastry filled with meat and cheese).

Soccer, volleyball, track, tennis, basketball, and boxing are favorite sports. A variety of museums and cultural sites offer recreation to many people. Villagers gather in open-air markets to conduct business, talk with friends, and celebrate with music and dance.

IT'S A FACT!

Chimborazo Volcano - the country's highest point, is located in the Andes Mountains and rises 20,561 ft. (6,267 m) above sea level.

DID YOU KNOW...

• Ecuador is the Spanish word for equator?
• Panama hats (straw hats woven by hand) are made in Ecuador?
• Many Ecuadorians place bread-dough dolls on gravestones to honor the dead on All Souls Day (November 25)?
• Charles Darwin conducted studies on the unique plant and animal life found on the Galapagos Islands? These studies led to the writing of his book *The Origin of Species* which discusses his theory of evolution.

EGYPT

OFFICIAL NAME: Arab Republic of Egypt
LOCATION: Northeast Africa
AREA: 386,662 sq. mi. (1,001,449 sq. km)
POPULATION (Est. 1995): 58,519,000
CAPITAL: Cairo
LARGEST CITIES: Cairo, Giza, Alexandria
GOVERNMENT: Republic governed by a prime minister.
FLAG: Three vertical stripes of red, white, and black. A golden eagle is centered on the white stripe.
ETHNIC GROUP: Arab
LANGUAGE: Arabic
RELIGION: Islam
BASIC MONETARY UNIT: Pound

GEOGRAPHY

Egypt is fairly square in shape and is bordered on the north by the Mediterranean Sea and on the east by the Red Sea, and is cut from north to south by the Nile River. It lies primarily in Africa, however its Sinai Peninsula is located in Asia. Much of Egypt is covered by desert. Most of its population live along its two major waterways—the Nile and the Suez Canal. Egypt has four main land regions: 1) the Nile Valley and Delta, 2) the Western Desert, 3) the Eastern Desert, and 4) the Sinai Peninsula.

The Nile Valley and Delta region follows the course of the Nile River. This region contains most of the farmland in Egypt.

The Western Desert, also called the Libyan Desert, covers about two-thirds of Egypt. It is part of the Sahara Desert. It is mainly a large, sandy plateau with some ridges and basins and pit-shaped areas called *depressions*.

The Eastern Desert, or Arabian Desert, is also a part of the Sahara Desert. It spreads eastward from the Nile as a sloping, sandy plateau. The land is impossible to cultivate because of the *wadis*, a series of rocky hills and deep valleys.

The Sinai Peninsula is largely a desert area east of the Suez Canal and the Gulf of Suez. It contains a flat, sandy, coastal plain in the north, a huge limestone plateau in the center, and mountains in the south. Jabal Katrinah, Egypt's highest elevation, is found here at 8,651 ft. (2,637 m) above sea level. Rich oil deposits are also located in the Sinai Peninsula.

CLIMATE

Egypt has primarily a desert climate with extremely hot summers and mild winters. Summer lasts from about May to October and winter lasts from about November to April. Daily temperatures in the deserts vary greatly. The average daytime temperature is 104°F (40°C), while the nighttime temperature may be as low as 45°F (7°C) after sunset. Average high temperatures in January range from 65°F (18°C) in Cairo to 74°F (23°C) in Aswan, while average high temperatures in July range from 96°F (36°C) in Cairo to 106°F (41°C) in Aswan. There is almost no rainfall in most of Egypt. The Mediterranean coast gets an occasional storm in the wintertime, where an average of 8 in. (20 cm) of rain falls annually. Around the month of April, a hot windstorm called the *khamsin* strikes Egypt. Its driving winds blow large amounts of sand and dust at high speeds. The khamsin may raise temperatures as much as 68°F (38°C) in two hours and can damage crops.

ECONOMY

Egypt is a developing country with a huge foreign debt, due to the fact that it has to import most of its food and its petroleum exports are incurring falling prices. Agriculture provides the most jobs. Because of its warm, dry climate and ancient attractions, Egypt's tourist industry has contributed significantly to its economy. However, due to possible violence, many travelers have avoided Egypt and thus, the tourist industry has suffered.

Agriculture - corn, cotton, oranges, potatoes, rice, sugar cane, tomatoes, and wheat
Manufacturing - chemicals, cotton textiles, fertilizers, processed foods, and steel
Mining - petroleum
Exports - cotton fibers and products, fruits, and petroleum
Imports - food, machinery, and transportation equipment

LIFE-STYLE

About half of all Egyptians live in cities. They cope with the same problems as other city dwellers—crowding and congested streets. There are great extremes of wealth and poverty in Egyptian cities. There are slum areas flanked by well-to-do residential areas. Because there is a serious lack of housing, people live in shacks they build on other people's land or on the roofs of apartment buildings.

The other half of Egypt's population live in the countryside. They are known as *fellahin* and most of them farm small plots of land or tend animals. They live in huts made of mud bricks or stone and have straw roofs. A small minority of Egypt's rural people are Bedouin nomads who wander the deserts with their herds of camels, goats, and sheep.

The styles of clothing in Egypt reflect the varied ways of life. Many city dwellers wear Western-style clothing. Poor people in rural areas wear the traditional clothing, which consists of a *galabiyaha* (a long shirtlike garment) and pants for the men and long, dark or bright gowns for the women. Men who follow Islamic customs grow beards and wear long, light-colored gowns and skullcaps, while the women wear robes and cover their hair, ears, and arms with a veil.

Most Egyptians eat a simple diet based on bread and broad beans. *Tahina* (sesame seed paste), cucumbers, tomatoes, and yogurt are typical Egyptian foods.

Around 45 percent of adult Egyptians are illiterate. Children ages six to 15 are required to attend school. This law is only enforced, however, for ages six through 12.

Egypt has long been the focus for much unrest, not only because of its relationship with Israel, but also due to factions from within. Fundamentalists seeking an Islamic state have made Egypt unsafe for government officials and tourists.

Soccer is very popular in Egypt, but the main form of recreation in both cities and towns is socializing. People enjoy going to the *bazaar* (outdoor market) to do business and to visit with friends. Egypt also has a rich artistic tradition. The ancient Egyptians created many fine paintings and statues.

IT'S A FACT!

Aswan High Dam - opened over 2 million acres of Egypt's land to cultivation and doubled its agricultural production. It measures 364 ft. (111 m) high and 2 1/3 mi. (3.7 km) long. The dam, located on the northern shore of Lake Nasser in southeastern Egypt, began operating in 1968.

The Great Sphinx - an enormous limestone statue with the head of a human and the body of a lion, was built about 4,500 years ago and stands 66 ft. (20 m) high and is 240 ft. (73 m) long.

Lake Nasser - a huge lake which covers 1,550 sq. mi. (4,014 sq. km), was formed when the Aswan High Dam opened to block the Nile River.

Nile River - the longest river in the world, measures 4,145 mi. (6,671 km). It runs north and south through Egypt for 900 mi. (1,448 km).

Qattara Depression - located in the Sahara Desert, is a place of limited plant life and coarse sand and gravel. The depression covers 7,000 sq. mi. (18,200 sq. km) and is the lowest point in Egypt at 436 ft. (133 m) below sea level.

Sahara - is the world's largest desert. It consists almost entirely of a large, sandy plateau with some ridges and basins, but it also includes a few mountain ranges and rocky plateaus. The Sahara extends more that 3,500 mi. (5,630 km) across northern Africa from the Atlantic Ocean to the Red Sea. It covers about 3.5 million sq. mi. (9 million sq. km), an area roughly equal in size to the United States.

Suez Canal - a narrow artificial waterway in Egypt that extends about 118 mi. (190 km) to join the Mediterranean and Red Seas. It was the busiest interocean waterway in the world until 1967, when it was closed due to war.

Valley of the Kings - a gorge used as a cemetery by Egypt's pharaohs between 1550 and 1100 B.C. The hieroglyphic texts and religious scenes that cover the walls of the tombs portray the kings' activities in the hereafter. Tutankhamen and Ramses II are among the many tombs located there.

 DID YOU KNOW...
- Village life and many Egyptian customs have not changed for hundreds of years?
- Some people in Egypt still use camels to travel in rural areas?
- Cairo, Egypt's capital, is the largest city in Africa?

EL SALVADOR

OFFICIAL NAME: República de El Salvador (Republic of El Salvador)
LOCATION: Central America
AREA: 8,124 sq. mi. (21,041 sq. km)
POPULATION (Est. 1993): 5,651,000
CAPITAL: San Salvador
LARGEST CITIES: San Salvador, Santa Ana
GOVERNMENT: Representative democracy governed by a president.
FLAG: Three horizontal stripes of blue, white, and blue. Blue represents unity and white represents peace. The coat of arms—which is encircled by the words *Republica de El Salvador en La America Central*—is centered on the white stripe.
ETHNIC GROUP: Mestizo
LANGUAGE: Spanish
RELIGION: Roman Catholic
BASIC MONETARY UNIT: Salvadoran Colón

GEOGRAPHY

El Salvador, the smallest Central American country in area, measures 88 mi. (142 km) from north to south and 163 mi. (262 km) from east to west at its greatest distances. It has 189 mi. (304 km) of coastline along the Pacific Ocean.

El Salvador is a tropical land of mountains, volcanoes, valleys, and lakes. It has three main land regions: 1) the Coastal Lowlands, 2) the Central Region, and 3) the Interior Highlands.

The Coastal Lowlands are a narrow, fertile plain along the ocean shore. The Central Region contains most of the country's industry and fertile farmland. A band of rugged mountains and inactive volcanoes form the southern border of this region. The Interior Highlands cover northern El Salvador. The Sierra Madre, a low mountain range of hardened volcanic material, spans most of this region.

CLIMATE

El Salvador has a tropical climate. Average temperatures range from 80°F (27°C) on the Pacific coast to 73°F (23°C) in the mountains. Annual rainfall averages 85 in. (216 cm) along the coast to less than 60 in. (150 cm) in the northwest.

ECONOMY

El Salvador's rich volcanic soil is its main natural resource. The economy depends mainly on agriculture, especially coffee.

Agriculture - beans, coffee, corn, cotton, rice, and sugar cane

Manufacturing - chemicals, cigarettes, processed food and beverages, leather goods, and textiles

Exports - coffee, cotton, sugar, and textiles

Imports - chemicals, food, machinery, and petroleum

LIFE-STYLE

El Salvador is the most heavily populated nation on the mainland of the Americas. It holds about ten times as many people per square mile as the United States.

Close to half of El Salvador's population lives in rural areas, mostly on farms. Some live in adobe houses. The poorer farmers live in *wattle huts,* with walls of interwoven branches covered with mud. The wealthy live on plantations in huge homes.

In urban areas, the poor live in crowded one-room apartments, the middle-class in row houses or apartments, and the wealthy in beautiful suburban homes.

Most Salvadorans primarily eat beans, bread, corn, and rice. In late afternoon, many people snack on *pupusas*, cornmeal cakes stuffed with chopped meat, beans, and spices.

About two-thirds of the country's adults are literate, but the country's public education system is inadequate. Many rural areas lack schools.

Soccer, the national sport, is also the most popular sport. Many Salvadorans spend weekends at resorts near lakes or on the beaches of the Pacific coast.

IT'S A FACT!

Lempa River - the country's longest river, rises in the Sierra Madre and flows 200 mi. (320 km) to the Pacific Ocean.

Monte Cristo - the country's highest point, rises 7,933 ft. (2,418 m) above sea level.

 DID YOU KNOW...
- During the rainy season—May to October—rain showers fall every afternoon?
- El Salvador is the third largest country in population in Central America, ranking after Guatemala and Honduras?
- Los Chorros, a popular national park, has swimming pools, waterfalls, and tropical gardens?

ENGLAND
Division of the United Kingdom

OFFICIAL NAME: England
LOCATION: Northwestern Europe
AREA: 50,378 sq. mi. (130,478 sq. km)
POPULATION (Est. 1995): 48,367,000
CAPITAL: London
LARGEST CITIES: London, Birmingham, Leeds
GOVERNMENT: Constitutional monarchy.
FLAG: White field with a red cross extending to all edges. It has been in use for over 700 years but never officially adopted.
ETHNIC GROUP: English
LANGUAGE: English
RELIGION: Christianity
BASIC MONETARY UNIT: Pound

GEOGRAPHY

England is located on the southeastern portion of the island of Great Britain in the British Isles. England is the largest in area of the four political components that make up the United Kingdom of Great Britain and Northern Ireland. At its greatest distances, England measures about 360 mi. (579 km) from north to south and about 270 mi. (435 km) from east to west. It has about 1,150 mi. (1,851 km) of coastline along the North Sea, the English Channel, the Bristol Channel, and the Irish Sea.

England is made up of three main land regions: 1) the Pennines, 2) the Southwest Peninsula, and 3) the English Lowlands.

The Pennines, a mountain chain often referred to as the "backbone of England," extend from the Scottish border down to about the middle of England. The Lake District, an area containing many lakes and mountains, lies west of the Pennines.

The Southwest Peninsula contains highlands rising above a low plateau. This plateau ends abruptly along much of the coast, creating steep cliffs.

The English Lowlands include all land not accounted for in the two other regions, and contain most of the country's farmland, industry, and population. The lowlands along the English Channel end sharply in cliffs. The country's white cliffs of Dover, on the Strait of Dover, are world-renowned.

England's area also comprises offshore islands, including the Isle of Wight and the Isles of Scilly. England's longest rivers include the Thames, Trent, and Severn. The country has over 2,000 mi. (3,200 km) of inland waterways.

CLIMATE

England has a temperate climate with cooler, wetter weather occurring in the north. Annual temperatures rarely fall below 25°F (-4°C) in winter and seldom rise above 75°F (24°C) in summer. The climate is greatly influenced by southwest winds that blow across warm Gulf Stream currents. These breezes bring warmth in the winter and cool breezes in the summer, along with heavy precipitation.

ECONOMY

Manufacturing has played a major role in England's economy since the Industrial Revolution, which began in the 1700s in England. Service industries, predominately banking and insurance, employ about 70 percent of the people. London's stock exchange is one of the world's busiest, and Lloyd's insurance society operates worldwide.

Agriculture - barley, cattle, chickens and eggs, fruit, milk, potatoes, sheep, sugar beets, and wheat

Fishing - cod, haddock, and mackerel

Manufacturing - aircraft engines, beverages, chemicals, clothing, electronic equipment, fabricated steel products, footwear, leather goods, paper, printed materials, processed foods, tobacco, wool and other textiles

Mining - chalk, china clay, coal, natural gas, and petroleum

Exports - consumer goods, crude oil, fine pottery, and manufactured goods

LIFE-STYLE

England's population is about 95 percent urban, and the country's seven large metropolitan areas account for about 35 percent of that. Prior to the mid-1800s, England's population was primarily rural. Urban growth stemmed from the Industrial Revolution.

England's urban areas are crowded with modern buildings related to business and entertainment. The suburban areas surrounding the crowded city centers are made up of neat brick houses. As gardening is a favorite English hobby, most homes have a garden. The urban and suburban areas are divided by rows of identical houses, called *terraced houses*, and abandoned or semi-used factories. Living conditions in these areas are often substandard.

England's small rural population makes a living by farming. Rural areas can be found largely on the southwest peninsula, in an area near the Wash, a bay of the North Sea, and in the Pennines in the north. Villages, towns, or isolated dwellings serve as homes to rural inhabitants.

The English wear Western-style clothing similar to that worn by people in the United States, though it is influenced more by European styles.

English food is generally simple with few spices and sauces. Roasted and grilled meats are often eaten with potatoes, another vegetable, and a dessert. Popular dishes include *shepherd's pie* (ground meat and mashed potatoes served as a casserole), and *steak and kidney pie* (pastry-crust topped stew). *Yorkshire pudding* (cake batter baked in meat fat) is commonly served with beef. *Fish and chips* is also popular. Preferred alcoholic beverages include beer and Scotch whiskey. Squash, a nonalcoholic drink made of water and orange or lemon concentrate, is also enjoyed.

Children ages five to 16 are required to attend school. About 90 percent of the children attend schools supported by public funds. The remaining children attend private schools, which the English call *public schools.* Two of England's universities are world-famous—Cambridge and Oxford. Almost all English residents are literate.

Popular team sports include *football* (similar to American soccer), cricket, and *rugby* football (similar to American football). Recreational activities include *bowls* (similar to bowling), darts, dominoes, golf, horseback riding, rowing, sailing, swimming, and tennis. Despite controversy, some British aristocrats still participate in the traditional fox hunt, in which hunters on horseback follow a pack of hounds as they chase a wild fox through the countryside.

Socializing at *pubs* (neighborhood taverns) is a common leisure activity, as well as spending an evening in front of the television. In addition, attending concerts, plays, and motion pictures are frequent pastimes.

England's *motorways* (expressways) are extensive. The country's system of inland waterways are used mainly for recreational boating. Ferry and hovercraft services offer passage across the English Channel to France. An underground tunnel built beneath the English Channel, connecting England with France, opened in 1994.

IT'S A FACT!

Hadrian's Wall - built in the 120s, extended from Solway Firth to the North Sea as protection against northern raiders. Portions of the wall still stand.

Scaffell Pike - the country's highest point, rises 3,210 ft. (978 m) above sea level.

Stonehenge - located near the city of Salisbury, is a series of large stone monuments that dates back to the early 1000s B.C.

 DID YOU KNOW...

- In England, the word for elevator is *lift* and the word for cookies is *biscuits*?
- England is the birthplace of such renowned historic personalities as Geoffrey Chaucer, Charles Dickens, Sir Christopher Wren, Sir Isaac Newton, and William Shakespeare?
- Today's rock music was heavily influenced by such English groups as the Beatles and the Rolling Stones?
- The Great Fire of London, which occurred in 1666, destroyed many buildings, including St. Paul's Cathedral which was eventually rebuilt by Sir Christopher Wren?
- The term for a late afternoon meal is *tea*?
- England's Lake District contains 16 lakes within a 30 mi. (48 km) diameter?
- Piccadilly Circus is not a circus at all, but rather a busy intersection in London where six streets come together?

EQUATORIAL GUINEA

OFFICIAL NAME: República de Guinea Ecuatorial
(Republic of Equatorial Guinea)
LOCATION: Western Africa
AREA: 10,831 sq. mi. (28,051 sq. km)
POPULATION (Est. 1993): 380,000
CAPITAL: Malabo
LARGEST CITIES: Bata, Malabo
GOVERNMENT: Republic in transition to multiparty democracy.
FLAG: Three horizontal stripes of green, white, and red overlapped by a blue triangle based on the hoist side. The coat of arms is centered on the white stripe.
ETHNIC GROUPS: Fang, Bubi
LANGUAGES: Spanish, Fang, Bubi
RELIGION: Christianity
BASIC MONETARY UNIT: CFA Franc

GEOGRAPHY

Equatorial Guinea is located in western Africa. The country includes a small area on the continent and five offshore islands in the Gulf of Guinea. Most of the population lives on the continental area called Río Muni. Bioko is the largest of the islands and is located northwest off the mainland. The other islands—Corisco, Elobey Chico, Elobey Grande, and Annobon—lie southwest of Río Muni. Most of the country is covered by dense tropical rainforests with plains along the coasts of Río Muni and Bioko.

CLIMATE

The country has a hot and humid equatorial climate. Temperatures generally average above 80°F (27°C). Annual rainfall ranges from 76 in. (193 cm) in Malabo to 430 in. (1,090 cm) in Ureca on the opposite end of the island of Bioko.

ECONOMY

Equatorial Guinea's economy is based primarily on agriculture with 90 percent of the people engaged in subsistence farming. Forestry and fishing are also important economic activities.

Agriculture - bananas, cacao, cassava, coffee, sweet potatoes, and timber

Exports - cacao, coffee, and timber

LIFE-STYLE

Over 70 percent of the population of Equatorial Guinea live in rural areas and the majority of this group farm for a living. Others work in lumber camps or fish. Most of the remaining population live in urban areas and make their living working in small industries or in import-export businesses.

Cassava and other starchy roots, along with various nut dishes, are the main foods eaten by Equatoguineans. Fish and meat sources, such as chickens, rodents, monkeys, and snakes, are also eaten.

Schooling is compulsory for all children until the age of 12. But, due to a severe shortage of teachers, many are not able to receive an education. There are no colleges or universities in the country.

A major social concern is the poor health services available in the country. Due to a shortage of physicians, diseases such as malaria and measles are widespread.

IT'S A FACT!

Santa Isabel Mountain - the country's highest point, rises 9,869 ft. (3,008 m) above sea level.

Río Mbini - divides the continental portion of the country in half.

DID YOU KNOW...

- The country's most important tree for timber, the *okoume tree*, is used to make plywood?
- Pygmies were probably the earliest people who lived in the area around Río Muni?

ERITREA

OFFICIAL NAME: State of Eritrea
FORMERLY: Eritrea Autonomous Region in Ethiopia (until 1993)
LOCATION: Northeastern Africa
AREA: 45,405 sq. mi. (117,598 sq. km)
POPULATION (Est. 1995): 3,651,000
CAPITAL/LARGEST CITY: Asmara (formerly Asmera)
GOVERNMENT: In transition; headed by a president elected by a 136-member National Assembly.
FLAG: Red triangle based on the hoist side divides the flag into two triangles of green (top) and blue. Centered on the red triangle is a yellow olive branch surrounded by a yellow wreath.
ETHNIC GROUPS: Tigray, Tigre, and Kunama
LANGUAGES: Tigrinya, Tigre, Arabic, Afar
RELIGIONS: Christianity, Islam
BASIC MONETARY UNIT: Birr

GEOGRAPHY

The newly independent, small country of Eritrea measures 510 mi. (821 km) from northwest to southeast and 290 mi. (467 km) from northeast to southwest at its greatest distances. Its coastline stretches about 620 mi. (1,000 km) along the Red Sea.

Eritrea has a coastal plain that rises to central highlands. West of the central highlands are lowlands, and the southeast is home to the Denakil Desert. Eritrea's main rivers include the Baraka and the Gash. A portion of the Gash is referred to as the Marab.

CLIMATE

Eritrea's climate varies. The coastal region is generally hot and dry, whereas the central highlands are usually cooler and wetter. The western hills and lowlands are semiarid. The average temperature ranges from 60°F (16°C) in the central highlands to 80°F (27°C) along the coast. The average rainfall is about 6-10 in. (15-25 cm) along the coast and up to 24 in. (61 cm) in the highlands. The heaviest rains fall in June and July in most areas. Drought, a frequent problem in Eritrea, has been somewhat relieved by irrigation.

ECONOMY

Eritrea's main economic activities include subsistence farming and herding. Most of Eritrea's few industrial facilities were shut down or damaged during the civil war; however, petroleum refinery operates near Assab, one of Eritrea's chief ports.

Agriculture - barley, cattle, dairy products, goats, lentils, millet, sheep, sorghum, teff, and wheat

Manufacturing - construction materials, leather goods, processed foods, and salt

LIFE-STYLE

Eritrea's population is over 85 percent rural. Most Eritreans are farmers or herders. Farming occurs primarily in the central highlands region, while herding takes place in the western lowlands region and along the coast. Eritrean farm families generally live in enclosed settlements that contain peaked, corrugated-iron or flat, thatched-roof homes. Farm households may include up to several dozen members of an extended family. Farmers socialize with others on market days, at festivals, or at regional village towns. Herders move their livestock from one place to another.

The educational system was disrupted during Eritrea's long civil war. Few children have received a formal education and the literacy rate is very low due to this and the country's frequent famines.

IT'S A FACT!

Denakil Depression - the country's lowest point of elevation, is located 360 ft. (110 m) below sea level.

Mount Soira - the country's highest point, rises 9,885 ft. (3,013 m) above sea level.

 DID YOU KNOW...

- Eritrea was settled by Africans from the heart of the continent around 2000 B.C. and by those from the Arabian Peninsula around 1000 B.C.?
- At independence, Eritrea inherited Ethiopia's coastline; now Ethiopia's economy is dependent upon Eritrea's ports for foreign trade?
- Teff, one of Eritrea's chief agricultural products, is a grain typically grown only in Eritrea and Ethiopia?
- Coptic Christianity, a form of Christianity that originated in Egypt, came to the Eritrean area in the A.D. 300s?
- Civil war between Eritrean rebels, who wanted independence, and Ethiopian government troops began in 1961 and lasted until 1991?

ESTONIA

OFFICIAL NAME: Eesti Vabariik (Republic of Estonia)
FORMERLY: Estonian Soviet Socialist Republic
LOCATION: Northern Europe
AREA: 17,413 sq. mi. (45,100 sq. km)
POPULATION (Est. 1993): 1,616,000
CAPITAL: Tallinn
LARGEST CITIES: Tallinn, Kohtla-Järve, Narva, Tartu
GOVERNMENT: Republic governed by a chief executive and a 101-member legislative body called the Supreme Council.
FLAG: Three horizontal stripes of blue, black, and white representing the sky, the land, and the future, accordingly.
ETHNIC GROUPS: Estonian, Russian, other
LANGUAGES: Estonian, Latvian, Lithuanian, Russian, other
RELIGIONS: Lutheran, Eastern Orthodox
BASIC MONETARY UNIT: Estonian Kroon

GEOGRAPHY

At its greatest distances, Estonia measures 150 mi. (240 km) from north to south and 230 mi. (370 km) from east to west. It has a coastline of 481 mi. (774 km) along the Baltic Sea, the Gulf of Finland, and the Gulf of Riga. About ten percent of the country's area includes more than 1,500 Baltic islands. The two largest islands are Saaremaa and Hiiumaa, both of which are inhabited.

Estonia is mainly a low plain containing about 40 percent farmland, 30 percent forest, and 20 percent swamps. It has a sandy western coast, which is a popular vacation spot.

CLIMATE

Estonia has a mild climate, unusual for such a northern area, because the air is affected by ocean breezes. Average annual temperatures range from 19° to 28° F (-7° to -2° C) in January and from 61° to 64° F (16° to 18° C) in July. The average annual rainfall is 19-23 in. (48-58 cm).

ECONOMY

Estonia's economy is based mainly on manufacturing and mining.

Agriculture - barley, beef cattle, butter, chickens, eggs, fruits, hogs, milk, potatoes, rye, and vegetables

Fishing - cod, herring, perch, pike, salmon, and sole

Manufacturing - cement, chemical fertilizer, clothing, electric motors, excavators, furniture, paper, phosphates, processed foods, shipbuilding, shoes, and textiles

Mining - oil shale

Exports - dairy products, textiles, timber, and wood products

Imports - chemicals, machinery, and oil

LIFE-STYLE

Estonia's population is approximately three-fourths urban and one-fourth rural. Prior to Estonia's industrialization by the Soviet Union, about two-thirds of the population was rural and made a living by farming. Now, many Estonians live in urban apartments and are employed in manufacturing and mining.

Dairy products are staples of the diet. Other commonly eaten foods include apples, beans, cabbage, carrots, cherries, dark rye bread, fish (mainly cod, herring, salmon, sole, perch, pike, and whitefish), meat (mainly beef, chicken, lamb, pork, and veal), pears, potatoes, and wild berries. Popular dishes include *pirukad* (meat- and vegetable-filled pastry) and *rosolje* (pink potato salad with beets and herring). *Sült* (head cheese) and *verivorst* (blood sausage) are commonly eaten at Christmastime. Commonly consumed beverages include coffee and tea.

Popular sports include basketball, cycling, ice boating, ice skating, sailing, swimming, and volleyball. Popular leisure activities include walking in gardens and picking mushrooms and wild berries. Music is an important aspect of Estonian culture. About every five years a song festival is held, attracting thousands of singers and hundreds of thousands of visitors.

Children ages six to 14 are required to attend school. Day care centers and kindergartens provide preschool education. After age 14, a student may either attend high school or a technical school. Following high school, many students continue on to a technical school or a university.

IT'S A FACT!

Suur Munamägi (Great Egghill) - the country's highest point, rises 1,043 ft. (318 m) above sea level.

 DID YOU KNOW...

- Estonia was an independent country between 1918 and 1940, was occupied by the Soviet Union for over 50 years, and then regained its independence in 1991?
- As early as 7000 B.C., people lived in the area now known as Estonia?
- Estonia was one of the last European nations to convert to Christianity?
- Tallinn's Old Town is one of the best-preserved European medieval villages and features cobblestone streets, defense towers, and Gothic buildings?
- The government restricted religious freedom from 1940 through the late 1980s, when the restrictions were lifted?

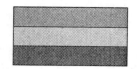

ETHIOPIA

OFFICIAL NAME: Federal Democratic Republic of Ethiopia
LOCATION: Eastern Africa
AREA: 426,373 sq. mi. (1,104,302 sq. km)
POPULATION (Est. 1995): 53,711,000
CAPITAL/LARGEST CITY: Addis Ababa
GOVERNMENT: Transitional.
FLAG: Three horizontal stripes of green, yellow, and red.
ETHNIC GROUPS: Afar, Amhara, Gurage, Oromo, Somali, Tigrean
LANGUAGES: Amharic, English
RELIGIONS: Islam, Ethiopian Orthodox Christianity
BASIC MONETARY UNIT: Birr

GEOGRAPHY

At its greatest distances, Ethiopia, a landlocked country, measures 800 mi. (1,290 km) from north to south and 1,035 mi. (1,666 km) from east to west.

The Ethiopian Plateau covers about two-thirds of the western and central parts of the country. The Great Rift Valley divides the plateau in half. The other one-third of the country consists of lowlands, which surround the plateau. In the northeastern part of the lowlands are hot deserts. Tropical rainforests can be found in parts of the southwest.

CLIMATE

The average annual temperature on the plateau ranges from 60° to 72°F (16° to 22°C). Rainfall on the plateau averages 40 in. (102 cm) per year. The lowland areas have an average annual temperature of 80°F (27°C). Rainfall in the lowlands is less than 20 in. (51 cm) per year. In the desert region, temperatures may climb to above 120°F (49°C).

ECONOMY

Ethiopia has a developing economy based mainly on agriculture. Agriculture employs 85 percent of the labor force. Five percent of the workers are employed in manufacturing with the remaining ten percent employed in service industries.

Agriculture - coffee, corn, oilseeds, sorghum, sugar cane, teff, and wheat
Manufacturing - cement, processed foods, shoes, and textiles
Exports - coffee, hides and skins, livestock, and oilseeds
Imports - chemicals, crude petroleum, and machinery

LIFE-STYLE

The majority of Ethiopians are farmers who work the land using wooden plows pulled by oxen. A small group of nomads make a living by raising livestock.

Much poverty can be found in rural areas, and although it exists in urban areas as well, it is not as widespread. In the rural areas, people live in round-shaped mud houses with cone-shaped thatched roofs. Sometimes the roofs are made of metal sheeting. In some areas, rectangular stone houses serve as shelters. Traditional housing, as well as modern apartment buildings, exist in towns and cities.

Many urban Ethiopians favor Western-style clothing. The rural population, both men and women, prefer a one-piece garment made of thin, white cotton called a *shamma*.

The Ethiopian diet includes fowl, goat, and lamb. As a general rule, Ethiopians do not eat ham, pork, or turkey. Two common foods are *injera* (a fermented pancake-shaped bread made of teff flour) and *wat* (a thick, spicy stew made with beef or chicken). For those in extreme poverty, the diet consists of grains and supplies from relief agencies.

Soccer, tennis, and volleyball are some of the more popular sports. Ethiopians also enjoy board games, card games, and a type of chess.

IT'S A FACT!

Denakil Depression - the country's lowest point, is located 381 ft. (116 m) below sea level.

Ras Dashen - the country's highest point, rises 15,158 ft. (4,620 m) above sea level.

Tisissat Falls - located on the Ethiopian Plateau, is formed by waters of the Blue Nile River.

 DID YOU KNOW...

- The name *Ethiopia* comes from a Greek word meaning "sunburned faces"?
- Ethiopian children are not required by law to attend school?
- Wild animals found in Ethiopia include antelope, giraffes, elephants, lions, monkeys, and rhinoceroses?
- Severe droughts have taken place in the last twenty years, causing widespread famine?
- Three or more generations of families, from the male line, often live in one house?
- Around 200 dialects and 70 languages are used in Ethiopia?

FAEROE ISLANDS
Overseas Division of Denmark

OFFICIAL NAME: Faeroe Islands
LOCATION: North Atlantic Ocean
AREA: 540 sq. mi. (1,399 sq. km)
POPULATION (Est. 1993): 48,065
CAPITAL/LARGEST CITY: Tórshavn
GOVERNMENT: Self-governing division of Denmark.
FLAG: White field with a red cross outlined in blue.
ETHNIC GROUP: Scandinavian
LANGUAGES: Faroese, Danish
RELIGION: Evangelical Lutheran
BASIC MONETARY UNIT: Danish Krone

GEOGRAPHY

Faeroe Islands (also spelled *Faroe* or *Føroyar)* are a group of 18 inhabited islands and some reefs in the North Atlantic Ocean that lie between Iceland and the Shetland Islands. The country's major islands are Streymoy, Eysturoy, Vágar, Sudhuroy, and Sandoy.

The country has 140 mi. (225 km) of coastline, which is steep and deeply indented. Navigation along the coast is difficult because of dangerous ocean currents. The land is high, rugged, rocky, and naturally treeless due to the strong winds and gales.

CLIMATE

The Faeroe Islands have mild winters and cool overcast summers. They are frequently foggy and windy. About 60 in. (150 cm) of rain fall annually.

ECONOMY

Fishing and related industries are the basis of the country's economy. The people still raise sheep, though sheepherding is not as important economically as in prior years. The islands also receive a subsidy from Denmark.

Agriculture - potatoes, sheep, and vegetables
Manufacturing - fish processing, handicrafts, and ship-building
Exports - animal feedstuffs, fish and fish products, and transport equipment (ships)
Imports - chemicals, food and livestock, fuels, machinery and transport equipment

LIFE-STYLE

Most of the people on Faeroe Islands are sheepherders or fishermen. The people do little farming.

The Faeroese are descendants of the Norwegian Vikings who inhabited the islands in the 800s. They primarily live in small settlements along the coast.

 DID YOU KNOW...
- The country's name first appeared as Faereyiar, meaning "sheep islands"?
- The people collect the eggs and feathers of sea birds, which nest on the steep cliffs, and sell them?
- The islanders have their own parliament and send representatives to the Danish parliament in Copenhagen?

FALKLAND ISLANDS
Dependency of the United Kingdom

OFFICIAL NAME: Colony of the Falkland Islands
LOCATION: South Atlantic Ocean
AREA: 4,699 sq. mi. (12,170 sq. km)
POPULATION (Est. 1993): 2,206
CAPITAL/LARGEST CITY: Stanley
GOVERNMENT: Dependent territory of the United Kingdom.
FLAG: Blue field with the flag of the United Kingdom in the upper, hoist-side quadrant and the Falkland Island coat of arms centered on the flag's outer half. The coat of arms features a white ram above the sailing ship *Desire* with a scroll at the bottom bearing the motto "DESIRE THE RIGHT."
ETHNIC GROUP: British
LANGUAGE: English
RELIGION: Christianity (mainly Anglican)
BASIC MONETARY UNIT: Falkland Island Pound

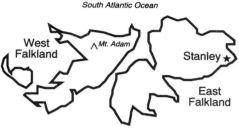

FALKLAND ISLANDS

GEOGRAPHY

The Falkland Islands lie about 320 mi. (515 km) east of Argentina's southern coast. The dependency includes two large islands—East and West Falkland—and 200 smaller ones. East Falkland covers 2,580 sq. mi. (6,682 sq. km) and West Falkland covers 2,038 sq. mi. (5,278 sq. km). The islands have a combined coastline of about 610 mi. (982 km). Most of the islands are treeless and rocky. Layers of black peat form the soil.

CLIMATE

The climate is damp and cool. Strong, almost constant, winds contribute to the lack of trees on the islands. The average annual temperature ranges from 22° to 70°F (-5.6° to 21°C). Snow falls in the winter, but it does not stay for long.

ECONOMY

The Falkland Islands are self-supporting. The main source of government income comes from selling fishing licenses to foreign fishing fleets. Sheep raising is the chief industry. In fact, wool is the basis for the entire economy. Also contributing to government revenues are the sales of postage stamps and coins, mainly to collectors.

Agriculture - oats and sheep
Manufacturing - wool processing
Exports - hides, skins, and wool
Imports - food, machinery, and manufactured goods

LIFE-STYLE

About half of the country's population lives in the city of Stanley. The rest of the people reside in the countryside, referred to as the *Camp*. It is here that hundreds of thousands of sheep are found grazing on farms and stations. The people are very busy during the summer months—November to February. Shearing must be done and, because most people grow their own vegetables, gardens must be planted, tended, and harvested. Most other foodstuffs are imported.

Travelers in the countryside often use horses to go from place to place. Contact between the farms and outlying islands with the city of Stanley is accomplished through the use of two-way radiotelephone sets.

Contact with the outside world is maintained by airplanes and ships. A ship from the Falkland Islands Company makes a round trip between the Falklands and Great Britain several times a year. Seaplanes bring supplies, doctors, passengers, and mail to the various settlements.

Children ages five to 14 are required to attend school. Those who live in isolated areas are instructed by traveling teachers. Students desiring higher education must go to Great Britain.

IT'S A FACT!

Mount Adam - the country's highest point, rises 2,315 ft. (706 m) above sea level.

 DID YOU KNOW...
- Ownership of the Falkland Islands is also claimed by Argentina? Argentinians call the islands *Las Islas Malvinas.*
- Argentinian troops invaded and occupied the islands in April, 1982, but these troops were forced by British troops to surrender in June, 1982?

FIJI

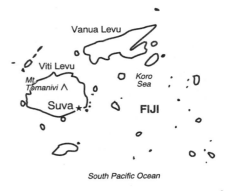

OFFICIAL NAME: Republic of Fiji
LOCATION: South Pacific Ocean
AREA: 7,056 sq. mi. (18,274 sq. km)
POPULATION (Est. 1994): 811,000
CAPITAL/LARGEST CITY: Suva
GOVERNMENT: Republic governed by prime minister. A president is head of state.
FLAG: Light blue field with the flag of the United Kingdom in the upper, hoist-side quadrant. The Fijian shield is centered on the flag's outer half. It depicts sugar cane, coconut palms, bananas, and a dove of peace divided by St. George's cross and set under the British lion.
ETHNIC GROUPS: Indigenous Fijian (Melanesian), Indian
LANGUAGES: English, Fijian, Hindi
RELIGIONS: Christianity, Hinduism, Islam
BASIC MONETARY UNIT: Fiji Dollar

GEOGRAPHY

Fiji's 800 plus islands are located north of New Zealand in the South Pacific Ocean. The two main islands are Viti Levu (Big Fiji) and Vanua Levu (Big Land). Viti Levu occupies about half of Fiji's land area. It is the location of Suva, Fiji's capital and largest city. Vanua Levu covers about one-third of Fiji's land area. Most of Fiji's islands are made from lava built up from the ocean floor; the volcanoes which formed the islands are no longer active. Heat from inactive volcanoes trapped under the islands gives birth to numerous flowing hot springs. Coral reefs surround most of the islands. The bigger islands have tall, volcanic peaks, rivers, grasslands, and rolling hills. The soil is fertile. Thick, tropical rainforests, located on the rainy, southeastern island slopes, together cover over half of Fiji's area.

Only about 100 of Fiji's islands are inhabited. The smaller islands consist of low, coral atolls with sandy beaches and perhaps a few palm trees.

CLIMATE

Fiji has a tropical climate. Temperatures range from 60° to 90°F (16° to 32°C), and trade winds blowing from the east have a pleasant cooling affect. Heavy rains and tropical storms occur during the rainiest months of November to April.

ECONOMY

Fiji's economy is based largely on agriculture. Tourism has become increasingly important.

Agriculture - bananas, cassava, coconut, forest products, sugar cane, and taro
Manufacturing - beer, building materials, cement, and cigarettes
Mining - gold
Exports - copra, gold, sugar, and timber
Imports - food, fuel, and machinery

LIFE-STYLE

About one-fifth of the population live in Suva, the capital. Urban dwellers live in Western-style homes.

Approximately two-thirds of Fiji's indigenous people live in the rural areas, mostly in small farming or fishing villages where they grow and live on their own food. They exist much as did their ancestors from centuries past, celebrating births and marriages by traditional feasting, singing, and dancing. One important ceremony involves drinking *kava* (a beverage derived from pepper plants). Village chiefs advise and lead their villages of 50-400 people. Food and farm tools are shared by villagers. Many men still wear cloth skirts called *sulus*, and some of the women wear cotton dresses. Most native Fijians practice Christianity. A traditional Fijian house, called a *bure*, is one large room having four doors. It is made of wood, a thatched roof, and woven floor covers.

Indians, the other major group in Fiji, live separate lives from native Fijians. Most are descended from laborers brought from India to work on sugar plantations. Some Indian Fijians live in cities where they run shops and small businesses. Indians run much of Fiji's industry and business. Many still work in the cane fields. Indian women wear the traditional dress of India, the sari. Most Indians are Muslims or Hindus. Most Indians live in tin, cement, or wood homes.

Fijian children are not required by law to attend school, yet over 85 percent of children ages six to 13 do attend. About 85 percent of the adult population is literate.

Boiled taro and cassava form the base of the Fijian diet. Also eaten are leafy vegetables, tropical fruits, and various meats. Indian food is often spicy and is made with curry.

IT'S A FACT!

Mount Tomanivi - the islands' highest point, is located on Viti Levu and rises 4,341 ft. (1,323 m) above sea level.

 DID YOU KNOW...

- It is considered rude to touch a Fijian's head?
- Fiji was once known as the "Cannibal Isles"?
- Fiji has been called the "crossroads of the South Pacific" because of its location on major shipping routes, its airport, and its excellent harbors?

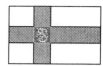

FINLAND

OFFICIAL NAME: Suomen Tasavalta (Republic of Finland)
LOCATION: Northern Europe
AREA: 130,559 sq. mi. (338,145 sq. km)
POPULATION (Est. 1993): 5,008,000
CAPITAL: Helsinki
LARGEST CITIES: Helsinki, Tampere, Turku
GOVERNMENT: Republic governed by a president.
FLAG: A blue cross is positioned to the left on a white field. A yellow-trimmed, red square at the center of the cross features the coat of arms.
ETHNIC GROUPS: Finns, Swedes, Lapps
LANGUAGES: Finnish, Swedish
RELIGION: Evangelical Lutheran
BASIC MONETARY UNIT: Markka

GEOGRAPHY

Finland is famous for its scenic beauty. Thousands of lakes dot the landscape and thick forests cover two-thirds of the land. Thousands of picturesque islands lie off a coast that features colorful gray and red granite. The country measures 640 mi. (1,030 km) from north to south and 320 mi. (515 km) from east to west at its greatest distances. Finland's total area includes 12,943 sq. mi. (33,522 sq. km) of inland water. The country's main land regions are: 1) the Coastal Lowland, 2) the Lake District, 3) the Upland District, and 4) the Coastal Islands.

CLIMATE

Finland's climate is much milder than other areas lying as far north. The climate is influenced by the Gulf Stream (a warm ocean current) and by its many lakes and nearby gulfs. July temperatures average 55° to 63°F (13° to 17°C). The coldest month is generally February, with an average temperature range of -7° to 26°F (-22° to -3°C). Precipitation varies from north to south. The north averages 16 in. (41 cm), while the south averages 27 in. (69 cm) per year. Snow covers the ground from December to April in southern Finland and from October to April in northern Finland. In southern Finland, where the majority of the population live, days last 19 hours in the summer and six hours in the winter. The aurora borealis brilliantly lights up the sky on winter nights.

ECONOMY

Finland's economy is based mainly on private ownership. Most of the country's wealth comes from its vast forests.
Agriculture - barley, beef cattle, hogs, milk, oats, potatoes, and sugar beets
Forestry - birch, pine, and spruce
Manufacturing - chemicals, machinery, paper products, ships, and wood products
Mining - copper, iron ore, and zinc
Exports - machinery, paper, pulp, ships, and wood products
Imports - fruits, industrial raw materials, manufactured goods, petroleum and petroleum products, and vegetables

LIFE-STYLE

Over 60 percent of Finns live in urban areas and rent or own apartments. About a fifth of the population live in Helsinki or its suburbs. People in rural areas usually live in single-family homes in villages or on farms.

Fish are an important part of the Finns' diet. Popular meats are beef, veal, and pork. Boiled potatoes covered with butter and dill sprigs are often served as a side dish.

Virtually all adult Finns are literate. Most children attend public schools. Finland has a comprehensive school system. Children, beginning at age seven, are required to attend *basic schools* for nine years, after which they may enter an *upper secondary* or *vocational school*. Graduates may continue their education at a vocational institute or a university.

The people of Finland love outdoor sports. In winter, they enjoy ice hockey, ice-skating, ski-jumping, and cross-country and downhill skiing. Summer sports include *pesäpallo* (Finnish baseball), swimming, boating, and hiking. Camping vacations are popular, as are escapes to cottages. The Finns also enjoy ballets, concerts, movies, plays, and operas. The most famous feature of Finnish life is a kind of bath called a sauna. Most people take a sauna once a week for cleansing and relaxation. When the bathers begin to sweat, they slap themselves with twigs to encourage circulation, and then shower in cold water.

IT'S A FACT!

Aland - Finland's largest island, covers 285 sq. mi. (738 sq. km). It is an important tourist and shipping center.
Mount Haltia - the country's highest point, rises 4,344 ft. (1,324 m) above sea level.
Pyhä Falls - located on the Oulujoki River, drop 105 ft. (32 m) and provide power for a major hydroelectric plant.
Saimaa - the largest lake in Finland, covers 680 sq. mi. (1,760 sq. km).

 DID YOU KNOW...
- About 6,000 gypsies live in Finland?
- Northern Finland lies in the "Land of the Midnight Sun" with constant daylight for 2.5 months out of each year?
- Smoked reindeer is a special treat for Finns?
- Most of Finland is icebound in the winter, but icebreaking boats keep major ports open to traffic?
- Finnish glassware, ceramics, furniture, and textiles are world famous because of their simplicity of line and shape?
- Finland is known as the "Land of 10,000 Lakes," although the actual number of lakes is much higher?

FRANCE

OFFICIAL NAME: French Republic
LOCATION: Western Europe
AREA: 212,935 sq. mi. (551,500 sq. km)
POPULATION (Est. 1995): 57,769,000
CAPITAL: Paris
LARGEST CITIES: Paris, Marseille, Lyon, Toulouse, Nice
GOVERNMENT: Parliamentary democracy headed by a prime minister.
FLAG: Three equal vertical bands of blue, white, and red.
ETHNIC GROUPS: French
LANGUAGE: French
RELIGION: Christianity
BASIC MONETARY UNIT: Franc

GEOGRAPHY

France lies in western Europe and shares borders with eight other countries. It has coastlines along the English Channel, the Bay of Biscay, and the Mediterranean Sea. The country's landscape varies from snow-covered mountain ranges to long, sandy beaches. In area, France is Western Europe's largest country.

France is divided into ten main geographic regions: 1) the Brittany-Normandy Hills, 2) the Northern France Plains, 3) the Northeastern Plateaus, 4) the Rhine Valley, 5) the Aquitanian Lowlands, 6) the Central Highlands, 7) the French Alps and Jura Mountains, 8) the Pyrenees Mountains, 9) the Mediterranean Lowlands and Rhône-Saône Valley, and 10) Corsica.

The Brittany-Normandy Hills, with rolling plains and low, rounded hills, consists of poor soil with a few coastal areas that are fertile. The Northern France Plains have flat or rolling plains, with hills and plateaus covered by forests. The Northeastern Plateaus are part of the Ardennes Mountains. The area is very wooded with rich deposits of iron ore. The Rhine Valley has steep slopes covered with trees and vines. Fertile farmland makes up the flat land that lies along the Rhine River. The Aquitanian Lowlands consist of beaches, pine forests, rolling plains, and sand dunes. Many vineyards are located in this region. The Central Highlands has poor soils except in some valley areas. The region also has grassland areas and forests in the higher areas. The French Alps and Jura Mountains attract scores of tourists because of their many ski resorts. The Pyrenees Mountains form France's border with Spain. The mountains have few inhabitants and poor soil. The Mediterranean Lowlands and Rhône-Saône Valley region has fertile soil and therefore boasts much productive farming. Corsica is an island that lies about 100 mi. (160 km) southeast of mainland France in the Mediterranean. Hills and mountains make up its landforms in addition to a steep, rocky coastline.

CLIMATE

France has a wide variation in climate depending on the influence of the Atlantic Ocean or the Mediterranean Sea. The temperatures range from 32°F (0°C) in January to 83°F (28°C) in August in Marseille. Western France is greatly affected by the westerly winds that blow in off the Atlantic. The climate there is rainy with cool winters and mild summers. The inland regions have hot summers and cold winters with moderate rainfall throughout the year. The highest amount of precipitation occurs in the mountainous regions. Lowlands, located along the Mediterranean Sea, experience hot, dry summers and mild winters with moderate rainfall. Southern France is affected by cold north winds called *mistrals* that sometimes cause crop damage. The resort area of the Riviera is protected from the cold north winds by the Alps.

ECONOMY

Previous to World War II, France's economy was primarily based on small farms and businesses. Since the war, France has worked to modernize production methods in order to be a major player in world economy and trade. Their efforts have succeeded, since the people enjoy a high standard of living and the country as a whole is prosperous.

Agriculture - apples, beef cattle, chickens, eggs, grapes, hogs, milk, potatoes, sugar beets, and wheat

Manufacturing - aerospace equipment, automobiles, chemicals, electronic goods, iron and steel, processed foods and beverages, railway equipment, and textiles and clothing

Mining - iron ore

Exports - aircraft, automobiles, chemical products, electrical equipment, grains, iron and steel, machinery, weapons, and wine

Imports - automobiles, chemicals, machinery, and petroleum products

LIFE-STYLE

Nearly three-fourths of the French people live in urban areas. In larger cities, many people prefer the older apartment buildings over the newer, more modern apartments, especially in Paris. Tenants tolerate outdated plumbing and other inconveniences so that they can enjoy the more ornate antique architecture found in these older buildings.

Rural residents live much the same as city dwellers. They have the same modern conveniences—televisions, automobiles, and washers and refrigerators. Because most rural residents live on farms, they live in single-family homes. Although some farm families are wealthy, many require a second source of income to supplement their farm income.

The French look upon cooking as an art and, since the 1700s, their gourmet cooking has been the standard for many parts of the world. Enjoying rich foods and fine wines is a normal, everyday occurrence for the French. Although breakfasts tend to be very light, main meals include several courses, and wine is frequently consumed during both lunch and dinner. Pâtés, crêpes, quiches, and croissants are a few of the foods that originated in France.

In France, children ages six to 16 are required to attend school. Parents may also send their children aged two to six to free nursery schools.

Paris, the capital of France, is one of the most beautiful cities in the world. Its nickname, "City of Light," comes from the many lights that shine on Paris's palaces and monuments at night. It's known for its high-fashion women's clothing, perfumes, and pricey jewelry. Beautiful gardens and parks, statues, and fountains are found throughout this spectacular city.

A bicycle race called the *Tour de France* is a national sporting event that draws cyclists from around the world. The event lasts for nearly a month and takes the cyclists on a grueling race throughout the country. The French enjoy participating in such sports as ice skating, fishing, swimming, skiing, and tennis, as well as watching the popular team sport of soccer. French law guarantees workers five weeks of paid vacation each year. So the resorts are very busy, especially during the months of July and August, the most popular vacation time.

Cafés are a popular meeting place for friends to enjoy food and/or drink and visit. Tourists also find the cafés an interesting feature of French culture.

French architects, writers, artists, and composers have long been noted among Europe's greatest. *Carmen*, an opera written in 1875 by Georges Bizet, is possibly the world's most famous opera. Monet, Renoir, Picasso, and Degas, only a few of France's most famous artists, are well-known names throughout the world.

IT'S A FACT!

The Arc de Triomphe - located in Paris, houses the tomb of France's Unknown Soldier of World War I. Napoleon Bonaparte initiated the construction of the arch in 1806 and King Louis Phillippe saw to its completion in 1836.

Bastille Day - the French national holiday, commemorates the capture of the Bastille (a fortified prison) by the people of Paris during the French Revolution. It is celebrated on July 14.

The Cathedral of Notre Dame - one of Paris's most famous sights, is known for its stone carvings and majestic stature.

Eiffel Tower - the most famous landmark in Paris, dominates the skyline at 984 ft. (300 m). The tower commemorates the 100th anniversary of the French Revolution.

The Loire - the longest river in France, is 650 mi. (1,050 km) long.

Mont Blanc - the country's and Europe's highest point, rises 15,771 ft. (4,807 m) above sea level.

Mont-St.-Michel - is actually a large rock off the coast of Normandy. A town and a medieval abbey are perched on the top of the rock.

Musée d'Orsay (Orsay Museum) - located in a building that used to be a railroad station, houses some of the world's finest paintings from the 1800s and 1900s.

Pyrenees Mountains - located along France's border with Spain, has many peaks that rise more than 10,000 ft. (3,000 m) above sea level.

Riviera - located along the Mediterranean Sea, is a world-famous resort area that attracts many tourists because of its mild climate throughout the year.

DID YOU KNOW...

- More than half of France's electricity is supplied by nuclear power?
- It is now possible to travel by rail from France to England by means of a tunnel built beneath the English Channel? The tunnel was begun in 1987 and completed in 1994.
- Louvre Museum, one of the largest in the world, displays the famous *Mona Lisa* by Leonardo da Vinci?
- French Renaissance architecture is best typified through castles called *châteaux?*

FRENCH GUIANA
Overseas Department of France

OFFICIAL NAME: French Guiana
LOCATION: Northeastern South America
AREA: 35,135 sq. mi. (91,000 sq. km)
POPULATION (Est. 1993): 133,376
CAPITAL/LARGEST CITY: Cayenne
GOVERNMENT: Overseas department of France headed by a president who is chosen by a 16-member elected general council.
FLAG: Uses the flag of France.
ETHNIC GROUPS: Black, Creole
LANGUAGES: French, Creolese dialect (French/English mix)
RELIGION: Roman Catholic
BASIC MONETARY UNIT: French Franc

GEOGRAPHY

French Guiana has three main land regions: 1) a northern coastal plain, 2) a hilly central plateau, and 3) the Tumuc-Humac Mountains in the south. All but the coastline—about four-fifths of the country's area—is heavily forested. The country has about 235 mi. (378 km) of coastline along the North Atlantic Ocean. The country has many rivers, the most important of which are the Maroni and the Oyapock.

CLIMATE

French Guiana has a hot, humid tropical climate. The average temperature is 80°F (27°C) with little temperature variation throughout the year. The average annual rainfall is 130 in. (330 cm), most of which falls from December to June.

ECONOMY

French Guiana's interior has rich, but mostly undeveloped, forests, soil, and bauxite resources. The main economic activities are fishing and forestry. The space center at Kourou is also important to the economy. Agriculture products are raised solely for the people's consumption. French Guiana is heavily dependent upon financial assistance from France.

Agriculture - bananas, cassava, cattle, cocoa, corn, manioc, pigs, pineapples, poultry, rice, sugar cane, and yams

Fishing - shrimp

Manufacturing - forest products

Mining - gold

Exports - rosewood essence, rum, shrimp, and timber

Imports - consumer goods, food, petroleum, and producer goods

LIFE-STYLE

Most of French Guiana's population lives in coastal areas and about half of the people reside in the capital city of Cayenne. Most residents are employed by the government. The country's small Indian population lives mainly in the heavily wooded interior.

Children ages six to 16 are required to attend school. The literacy rate of those aged 15 and older is over 75 percent.

The culture of the French Guianese reflects heavily upon ethnic black and Indian populations. In urban areas, festivals reflect the influence of Africa, East India, and France through costume and dance. The pre-Lenten Carnival is the largest celebration—involving most residents—and features colorful costumes, music, and dance competitions.

IT'S A FACT!

Devil's Island - an isle located northwest of the city of Cayenne, was formerly used as a camp for political prisoners.

Mana - was the site of a community that established educational centers for freed black slaves and women. It was founded by a mother superior and a father.

 DID YOU KNOW...

- For about 150 years, French Guiana had several penal colonies for French convicts? The cruelty of the country's prison camps was notorious.
- Kourou, a former prison camp, is now a space research center?
- Most French Guianese descended from slaves brought to the country in the 1600s and 1700s?
- Though founded in 1643, the capital city of Cayenne was not permanently settled until 21 years later?
- American Indians were French Guiana's first settlers?
- French Guianese wildlife includes armadillo, caiman, great anteater, ocelot, sloth, and tapir?

FRENCH POLYNESIA
Overseas Territory of France

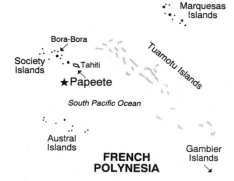

OFFICIAL NAME: Territoire de la Polynesie Francaise (Territory of French Polynesia)
LOCATION: South Pacific Ocean
AREA: 1,513 sq. mi. (3,941 sq. km)
POPULATION (Est. 1993): 210,333
CAPITAL: Papeete
GOVERNMENT: Overseas territory of France. (French Polynesians may vote for the French president and elect representatives to the French parliament.)
FLAG: Uses the flag of France
ETHNIC GROUPS: Polynesian, Asian, European
LANGUAGES: French, Tahitian
RELIGION: Christianity
BASIC MONETARY UNIT: CFP Franc

GEOGRAPHY

French Polynesia is a territory made up of over 120 islands covering an area in the South Pacific Ocean close to the size of Western Europe. The islands are divided into five groups: 1) Austral, 2) Gambier, 3) Marquesas, 4) Society, and 5) Tuamotu.

Formed by volcanoes, the ten Marquesas Islands have high mountains that drop abruptly to the ocean and lush, green valleys filled with streams and waterfalls. The Society Islands, located southwest of the Marquesas, consist of 14 islands also formed by ancient volcanoes. Rugged mountains cover most of this group; some are low coral atolls. The Tuamotu Islands extend over 1,000 mi. (1,600 km) of the Pacific Ocean and consist of 75 reef islands and atolls. The Austral Islands lie south of the Society Islands and the Gambier Islands lie southeast of the Tuamotus.

CLIMATE

The tropical climate of French Polynesia is generally hot and humid. Because the territory lies south of the equator, the warmest months are November through April. These months also have the most rain. The higher-altitude volcanic islands, especially the eastern slopes, receive the greatest amounts of precipitation. Trade winds blowing from the southeast cool French Polynesia from May to October. Cyclones occasionally hit in January.

ECONOMY

French Polynesia's largest industry is tourism. The islands of Tahiti and Bora-Bora, both located in the Society Islands group, are among the territory's most popular tourist attractions. Agriculture and fishing are also important economic activities.

Agriculture - bananas, beef, breadfruit, cassava, coconut, dairy products, hogs, poultry, sweet potatoes, taro, tropical fruits, vanilla, and yams

Manufacturing - handicrafts and processed agricultural products

Exports - copra and coconut products, pearls, shark meat, tropical fruits, and vanilla

Imports - equipment, foodstuffs, and fuel

LIFE-STYLE

Although most Polynesians make their living working for the French government or in the tourist trade, vestiges of traditional life remain. Many Polynesians fish and raise their own crops. Some dive for pearls. Others work abroad in such places as Australia, New Zealand, New Caledonia, and the United States, sending much-needed income home to their families.

Some French Polynesian houses and resorts are built on stilts in lagoons.

Education is free and compulsory and the literacy rate is high.

IT'S A FACT!

Bora-Bora - one of the territory's most beautiful islands, is located about 170 mi. (270 km) northwest of Tahiti. A barrier reef and many tiny islands surround it.

Tahiti - the territory's largest and most populous island. It is a popular vacation spot and home to Papeete, the territory's capital and a bustling seaport.

 DID YOU KNOW...

- In many traditional Polynesian societies, it was considered taboo for the most powerful chiefs to have contact with common people? Chiefs fished or grew their own food, making it unnecessary for them to live off the work of others.
- Between 1975 and 1989, France conducted 110 underground nuclear tests on one of Tuamotu's atolls?
- While bird and marine life abounds in French Polynesia, there are no indigenous mammals?
- Tahiti became famous as a tropical paradise through the works of many authors and artists, including artist Paul Gauguin and authors Herman Melville, James Michener, and Robert Louis Stevenson?

GABON

OFFICIAL NAME: République Gabonaise (Gabonese Republic)
FORMERLY: Part of French Equatorial Africa
LOCATION: West Africa
AREA: 103,347 sq. mi. (267,667 sq. km)
POPULATION (Est. 1993): 1,292,000
CAPITAL: Libreville
LARGEST CITIES: Libreville, Lambaréné, Franceville
GOVERNMENT: Republic governed by a president.
FLAG: Three horizontal stripes of green, yellow, and blue.
ETHNIC GROUPS: Fang, Omyéné, Pygmy
LANGUAGES: French, Bantu dialects
RELIGIONS: Christianity, Traditional African Religions
BASIC MONETARY UNIT: CFA Franc

GEOGRAPHY

Gabon, located on Africa's west coast, straddles the equator. The country makes up the drainage basin of the Ogooué River.

Palm-lined beaches, lagoons, and swamps line Gabon's 500 mi. (800 km) of coast along the Atlantic Ocean. Inland, the land rises gradually to rolling hills and low mountain ranges. Most of the country is covered by thick rainforests.

CLIMATE

The country's location on the equator gives it a hot, humid climate throughout the year. The average annual temperature is 79°F (26°C). Rainfall is heavy throughout Gabon, especially on the northern coast. Many regions receive up to 100 in. (250 cm) of rainfall yearly.

ECONOMY

Gabon is rich in natural resources. It is noted for its high-quality timber and its rich iron and manganese deposits. Gabon's forests are its chief source of wealth.

Agriculture - bananas, cacao, cassava, coffee, palm oil, tropical fruits, rubber, and yams

Forestry - ebony, mahogany, and okoumé

Mining - gold, iron ore, manganese, petroleum, and uranium

Exports - lumber, cacao, coffee, iron, manganese, petroleum, and uranium

Imports - electrical equipment, food, mining and road-building machinery, textiles, and transport vehicles

LIFE-STYLE

Gabon is one of the least populated countries in Africa. More than half of its people live in small villages along the rivers or coast, or in thinly forested areas in the north. The villagers must clear the surrounding forests and plant their main food crops. Some also fish, hunt, or raise livestock.

Most Gabonese once lived in houses with walls made of mud-covered branches and roofs of woven grass. Reed mats hung at windows and doors. Now the roofs are made of corrugated metal and some houses have cement walls. Most villages have a meeting place where the older men discuss village affairs.

Fang is the most important ethnic group in Gabon. Once fierce warriors, they now dominate the national government. The Omyéné, a small group of related peoples, live along the coast. Pygmies live in small, isolated groups in the thick southern forests. They live on the animals they hunt and trap, and on the food they gather.

In rural areas, food is eaten with the right hand or a spoon. In general, men and older boys eat at the table, while women and young children eat near the cooking fire. A typical meal consists of either plantain bananas or *baton de manioc*, a dough-like paste made from cassava. It is often served with meat or fish, and a green leaf vegetable. Water is the usual drink, but beer is also a favorite. Tropical fruits, such as avocados, mangoes, and pineapples, are also popular food items. *Atangas*, a bitter fruit about the size of a golf ball, is often boiled and spread on bread or rice.

Extended families are the rule. Traditionally, the family lives in a compound of several buildings with each nuclear family having its own separate house and kitchen. Cooking, child care, and chores are often shared by the group.

About two-thirds of the people of Gabon are literate. Approximately 90 percent of the children attend primary schools. Attendance in secondary schools is rising.

Soccer and basketball are the most popular sports. In the capital city, people enjoy movies, dancing, and swimming. Visiting is the most common leisure activity throughout the country. Tag and tug-of-war are also enjoyed by many Gabonese.

IT'S A FACT!

Mount Iboundji - the country's highest point, rises 5,167 ft. (1,575 m) above sea level.

 DID YOU KNOW...

- The city of Lambaréné is home to a hospital and leper colony founded in 1913 by Albert Schweitzer—physician, missionary, and musician—on the banks of the Ogooué River?
- The earliest inhabitants of Gabon were the Pygmies?
- Insects, such as termites, are a common part of the diet in remote areas of Gabon?

THE GAMBIA

OFFICIAL NAME: Republic of The Gambia
LOCATION: Western Africa
AREA: 4,361 sq. mi. (11,295 sq. km)
POPULATION (Est. 1993): 932,000
CAPITAL/LARGEST CITY: Banjul
GOVERNMENT: Republic governed by a president.
FLAG: Three horizontal stripes of red, blue, and green divided by two narrow white bands.
ETHNIC GROUPS: Mandingo, Fulani, Wolof, Serahuli, Jola
LANGUAGES: English, Mandinka, Wolof, Fula
RELIGION: Islam
BASIC MONETARY UNIT: Dalasi

GEOGRAPHY

The Gambia, one of Africa's smallest independent countries, is located on the Atlantic coast, near the westernmost tip of Africa. The country extends inward from the Atlantic Ocean for 180 mi. (290 km). It is only 15 to 30 mi. (24 to 48 km) wide.

Narrow strips of mangrove swamps run along each side of the Gambia River, which flows from east to west through the country. Beyond the swamps are *banto faros*, areas of land that are firm ground in the dry season, but turn into swamps during the rainy season. Beyond the banto faros, plateaus extend to the borders with Senegal.

CLIMATE

Gambia's climate is basically tropical with hot, rainy weather during the summer months of June through October. From November through May, the winter months, the weather is cooler and drier. The land near the coast averages 40 in. (100 cm) of rainfall annually. Inland regions receive less.

ECONOMY

Gambia's economy is based primarily on growing and processing peanuts.

Agriculture - bananas, cassava, corn, hides and skins, limes, livestock, mangoes, millet, oranges, palm kernels, papayas, peanuts, rice, and vegetables

Manufacturing - peanut processing

Exports - fish, palm kernels, and peanuts and peanut products

Imports - foodstuffs, fuel, machinery, and transportation equipment

LIFE-STYLE

There are five major ethnic groups, all of whom are black Africans, which make up almost the entire population of Gambia. The Mandingo, the largest in number, earn their living as peanut farmers and traders. A music-loving people, they are distinguished by their height and are found throughout the country.

The Fulani are nomadic cattle herders who live in eastern Gambia. The Wolof are farmers who live near the northern border or are city dwellers inhabiting Banjul. They are also music-lovers who enjoy dancing and whose city-dwelling women like to dress elegantly and with much ornamentation.

The Serahuli are farmers who must contend with very poor soil in eastern Gambia. Farmers from Senegal, called *strange farmers*, help the Serahuli with the difficult tasks of planting and

harvesting in exchange for an agreed upon portion of the crop and a small plot of land on which to grow their own crop.

The last ethnic group, the Jola, live south of the Gambia River near the coast and also make a living by farming. The Jola live in small villages and practice the African religions handed down by their ancestors.

Rice is the main staple of the diet. For lunch, Gambians eat a type of stew made using spices, vegetables, and some type of meat. Popular dishes are *Benachin* (jollof rice), *Domoda* (peanut butter stew), and *Superkanja* (okra soup). Leftover rice from lunch may be served at dinner along with *Chereh* (millet couscous), fried fish, bread with beef sauce, or chicken or beef served with salad and potatoes.

Soccer is the most popular sport. Gambians also enjoy basketball, cricket, running, tennis, and wrestling.

IT'S A FACT!

James Island - located in the Gambia River, was once a slave trading center.

Trans-Gambia Highway - runs north and south through Gambia, connecting northern and southern Senegal.

 DID YOU KNOW...

- Except for a very short coastline, Gambia is entirely surrounded by the country of Senegal?
- The main transportation route for the country is the Gambia River?
- Most farmers in Gambia earn a living by growing peanuts?
- Up until 1973, the capital city of Banjul was known as Bathurst?

GEORGIA

OFFICIAL NAME: Sakartvelo Respublika
(Republic of Georgia)
FORMERLY: Part of the Soviet Union
LOCATION: Southeastern Europe/Western Asia
AREA: 26,911 sq. mi. (69,700 sq. km)
POPULATION (Est. 1993): 5,599,000
CAPITAL: Tbilisi
LARGEST CITIES: Tbilisi, Kutaisi, Rustavi, Sukhumi
GOVERNMENT: Republic headed by prime minister.
FLAG: Red field with a canton in the upper hoist-side corner divided into two horizontal stripes of black and white.
ETHNIC GROUPS: Georgian, Armenian, Russian, Azerbaijan
LANGUAGE: Georgian
RELIGIONS: Georgian Orthodox, Russian Orthodox, Islam
BASIC MONETARY UNIT: Coupon (Ruble also used)

GEOGRAPHY

Georgia is located primarily in Asia, but part of the country lies in Europe. At its greatest distances, Georgia measures 175 mi. (280 km) from north to south and 350 mi. (565 km) from east to west. It has 192.5 mi. (310 km) of coastline along the Black Sea.

Much of Georgia's northern part is covered by the Caucasus Mountains. The Little Caucasus Mountains cover much of the southern part. Western Georgia includes the Rioni Valley and other lowlands near the Black Sea. Eastern Georgia includes part of the upper Kura Valley. Forests cover about a third of the country.

CLIMATE

Georgia's climate ranges from subtropical along the Black Sea to continental in the east. The lower mountain slopes facing the Black Sea have a mild, wet climate. Inland mountains and slopes facing away from the sea have colder and drier climates. The highest mountain peaks are snow-covered year-round. Western Georgia has a warm, humid climate with heavy rainfall. Eastern Georgia is dry, requiring farmers to irrigate some crops.

ECONOMY

Georgia's greatest natural resources are its fertile soil and mild climate. Like all other former Soviet republics, the country's economy has suffered since independence.

Agriculture - cattle, citrus fruits, corn, grapes, sheep, silk, sugar beets, tea, tobacco, tung oil, and wheat
Manufacturing - food products
Mining - barite, coal, copper, and manganese
Exports - chemicals, cognac and wine, and machines
Imports - foodstuffs, fuel, light manufactures, and wheat

LIFE-STYLE

More than half of the people live in urban areas. Houses in these areas are generally one- or two-story structures that are closely grouped. In the villages, houses are large, spacious two-story homes. Villagers often have a garden or an orchard.

Georgian food is generally highly seasoned with a variety of herbs and garlic. Mutton and chicken are some favorite foods. Two popular dishes are *shashlik* (a type of shish kebab) and

chicken tabaka (pressed fried chicken). The country is also famous for its wines.

Almost all of the people of Georgia can read and write. Children must attend school through the tenth grade.

Family gatherings and celebrations are important events. One traditional feast is called *tamada*, with its purpose being the reconciliation of enemies.

Georgia has a rich literary tradition. Poetry and music are particularly popular among the people. Georgia's national treasure is a heroic poem, *The Man in the Tiger's Skin*, by Shota Rustaveli, a great medieval writer.

IT'S A FACT!

Monasteries at *Ikalto* and *Gelati* - built during the medieval period, are important educational centers.

Mount Shkhara - the country's highest point, rises 17,163 ft. (5,201 m) above sea level.

 DID YOU KNOW...
- The cliff dwellings in Vardzia, Georgia, were used during the 12th century as places to hide from invading armies?
- During the Soviet rule, Georgia was developed as a center for silk textiles and automobile industries?
- The shortest route crossing the Caucasus Mountains is a road called the Georgian Military Highway, which connects Tbilisi with Vladikavkaz in Russia?
- Some vineyards in Georgia have their beginnings traced to prehistory?
- Georgia became independent in 1991 after 200 years of Russian and Soviet rule?
- The infamous dictator, Joseph Stalin, was born in Georgia?

GERMANY

OFFICIAL NAME: Bundesrepublik Deutschland
(Federal Republic of Germany)
LOCATION: Central Europe
AREA: 137,358 sq. mi. (355,754 sq. km)
POPULATION (Est. 1993): 77,425,000
CAPITAL: Berlin
LARGEST CITIES: Berlin, Hamburg, Munich
GOVERNMENT: Federal republic governed by a federal chancellor
FLAG: Three horizontal stripes of black, red, and gold.
ETHNIC GROUP: German
LANGUAGE: German
RELIGION: Christianity
BASIC MONETARY UNIT: Deutsche Mark

GEOGRAPHY

At its greatest distances, Germany measures 540 mi. (869 km) from north to south and 390 mi. (628 km) from east to west. It has 574 mi. (924 km) of coastline along the North and Baltic Seas. Germany has five main land regions: 1) the North German Plain, 2) the Central Highlands, 3) the South German Hills, 4) the Black Forest, and 5) the Bavarian Alps.

The North German Plain, the largest region, covers all of northern Germany. The plain predominantly lies less than 300 ft. (91 m) above sea level. The region is drained by the Elbe, Ems, Oder, Rhine, and Weser Rivers, which are important commercial waterways.

The Central Highlands are a series of plateaus that lie 1,000 to 2,500 ft. (300 to 760 m) above sea level. The steep, narrow valleys provide some of the most beautiful scenery in Germany.

The South German Hills include a series of escarpments (long, parallel ridges). Most of the area rises 500 to 2,500 ft. (150 to 762 m) above sea level.

The Black Forest is a mountainous region covered with thick forests of dark fir and spruce trees. The region lies 2,500 to 3,000 ft. (762 to 910 m) above sea level. It is famous for its mineral springs.

The Bavarian Alps are part of the largest mountain system in Europe, the Alps. These snow-capped mountains rise more than 6,000 ft. (1,800 m) above sea level. The mountains' beautiful landscape makes them a year-round vacation spot. The region also has many lakes formed by ancient glaciers.

CLIMATE

Germany's location near the sea creates a mild climate. The coldest month of the year is January, with an average temperature above 30°F (-1°C). July, the hottest month, has a temperature average of about 64°F (18°C). The average annual precipitation is 20-40 in. (50-100 cm) In the northwest, rain falls evenly throughout the year. Inland, most rain falls in summer. Deep snow blankets some mountain peaks all year long.

ECONOMY

At the end of World War II, Germany's economy was almost in total ruin. Under the Marshall Plan, the United States's aid helped to rapidly rebuild West Germany's economy. East Germany's economy was controlled by the Soviet Union, which set up a strong Communist state. The unification of Germany occurred on October 3, 1990. The first step in the process was economic unification, beginning July 1,1990. Today, Germany is one of the top five economic powers in the world.

Agriculture - barley, beef cattle, hogs, milk, potatoes, sugar beets, and wheat

Manufacturing - chemicals and pharmaceuticals, electrical equipment, machinery, motor vehicles, processed foods and beverages, and steel

Mining - coal

Exports - chemicals, iron and steel products, machinery, and motor vehicles

Imports - food products, industrial raw materials, petroleum, and petroleum products

LIFE-STYLE

Approximately 84 percent of Germans live in urban areas. About six percent of Germans work as farmers. In western Germany, most farms are small and privately owned. In eastern Germany, most farms were large collectives run by the government. This land is now being returned to private ownership.

Germany was among the first countries in the world to set up a public education system for all children. By the 1900s, almost all Germans over age 15 were literate. All children must attend school for 9-10 years, beginning at age six. The length of education varies among states.

The German people enjoy good food in large amounts. Meats, such as veal, pork, beef, or chicken, are often served. Noodles, dumplings, potatoes, beets, carrots, onions, or turnips may also be served. Many well-known German dishes were created hundreds of years ago as a method of preservation. Sauerkraut, sauerbraten, and sausage are examples. Cheeses such as Limburger, Münster, and Tilsiter originated in Germany. Germany is also known for its beer and wine.

The German people enjoy hiking, reading, gardening, swimming, and watching television. Young people often take bicycling and hiking trips and spend nights in the open or at youth hostels (inexpensive inns). Snow skiing, canoeing, and sailing are also popular. Soccer is the most important organized sport in Germany.

A few of the greatest composers of all time were from Germany: Bach, Handel, Beethoven, and Mendelssohn.

IT'S A FACT!

Adolf Hitler - leader of the Nazi Party, began to rebuild Germay's military power in 1933. He started World War II in 1939 and was defeated in 1945.

The Berlin Wall - built in 1961, this 26 mi. (42 km) wall closed the escape route between East and West Germany. It was opened when the unification of Germany took place.

Neuschwanstein Castle - located in the Bavarian Alps, was built by King Louis II, known as "Mad King Ludwig."

The University of Heidelberg - founded in 1386, is Germany's oldest university.

Zugspitze - the country's highest point, rises 9,721 ft. (2,963 m) above sea level.

 DID YOU KNOW...

- Hundreds of years ago, German cooks soaked meat in vinegar and spices to preserve it?
- The Bradenburg Gate, completed in 1791, stands as a symbol of Berlin?
- Germany's highway system includes 6,500 mi. (10,500 km) of four-lane highways called *autobahns* which have no speed limits?
- Oktoberfest is a festival that has been held in Munich each fall since the 1800s?
- There is such a variety of dialects in Germany that people from different areas may have trouble understanding each other?
- The Danube River is the only major river in Germany that flows eastward?
- The Black Forest was the setting of many old German legends and fairy tales?

GHANA

OFFICIAL NAME: Republic of Ghana
FORMERLY: The Gold Coast
LOCATION: Western Africa
AREA: 92,098 sq. mi. (238,533 sq. km)
POPULATION (Est. 1992): 15,966,000
CAPITAL: Accra
LARGEST CITIES: Accra, Kumasi, Tamale
GOVERNMENT: Constitutional democracy headed by the military leader, who serves as chairman of the Provisional National Defense Council.
FLAG: Three horizontal stripes of red, yellow, and green with a five-pointed, black star, symbolizing freedom, centered on the yellow stripe.
ETHNIC GROUPS: Akan (comprised of Ashanti and Fante), Ewe, Ga, Moshi (Mossi)-Dagomba, others (about 100 groups total)
LANGUAGES: English, various African languages
RELIGIONS: Traditional African Religions, Christianity, Islam
BASIC MONETARY UNIT: Cedi/New Cedi

GEOGRAPHY

Ghana measures 445 mi. (716 km) from north to south and 310 mi. (499 km) from east to west at its greatest distances. It has 335 mi. (539 km) of coastline along the Gulf of Guinea.

Ghana's coastline consists of a plain that rises to the Kwahu Plateau in south-central Ghana. The southwest is covered by a thick forest and the north is made up of a savanna and grassland.

Ghana has many rivers: the White Volta in the north; the Black Volta in the east; and the Ankobra, the Pra, and the Tano in the southwest.

CLIMATE

Ghana has a tropical climate that is hot and dry in the north, warm and dry in the southeast, and hot and humid in the southwest. In the south, near the country's capital of Accra, the average annual temperature is 80°F (27°C). Temperatures are higher in the north. The average annual rainfall ranges from 40-60 in. (100-150 cm) with the heaviest rains falling in the southwest. Northern and eastern Ghana suffer severe droughts during the months of November to March.

ECONOMY

Ghana's economy is based on agriculture—especially the growing and exporting of cacao—and its mineral deposits.

Agriculture - cacao, cassava, coconuts, coffee, corn, goats, kola nuts, millet, palm oil and kernels, peanuts, rice, shea nuts, sheep, sorghum, taro, and yams

Forestry - mahogany and other tropical hardwoods

Manufacturing - aluminum, beverages, cement, and clothing

Mining - bauxite, diamonds, gold, and manganese

Exports - cacao, diamonds, gold, manganese, and timber

Imports - capital equipment, food, and petroleum

LIFE-STYLE

About two-thirds of Ghana's population live in rural areas and are farmers who live in houses constructed with mud walls and thatched or tin roofs. The other one-third of the population are urban dwellers, often government workers, who live in modern buildings or rural-type houses.

Staples of the diet consist of yams, cassava, corn, millet, and rice. Ghanaian food is generally hot and spicy, and most meals are served with a pepper sauce containing meat, fish, or chicken. Popular dishes include *ampesi* (a green vegetable dish), *fufu* (a dough-like mixture of plantain and cassava), and soups and sauces made from palm or peanut oils.

National dress consists of brightly colored cloth, which is worn as a wraparound by men and as blouses and narrow skirts by women.

Education—at the primary, secondary, and technical levels—is free, but most children only attend school up to the age of 12. Health conditions are improving, but Ghanaians are still susceptible to malaria and other tropical diseases.

The most common forms of transportation include walking and riding in buses or flat-bed trucks.

Popular sports include soccer, field hockey, horse racing, track and field, tennis, and boxing. Other leisure activities include the theater, movies, and festivals.

Ghana's culture varies from region to region, but such events as harvest, marriage, birth, puberty, and death are often celebrated or observed. Ghanaian art includes dance and music, pottery, wood carving, gold and silver work, and textiles.

IT'S A FACT!

Lake Volta - located in east-central Ghana, is one of the world's largest artificially created lakes. It extends 250 mi. (402 km) north of the Akosombo Dam and covers an area of 3,275 sq. mi. (8,482 sq. km)

 DID YOU KNOW...

- When Portuguese explorers landed in what is now Ghana in 1471, they found so much gold that they named the area *Gold Coast*?
- When Gold Coast gained its independence in 1957, its name was changed to *Ghana*, which is the name of an ancient African kingdom?
- Less than one percent of the population owns an automobile or a television set and only about ten percent of the population owns a radio?

GIBRALTAR
Dependency of the United Kingdom

SPAIN
Bay of Gibraltar
Gibraltar
Gibraltar Harbor
The Rock
Mediterranean Sea
GIBRALTAR
Strait of Gibraltar

OFFICIAL NAME: Gibraltar
LOCATION: Peninsula in Southern Spain
AREA: 2.3 sq. mi. (6 sq. km)
POPULATION (Est. 1993): 31,508
CAPITAL/LARGEST CITY: Gibraltar
GOVERNMENT: British dependency headed by a governor.
FLAG: Two horizontal stripes of white and red with a red castle centered on the white stripe.
ETHNIC GROUPS: Italian, Maltese, Portuguese, Spanish
LANGUAGES: English, Spanish
RELIGIONS: Roman Catholic, Protestant
BASIC MONETARY UNIT: Gibraltar Pound

GEOGRAPHY

Gibraltar is a small peninsula—about 3 mi. (5 km) long and 0.75 mi. (1.2 km) wide—located on Spain's southern coast. It lies near the entrance to the Mediterranean Sea. Most of the peninsula is occupied by a huge limestone mass, named the Rock of Gibraltar. None of Gibraltar's land is arable and it has no rivers or springs.

CLIMATE

Gibraltar has a mild, Mediterranean climate with an average annual temperature of 55° to 84°F (13° to 29°C). It receives an adequate amount of rain only in the winter.

ECONOMY

Gibraltar has no agriculture and very little industry. The economy is mainly dependent on shipping services fees and on revenues from tourism and banking and finance activities.
Exports - manufactured goods and petroleum
Imports - food, fuels, manufactured goods

LIFE-STYLE

Almost all of the people live in apartments in the town of Gibraltar. Most work for the government or in the dockyards servicing ships that use the port. Increasing numbers of workers are employed in the tourist industry.

Children ages five to 15 must attend school, which is free. Classes are taught in English, but many families speak Spanish in their homes. There is no higher education available in the country.

IT'S A FACT!

Rock of Gibraltar - the country's highest point, rises 1,398 ft. (426 m).

DID YOU KNOW...

- In 1713, at the end of the War of the Spanish Succession, Spain ceded Gibraltar to Britain under the terms of the Treaty of Utrecht?
- Gibraltar is considered one of the Pillars of Hercules, which established the western limits of navigation for the ancient Mediterranean world?
- In a 1967 referendum allowing the people to choose between Spain and Britain, the people chose to remain under the government of Britain?
- Excavations of caves in the Rock have proven that Gibraltar was inhabited in prehistoric times?
- Gibraltar is home of the Barbary apes, the only monkeys native to Europe?

GREECE

OFFICIAL NAME: Elliniki dimokratia (Hellenic Republic)
LOCATION: Southeastern Europe
AREA: 50,962 sq. mi. (131,990 sq. km)
POPULATION (Est. 1995): 10,322,000
CAPITAL: Athens
LARGEST CITIES: Athens, Thessaloniki
GOVERNMENT: Parliamentary republic headed by a president.
FLAG: Nine horizontal stripes: five blue alternating with four white. The upper hoist-side corner features a blue field with a white cross, which symbolizes Greek Orthodoxy. Blue stripes represent the sea and sky, and white stripes the purity of the country's independence struggle.
ETHNIC GROUP: Greek
LANGUAGE: Greek
RELIGION: Greek Orthodox
BASIC MONETARY UNIT: Drachma

GEOGRAPHY

Greece is a small country in southeastern Europe whose mainland juts out into the Mediterranean Sea. Approximately one-fifth of the country is made up of over 2,000 islands. Only 166 are suitable to live on. Crete, the largest island, has an area of 3,218 sq. mi. (8,336 sq. km). The country's mainland stretches 365 mi. (587 km) from north to south and 345 mi. (555 km) from east to west at its greatest distances. Mountains and water divide Greece into many land areas. High peaks separate valleys and plains, and the sea pushes into the coasts, forming many peninsulas.

Greece has nine main land regions: 1) Central Greece and Euboea, 2) Thessaly, 3) Epirus, 4) Macedonia, 5) Thrace, 6) the Peloponnesus, 7) the Ionian Islands, 8) Crete, and 9) the Aegean Islands. Central Greece and Euboea is an area of hills and mountains, small valleys, and numerous islands. It makes up one-fifth of Greece and holds nearly half the population. Athens is part of this area. Thessaly, which lies east of the Pindus Mountains, is a large plain almost completely surrounded by mountains, most notably Mount Olympus. Epirus, located south of Albania, is a very mountainous area. Macedonia, west of Albania and south of the country of Macedonia, has mountains and the country's most fertile farmland. Thrace, located in the extreme northeast, is covered by mountains and has a narrow coastal plain. Peloponnesus has mountains, small valleys, and rugged coastlines. The Ionian Islands, west of the Greek mainland, have mountains and some arable land. Crete is covered with mountains and hills with some valleys. Its northern coast contains a narrow plain. The Aegean Islands are rocky and sparsely populated.

CLIMATE

Greece has a Mediterranean climate with mild, wet winters and hot, dry summers. In much of Greece, most of the rainfall occurs in winter. Nearly all of Greece's rivers dry up in the summertime. The amount of precipitation in Greece is greater in the northwest than it is in the southeast. It ranges from more than 60 in. (150 cm) a year in northern areas of the Pindus Mountains to less than 15 in. (38 cm) on the islands just southeast of Athens. The average coastal temperature ranges from 75°F (24°C) in summer to 40°F (4°C) in winter.

ECONOMY

Greece's economy was almost devastated during World War II and the following Greek Civil War, but it has expanded greatly since then. Economic expansion has largely resulted from government programs, United States assistance, and trade with the Middle East and European nations.

Athens is the most visited city because of its many historic structures. It draws in over 90 percent of the country's tourists.

Agriculture - corn, cotton, grapes and raisins, olives, poultry, sheep, sugar beets, tobacco, and wheat

Manufacturing - cement, chemicals, cigarettes, clothing, metal products, petrochemicals, processed foods, and textiles

Mining - bauxite, chromite, iron ore, lignite, and magnesite

Exports - cement and its products, clothing, metal products, olive oil, petroleum products, prepared fruit, and textiles

Imports - chemicals, machinery, manufactured goods, meat, petroleum and its products, and transportation equipment

LIFE-STYLE

About two-thirds of the Greek people live in urban areas and have life-styles resembling those in other Western nations. The rural population has declined since the 1960s. Many small farms in the mountains have been abandoned. The largest farms are in the coastal and interior plains, which are irrigated.

Lamb is the most popular type of meat consumed in Greece. Greeks also eat a wide variety of fish and other seafood. Olive oil, oregano, garlic, onions, and fennel are used to prepare many Greek dishes. Popular meals include *moussaka* (eggplant and ground meat), *souvlaki* (shish kebab), and *dolmathes* (grape leaves stuffed with rice and ground meat). Various sweet pastries are enjoyed.

Children ages six to 15 are required to attend school. About 90 percent of the adults are literate.

Soccer, a national sport, is particularly popular in Greece. Basketball, swimming, and sailing are other popular forms of recreation. Socializing, especially in outdoor coffee houses and restaurants, is also enjoyed.

Religious festivals are an important part of Greek culture. Every major area has a patron saint. The people attend church the evening before the saint's yearly feast day, then eat, dance, and sing far into the night.

Many Greeks are skilled weavers, silversmiths, and embroiderers. Greeks are known for their folk dances.

IT'S A FACT!

Acropolis - a hill which was the center of ancient Athens. It includes the ruins of the Parthenon, an ancient white marble temple built to honor Athena, the city's patron goddess.

Mount Olympus - the country's highest point, rises 9,570 ft. (2,917 m) above sea level.

Mycenae - a leading cultural and political center in Greece from about 1400 to 1200 B.C. It is known for its royal palace, walled fortress, and beehive-shaped tombs.

National Archaeological Museum - one of the world's greatest museums, contains ancient jewelry, pottery, and sculptures.

Peloponnesus - one of the most historically famous areas of Greece, includes ruins from Corinth, Olympia (a valley where the ancient Olympic games were held), and other ancient sites.

 DID YOU KNOW...

- The famous artist, El Greco, was born in Greece?
- The open-air theater of Epidaurus has such excellent acoustics that an actor's breathing can be heard from 100 yds. (91 m) away, in the last row of seats?

GREENLAND

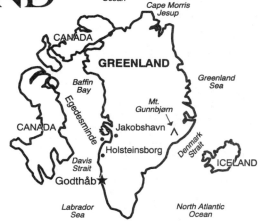

OFFICIAL NAME: Kalaallit Nunaat (Greenlandic); Gronland (Danish) (Greenland)
LOCATION: North Atlantic Ocean
AREA: 840,000 sq. mi. (2,175,600 sq. km)
POPULATION (Est. 1994): 58,000
CAPITAL: Godthåb
LARGEST CITIES: Godthåb, Holsteinsborg, Jakobshavn, Egedesminde
GOVERNMENT: Danish possession with local self-goverment.
FLAG: Two horizontal stripes of white (top) and red with a disk, slightly off-center, of red (top) and white.
ETHNIC GROUP: Greenlander (Danish and Eskimo ancestry)
LANGUAGES: Danish, Greenlandic (form of Eskimo)
RELIGION: Evangelical Lutheran
BASIC MONETARY UNIT: Danish Krone

GEOGRAPHY

Greenland, the world's largest island, lies an average of 1,300 mi. (2,090 km) east of North America, although at one point it lies only 10 mi. (16 km) away from Canada. At its greatest distances, Greenland measures 1,660 mi. (2,670 km) from north to south and 750 mi. (1,210 km) from east to west. It has 8,650 mi. (13,920 km) of coastline along the North Atlantic Ocean, the Greenland Sea, the Labrador Sea, Davis Strait, Denmark Strait, and Baffin Bay.

Greenland consists of a low, inland, ice-covered plateau surrounded by coastal mountains. The icecap covers about 708,073 sq. mi. (1,833,900 sq km), or more than four-fifths, of the country's area and has an average thickness of 1-2 mi. (1.6-3.2 km). *Fiords* (long, narrow, sea inlets) cut through the coast. Icebergs are commonly found in the fiords. The country has no forests and few trees. Only during the country's short summer season are the coastal areas green.

CLIMATE

Greenland experiences cool summers and cold winters. The warmest region is along the southwestern coast, with an average annual temperature of 18°F (-8°C) in February and 50°F (10°C) in July. The coldest region is the center of the icecap, with an average annual temperature of -53°F (-47°C) in February and 12°F (-11°C) in July. The country experiences very little rain or snow, and most of what it does receive falls in the south. Because the country lies so far north, Greenland experiences periods of 24-hour sunshine, called "midnight sun," during the summer and periods of continuous darkness during the winter.

ECONOMY

Greenland's economy is based mainly on fishing. Though there are deposits of coal, graphite, lead, uranium, and zinc, little mining takes place.
Agriculture - hay, potatoes, sheep, and vegetables
Fishing - cod, halibut, salmon, shrimp, and wolf fish
Hunting - arctic hares, foxes, polar bears, reindeer, and seals
Exports - cod, halibut, salmon, shrimp, and wolf fish
Imports - food, live animals, machinery, manufactured goods, petroleum products, and transport equipment

LIFE-STYLE

Greenland's population is about three-fourths urban and one-fourth rural, with almost all of the population living on the southwestern coast. About one-third of all Greenlanders are employed in the fishing industry—either catching or processing fish. Shelters in towns and villages are constructed of wood. Most families keep one room warmer than the others and use this room the most in order to conserve coal. The few Greenlanders of total Eskimoan ancestry live in the far northwest and make a living hunting seals and other animals, eating their meat, using their blubber for fuel, and making their skins into clothes, kayaks, and summer tents. Eskimoan winter homes are made of earth and stone.

Greenlanders mainly wear European-style clothing, with colorful traditional costumes reserved for special occasions.

The Greenlandic diet consists of seal meat, fish, mutton, potatoes, vegetables, and canned foods.

Children ages seven to 14 are required to attend school. Greenland has over 120 elementary schools.

IT'S A FACT!

Cape Morris Jesup - located about 440 mi. (708 km) from the North Pole, is the world's northernmost land.

Mount Gunnbjørn - the country's highest point, rises 12,139 ft. (3,700 m) above sea level.

 DID YOU KNOW...

- The lowest recorded North American temperature—at -87°F (-66°C)—occured in Greenland in 1954?
- Scientists use Greenland as a location for forecasting North Atlantic storms?
- Although Greenland is about 50 times larger than Denmark in area, Denmark's population is almost 90 times that of Greenland?
- The United States has military bases on Greenland?
- It is believed that Norwegian Vikings sighted what is now known as Greenland about A.D. 875, and the early Viking explorers may have given the icy land its misleading name—Greenland—in order to attract settlers?

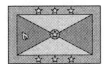

GRENADA

Carriacou Petite Martinique

North Atlantic Ocean

Caribbean Sea

GRENADA

∧ Mt. St. Catherine

Grand Etang ○

★ St. George's

OFFICIAL NAME:	Grenada
LOCATION:	Caribbean Sea
AREA:	133 sq. mi. (344 sq. km)
POPULATION (Est. 1993):	84,000
CAPITAL/LARGEST CITY:	St. George's
GOVERNMENT:	Parliamentary government.
FLAG:	Red border surrounding four triangles, two each of yellow and green, which form a smaller rectangle. Six yellow stars are in the red border: three along the top edge and three along the bottom. Another star is centered on a red circle in the flag's center. A small nutmeg is on the hoist-side green triangle.
ETHNIC GROUP:	Black African
LANGUAGES:	English, French patois
RELIGIONS:	Roman Catholic, Anglican
BASIC MONETARY UNIT:	East Caribbean Dollar

GEOGRAPHY

Grenada is an island nation in the West Indies. It is located in the Caribbean Sea about 90 mi. (140 km) north of Venezuela. The country includes Grenada (the main island), Carriacou, Petite Martinique, and smaller islets northeast of the main island.

Grenada was formed by volcanic activity. The country is dominated by a ridge of thickly forested mountains running from north to south. The main island of Grenada abounds with waterfalls and gorges. The country also has many white sandy beaches, beautiful streams, and green valleys. Tropical flowers add vivid color to the countryside.

CLIMATE

Grenada has just two seasons: one wet (June to December) and one dry (January to May). Temperatures range from 69°F (21°C) in winter to 90°F (32°C) in the summer. Annual rainfall averages 60 in. (150 cm) along the coast and up to 200 in. (510 cm) in the mountains.

ECONOMY

The economy is based primarily on agriculture and tourism. Few factories exist. Grenada is the only island in the West Indies that produces nutmeg and mace, both of which are vitally important to the economy of the island.

The country's beautiful scenery and beaches and pleasant climate beckon many tourists to its shores.

Agriculture - bananas, cocoa, coconut, cotton, limes, mace, nutmeg, and sugar cane

Manufacturing - lime juice and sugar

Exports - bananas, cocoa beans, mace, and nutmeg

Imports - foodstuffs, machinery, manufactured goods, and petroleum

LIFE-STYLE

Arawak Indians were Grenada's first inhabitants. During the 1400s, Carib Indians from South America took over the main island. The Caribs were later wiped out by European settlers. Most of today's inhabitants are descendants of slaves brought to the islands before the British stopped this practice in 1834.

The standard of living is low because of high unemployment and low-paying jobs. Most Grenadians work in either agriculture or the tourist industry.

Grenada has about 60 elementary schools and ten high schools. Children are required to attend school for six years. The literacy rate is 95 percent.

Most of Grenada's 600 mi. (970 km) of roads are surfaced. The country has two airports and a bus service but no railroads. A radio station and five newspapers provide the nation with news and entertainment.

IT'S A FACT!

Grand Etang - a lake formed in the crater of an extinct volcano, lies high in the mountains near the center of the island.

Mount St. Catherine - the country's highest point, rises 2,757 ft. (840 m) above sea level.

 DID YOU KNOW...

- In 1498, Christopher Columbus was the first European to land on the island? He named it *Concepcion*.
- Some say that sailors in the past could find Grenada by the fragrance that drifted out to sea from the island's nutmeg trees?
- Grenada calls itself the "isle of spice"?

GUADELOUPE
Overseas Department of France

OFFICIAL NAME:	Department of Guadeloupe
LOCATION:	West Indies
AREA:	658 sq. mi. (1,074 sq. km)
POPULATION (Est. 1993):	422,114
CAPITAL:	Basse-Terre
LARGEST CITIES:	Basse-Terre, Pointe-à-Pitre
GOVERNMENT:	Department of France governed by a general council. Three deputies represent the council in the French National Assembly.
FLAG:	Uses the flag of France.
ETHNIC GROUP:	Black, Mulatto
LANGUAGES:	French, Creole patois
RELIGION:	Roman Catholic
BASIC MONETARY UNIT:	French Franc

GEOGRAPHY

Guadeloupe is a group of islands in the West Indies. The country consists of two main islands (Basse-Terre and Grande-Terre), a small island group called Îles des Saintes, and five small islands.

Basse-Terre is mountainous with dense forests. It is 27 mi. (43 km) long and 15 mi. (24 km) wide. The Goyaves River runs for 15 miles through the island. The coastline is lined with beaches and bays.

Grande-Terre is 21 mi. (34 km) long and 20 mi. (32 km) wide. It is a limestone island with low hills. Coral reefs follow the coastline.

The Riviére Salée channel separates Basse-Terre and Grande-Terre. It is only 16 ft. (5 m) deep, 4 mi. (6 km) long, and very narrow.

CLIMATE

The islands have a hot, damp climate from June to December. Though trade winds help to moderate the heat, cool, dry weather occurs between January and May. The average temperature is 80°F (27°C) on the coast. The average annual precipitation ranges from approximately 50 in. (130 cm) on the coast to over 300 in. (800 cm) at Mount Soufrière's summit.

ECONOMY

Guadeloupe's economy is dependent on agriculture, tourism, light industry, and services. It also receives subsidies from France.

Agriculture - bananas, cocoa, coffee, eggplant, flowers, sugar cane, tobacco, and vegetables

Manufacturing - construction, rum distilleries, and sugar processing

Exports - bananas, cocoa, coffee, eggplant, flowers, rum, and sugar

Imports - clothing, construction materials, foodstuffs, petroleum products, vehicles

LIFE-STYLE

The majority of the people in Guadeloupe are of mixed black and white ancestry. However, the inhabitants of Îles des Saintes are primarily white French descendants. Close to half of Guadeloupe's population live in urban areas.

About 90 percent of the adult population is literate. Children ages six to 16 must attend school.

IT'S A FACT!

Mount Soufrière - a volcano on Basse-Terre, rises 4,813 ft. (1,467 m) above sea level.

 DID YOU KNOW...
- In 1989, Hurricane Hugo killed six people on Basse-Terre and Grande-Terre and left 10,000 people homeless?
- The Carib Indians were living on Guadeloupe when the first French settlers arrived in 1635?

GUAM
Territory of the United States

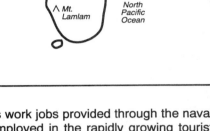

OFFICIAL NAME: Territory of Guam
LOCATION: North Pacific Ocean/Philippine Sea
AREA: 209 sq. mi. (541 sq. km.)
POPULATION (Est. 1993): 133,000
CAPITAL: Agana
LARGEST CITY: Tamuning
GOVERNMENT: Self-governing territory of the United States headed by an elected governor.
FLAG: Red-trimmed blue field on which is centered a red-trimmed, pointed, vertical ellipse featuring a beach scene, an outrigger canoe with a sail, and a palm tree. The word "GUAM" is centered on the scene in red letters.
ETHNIC GROUPS: Chamorro, Filipino, White, Micronesian
LANGUAGES: English, Chamorro
RELIGION: Roman Catholic
BASIC MONETARY UNIT: United States Dollar

GEOGRAPHY

Guam, a territory of the United States, is located at the south end of the Mariana Islands, about 1,300 mi. (2,100 km) east of the Philippines. The country measures about 30 mi. (48 km) from north to south and about 4-10 mi. (6.4-16 km) from east to west. It has about 78 mi. (125.5 km) of coastline along the North Atlantic Ocean and the Philippine Sea.

Coral reefs are found off the coast of Guam. On the northern part of the island is a limestone plateau. The southern half of Guam has a range of volcanic mountains.

CLIMATE

Guam's generally warm and humid climate is tempered by northeast trade winds. The average annual temperature ranges from 68° to 90°F (20° to 32°C). Rainfall averages 90 in. (230 cm) per year. Earthquakes and typhoons occasionally hit the island. Typhoons can be very destructive.

ECONOMY

Most of Guam's income is generated by tourism. The country is also dependent on money provided by the United States military.

Agriculture - bananas, beans, cabbages, canteloupe, cattle, coconuts, cucumbers, eggplants, hogs, maize, papayas, sweet potatoes, taro, tomatoes, watermelon, and yams

Manufacturing - concrete products, processed foods, and textiles

Exports - construction materials, fish, food and beverage products, and transshipments of refined petroleum products

Imports - food, manufactured goods, and petroleum and petroleum products

LIFE-STYLE

About 40 percent of the Guamanian people are Chamorros, descendents of the island's original inhabitants and other Micronesian islanders, and of Filipinos and Spaniards. About one-sixth of the population are U.S. military personnel and their dependents.

Many Guamanians work jobs provided through the naval facilities. Others are employed in the rapidly growing tourist industry. Farmers on Guam grow coconuts, sweet potatoes, and taro. Tuna is the most important fish. Some farmers raise chickens and pigs.

Children ages six to 16 are required to attend school.

IT'S A FACT!

Mount Lamlam - the country's highest point, rises 1,334 ft. (407 m) above sea level.

The War in the Pacific National Historical Park - commemorates the U.S. troops who fought in the Pacific during World War II.

 DID YOU KNOW...
- The people of Guam are citizens of the United States?
- Guam is allowed to elect one delegate to the U.S. House of Representatives, who can vote in committees, but not on the House floor?
- The national bird of Guam is the toto (fruit dove)?
- The U.S. military maintains Andersen Air Force Base and Agana Naval Air Station and several other naval facilities on Guam?
- About one-third of Guam's land is owned by the U.S. armed forces?
- Spain made Guam a possession in 1565 and ceded it to the United States in 1898, the latter of which made Guam a territory in 1950?
- Most of Guam's 500,000 annual tourists are Japanese?

GUATEMALA

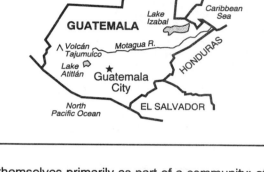

OFFICIAL NAME: República de Guatemala (Republic of Guatemala)
LOCATION: Central America
AREA: 42,042 sq. mi. (108,889 sq. km)
POPULATION (Est. 1993): 10,015,000
CAPITAL/LARGEST CITY: Guatemala City
GOVERNMENT: Republic governed by a president.
FLAG: Three vertical stripes of light blue, white, and light blue. The two light blue stripes represent the Atlantic and Pacific Oceans. A coat of arms is centered on the white stripe.
ETHNIC GROUPS: Ladino, Indian
LANGUAGES: Spanish, Maya Indian languages
RELIGION: Christianity
BASIC MONETARY UNIT: Quetzal

GEOGRAPHY

Guatemala is the most heavily populated country in Central America. The country measures 283 mi. (455 km) from north to south and 261 mi. (420 km) from east to west at its greatest distances. The Pacific coastline is 152 mi. (245 km), and the Caribbean coastline is 53 mi. (85 km). There are three land regions in Guatemala: 1) the Northern Plain, 2) the Highlands, and 3) the Pacific Lowland. Tropical rainforests and some grasslands cover the Northern Plain. The Highlands are a mountain chain that extends east to west across Guatemala. Earthquakes are common in the Highlands, and the region contains many volcanoes. Most Guatemalans live in the Highlands. The Pacific Lowland mainly consists of farmlands.

CLIMATE

Guatemala's climate is tropical. Temperatures vary according to altitude. The plains and lowlands have an average yearly temperature of 80°F (27°C). Mountain valleys at 4,000-6,000 ft. (1,200-1,800 m) above sea level average 60° to 70°F (16° to 21°C). Higher valleys often have frost and average temperatures of 40°F (4°C). The Pacific Lowland and western Highlands receive 30-60 in. (76-150 cm) of rain yearly, while the eastern Highlands receive 20-30 in. (51-76 cm). Most of the Northern Plain receives 80-150 in. (200-381 cm) of rain annually.

ECONOMY

Guatemala is a developing country. Its major natural resource is fertile soil. Guatemala's main sources of income are exported farm products, particularly coffee.

Agriculture - bananas, beans, beef cattle, cardamon, coffee, corn, cotton, and sugar cane

Manufacturing - clothing and textiles, handicrafts, and processed foods and beverages

Exports - bananas, beef, cardamon, coffee, cotton, and sugar

Imports - fertilizers, fuel and petroleum products, grain, machinery, and motor vehicles

LIFE-STYLE

Guatemala has two main population groups—Indians and Ladinos (people of mixed Spanish and Indian ancestry). Being a Ladino or an Indian, however, depends more on life-style than on ancestry.

Most Indians speak an Indian language, wear colorful Indian clothing, and live in an Indian peasant or farm community.

They think of themselves primarily as part of a community; affairs outside the community are given little attention. About 45 percent of Guatemalans are Indians. Most are uneducated and very poor. Indians often travel great distances from their community to trade in markets or to obtain work.

Ladinos typically speak Spanish and follow Spanish-American customs and beliefs. Many are poor farmworkers, but others control the government and the economy. Most live in towns or cities.

In Guatemala, tortillas are eaten at each meal. Black beans, rice, tamales, and fried *plátanos* (bananas) are common food items. Beef, pork, and chicken are often stewed. Common fruits include papaya and breadfruit.

Children ages seven to 13 are required to attend school. About 55 percent actually attend primary school and only about 15 percent go on to high school. School attendance is much higher in the cities and among Ladinos than in rural areas and among Indians.

The most popular sports are soccer, basketball, and volleyball. Other recreational activities are centered around festivals and holidays. The *marimba*, a musical instrument most often connected with Guatemala, can be heard at many festivals.

IT'S A FACT!

Lake Izabal - the country's largest lake, lies near the Caribbean Coast and has an area of 228 sq. mi. (1,591 sq. km).

Motagua River - the country's longest river, flows 250 mi. (402 km) from the Highlands to the Caribbean Sea.

Tikal - the site of ancient Mayan ruins, lies in the rainforests of the Northern Plain.

Volcán Tajumulco - the country's highest point, rises 13,845 ft. (4,220 m) above sea level.

 DID YOU KNOW...
- The national bird of Guatemala is the quetzal?
- The bed of Lake Atitlán is believed to be an ancient valley dammed by volcanic ash?
- The Mayan empire flourished in what is now Guatemala for over 1,000 years?
- Black beans are as common in Guatemala as hamburgers are in the United States?

GUINEA

OFFICIAL NAME: République de Guinée (Republic of Guinea)
FORMERLY: French Guinea
LOCATION: Western Africa
AREA: 94,926 sq. mi. (245,857 sq. km)
POPULATION (Est. 1992): 7,230,000
CAPITAL/LARGEST CITY: Conakry
GOVERNMENT: Republic controlled through the *Military Committee for National Reform* and headed by the military leader, who serves as president.
FLAG: Three vertical stripes of red, gold, and green representing the spirit of sacrifice, the sun and wealth, and the forests.
ETHNIC GROUPS: Fulani (Peul), Malinke, Susu, and others
LANGUAGES: Eight African languages, French
RELIGIONS: Islam, Christianity, Traditional African Religions
BASIC MONETARY UNIT: Franc/Guinean Franc

GEOGRAPHY

Guinea measures 350 sq. mi. (565 sq. km) from north to south and 450 mi. (725 km) from east to west at its greatest distances. It has 190 mi. (305 km) of coastline along the Atlantic Ocean.

Guinea has four main land regions: 1) Lower Guinea, 2) Fouta Djallon (Middle Guinea), 3) Upper Guinea, and 4) the Guinea Highlands. Lower Guinea consists of a swampy, coastal area; Fouta Djallon is a hard, crusty plateau in central Guinea; Upper Guinea is a northern savanna; and the Guinea Highlands is a region of forests and hills in the southeast.

CLIMATE

Guinea enjoys a tropical climate with monsoon-type rains during the months of June through September. Lower Guinea has an average annual temperature range of 73° to 84°F (23° to 29°C) and receives about 110 in. (279 cm) of rain per year. Fouta Djallon is cooler than Lower Guinea and receives 60-100 in. (152-254 cm) of rain per year. Greater temperature variances occur in Upper Guinea and the Guinea Highlands. Of the four regions, Upper Guinea receives the least amount of rain.

ECONOMY

Guinea is one of the world's most underdeveloped countries, but it has an abundance of natural resources.

Agriculture - bananas, cassava, cattle, coffee, corn, goats, palm products, peanuts, pineapples, plantains, rice, sheep, and sweet potatoes

Manufacturing - food products and textiles

Mining - bauxite, diamonds, gold, iron ore, and uranium

Exports - alumina, bauxite, bananas, coffee, diamonds, palm products, and pineapples

Imports - building materials, consumer products, food, machinery, metals, petroleum products, textiles, and transportation equipment

LIFE-STYLE

About three-fourths of all Guineans are farmers, many of whom raise only enough crops to feed their families. These people live in round huts made of mud bricks with thatched roofs. The other one-fourth of the population works in cities or towns in business, manufacturing, or service industries and lives in one-story rectangular mud or wooden homes.

Many Guineans wear modern clothing. However, most Guineans still wear traditional clothing, which consists of a *boubou* (loose robe) for men and a blouse and a brightly-colored skirt for women.

The Guinean diet is usually poor in protein and vitamins. The staple for coastal Guineans is rice. The staples of northern Guineans are corn and millet, which are eaten in a porridge and served with a hot, spicy sauce. On occasion, meals may include vegetables, such as cassava and plantains; fruits, such as bananas, oranges, or pineapples; and meat or fish. Beverages include homemade beer, palm wine, and milk mixed with water.

Guinea's government provides free public school education and requires children ages seven to 19 to attend. Because of classroom and teacher shortages, however, only about one-third of the children actually attend. Few continue on to college, although Guinea does have universities in Conakry and Kankan.

Guineans have a culture rich in music, oral folk tales, and drama. *Griots* (storytellers) are an important part of culture as they recite history. Crafts include woven baskets, metal jewelry, and leather products.

IT'S A FACT!

Mount Nimba - the country's highest point, is located in the Guinea Highlands and rises 5,748 ft. (1,752 m) above sea level.

 DID YOU KNOW...

- Most of Guinea's roads are unpaved and less than one percent of the population owns an automobile?
- Few homes in Guinea have electricity or indoor plumbing; less than one percent of the population owns a television set, and less than three percent of the population owns a radio?
- Guinea is home to about one-third of the world's bauxite reserves?
- Guinea was a French colony from the late 1800s to 1958, at which time the country gained its independence?

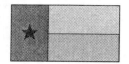

GUINEA-BISSAU

OFFICIAL NAME: Republica de Guine-Bissau (Republic of Guinea-Bissau)
FORMERLY: Portuguese Guinea
LOCATION: Western Africa
AREA: 13,948 sq. mi. (36,125 sq. km)
POPULATION (Est. 1993): 1,027,000
CAPITAL/LARGEST CITY: Bissau
GOVERNMENT: Republic governed by a president, who is elected by a 150-member National People's Assembly.
FLAG: Two horizontal stripes of yellow and green edged by a red vertical stripe on the hoist side. A five-pointed, black star is centered on the red stripe.
ETHNIC GROUPS: Black (20 ethnic groups, the main ones being Balante, Fulani, Manjaca or Manjako, and Malinke or Mandingo), Mestizo
LANGUAGES: Portuguese, Crioulo
RELIGIONS: Animism, Islam, Christianity
BASIC MONETARY UNIT: Guinea-Bissauan Peso

GEOGRAPHY

At its greatest distances, Guinea-Bissau measures 120 mi. (193 km) from north to south and 200 mi. (322 km) from east to west. It has 247 mi. (398 km) of coastline along the North Atlantic Ocean. The country's area includes the Bijagós (Bissagos) Islands, an archipelago that extends 30 mi. (48 km) out into the ocean. The islands are heavily forested.

Guinea-Bissau's coast is covered by rainforests, thick swamps, and mangrove-covered wetlands. The rest of the land is mainly covered by savannas. The country's main rivers include the Cacheu, the Corubal, and the Geba.

CLIMATE

Guinea-Bissau has a tropical climate. The average annual temperature ranges from 74°F (23°C) during the dry season—December to May—to 83°F (28°C) during the wet season—June to November. The average annual rainfall ranges from 95 in. (241 cm) along the coast to 55 in. (140 cm) inland. The heaviest rains fall in July and August.

ECONOMY

Guinea-Bissau's economy—one of the world's poorest—is based mainly on agriculture.

Agriculture - beans, cashews, cassava, coconuts, corn, cotton, palm kernels, peanuts, and rice

Fishing - shrimp

Manufacturing - building construction, and processed foods and beverages

Exports - cashews, coconuts, palm kernels, peanuts, and shrimp

Imports - capital equipment, consumer goods, fuels, rice, and textiles

LIFE-STYLE

Guinea-Bissau's population is about four-fifths rural, with most of the population making a living by farming. Rural shelters are mainly straw huts with thatched roofs. Urban Guinea-Bissauans wear Western-style clothing. In rural areas, traditional clothing is common.

The staple of the diet is rice, and a typical meal consists of rice or millet, a sauce made of palm oil or peanut paste, and fish or meat. Peanuts, tropical fruits, and vegetables are eaten in season. Fish is generally eaten only in coastal areas. In rural areas, the main dish is typically served in large bowls placed on floor mats. Most Guinea-Bissauans eat with the fingers of the right hand. Others use utensils.

Soccer is the most popular sport. In rural areas, *luta livre* (traditional wrestling) is popular. Some who live in urban areas enjoy basketball and tennis. Popular leisure activities include socializing, listening to music, and dancing.

Most Guinea-Bissauans received little education under Portuguese rule, and it wasn't until the quest for independence that schools and education were implemented. After the country gained independence, several military buildings were turned into schools.

Guinea-Bissau has inadequate medical facilities and impotable water. Bilharzia and tuberculosis are widespread, and the major causes of death include gastrointestinal infections and malaria. Malnutrition is also a serious problem. The average life expectancy is from 44 to 48 years.

Rivers are the main means of transportation; the country has few paved roads and no railroads. *Bush-taxis* (pickup trucks with seats and a baggage roof) are used for long-distance travel.

IT'S A FACT!

Amilcar Cabral Avenue - a street in Bissau, is named for the man who led the African Party for the Independence of Guinea and Cape Verde (PAIGC) from 1956 until his assassination in 1973.

 DID YOU KNOW...

- Polygamy is still commonly practiced in Guinea-Bissau because a man's status is often based on the number of wives he has?
- Guinea-Bissau was discovered by Europeans in 1446 by Portuguese explorer Nuno Tristao?
- Guinea-Bissau was under Portuguese rule from 1879 to 1974, when the country gained its independence?
- Some rural Guinea-Bissauans may use their tongues to point directions?
- Guinea-Bissauans consider it bad manners to stretch in public?

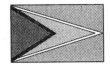

GUYANA

OFFICIAL NAME: Cooperative Republic of Guyana
FORMERLY: British Guiana
LOCATION: Northeastern South America
AREA: 83,000 sq. mi. (214,969 sq. km)
POPULATION (Est. 1993): 815,000
CAPITAL/LARGEST CITY: Georgetown
GOVERNMENT: Republic governed by a president and a 53-member legislature called the National Assembly.
FLAG: Green field with a yellow arrowhead edged in white overlapped by a red isosceles triangle edged in black.
ETHNIC GROUPS: East Indian, Black, Amerindian, European, Chinese
LANGUAGES: English, Hindi, Urdu, Amerindian dialects
RELIGIONS: Christianity, Hinduism, Islam
BASIC MONETARY UNIT: Guyanese Dollar

GEOGRAPHY

At its greatest distances, Guyana measures 495 mi. (797 km) from north to south and 290 mi. (467 km) from east to west. It has 270 mi. (435 km) of coastline along the North Atlantic Ocean.

Guyana has three main regions: 1) the coastal plain, 2) the inland forest, and 3) the highland. The coastal plain is a strip of land on the Atlantic Ocean that varies from 2-30 mi. (3.2-48 km) in width and is mainly used for farmland. Because of the plain's low elevation, the Guyanese have had to build dikes, drainage canals, and sea walls to keep out the sea. The inland forest region lies south of the coastal plain, covers a plateau, and accounts for about 85 percent of the country's area. It is covered with about a thousand different types of timber. The highland region is mountainous in the south and southwest. It has a large savanna in the southwest—about 6,000 sq. mi. (16,000 sq. km) in area—and a small savanna in the northeast.

The country has four main rivers—Essequibo, Demerara, Berbice, and Courantyne—and several waterfalls.

CLIMATE

Guyana's climate is tropical with two rainy seasons: May to mid-August and mid-November to mid-January. The coastal plain has an average annual temperature of 80°F (27°C) and an average rainfall of about 90 in. (230 cm) per year. The forest and highland regions experience higher temperatures and the forest region generally receives more rain.

ECONOMY

Guyana has one of the world's poorest economies. The economy is mainly based on agriculture and mining. .

Agriculture - citrus fruits, cocoa, coconuts, coffee, plantains, rice, and sugar cane
Fishing - shrimp
Forestry - greenheart wood
Manufacturing - textiles and timber
Mining - bauxite, diamonds, gold, and manganese
Exports - bauxite, gold, molasses, rice, rum, shrimp, sugar, and timber
Imports - food, machinery, manufactures, and petroleum

LIFE-STYLE

Guyana's population is about 65 percent rural. About 90 percent of the population lives in the coastal plain region. The East Indians descended from those who were brought from India to work on the plantations. Most live in rural areas and work on sugar plantations or grow rice and vegetables on small farms. Others have urbanized and are doctors, lawyers, or merchants.

Guyana's black population descended from those who were brought from Africa as slaves. They mainly live in urban areas and are employed as government employees, police officers, and teachers or work in bauxite mines and sugar mills.

The Amerindians (American Indians) generally make a living by farming, hunting, or lumbering. Some live by traditional means in remote forest areas. The Chinese and Europeans are mainly employed in business.

Most schools are government-operated and children ages six to 14 are required to attend. For those ages five to 16, most education is free. The country has one university, the University of Guyana, located in Georgetown.

IT'S A FACT!

King George VI Falls - one of the world's highest waterfalls, was discovered in 1938 by scientist Paul A. Zahl, is located on the Utashi River, and drops 1,600 ft. (488 m).

 DID YOU KNOW...
- Because Guyana's mountains and dense forests make travel difficult, some of the country's areas have gone unexplored?
- *Guyana* is Amerindian for "Land of Waters"?
- Guyana became an independent nation in 1966?
- The area now known as Guyana was one of the first western areas to be settled?

HAITI

OFFICIAL NAME: République d'Haiti (Republic of Haiti)
LOCATION: Northern Caribbean Sea
AREA: 10,714 sq. mi. (27,750 sq. km)
POPULATION (Est. 1993): 6,922,000
CAPITAL: Port-au-Prince
IMPORTANT SEAPORTS: Port-au-Prince, Cap-Haïtien, Les Cayes, Saint-Marc
GOVERNMENT: Republic alternatively governed by dictators, the military, a president, a prime minister, and others.
FLAG: Two horizontal stripes of blue and red with a white rectangle featuring the coat of arms in the center. Coat of arms includes a palm tree flanked by flags and two cannons, all resting above a scroll which reads "L'UNION FAIT LA FORCE" (Union Makes Strength).
ETHNIC GROUPS: Black, Mulatto, European
LANGUAGES: French, Haitian Creole
RELIGIONS: Roman Catholic mixed with voodoo, Protestant
BASIC MONETARY UNIT: Gourde

GEOGRAPHY

Haiti makes up the western one-third of Hispaniola Island, which it shares with the country of Dominican Republic. At its greatest distances, Haiti measures 135 mi. (217 km) from north to south and 180 mi. (290 km) from east to west. It has 672 mi. (1,081 km) of coastline including offshore islands.

Haiti has two mountain chains—one in the north and one in the south. The mountains form two peninsulas at the west end of the island. The northern peninsula extends about 100 mi. (161 km) into the Atlantic Ocean, and the southern peninsula extends about 200 mi. (320 km) into the Caribbean Sea. Golfe de la Gonâve lies between the two peninsulas.

CLIMATE

Haiti has a tropical climate. Average annual coastal temperatures range from 70° to 95°F (21° to 35°C) and average annual mountain temperatures range from 50° to 75°F (10° to 24°C). Average annual rainfall ranges from 80 in. (200 cm) in the northern region to less than 40 in. (100 cm) along the southern coast. Severe storms and hurricanes are common from June to October. The country occasionally suffers from flooding and earthquakes.

ECONOMY

Haiti's economy, which is based on agriculture, is one of the least developed of all Western countries.
Agriculture - coffee, corn, fruits, mangoes, rice, sisal, sorghum, and sugar cane
Forestry - mahogany
Manufacturing - cement, flour milling, handicrafts, sugar refining, and textiles
Exports - coffee, light manufactures, and sugar
Imports - beverages, chemicals, cotton goods, fats and oils, food, grain, machinery, manufactures, and petroleum products

LIFE-STYLE

Haiti's population is about three-fourths rural and one-fourth urban; Haiti is one of the most densely populated Western countries. Most Haitians are farmers who work a piece of land no larger than 2 acres (0.8 hectare) and barely raise enough food to feed their families. Their main crops usually include beans, corn, rice, and yams. Some are fortunate enough to own livestock in the form of chickens or a goat or pig. They mainly live in small, one-room huts with thatched roofs and walls constructed of dried, mud-covered sticks.

Haiti's mulatto population mainly belongs to the middle and upper classes and are doctors, lawyers, or merchants. Many received their education in France, and most of them live in modern houses.

At least 50 percent of Haitians are illiterate. Most children do not attend primary school because of the lack of trained teachers and adequate facilities.

Haiti has a shortage of doctors and medical facilities, and many Haitians suffer from a poor diet.

IT'S A FACT!

Pic La Selle - the country's highest point, rises 8,783 ft. (2,677 m) above sea level.

DID YOU KNOW...

- *Haiti* is Indian for "high ground"?
- Haiti is the world's oldest black republic and the second oldest independent Western nation (independent since 1804, second only to the United States)?
- Haiti was discovered by Christopher Columbus in 1492 and became a French possession—known as Saint Domingue—in 1697?
- Of Haiti's 2,500 mi. (4,000 km) of road, only about 375 mi. (600 km) can be used in all weather conditions?

HONDURAS

OFFICIAL NAME: República de Honduras (Republic of Honduras)
LOCATION: Central America
AREA: 43,277 sq. mi. (112,088 sq. km)
POPULATION (Est. 1993): 5,614,000
CAPITAL: Tegucigalpa
LARGEST CITIES: Tegucigalpa, San Pedro Sula
GOVERNMENT: Republic governed by a president.
FLAG: Adopted in 1866. Three horizontal stripes of blue, white, and blue. Five blue stars are arranged in an "X" pattern and centered on the white stripe.
ETHNIC GROUP: Mestizo
LANGUAGE: Spanish
RELIGION: Roman Catholic
BASIC MONETARY UNIT: Lempira

GEOGRAPHY

Honduras is a Central American country that borders both the Caribbean Sea and Pacific Ocean. The Caribbean coastline is 382 mi. (615 km) and the Pacific coast is 48 mi. (77 km). At its greatest distances, Honduras measures 240 mi. (386 km) from north to south and 405 mi. (652 km) from east to west.

The country has four land regions: 1) the Mountainous Interior, 2) the Northern Coast, 3) the Northeastern Plain, and 4) the Southern Coast. The mountainous interior is Honduras's largest region. It includes over 60 percent of this country's land, much of which is covered with forests.

The Northern Coast is an important banana-producing area.

CLIMATE

Honduras has a tropical climate., however the mountain areas are much cooler. The temperature of the coastal lowlands averages 88° F (31°C). The capital, which is 3,070 ft. (936 m) above sea level, has an average temperature of 74°F (23°C).

The southern and central highlands receive an average of 30-60 in. (76-152 cm) of rain annually. The tropical rainforest receives more than 100 in. (250 cm) of rain per year.

ECONOMY

Honduras has one of the most underdeveloped economies in Latin America. Banana and coffee exports account for most of its income.

Agriculture - bananas, beans, beef and dairy cattle, coffee, corn, cotton, milk, sugar cane, rice, and tobacco

Manufacturing - clothing and textiles, cigarettes, lumber, and processed food and beverages

Mining - lead, silver, and zinc

Exports - bananas, beef, coffee, shrimp, timber

Imports - chemical products, foodstuffs, fuel and oil, machinery and manufactured goods

LIFE-STYLE

A little over half of Honduras's population live in rural areas. Most are poor farmers who live in homes constructed of adobe, boards, or poles or of dirt and stones packed into a wooden frame.

Children ages seven to 12 are required to attend school. Many do not attend due to a shortage of schools. Over 40 percent of the adults cannot read or write.

Beans, corn, *tortillas*, and rice are staples of Hondurans' diet. Fruits and vegetables include bananas, pineapples, mangoes, avocados, yams, and potatoes. Traditional Honduran dishes include *mondongo* (tripe with beef knuckles), *nacatamales* (pork tamales), and *tapado* (stew with beef, vegetables, and coconut milk).

Soccer is the national sport, however girls are more likely to play basketball.

IT'S A FACT!

Cerro Las Minas - the country's highest point, rises 9,347 ft. (2,849 m) above sea level.

Copán - is an ancient center of Mayan civilization which once had beautiful palaces, pyramids, and temples.

Mosquito Coast - also called *Mosquitia*, is an area of tropical rainforests on the northeastern plain.

 DID YOU KNOW...

- Honduras was the first Latin American country to be referred to as a "banana republic"?
- Every city and town has a patron saint and holds an annual festival to honor that saint?
- To show they're excited about something, Hondurans place the middle finger and thumb together and shake the hand, producing a snapping sound?
- At 15 years, girls are given a grand party *(La Fiesta Rosa)* to recognize their coming of age?
- *Torrejas* (similar to French toast) is served at Christmastime?
- In 1502, Christopher Columbus arrived at Honduras?

HONG KONG
Dependent Territory of the United Kingdom

OFFICIAL NAME: Hong Kong
LOCATION: Southeastern Asia
AREA: 400 sq. mi. (1,045 sq. km)
POPULATION (Est. 1994): 5,724,000
CAPITAL: Victoria
LARGEST CITIES: Kowloon (includes Kowloon and New Kowloon), Hong Kong City (includes Victoria), Tsuen Wan, Tuen Mun, Sha Tin
GOVERNMENT: Constitutional monarchy headed by a British-appointed governor. In 1997, Hong Kong will become a special administrative region of China.
FLAG: Blue field with the United Kingdom's flag in the upper, hoist-side quadrant. The coat of arms is centered on the flag's outer half.
ETHNIC GROUP: Chinese
LANGUAGES: Chinese (mainly Yue, a Cantonese dialect), English
RELIGIONS: Buddhism, Taoism, Christianity, Hinduism, Judaism, Islam
BASIC MONETARY UNIT: Hong Kong Dollar

GEOGRAPHY

Hong Kong's area consists of a peninsula and more than 235 islands. The country has 455 mi. (733 km) of coastline along Hau Hoi Bay, the South China Sea, and Tai Pang Bay.

Hong Kong lies near the mouth of the Zhu Jiang (Pearl River), and the country's northern border with China follows the Sham Chun River. Hong Kong's peninsula consists of the New Territories in the north and the Kowloon Peninsula in the south. Hong Kong Island is separated from Kowloon Peninsula by Victoria Harbor. Most of the land—only ten percent of which is arable—is covered by mountains and rolling hills.

CLIMATE

Hong Kong has a semitropical climate with cool, dry winters and hot, rainy summers. The average annual temperature rarely falls below 40°F (4°C) in the winter; it often reaches 95°F (35°C) or higher in the summer. The average annual rainfall is 88 in. (224 cm). About 75 percent of the rain falls in the summer, often causing flooding and mudslides. The country is occasionally plagued by typhoons.

ECONOMY

Hong Kong has one of Asia's strongest economies—based mainly on finance, international trade, manufacturing, and tourism—and is among Asia's major ports.

Agriculture - dairy products, poultry, rice, and vegetables
Fishing - eels, sardines, and other seafood
Manufacturing - clocks and watches, clothing and textiles, electronics, plastics, and toys
Exports - clocks and watches, clothing and textiles, electronics, footwear, metal goods, plastic products, and toys
Imports - food, iron and steel, machinery, raw materials, petroleum, semi-manufactures, and transport equipment

LIFE-STYLE

Hong Kong's population was about 5,000 in 1842. Fantastic growth resulted from five major immigration waves. Today, Hong Kong is one of the world's most crowded places, and Hong Kong City—the world's most densely populated city—averages 247,501 persons per sq. mi. (94,053 persons per sq. km). Parts of Victoria Harbor have been filled with earth to create new land.

Hong Kong's population is employed mainly in commerce, government, or manufacturing. A small percent makes a living by farming or fishing. Hong Kong's wealthy urban population lives in luxury apartment buildings and elegant houses with gardens. The middle- and low-income urban population lives in high-rise apartment buildings where several poor families may share one or two small rooms. Some urban residents still live in wood and tin shacks or on boats in the harbor. The rural population lives mainly in one- or two-story shelters constructed of brick or straw with tile or tin roofs. Most Chinese wear Western-style clothing. Others wear traditional Chinese clothing that includes dark-colored pants and shirts and long robes.

Rice, the staple of the diet, is often eaten with chicken, fish, pork, or vegetables. Because of winter water shortages, Hong Kong must import millions of gallons of water from China each year.

Children are required to attend school for nine years—six at the elementary level and three at the high school level. Public schools are government-supported and classes are taught in Chinese. Some private schools teach classes in English. About 77 percent of the population is literate.

Popular sports include basketball, boating, horse racing, ping pong, skating, soccer, squash, swimming, and tennis. Popular leisure activities include socializing, watching movies and television, and playing *mahjong* (a tile game that is a cross between cards and dominoes).

A tunnel that runs under Victoria Harbor connects Hong Kong City and Kowloon, allowing about 85,000 motor vehicles to travel daily between the two cities. An underground subway also links the two.

IT'S A FACT!

Tai Mo Mountain - the country's highest point, is located in the New Territories and rises 3,144 ft. (958 m) above sea level.

 DID YOU KNOW...
- In Hong Kong, the average life expectancy is 76 to 83 years, which is one of the highest in the world?
- In Chinese, *Hong Kong* means "fragrant harbor"?
- Hong Kong was once used as a land base by pirates?

HUNGARY

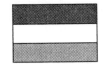

OFFICIAL NAME: Magyar Köztársaság (Republic of Hungary)
LOCATION: Central Europe
AREA: 35,920 sq. mi. (93,032 sq. km)
POPULATION (Est. 1993): 10,527,000
CAPITAL: Budapest
LARGEST CITIES: Budapest, Miskolc, Debrecen
GOVERNMENT: Republic governed by a president.
FLAG: Three horizontal stripes of red, white, and green.
ETHNIC GROUP: Magyar
LANGUAGE: Magyar (Hungarian)
RELIGIONS: Roman Catholic, Protestant
BASIC MONETARY UNIT: Forint

GEOGRAPHY

At its greatest distances, Hungary, a landlocked country, measures 193 mi. (311 km) from north to south and 312 mi. (502 km) from east to west. The country's chief natural resources are fertile soil and a climate favorable for farming. Most of the country is low-lying: two-thirds of the land rises less than 650 ft. (198 m) above sea level.

Hungary has four land regions: 1) the Great Plain, 2) Transdanubia, 3) the Little Plain, and 4) the Northern Highlands. The Great Plain lies east of the Danube River. It is made up of rich soil primarily used for farming. Transdanubia, which includes the land west of the Danube, is comprised of hills and mountains. The Little Plain is the smallest region. It is located in the northwest corner of Hungary, and is mostly flat. Northeast of the Danube lies the Northern Highlands area which has streams, lush forests, and incredible rock formations.

CLIMATE

There is very little variation in Hungary's climate due to its small size and similar land features throughout. The winters are cold with an average January temperature of 29°F (-2°C). Summers are hot with an average July temperature of 70°F (21°C). Approximately 24 in. (60 cm) of precipitation falls annually.

ECONOMY

Prior to World War II, Hungary was primarily an agricultural country. After the Communists rose to power in the late 1940s, industrial development was emphasized. Today, industry accounts for almost 40 percent of the gross domestic product.

Agriculture - chickens and eggs, corn, grapes, hogs, milk, potatoes, sugar beets, and wheat

Manufacturing - buses and railroad equipment, electrical and electronic goods, food products, medical and scientific equipment, pharmaceuticals, steel, and textiles

Mining - bauxite

Exports - alumina, livestock, machinery, medicines, processed foods and beverages, and steel

Imports - automobiles, buses, coal, cotton, electric power, fertilizers, iron ore, livestock feed, machinery, and oil

LIFE-STYLE

More Hungarians now work in industry than on farms. The urban population, which is made up of about 60 percent of the people, live in apartments or one-family homes. Many rural dwellers live in *stucco* houses with tile roofs.

Good food in large quantities is important to Hungarians. A famous Hungarian soup is *goulash*. Many Hungarian dishes are seasoned with paprika. Pork is the favorite meat. Hungary is also known for its *strudel* pastry and many fine wines.

Children ages six to 15 are required to attend school. Most adults are literate.

A favorite activity among the people is visiting coffee houses to read or talk with friends. Hungarians also enjoy art exhibits, the theater, concerts, and operas. Soccer is the most popular sport. Other recreational sports are basketball, boating, fencing, fishing, swimming, and volleyball. Horseback riding, for fun or while hunting, is also enjoyed.

Franz Liszt and Béla Bartók are two world-famous composers. Hungary also has many famous writers.

IT'S A FACT!

Lake Balaton - the country's and Central Europe's largest lake, covers 230 sq. mi. (596 sq. km).

Mount Kékes - the country's highest point, rises 3,330 ft. (1,015 m) above sea level.

Tisza - the country's longest river, flows 360 mi. (579 km) from north to south.

 DID YOU KNOW...

- On December 26 Hungarians celebrate Boxing Day, a holiday originating from an old British tradition of giving gifts to servants and tradesmen the day after Christmas?
- Hungary has many health resorts called "spas" which offer medicinal bathing in mineral waters?
- At Easter, boys "sprinkle" girls with water or cologne, showing that the girl is a flower that should not fade?
- Laborers' average work week is 42 hours, but many also have part-time jobs? Three weeks of vacation a year are usually guaranteed.
- Budapest, the capital, was formed in 1873 when the cities of Buda, Pest, and Obuda, and Margaret Island, joined? Buda and Pest were on opposite sides of the Danube River.

ICELAND

OFFICIAL NAME: Lyoveldio Island (Republic of Iceland)
LOCATION: North Atlantic Ocean
AREA: 39,769 sq. mi. (103,000 sq. km)
POPULATION (Est. 1993): 259,000
CAPITAL: Reykjavík
LARGEST CITIES: Reykjavík, Akureyrí
GOVERNMENT: Republic governed by a president.
FLAG: Blue field with a white-trimmed red cross shifted slightly to the hoist side.
ETHNIC GROUP: Icelander
LANGUAGE: Icelandic
RELIGION: Evangelical Lutheran
BASIC MONETARY UNIT: Icelandic Krona

GEOGRAPHY

Iceland is an island with many natural wonders. Over 200 volcanoes, some of which are still active, have erupted here. Iceland has more sulfur steam areas and hot springs than any other place in the world. Moreover, one-eighth of its land area is covered by glaciers.

Iceland is located just below the Arctic Circle in the North Atlantic Ocean. At its greatest distances, Iceland measures 190 mi. (306 km) from north to south and 300 mi. (483 km) from east to west. It has a total of 1,243 mi. (2,000 km) of coastline.

Iceland's two main land regions are the coastal lowlands and the inland plateau. The lowland region provides the only livable area in the country. The Icelanders raise sheep and some crops in this area.

The inland plateau is a barren region about 2,500 ft. (762 m) above sea level. The fault line crosses this region.

CLIMATE

Despite its location, Iceland has a relatively mild climate. Part of the Gulf Stream flows around the southern and western and parts of the northern coasts. This allows Iceland's ports to be ice-free all year. In Reykjavík, the average temperature is 52°F (11°C) in July and 30°F (-1°C) in January. It receives about 30 in. (76 cm) of rain annually. Some glacial areas receive 180 in. (457 cm) of rain each year.

ECONOMY

Iceland has few natural resources and only one percent of the land is arable. It depends heavily on the fishing industry.
Agriculture - cattle, hay, market gardening, and sheep
Fishing - capelin, cod, haddock, and herring
Manufacturing - aluminum, book binding, cement, clothing, electrical equipment, fertilizer, food processing, and printing
Exports - aluminum, diatomite, animal products, fish and fish products
Imports - appliances, fruits and vegetables, heavy equipment, and raw materials

LIFE-STYLE

The people of Iceland do not have family names. They have first names and a second name that is a combination of the father's first name and -*son* for a male or -*dóttir* for a female. All people are greeted by their first names. Women do not change their name when they marry.

Most Icelandic homes are built of reinforced concrete to withstand earthquakes and high winds. Pastel colors adorn the outside of many of these homes. Water from the hot springs is used to heat the homes and to provide hot tap water.

School is required for all children ages seven to 15. In some of Iceland's isolated areas, teachers travel from farm to farm, staying several weeks in a home to teach the children.

Staples of the Icelander's diet include fish and lamb. Two popular dishes are *hangikjöt* (smoked mutton) and *skyr* (yogurt-like dessert).

Icelanders enjoy swimming in pools year round. Hot springs are used to heat the outdoor pools. The people also participate in basketball, handball, skiing, soccer, and *glima* wrestling.

IT'S A FACT!

Geysir - Iceland's most famous hot spring, spouts water 195 ft. (59 m) into the air.

Hvannadalshnúkur - the country's highest point, rises 6,952 ft. (2,119 m) above sea level.

Mount Hekla - is an active volcano that last erupted in 1980 and 1981.

Thjórsá - the country's longest river, flows 150 mi. (241 km) in southern Iceland.

Vatnajökull - the country's largest glacier, covers 3,140 sq. mi. (8,133 sq. km). It's as big as all the glaciers in Europe put together.

 DID YOU KNOW...

- Iceland has little crime and very little pollution?
- Iceland is sometimes called the "Land of Ice and Fire" because glaciers are found near hot springs, geysers, and volcanoes?
- Telephone directories list one's occupation as well as one's name and address because so many Icelanders have the same name?

INDIA

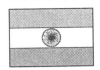

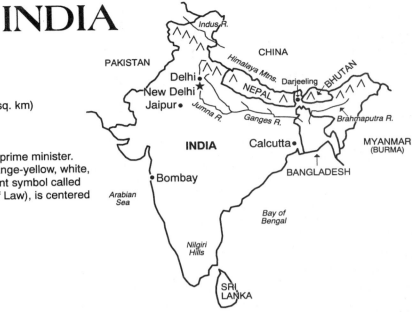

OFFICIAL NAME: Bharat (Union of India)
LOCATION: Southern Asia
AREA: 1,269,346 sq. mi. (3,287,590 sq. km)
POPULATION (Est. 1995): 931,044,000
CAPITAL: New Delhi
LARGEST CITIES: Bombay, Delhi, Calcutta,
GOVERNMENT: Federal republic headed by a prime minister.
FLAG: Three horizontal stripes of orange-yellow, white, and green. A wheel, an ancient symbol called the *Dharma Chakra* (Wheel of Law), is centered on the white stripe.
ETHNIC GROUPS: Indo-Aryans, Dravidians
LANGUAGES: Hindi, English, Sanskrit
RELIGIONS: Hinduism, Islam
BASIC MONETARY UNIT: Indian Rupee

GEOGRAPHY

India, located in southern Asia, is about one-third the size of the United States. It reaches 2,000 mi. (3,200 km) north to south and 1,700 mi. (2,746 km) east to west. It is the second largest country in the world in terms of population. Approximately one out of every six of the world's inhabitants lives in India. The varied landforms include a desert, jungles, one of the world's rainiest areas, broad plains, mighty rivers, the tallest mountains in the world, and tropical lowlands. Most of northern India is separated from the rest of Asia by large mountains. The Arabian Sea touches India on the west and the Bay of Bengal on the east. The coastline stretches 4,252 mi. (6,843 km).

India has three main land regions: 1) the Himalaya, 2) the Northern Plains, and 3) the Deccan, or Southern Plateau.

The Himalaya is the highest mountain system in the world. Located partly in India and partly in China, it runs about 1,500 mi. (2,410 km) from northernmost India to northeastern India and is 200 mi. (320 km) wide in some areas.

The Northern Plains extend across northern India about 1,500 mi. (2,410 km) and have an average width of about 200 mi. (320 km). The region is comprised of the valleys and branches of the Brahmaputra, Ganges, and Indus Rivers. It contains the world's largest alluvial plain (land formed by soil left by rivers). The soil is some of the richest in the world.

The Deccan, or Southern Plateau, is a huge plateau which makes up most of the southern peninsula. It contains two mountain ranges, the Western Ghats and the Eastern Ghats which meet in the Nilgiri Hills. The Deccan also has farming and grazing land, most of India's ores, forests, and several major rivers.

CLIMATE

Most of India has three seasons: 1) cool, 2) hot, and 3) rainy. The cool season extends from October through February. Usually the mountain areas get snow during these months.

The hot season runs from March to the end of June. The northern plains are the warmest. Temperatures are known to rise to 120°F (49°C). Temperatures on the coastal plains are 85°F to 90°F (29°C to 32°C). The northern mountains remain cool or cold during this season.

The rainy season extends from the middle of June through September. Monsoons blow across the Indian Ocean, bringing almost all the rain that falls in India. Some areas in northeastern India get about 450 in. (1,140 cm) of rain yearly.

ECONOMY

Poverty is widespread in India. India has a large economy based on its gross national product (GNP), but because of its large population, it has one of the lowest *per capita* incomes in the world. Agriculture provides about a third of India's national income.

Agriculture - bananas, beans, chickpeas, cotton, jute, mangoes, millet, peanuts, pepper, potatoes, rice, sesame seeds, sorghum, sugar cane, tea, and wheat

Manufacturing - brassware, cement, chemicals, clothing, electric motors, fertilizer, iron, jute bags, leather goods, machinery, medicines, motor vehicles, paper, rope, rugs, silverware, steel, sugar, textiles, and wood products

Mining - iron ore and petroleum

Exports - cashews, coffee, cotton textiles and clothing, cut diamonds, handicrafts, industrial goods, iron ore, jute products, leather goods, shrimp, tea, and tobacco

Imports - edible oils, fertilizer, food grains, industrial machinery, iron and steel, petroleum, and transportation equipment

LIFE-STYLE

Approximately 73 percent of India's population live in rural areas. Indian farmers live in villages, not on their own land. Most Indian villages are comprised of huts made of mud and straw. The homes, which are situated close together, have mud floors and only one or two rooms. Many have no running water or electricity.

Cities encompass a combination of high-rise apartment and office buildings and areas of narrow, winding streets with small open-front shops. The cities of India also have slums. Thousands of people sleep in the streets and others live in shelters made of scraps of wood or metal.

Clothing worn by Indians varies by region. The majority of

 IF8201 Comprehensive World Reference Guide

Indians wear light, loose clothing because of the hot climate. Many men wear a *dhoti,* which is a type of loose pant. The women may wear a *sari,* which is a long piece of material wrapped around the body to form a long dress. Many women also may wear a round dot in the middle of their forehead called a *kumkum.* City dwellers are more likely to wear Western-style clothing.

The principal foods of India include rice, millet, wheat, and *pulses* (seeds of vegetables such as beans, chickpeas, pigeon peas, and lentils). Rice and *dal,* a porridge made of pulses, is a traditional Indian meal. Indians also eat wheat-flour *chapatties,* thin, flat, baked breads that look like tortillas.

Only about one-third of India's adults are literate. Education is provided for children ages six to 14. School attendance declines from sixth grade up because many start working to help support their families.

Indians regard marriage as more of a union between two families than just between two people. Most marriages are arranged, but often the two people involved have the right to turn down the parents' choice.

Some of the oldest types of Indian architecture are found in the ruins of Buddhist monasteries and shrines at Ajanta. Some of the world's loveliest frescoes are found here. There are two types of Indian paintings—wallpaintings and miniatures. They tell stories of the ruling classes or illustrate Hindu legends.

Indian musicians play primarily stringed instruments and drums. They use different musical chords than Westerners use.

For recreation people also enjoy soccer, hockey, and cricket. The most popular form of entertainment is the movies. The film industry in India is one of the world's largest. Every major city has over 100 movie theaters, some of which have restaurants and elevators.

IT'S A FACT!

Bombay - India's largest city and chief western seaport, is an island city located off India's west coast.

Darjeeling - the summer capital of West Bengal, is known for the Darjeeling tea which grows nearby.

Ganges River - considered sacred by the Hindus, is one of the longest in the world.

The Himalaya - is the highest mountain system in the world. It is often referred to as the "top of the world" because many peaks rise more than 20,000 ft. (6,096 m) above sea level.

Kanchenjunga - the country's highest point, rises 28,208 ft. (8,598 m) above sea level.

Taj Mahal - one of the most famous and beautiful buildings in the world, was built between 1632 and 1653. It is the tomb for an Indian ruler and his wife.

 DID YOU KNOW...

- Jaipur is known as the "pink city" because in 1883 the ruling maharaja ordered its buildings to be painted pink, the traditional color of welcome in India?
- Sixteen major languages and over 1,000 minor dialects and languages are spoken by Indians?
- Cows are sacred in the Hindu religion? Because of this, they freely wander around, often in the busy business districts.
- About 16 percent of the total world population live in India?
- Sanskrit classics date back to 1500 B.C. and are known as some of the world's greatest pieces of literature?

INDONESIA

OFFICIAL NAME: Republik Indonesia
(Republic of Indonesia)
FORMERLY: Netherlands East Indies;
Dutch East Indies
LOCATION: Southeast Asia
AREA: 741,101 sq. mi. (1,919,443 sq. km)
POPULATION (Est. 1995): 201,477,000
CAPITAL: Jakarta
LARGEST CITIES: Jakarta, Surabaya, Medan, Bandung
GOVERNMENT: Republic governed by a president.
FLAG: Two equal horizontal stripes of red and white.
The red half stands for courage, the white for purity.
ETHNIC GROUPS: Javanese, Sundanese, Madurese
LANGUAGES: Bahasa Indonesia, English, Dutch, Javanese
RELIGIONS: Islam, Christianity, Bali-Hinduism
BASIC MONETARY UNIT: Rupiah

INDONESIA

GEOGRAPHY

Indonesia consists of a vast chain of islands lying along the equator. The archipelago, made up of more than 13,600 islands, creates a broken bridge of over 3,000 mi. (4,800 km) between Australia and Asia's mainland. Some of Indonesia's islands are less than 1 sq. mi. (2.6 sq. km). Others, such as New Guinea and Borneo, both of which only partly belong to Indonesia, are among the largest islands in the world. The islands of Indonesia can be divided into three groups: 1) the Greater Sunda Islands, 2) the Lesser Sunda Islands, and 3) the Moluccas.

Numerous mountains, including 60 active volcanoes, tower above abundant tropical rainforests on much of Indonesia. Most of the islands have coastal lowlands. The Moluccas include hundreds of small coral islands and atolls.

CLIMATE

Indonesia's location near the equator dictates a tropical climate that is generally hot and humid, although temperatures vary depending on the altitude. In the lowlands, temperatures average 80°F (27°C) throughout the year.

Since year-round temperatures are relatively constant, rainfall plays the largest role in determining Indonesia's seasons. Most of Indonesia's rainfall is distributed evenly throughout the year, with slightly heavier rainfall during the wet season. Two major winds, called monsoons, are largely responsible for the wet and dry seasons.

ECONOMY

Although much of it is undeveloped, Indonesia is rich in natural resources. Agriculture employs over 50 percent of Indonesia's people.

Agriculture - bananas, cassava, coconuts, coffee, corn, palm products, poultry and eggs, rice, rubber, spices, sugar cane, sweet potatoes, tea, and tobacco

Fishing - (one of the world's largest industries) anchovies, mackerel, prawns, sardines, and tuna

Forestry - ebony and teak

Manufacturing - aluminum, cement, cigarettes, fertilizer, glassware, petroleum products, processed foods, steel, textiles, and wood products

Mining - bauxite, coal, copper, natural gas, nickel, petroleum, and tin

Exports - animal and vegetable oils, coffee, copper, natural gas, palm oil, petroleum, rubber, sugar cane, tea, timber, tin, and tobacco

Imports - cereal products, chemicals, iron and steel products, machinery, and transportation equipment

LIFE-STYLE

Indonesia is the fifth most populated country in the world. Three-fifths of Indonesia's people live on the island of Java, which makes up only seven percent of the country's total area. Most Indonesians adhere to many traditional customs, such as the important Javanese feast called a *selametan*, in which family events are celebrated through spirit worship, Muslim prayer, and the offering of special foods to spirits. Just over half of all Indonesians live in small rural villages and are farmers or agricultural workers. Most villages are controlled by traditional leaders who govern by local customs emphasizing cooperation.

Indonesian houses vary widely. The Javanese build their houses on the ground. Most other Indonesians build their houses on 6-ft.- (1.8-m-) high stilts. Floors and walls are constructed of bamboo or timber and roofs are constructed of clay tiles or palm leaves. Chicken coops, cattle stalls, or storage areas occupy the space underneath the houses. In Sumatra, some houses have steep roofs that curve up like buffalo horns at both ends. Other groups construct *long houses* where as many as 100 people may live. Some Indonesians adorn the walls of their homes with intricately carved wood panels.

Although the majority of city dwellers have adopted Western clothing styles, many still prefer to wear traditional clothing like that of their rural counterparts. Rural women wear long-sleeved blouses with *sarongs* or *kains* (brightly colored skirts) that wrap around the body. Instead of the veil worn in other Muslim countries, Indonesian women simply drape a shawl over their shoulders or head. Men wear a special cap or hat and a shirt with either trousers or a *sarong*.

Children are required to attend school for six years, usually beginning at age six. Literacy has risen rapidly since 1945, when only about ten percent of the people could read or write.

Among the arts, Javanese dancing is known for its use of slow, complex movements in which even movements made by the fingers have special meaning. Balinese dancing, based on ancient Hindu folk themes, incorporates strong rhythms and movements. In Bali and Java, shadow plays, called *wayang*, are performed with leather puppets. The puppets cast shadows on lighted screens while a narrator speaks and an orchestra of traditional instruments provides accompaniment. *Batik*, an Indonesian craft involving the waxing and dyeing of cloth, is used to make beautiful fabrics.

Rice is the main staple of the Indonesian's diet. It is served alone or as an accompaniment to meat, fish, or vegetables. Corn is a staple in some areas. Coffee and tea are favorite drinks.

Badminton, soccer, and basketball are popular sports. The people also enjoy the traditional *pencak silat*, which is a combination of dance and self-defense.

IT'S A FACT!

Bali - is an island known for its rare beauty and ancient Hindu culture.

Borobudur - an ancient Buddhist monument in Java, serves as a reminder of the Buddhist Saliendra kingdom that came to power in the 700s.

Jakarta - the country's largest city, has about 9 million people. With its six-lane highways, modern buildings, and thriving seaport, it is one of Asia's busiest trade and communication centers.

Komodo Dragon - the world's largest lizard—known to grow over 10 ft. (3 m) long—is found on the island of Komodo and other Indonesian islands. The lizard can overpower deer, wild pigs, and water buffalo, and has even been known to attack humans.

Krakatau - an active volcano, is located on the island of the same name between Java and Sumatra. Its 1883 eruption caused a gigantic wave, called a *tsunami*, to strike neighboring islands and kill over 36,000 people.

Puncak Jaya - the country's highest mountain, rises 16,503 ft. (5,030 m) above sea level and is located in the province of Irian Jaya.

 DID YOU KNOW...

- Hundreds of years ago the Moluccas were known as the "Spice Islands"? The spices obtained there were sold in Europe.
- Indonesia has over 300 different ethnic groups, each with their own customs and languages?
- An imaginary line from north to south, called the Wallace Line, divides Indonesia's plants and animals into two totally different groups? Those found west of the line—including orangutans, tigers, and water buffalo—are much like those found in Southeast Asia. Those found east of the line—including kangaroos—have more in common with Australia.
- Many Indonesians have only one name, such as Sukarno (the name of the country's first president) and Suharto (president in the late 1960s)?

IRAN

OFFICIAL NAME: Jomhuri-ye Eslami-yeIran (Islamic Republic of Iran)
FORMERLY: Persia (until 1935)
LOCATION: Southwestern Asia/Middle East
AREA: 636,296 sq. mi. (1,648,000 sq. km)
POPULATION (Est. 1993): 57,966,000
CAPITAL: Teheran
LARGEST CITIES: Teheran, Isfahan, Meshed, Tabriz
GOVERNMENT: Theocratic republic.
FLAG: Three horizontal stripes of green, white, and red. The Arabic inscription *God Is Great* appears 22 times, 11 each on the green and red stripes. The coat of arms—which is Arabic script for *Allah* (God)—is centered on the white stripe.
ETHNIC GROUPS: Persian, Azerbaijani, Kurd, others
LANGUAGES: Persian (Farsi), Turkic, Kurdish, Arabic, Baluchi
RELIGION: Islam
BASIC MONETARY UNIT: Iranian Rial

GEOGRAPHY

At its greatest distances, Iran measures 1,375 mi. (2,213 km) from northwest to southeast, and 850 mi. (1,370 km) from northeast to southwest. It has 1,650 mi. (2,655 km) of coastline along the Persian Gulf, the Gulf of Oman, and the Caspian Sea.

Iran has four land regions: 1) the Interior Plateau, 2) the Mountains, 3) the Caspian Sea Coast, and 4) the Khuzistan Plain. The Interior Plateau makes up about half of Iran's total land area. The arid deserts of Dasht-e Kavir and Dasht-e Lut occupy much of this land region. The Mountain region contains the Elburz and the Zagros ranges. The rich land of the Caspian Sea Coast produces a variety of crops. This is also the most populated region. Iran's Khuzistan Plain, which lies north of the Persian Gulf near Iraq's border, contains rich petroleum deposits.

CLIMATE

Iran's climate varies by region. Long, severe winters followed by mild summers occur in the mountains. The Khuzistan Plain has hot, humid summers with an average temperature of 95°F (35°C) and mild winters. Teheran in the Interior Plateau averages temperatures of 35°F (2°C) in January and 85°F (29°C) in July. The average rainfall there is 9 in. (23 cm). On the Caspian Sea Coast, temperatures rarely rise above 90°F (32°C) or drop below freezing. The region receives approximately 40 in. (100 cm) of rain per year.

ECONOMY

The revolution of 1979 badly damaged Iran's economy. Today, economic growth in Iran is low. The country is experiencing high unemployment and an extremely high inflation rate.

Agriculture - barley, nuts, rice, sugar beets, and wheat
Fishing - caviar
Manufacturing - brick, cement, food products, petroleum products, and textiles
Mining - petroleum
Exports - caviar, cotton, dried fruits, hides, mineral ores, nuts, Persian rugs, petroleum, and spices
Imports - electrical appliances, food, industrial machinery, medicine, and military equipment

LIFE-STYLE

A little over half of the Iranian population live in urban areas. Blue-domed *mosques* (houses of worship) and bazaars are seen throughout the cities. Urban housing includes modern apartment buildings and traditional houses made of mud or brick, each one opening onto a central courtyard.

Most rural villages are farming communities. The villagers live in traditional homes with no modern conveniences. A small segment of rural Iranians are nomads. They travel with their livestock and live in small tents.

Many urban Iranian women wear *chadors* (long, black body veils) over their clothing. Most rural men and women wear black pants and loose cotton tops. The women wear scarves to cover their head.

Staples of the diet are rice and bread. Rice is often combined with meat and vegetables, and mixed with a thick, spicy sauce. Traditional dishes are *abgusht* (thick, meat and bean soup), *dolmeh* (vegetables stuffed with meat and rice), and *kebab* (lamb roasted on a skewer). Yogurt, fresh fruit, and white cheeses are also popular.

The extended family is very important in Iranian society. The father is the head of the household and large families are common. Most marriages are arranged. Men and women rarely make eye contact when conversing.

Most leisure time is spent visiting and entertaining. Popular sports are basketball, soccer, volleyball, and weight-lifting. Movies are popular in urban areas.

Only about half of Iranians aged 15 or older are literate. Although children ages seven to 13 are required to attend school, many children, especially in rural areas, do not attend because of the shortage of teachers and classrooms.

IT'S A FACT!

Mount Damavand - the country's highest point, rises 18,386 ft. (5,604 m) above sea level.

 DID YOU KNOW...
- Iran's history dates back almost 5,000 years and includes the days of the great Persian Empire?
- About 70 percent of Iran is almost uninhabited?

IRAQ

OFFICIAL NAME: Al-Jumhuriya Al-Iraqiya (Republic of Iraq)
LOCATION: Southwestern Asia
AREA: 169,235 sq. mi. (438,317 sq. km)
POPULATION (Est. 1993): 20,910,000
CAPITAL: Baghdad
LARGEST CITIES: Baghdad, Mosul, Al Basrah
GOVERNMENT: Republic ruled by a dictator.
FLAG: Three horizontal stripes of red, white, and black with three green stars and the Arabic inscription "God is great" on the white stripe.
ETHNIC GROUPS: Arabs, Kurds
LANGUAGES: Arabic, Kurdish
RELIGION: Islam
BASIC MONETARY UNIT: Iraqi Dinar

GEOGRAPHY

Iraq is an Arab nation which occupies the eastern part of the Fertile Crescent, the area referred to as *Mesopotamia* by the ancient Greeks. At its greatest distances, Iraq measures 530 mi. (853 km) from north to south and 495 mi. (797 km) from east to west. It has 40 mi. (64 km) of coastline along the Persian Gulf.

There are four main land regions: 1) the northern plain, an area of dry, rolling land that lies between the Tigris and Euphrates Rivers; 2) the southern plain, which includes the fertile delta between the Tigris and Euphrates Rivers; 3) the mountains in the northeast; and 4) the desert, most of which is part of the Syrian Desert.

CLIMATE

Iraq's climate ranges from semitropical in the east and southeast to mild in the north. Desert climate, warm days and cool nights, can be found in the west and southwest. High temperatures in the summer average more than 100°F (38°C). Low temperatures in the winter may fall to 35°F (2°C).

Iraq receives relatively small amounts of precipitation. Average annual amounts range from 5 in. (13 cm) in the desert areas to 15 in. (38 cm) in the mountains.

ECONOMY

Until the trade embargo of 1990, Iraq's economy prospered from the export of oil and petroleum products. The war with Iran and the Persian Gulf War severely damaged the economy. Trade routes were disrupted, ports were closed, and factories were destroyed. (Export and import information applies to the years prior to the 1990 Trade Embargo imposed by the United Nations.)

Agriculture - barley, cotton, dates, grapes, rice, tomatoes, and wheat

Manufacturing - building materials, chemicals, flour, iron and steel, leather goods, petroleum refining, and textiles

Mining - petroleum, phosphates, natural gas, and sulfur

Exports - dates, fertilizer, natural gas, and oil

Imports - cotton, military weapons, motor vehicles, sugar, tea, textiles, and timber

LIFE-STYLE

Almost three-fourths of Iraq's people live in cities and towns located in the fertile plain that extends south from Baghdad along the Tigris and Euphrates Rivers. Iraq has a population growth rate of 3.5 percent, one of the highest in the world. Its population explosion has contributed to severe unemployment and housing shortages found in some cities. Village houses in central and southern Iraq are flat-roofed, rectangular, and made of dried mud and brick; in the north, they are built of stone.

In urban areas, the middle-class and wealthy wear Western-style clothing. Members of the laboring class wear more traditional clothing. Men generally wear long cotton gowns and jackets. Women wear a long, concealing dress and a scarf that covers most of the head.

The Iraqi diet consists of bread, dates, fish, flat bread, meat (chicken, fish, and grilled lamb), rice, and vegetables. Also consumed are large amounts of beans, plain yogurt, and fresh fruits, especially melons. A traditional dish is *sanbusak* (moon-shaped dough filled with cheese or meat). Popular beverages are coffee, fruit juices, and tea.

For sports and recreation, the Iraqis favor backgammon, chess, horse racing, and soccer. Leisure activities are generally centered around family events.

School is compulsory until the age of 12. The country's adult literacy rate is over 55 percent.

IT'S A FACT!

Great Mosque of Samarra - built in the 9th century; though it lies in ruins, its spiral minaret still stands.

Monument of Saddam's Qadissiya - a 150-foot-high tiled split dome which commemorates the Arab defeat of Persia in A.D. 637, and the thousands of Iraqis killed during the recent war with Iran.

Ninevah - site of the ancient ruins of the Assyrian Empire, it is located north of the city of Mosul.

 DID YOU KNOW...

- Iraq occupies an area once known as *Mesopotamia*, the legendary site of the biblical Garden of Eden?
- Iraq's oil reserves are second only to those of Saudi Arabia?
- In rural areas, people use buses, donkeys, and camels for transportation?
- *Wadis* are valleys in the desert that are dry the majority of the year but turn into rivers after a rain?

IRELAND

OFFICIAL NAME: Ireland
LOCATION: Northwestern Europe
AREA: 27,137 sq. mi. (70,284 sq. km)
POPULATION (Est. 1994): 3,863,000
CAPITAL: Dublin
LARGEST CITIES: Dublin, Cork
GOVERNMENT: Republic governed by a president and a prime minister.
FLAG: Three vertical stripes of green, white, and orange, representing the country's Roman Catholics, unity, and the Protestants of Ulster, accordingly.
ETHNIC GROUPS: Irish (descendents of British, Celtic, Norman and Viking settlers)
LANGUAGES: English, Gaelic (generally called Irish)
RELIGION: Roman Catholic
BASIC MONETARY UNIT: Irish Pound

GEOGRAPHY

Ireland covers about five-sixths of the island of Ireland in the British Isles. Ireland is often referred to as the Republic of Ireland to distinguish it from Northern Ireland, which occupies the northeastern one-sixth of the island.

At its greatest distances, Ireland measures 289 mi. (465 km) from north to south and 177 mi. (285 km) from east to west. It has 1,738 mi. (2,797 km) of coastline along the North Atlantic Ocean, St. George's Channel, and the Irish Sea.

Ireland's lush, green countryside has earned it the name *Emerald Isle*. Over two-thirds of the country's land is used for farming. Ireland's topography consists of lowlands, mountains, and coasts. The lowlands comprise most of central Ireland and feature peat bogs, some wooded areas, and most of the country's farmland. Mountains are found mainly near the coast and near the lowland borders. The main mountain ranges include the Mountains of Connemara, the Donegal Mountains, the Mountains of Mayo, the Mountains of Kerry, and the Wicklow Mountains.

The island's western coast has high cliffs and inlets and bays which cut deeply inland. Straighter, less rugged coasts are found to the south and east. No part of Ireland is more than 70 miles (110 km) from the sea.

Off the west coast of Ireland lie the islands of Achill, Aran, and Valentia—along with hundreds of other small islands.

CLIMATE

Ireland's climate has mild winters and cool summers partly as a result of the North Atlantic Current which flows past the British Isles. The average temperature is about 41°F (5°C) in winter to about 59°F (15°C) in summer. The average rainfall in the lowlands is about 35 in. (90 cm) and about 60-100 in. (150-250 cm) along the mountainous west coast. Because of the heavy rainfall and the cool year-round temperatures, humidity is constant. Some areas suffer from flooding.

ECONOMY

Prior to the 1920s, agriculture was the primary economic activity. Today, service industries and manufacturing dominate.

Agriculture - barley, beef and dairy cattle, hay, hogs, milk, potatoes, poultry, sheep, sugar beets, turnips, and wheat

Fishing - cod, haddock, herring, lobsters, mackerel, plaice, prawns, rays, salmon, and whiting

Manufacturing - alcoholic beverages, chemicals, clothing, computers, crystal and glass, machinery, medicines, metal products, paper, pharmaceuticals, printed materials, processed foods, textiles, and transportation equipment

Mining - lead, marble, natural gas, peat, and zinc

Exports - chemicals, computers, dairy products, industrial machinery, livestock, meat, stout, and textiles

Imports - clothing and textiles, fruits, grains, machinery, motor vehicles, petroleum, and plastics

LIFE-STYLE

Ireland's population is approximately three-fifths urban. Most urban dwellers live in houses, and others in apartment buildings. The houses are constructed of brick or concrete. Rural dwellers live in small towns or villages in modern houses, though some still dwell in traditional, thatch-roofed cottages. Over half of the people are employed in service industries.

Conservative European-style clothing is commonly worn. Because of the country's cool, humid climate, residents often wear sweaters and woolen clothing.

Irish fare is generally simple. Staples of the diet include beef, bread, chicken, fruit, mutton, pork, and potatoes and other vegetables. A popular dish is *Irish stew* (potatoes, onions, and mutton pieces boiled in a covered pot). Another dish consists of cabbage, potatoes, and boiled salt pork. Tea is the preferred beverage, and beer is the most popular alcoholic drink, especially a type called *stout*. *Irish whiskey,* a liquor made from barley malt, and *Irish coffee,* a coffee mixed with brown sugar, cream, and Irish whiskey, are other popular drinks.

Children ages six to 15 are required to attend school. Private organizations, such as the Church of Ireland (Protestant) and the Roman Catholic Church, control nearly all of the schools.

Most primary and secondary education is free. Boys and girls usually attend separate secondary schools. The country's schools teach English and Gaelic, though only about 30 percent of the people say they are fluent enough in Gaelic to use it for everyday conversation. The government uses both languages for official business.

Horseback riding and horse shows are popular recreational activities in Ireland. The two biggest horse races are the Irish Derby and the Irish Grand National. The Royal Dublin Society Horse Show boasts of international participation.

Popular team sports include *cricket* (played with a ball and bat), *football* (similar to North American soccer), *Gaelic football* (which also resembles soccer), *hurling* (similar to field hockey), *camogie* (the women's version of hurling), and Rugby football. Leisure activities include boxing, cycling, fishing, golf, sailing, swimming, tennis, and walking. Socializing at *pubs* (public houses) is also popular.

Ireland is known for its many famous authors. James Joyce, George Augustus Moore, George Bernard Shaw, and William Butler Yeats are a few of the most famous. Celtic crosses, Donegal tweed, Waterford crystal, folk music, and energetic dances such as jigs and reels are also part of Ireland's rich artistic culture.

IT'S A FACT!

Abbey Theatre - considered the national theater of Ireland, opened in Dublin in 1904 by the authors William Butler Yeats, and Lady Gregory. The theater presents plays written by Ireland's finest dramatists.

Carrauntoohill - the country's highest point, is located in the Mountains of Kerry and rises 3,414 ft. (1,041 m) above sea level.

River Shannon - the longest river in the British Isles, flows 230 mi. (370 km) southwest to the Atlantic Ocean.

 DID YOU KNOW...

- About 750,000 Irish residents died in the 1840s as a result of a potato famine? This famine also caused hundreds of thousands of people to emigrate. There are only a little more than half as many people now living in Ireland as there were in 1845.
- The Roman Catholic Church plays a major role in Irish life and the country's law? For example, since abortion and divorce are opposed by the Catholic Church, the Irish government considers them illegal.
- St. Patrick, the patron saint of Ireland, converted the Irish to Christianity in the A.D. 400s? He also introduced the people to Latin literature and the Roman alphabet.
- Ireland is known in Gaelic as *Éire*? It is also known by the poetic name *Erin* (as in *Erin go bragh*, meaning "Ireland forever").
- One of the world's largest lead-zinc mines is located near the city of Navan?
- Because of economic conditions in the past, it was common practice for young people to stay single and to live with their parents until they were over the age of 30?
- Ireland was part of Britain until 1921 when Ireland became a self-governing country of the British Commonwealth? In 1948, Ireland declared itself an independent republic.

- Ireland has a censorship board which prohibits "improper" works? Throughout history, many famous Irish writers had their works banned in their own country.
- It is believed that people first settled in Ireland as early as 6000 B.C.?
- In Ireland, peat functions as a fuel to make electricity and is also used for heating and cooking? Natural gas is also used, but Ireland has little coal.

ISLE OF MAN
Dependency of the United Kingdom

OFFICIAL NAME: Isle of Man
LOCATION: Irish Sea
AREA: 227 sq. mi. (588 sq. km)
POPULATION (Est. 1993): 65,000
CAPITAL/LARGEST CITY: Douglas
PRINCIPAL TOWNS: Douglas, Peel, Castletown, Ramsey
GOVERNMENT: Self-governing dependency of the United Kingdom.
ETHNIC GROUP: Celtic
LANGUAGE: English
BASIC MONETARY UNIT: Isle of Man Pound

GEOGRAPHY

The Isle of Man is located in the Irish Sea about halfway between England, Ireland, and Scotland.

There is a chain of low mountains that runs the length of the island. Farmland and moors (wastelands of coarse grasses and evergreen shrubs called *heather*) cover most of the country. It is also marked by a rocky, indented coastline.

CLIMATE

Despite its location in the far northern latitudes, the country has a relatively mild climate due to the warm Gulf Stream. The average annual temperature ranges from 40° to 50°F (4° to 10°C). The average annual rainfall is 45 in. (115 cm).

ECONOMY

The country's economy is based on agriculture, fishing, and tourism.

Agriculture - barley, oats, potatoes, turnips, and wheat
Fishing - kippers and scallops
Exports - beef, fish, lamb, and livestock

LIFE-STYLE

Increasing numbers of people are working in the growing tourist industry. The people of the British Isles have chosen the island as a popular place to spend summer vacations. Motorcycle races in the summer attract many tourists, as well.

Although technically ruled by Great Britain, the people elect representatives to a 1,000-year-old parliament called Tynwald Court, which regulates the island's internal affairs. It enjoys a considerable amount of self-government, and British laws do not apply unless they specifically name the Isle of Man.

IT'S A FACT!

Calf of Man - an islet in the southwest, is home to a bird sanctuary and a farm.

Snaefell - the country's highest point, rises 2,034 ft. (620 m) above sea level.

 DID YOU KNOW...
- Great Britain has controlled the Isle of Man since 1765?
- The *Manx* cat, a tailless breed, is believed to have originated on the Isle of Man?
- It is thought that the island's name, *Man*, originates from the Celtic word *monadh*, meaning "mountain"?

ISRAEL

OFFICIAL NAME:	Medinat Yisra'el (State of Israel)
LOCATION:	Southwestern Asia
AREA:	8,019 sq. mi. (20,770 sq. km)
POPULATION (Est. 1993):	4,810,000
CAPITAL:	Jerusalem
LARGEST CITIES:	Jerusalem, Tel Aviv, Haifa
GOVERNMENT:	Democratic republic headed by a prime minister.
FLAG:	White field with the Star of David in the center and horizontal stripes of blue near the top and the bottom.
ETHNIC GROUPS:	Jewish, Arab
LANGUAGES:	Hebrew, Arabic
RELIGIONS:	Judaism, Islam
BASIC MONETARY UNIT:	New Israeli Shekel

GEOGRAPHY

Located in southwestern Asia, Israel is a small country occupying a narrow strip of land on the eastern shore of the Mediterranean Sea.

The country has four main land regions: 1) the Coastal Plain, a narrow strip of land along the Mediterranean Sea; 2) the Judeo-Galilean Highlands, a group of mountains that stretch from Galilee to the edge of the Negev Desert; 3) the Rift Valley, in eastern Israel, a long narrow strip of land that is part of the Great Rift Valley that extends into southern Africa; and 4) the Negev Desert, a dry area of flatlands and mountains located in the south-central part of the country.

Two Arab territories—the West Bank, west of the River Jordan, and the Gaza Strip, on the Mediterranean coast—have been occupied by Israeli troops since 1967. Violence has erupted numerous times because Palestinian Arabs protest Israeli occupation. Pending a negotiated settlement, the territory remains in a state of uncertainty as to its final political destination.

CLIMATE

Altitude causes Israel's climate to vary somewhat by region. Generally, the country experiences hot, dry summers and cool, mild winters. In August, the hottest month, temperatures may reach 120°F (49°C) near the Dead Sea. In July, average temperatures range from 73° to 81°F (23° to 27°C). In January, the coldest month, average temperatures range from 48° to 57°F (9° to 14°C). Most of Israel's rain falls between November and March. In the southern Negev Desert, average rainfall is only 1 in. (2.5 cm) annually. In the wettest part of the country, Upper Galilee, average yearly rainfall is 42.5 in. (108 cm). Light snow falls occasionally in the hill regions.

ECONOMY

In 1948, when the modern nation of Israel was established, the economy was poor. Today, the economy is well-developed and modern. Israelis enjoy a relatively high standard of living.

Agriculture - citrus and other fruits, cotton, eggs, grains, poultry, and vegetables

Manufacturing - chemical products, clothing, electronic equipment, fertilizer, finished diamonds, paper, plastics, processed foods, scientific and optical instruments, and textiles

Mining - bromine, phosphates, potash, and salt

Exports - chemicals, electronic equipment, meats, polished diamonds, scientific instruments, and textiles

Imports - chemicals, computer equipment, dairy products, fertilizers, grains, military equipment, motor vehicles, paper, petroleum products, rough diamonds, and textiles

LIFE-STYLE

Israel is about 90 percent urban. Like most rapid-growing urban centers, Israelis face problems such as traffic congestion, pollution, and a shortage of housing. Of the ten percent of the population who live in rural areas, over half live in collective communities called *kibbutzim*. Inhabitants in a kibbutz receive food, housing, education, child care, and medical care in exchange for agricultural or industrial labor. All property is shared.

Israel's ethnic diversity is reflected in its many different types of food and drink. Common European Jewish dishes are gelfille fish and chopped liver. *Felafel*, a traditional Middle Eastern dish consisting of ground chickpeas, is also a popular meal in Israel.

Children ages five to 16 are required to attend school. Israel has both Jewish schools, where the lessons are taught in Hebrew, and Arab/Druse school systems, where Arabic is used. There is a high priority given to education which accounts for Israel's high literacy rate.

IT'S A FACT!

Jerusalem - the capital and largest city, is the spiritual center of the Jewish religion and a holy city for Christians and Muslims.

Mount Meron - the country's highest point, rises 3,963 ft. (1,208 m) above sea level.

Dead Sea shore - the country's lowest point of elevation, is located 1,310 ft. (399 m) below sea level.

 DID YOU KNOW...

- Israel requires mandatory military service for both men and women?
- Most Israelis observe Jewish dietary laws which prohibit milk and meat being eaten together?
- Israel does not have a written constitution?
- Most Israeli students wear uniforms for school?
- Israel makes up most of the Biblical Holy Land; Jerusalem played a major role in the development of Christianity, Judaism, and Islam?
- Israelis use the term *Shalom*, meaning "Peace," as a greeting and a way of saying "Good-bye"?

ITALY

OFFICIAL NAME: Repubblica Italiana (Italian Republic)
LOCATION: Southern Europe
AREA: 116,320 sq. mi. (301,268 sq. km)
POPULATION (Est. 1995): 57,910,000
CAPITAL: Rome
LARGEST CITIES: Rome, Milan, Naples, Turin
GOVERNMENT: Parliamentary democracy governed by a premier.
FLAG: Three vertical stripes of green, white, and red.
ETHNIC GROUPS: Italian, German, Slovene
LANGUAGE: Italian
RELIGION: Roman Catholic
BASIC MONETARY UNIT: Italian Lira

GEOGRAPHY

Italy is a boot-shaped peninsula that extends into the Mediterranean Sea. Within its borders are two independent states: the Republic of San Marino and Vatican City. The majestic mountain ranges of the Alps and the Apennines dominate Italy's landscape. The islands of Sicily and Sardinia are also part of Italy. Italy measures 708 mi. (1,139 km) from north to south and 320 mi. (515 km) from east to west at its greatest distances.

Italy has eight land regions: 1) the Alpine Slope, 2) the Po Valley, 3) the Adriatic Plain, 4) the Apennines, 5) Apulia and the Southeastern Plains, 6) the Western Uplands and Plains, 7) Sicily, and 8) Sardinia. Located in the northernmost part of Italy, the Alpine Slope has huge mountains and deep valleys. The Po Valley is a broad plain that stretches between the Alps and the Apennines. It is the most densely populated region of Italy. Almost all of its rich soil is cultivated. The Adriatic Plain is a small area north of the Adriatic Sea. The Apennines stretch almost the whole length of the country. Most of the lower and middle levels are covered by forests. Apulia and the Southeastern Plain form the "heel" of the boot. This region has large farming estates that produce more olive oil than any other region. The Western Uplands and Plains stretch along the western coast from the city of La Spezia to Salerno. Rome and Naples are both found here. It is also the location of many of Italy's vineyards. Sicily is the largest island in the Mediterranean Sea. Mountains and plains form the landscape. It has the largest fishing industry in Italy. The island of Sardinia is west of Italy in the Tyrrhenian Sea. Its landscape is made up of mountains and plateaus.

CLIMATE

Italy's reputation as a sunny land is only partly true. Spring, summer, and fall are usually sunny, but winter is cloudy and rainy. The climate does not vary much between the north and south except in winter. Northern Italy is protected from intense cold by the Alps. In January, temperatures average from 29° to 54°F (-20° to 12°C). July temperatures average 64° to 88°F (18° to 31°C). Northern Italy averages 30 in. (76 cm) of rain per year. Average rainfall in the south is 15 in. (38 cm) per year.

ECONOMY

Italy's economy is primarily dependent on service industries. The approximately 50 million tourists who visit Italy annually contribute billions of dollars to the economy each year. They account for over 65 percent of Italy's gross domestic product. Manufacturing accounts for almost 30 percent of economic activity.

Agriculture - apples, artichokes, beef cattle, corn, grapes, hogs, olives, oranges, peaches, potatoes, rice, sugar beets, tomatoes, and wheat

Manufacturing - chemicals, clothing and shoes, foods and beverages, machinery, motor vehicles, and petroleum products

Mining - granite, marble, and natural gas

Exports - chemicals, clothing and shoes, fruits, machinery, motor vehicles, and vegetables

Imports - machinery, metals, motor vehicles, petroleum, and textile yarns

LIFE-STYLE

Life in northern Italy is very different from life in the south. In general, the north is richer, more urbanized, and more industrialized. The percentage of people employed in agriculture is much higher in the south.

Italy has several world-renowned cities. The largest is also the capital city, Rome. Two thousand years ago it was the center of the Roman Empire. Florence boasts being the home of many Renaissance artists. Romantic Venice is a famous vacation spot with its numerous gondolas winding along its many canals. Vatican City is the headquarters of the Roman Catholic Church. Even though it is within the city of Rome, it is self-governed and independent from Italy.

The majority of Italy's population live in apartment buildings in urban areas. Many apartments are bought, not leased. Quite often in rural areas you'll find single-family homes built around a community center.

Italians are very proud of their cooking abilities. The main meal is usually at midday. Oftentimes, *antipasto* (appetizer) is served first. Antipasto may include a variety of cold meats and vegetables. In the north, pasta with cream sauces is popular. In the south, tomato-based pasta is dominant. The most popular meats are veal and pork. Cheeses are also important parts of the diet. Fresh fruit is often served as dessert. Wine is served with every meal, except breakfast.

Italy has a well-developed public school system. Children ages six to 14 are required to attend school. Many elementary, junior high and senior high schools, and universities are available for enrollment.

Popular professional sports in Italy are soccer and basketball. Both sports—as well as fishing, hunting, cycling, roller skating, and baseball—are popular activities for all ages. Families enjoy taking strolls, driving to the mountains or coast, and watching television.

Italy is known as one of the world's greatest centers of the arts. Many of the best-known artists, sculptors, architects, and composers in history were Italian. Several famous *basilicas* can be seen throughout Italy. Probably the most famous is the Basilica of St. Mark in Venice. Also, the Colosseum in Rome is evidence of the architecture style of the Roman Empire. The world's first operas were composed in the 1590s in Florence. Since that time many well-known Italian composers, such as Monteverdi, Verdi, Puccini, and Rossini, have produced many famous works. Florence is also known for the many painters and sculptors who lived there. Leonardo da Vinci's *Mona Lisa* and *The Last Supper* are two of the most recognized paintings in the world. Another famous Italian painter, Michelangelo, was equally well-known as a sculptor. His painting on the ceiling of the Sistine Chapel in the Vatican and his sculpture *Pietá* in St. Peter's Cathedral are just two of his many famous works. The Arch of Constantine, the Pantheon, and the Roman Forum are just three of the many remaining architectural works that date from the Roman Empire.

IT'S A FACT!

Leaning Tower of Pisa - located in the city of Pisa, is the Pisa Cathedral's bell tower. It was constructed between 1173 and about 1360 or 1370, and rises 180 ft. (55 m) above sea level. The tower leans as a result of its unstable foundation.

Mont Blanc - the country's highest point, rises 15,571 ft. (4,807 m) above sea level.

Mount Etna - located in Sicily, it is one of the largest active volcanoes in the world.

Po River - is the country's longest river.

 DID YOU KNOW...
- Tunnels through the Alps link Italy's highway system with those of other countries?
- Contrary to popular belief in the United States, spaghetti and meatballs are not served together at Italian meals?
- *The Divine Comedy* was written by the Italian poet Dante in the 1300s and is still studied in classrooms around the world?

IVORY COAST

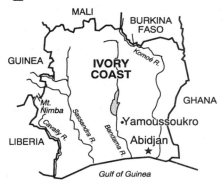

OFFICIAL NAME: République de Côte d'Ivoire
(Republic of the Ivory Coast)
LOCATION: Western Africa
AREA: 124,504 sq. mi. (322,463 sq. km)
POPULATION (Est. 1992): 13,600,000
CAPITAL/LARGEST CITY: Abidjan
GOVERNMENT: Republic governed by a president and
a legislature called the National Assembly.
FLAG: Three vertical stripes of orange, white, and green.
ETHNIC GROUPS: Akan, Kru, Mandingo, Voltaic
LANGUAGES: Over 60 African languages, French
RELIGIONS: Traditional African Religions, Islam, Christianity
BASIC MONETARY UNIT: CFA Franc

GEOGRAPHY

The Ivory Coast measures 420 mi. (676 km) from north to south and 411 mi. (661 km) from east to west at its greatest distances. It has 315 mi. (507 km) of coastline along the Gulf of Guinea.

The coast is flat and sandy to the east and has small, rocky cliffs to the west. A sand bar stretches along 180 mi. (289 km) of the coast, behind which lie deep lagoons. Behind the coastal area is a tropical forest region that ranges from 95 to 185 mi. (153 to 298 km) wide. The northern portion of Ivory Coast is a savanna while the west is made up of the Guinea highlands. The country's major rivers include the Bandama, the Cavally, the Komoé, and the Sassandra.

CLIMATE

Ivory Coast's climate ranges from tropical along the coast to semiarid in the savanna. The country has three seasons. It is warm and dry from November to March, hot and dry from March to May, and hot and wet from June to October. Average annual temperatures in the coastal area range from 76° to 83°F (24° to 28°C) with an average rainfall of 79-128 in. (201-325 cm) per year. Average annual temperatures in the central forest region range from 57° to 103°F (14° to 39°C) with an average rainfall of 39-98 in. (99-249 cm) per year. Average annual temperatures in the northern savanna may reach as high as 120°F (49°C) with an average rainfall of 60-80 in. (150-200 cm) per year.

ECONOMY

Prior to 1960, Ivory Coast's economy was primarily dependent on its coffee and cacao seed exports. Now its export income has expanded to include palm oil and other goods as well.

Agriculture - bananas, cacao, cassava, coffee, corn, manioc, palm kernels, pineapples, rice, rubber, and yams

Forestry - tropical woods

Manufacturing - processed foods (including palm oil, pineapples, sugar, and tuna), refined petroleum products, textiles, and timber products

Mining - bauxite, cobalt, copper, crude oil, diamonds, iron ores, and manganese

Exports - bananas, cacao seeds, coffee, cotton, palm oil, rubber, and timber

Imports - capital goods, consumer goods, food, and fuel

LIFE-STYLE

Ivory Coast is approximately 50 percent rural and 50 percent urban. The younger Ivorians are moving to cities to find work, however, most Ivorians are farmers who live in village-like *compounds* (groups of huts). The villagers' huts are constructed of mud walls and thatched or metal roofs. Many urban Ivorians also live in huts, however, a few wealthy Africans, and most all non-Africans, live in modern houses or apartment buildings.

Ivorian children are required to attend primary and elementary school if one is near their home. But due to the limited number of teachers and schools, only about 75 percent of Ivorian children actually attend school and only about 20 percent continue on to high school. Ivory Coast has one university—the National University of Ivory Coast—but many Ivorians attend college in other countries.

The country's health conditions are poor and a large number of people suffer from malaria, dysentery, yaws, tuberculosis, and venereal disease.

IT'S A FACT!

Mount Nimba - the country's highest point, is located in the Guinea Highlands and rises 5,748 ft. (1,752 m) above sea level.

Bandama River - the country's longest river, stretches 500 mi. (800 km) and contains many rapids and waterfalls, making only about 40 mi. (64 km) of it traversable.

 DID YOU KNOW...
- Yamoussoukro has been the country's capital since 1983, but some sources still recognize Abidjan as the country's capital because it is the country's administrative center and the place of residence for foreign governments?
- A Christian church in Yamoussoukro is Africa's largest Church? Completed in 1989, it is also one of the world's largest.
- Ivory Coast was named for the great amounts of ivory found there by French sailors in the late 1400s?
- Ivory Coast has only one railroad system, which connects Abidjan to Ouagadougou, in Burkina Faso?

JAMAICA

OFFICIAL NAME: Jamaica
LOCATION: Caribbean Sea
AREA: 4,243 sq. mi. (10,990 sq. km)
POPULATION (Est. 1993): 2,543,000
CAPITAL/LARGEST CITY: Kingston
GOVERNMENT: Constitutional monarchy headed by a prime minister.
FLAG: Adopted in 1962. Gold diagonal cross with black triangles on the hoist and fly sides and green triangles at the top and bottom. Gold, black, and green represent sunlight, hardships, and hope and agricultural wealth, accordingly.
ETHNIC GROUPS: African, African-European, European, Asian (mainly Chinese and Indian), Syrian
LANGUAGES: English, Jamaican Creole
RELIGIONS: Anglican, Baptist, Church of God, Roman Catholic, Rastafarian
BASIC MONETARY UNIT: Jamaican Dollar

GEOGRAPHY

Jamaica is a West Indian island located about 480 mi. (772 km) south of Florida, United States. At its greatest distances, Jamaica measures 51 mi. (82 km) from north to south and 146 mi. (235 km) from east to west. It has 635 mi. (1,022 km) of coastline along the Caribbean Sea.

Jamaica has coastal plains, a plateau and hills in the central region, and the Blue Mountains in the east. The country has many springs, streams, and waterfalls. *Cockpits* (deep depressions) in the northwest have lent that area the name of Cockpit Country.

CLIMATE

Jamaica has a tropical climate that is cooled by winds off the Caribbean. The average annual temperature ranges from about 75°F (24°C) in the winter to about 80°F (27°C) in the summer, though temperatures may drop to 40°F (4°C) in the mountains. The country has two rainy seasons—May to June and September to November—with the most rain falling during the months of May and October. The average annual rainfall ranges from about 30 in. (76 cm) along the coast to about 200 in. (510 cm) in the mountains. The country may experience hurricanes, especially between the months of July and November.

ECONOMY

Jamaica's economy is based primarily on mining and tourism. The country is one of the world's leading bauxite producers.
Agriculture - allspice, bananas, cacao, citrus fruits, coconuts, coffee, livestock (goats and poultry), milk, potatoes, sugar cane, vegetables, and yams
Manufacturing - alumina, cement, chemicals, cigars, clothing, fertilizer, footwear, machinery, molasses, petroleum products, processed foods, refined sugar, rum, and textiles
Mining - alumina, bauxite, and gypsum
Exports - alumina, bananas, bauxite, gypsum, rum, and sugar
Imports - construction materials, food, fuel, raw materials, and transport equipment

LIFE-STYLE

Jamaica's population is almost equally rural and urban. Most of the African and Asian populations work as farm laborers while most of the Europeans and African-Europeans hold business and professional positions. The Chinese and Syrians mainly operate small shops.

Jamaicans generally eat very spicy food. Commonly eaten foods include fish, rice with beans or peas, and stews. Popular foods include *jerk* (roasted, spicy hot piece of barbecued chicken or pork) which is often served with hard-dough bread, and *bammy* (cassava/manioc bread) or *festival* (fried dough), both of which are also eaten with fish. Commonly consumed beverages include alcohol (of which beer and white rum are most popular), coffee, fruit juices, herbal teas, tea, and drinks made from boiled roots.

Popular sports include cricket, field hockey, football (similar to North American soccer), tennis, and track and field. Leisure activities include attending theater, dancing and listening to music (of which reggae and calypso are most popular), dominoes, and table tennis. *Carnival* is a grand festival celebrated in the spring, involving costumes, parades, and parties.

Education is free for children ages six to 15. Over 90 percent attend primary school, but little more than 55 percent attend high school.

IT'S A FACT!

Blue Mountain Peak - the country's highest point, rises 7,402 ft. (2,256 m) above sea level.

 DID YOU KNOW...

- Jamaica is the third largest island in the Caribbean Sea, following Cuba and Hispaniola?
- Jamaica's first inhabitants, the Arawak Indians, originally called the island *Xaymaca*, meaning "land of wood and water," and when Christopher Columbus landed on Jamaica in 1494, he named it St. Iago?
- Kingston—founded in 1693 after an earthquake destroyed the nearby city of Port Royal—has suffered a number of disasters, including an earthquake in 1907, a fire in 1882, and hurricanes in 1880, 1951, and 1980?
- Jamaica gained its independence in 1962, after about 300 years as a British colony?
- During the 1670s, Jamaica was used as a base by British pirates to attack Spanish ports and ships?

JAPAN

OFFICIAL NAME: Japan
LOCATION: North Pacific Ocean
AREA: 145,870 sq. mi. (377,801 sq. km)
POPULATION (Est. 1993): 124,110,000
CAPITAL: Tokyo
LARGEST CITIES: Tokyo, Yokohama, Osaka, Nagoya
GOVERNMENT: Constitutional monarchy headed by a prime minister chosen from among a 764-member, two-house *Diet* (the law-making body).
FLAG: Features a red sun on a white background.
ETHNIC GROUP: Japanese
LANGUAGES: Japanese (written), Tokyo dialect (standard form of spoken Japanese)
RELIGIONS: Shinto, Buddhism
BASIC MONETARY UNIT: Yen

GEOGRAPHY

Japan lies in the North Pacific Ocean off the northeast coast of mainland Asia. The country is actually a chain of hilly or mountainous islands that are covered with forests. It includes four large and thousands of smaller islands that extend for a distance of about 1,200 mi. (1,900 km).

Japan's four main islands, from largest to smallest in area, are Honshu, Hokkaido, Kyushu, and Shikoku. The country has 5,857 mi. (9,426 km) of coastline along the North Pacific Ocean and the Sea of Japan. The Ryukyu and Bonin island chains are also part of Japan.

Honshu is home to about 80 percent of Japan's people. It has a number of mountain ranges—including Kitakami and Ou in the north; Abukuma, Mikuni, and Kanto in the central region; the Japanese Alps in the west-central region; Kii in the south; and Chugoku in the southwest—and plains along the eastern and southern coasts. The Kanto Plain is the country's largest lowland area and is home to the country's capital.

Much of Hokkaido is forested and mountainous. It includes the Kitami and Hidaka Mountains. It is home to about five percent of Japan's people. The Ishikari Plain, Hokkaido's main agricultural region, lies just north of a curved peninsula.

Kyushu comprises about 11 percent of Japan's people. The island's central region features the Kyushu Mountains. Most farming is done along Kyushu's west coast. The island's northeastern and southern regions are covered by volcanoes, high lava plateaus, and volcanic ash deposits.

Shikoku is home to about three percent of Japan's people, most of whom live along the island's northern coast. Central Shikoku features the Shikoku Mountains. The western and southern coastal regions are used for farming.

The Ryukyu island chain contains over one million people. The chain is composed of over 100 islands—some of which have active volcanoes—extending from Kyushu to the country of Tai-

wan. The Bonin island chain is home to about 1,900 people. It consists of about 97 volcanic islands, which lie about 600 mi. (970 km) southeast of Japan's main islands.

CLIMATE

Japan's climate is influenced by monsoons and by the Japan and Oyashio currents off the Pacific Ocean. A northwestern winter monsoon brings cold air to northern Japan, while a southeastern summer monsoon brings hot, humid weather to central and southern Japan.

Honshu has warm, humid summers and experiences balmy weather in spring and autumn. Its winters range from cold and snowy in the north to mild in the south. Hokkaido has cool summers and cold, snowy winters. Kyushu and Shikoku have long, hot summers and mild winters.

Japan has two rainy seasons: mid-June to early July and September to October. An average rainfall of 40 in. (100 cm) falls on all of the islands except eastern Hokkaido. Typhoons are common, often striking in late summer and early fall.

The Ryukyu Islands generally have a warm, wet climate. However, cloudy, chilly, and drier weather is common in winter. The average temperature is about 70°F (21°C) and the average rainfall is 53-120 in. (135-305 cm). The Bonin Islands have a mild, warm climate.

Earthquakes are common in Japan with an average of 1,500 per year. Most of the earthquakes are minor, but every few years severe quakes occur. The country's coastal areas also suffer from *tsunami* (destructive tidal waves) caused by undersea earthquakes. Japan has over 150 major volcanoes, more than 60 of which are active.

ECONOMY

Following only the United States, Japan is the world's sec-

---

ond largest economic power in terms of *gross domestic product* (GDP). Japan has few natural resources, so the country's economy is heavily dependent upon imported raw materials and foreign trade. Manufacturing, specifically the production of transportation equipment, is Japan's most important economic activity. Japan ranks first among the world's shipbuilding and car-making countries. The country also ranks high among the world's leaders in energy production.

Though only employing about one percent of the nation's people, Japan's fishing industry is the world's largest. Agriculture represents only a small portion of the economy. However, over half of Japan's arable land is devoted to the growth of rice, making it one of the world's leading rice-producers. Service industries account for over three-fifths of the country's economy and employ more than half the people.

Agriculture - cabbage, Chinese cabbage, eggs, hogs, mandarin oranges, milk, potatoes, poultry, rice, strawberries, tea, and white radishes

Fishing - clams, flatfish, mackerel, oysters, pollock, salmon, sardines, scallops, squid, and tuna

Manufacturing - automobiles, calculators, cameras, cement, chemicals, clocks and watches, clothing and textiles (including raw silk and synthetic fibers), computers, iron and steel, optical equipment, paper and newsprint, phonographs, processed foods, radios, tape recorders, and television sets

Mining - coal, copper, lead, limestone, manganese, silver, tin, and zinc

Exports - electronic equipment, iron and steel, machinery, motorcycles and trucks, passenger cars, plastics, precision instruments, ships, and synthetic fiber fabrics

Imports - bauxite, chemicals, coking coal, copper, food, iron ore and other minerals, meat, natural gas, petroleum, raw materials, timber, and wheat

LIFE-STYLE

Japan is the eighth largest country in population and one of the world's most densely populated countries with an average of about 851 persons per sq. mi. (329 per sq. km), though some areas are much more crowded. Japan's population is about three-fourths urban. These urban areas contain both Western and traditional Japanese features: tall, concrete and steel office buildings, as well as traditional Japanese homes; restaurants serving American fast foods as well as traditional Japanese fare; and modern plays, movies, and music, as well as traditional Japanese theater. Most urban residents live comfortably in modern apartment buildings or one- to two-story, tile-roofed, wooden buildings enclosed by a walled garden. Traditional Japanese homes feature sliding paper screens, as well as *tatami* (straw floor coverings), *futons* (padded quilts used as beds), and cushions for seats.

Most of the rural population and the inhabitants of the Bonin and Ryukyu island groups make a living by farming. Some of those in coastal areas make a living by fishing or harvesting seaweed. At least one member of most rural families supplement the family income by holding a part-time job in an urban area. Most rural shelters are similar to traditional urban homes.

Japan has a number of minority groups, including a people known as the *burakumin* or *eta*. The burakumin were traditionally responsible for such tasks as criminal execution, cattle slaughter, and leather tanning, activities which violate the Buddhist code of "cleanliness." Many live in special villages or segregated urban slums.

Most Japanese wear Western-style clothing. Traditional clothing is generally reserved for special occasions, though some older Japanese wear traditional clothing at home. It consists of a kimono tied around the waist with an *obi* (sash) and worn with *geta* (wooden clogs) or *zori* (flat sandals).

Rice is eaten at almost every meal and is often served with pickled vegetables, such as cabbage, cucumbers, eggplant, or radishes. Fish and soybeans are the main source of protein, though meat and dairy products are increasingly being consumed. Fruit and seaweed are also eaten. Favorite dishes include *sashimi* (thinly sliced raw fish), *sukiyaki* (beef cooked with vegetables), *sushi* (vinegar-flavored rice usually topped by raw fish, sliced vegetables, shellfish, or seaweed), and *tempura* (fish and vegetables fried in batter). Tea is the favorite drink. Common alcoholic beverages include beer and *sake* (a winelike beverage made from rice).

Education is free and compulsory for children ages six to 14, and most go on to high school. The country's literacy rate is almost 100 percent.

Baseball and *sumo* (a Japanese wrestling style) are the favorite spectator sports. Other popular sports include bowling, golf, ice-skating, skiing, table tennis, and volleyball. Martial arts, including aikido, judo, and karate, are practiced by many. *Kendo* (a Japanese form of fencing that uses bamboo or wooden sticks) is also popular.

Popular leisure activities include calligraphy, chanting and dancing, and poetry writing, specifically *haiku* and *tanka*. Many urban residents play a pinball game called pachinko. Traditional Japanese theater includes *no* and *kabuki* plays, and *puppet* theater. No plays are serious renditions of legends and historical events. Kabuki plays are melodramatic renditions of domestic and historical events. In puppet theater, lifelike puppets act out a story recited by a narrator.

IT'S A FACT!

Great Buddha - located in Kamakura, a city near Tokyo, is a huge bronze statue of the founder of Buddhism.

Mount Fuji (or Fujiyama) - the country's highest point and an inactive volcano, is located in the Japanese Alps and rises 12,388 ft. (3,776 m) above sea level.

 DID YOU KNOW...

- The Japanese call their country *Nippon* or *Nihon*, meaning "source of the sun"?
- *Zipangu* was the name given to the country by the Venetian traveler Marco Polo?
- Tokyo, Japan, is the world's fourth largest city with an average of 36,000 persons per sq. mi. (14,000 per sq. km)?
- Prior to 1945, marriages were prearranged, and in some cases the couple did not meet until the wedding?
- All outdoor footwear is removed prior to entering a Japanese home? Slippers are the only indoor footwear.
- Some traditional restaurants feature entertainment by *geisha*, young women trained since childhood in the arts of conversation, dance, and music?
- Japan is one of the world's leading motion-picture producers?
- Japan's population more than tripled between 1870 and 1970?
- Most of central Tokyo was destroyed during an earthquake in 1923? It took about 20 years to rebuild.

JORDAN

OFFICIAL NAME: Al-Mamlakah Al-Urdiniyah Al-Hashimiyah
(Hashemite Kingdom of Jordan)
FORMERLY: Transjordan (until 1949)
LOCATION: Middle East
AREA: 35,475 sq. mi. (91,880 sq. km)
POPULATION (Est. 1993): 3,362,000
CAPITAL: Amman
LARGEST CITIES: Amman, Az Zarqa, Irbid
GOVERNMENT: Constitutional monarchy headed by a king-appointed prime minister.
FLAG: Three horizontal stripes of black, white, and green. A red, isosceles
triangle—based on the hoist side—features a seven-pointed, white star.
ETHNIC GROUPS: Jordanian Arab, Palestinian Arab, others
LANGUAGES: Arabic, English, others
RELIGIONS: Islam (mainly Sunni Muslim), Christianity
BASIC MONETARY UNIT: Jordanian Dinar

GEOGRAPHY

Jordan is an Arab country on the East Bank of the River Jordan. It has three main land regions: 1) the Jordan River Valley, 2) the Transjordan Plateau, and 3) the Syrian Desert.

The Jordan River Valley—which is part of the Great Rift Valley—runs from south of the Sea of Galilee to the Dead Sea. East of this region, the Transjordan Plateau extends from Syria to south-central Jordan. The plateau—with its broad rolling plains and steep valleys—is home to most of the country's farmland. The Syrian Desert—also known as the northern Arabian Desert— is both south and east of the Transjordan Plateau. The River Jordan is Jordan's only important river.

CLIMATE

Jordan has a warm, generally dry climate. A rainy season in western Jordan lasts from about November to April. The Jordan River Valley receives little rain, and the average summer temperature often exceeds 100°F (38°C). The average annual temperature on the Transjordan Plateau ranges from 64° to 86°F (18° to 30°C) in the summer and from 40° to 52°F (4° to 11°C) in the winter. The average annual rainfall ranges from 25 in. (64 cm) in the north to 10-15 in. (25-38 cm) in the south. Summer temperatures in the Syrian Desert may reach as high as 120°F (49°C); the average annual rainfall in the desert is less than 10 in. (25 cm).

ECONOMY

Jordan has a developing economy based on the free enterprise system. Service industries contribute most to the economy.

Agriculture - barley, cabbage, citrus fruit, cucumbers, egg-plants, grapes, melons, nuts, olives, tomatoes, and wheat

Manufacturing - batteries, cement, ceramics, cigarettes, detergents, fertilizer, food products, leather goods, petroleum products, pharmaceutical products, and textiles

Mining - phosphate and potash

Exports - chemicals, fertilizers, fruits and vegetables, manu-factured products, phosphates, and potash

Imports - food, grain, livestock, machinery, manufactured goods, meat, petroleum, and transport equipment

LIFE-STYLE

Jordan's population is about two-thirds urban, with most residents living in the northwest. Urban Jordanians mainly work in such service industries as commerce and government, and live in apartment buildings and homes, most of which have electricity and running water. The rural population makes a living by farming or mining and lives in concrete, mud, or stone shelters. The small nomadic population herds livestock and lives in tents. About ten percent of the population live in crowded Palestinian refugee camps in one- or two-story concrete shelters.

Jordanians usually wear Western-style clothing. Some men wear a *kaffiyeh* (cloth that covers the head), and some women wear long, loose-fitting dresses.

Staples of the diet include bread, cheese, cracked wheat, flat bread, meat (mainly chicken and lamb), rice, seasonal fruits and vegetables, and yogurt. Popular dishes include *mahshi* (stuffed vegetables), *mansef* (rice covered with chunks of stewed lamb and a yogurt sauce), and *musakhan* (chicken with onions, olive oil, pine seeds, and seasonings). Common beverages include coffee, fruit juices, mineral water, soft drinks, and tea.

Popular sports include basketball, camel racing, horse racing, martial arts, and soccer. Leisure activities include cultural activities (such as folk dancing), attending festivals, and socializing with relatives.

Jordanian craftworkers make coffeepots, daggers, jewelry, and Islamic prayer beads. They also create beautiful cross-stitch embroidery and Arabic calligraphy.

Jordanian children are required to attend school through the ninth grade, and most attend government schools. Around 80 percent of the population is literate.

IT'S A FACT!

Dead Sea shore - the country's lowest point of elevation, is located 1,310 ft. (399 m) below sea level.

Jabal Ramm - the country's highest point, rises 5,755 ft. (1,754 m) above sea level.

 DID YOU KNOW...
- The area now known as Jordan was mentioned in historical references as early as 2000 B.C.?
- In July of 1994, a declaration was signed, ending the state of war that existed between Israel and Jordan since 1948?

KAZAKSTAN

OFFICIAL NAME: Qazaqstan Respublikasy (Republic of Kazakstan)
FORMERLY: Kazak Soviet Socialist Republic
LOCATION: West-central Asia
AREA: 1,049,156 sq. mi. (2,717,300 sq. km)
POPULATION (Est. 1993): 16,992,000
CAPITAL/LARGEST CITY: Alma-Ata
GOVERNMENT: Republic governed by a president.
FLAG: Blue background with a yellow sun and eagle in the center and a yellow stripe of national ornamentation on the hoist side.
ETHNIC GROUPS: Kazak, Russian
LANGUAGES: Kazak, Russian
RELIGIONS: Islam, Orthodox Christianity
BASIC MONETARY UNIT: Russian Ruble

GEOGRAPHY

At its greatest distances, Kazakstan, a landlocked country, measures 1,000 mi. (1,600 km) from north to south and 1,800 mi. (2,900 km) from east to west. Kazakstan lies primarily in west-central Asia. A small part of the country lies west of the Ural River on the European continent. Of all the former Soviet republics, Kazakstan is second only to Russia in size.

Due to its size, the country's landscape varies greatly from west to east. Dry plains and lowlands are found in the west. *Steppes* (high, grassy plains) cover the northern part of the country. Much of the south consists of sandy deserts. Mountain ranges form the eastern and southeastern borders. Lake Balkhash is the country's largest lake.

CLIMATE

The country has extremely cold winters and long, hot summers. January temperatures average 0°F (-18°C) in the north and 23°F (-5°C) in the south. July temperatures average 68°F (20°C) in the north and 81°F (27°C) in the south. The average annual rainfall is only about 4-16 in. (10-40 cm).

ECONOMY

Agriculture makes up two-fifths of the value of Kazakstan's economic production.

Agriculture - grain, livestock, and wool
Manufacturing - chemicals, food products, and heavy machinery
Mining - coal, copper, lead, natural gas, and petroleum
Exports - agricultural products, and mineral resources
Imports - consumer goods and machinery

LIFE-STYLE

For hundreds of years, Kazaks were nomads who raised their livestock on the plains of the country. When the Russian Empire conquered the Kazak region in the 1800s, this changed and the people settled in permanent villages. Today, the population is almost three-fifths urban. Most people live in houses in the villages, or apartments or houses in the cities. Some villagers, however, still live in tent-like dwellings called *yurts*. These portable homes are made of a wooden circular frame covered with felt. Few rural villages have running water or electricity.

Extended families are the rule, with Kazak men and their children remaining part of their parents' households. Married women become part of their husband's parents' household. Kazaks enjoy socializing at the bazaar, the place people buy food and other goods.

Most Kazak foods include meat dishes and milk products, such as cheese and curds. One popular dish is *besh barmak* (thinly sliced meat and noodles boiled in broth). *Kumiss*, a traditional Kazak beverage, is made from fermented mare's milk.

Children ages six to 17 are required to attend school. Almost all of Kazakstan's citizens can read and write.

Popular sports are skating, volleyball, and wrestling. A traditional Kazakstani game is *kopkar* (game in which skilled horsemen try to carry the carcass of a goat or a sheep across a goal). Cultural activities include singing folk songs and reciting legends and epic poems.

IT'S A FACT!

Karagiye Depression - the country's lowest point of elevation, is located 433 ft. (132 m) below sea level.

Mount Tengri - country's highest point, rises 20,991 ft. (6,398 m) above sea level.

 DID YOU KNOW...
- Kazakstan's land area is twice that of Alaska?
- The Aral Sea, part of which lies in Kazakstan, is too salty and polluted to support fish?
- Chevron, an American oil company, is investing $10 billion to develop the Tengiz oil field near the Caspian Sea?
- Kazakstan is one of four former Soviet republics with large stockpiles of nuclear weapons?
- Temperatures in Kazakstan have fallen as low as -49°F (-45°C)?
- The word *Kazak* is found in historical records from the 11th century and roughly means "riders of the steppe"?

KENYA

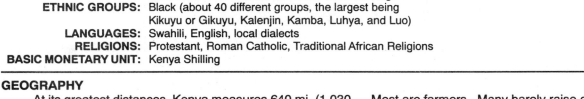

OFFICIAL NAME: Jamhuri ya Kenya (Republic of Kenya)
FORMERLY: British East Africa (1895-1963)
LOCATION: Eastern Africa
AREA: 224,081 sq. mi. (580,367 sq. km)
POPULATION (Est. 1993): 26,829,000
CAPITAL: Nairobi
LARGEST CITIES: Nairobi, Mombasa
GOVERNMENT: Republic governed by a president.
FLAG: Adopted in 1963. Three horizontal stripes of black, red, and green divided by two narrow white bands. The colors represent the Kenyan people, the struggle for independence, and agriculture, accordingly. A shield and spears, representing the defense of freedom, are centered on the flag.
ETHNIC GROUPS: Black (about 40 different groups, the largest being Kikuyu or Gikuyu, Kalenjin, Kamba, Luhya, and Luo)
LANGUAGES: Swahili, English, local dialects
RELIGIONS: Protestant, Roman Catholic, Traditional African Religions
BASIC MONETARY UNIT: Kenya Shilling

GEOGRAPHY

At its greatest distances, Kenya measures 640 mi. (1,030 km) from north to south and 560 mi. (901 km) from east to west. It has 284 mi. (457 km) of coastline along the Indian Ocean. The equator runs through the center of Kenya.

Kenya has three main land regions: 1) a tropical coastal area, 2) a dry plains area, and 3) a fertile highland. About three-fourths of the country's land is a dry plain. The only land suitable for farming is along the narrow coast and in the southwestern highland. The Chalbi and Dida Galgalu Deserts lie in the north.

CLIMATE

Kenya's climate varies by region. The coastal area has a hot, humid climate. The average temperature is 80°F (27°C) and rainfall averages 40 in. (100 cm) per year. The plains region experiences a temperature range of 60° to 80°F (16° to 27°C), depending on the altitude. Most of the area receives 10-30 in. (25-76 cm) of rainfall annually. The northern desert area receives less than 10 in. (25 cm). The average temperature in the highland region is 67°F (19°C). Rainfall averages 40-50 in. (100-130 cm) per year.

ECONOMY

Kenya has a developing economy largely based on agriculture. The country's abundant wildlife—including elephants, giraffes, lions, rhinoceroses, and zebras—attracts tourists, making tourism a major economic activity.

Agriculture - bananas, beans, beef, cashews, cassava, coffee, corn, cotton, pineapples, potatoes, pyrethrum, sisal, sugar cane, sweet potatoes, tea, and wheat

Manufacturing - cement, chemicals, household utensils, light machinery, motor vehicles, paper and paper products, petroleum products, processed foods, and textiles

Mining - fluorite, gemstones, salt, and soda

Exports - cement, coffee, flowers, meat, petroleum products, pineapples, sisal, and tea

Imports - industrial machinery, iron and steel, and petroleum

LIFE-STYLE

About three-fourths of Kenya's people are rural dwellers.

Most are farmers. Many barely raise enough food to feed their families, so they also work part-time in a trade or on a large plantation. Urban Kenyans work in businesses, government offices, factories, or stores. The country's nomadic population is small.

Shelters in rural areas and city slums usually have thatched roofs and are of mud or stick construction. Urban areas feature apartment buildings and modern homes built of cement or stone.

Clothing is simple and consists of a cotton shirt with shorts or trousers for men, and cotton dresses or blouses and skirts for women. A one-piece cloth that wraps around the body serves as clothing for some rural Kenyans and most nomads.

The staple of the diet is corn, which is often ground into a porridge and mixed with other vegetables. Fish and meat are eaten when affordable. Beer is a popular beverage.

Elementary education is provided at no charge by the government. Although children are not required to attend, about 80 percent receive at least an elementary education. In places where no schools exist, residents have initiated *harambee*, Swahili for "pulling together" or "self-help," schools.

Soccer and track and field are the national sports. Popular recreational activities include cricket, croquet, field hockey, tug-of-war, and wrestling. Dance, especially in celebration, is an important part of Kenyan life.

Most Kenyans travel by bus or by crowded *matatus* (taxis). The majority of Kenyan roads are unpaved.

IT'S A FACT!

Lake Turkana (Lake Rudolf) - the country's largest lake, is located in the north and covers 2,473 sq. mi. (6,405 sq. km).

Mount Kenya - the country's highest point and the second highest point in Africa, rises 17,058 ft. (5,199 m) above sea level.

 DID YOU KNOW...

• Evidence found near the Great Rift Valley indicates that people may have lived in the area now known as Kenya as early as two million years ago?

KIRIBATI

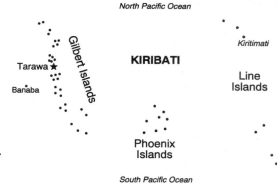

OFFICIAL NAME: Republic of Kiribati
FORMERLY: Gilbert Islands
LOCATION: Central Pacific Ocean
AREA: 280 sq. mi. (726 sq. km)
POPULATION (Est. 1993): 76,320
CAPITAL: Tarawa
GOVERNMENT: Republic headed by a president.
FLAG: Top half is red with a yellow frigate bird flying over a yellow rising sun. The bottom half is blue with three horizontal, wavy, white stripes representing the ocean.
ETHNIC GROUPS: Micronesian, others
LANGUAGES: English, Gilbertese
RELIGIONS: Protestant, Roman Catholic, others
BASIC MONETARY UNIT: Australian Dollar

GEOGRAPHY

Kiribati is composed of 33 islands—20 of which are inhabited—belonging to three island groups: the 16 Gilbert Islands and Banaba (formerly called Ocean Island), the eight Phoenix Islands, and eight of the Line Islands. The islands are spread out over an area of about 2 million sq. mi. (5 million sq. km.), and have a combined coastline of 710 mi. (1,143 km) along the North and South Pacific Oceans. More than half of the country's total land area consists of the island of Kiritimati Atoll in the Line Islands group. Most of the islands are coral atolls.

CLIMATE

The country's central islands have a maritime equatorial climate, with a more tropical climate found on the northern and southern islands. The average annual temperature is about 80°F (27°C). Typhoons can occur at any time, but are more common during the rainy season, which generally lasts from November to April. The average annual rainfall ranges from about 120 in. (300 cm) on the northern islands to about 40 in. (100 cm) on the other islands. Some islands experience periodic droughts.

ECONOMY

Kiribati has a developing economy.
Agriculture - *babai* (giant taro), bananas, breadfruit, coconuts, pandanus fruit, papaya, sweet potatoes, other vegetables
Manufacturing - fishing and handicrafts
Exports - copra, fish, and seaweed
Imports - food, fuel, machinery and equipment, and miscellaneous manufactured goods

LIFE-STYLE

Kiribati's islanders are known as *I-Kiribati*. Most live in rural villages where houses—ranging from a few to over 100—are clustered around a church and a *maneaba* (meeting house). Many shelters are made of wood and the leaves of coconut trees, though those constructed of cement block with iron roofs are becoming more common.

I-Kiribati are dependent upon the sea, with fishing, constructing canoes, and sailing important to their way of life. They catch such fish as kingfish, snapper, and tuna. They also grow most of their own foods—except on Tarawa, where most of the food is imported—and raise chickens and pigs.

Traditionally, the I-Kiribati wore clothing of soft, finely woven mats. Today, they wear light cotton clothing.

DID YOU KNOW...

- *Kiritimati* is Gilbertese for "Christmas," thus Kiritimati Atoll is also known as Christmas Island?
- Kiritimati Atoll and Tarawa Island became part of Kiribati in 1979?
- About 90 percent of Kiribati's population lives in the Gilbert Islands?
- Much of what is now known as the country of Kiribati was ruled by Great Britain from 1892-1979, after which time the country gained its independence?
- Kiritimati Atoll was used as a nuclear test site by the British from 1957-1962 and by the United States in 1962?
- Banaba Island (Ocean Island) is one of the three phosphate-rock islands in the Pacific Ocean and is uninhabitable because of extensive mining?
- Tarawa Island has an "earth station," which transmits and receives international messages via a space satellite?

KUWAIT

OFFICIAL NAME: Dowlat al Kuwait (State of Kuwait)
LOCATION: Southwestern Asia
AREA: 6,880 sq. mi. (17,818 sq. km)
POPULATION (Est. 1993): 2,216,000
CAPITAL/LARGEST CITY: Kuwait
GOVERNMENT: Constitutional monarchy.
FLAG: Three horizontal stripes of green, white, and red, with a black trapezoid based on the hoist side.
ETHNIC GROUPS: Kuwaiti, other Arabs, Iranian, Indian, Pakistani
LANGUAGES: Arabic, English
RELIGIONS: Islam, Christianity, Hinduism
BASIC MONETARY UNIT: Kuwaiti Dinar

GEOGRAPHY

Kuwait is a small Arab country at the north end of the Persian Gulf. It measures 90 mi. (145 km) from north to south and 95 mi. (153 km) from east to west at its greatest distances. It has 120 mi. (193 km) of coastline along the Persian Gulf.

The country is primarily desert with very little vegetation. Kuwait is made up of a mainland and nine islands. The islands of Faylakah and Bubiyan are the two largest. Although Bubiyan is the larger of the two, it is virtually uninhabited. There are no rivers or lakes in the country. Until 1950, fresh drinking water was brought in on ships from Iraq. Then engineers developed a distillation system for turning salt water into fresh water. Also, an underground freshwater supply was found in 1960.

CLIMATE

Kuwait's climate is very hot and dry. Between October and March, an average of 2-6 in. (5-15 cm) of rain falls. Although the temperature may exceed 120°F (49°C) from April to September, it is not truly uncomfortable until combined with high humidity during the months of August and September. During January, the temperature ranges from 50° to 60°F (10° to 16°C).

ECONOMY

Kuwait was a very poor country until the development of the petroleum industry. After World War II, Kuwait became a major exporter of oil and natural gas. The country has over one-tenth of the world's known oil reserves. But since the oil industry does not require many workers, the Kuwaiti government is trying to promote other economic activities in order to provide more jobs for its people.

The government also receives large amounts of money from its investments in the United States and other foreign countries.

Agriculture - camels, dates, goats, sheep, and tomatoes
Mining - petroleum and natural gas
Exports - natural gas, oil, and shrimp
Imports - clothing, construction materials, food, and vehicles and parts

LIFE-STYLE

Two-thirds of the country's people live in the capital city of Kuwait. Over half of the people living in Kuwait today are not citizens. They are Iranians, Indians, Pakistanis, and Arabs from other countries.

Kuwait's rulers have used the income from oil to provide free education, health, and social services. Prior to the 1950s, few Kuwaiti children attended school. Today, more than 85 percent attend. The government provides special schools for the disabled and for adults who wish to learn to read and write.

The role of women in Kuwaiti society has changed since the 1900s. Many women now receive a college education and work outside of the home.

DID YOU KNOW...
- Kuwait is one of the richest nations in the world in terms of national income per person?
- Kuwait has no income tax?
- Scientists are trying to produce crops in Kuwait by *hydroponic farming*? They use trays of sand for planting and feed plants with water and plant foods.

KYRGYZSTAN

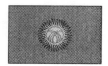

OFFICIAL NAME: Kyrgyz Respublikasy (Republic of Kyrgyzstan)
FORMERLY: Kirghiz, part of the Soviet Union
LOCATION: Central Asia
AREA: 76,641 sq. mi. (198,500 sq. km)
POPULATION (Est. 1993): 4,409,000
CAPITAL/LARGEST CITY: Bishkek
GOVERNMENT: Republic governed by a president.
FLAG: Red background with a yellow sun in the center. Within the sun is a yellow disk with two intersecting sets of three curved red bands.
ETHNIC GROUPS: Kyrgyz, Russian, Uzbek, Ukrainian, German
LANGUAGES: Kyrgyz, Russian
RELIGION: Islam
BASIC MONETARY UNIT: Som

GEOGRAPHY

At its greatest distances, Kyrgyzstan, a landlocked country, measures 270 mi. (435 km) from north to south and 580 mi. (935 km) from east to west. Most of the country is covered by the Tian Shan and Alay Mountains. Three-fourths of Kyrgyzstan reaches altitudes of more than 4,950 ft. (1,500 m) above sea level. About 15 percent of the country is below 3,000 ft. (915 m) above sea level. Plains and mountain valleys are found in these areas.

CLIMATE

Kyrgyzstan's climate varies with the altitude. Summers are warm and dry in the lowlands and cool in the mountains. July temperatures range from 60° to 75°F (16° to 24°C) in the lowlands to 41°F (5°C) in the mountains. Winters are bitterly cold, and January temperatures range from 7° to 23°F (-5° to -14°C) in the lowlands to -18°F (-28°C) in the mountains.

ECONOMY

Kyrgyzstan is one of the poorer republics of Central Asia. Agriculture provides two-fifths of the value of the country's economic production.

Agriculture - cotton, eggs, fruit, grain, livestock, milk, vegetables, and wool

Manufacturing - construction materials, food products, machinery, metals, and textiles

Mining - antimony, coal, and mercury

Exports - antimony, coal, and mercury

Imports - foodstuffs, fuel, and machinery

LIFE-STYLE

About half of the population belongs to the Kyrgyz ethnic group. The majority live in rural areas and make a living by herding livestock and farming. Among this group, tribal organizations and large kinship units, called *clans*, play important roles in the lives of the people. There are several clans in each tribe. A clan includes all people descended from a common ancestor on the father's side of the family. Kyrgyz tend to marry only people from their own clan.

The basis of society is the extended family. Households often include parents, children, married sons and their families, plus other relatives.

Both Western-style and traditional clothing are worn. Traditional clothing for men consists of a padded or sheepskin coat, boots, and a white felt hat with black flaps. Some married women wear a white turban fashioned from a long scarf.

Two common dishes are *shurpa* (mutton and vegetable soup) and *besh barmak* (lamb and noodles in broth). Popular milk products include cheese, *ayran* (a yogurt-like drink), and *kumiss* (fermented mare's milk).

Horseback riding is a popular recreational activity. The people also enjoy folk songs and dancing. Reciting epic poems is a traditional activity.

Soviet rule made education compulsory, and children ages seven to 17 are required to attend school. The country has an extremely high literacy rate.

IT'S A FACT!!

Inylchek Glacier - one of the largest glaciers in the world, measures 37 mi. (60 km) long.

Peak Pobedy - the country's highest point, rises 24,406 ft. (7,439 m) above sea level.

 DID YOU KNOW...

- Until the period of Soviet domination, the Kyrgyz were nomads?
- Issyk-Kul Lake is believed by some to harbor a monster trout?
- A traditional game played by the Kyrgyz is called *keshkumai*, in which a man chases a girl on horseback and tries to kiss her?
- One of the country's most famous poems is *Manas*, which describes the history of the Kyrgyz people?
- The Kyrgyz language belongs to the Turkish family of languages?
- The trade route known as the *Silk Road* that joined Europe with China was adjacent to the area of present-day Kyrgyzstan?

LAOS

OFFICIAL NAME: Sathalanalat Paxathipatai Paxaxon Lao
(Lao People's Democratic Republic)
LOCATION: Southeast Asia
AREA: 91,429 sq. mi. (236,800 sq. km)
POPULATION (Est. 1994): 4,644,000
CAPITAL/LARGEST CITY: Vientiane
GOVERNMENT: People's democratic republic governed by a president.
FLAG: Adopted in 1975. Three horizontal stripes of red, blue, and red with a white circle centered on the blue stripe. Red, blue, and white represent the blood and soul of all Laotians, prosperity, and the promise of a bright future, accordingly.
ETHNIC GROUPS: Lao, Kha or Phoutheung, tribal Thai, Meo, Hmong, Yao, others
LANGUAGES: Lao, French, English
RELIGIONS: Buddhism, Animism, others
BASIC MONETARY UNIT: New Kip

GEOGRAPHY

Laos, a landlocked country, is located on the northwest portion of the Indochinese Peninsula. At its greatest distances, Laos measures 650 mi. (1,046 km) from northwest to southeast and 315 mi. (510 km) from northeast to southwest.

Laos lies in the Mekong Basin, bordered by the Mekong River in the west and the Annamite Range in the east. The country is mountainous and forest-covered. It has many valuable mineral deposits and its most fertile soil lies along the Mekong River and its tributaries.

CLIMATE

Laos has a tropical climate. During the rainy season—May to November—the average temperature is 82°F (28°C) and the average rainfall is 10 in. (25 cm) per month. During the dry season—December to April—the average temperature is 70°F (21°C) and the average rainfall is less than 1 in. (2.5 cm) per month. Laos is subject to flooding during the rainy season.

ECONOMY

Laos has one of the world's most undeveloped economies. It is based mainly on agriculture, with little manufacturing or mining.

Agriculture - cardamom, citrus fruits, coffee, corn, cotton, livestock (buffalo, cattle, hogs, and poultry), opium, rice, tea, tobacco, sweet potatoes, and sugar cane

Forestry - bamboo, benzoin, cinchona, and teak

Manufacturing - leather goods, pottery, processed foods, silk weaving, and silver work

Minerals - gold, gypsum, lead, silver, tin, and zinc

Exports - coffee, electricity, livestock, opium, raw materials, spices, tea, tin, and wood products

Imports - consumer goods, cotton, food, fuel, machinery and transport equipment, and steel

LIFE-STYLE

Laos's population is about four-fifths rural. Most Laotians live in the floodplains of the Mekong River and make a living by using traditional means to raise rice. Rural Laotians live in thatch-roofed, bamboo houses that are raised up on stilts 6-8 ft. (1.8-2.4 m) above the ground. Residents of hilly or mountainous areas practice slash-and-burn agriculture.

Rice is the staple of the diet and is usually served with chili sauce or a spicy sauce made with fermented fish. A typical Lao food is *lap* (sautéed buffalo innards, onions, lemon grass, and spices served with a rice-flour sauce). Other commonly consumed foods include chicken, eggs, fish, and pork. Beef is eaten on occasion. Commonly consumed beverages include coffee and tea.

Social and occupational activities of Laotians are tied to weather, with dry months after harvest used for visiting friends and relatives, May and June used for intensive planting, and July and August—the months of heaviest rain—used for rest. Popular sports include badminton, soccer, table tennis, volleyball, and *kato* (a game in which players try to keep a rattan ball in the air without the use of their hands). Buddhist festivals and holidays are also integral to the Laotian social life.

The Laotian government provides education—five years at the elementary level and six years at the secondary level—free. However, many villages lack schools.

Few medical facilities exist in Laos, with almost none in rural areas. Water is not potable and must be boiled prior to consumption. Laotian residents in some areas suffer from dysentery, hepatitis, malaria, trachoma, tuberculosis, and typhoid.

The country has no railroads, and most roads are only passable during the country's dry season. The main means of transportation is via the Mekong River and its tributaries.

IT'S A FACT!

Mount Bia - the country's highest point, rises 9,242 ft. (2,817 m) above sea level.

 DID YOU KNOW...
- Laos gained its independence in 1954 after more than 50 years under French rule as part of French Indochina?
- Laos is the world's third-largest producer of opium?
- Laotians can be divided into 68 distinct ethnic groups?
- Laos's government once ruled parts of what are now China, Cambodia, Myanmar (Burma), Thailand, and Vietnam?
- In many areas of Laos, supplies can only be transported by airplane?

LATVIA

OFFICIAL NAME: Latvijas Republika (Republic of Latvia)
LOCATION: Northern Europe
AREA: 24,595 sq. mi. (63,700 sq. km)
POPULATION (Est. 1993): 2,775,000
CAPITAL: Riga
LARGEST CITIES: Riga, Daugavpils, Liepāja
GOVERNMENT: Republic governed by a president. A 201-member parliament, called the Supreme Council, is elected by the people. The Supreme Council chooses a chairperson, who serves as president.
FLAG: Dates back to the 1200s, when it served as a tribal war banner. Two horizontal stripes of red separated by a narrow, white band.
ETHNIC GROUPS: Latvian (also called Letts), Russian, Belarusian, Polish, Ukrainian, Lithuanian, Jewish
LANGUAGES: Latvian, Russian
RELIGIONS: Lutheran, Roman Catholic, Russian Orthodox
BASIC MONETARY UNIT: Lat

GEOGRAPHY

At its greatest distances, Latvia measures 170 mi. (270 km) from north to south and 280 mi. (450 km) from east to west. It has 293 mi. (472 km) of coastline along the Gulf of Riga and the Baltic Sea.

Latvia consists mainly of low hills and shallow valleys, and has about 4,000 small lakes and swamps. About 40 percent of the land is covered by forests. The country's main river is the Western Dvina (or Daugava).

Because of heavy industrial development, Latvian lakes and rivers, as well as the Baltic Sea, suffer from serious pollution.

CLIMATE

Latvia's climate is very humid. Days are usually cloudy, and the country averages only 30-40 sunny days per year. The average annual temperature ranges from 19° to 27°F (-7° to -3°C) in January and from 61° to 64°F (16° to 18°C) in July. The average annual rainfall is 20-31 in. (51-80 cm).

ECONOMY

Latvia's economy is based primarily on manufacturing.
Agriculture - barley, eggs, flax, meat, milk, oats, potatoes, rye, sugar beets, and vegetables

Manufacturing - appliances, electrical equipment, fertilizers, food products, machinery, pharmaceuticals, primary metals, processed foods, processed metals, radios, textiles, transportation equipment, and washing machines

Exports - appliances, radios, scientific instruments, shoes, and textiles

Imports - chemicals, fuel, grain, machinery, and petroleum products

LIFE-STYLE

Latvia's population is about 70 percent urban, with most people employed by industry and living in apartment buildings built after World War II. Those who live in rural areas work on dairy or cattle farms, which are increasingly privately owned.

Most Latvians wear Western-style clothing, though traditional dress is still worn for holiday festivals.

Popular sports include basketball and soccer, and popular leisure activities include attending ballet, dramatic productions, and the opera. The people have a rich tradition of folklore, which is evident in their folk songs. Choral singing is a popular activity with many Latvians participating in annual song festivals.

From 1940 to 1988, the Soviet Union restricted religion in Latvia. The people were able to attend religious services, but not allowed to teach religion. Those who did attend religious services were often barred from good educational and job opportunities. The restrictions were temporarily lifted in 1988, and fully lifted in 1990.

IT'S A FACT!

Gaizina (mountain) - the country's highest point, rises 1,020 ft. (311 m) above sea level.

Latvian State University - located in Riga, is the largest of the country's ten universities.

 DID YOU KNOW...

- The Latvian language—one of Europe's oldest—is related to Sanskrit, a language of ancient India?
- People lived in what is now known as Latvia as early as 7000 or 8000 B.C.?
- Riga, the country's capital, dates back to 1158, when it was used as a depot for merchants from Bremen, and was founded in 1201 by German crusaders?
- Latvia was independent during 1918-1940, was under Soviet rule for 51 years, and regained independence in 1991?

LEBANON

OFFICIAL NAME: Al Jumhuriya al Lubnaniyah (Republic of Lebanon)
LOCATION: Western Asia
AREA: 4,015 sq. mi. (10,400 sq. km)
POPULATION (Est. 1993): 2,883,000
CAPITAL: Beirut
LARGEST CITIES: Beirut, Tripoli
GOVERNMENT: Republic governed by a president.
FLAG: Adopted in 1943. Three horizontal stripes of red, white, and red, with a cedar tree centered on the white stripe.
ETHNIC GROUP: Arab
LANGUAGES: Arabic, French
RELIGIONS: Islam, Christianity
BASIC MONETARY UNIT: Lebanese Pound

GEOGRAPHY

Lebanon is located on the eastern end of the Mediterranean Sea at the western end of Asia. At its greatest distances, Lebanon measures 120 mi. (193 km) from north to south and 50 mi. (80 km) from east to west. The country has 130 mi. (210 km) of coastline.

A low coastal plain covers the western part of Lebanon. The Lebanon Mountains extend down most of the center of the country. Between the Lebanon and Anti-Lebanon Mountains on the east is the fertile Bekaa Valley.

CLIMATE

Lebanon has a Mediterranean climate with mild, wet winters and hot, dry summers. The average annual temperature on the coast ranges from about 55°F (13°C) in January to about 84°F (29°C) in June. The average annual rainfall along the coast is 35 in. (89 cm).

The mountains and the Bekaa Valley have slightly cooler temperatures and lower humidity. The average rainfall in the mountains is from 50-60 in. (130-150 cm) annually. The mountains also receive large amounts of snow during the winter.

ECONOMY

Since the 1800s, Lebanon has been a major banking and trade center. Much of the labor force is employed in service industries, such as trade and finance.

Agriculture - apples, cherries, cucumbers, grapes, lemons, oranges, peaches, sugar beets, and tomatoes

Manufacturing - cement, chemicals, electric appliances, furniture, processed foods, and textiles

Exports - agricultural products, chemicals, and textiles

Imports - foodstuffs, machinery, and metals

LIFE-STYLE

The majority of Lebanese people live in urban areas. Cities are also home to the middle-class and wealthy segments of society. The poorer people live in the rural areas and in run-down sections of the cities.

Western culture and dress have had a great deal of influence on the Lebanese people, as is evident in their dress and taste in literature, art, and music.

Chief foods of the Lebanese include grains, fruits, meat, vegetables, and yogurt. Favorite beverages include Arabic coffee, beer, soft drinks, wine, and a liquor called *arak*.

Soccer, basketball, skiing, table tennis, and volleyball are the most popular sports. Attending movies is also a favorite leisure activity. People who live near the coast enjoy the beautiful beaches on the Mediterranean.

IT'S A FACT!

Baalbek - ruins of the ancient city built by the Romans around 64 B.C.

Qurnat as Sawda - the country's highest point, rises 10,115 ft. (3,083 m) above sea level.

 DID YOU KNOW...

- Farmers use irrigated terraces built on the slopes of the Lebanon Mountains to grow fruit?
- Today, Lebanon's inflation rate is 100 percent and unemployment is over 30 percent?
- One-fourth of Lebanon's population lives in and around the city of Beirut?
- Lebanon was once a tourist mecca, but a civil war between Christians and the Muslim-PLO alliance damaged large portions of Beirut and surrounding areas, putting a hold on the tourist trade?

LESOTHO

OFFICIAL NAME: Kingdom of Lesotho
FORMERLY: Basutoland, a British protectorate
LOCATION: Southern Africa
AREA: 11,720 sq. mi. (30,355 sq. km)
POPULATION (Est. 1993): 1,934,000
CAPITAL/LARGEST CITY: Maseru
GOVERNMENT: Constitutional monarchy run by a six-member Military Council.
FLAG: Adopted in 1987. A white triangle in the upper, hoist-side corner and a green triangle in the lower, fly-side corner separated by a blue diagonal stripe. The white triangle features a brown shield.
ETHNIC GROUP: Basotho (or Basuto)
LANGUAGES: English, Sesotho
RELIGION: Christianity
BASIC MONETARY UNIT: Loti

GEOGRAPHY

Lesotho is totally surrounded by the country of South Africa. It is located about 200 mi. (320 km) inland from the Indian Ocean. Most of the country is mountainous. Plains are found in the western part of Lesotho.

CLIMATE

The country has a moderate, moist climate because most of the land lies over 5,000 ft. (1,500 m) above sea level. The average temperature ranges from 90°F (32°C) in the summer to 20°F (-7°C) in the winter. Snow falls in the highlands where temperatures are often below freezing during the winter. The average annual rainfall is 28 in. (71 cm). Most rain falls between October and April.

ECONOMY

Lesotho is a very poor country whose male citizens travel to South Africa to find work in the factories and mines. Over 85 percent of the residents are engaged in subsistence farming. At one time, diamonds were an important export. But in the early 1980s, diamond mining was discontinued because of a big drop in the price of diamonds worldwide. The most important economic activity within Lesotho is raising livestock.

Agriculture - asparagus, beans, cattle, corn, goats, peas, sheep, sorghum, wheat, and wool

Manufacturing - clothing and textiles, furniture, and food processing

Exports - baskets, beans, cattle, corn, hides, mohair, peas, skins, wheat, and wool

Imports - building materials, clothing, corn, machinery, medicines, petroleum, and vehicles

LIFE-STYLE

Lesotho's population is about four-fifths rural. Traditional rural shelters consist of mud or sod walls with thatched roofs. Stone houses with tile or tin roofs serve as shelters for wealthier Basotho. Since Lesotho does not have enough jobs for its people, many men spend months or years working in mines, factories, farms, or households in South Africa. As a result, women make many of the family decisions and do most of the heavy work. On farms, they hoe and weed the land, harvest the crops, and build the houses. When men are at home, they plow the land and look after the livestock.

From the time boys are five or six years old, they herd livestock. Since the boys are working, three-fourths of school children are girls.

Corn, milk, sorghum, and vegetables are staples of the diet. A typical meal may consist of a *mealie meal* (cornmeal), rice, potatoes, vegetables, and fruit. Popular meats are beef, chicken, and pork. Though the continental style of eating—with the fork in the left hand and the knife in the right—is prevalent in Maseru, the capital, most villagers eat with their hands. Tea, often a full meal that takes place between lunch and dinner, is served to visitors in rural areas.

IT'S A FACT!

Thabana Ntlenyana - the country's highest point, is located in the Drakensberg Mountains and rises 11,425 ft. (3,482 m) above sea level.

 DID YOU KNOW...

- Because of its beautiful mountain scenery, Lesotho is sometimes referred to as the "Switzerland of Southern Africa"?
- The wealth of a Basotho family is often measured by the number of cattle it owns?
- The Basotho often paint designs in bright colors on the walls and doors of their homes?
- The traditional hat of Lesotho is the *Makorotlo*, which is conical in shape (like the roof of a house) and has an intricately designed knob on top?
- The legal working age in Lesotho is 12?
- Lesotho's overall literacy rate is over 60 percent, one of the highest in Africa?
- Over 40 percent of the population is under the age of 15?
- Women make up over 43 percent of the work force?
- In Lesotho, it is considered very rude to enter someone's home without speaking, even if the door is open and you are expected?

LIBERIA

OFFICIAL NAME: Republic of Liberia
LOCATION: Western Africa
AREA: 43,000 sq. mi. (111,369 sq. km)
POPULATION (Est. 1993): 2,835,000
CAPITAL/LARGEST CITY: Monrovia
GOVERNMENT: Republic headed by a president.
FLAG: Adopted in 1847. Eleven horizontal stripes—six red and five white—represent the 11 signers of the Liberian Declaration of Independence. A blue canton featuring a white, five-pointed star is in the upper hoist-side corner.
ETHNIC GROUPS: Black (indigenous African), Americo-Liberian, Western European, Lebanese, Asian Indian
LANGUAGES: English, African languages and dialects
RELIGIONS: Traditional African Religions, Islam, Christianity
BASIC MONETARY UNIT: Liberian Dollar

GEOGRAPHY

At its greatest distances, Liberia measures 210 mi. (338 km) from north to south and 230 mi. (370 km) from east to west. It has 315 mi. (507 km) of coastline along the North Atlantic Ocean. It has a narrow coastal plain backed by a plateau region. The plateau region contains the Bomi Hills and the Bong Range, has grasses and scattered trees in its valleys, and has forests at higher elevations. North and northeast Liberia are highland regions and include the Wologizi and Nimba mountain ranges. The country's main rivers include the Cavally and the St. Paul.

CLIMATE

Liberia has a tropical climate. The coastal region's average annual temperature is 80°F (27°C) with an average rainfall of 200 in. (510 cm) per year. Rainfall farther inland averages 85 in. (220 cm) per year. Most of Liberia has a dry season and a rainy season.

ECONOMY

Liberia's economy is based on service industries, agriculture, mining, manufacturing, and construction.

Agriculture - bananas, cacao, cassava, coffee, goats, pigs, rubber, rice, sheep, sugar cane, and tropical fruits

Forestry - mahogany

Manufacturing - beverages, construction materials, explosives, furniture, oil refinement, palm oil, processed foods, mining products, rubber, and soap

Mining - diamonds, gold, and iron ore

Exports - cacao, coffee, iron ore, rubber, and timber

Imports - chemicals, food, fuel, machinery, rice, and transportation equipment

LIFE-STYLE

More than half of Liberia's population lives in rural areas. The black population can be divided into two groups: indigenous Africans whose ancestors have lived in the area for hundreds of years, and Americo-Liberians who are descendents of former American slaves who were sent to Liberia in order to colonize it. Indigenous Africans can be divided into 16 ethnic groups, each of which has its own customs, history, language, and territory. The largest of these groups are the Kpelle and the Bassa. Some other groups are the Gio, the Krahn, the Kru, the Mandingo, and the Mano. Americo-Liberians mainly live in coastal urban areas.

Liberia's rural population lives mainly in small villages of mud houses with thatched roofs. Unlike urban homes, rural homes do not generally have electricity or running water. Most rural Liberians are farmers, although those living near the coast may make a living by fishing or working aboard ships.

Most of Liberia's urban population lives in small, tin-roofed, wooden houses, many of which have electricity and running water. Wealthier urban Liberians live in more expensive houses. Urban Liberians work in government offices, factories, schools, or stores, or as carpenters, doctors, servants, or taxi drivers. Many urban women travel to rural farms on a daily basis to work. Extended family living arrangements are common in both rural and urban areas.

Children are required by law to attend school for 12 years—six years each at the elementary and secondary levels. Because of a lack of schools, teachers, and teaching materials, only about 60 percent actually attend. Less than one percent of Liberians continue their education past the secondary level.

IT'S A FACT!

Nimba Mountains - the country's highest point, rises 4,528 ft. (1,380 m) above sea level.

 DID YOU KNOW...

- Monrovia, Liberia's capital, was named for former United States president James Monroe?
- Liberia is the world's second oldest predominantly black independent nation (independent since 1822, it is second only to Haiti in age)?
- *Liberia* is Latin for "free land"?
- Most Liberian roads are unpaved, and few Liberians own automobiles, making buses, taxis, and walking the predominant modes of transportation?
- Liberia once had a lot of wildlife, but most of it has been killed off by hunters?

LIBYA

OFFICIAL NAME: Socialist People's Libyan Arab Jamahiriya
LOCATION: Northern Africa
AREA: 679,362 sq. mi. (1,759,540 sq. km)
POPULATION (Est. 1993): 5,057,000
CAPITAL: Tripoli
LARGEST CITIES: Tripoli, Benghazi
GOVERNMENT: Military dictatorship whose head of state holds no official title; in theory, governed by the populace through local councils.
FLAG: Adopted in 1977. Totally green, the traditional color of Islam.
ETHNIC GROUP: Arab/Berber
LANGUAGES: Arabic, English, Italian
RELIGION: Islam (mainly Sunni Muslim)
BASIC MONETARY UNIT: Libyan Dinar

GEOGRAPHY

Libya is an Arab country that measures 930 mi. (1,497 km) from north to south and 1,050 mi. (1,690 km) from east to west at its greatest distances. It has 1,047 mi. (1,685 km) of coastline along the Gulf of Sidra and the Mediterranean Sea.

Only about five percent of Libya's land is inhabitable and arable. This includes the land along the Mediterranean Sea and a few desert oases. The remaining 95 percent is desert. The coastal region is divided into eastern and western sections by the Sahara Desert, which extends to the Gulf of Sidra. Part of the coastal region is made up of a fertile plain that measures about 200 mi. (320 km) long. Behind this region is part of the Sahara Desert, the eastern portion of which is called the Libyan Desert. The desert region starts at low elevations near the coast and gradually rises to form mountains near the southern border. The inland desert in large part is made up of huge sand dunes.

CLIMATE

Libya's climate is influenced by the Mediterranean near the coast and is dry and extremely desertlike in the interior. Average coastal temperatures near Tripoli range from 52°F (11°C) in January to 81°F (27°C) in July with an average annual rainfall of about 16 in. (41 cm). Average desert temperatures range from daytime highs of 100°F (38°C) to nighttime lows of 50°F (10°C). The average annual rainfall in the desert is less than 2 in. (5 cm).

ECONOMY

Libya has a developing economy that relies heavily on petroleum. The discovery of oil in 1959 helped Libya move from a poverty-stricken country to one of the wealthiest in the world. Yet most Libyans work in service industries and agriculture.

Agriculture - barley, citrus fruits, dates, livestock (such as cattle, chickens, and sheep), olives, potatoes, tomatoes, and wheat

Manufacturing - cement, petrochemicals, petroleum products, processed foods, and steel

Mining - gypsum, iron ore, lime, natural gas, petroleum, and sulfur

Exports - crude oil, natural gas, and refined petroleum

Imports - food, machinery, manufactured goods, textiles, and transportation equipment

LIFE-STYLE

The majority (80 percent) of Libya's people live near or along the coast. Libya's population is approximately 70 percent urban. The 30 percent rural population lives mainly in villages or desert oases—though its members continue to migrate to urban areas. Rural residents largely make a living by farming. Most farmland is owned by families, and the average farm is 27 acres (11 hectares). Traditional farming methods are used on small farms while modern, mechanized equipment is used on large farms. Most rural Libyans live as extended families and occupy single-room houses constructed of stone or mud-brick with a nearby shelter for their animals. Those moving to urban areas are finding it impossible to live as an extended family due to overcrowding. Cities are characterized by modern high-rise office and apartment buildings. Suburban areas feature single-family homes.

Rural Libyans usually wear traditional clothing. Men generally wear loose, cotton shirts, trousers, an outer cloak, and a brimless, tight-fitting cap. Women wear a full-length robe. Most urban Libyans wear Western-style clothing.

Education is free, and children ages six to 15 are required to attend school. About 64 percent of the population is literate.

IT'S A FACT!

Bette Peak - the country's highest point, rises 7,500 ft. (2,286 m) above sea level.

 DID YOU KNOW...
- At one time, Libyan women rarely left home and received little or no education, while today they have the legal status to participate fully in society?
- Libyan newspapers and periodicals fall under strict government supervision?
- Libya still has some nomads who travel with their herds of camels, goats, and sheep looking for grazing land?

LIECHTENSTEIN

OFFICIAL NAME: Fürstentum Liechtenstein (Principality of Liechtenstein)
LOCATION: South-central Europe
AREA: 62 sq. mi. (160 sq. km)
POPULATION (Est. 1993): 28,000
CAPITAL/LARGEST TOWN: Vaduz
GOVERNMENT: Hereditary constitutional monarchy ruled by the head of the House of Liechtenstein, a prince.
FLAG: Two horizontal stripes of blue and red representing the sky and the glow of evening fires, accordingly. A crown in the upper hoist-side corner represents the prince.
ETHNIC GROUP: Alemannic (Germanic)
LANGUAGE: German
RELIGION: Roman Catholic
BASIC MONETARY UNIT: Swiss Franc

GEOGRAPHY

Liechtenstein is one of the world's smallest countries. At its greatest distances, it measures 17.4 mi. (28 km) from north to south and 7 mi. (11 km) from east to west.

Following the Rhine River, which flows along the western border, is a narrow strip of flat farmland. The eastern and southern sections of the country are predominantly covered with snow-capped mountains whose slopes contain meadows and pine forests.

CLIMATE

Liechtenstein's climate includes cold, cloudy winters and warm, cloudy, humid summers. The average temperature is 47°F (8°C). The country receives about 35 in. (89 cm) of precipitation annually.

ECONOMY

Liechtenstein has a highly industrialized economy and one of the highest living standards in the world. Because it offers low business and income taxes, many foreign businesses have set up their home office in Liechtenstein. Government revenues are also generated by the sales of postage stamps to collectors around the world. Tourism is one of the country's biggest service industries.

Agriculture - beef and dairy cattle, corn, grapes, potatoes, wheat, and other fruits and vegetables

Manufacturing - ceramics, cotton textiles, electronics, food products, heating appliances, metal manufacturing, pharmaceuticals, and precision instruments

Exports - dental products, hardware, pottery, small specialty machinery, and stamps

Imports - foodstuffs, machinery, metal goods, motor vehicles, and textiles

LIFE-STYLE

Liechtenstein's population is about four-fifths rural but less than ten percent of the people make a living in agriculture. Most Liechtensteiners work in factories or as craftworkers.

Liechtensteiners enjoy wearing colorful European-style clothing. Traditional clothing is reserved for special occasions.

The country's national dish is *Riebel* (cornmeal stirred in a frying pan with milk, water, and salt), which is often eaten with elderberry purée. Other traditional dishes include *Käsknöpfle*

(pasta with sharp cheese) and *Rösti* (fried, grated potatoes).

Primary and secondary education is free, and children are required to attend school for eight years. The people are 100 percent literate.

Popular group activities include gymnastics, choral singing, playing in a band, and soccer. Favorite leisure activities include cycling, hiking, and skiing.

The country's royal family owns an art collection that features works by such famed artists as Pieter Bruegel the Elder, Sandro Botticelli, Rembrandt, and Peter Paul Rubens. Many of the stamps sold by Liechtenstein's government feature replicas of paintings from this collection.

IT'S A FACT!

Vorder-Grauspitz - the country's highest point, rises 8,527 ft. (2,599 m) above sea level.

 DID YOU KNOW...

- Politically neutral Liechtenstein has remained undamaged in European wars since 1866?
- Liechtenstein's postal, telegraph, and telephone services are operated by Switzerland, who also represents the country in diplomatic and trade relations?
- One of Liechtenstein's legends tells of the *Wildmannli* (little wild men), shy dwarfs who came out at night to do chores for sleeping villagers?
- Three southeastern mountains were named the "Three Sisters" for a Liechtenstein legend about three heartless sisters who were transformed into mountains by an angry god?
- High German is taught in schools and used for written language while an Alemannic dialect is used for oral language?
- The area now known as Liechtenstein has been inhabited since about 3,000 B.C.?
- Many buildings in the capital city of Vaduz date back to the Middle Ages?
- The country's women were not given the right to vote in national elections until 1984?

LITHUANIA

OFFICIAL NAME: Lietuvos Respublika (Republic of Lithuania)
LOCATION: Eastern Europe
AREA: 25,174 sq. mi. (65,200 sq. km)
POPULATION (Est. 1992): 3,742,000
CAPITAL: Vilnius
LARGEST CITIES: Vilnius, Kaunas, Klaipeda, Šiauliai
GOVERNMENT: Republic headed by a president.
FLAG: Three horizontal stripes of yellow, green, and red representing fields of ripening grain, evergreen forests, and the blood shed for freedom.
ETHNIC GROUPS: Lithuanian, Russian, Polish, Byelorussian, Ukrainian
LANGUAGES: Lithuanian, others
RELIGION: Christianity
BASIC MONETARY UNIT: Litas

GEOGRAPHY

Lithuania measures 175 mi. (280 km) from north to south and 235 mi. (375 km) from east to west at its greatest distances. It has 67 mi. (108 km) of coastline on the Baltic Sea.

Lithuania consists mainly lowlands and gently sloping hills with its highest points in the southeast. It has hundreds of rivers and about 3,000 small lakes. Forests cover approximately one-fourth of the land. Its seacoast is covered with white sand dunes.

CLIMATE

Lithuania has cold, foggy winters and short summers. Rain falls throughout the year, but less so in the summer. The average January temperature ranges from about 27°F (-3°C) on the seacoast to about 21°F (-6°C) in the east. Average July temperatures range from about 61°F (16°C) on the seacoast to about 64°F (18°C) in the east. Precipitation levels average 21-34 in. (53-86 cm) per year.

ECONOMY

Lithuania's economic output is about two-thirds industrial and one-fourth agricultural. Under Soviet control, the government owned most of the businesses, factories, and farmlands. Today, Lithuania's government supports free enterprise.

Agriculture - beef cattle, dairy products, eggs, grain, hogs, meat, milk, potatoes, sugar beets, and vegetables

Manufacturing - chemicals, electrical equipment, fabricated metal products, food products, machinery, oil refining, and petroleum products

Exports - chemicals, eggs, electronics, food, meat, milk, and petroleum products

Imports - chemicals, grain, machinery, and oil

LIFE-STYLE

Prior to Soviet rule, three-fourths of Lithuania's people lived in rural areas. Now, however, as a result of industrialization, two-thirds of the people live in urban areas and one-third live in rural areas. Most urban Lithuanians live in apartments, while many rural Lithanians live in single-family homes.

Under Soviet rule, Lithuanians weren't allowed to teach or publish religious ideas, or do charity work. Church attendance was also discouraged and those who did attend were not offered good educational or job opportunities.

Lithuanians mainly wear modern clothing, but don their decorative national costumes for celebrations and festivals.

The Lithuanian diet includes soup, cheeses, fruits, vegetables, rye bread, and dairy products. Popular dishes include smoked sausage, *cepelinai* (potato dough filled with meat and served with a sauce) and *vedarai* (pig intestines stuffed with potatoes and sausage). Beverages most frequently consumed include coffee, milk, and tea.

Recreational activities include basketball, cycling, rowing, skiing, soccer, tennis, and volleyball. The country's forests and seacoast of white sand dunes offer vacationers beautiful camping and resort areas.

Lithuania is well-known for its choral singing, especially at its annual festivals. The country's *dainos* (ancient songs) and folk tales are vocally passed down through generations. The country also has 13 theaters featuring ballet, drama, and opera and a motion-picture industry.

Children ages six to 17 are required to attend school.

IT'S A FACT!

Neman (Nemunas) - the country's largest and longest river, begins in the southeast and flows into the Baltic Sea.

Juozapines - the country's highest point, rises 958 ft. (292 m) above sea level.

 DID YOU KNOW...

- Lithuania regained its independence in 1991 after 50 years of Soviet control?
- Lithuania's State University, located in Vilnius, was established in 1579?
- Under Soviet rule, private land was taken away and smaller farms were combined to form large state-owned farms?

LUXEMBOURG

OFFICIAL NAME: Grand-Duché de Luxembourg (Grand Duchy of Luxembourg)
LOCATION: Northwestern Europe
AREA: 998 sq. mi. (2,586 sq. km)
POPULATION (Est. 1992): 367,000
CAPITAL/LARGEST CITY: Luxembourg
GOVERNMENT: Constitutional monarchy headed by the grand duke, or duchess, of the House of Nassau who serves as monarch and chief executive.
FLAG: Three horizontal stripes of red, white, and blue.
ETHNIC GROUPS: Luxembourgers (French and German mix), Portuguese, Italian
LANGUAGES: French, German, Letzeburgesch (a German dialect)
RELIGION: Roman Catholic
BASIC MONETARY UNIT: Luxembourg Franc

GEOGRAPHY

Luxembourg, a landlocked country, measures 55 mi. (89 km) from north to south and 35 mi. (56 km) from east to west at its greatest distances.

The country has two regions: 1) the Ardennes, and 2) the Bon Pays (Good Land). Northern Luxembourg is home to the Ardennes, part of a mountain range that stretches from Germany's Rhineland in the east to Luxembourg and Belgium in the west. The Bon Pays makes up the rest of Luxembourg and consists of a hilly, rolling plateau and such rivers as the Attert, the Alzette, the Moselle, and the Sûre.

CLIMATE

Luxembourg has a cool, moist climate with cool summers and mild winters. Temperatures in the capital city of Luxembourg average 32°F (0°C) in January and 63°F (17°C) in July, with cooler temperatures in the mountain region. The annual rainfall averages 40 in. (100 cm) in the southwest and 12-16 in. (30-41 cm) in the southeast. Most of the country's snowfall occurs high in the Ardennes and the country's sunniest months are usually May and June.

ECONOMY

Luxembourg is one of the most industrialized countries in the world and one of Europe's leading producers of steel. Their economy also includes advanced technology, international finance, and tourism.

Agriculture - barley, cattle, fruits, grapes, livestock, oats, pigs, potatoes, poultry, sheep, and wheat

Manufacturing - chemicals, glass, metal products, plastics, processed foods, steel, tires, and wine

Mining - iron ore

Exports - aluminum, chemicals, glass, industrial products, iron ore, rubber products, steel products, and wine

Imports - consumer goods, food, machinery, metals, and minerals

LIFE-STYLE

Luxembourg is over 80 percent urban and about 25 percent of the country's population live in the capital city. Urban areas have many modern apartments and office buildings. Small towns and villages, however, often nestle around medieval castles and churches and have an architectural mix spanning from the 1100s to the 1900s.

Staples of the diet include sausages, potatoes, sauerkraut, seasonal fruits and vegetables, and cheeses. Popular dishes include *Bouneschlupp* (bean soup); *Fritten, Ham an Zalot* (french fries, ham and salad); *Judd mat Gaardebounen* (smoked pork collar with broad beans); *Kachkéis* (a soft cheese); *Quetschentaart* (plum tart); *Träipen* (black pudding); and freshwater fish, such as trout. Popular beverages include beer, coffee, juice, and wine.

Children ages six to 15 are required to attend school. Continued education is available at Luxembourg's International University of Comparative Science and at technical and vocational schools.

Popular recreational activities include cycling, golf, hiking, jogging, soccer, squash, tennis, soccer, volleyball, and water sports. Hunting and fishing are popular during the appropriate seasons, and other leisure activities include gardening, and attending theaters and museums.

IT'S A FACT!

Buurgplatz - the country's highest point, rises 1,835 ft. (559 m) above sea level.

Institut Grand-Ducal - is Luxembourg's main cultural institution of arts and humanities with exhibits on arts and letters, folklore, languages, and the natural sciences.

 DID YOU KNOW...

- Luxembourg is home to two of Europe's oldest daily newspapers—founded in 1848 and 1880—and has one of the world's highest circulation rates?
- Although about one-half of Luxembourg's land is farmed, only about six percent of its workers are farmers?
- Of Luxembourg's three languages, French is most commonly used in high schools and legal/political settings, German is most commonly used in elementary schools and newspapers, and Letzeburgesch is most commonly used as the everyday language?

MACAO
Overseas Territory of Portugal

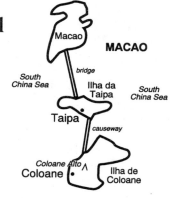

MACAO

OFFICIAL NAME: Macao
LOCATION: Southeast Coast of China
AREA: 6.5 sq. mi. (17 sq. km)
POPULATION (Est. 1993): 477,850
CAPITAL/LARGEST CITY: Nome de Deus de Macao (Macao)
GOVERNMENT: Dependency of Portugal with an appointed governor.
FLAG: Uses the flag of Portugal.
ETHNIC GROUPS: Chinese, Portuguese
LANGUAGES: Portuguese, Cantonese
RELIGION: Buddhism
BASIC MONETARY UNIT: Pataca

GEOGRAPHY

Macao (also spelled Macau) is located on the southeast coast of China and lies at the mouth of China's Pearl River. The territory is made up of the city of Macao, which lies on a peninsula, and two small islands, Taipa and Coloane. The terrain is generally low and flat. The territory has 25 mi. (40 km) of coastline along the South China Sea.

CLIMATE

The country is located just within the Tropic of Cancer. Average annual precipitation is 40-100 in. (102-254 cm). This results in hot, humid summers and cool winters.

ECONOMY

Macao's economy is based on tourism, gambling, and light industry.

Agriculture - rice and vegetables
Manufacturing - fireworks, plastic products, textiles, and toys
Exports - fireworks, textiles, and toys
Imports - consumer goods, food, fresh water, and raw materials

LIFE-STYLE

Chinese make up 95 percent of the population; the remainder are mostly Macanese—Macao-born Portuguese and Eurasians. A large number of Chinese citizens travel across the Macao-Chinese border every day to work in Macao.

Some residents of Macao live in areas with old, pastel-colored houses lining cobblestone streets. Others live in modern apartment buildings.

Most of the country's people live on the peninsula. The rest of the people live on the two islands, which are connected to each other by a causeway and to the mainland by a bridge.

Staples of the diet are fish, rice, and vegetables.

IT'S A FACT!

Coloane Alto - the territory's highest point, is located on Coloane and rises 571 ft. (174 m) above sea level.

DID YOU KNOW...

• Control of Macao will be transferred from Portugal to China in December 1999?

• In reality, the Chinese government dominates the government of Macao; China has veto power over any policies or laws concerning Macao?

• Macao is Asia's oldest surviving European settlement?

• Macao is sometimes called "Latin Orient" for its mix of Portuguese and Chinese cultures, and the "Las Vegas of the East" for its many gambling casinos?

• The name *Macao* comes from the Cantonese word *A-Ma-Gau*, meaning "City of God"?

MACEDONIA

OFFICIAL NAME: Republika Makedonija (Republic of Macedonia)
FORMERLY: Part of Yugoslavia (until 1991)
LOCATION: Southeastern Europe
AREA: 9,928 sq. mi. (25,713 sq. km)
POPULATION (Est. 1993): 2,141,000
CAPITAL/LARGEST CITY: Skopje
GOVERNMENT: Republic governed by a president.
FLAG: Adopted in 1992. A yellow disk with 16 yellow rays, centered on a red field.
ETHNIC GROUPS: Macedonian, Albanian
LANGUAGES: Macedonian, Albanian
RELIGIONS: Christianity (Eastern Orthodox), Islam
BASIC MONETARY UNIT: Denar

GEOGRAPHY

Macedonia, a landlocked country, lies on southeastern Europe's Balkan Peninsula. At its greatest distances, Macedonia measures 105 mi. (170 km) from north to south and 135 mi. (215 km) from east to west.

A large portion of the country is composed of mountains and hills. A plateau, which lies 2,000-3,000 ft. (600-900 m) above sea level, covers much of Macedonia.

CLIMATE

Macedonia has a Mediterranean-like climate of hot, dry summers and rather cold winters with heavy snowfall.

ECONOMY

Most factories and businesses in Macedonia are owned by the government.

Agriculture - apples, cattle, corn, cotton, grapes, hogs, peaches, plums, poultry, sheep, tobacco, and wheat

Manufacturing - cement, iron and steel, refrigerators, sulfuric acid, textiles, and tobacco products

Mining - chromium, copper, iron ore, lead, manganese, uranium, and zinc

Exports - fruit, machinery, manufactured goods, and textiles

Imports - consumer goods and oil

LIFE-STYLE

About 55 percent of the people live in urban areas in high-rise apartment buildings. The other 45 percent live in rural areas in homes built of concrete blocks, red brick, or stone.

Popular Macedonian dishes include cold cucumber soup, garlic soup, stuffed grape leaves, and *sataraš* (a pork and veal dish flavored with onions and red peppers). *Šljivovica*, a plum brandy, is the national drink.

Children ages seven to 15 are required to attend school. Macedonia has a 90 percent literacy rate.

The most popular sport is soccer. Macedonians also enjoy folk dances, like the *oro* (a type of circle dance). Many people enjoy carpet weaving, wood carving, and embroidery as pastimes.

IT'S A FACT!

Mount Korabit - the country's highest point, rises 9,026 ft. (2,751 m) above sea level.

Ohrid - once an important religious center, is now the most frequented tourist spot in Macedonia.

Stone Bridge - located in Skopje across the Vardar River, was originally built in the 15th century.

 DID YOU KNOW...

- In July of 1963, an earthquake damaged or destroyed about 80 percent of the buildings in Skopje and killed more than 1,000 people?
- Macedonia has an average of only one automobile for every nine people?
- Macedonia is one of the world's seven legal cultivators of the opium poppy for the pharmaceutical industry?
- The United States and most European nations, at the request of the government of Greece, have not recognized the independence of Macedonia because it refuses to change its historical, Greek-linked name and flag?
- Ancient Macedonia, a greater land area which included Macedonia, was the birthplace of Alexander the Great?

MADAGASCAR

MADAGASCAR

OFFICIAL NAME: Republique Démocratique de Madagascar
(Democratic Republic of Madagascar)
FORMERLY: Malagasy Republic
LOCATION: Indian Ocean
AREA: 226,658 sq. mi. (587,041 sq. km)
POPULATION (Est. 1993): 13,186,000
CAPITAL/LARGEST CITY: Antananarivo
GOVERNMENT: Republic governed by a president and prime minister.
FLAG: Two horizontal stripes of red and green edged by a vertical white stripe on the hoist side. White, red, and green represent purity, sovereignty, and hope, accordingly.
ETHNIC GROUPS: Mixed Indonesian and Black African descent
LANGUAGES: Malagasy, French
RELIGIONS: Christianity, Islam, Traditional African Religions
BASIC MONETARY UNIT: Malagasy Franc

GEOGRAPHY

Madagascar is an African country that consists of one large island—also called Madagascar—and several tiny islands. It is located about 240 mi. (386 km) off mainland Africa's southeastern coast.

At its greatest distances, Madagascar measures 980 mi. (1,580 km) from north to south and 360 mi. (579 km) from east to west. It has 2,600 mi. (4,180 km) of coastline along the Indian Ocean and the Mozambique Channel.

Central Madagascar is covered by mountains with altitudes of 2,000-4,000 ft. (610-1,200 m) above sea level. This area—the most densely populated of all—suffers from deforestation and soil erosion. North of the mountains is an area of fertile soil, while the south is mainly desert. The west coast has wide plains and some fertile river valleys, while the east coast has a narrow plain. Reefs and storms off the east coast make it dangerous for ships.

CLIMATE

Madagascar's coastal regions have a tropical climate while the southern desert region is hot and dry. The highlands region has a cool climate. The average temperature at Antananarivo ranges from 55° to 67°F (13° to 19°C). The average annual rainfall is 40-60 in. (100-150 cm) with greater amounts falling in the coastal regions. The country experiences cyclones periodically, and during the rainy season many of Madagascar's roads become impassable.

ECONOMY

Madagascar has a poor but developing economy. It is the world's greatest producer of cloves and vanilla. Agriculture is the mainstay of the economy.

Agriculture - bananas, beans, cassava, cattle, cloves, cocoa, coffee, peanuts, rice, sugar cane, sweet potatoes, and vanilla

Manufacturing - agricultural processing (meat, sugar), cement, hides, paper, petroleum, and sisal

Mining - bauxite, chromite, coal, and graphite

Exports - cloves, coffee, hides, meat, petroleum products, sisal, sugar, and vanilla

Imports - capital goods, consumer goods, food, intermediate manufactures, and petroleum

LIFE-STYLE

About three-fourths of the Malagasy are farmers and herders. Central and southern Malagasy largely make a living by raising rice in irrigated fields, while coastal Malagasy mainly herd cattle. Most Malagasy homes are several stories high and constructed of brick with tile or thatched roofs. Much of the population wears European-style clothing. On special occasions, people from one region can be distinguished from another region by the distinctive straw hats they don. Members of isolated southern tribes often wear little clothing.

Staples of the diet include fruit, rice, and vegetables. Fish and meat are eaten on occasion.

Almost all children attend primary school, but only about a fifth of the children attend secondary school. Approximately 75 percent of the population is literate.

IT'S A FACT!

Maromokotro - the country's highest point, rises 9,436 ft. (2,876 m) above sea level.

 DID YOU KNOW...

- During the 1600s and 1700s, Madagascar was a favorite hideout for sea pirates, including the well-known Captain William Kidd?
- Madagascar Island is the world's fourth largest island?
- Antananarivo, the country's capital, was formerly called Tananarive?
- Madagascar was formerly a French colony, but gained its independence in 1960?
- Madagascar publishes seven daily newspapers whose content is sometimes restricted by the government?
- The majority of Madagascar's plants and animals, such as lemurs, are found nowhere else in the world, other than on nearby Comoros?
- The elephant bird, which has been extinct about 1,000 years, was native only to Madagascar? (This flightless bird measured up to 10 ft. {3 m} tall and weighed about 1,000 lb. {450 kg}.)

MADEIRA ISLANDS
Dependency of Portugal

OFFICIAL NAME: Arquipélago da Madeira (Madeira Islands)
LOCATION: Atlantic Ocean
AREA: 307 sq. mi. (794 sq. km)
POPULATION (Est. 1993): 271,000
CAPITAL/LARGEST CITY: Funchal
GOVERNMENT: Dependency of Portugal.
FLAG: Uses the flag of Portugal.

GEOGRAPHY

The Madeira Islands, also referred to as the Funchal Islands, are located off the northwest coast of mainland Africa. The country's area includes the islands of Madeira and Porto Santo and the uninhabited Desertas and Selvagens (Salvage) island groups. Madeira consists of a dramatic ocean mountain range, and Porto Santo boasts many beautiful sandy beaches. The Desertas Island Group includes the islets of Bugio, Chão, and Deserta Grande. The Selvagens Island Group is located about 156 mi. (251 km) south of Madeira.

ECONOMY

Wine production is the chief industry of Madeira.
Agriculture - bananas, grapes, mangoes, oranges, pomegranates, sugar cane, and vegetables
Industry - fishing, embroidery, willow wicker baskets and furniture, and wine production
Exports - embroidered items, fruits, wicker furniture, vegetables, and wine

LIFE-STYLE

Madeira is known as the "Rock Garden of the Atlantic" because its towns and farms are terraced on its mountain range and covered with exotic flowers and trees. Farmers use *levadas* (stone aqueducts) to ration and distribute the small amount of rain that falls on the island.

The country uses several unusual types of transportation. Ox-drawn sleighs maneuver over the steep streets and roads. Some people use basket sleds for a fast, thrilling downhill mode of transportation. To reach remote areas, tourists can travel in hammocks carried on poles by two people.

IT'S A FACT!

Pico Ruivo de Santana - the islands' highest point, is located on Madeira Island and rises 6,104 ft. (1,860 m) above sea level.

 DID YOU KNOW...

- Exotic flowers grown on the islands include bignonia, bougainvillea, camellias, hibiscus, hydrangeas, jacaranda, orchids, and wisteria?
- The large variety of trees found on the Madeira Islands includes bamboo, Brazilian araucaria, eucalyptus, Indian fig, Japanese camphor, laurel, mimosa, palm, and West Indies coral?
- The Portuguese named the island *Madeira,* meaning "wood," because of its heavy forestation?
- The islands supply most of Europe's culinary vegetables?

MALAWI

OFFICIAL NAME: Republic of Malawi
FORMERLY: Nyasaland, a British protectorate
LOCATION: Southeastern Africa
AREA: 45,747 sq. mi. (118,484 sq. km)
POPULATION (Est. 1994): 10,096,000
CAPITAL: Lilongwe
LARGEST CITY: Blantyre
GOVERNMENT: Republic governed by a president.
FLAG: Adopted in 1964. Three horizontal stripes of black, red, and green with a radiant rising red sun on the black stripe. Black, red, and green represent the African people, the blood of those who fought for freedom, the land's fertility, accordingly. The sun symbolizes a new era for the entire African continent.
ETHNIC GROUPS: Black (belonging to such Bantu groups as Angoni or Ngoni, Cewa or Chewa, Lomwe, Ngonde, Nyanja, Sena, Tonga, Tumbuko, and Yao), Asian, European
LANGUAGES: Chichewa, English, others
RELIGIONS: Traditional African Religions, Christianity, Islam
BASIC MONETARY UNIT: Malawian Kwacha

GEOGRAPHY

Malawi, a landlocked country, measures about 520 mi. (837 km) from north to south and about 50-100 mi. (80-160 km) from east to west.

The Great Rift Valley lies along Malawi's eastern border. Lake Malawi, also referred to as Lake Nyasa, lies within the Great Rift Valley and accounts for about one-fifth of the country's area. Lake Malawi is Africa's third largest lake. West of the lake, the land consists of steep plateaus. Grassland and savanna cover a lot of the land. The Shire River is the country's main river.

CLIMATE

The lowlands along the shores of Lake Malawi and in the Shire River Valley have a hot, humid, tropical climate with temperatures averaging 74° to 78°F (23° to 26°C). The average annual temperature on the plateaus ranges from 58° to 65°F (14° to 18°C). The average annual rainfall ranges from 70 in. (180 cm) in the north to 30 in. (76 cm) in the south. The country has a rainy season which lasts from November to May. A dry season predominates throughout the remainder of the year.

ECONOMY

Malawi has one of the world's least developed economies. It is based mainly on agriculture, but only about one-third of its land is suitable for farming. Fishing in Lake Malawi has become an important industry, too. Though parts of the northwest are covered by forests containing valuable hardwoods, trucks are unable to reach and harvest the trees.

Agriculture - cattle, corn, cotton, goats, peanuts, sorghum, sugar cane, tea, and tobacco

Manufacturing - bricks, cement, consumer goods, cotton goods, hides and skins, and processed foods

Exports - coffee, sugar, tea, tobacco

Imports - food, fuels, semimanufactures, and transport equipment

LIFE-STYLE

Malawi's population is over 85 percent rural. Most Malawians are native Africans who live in small, rural villages. Their traditional homes have mud walls and thatched roofs. Residents of European descent live in the larger towns and work for the government, Christian missions, and industry. Some also run tea plantations outside of the cities. Most of Malawi's Asians own or work in small town shops.

For years, the women of Malawi raised the family's crops, while the men supplied the family with meat and fish. Today, both women and men farm, with women growing food for their families and men raising crops—such as sugar cane, tea, and cotton—to sell.

About 70 percent of the boys and 50 percent of the girls attend primary school. An even smaller percentage attend secondary school.

IT'S A FACT!

Mount Sapitwa - the country's highest point, rises 9,843 ft. (3,000 m) above sea level.

 DID YOU KNOW...
- Malawian families typically have 9-10 members?
- The father is not the head of the Malawian household; most native Malawians determine descent through their mothers, with new families setting up households near their mother or her relatives?
- Each October, Malawi turns into a "land of fire" when its grass is burned to fertilize and make way for new crops?
- Malawi gained its independence in 1964?
- Originally, the Yao sold slaves to Arabs along Africa's eastern coast?
- *Malawi* is the modern spelling of the word *Maravi*, meaning "land of flames"?

MALAYSIA

OFFICIAL NAME: Malaysia
LOCATION: Southeast Asia
AREA: 127,317 sq. mi. (329,749 sq. km)
POPULATION (Est. 1993): 19,346,000
CAPITAL/LARGEST CITY: Kuala Lumpur
GOVERNMENT: Constitutional monarchy headed by a prime minister.
FLAG: Background of 14 alternating red and white horizontal stripes. A blue rectangle in the upper hoist-side corner features a yellow crescent and a 14-pointed star.
ETHNIC GROUPS: Malay, Chinese, Asian Indian
LANGUAGES: Bahasa Malaysia, Chinese, Tamil, English
RELIGIONS: Islam, Buddhism, Hinduism
BASIC MONETARY UNIT: Ringgit

GEOGRAPHY

Malaysia consists of two distinct land regions located in Southeast Asia. The two regions are approximately 400 mi. (664 km) apart. Peninsular Malaysia covers the southern part of the Malay Peninsula. Sarawak and Sabah are located on the northern portion of the island of Borneo. The two regions are separated by the South China Sea.

Thick, tropical rainforests cover the mountains that run down the center of Peninsular Malaysia. East and west of the mountainous areas are low, swampy plains. The coastal areas of Sarawak and Sabah are also low and swampy with tropical rainforests covering inland mountain areas.

CLIMATE

Both of Malaysia's regions have tropical climates. The average annual coastal temperature ranges from 70° to 90°F (21° to 32°C). In the mountains, the average annual temperature ranges from 55° to 80°F (13° to 27°C). Peninsular Malaysia receives an average of 100 in. (250 cm) of rain per year. Sarawak and Sabah receive an average of 150 in. (381 cm) of rain per year.

ECONOMY

One of the strongest economies in Southeast Asia thrives in Malaysia. It is the world's major producer of natural rubber and palm oil.

Agriculture - cacao, coconuts, palm oil, pepper, pineapples, rice, rubber, and timber

Fishing - anchovies, mackerel, and shrimp

Manufacturing - air conditioners, cement, processed foods, rubber goods, semiconductors, and textiles

Mining - bauxite, copper, gold, iron ore, natural gas, petroleum, and tin

Exports - electronic equipment, machinery, palm oil, petroleum, rubber, timber, and tin

Imports - chemicals and machinery

LIFE-STYLE

Peninsular Malaysia is composed of diverse ethnic groups. The majority of Malays, which make up the largest group, live primarily in rural areas on the peninsula. They work as farmers and live in wood houses with thatched roofs. Some of the houses are built on stilts because of the swampy ground. The Malays hold much of the political power.

The Chinese, on the other hand, reside mostly in the cities and earn their living working in stores, banks, or offices and live in suburban homes or high-rise apartment buildings. The Chinese run most of the nation's financial dealings. They also own a large portion of the businesses.

One other sizable ethnic group, the Asian Indians, are found in great numbers working on rubber plantations. Some hold jobs in the cities. Both the Asian Indians and the Malays who live in the cities, as well as low-income Chinese, live in poor, crowded areas.

A strong Western influence can be seen in the clothing worn by Malaysia's Chinese. However, traditional dress or a combination of traditional and Western-style clothing is very evident as well. Many of the rural Malay men and women wear a skirt known as a *sarong*.

Rice is a staple of the Malaysian diet. It is often served with fish or a fish sauce, meat, or fruit or vegetables. A popular dish is *satay*, consisting of small chunks of meat placed on a skewer, grilled, and dipped in a hot sauce.

Soccer is the most popular sport. Other favorite sports are badminton, cricket, field hockey, rugby, squash, swimming, table and outdoor tennis, and volleyball. Competitive sports include *main gasing* (game which requires spinning heavy tops for long periods of time), martial arts, and *sepaktakraw* (a team sport played with a rattan ball).

IT'S A FACT!

Mount Kinabalu - the country's highest point and the highest peak in Southeast Asia, rises 13,341 ft. (4,094 m) above sea level.

National Mosque - an Islamic house of worship located in Kuala Lumpur.

DID YOU KNOW...

- Malaysia's land area is about 63 percent forested?
- Four-fifths of Malaysian farms measure only 5 acres (2 hectares), or less?
- Malaysia is home to a number of valuable trees—ebony, fig, camphor, mahogany, rubber, and sandalwood?
- Malaysia's abundant animal life includes civets, cobras, crocodiles, elephants, lizards, monkeys, pythons, tigers, 500 species of birds, and numerous butterflies?

MALDIVES

OFFICIAL NAME: Republic of Maldives
LOCATION: Indian Ocean, off India's south coast
AREA: 115 sq. mi. (298 sq. km)
POPULATION (Est. 1993): 230,000
CAPITAL/LARGEST CITY: Malé (on Malé Island in Malé Atoll)
GOVERNMENT: Republic governed by a president.
FLAG: Adopted in 1965. A green rectangle, featuring a white crescent, centered on a red field.
ETHNIC GROUPS: Sinhalese, Dravidian
LANGUAGES: Divehi, English
RELIGION: Islam (mainly Sunni Muslim)
BASIC MONETARY UNIT: Rufiyaa

MALDIVES

GEOGRAPHY

Maldives is composed of over 1,200 small coral islands which form a chain 475 mi. (764 km) long and 80 mi. (129 km) wide in the Indian Ocean. This archipelago is grouped into 19 atolls. No one island is larger than 5 sq. mi. (13 sq. km). The atolls are surrounded by barrier reefs, protecting them from the sea. The islands have clear lagoons and white sandy beaches. Grass and low-growing tropical plants cover the land.

CLIMATE

The climate is tropical—hot and humid. Daytime temperatures average 80°F (27°C). The northern islands receive an average of 100 in. (250 cm) of rain per year; the southern islands receive nearly 150 in. (381 cm) per year. Monsoonal winds, blowing over the islands twice a year, bring most of the rain.

ECONOMY

The country's leading economic activities are fishing and tourism. Another key industry is the cultivation of coconuts and products derived from coconuts.

Agriculture - chili peppers, coconuts, millet, and sweet potatoes

Fishing - bonito and tuna

Handicrafts - coir yarn, shirts and sweaters, and woven mats

Exports - coir yarn, copra, cowrie shells, and fish and fish meal

Imports - manufactured goods, rice, sugar, and wheat flour

LIFE-STYLE

With the exception of Malé, the only relatively large settlement, most of the population lives in villages on the small islands scattered throughout the atolls. Only about 210 of the more than 1,200 islands are inhabited.

The Maldivians are a skilled seafaring people. Maldivian men often go to sea every day to fish. They build their own boats of coconut palms or other timbers. Each boat holds about 12 fishermen. Fishermen use rods and reels to catch bonito, tuna, and other fish. The women prepare the fish by cooking and smoking it over a fire. Fish is the country's greatest natural resource, and much of it is exported to countries such as Sri Lanka and Japan.

In addition to fish, other diet staples of the Maldivians include coconuts, papayas, pineapples, pomegranates, and sweet potatoes.

Women use coconut husk fibers, called *coir*, to make yarn and rope for export. They also export cowrie shells collected from the shore. Weaving reed mats is another frequent activity.

The most common form of transportation is the sailboat. Steamships regularly ply the waters between the port of Malé and Sri Lanka. On land, many people ride bicycles.

IT'S A FACT!

Rat Point - the country's highest point, is located on Wilingili Island and rises 80 ft. (24 m) above sea level.

DID YOU KNOW...

- The low-lying islands are generally no more than 8 ft. (2.5 m) above sea level, and a majority are only 6 ft. (1.8 m) above sea level?
- The term *atoll*, meaning a coral island or group of islands enclosing a lagoon, comes from the Maldivian word *atolu*?
- Maldivian-made fishing boats measure 36 ft. (11 m) long and 8-9 ft. (2.4-2.7 m) wide?
- Only about two-thirds of the school-age population is enrolled in school?
- Magnificent tortoises can be found in abundance in the waters around Maldives?

MALI

OFFICIAL NAME: République de Mali (Republic of Mali)
FORMERLY: French Sudan
LOCATION: Western Africa
AREA: 478,841 sq. mi. (1,240,192 sq. km)
POPULATION (Est. 1993): 10,080,000
CAPITAL/LARGEST CITY: Bamako
GOVERNMENT: Republic governed by a president.
FLAG: Three vertical stripes of green, gold, and red.
ETHNIC GROUPS: Fulani, Toucouleur, Mandingo, Dogon, Songhai, Voltaic
OFFICIAL LANGUAGE: French
MAJOR LANGUAGES: Fulani, Bambara
RELIGIONS: Islam, Traditional African Religions
BASIC MONETARY UNIT: CFA Franc

GEOGRAPHY

Mali, a landlocked country, is the seventh largest country on the African continent. At its greatest distances, Mali measures 1,000 mi. (1,609 km) form north to south and 1,150 mi. (1,851 km) from east to west.

Mali has three main land regions: 1) the Sahara, a desert which covers northern Mali; 2) the Sahel, a semidesert located in central Mali; and 3) grasslands, found in southern Mali.

CLIMATE

Mali has three seasons. From March to May, the climate is hot and dry; from June to October, it is warm and rainy; and from November to February, Mali is cool and dry. Throughout most of the country, the average annual temperature ranges from 80° to 85°F (27° to 29°C). In the desert region, daytime temperatures may exceed 110°F (43°C). The Sahara receives about 10 in. (25 cm) of rain per year, while southern Mali averages about 35 in. (89 cm) of rain per year.

ECONOMY

Mali is a very poor country trying to develop a sound economy. More than three-fourths of the workers are involved in agriculture, but only one-fifth of the land is fertile. This creates severe economic problems.

Agriculture - cassava, corn, cotton, livestock, millet, peanuts, rice, sorghum, sugar cane, and yams

Fishing - carp, catfish, and perch

Manufacturing - food products, leather products, and textiles

Mining - gold and salt

Exports - cotton, fish, leather products, livestock, meat, and peanuts

Imports - chemicals, food, machinery, petroleum, and textiles

LIFE-STYLE

Most of Mali's people are black Africans, living in rural areas and growing farm crops for a living. Most of the farmers cannot afford agricultural machinery, so the work is done with hand tools. Their shelters are small houses made of mud or branches. These are clustered in small villages.

The Fulani, people who are descendents of blacks and whites, farm for a living, but some raise cattle in the semidesert Sahel and in the southern grasslands.

Nomads are found among the Arabs, Moors, and Tuareg, herding their livestock back and forth across the desert regions in search of water and grazing pasture. These nomads live in portable camel hair tents and travel in groups.

European descendents live in Bamako and other urban areas. These are the people who own businesses or hold government or professional positions.

Because Mali is considered a developing nation, it faces major social problems, such as lack of education and poor health conditions. The majority of the adult population cannot read or write, and only about 27 percent of school-age children actually attend school. Malaria is a frequent cause of death among children, and there are too few doctors to serve the population.

Millet is the staple of the diet. It is often served with a leaf or vegetable sauce. Other important foods are cassava, corn, rice, sorghum, and yams.

Soccer is the most popular sport.

IT'S A FACT!

Hombori Tondo - the country's highest point, rises 3,789 ft. (1,155 m) above sea level.

Timbuktu - a small trading center in central Mali, was once the center of Muslim learning in Africa.

 DID YOU KNOW...

- Only ten percent of Mali's 11,200 mi. (18,000 km) of roads are paved?
- Street markets serve not only as places to buy food and other goods, but also as centers for socializing?
- Wild animals, includinxg elephants, gazelles, giraffes, hyenas, leopards, and lions roam across the southern grasslands; crocodiles and hippos are found in the river areas?

MALTA

MALTA

OFFICIAL NAME: Republic of Malta
LOCATION: Mediterranean Sea
AREA: 122 sq. mi. (316 sq. km)
POPULATION (Est. 1994): 359,000
CAPITAL/CHIEF PORT: Valletta
GOVERNMENT: Republic headed by a president.
FLAG: Two vertical bands of white and red. The upper hoist-side corner features the George Cross—awarded to Malta for bravery during World War II—edged in red.
ETHNIC GROUPS: Arab, Sicilian, Norman, Spanish, Italian, English
LANGUAGES: Maltese, English
RELIGION: Roman Catholic
BASIC MONETARY UNIT: Maltese Lira

GEOGRAPHY

Malta is an archipelago of five islands located about 60 mi. (97 km) south of Sicily. The largest and only inhabited islands include Malta, with an area of 95 sq. mi. (246 sq. km); Gozo, with an area of 26 sq. mi. (67 sq. km); and Comino, with an area of 1 sq. mi. (3 sq. km). The other two islands are Cominotto and Filfla. The islands have a combined coastline of 87 mi. (140 km) along the Mediterranean Sea.

The islands mainly consist of rocky soil with bays, beaches, harbors, and rocky caves. Elevations are low, with the highest point rising 829 ft. (253 m) above sea level. The islands have no permanent lakes or rivers, making fresh water scarce. Natural resources are also scarce, with the main minerals being limestone and salt.

CLIMATE

Malta enjoys a Mediterranean climate with mild, rainy winters and hot, dry summers. The average annual temperature ranges from 55°F (13°C) in January to 79°F (26°C) in July. The average annual rainfall is about 21 in. (53 cm).

ECONOMY

Much of Malta's population is employed in shipbuilding and repair, though the country's economy is becoming more dependent on tourism. The country imports more than it exports.

Agriculture - barley, cauliflower, citrus fruits, flowers, grapes, green peppers, milk, onions, pork, potatoes, poultry, tomatoes, and wheat

Manufacturing - beverages, clothing, electronics, footwear, processed foods, shipbuilding and repair, textiles, and tobacco

Exports - clothing, flowers, footwear, ships, and textiles

Imports - food, machinery, petroleum, and semi-manufactured goods

LIFE-STYLE

Malta is almost 90 percent urban. Most of the population is employed in the building industry or works in the dockyards. Some residents farm, but crops are often small because of the rocky soil. Terraced farming—which gives the country the appearance of having giant steps—covers much of the land.

Public education is free, and children ages six to 16 are required to attend elementary school. Catholic education is also offered, and by law, teachings of the Roman Catholic Church taught at the Catholic school must also be taught at the public

schools. Both the English and Maltese languages are used in instructing.

Many of Malta's folk traditions evolved around the *festa*, which celebrates a village's patron saint through fireworks and processions.

 DID YOU KNOW...
- Malta has some of the world's best examples of Baroque and Renaissance art and architecture?
- Remains of late Bronze Age and Stone Age people have been found in some of Malta's limestone caverns?
- During World War II, Malta's deep inlets concealed submarine bases?
- Malta was once a British colony, which gained independence in 1964?
- Valletta has been Malta's capital since 1571?
- Tradition holds that Malta's inhabitants were converted to Christianity by St. Paul the Apostle after he was shipwrecked near the country in A.D. 60?
- Malta is one of the world's most densely populated countries with an average of 2,943 persons per sq. mi. (1,136 per sq. km)?

MARIANA ISLANDS
Commonwealth of the United States

MARIANA ISLANDS

OFFICIAL NAME: Commonwealth of the Northern Mariana Islands
LOCATION: Philippine Sea/North Pacific Ocean
AREA: 183 sq. mi. (477 sq. km, excluding Guam)
POPULATION (Est. 1993): 48,581 (excluding Guam)
CAPITAL/LARGEST CITY: Saipan (on Saipan Island)
GOVERNMENT: Self-governing commonwealth of the United States headed by a governor. The commonwealth relies on the United States to take care of defense and foreign affairs.
FLAG: White five-pointed star superimposed on the gray silhouette of a latte stone, all of which is centered on a blue field.
ETHNIC GROUP: Chamorro
LANGUAGES: English, Chamorro
RELIGION: Christianity (mainly Roman Catholic)
BASIC MONETARY UNIT: United States Dollar

GEOGRAPHY

The Mariana Islands are the northernmost islands in Micronesia. They are an archipelago formed by the summits of volcanic mountains. The Marianas make up the southern portion of a submerged mountain range that extends from Guam almost to Japan, a distance of 1,565 mi. (2,519 km). The islands have a combined coastline of about 920 mi. (1,482 km) on the Philippine Sea and the North Pacific Ocean.

The 15 islands that make up the Marianas can be divided into two smaller groups: ten northern and five southern. Only six of the islands are inhabited. The largest islands in the northern group are Agrihan, Anatahan, and Pagan. Some of these northern islands have active volcanoes. The largest islands in the southern group are Guam, Rota, Saipan, and Tinian. Volcanic slopes with limestone or reef rock terraces make up the land in the southern islands.

Although Guam is the southernmost Marianas island, it is a separate territory of the United States.

CLIMATE

The Mariana Islands have a tropical climate with little temperature variation. The rainy season generally lasts from July to October. Dry weather occurs throughout most of the rest of the year. The islands are subject to typhoons especially from August to November.

ECONOMY

The Marianas Islands' economy is dependent upon monetary assistance from the United States. Tourism is a main source of revenue.

Agriculture - cattle, coconuts, fruits, and vegetables
Manufacturing - handicrafts, and light manufacturing
Exports - bread, concrete blocks, garments, light iron work, manufactured goods, and pastries
Imports - construction equipment, food, and materials

LIFE-STYLE

Saipan is home to a majority of the islands' population. Chamorros, though native to the Mariana Islands, have intermarried with other cultures and mainly follow Western customs. The islanders have a literacy rate of more than 95 percent.

IT'S A FACT!

Mount Okso' Takpochao - the islands' highest point, is located on Saipan and rises 293 mi. (471 km) above sea level.

 DID YOU KNOW...

- More than 85 percent of the Mariana Islands' residents speak a language other than English while at home?
- *Islas de los Ladrones*, meaning "Islands of Thieves," was the name originally given to the Mariana Islands by Ferdinand Magellan's sailors because the natives, after supplying the sailors with food and water, helped themselves to the ships' goods?
- The people of the Marianas have been citizens of the United States since 1986?

MARSHALL ISLANDS
Dependency of the United States

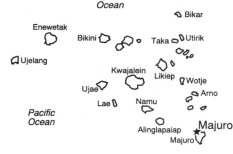

OFFICIAL NAME: Republic of the Marshall Islands
LOCATION: Central Pacific Ocean
AREA: 70 sq. mi. (181 sq. km.)
POPULATION (Est. 1993): 42,000
CAPITAL/LARGEST CITY: Majuro (on Majuro Atoll)
GOVERNMENT: Republic in free association with the United States.
FLAG: Blue field with two diagonal stripes of orange (top) and white extending from the lower, hoist-side corner to the upper, fly-side corner. A white star with four large rays and 20 small rays appears in the upper, hoist-side corner.
ETHNIC GROUP: Marshallese
LANGUAGES: Marshallese, English
RELIGION: Christianity (mainly Protestant)
BASIC MONETARY UNIT: United States Dollar

GEOGRAPHY

The Marshall Islands are a group of low-lying coral atolls and islands in the central Pacific Ocean. They are located in a part of the Pacific known as *Micronesia*, which means "small islands."

There are two chains of atolls about 130 mi. (200 km) apart. The Ratak (*eastern* or *sunrise*) chain is composed of 15 atolls; the Ralik (*western* or *sunset*) chain is made up of 16 atolls. In all, there are more than 1,200 islands and islets, with a combined coastline of about 230 mi. (370 km).

Atoll islands are coral based, flat, and narrow with a thin layer of sandy soil.

CLIMATE

The Marshall Islands have a hot and humid climate, with ocean breezes cooling the air. The average temperature is 84°F (29°C). More rainfall occurs on the southern islands. The typhoon season occurs between August and November.

ECONOMY

Revenues on the islands are generated by farming, fishing, and the raising of pigs and poultry. Other major sources of revenue come from the production of copra cake and coconut oil for exporting, and the leasing of land to the U.S. for a missile range.

Agriculture - coconuts, bananas, breadfruit, limes, taro, pumpkins, and papayas
Manufacturing - coconut oil production and handicrafts
Exports - coconut oil, handicrafts, and fish
Imports - rice, flour, sugar, coffee, tea, and canned meat

LIFE-STYLE

The extended family is the center of Marshallese life. It is the basis of relationships and land ownership. The society is matrilineal, meaning that land is passed down through women. Men have a lot of day-to-day power.

Most Marshallese lead casual, carefree lives. The people are friendly and non-confrontational. Rudeness is very rare. Personal time is not as important as that spent with family and friends. Sharing and borrowing are much more common than owning and having.

A common greeting is *Itok im mona*, or "Come and eat." When addressing another, names are generally not used. A more common term, such as "friend," will follow a "hello" or a good-bye." During conversations, prolonged eye contact is avoided; it is considered more respectful to look down than it is to look into a person's eyes. Since the head is considered the most sacred part of the body, it is considered improper to point at or touch another person's head. A quick hissing noise may be used to get someone's attention.

Most foods are eaten with the fingers. Young children are generally fed first. Sharing of food with others is an obligation, even when there may not be enough for the family. If a plate of food, such as fish, is taken to friends or a relative, a few days later the plate might return filled with bananas or some other food. Popular Marshallese dishes are *jaajmi* (raw fish), *kwanjin* (breadfruit baked on coals and scraped), and *taituuj* (fried banana pancakes).

Popular sports are baseball, basketball, canoe racing, swimming, and volleyball. Many people enjoy storytelling. Visiting is an important leisure activity. *Jambo* (the art of walking around to visit and chat) is a national pastime.

IT'S A FACT!

Bikini and Enewetak Atolls - the sites of 66 controversial atomic tests conducted by the United States between 1946 and 1958.

Kwajalein Atoll - is the site of a missile range maintained by the United States?

 DID YOU KNOW...
- When the Marshallese shake hands, they may continue to do so for a long period, possibly even the length the conversation?
- Many Marshallese lie down when they converse, propping their heads with a stone, coconut, or a window sill?
- The original Marshallese were renowned for developing an elaborate system of navigation, using wave and current patterns rather than specific landmarks?
- None of the atolls or islands rise more than 20 ft. (6 m) above high tide?
- It is considered bad manners for a guest to refuse food offered by a host; it is better to wrap up the food and take it home than to give it back?

MARTINIQUE
Overseas Department of France

OFFICIAL NAME: Département de la Martinique
(Department of Martinique)
LOCATION: Caribbean Sea
AREA: 425 sq. mi. (1,100 sq. km)
POPULATION (Est. 1993): 387,656
CAPITAL/LARGEST CITY: Fort-de-France
GOVERNMENT: Overseas department of France with a regional council responsible for economic and social planning.
FLAG: Uses the flag of France.
ETHNIC GROUPS: Black, Black-European-Indian mix, European (mainly French), East Indian, Lebanese, Chinese
LANGUAGES: French, Creole patois
RELIGIONS: Roman Catholic, Hinduism, Traditional African Religions
BASIC MONETARY UNIT: French Franc

GEOGRAPHY

Martinique is an oval-shaped island that measures about 50 mi. (80 km) from north to south and about 22 mi. (35 km) from east to west at its greatest distances. It has 180 mi. (290 km) of coastline along the Caribbean Sea.

Martinique consists mainly of mountains and volcanic rock with so many indented areas that no point on the island is over 7 mi. (11 km) away from the sea. The only flat land, besides the narrow coastal plains, is the Lamentin Plain (Lézarde River basin) in the central southwest. About one-fourth of the island's area is covered by both European and tropical forests.

CLIMATE

Martinique has a sunny, tropical climate. The average annual temperature is 79°F (26°C). The island's rainy season usually lasts from June to October, and the average annual rainfall ranges from 160-200 in. (400-500 cm) in the mountainous north to less than 40 in. (100 cm) in the south. Martinique experiences floods, hurricanes, and volcanic activity, and between the three, averages one national disaster every five years.

ECONOMY

Martinique's economy is based mainly on agriculture and tourism.

Agriculture - avocados, bananas, cotton, flowers, pineapples, sugar cane, tobacco, and vegetables

Manufacturing - cement, construction, petroleum refining, rum distilling, and sugar

Exports - bananas, pineapples, refined petroleum products, and rum

Imports - clothing, construction materials, crude oil, food, petroleum products, and vehicles

LIFE-STYLE

Staples of the diet include those foods grown on the island, various fish and prawns caught in the Caribbean Sea, and the grains, meats, and vegetables that have been imported.

The island's major event is the carnival of Fort-de-France.

IT'S A FACT!

Fort-de-France - founded in 1675, is Martinique's central port and financial center. It became the island's capital in 1692 and was known as Fort Royal until the late 1700s.

Mont Pelée - the island's highest point and an active volcano, rises 4,583 ft. (1,397 m) above sea level.

 DID YOU KNOW...

• When Mont Pelée erupted in 1902, its gaseous clouds and lava avalanche killed all but one of Saint-Pierre's residents, who was in the city's dungeon?
• Fort-de-France was partially destroyed by an earthquake in 1839 and a fire in 1890?
• Martinique was reached by Christopher Columbus in 1502 while on his fourth voyage, and began being colonized by the French in 1635?
• The French government maintains a volcano observatory on Mont Pelée?

MAURITANIA

OFFICIAL NAME: République Islamique de Mauritanie (Islamic Republic of Mauritania)
LOCATION: Northwestern Africa
AREA: 397,956 sq. mi. (1,030,700 sq. km)
POPULATION (Est. 1993): 2,194,000
CAPITAL: Nouakchott
LARGEST CITIES: Nouakchott, Nouadhibou
GOVERNMENT: Islamic republic.
FLAG: A five-pointed, yellow star above a yellow crescent, both of which are centered on a green field.
ETHNIC GROUPS: Moors, Black Africans
LANGUAGES: Arabic, French
RELIGION: Islam
BASIC MONETARY UNIT: Ouguiya

GEOGRAPHY

At its greatest distances, Mauritania measures 800 mi. (1,287 km) from east to west and 780 mi. (1,255 km) from east to west. It has 414 mi. (666 km) of coastline along the Atlantic Ocean.

Mauritania stretches east from the Atlantic into the Sahara Desert. Because the ocean and the desert meet in Mauritania, the country is sometimes referred to as the *Atlantic Sahara*. The northern two-thirds of the country is covered by the Sahara. A narrow plain lies along the Sénégal River in the southern one-third. Savanna covers the southeast.

CLIMATE

Mauritania's climate is hot, but there is a vast difference between daytime and nighttime temperatures. Between November and March, desert temperatures range from freezing to over 100°F (38°C). Between April and October, the daily temperature ranges from 60° to 120°F (16° to 49°C). Temperature variances are not as great in the country's southern portion.

The northern two-thirds of the country receives little, if any, rainfall. The southern one-third receives more than 20 in. (51 cm) of rainfall annually. Hot, sandy sirocco winds blow in March and April.

ECONOMY

Mauritania's economic base is agriculture.
Agriculture - corn, dates, livestock, millet, and rice
Fishing - ocean and freshwater fish
Mining - iron ore
Exports - fish products, gum arabic, and iron ore
Imports - consumer goods, foodstuffs, machinery and equipment, and petroleum products

LIFE-STYLE

Mauritania has two major ethnic groups: the Moors, who inhabit the desert and semidesert regions of the north; and the black Africans, who live primarily in the south. Each has its own distinct customs and traditions. The one common bond is their Muslim religion.

Moors are herdsmen who drive their herds of camels, goats, or sheep from water point to water point in the desert regions. They set up camel's hair tents at night. Hospitality is an important tradition among the Moors because they understand the needs of someone who is constantly moving from place to place. Therefore, most chance meetings in the desert involve an invitation to a meal. The most popular dish is *meshwi* (barbecued lamb, goat, or antelope). Traditional meals begin and end by drinking three short glasses of tea.

To survive harsh desert life, the Moors have developed a keen sense of direction and fantastic eyesight. Many can also tell location by sniffing the air.

A tradition of oral history relates to the Moors' highly developed memory. They are often able to recite the family histories of all the Moorish tribes. Because the Moors prefer desert living, those who live in cities still set up their tents in the town.

Mauritania's black Africans belong to three groups: the Fulani, the Tukulor, and the Sarakole. The Fulani are cowherders who drive their herds from place to place in the savanna. Their homes are temporary beehive huts called *ruga*. Their diet consists of milk, milk products, and millet. Cows are rarely slaughtered, so black Africans eat very little meat.

The Tukulor are the most numerous group. They live primarily by farming or fishing. Because they believe in large extended families, they live in large family compounds, with each household having its own separate dwelling.

The Sarakole may have once been a ruling class and the first inhabitants of Mauritania. Their life-style is similar to that of the Tukulor.

Black Africans were the first to obtain a modern education, thus allowing them to obtain jobs in government or as teachers. Very few children attend school in Mauritania and the literacy rate is below 20 percent. To combat the problem of children living on the move, portable classrooms have been devised that can be packed up to follow herders.

IT'S A FACT!

Kediet Ijill- the country's highest point, rises 3,002 ft. (915 m) above sea level.

 DID YOU KNOW...
- Like their ancestors, desert residents wear turbans and long flowing robes as protection from the sun and heat?
- Less than one-fifth of the country's roads are paved?
- During the Stone Age, well-watered fields covered the land in Mauritania that is now desert?
- Mauritania has rich offshore fishing grounds?

MAURITIUS

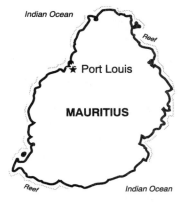

Indian Ocean

Reef

★ Port Louis

MAURITIUS

Reef

Indian Ocean

OFFICIAL NAME: Republic of Mauritius
LOCATION: Indian Ocean
AREA: 788 sq. mi. (2,040 sq. km)
POPULATION (Est. 1993): 1,120,000
CAPITAL/LARGEST CITY: Port Louis
GOVERNMENT: Constitutional monarchy.
FLAG: Four horizontal stripes of red, blue, yellow, and green representing the struggle for freedom, the Indian Ocean, the light of independence, and agriculture, accordingly.
ETHNIC GROUPS: Indo-Mauritian, Creole
LANGUAGES: English, French, Creole
RELIGIONS: Hinduism, Christianity, Islam
BASIC MONETARY UNIT: Mauritian Rupee

GEOGRAPHY

Mauritius is a mountainous island nation in the Indian Ocean. The country consists of the main island of Mauritius, and several smaller uninhabited islands. Its chief island, Mauritius, is located approximately 500 mi. (800 km) east of Madagascar and about 2,450 mi. (3,943 km) southwest of India.

Mauritius was formed by volcanoes that covered the land with rocks and a layer of lava. A plateau, rising 2,200 ft. (671 m) above sea level, covers the center of the island. Mauritius is almost surrounded by coral reefs. Beaches and crystal-clear water provide tourists with a tropical paradise.

CLIMATE

Mauritius has a tropical climate. Winters—June to October—are warm and dry; summers—November to April—are hot, wet, and humid. The average temperature ranges from about 72°F (22°C) in the winter to about 79°F (26°C) in the summer. The plateau region receives as much as 200 in. (510 cm) of rain per year. In the southwestern part of the island, an average of only 35 in. (89 cm) of rain falls each year. The country is subject to cyclones during the winter months.

ECONOMY

The country has been dominated by the sugar cane industry since the 19th century.
Agriculture - sugar cane, tea, and tobacco
Industry - clothing, food processing, textiles, and tourism
Exports - sugar cane and sugar products, tea, and textiles
Imports - foodstuffs, chemicals, and manufactured goods

LIFE-STYLE

Mauritians are descendents of Asian Indians, Chinese, Africans, and French Europeans. While most Europeans live in towns, the rest of the population is divided between villages and other rural areas. The houses in the villages are constructed of concrete or wood, with corrugated iron roofs.

Because the economy depends so heavily on sugar cane, about one-third of the workers are involved in the industry, either as growers, harvesters, or processors. Some farms in the wet uplands grow tea, much of which is exported.

Most Mauritian men wear Western-style clothing, while Mauritian women prefer the traditional *sari*, a type of wraparound dress with one end draped over the shoulder. Rural Mauritian men wear a *langouti*, a wraparound garment that extends to the feet and ties at the waist.

Although people grow some vegetables and raise some livestock, most foodstuffs are imported. French ancestry resulted in French bread being a popular food item. The religious preferences of the Hindus and Muslims dictate much vegetarian cooking. As in many regions of the world, rice is a staple food item. Tea with milk and sugar is a popular beverage.

The government provides free primary and secondary education, but school attendance is not mandatory.

Soccer is the most popular participation sport and horse racing is the most popular spectator sport. The most important leisure activities are movies, and visiting friends and family. On the coast, many people engage in swimming and water sports.

DID YOU KNOW...

• Married Indian women wear a red *tika*, made from vermilion powder, on their forehead as a sign that their husbands are alive?
• Almost all Mauritians speak two or more languages?
• There are numerous examples of Hindu temples, Christian churches, Muslim mosques, and Buddhist pagodas throughout Mauritius?

MEXICO

OFFICIAL NAME: Estados Unidos Mexicanos (United Mexican States)
LOCATION: Northern Central America
AREA: 756,067 sq. mi. (1,958,201 sq. km)
POPULATION (Est. 1993): 94,545,000
CAPITAL: Mexico City
LARGEST CITIES: Mexico City, Guadalajara, Monterrey, Netzahualcóyotl
GOVERNMENT: Presidential democracy.
FLAG: Three vertical stripes of green, white, and red representing independence, religion, and union, accordingly. The coat of arms —which features an eagle perched on a cactus with a snake in its beak—is centered on the white stripe.
ETHNIC GROUPS: Mestizo, American Indian, Caucasian
LANGUAGES: Spanish, Indian (Maya, Mixtec, others)
RELIGION: Roman Catholic
BASIC MONETARY UNIT: New Peso

GEOGRAPHY

Mexico measures 1,250 mi. (2,012 km) from north to south and 1,900 mi. (3,060 km) from east to west at its greatest distances. It has 6,320 mi. (10,170 km) of coastline on the Gulf of Mexico, the Gulf of California, and the North Pacific Ocean.

The Rio Grande forms about 1,300 m (2,090 km) of the border between the United States and Mexico. Mexico has a wide variety of landscapes and climates in proximity. However, over two-thirds of the country is covered by high mountains and high, rolling plateaus. It contains six major land regions: 1) Pacific Northwest, 2) Plateau of Mexico, 3) Gulf Coastal Plain, 4) Southern Uplands, 5) Chiapas Highlands, and 6) Yucatán Peninsula.

The Pacific Northwest land region includes the Peninsula of California, which is mainly rolling or mountainous desert, and the mainland northwestern coastal strip, which holds some of Mexico's richest farmland. The largest region, the Plateau of Mexico, has a wide variety of land features, such as mountains, deserts, and rich farm land. The Gulf Coastal Plain consists mainly of thick masses of low trees and bushes. The Balsas River cuts through the mountains in the Southern Uplands on its way to the Pacific Ocean. Broad river valleys in the Chiapas Highlands are used to grow coffee, fruits, and a variety of other crops. The Yucatán Peninsula is primarily limestone. Rainforests cover the southern part of the peninsula.

CLIMATE

Mexico's climate varies greatly by region. This is particularly true in tropical Mexico, which is located south of the Tropic of Cancer. There are three temperature regions in the south: 1) *tierra caliente* (hot land) with long hot summers and mild winters; 2) *tierra templada* (temperate land) with temperatures staying between 50° to 80°F (10° to 27°C); and 3) *tierra fria* (cold land) with the possibility of frost at any time. The highest peaks are always snow-covered.

Northern Mexico is generally dry and consists of deserts and semideserts. Most rainfall occurs in the summer. During the summer, days are hot and nights are cool.

ECONOMY

Prior to the 1940s, Mexico's economy was based on agriculture and mining. Tourism is extremely important to Mexico's economy today, along with manufacturing. Mexico is also the world's primary source of silver.

Agriculture - beef cattle, coffee, corn, milk, and wheat
Fishing - anchovies, oysters, sardines, shrimp, and tuna
Manufacturing - iron and steel, motor vehicles, and processed foods
Mining - iron ore, natural gas, and petroleum
Exports - coffee, motor vehicles and engines, and petroleum
Imports - electrical and electronic equipment, industrial machinery, and motor vehicles and parts

LIFE-STYLE

The majority of Mexicans live in urban areas. Each city, no matter how large, is built around a *plaza* (public square). The plaza is a gathering place for young and old. High-rise buildings fill the city centers and the suburbs have modern houses and apartment buildings. Older sections of cities have rows of Spanish colonial-style homes. Most are made of stone or adobe and have a *patio* (courtyard), which is the center of family life. Houses in poor sections lack electricity and running water and are often made of scraps of wood, metal, and other materials. Population growth is high and air pollution is a problem in Mexico City.

Most rural residents live in villages or farms. Most of the villagers are extremely poor and have little access to health care and education. Most young people leave the villages to find work in the cities. Almost every village has a marketplace (similar to the plaza) where villagers gather weekly to buy, sell, or trade goods and chat with friends. Houses vary according to climate.

Most Mexicans wear Western-style clothing. The traditional Mexican clothing style, typically worn in central and southern Mexico, is easily recognized. Rural men often wear cotton shirts, trousers, *huaraches* (leather sandals), and *sombreros* (wide-brimmed hats). *Ponchos* (blankets with holes cut out for heads) are worn when the weather is rainy or cold.

Ancient Indians of Mexico were the first to cultivate corn. Today, corn is still the primary food of most Mexicans. Corn meal is shaped into *tortillas* (thin, flat bread cooked on an ungreased griddle). A tortilla is eaten plain or as part of the *taco*, *enchilada*, or *tostada*. Most of the people like their food highly seasoned with hot chili peppers. Bland foods, such as bread or rice, accompany spicy foods to relieve the burning sensation. Other popular foods are *frijoles* (refried beans), rice, and *pozole* (vegetable soup with pork). Favorite fruits are avocados, bananas, mangoes, oranges, papayas, and prickly pears. Many Mexicans also enjoy water flavored with fruit juice or cinnamon-flavored hot chocolate.

About 90 percent of all Mexican adults are literate. Children ages six to 14 are required to attend school. About 90 percent begin school but only about half of these finish elementary school.

Fiestas (festivals) are very popular in Mexico when celebrating holidays. Most begin with the firing of rockets, shooting of fireworks, and ringing of bells. Parades, gambling, dancing, and eating are also a big part of fiestas. *Piñatas* are an important part of holiday celebrations for the children. They are filled with candy, toys, and nuts, and hung up high. The children are blindfolded and take turns using a stick to hit the *piñata*. Eventually it breaks and the goodies are free for anyone to take. To celebrate the Christmas holiday, Mexicans act out Mary and Joseph's trip to Bethlehem. This takes place each of the nine nights before Christmas. These nine ceremonies are called *posadas*. Guadalupe Day, December 12, honors Mexico's patron saint, the Virgin of Guadalupe, and is Mexico's most important religious holiday. Other popular holidays are *Cinco de Mayo* on May 5, which observes Mexico's victory over the French in 1867, and All Saints Day, November 1, when the dead are memorialized.

Music and dancing are very prevalent in Mexico. *Mariachi* bands stroll through the streets and restaurants, singing, and playing spectators' requests. The Mexican hat dance is a folk dance performed at many fiestas. The music of a *marimba* (similar to xylophone) is also heard throughout Mexico.

Soccer is the most popular sport, followed closely by baseball. *Jai alai* (a type of handball), basketball, tennis, golf, and volleyball are also enjoyed by many. Watching bullfights is very popular among most Mexicans. Almost all of the large cities have bullrings. On Sundays, the only day off for most Mexicans, many families go to parks for picnics.

The ancient Indians of Mexico are responsible for much of the country's beautiful art. The murals painted by the Mayans and Toltecs in their beautiful temples and the music and poetry of the Aztecs are part of Mexico's history. Ancient Indian ruins are visited by thousands of tourists daily at Chichén Itzá and near Mexico City. The Spaniards' architectural feats and literary works are also important to Mexico's heritage. Diego Rivera, José Orozco, and David Siqueiros are well-known for their paintings on buildings of the 1910 Mexican Revolution.

IT'S A FACT!
Lake Chapala - the country's largest lake, covers 417 sq. mi. (1,080 sq. km).

The National Museum of Anthropology - located in Mexico City, houses priceless displays of Aztec and Mayan art.

Orizaba - the country's highest point, rises 18,701 ft. (5,700 m) above sea level.

The Palacio de Bellas Artes - located in Mexico City, is a beautiful performance and exhibition center known for its architecture and for Diego Rivera's murals which ornament its walls.

DID YOU KNOW...
- Mexico City is built on the site of Tenochtitlan, the ancient Aztec capital?
- Mexico City has the largest bullring in the world, with seats for 55,000 spectators?
- Tortillas are often used like a spoon when eating?
- Mexico's capital, Mexico City, is the world's largest city in terms of population?

MICRONESIA

North Pacific Ocean

MICRONESIA

OFFICIAL NAME: Federated States of Micronesia
LOCATION: North Pacific Ocean
AREA: 271 sq. mi. (702 sq. km)
POPULATION (Est. 1993): 122,000
FEDERATION CAPITAL: Palikir (on Pohnpei Island in the State of Pohnpei)
STATE CAPITALS: Colonio (Yap), Moen (Chuuk), Palikir (Pohnpei), Tofol (Kosrae)
LARGEST CITY: Weno (in the State of Chuuk)
GOVERNMENT: Republic governed by a president. Micronesia is in free association with the United States, which is responsible for Micronesia's defense and internal security.
FLAG: Blue field featuring four white, five-pointed stars arranged in a diamond pattern.
ETHNIC GROUP: Micronesian
LANGUAGE: English
RELIGION: Christianity (Protestant and Roman Catholic)
BASIC MONETARY UNIT: United States Dollar

GEOGRAPHY

Micronesia is located about 3,193 mi. (5,109 km) west-southwest of Hawaii in the North Pacific Ocean. Micronesia consists of four major island states totaling 607 islands, about 100 of which are inhabited. The four states are: Yap, Chuuk (formerly Truk), Pohnpei, and Kosrae.

Micronesia ranges from high, mountainous islands to low-lying atolls with sand covering a coral reef.

CLIMATE

Micronesia has a warm, tropical climate. The average annual temperature is 80°F (27°C). Year-round rainfall is heaviest in the eastern islands. Typhoons are a frequent occurrence, especially on the western islands.

ECONOMY

For most of the islanders, fishing and subsistence farming are the primary economic activities. U.S. financial assistance is the main source of revenue.

Agriculture - black pepper, chickens, coconuts, copra, pigs, sweet potatoes, and tropical fruits and vegetables

Manufacturing - copra, craft items (made from shell, wood, and pearls), and fish processing

Exports - black pepper and copra

Imports - beverages, building materials, food, fuels, and manufactured goods

LIFE-STYLE

Micronesia's population is about 70 percent rural, with rural residents relying on fishing and subsistence farming. Two-thirds of those in the labor force work for the government. Rural shelters have thatched roofs with walls constructed of palm branches or wood from local trees. Urban shelters have metal roofs and are constructed from imported concrete, lumber, and plywood. Land ownership is very important to Micronesians. Property in Micronesia is passed down from generation to generation through the mother. Although some Micronesians live and work as family groups, this traditional way of life is being replaced as residents adopt U.S. customs.

About 30 percent of Micronesia's population resides on Pohnpei Island. Other highly populated islands include Moen Island in the State of Chuuk and Yap Island in the State of Yap.

Staples of the diet include fish and such native foods as breadfruit, coconuts, and yams.

The country's literacy rate is about 90 percent. There is at least one primary school on each inhabited atoll and large island.

DID YOU KNOW...

- New industries in Micronesia are seaweed farming and the processing of sun-dried fish?
- Under the Compact of Free Association between Micronesia and the United States, Micronesia controls domestic and most foreign affairs with the U.S. responsible for defense?
- There is only one telephone for every 61 people in Micronesia?
- Micronesians are often called Carolinians because Micronesia covers almost all of the islands in the Caroline archipelago?

MIDWAY ISLAND
Territory of the United States

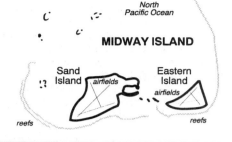

OFFICIAL NAME: Midway Island
LOCATION: Pacific Ocean
AREA: 2 sq. mi. (5 sq. km)
POPULATION (Est. 1993): 453 (U.S. military personnel)
CAPITAL: None; administered from Washington, D.C. (United States)
GOVERNMENT: Dependency of the United States managed by the United States Navy Department.
FLAG: Uses the flag of the United States.
LANGUAGE: English
BASIC MONETARY UNIT: United States Dollar

GEOGRAPHY

Midway Island is located about 1,300 mi. (2,090 km) northwest of Honolulu, Hawaii, in the Pacific Ocean. It is composed of two islands—Eastern and Sand—in an atoll 6 mi. (10 km) in diameter. The islands have a coastline of about 20 mi. (32 km).

CLIMATE

Midway Island has a tropical climate moderated by prevailing easterly winds.

ECONOMY

Midway Island's economy is based on providing support services for U.S. naval operations taking place on the island. Everything, from foodstuffs to manufactured goods, must be imported.

LIFE-STYLE

Midway Island has no indigenous population. All inhabitants are U.S. military personnel.

IT'S A FACT!

National Wildlife Preserve - established to protect the bird life found in abundance on the islands.

 DID YOU KNOW...
- The United States discovered Midway Island in 1859, and annexed it in 1867?
- The Battle of Midway was the first decisive U.S. Naval victory over the Japanese in World War II?

MOLDOVA

OFFICIAL NAME: Republica Moldova (Republic of Moldova)
FORMERLY: Soviet Socialist Republic of Moldova; Moldavia
LOCATION: South-central Europe
AREA: 13,012 sq. mi. (33,700 sq. km)
POPULATION (Est. 1995): 4,350,000
CAPITAL/LARGEST CITY: Chisinau (Kishinev)
GOVERNMENT: Republic with duties divided among a president, a parliament, and a council of ministers.
FLAG: Three vertical stripes of blue, yellow, and red. A Roman eagle emblem is centered on the yellow stripe.
ETHNIC GROUPS: Moldovan, Russian, Ukrainian
LANGUAGES: Romanian, Ukrainian, Russian
RELIGION: Christianity (Eastern Orthodox)
BASIC MONETARY UNIT: Leu

GEOGRAPHY

At its greatest distances, Moldova, a landlocked country, measures 210 mi. (340 km) from north to south and 165 mi. (265 km) from east to west.

Most of the country consists of low-lying hills broken by river valleys and steep, forested slopes. In the north and east are lush uplands and steppes. A large plain covers the south. Three-fourth of the area is covered with a rich, black soil, thus contributing to the mostly agricultural economy.

CLIMATE

The climate is moderately continental with cold winters and mild summers. The average temperature ranges from 25°F (-4°C) in January to 70°F (21°C) in July. Average annual precipitation is about 20 in. (50 cm).

ECONOMY

Moldova has a developing economy based primarily on agriculture.

Agriculture - eggs, grain, grapes, livestock, milk, and sugar beets

Manufacturing - construction materials, refrigerators, tractors, and washing machines

Exports - clothing, leather and fur, machinery, tobacco, and wine

Imports - automobiles, electronics items, and fuel

LIFE-STYLE

More than half of the Moldavian people live clustered in rural villages and work as farmers. About 47 percent of the people live in urban areas.

Children ages six to 18 are required to attend school. Almost every Moldovan over 15 years of age can read and write. Despite the repression during the Soviet era, gains were made in education, especially in technical fields.

Folk dancing and music are very popular in the country. Several orchestras and groups, such as the Doina Choir and the Zhok Folk Dance, have become internationally famous. Western music is very popular with young people.

IT'S A FACT!

Bendery - a city founded in the 15th century by Genoese traders, is currently an industrial center.

Mount Balaneshty - the country's highest point, is located in the Kodry Hills and rises 1,407 ft. (429 m) above sea level.

DID YOU KNOW...

• Moldova has over 3,000 rivers?

• Moldova is the most densely populated of the former Soviet republics, with 343 persons per sq. mi. (132 per sq. km)?

• Animals found in Moldova include wolves, badgers, wild boars, and Siberian stags?

• In Moldova, hares, muskrats, and foxes are hunted for their fur?

• One Moldovan orchestra, called Fluierash, uses rare ancient instruments, including a type of bagpipe and an ancient clarinet?

• As a member of the former U.S.S.R., Moldova was the leading food-processing republic?

• More than half of the buildings in the capital city were destroyed in World War II?

MONACO

OFFICIAL NAME: Principauté de Monaco (Principality of Monaco)
LOCATION: Western Europe
AREA: 0.58 sq. mi. (1.49 sq. km)
POPULATION (Est. 1993): 29,000
CAPITAL: Monaco
LARGEST CITIES: Monaco, Monte Carlo
GOVERNMENT: Principality headed by a prince.
FLAG: Two horizontal stripes of red and white.
ETHNIC GROUPS: French, Monégasque
LANGUAGES: French, Monégasque
RELIGION: Roman Catholic
BASIC MONETARY UNIT: French Franc

GEOGRAPHY

Monaco is one of the world's smallest independent countries. It lies at the foot of Mt. Agel on the southern edge of France. It has 2.55 mi. (4.1 km) of coastline along the French Riviera, which borders the Mediterranean Sea.

Monaco has a rugged, hilly terrain. It has four main sections: three towns—La Condamine, Monaco, and Monte Carlo—and one industrial center—Fontvieille.

CLIMATE

Monaco's climate includes mild, wet winters and hot, dry summers. Its average temperature ranges from 50°F (10°C) in January to 90°F (32°C) in the summer. The country averages about 62 rainy days per year, with an average annual rainfall of 30 in. (76 cm).

ECONOMY

The people of Monaco have a high standard of living. Monaco's economy is based mainly on commerce, manufacturing, and tourism. Its postage stamps—which are popular with collectors—serve as one of Monaco's income sources.

Manufacturing - beer, candy, chemicals, cosmetics, dairy products, glass, pharmaceuticals, precision instruments, and processed foods

Exports - olive oil, oranges, and perfumes

LIFE-STYLE

Monaco's population is entirely urban.

Primary schools are run by Monaco's churches. A high school and a music academy provide further education.

Popular attractions in Monaco include the Princess Caroline Library (which specializes in children's literature), the Oceanographic Museum, botanical gardens, and a museum where artifacts from prehistoric times are preserved. The Grand Theater of Monte Carlo features performances by world-famous ballet dancers and singers. The country also is renowned for such races as the Monaco Grand Prix and the Monte Carlo Rally.

IT'S A FACT!

Oceanographic Museum - founded by Prince Albert, who was known as the "Scientist Prince," features a lab for marine research, a collection of rare exhibits, and one of the world's leading aquariums.

 DID YOU KNOW...

- Monte Carlo has been a famous gambling center since the mid-1800s?
- Local citizens are forbidden to gamble at any of the country's gambling facilities?
- Part of the castle that Monaco's prince lives in was built in the 1200s?
- Under the terms of a treaty signed with France in 1918, Monaco's principality will come under French rule if no male heirs are produced?
- Many wealthy residents of foreign countries make their home in Monaco because the principality has no income tax, though since 1963 most French residents living in Monaco have had to pay income tax at French rates?

MONGOLIA

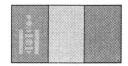

OFFICIAL NAME: Mongolia
LOCATION: East-central Asia
AREA: 604,829 sq. mi. (1,566,500 sq. km)
POPULATION (Est. 1995): 2,498,000
CAPITAL: Ulan Bator (Ulaanbaatar)
LARGEST CITIES: Ulan Bator, Darhan
GOVERNMENT: Republic governed by a president.
FLAG: Three vertical stripes of red, blue, and red with the national emblem in gold—called a *soyombo*—centered on the red, hoist-side stripe. The soyombo represents fire, sun, moon, earth, water, and the yin-yang symbol.
ETHNIC GROUP: Mongol
LANGUAGE: Mongolian
RELIGION: Buddhism
BASIC MONETARY UNIT: Tughrik

GEOGRAPHY

Mongolia is a landlocked country located in east-central Asia between China and Russia. All of the land in Mongolia rises at least 1,700 ft. (518 m) above sea level. Much of the land in the northwest is covered by plateaus and mountains. The barren Gobi Desert covers much of the southeastern region. Mongolia measures 790 mi. (1,271 km) from north to south and 1,500 mi. (2,414 km) from east to west at its greatest distances.

CLIMATE

Mongolia's climate is continental with long winters and short summers. In the capital city, extreme temperatures of -57° to 96°F (-49° to 36°C) have been recorded. Snow and rain usually amount to less than 15 in. (37 cm) annually. Earthquakes sometimes strike the country.

ECONOMY

Raising livestock is the backbone of the economy. Industry is gaining in importance.

Agriculture - camels, cattle, goats, grain, horses, meat, milk, potatoes, sheep, and vegetables

Manufacturing - building materials, felt, processed foods, soap, and textiles

Mining - coal, copper, gold, iron, and petroleum

Exports - cattle, dairy products, furs, hides, meat, and wool

Imports - building materials, chemicals, food products, fuels, industrial consumer goods, machinery and equipment, sugar, and tea

LIFE-STYLE

Most Mongolians live in nuclear families. Older parents usually live with the family of their youngest child. The youngest son inherits the family home and the remainder of the herd—after older sons have received equal shares.

Some people (particularly nomads) live in a circular tent called a *ger* or *yurt*. The average size is 18 ft. (5.5 m) in diameter. A wooden framework is covered with layers of wool felt and a white cloth. These dwellings are easy to put up and take down.

Approximately half of all Mongolians live and work on cooperative livestock farms set up by the government. The farms are like large ranches with small towns in the middle. The buildings in the center consist of homes, shops, offices, and medical posts for animals and for people. Few Mongolians still follow the traditional nomadic life-style.

The Mongolian diet includes dairy products, meat (mutton and beef), millet, barley, and wheat, and available vegetables, such as potatoes, cabbage, carrots, onions, and garlic. Boiled mutton and *buuz* (a dumpling stuffed with diced meat, onion, cabbage, garlic, salt, and pepper) are favorite meals.

Mongol wrestling, horse racing, and archery are the favorite sports, followed by boxing, soccer, volleyball, and table tennis.

Mongolia has a literacy rate of about 90 percent. Beginning at age seven, education is free and compulsory for eight years. Two additional years of school may be spent in general education or vocational training.

IT'S A FACT!

Altai Mountains - located in western Mongolia, rise over 14,000 ft. (4,270 m) above sea level.

Uvs Lake - Mongolia's largest lake, covers 1,300 sq. mi. (3,370 sq. km).

 DID YOU KNOW...

- In the 1200s, under Genghis Khan and Kublai Khan, the Mongols built the largest land empire in history?
- Some wandering nomads still exist on the plains?
- The whole country gets involved in annual wrestling championships?
- In the summer, *airag* (fermented mare's milk) is sometimes served to guests?
- On very special occasions, a younger person gives *khadag* (a blue silk band) and a silver bowl full of airag to an older person?

MONTSERRAT
Dependent Territory of the United Kingdom

Caribbean Sea

MONTSERRAT

★ Plymouth

OFFICIAL NAME: Montserrat
LOCATION: West Indies
AREA: 38 sq. mi. (98 sq. km)
POPULATION (Est. 1993): 11,900
CAPITAL/LARGEST CITY: Plymouth
GOVERNMENT: Dependent territory of the United Kingdom.
FLAG: Blue field with the United Kingdom's flag in the upper, hoist-side quadrant. The Montserratian coat of arms is centered on the flag's outer half. The coat of arms features a woman standing next to a yellow harp with her arm around a black cross.
ETHNIC GROUPS: Black African, White European
LANGUAGE: English
RELIGION: Christianity
BASIC MONETARY UNIT: East Caribbean Dollar

GEOGRAPHY

Montserrat is one of the Leeward Islands in the West Indies. It is located about 250 mi. (402 km) southeast of Puerto Rico, and has about 25 mi. (40 km) of coastline along the Caribbean Sea. The heavily forested country is composed of three groups of mountains. There are a number of streams and waterfalls which cut through the land. Montserrat has seven active volcanoes.

CLIMATE

Montserrat has a warm, tropical climate with very little seasonal change in temperature or rainfall. The average annual temperature ranges from 70° to 86°F (21° to 30°C). The average annual rainfall is 57 in. (145 cm). June to November is not only the warmest period, but also the season for hurricanes.

ECONOMY

Tourism has overtaken agriculture as Montserrat's economic base.

Agriculture - carrots, hot peppers, limes, sea-island cotton, onions, potatoes, and tomatoes

Manufacturing - light manufacturing (including electronic appliances, rum, and textiles)

Exports - apparel, cattle, cotton, electronic parts, lint, live plants, mangoes, plastic bags, potatoes, processed products (such as canned pineapples and preserved peppers), recapped tires, and tomatoes

Imports - foodstuffs, fuels, lubricants, machinery and transportation equipment, and manufactured goods

LIFE-STYLE

Education is free, and children are required to attend school until the age of 14.

IT'S A FACT!

Chances Peak - the country's highest point, rises 3,002 ft. (915 m) above sea level.

 DID YOU KNOW...
- Great Britain has controlled Montserrat since 1783?
- Christopher Columbus landed on the island now known as Montserrat while on his second voyage to the New World; he named it after a mountain in Spain?
- Irish settlers came to Montserrat in 1632, and many Montserratians still speak with a *brogue* (Irish accent)?
- Hurricane Hugo struck the island in 1989, causing much damage to the island and killing 10 people?

MOROCCO

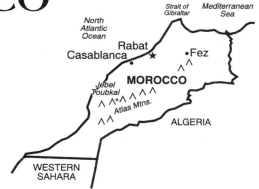

OFFICIAL NAME: al-Mamlaka al-Maghrebia (Kingdom of Morocco)
LOCATION: Northwestern Africa
AREA: 172,414 sq. mi. (446,500 sq. km)
POPULATION (Est. 1993): 27,051,000
CAPITAL: Rabat
LARGEST CITIES: Casablanca, Rabat, Fez
GOVERNMENT: Constitutional monarchy headed by a king.
FLAG: Red field with a green star in the center.
ETHNIC GROUP: Arab-Berber
LANGUAGES: Arabic, Berber
RELIGION: Islam
BASIC MONETARY UNIT: Moroccan Dirham

GEOGRAPHY

Morocco measures 565 mi. (910 km) from north to south and 730 mi. (1,170 km) from east to west at its greatest distances. It has 1,140 mi. (1,835 km) of coastline along the North Atlantic Ocean and the Mediterranean Sea.

Morocco has three main land regions: 1) the Coastal Lowlands, 2) the Atlas Mountain Chain, and 3) the Sahara. Fertile plains are found in the Coastal Lowlands. The Atlas Mountain Chain crosses the middle of Morocco from southwest to northeast. East and south of the mountains lies the barren, sun-baked Sahara.

CLIMATE

Most of the country has two seasons: rainy and dry. The coastal north and west have mild winters and hot, dry summers. In the mountains, winters are colder and wetter. Annual rainfall averages 9 in. (23 cm) in the mountains and 21 in. (53 cm) on the Atlantic coast. January temperatures average 63° to 66°F (19°C). June temperatures average 77° to 91°F (25° to 33°C).

ECONOMY

Morocco's economy is based mainly on agriculture and mining.

Agriculture - barley, citrus fruits, corn, potatoes, sugar beets, tomatoes, and wheat

Fishing - anchovies, mackerel, sardines, and tuna

Manufacturing - cement, chemicals, fertilizers, leather goods, petroleum products, processed foods, and textiles

Mining - phosphate rock

Exports - clothing, fish, fruits, leather goods, phosphate rock, phosphate products, rugs, and vegetables

Imports - consumer goods, food, industrial equipment, and oil

LIFE-STYLE

The most important element in Moroccan social life is the extended family. Normally, the household includes two parents, unmarried children, and married sons with their families. When the father dies, married sons establish their own households. In crowded urban areas, sons sometimes leave home before the father dies. Polygamy is legal in Morocco, but is rarely practiced.

Farming is the main occupation. Just over half the people live in rural areas. Many rural Moroccans in the south live in houses of dried mud bricks. In other rural areas, homes are built of stone and wood. Many homes consist of one large room that serves as kitchen, living room, sleeping quarters, and barn. Some Moroccans in desert areas are nomadic and live in tents. Urban dwellers often live in small attached homes. The wealthy live in modern apartment buildings or spacious homes while the poor live in sprawling slums called *bidonvilles* (tin can towns) on the outskirts of large cities.

Staples of the diet include foods made of barley and wheat. *Couscous* (steamed wheat served with vegetables, fish or meat, and a souplike sauce) is the national dish. Popular dishes include lemon chicken and *tajine* (a meat stew with vegetables). A pastry made with honey and almonds is a favorite of the people. The national drink is mint tea. Moroccans eat with their fingers from a large communal dish.

People in Morocco wear traditional clothing, though city dwellers often combine traditional with Western-style clothing. Men wear a *jellaba*, a loose-fitting hooded robe with long, full sleeves, outdoors. Rural men wear a similar, but heavier garment called a *burnoose*. Men usually wear a turban or brimless cap. A *fez*, which is a red flat-topped cap, is worn only on formal occasions.

Women also wear a jellaba as an outer garment. For social occasions and at home, women wear a long, beautiful *caftan* or robe. Some Islamic women still cover their face with a veil.

Elementary and secondary school is free. School is compulsory for children ages seven to 13, but less than 70 percent attend. Only about 50 percent of adult Moroccans are literate.

Soccer and basketball are the most popular spectator sports. Visiting family and gathering at cafes (the latter of which is done only by men) are important leisure activities.

IT'S A FACT!

Jebel Toubkal - the country's highest point, rises 13,665 ft. (4,165 m) above sea level.

Strait of Gibraltar - separates Morocco from Spain.

 DID YOU KNOW...

- The city of Casablanca provided the title and setting for the classic movie *Casablanca*, starring Humphrey Bogart and Ingrid Bergman?
- Farming communities existed in the Moroccan area about 8,000 years ago?

MOZAMBIQUE

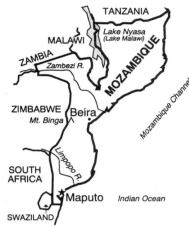

OFFICIAL NAME: República Popular de Moçambique (Republic of Mozambique)
LOCATION: Southeast Africa
AREA: 309,496 sq. mi. (801,590 sq. km)
POPULATION (Est. 1993): 16,934,000
CAPITAL: Maputo
IMPORTANT SEAPORTS: Maputo, Beira
GOVERNMENT: Republic headed by a president.
FLAG: Three horizontal stripes of green, black, and yellow separated by bands of white. A red isosceles triangle is based on the hoist-side and features a five-point, yellow star and a book with a hoe and a rifle crossed over it.
ETHNIC GROUPS: Black, Arab, European, Pakistani
LANGUAGES: Bantu, Portuguese, English
RELIGIONS: Traditional African Religions (mainly Animism), Christianity (mainly Roman Catholic), Islam
BASIC MONETARY UNIT: Metical

GEOGRAPHY

At its greatest distances, Mozambique measures 1,100 mi. (1,770 km) from north to south and 680 mi. (1,094 km) from east to west. It has 1,556 mi. (2,504 km) of coastline along the Mozambique Channel and the Indian Ocean.

Mozambique's coastline is made up of sand dunes and swamps. Extending westward from the coast is a flat plain, which makes up about half of Mozambique's area. Much of the country is covered with grasslands and tropical forests. High plateaus and mountains line the country's western border. Many large rivers run through Mozambique to the Indian Ocean, and the basins of these rivers contain very fertile soil.

CLIMATE

Mozambique's climate is basically tropical, but temperature and rainfall vary from region to region. Southern parts of the country suffer from severe droughts and flooding.

The average annual temperature ranges from 80°F (27°C) in January to 68°F (20°C) in July. The average rainfall is about 16-48 in. (41-122 cm) per year. The majority of the rain falls from November to March.

ECONOMY

Mozambique's economy is based mainly on agriculture, but it is not well-developed. The country is one of the leading cashew producers. Part of Mozambique's economy depends on payments from other countries for the use of its railroads and port facilities.

Agriculture - cashews, cassava, coconuts, corn, cotton, rice, sugar cane, tea, and tropical fruits
Fishing - shrimp
Manufacturing - beverages, chemicals (including fertilizers, paints, and soaps), nonmetallic mineral products (including asbestos, cement, and glass), oil refining, petroleum products, processed foods, textiles, and tobacco
Mining - coal
Exports - cashews, copra, shrimp, sugar, and tropical fruits
Imports - clothing, farm equipment, food, and petroleum

LIFE-STYLE

Mozambique's population is approximately three-fourths rural and one-fourth urban. Mozambicans are mainly farmers who use such simple farming methods as "slash-and-burn," in which an area is cleared for planting by cutting and burning. There are some farmers who use modern farming methods. Most urban centers are located near the coast. Many Mozambicans work in South Africa.

Only about 15 percent of the population over the age of 15 can read and write. The government is trying to improve education.

Most Mozambican roads are unpaved, but there are several railroads which link the country's ports to other African countries.

IT'S A FACT!

Mount Binga - the country's highest point, rises 7,992 ft. (2,436 m) above sea level.

Nossa Senhora da Conceição - fortress built in 1871, is one of Mozambique's most renowned landmarks.

 DID YOU KNOW...
- Mozambique was governed by Portugal from the early 1500s until 1975, when after a ten-year struggle it gained its independence?
- Maputo, Mozambique's capital, was founded by the Portuguese in 1780 and was originally known as *Lourenço Marques*, a name which was changed in 1976?

IF8201 Comprehensive World Reference Guide

MYANMAR
(Burma)

OFFICIAL NAME: Pyidaungzu Myanma Naingngandaw (Union of Myanmar)
FORMERLY: Burma
LOCATION: Southeast Asia
AREA: 261,288 sq. mi. (676,578 sq. km)
POPULATION (Est. 1993): 44,343,000
CAPITAL: Yangon (Rangoon)
LARGEST CITIES: Yangon (Rangoon), Mandalay
GOVERNMENT: Military council or military regime.
FLAG: Adopted in 1974. Red field with a blue rectangle in the upper hoist-side corner. The rectangle features 14 five-point, white stars encircling a cogwheel and rice plant.
ETHNIC GROUP: Burman
LANGUAGE: Burmese
RELIGION: Buddhism
BASIC MONETARY UNIT: Kyat

GEOGRAPHY

Myanmar is the largest country in mainland Southeast Asia. At its greatest distances, Myanmar measures 1,300 mi. (2,090 km) from north to south and 580 mi. (930 km) from east to west. It has 1,650 mi. (2,655 km) of coastline along the Bay of Bengal and the Andaman Sea.

Mountains form Myanmar's borders on the north, east, and west. These are the: 1) Eastern Mountain System, 2) Western Mountain Belt, and 3) Central Belt.

CLIMATE

With its proximity to the equator, Myanmar has a tropical monsoon climate. Temperatures average about 80°F (27°C) in the south and are slightly cooler in the north. Between March and May, temperatures may rise above 100°F (38°C). The average rainfall ranges from about 200 in. (500 cm) on the coast to about 30 in. (77 cm) in the central region. Myanmar is subject to cyclones, earthquakes, flooding, and landslides.

ECONOMY

Agriculture and forestry are the mainstays of Myanmar's economy. For example, rice and teakwood account for two-thirds of the country's exports.

Agriculture - corn, cotton, fruit, jute, millet, rice, rubber, sesame seeds, sugar cane, tobacco, vegetables, and wheat
Manufacturing - fertilizer, and processed foods
Mining - coal, jade, lead, natural gas, petroleum, rubies, sapphires, silver, tin, tungsten, and zinc
Exports - cement, minerals, rice, rubber, silver, and teakwood
Imports - iron and steel, machinery and transport equipment, paper, peanut oil, pharmaceuticals, and textiles

LIFE-STYLE

About three-fourths of the Burmese live in rural villages, primarily in the river valleys and delta floodplains of lower Myanmar. Burmese houses are constructed of bamboo with thatched roofs and are built on stilts as protection against floods and wild animals. Most villages have a Buddhist monastery which serves as a center for both social and religious activities. City dwellers live in small brick or concrete buildings and participate in more leisure and cultural activities than their country counterparts. Life moves at a quicker pace in cities.

Both men and women wear a long, tightly wrapped skirt called *longyis*. With the longyi, men wear a shirt and women wear a thin blouse.

Burmese women have more rights than women in a number of other Asian nations. They keep their names after marriage and share property ownership with their husbands. Women own or manage nearly all the bazaar stalls and shops in the local markets.

Rice is the staple of the diet. It is often flavored with chili peppers. Chicken, fish, shrimp, and vegetables are also popular. Red meats are rarely eaten. Favorite fruits are bananas, citrus fruits, and Southeast Asian fruits called *durians*.

Popular spectator sports are soccer and a type of boxing which allows hitting with any part of the body. A popular participant sport is *chinlon*, in which a ball of woven cane is passed from player to player by hitting it with the feet, knees, or head.

Although school is compulsory for only four years, education is valued highly and more than two-thirds of the population can read and write.

IT'S A FACT!

Hkakabo Razi - the country's highest point, rises 19,296 ft. (5,881 m) above sea level.

Shwe Dagon Pagoda - located in Yangon, is a famous golden-domed Buddhist shrine which rises 326 ft. (99 m) above a marble platform.

 DID YOU KNOW...

- Every five days, the Burmese gather in boats on Inle Lake for a "floating market"?
- The name *Myanmar* means "swift and strong"?
- During a Buddhist adulthood ceremony, the heads of boys are shaved as a symbol of their temporary rejection of the world?
- An oxcart is a common mode of transportation in Myanmar's rural areas?
- Elephants are used by the lumber industry to help move around heavy beams of teakwood?
- Myanmar is the world's largest illicit producer of opium poppy?

NAMIBIA

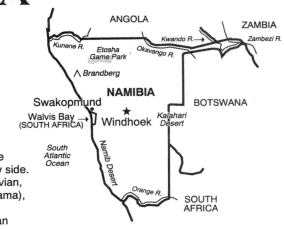

OFFICIAL NAME: Republic of Namibia
FORMERLY: South West Africa
LOCATION: Southwestern Africa
AREA: 317,827 sq. mi. (823,168 sq. km)
POPULATION (Est. 1992): 1,994,000
CAPITAL/LARGEST CITY: Windhoek
GOVERNMENT: Republic headed by a president.
FLAG: Features a blue triangle on the upper hoist side with a yellow sunburst, a red diagonal stripe bordered in white across the middle, and a green triangle on the lower fly side.
ETHNIC GROUPS: Black (including Ovambo or Owambo, Kavango, Caprivian, Damara, Herero, Tswana, San or Bushmen, Baster, Nama), White (South Africans), Coloreds (mixed ancestry)
LANGUAGES: English, about 15 African languages, Afrikaans, German
RELIGIONS: Lutheran, Roman Catholic, Anglican, Dutch Reformed
BASIC MONETARY UNIT: South African Rand

GEOGRAPHY

Namibia measures 820 mi. (1,320 km) from north to south and 880 mi. (1,420 km) from east to west at its greatest distances. It has 925 mi. (1,489 km) of coastline along the South Atlantic Ocean.

Although Namibia is bordered by many rivers—the Kunene and the Okavango in the north, the Kwando and the Zambezi in the northeast, and the Orange in the south—its land is dry and unfertile. The country's three regions include the Namib Desert along the coast, a grassy plain in the center, and the Kalahari Desert in the east.

CLIMATE

Average daytime temperatures range from 75°F (24°C) in January and 68°F (20°C) in June. The average annual rainfall is 20 in. (50 cm) in the north, 8-16 in. (20-40 cm) in the central region, and 1-6 in. (2.5-15 cm) in the south. Most rain falls during the months of December through March.

ECONOMY

Because Namibia receives little rainfall, the land barely yields enough food for its people. However, the land provides valuable minerals.

Agriculture - cattle, corn, millet, peanuts, sheep, sorghum, and vegetables

Fishing - anchovies, mackerel, and sardines

Mining - copper, diamonds, gold, lead, tin, uranium, and zinc

Exports - cattle, copper, diamonds, gold, karakul skins, lead, processed fish, uranium oxide, and zinc

Imports - food, fuel, and manufactured products, petroleum products, and wheat

LIFE-STYLE

Namibia's population is almost equally divided between urban and rural areas. The white and mixed population generally lives in or near urban areas. Whites hold most of the administrative jobs, therefore earning higher incomes. The majority of the northern rural Namibians fish, grow crops, and raise livestock, while many Ovambo and Kavango work in the copper and diamond mines near the country's southern border. Blacks make up a greater part of the rural population, and most struggle to make a living.

Public education is provided free-of-charge and children ages seven to 16 are required to attend school. Further education is offered at the University of Namibia.

Namibia's cultural traditions include dance, music, and the arts of engraving, rock painting and sculpting.

IT'S A FACT!

Brandberg - the country's highest point, rises 8,465 ft. (2,580 m) above sea level.

Cape Cross Seal Reserve - located about 80 mi. (129 km) north of the city of Swakopmund—near Walvis Bay—is home to about 100,000 seals.

Etosha Game Park - an animal reserve located in north central Namibia, is home to antelopes, cheetahs, elephants, giraffes, lions, rhinos, and zebras.

Walvis Bay - located on Namibia's west coast, is actually a district of South Africa, covering 434 sq. mi. (1,124 sq. km) and containing a population of 20,740.

 DID YOU KNOW...
• South Africa controlled Namibia from 1916 to 1990, after which time the country gained its full independence?

NAURU

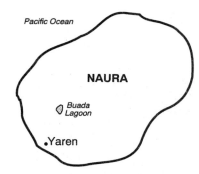
Pacific Ocean

NAURA

Buada Lagoon

.Yaren

OFFICIAL NAME: Republic of Nauru
LOCATION: Central Pacific Ocean
AREA: 8 sq. mi. (21 sq. km)
POPULATION (Est. 1993): 9,000
CAPITAL: No official capital; main government offices in Yaren.
GOVERNMENT: Parliamentary republic governed by a president.
FLAG: Two broad blue horizontal bars separated by a narrow yellow stripe. White starburst below the stripe to the left.
ETHNIC GROUPS: Nauruan, Pacific Islander
LANGUAGE: Nauruan, English
RELIGION: Christianity
BASIC MONETARY UNIT: Australian Dollar

GEOGRAPHY

Nauru is a small isolated island country in the central Pacific Ocean. It lies 40 mi. (65 km) south of the equator and halfway between Sydney, Australia, and Honolulu, Hawaii.

Nauru is an oval-shaped coral island. Most of the island is a plateau, 200 ft. (61 m) high. Near the center of the plateau is a lagoon surrounded by an area of fertile land. The country's 12 mi. (19 km) perimeter contains sandy beaches. The island contains no streams or rivers.

CLIMATE

Nauru has a tropical climate cooled by trade winds. Temperatures range from 76° to 93°F (24° to 34°C). Annually, about 80 in. (200 cm) of rain fall.

ECONOMY

Nauru's present economy is based on the mining of phosphates; however, these deposits are expected to be depleted by 1995.

Agriculture - coconuts
Mining - phosphate
Exports - phosphate
Imports - automobiles, food, furniture, machinery, medicines, shoes, and water

LIFE-STYLE

Nauru is one of the wealthiest countries in the world. The majority of native Nauruans work for the government or in phosphate-related activities. Most people live along a fertile strip of land along the perimeter of the island. Many live in low-rent, ranch-style homes provided by the government.

Children ages six to 17 are required to attend school. Tuition is provided free to those who wish to attend college in other countries.

Medical care is free for native Nauruans.

Most families own automobiles and many have power boats that they use for leisure activities.

DID YOU KNOW...

- The Nauruans have invested much of the revenue from the export of phosphate to help support themselves in various businesses after all of the phosphates have been mined?
- Nauru is the third smallest country in the world after Vatican City and Monaco?
- Since Nauru has no streams or rivers, most of its water is imported?
- Phosphate was formed from the droppings of huge prehistoric birds that over thousands of years turned into rock?

NEPAL

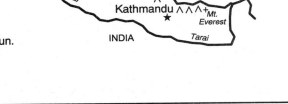

OFFICIAL NAME: Kingdom of Nepal
LOCATION: South-central Asia
AREA: 54,362 sq. mi. (140,797 sq. km)
POPULATION (Est. 1993): 20,519,000
CAPITAL/LARGEST CITY: Kathmandu
GOVERNMENT: Constitutional monarchy.
FLAG: Two overlapping crimson triangles trimmed in blue. The smaller, upper triangle features a white moon and the larger, lower triangle features a white, 12-pointed sun.
ETHNIC GROUPS: Nepalese, Bihari
LANGUAGE: Nepali
RELIGION: Hinduism
BASIC MONETARY UNIT: Nepalese Rupee

GEOGRAPHY

Nepal is a landlocked country in south-central Asia. Over 80 percent of the country is covered by the Himalaya Mountains. South of the Himalayas lie hills and valleys, with the Tarai—a flat, fertile river plain stretching along the border with India—making up the remainder of the country.

CLIMATE

Altitude plays an important role in Nepal's climate. Cool summers and severe winters in the northern mountains contrast with mild winters and subtropical summers in the lower elevations in the south.

ECONOMY

Nepal's economy depends predominantly on agriculture, with over 90 percent of the labor force employed in some aspect of farming. A number of people earn their living as craftworkers—blacksmiths, carpet weavers, tailors, and so on. The country's greatest natural resources are its forests and its rivers.

Agriculture - jute, rice, sugar cane, and wheat

Exports - carpets and textiles, herbs, jute, rice, spices, and wheat

Imports - machinery, metals and metal products, petroleum products, and textiles

LIFE-STYLE

The basic unit of Nepalese society is the extended family. Traditionally, families are large and several generations share the same home.

Most people live in rural settlements in the densely populated Kathmandu Valley. The government is trying to coax people to spread out by improving communication and transportation.

In urban, upper-class areas, rice with lentil soup and vegetable curry are the main dishes. Vegetarians are frequently found among people of higher social status. Millet and corn is the main diet in rural areas, where most people belong to the lower class. Meat is eaten in small quantities and only a few times a month. Fruit is eaten as a snack or dessert. The most popular beverage is tea with sugar and milk.

The most popular sports are badminton, soccer, and volleyball, but adults consider games and sports reserved for children's enjoyment. Movies from India are shown in theaters and some wealthy people have televisions and VCRs. Music and dance are much appreciated by the Nepalese. At most family and religious celebrations, devotional songs play and important part. Wind instruments and drums used for religious ceremonies have been handed down from ancient times.

IT'S A FACT!

Mount Everest - not only the country's highest point, but the world's highest point, it rises 29,028 ft. (8,848 m) above sea level on Nepal's border with Tibet.

 DID YOU KNOW...

• While Nepal's overall literacy rate is about 26 percent, only about 13 percent of females are literate?
• Polyandry, the practice of a wife having more than one husband, is practiced by some groups in northern Nepal?
• Nepal's health system is poorly developed, and many Nepalese consult *shamans* when they fall ill?
• Some people believe the *Abominable Snowman*, or *Yeti*, lives in the Himalaya Mountains?
• The Sherpas, a group of people who live in the Himalayas, have become world-renowned as guides and porters for mountain-climbing expeditions?
• *Pagodas*, many-storied Hindu and Buddhist temples, are prevalent in the city of Kathmandu?
• Nepal is the only country with a non-rectangular flag?
• Nepal is home to eight of the world's ten tallest points?
• The Hindus believe cows are sacred and therefore should not be killed?

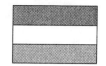

NETHERLANDS

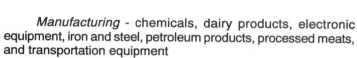

OFFICIAL NAME: Koninkrijk der Nederlanden (Kingdom of the Netherlands)
LOCATION: Northwestern Europe
AREA: 16,163 sq. mi. (41,863 sq. km)
POPULATION (Est. 1993): 15,222,000
CAPITAL: Amsterdam; The Hague is the seat of government.
LARGEST CITIES: Amsterdam, Rotterdam, The Hague
GOVERNMENT: Constitutional monarchy.
FLAG: Three horizontal stripes of red, white, and blue.
ETHNIC GROUP: Dutch
LANGUAGE: Dutch
RELIGIONS: Roman Catholic, Dutch Reformed
BASIC MONETARY UNIT: Netherlands Guilder, Gulden, or Florin

GEOGRAPHY

Netherlands is a small country. It measures 196 mi. (315 km) from north to south and 167 mi. (269 km) from east to west at its greatest distances. It has 228 mi. (367 km) of coastline along the North Sea. More than two-fifths of its land lies below sea level and was once covered with water. The people pumped the water off the land and built dikes to hold back the water. These drained lands, called *polders*, contain the richest farmlands and the largest cities in the country.

The Netherlands is generally flat and is crisscrossed by many canals that drain the land and act as waterways. The southwestern part of the Netherlands is made up of islands and peninsulas in the North Sea. This area is a delta formed by the Maas and Schelde Rivers, along with branches of the Rhine River.

The Netherlands has four main land regions: 1) the Dunes, 2) the Polders, 3) the Sand Plains, and 4) the Southern Uplands. The Dunes region curves a line along the North Sea coast and includes the West Frisian Islands in the north. This sandy region has few trees and no farmland. The Polders region contains flat, fertile areas that were once covered by water. Canals drain away water and irrigate the area. The Sand Plains region is low but rises slightly in the southwest.

CLIMATE

The Netherlands has a mild, damp climate due to its location on the sea. West winds from the North Sea warm the country in winter and cool it in summer. Winds also bring moisture from the sea that makes the skies very cloudy. Since there are no mountains, there is little variation in the climate from area to area. Precipitation falls fairly evenly throughout the year. The country's wettest area—the extreme southeast—receives an average of more than 34 in. (86 cm) of precipitation yearly. Temperatures generally range from 60° to 65°F (16° to 18°C) in summer and about 30°F (-1°C) in winter.

ECONOMY

The country's economy is technically advanced and highly industrialized. Dairy farming is the most important form of agriculture.

Agriculture - flowers and flower bulbs, hogs, milk, potatoes, sugar beets, and wheat
Fishing - eels, flatfish, herring, mackerel, mussels, and shrimp

Manufacturing - chemicals, dairy products, electronic equipment, iron and steel, petroleum products, processed meats, and transportation equipment
Mining - natural gas, petroleum, and salt
Exports - chemicals, dairy products, flowers and flower bulbs, food, natural gas, textiles and clothing, tobacco, and wooden shoes
Imports - consumer goods, iron ore, petroleum, raw materials, transportation equipment

LIFE-STYLE

The Netherlands is one of the most densely populated nations in the world with more than 1,000 people per sq. mi. (390 per sq. km). It also has one of the highest proportions of urban dwellers. About 90 percent of its population reside in cities. The Netherlanders are known for their friendliness and orderliness, despite their crowded conditions.

Most people in the Netherlands dress in styles common to the United States. *Klompen*, Dutch wooden shoes, are sometimes worn in rural areas and fishing villages. They offer good protection against damp ground.

Children ages six to 16 are required to attend school. Several varieties of high schools exist to train for special purposes, such as university work, advanced study in various institutes, or jobs in industry or business.

In the Netherlands, breakfast often consists of toast or bread with jelly, cheese or meats, and coffee or tea. *Krentebollen* (raisin rolls) are also favorites. For lunch, open-faced sandwiches or *kroket* (deep-fried sausage) are served. The main meal, dinner, usually includes potatoes and gravy, vegetables, and meat or fish. Favorite dishes are herring, smoked eel, pea soup, *poffertjes* (small, puffed pancakes), and *hutspot* (mashed potatoes mixed with various vegetables). Dutch pastries are world-famous.

Soccer is the favorite sport. Other popular sports are tennis, field hockey, swimming, sailing, ice skating, wind surfing, and cycling. Discos are popular with young people.

IT'S A FACT!

IJsselmeer - formerly a large bay named the Zuider Zee, is now a freshwater lake. A 20-mi.- (32-km-) long dike separates it from the sea.

Prins Alexander Polder - the country's lowest point, is located 22 ft. (6.7 m) below sea level.

Rijks Museum in Amsterdam - has a collection of some of the world's greatest masterpieces.

Vaalser Berg - the country's highest point, rises 1,053 ft. (321 m) above sea level.

 DID YOU KNOW...

- The city of Amsterdam has long been famous as a center for diamond cutting and polishing?
- The Royal Dutch Airline (KLM), established in 1919, is the world's oldest airline still in operation?
- Today, most *klompen* (wooden shoes) are exported?
- Flowers and bulbs (particularly tulips) grown in the Netherlands are exported to many countries around the world?
- The Netherlands contain over 600 museums, featuring works by such famous Dutch artists as Van Gogh and Rembrandt?

NETHERLANDS ANTILLES
Dependency of the Netherlands

OFFICIAL NAME: Nederlandse Antillen (Netherlands Antilles)
LOCATION: Caribbean Sea
AREA: 308 sq. mi. (798 sq. km)
POPULATION (Est. 1993): 196,000
CAPITAL/LARGEST CITY: Willemstad
GOVERNMENT: Self-governing dependency headed by a governor.
FLAG: White field with a centered horizontal blue stripe superimposed on a centered vertical red stripe. Five white, five-point stars are arranged in an oval pattern in the center of the blue band.
ETHNIC GROUP: Mixed European/Caribbean Indian
LANGUAGES: Dutch, English, Spanish, *Papiamento* (a mixture of Dutch, English, and Spanish)
RELIGION: Christianity
BASIC MONETARY UNIT: Netherlands Antillean Guilder, Gulden, or Florin

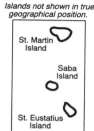

Islands not shown in true geographical position.

Caribbean Sea

Curaçao Island

Bonaire Island

★Willemstad

NETHERLANDS ANTILLES

St. Martin Island

Saba Island

St. Eustatius Island

GEOGRAPHY

The Netherlands Antilles, two groups of islands also known as the Dutch West Indies, are located in the Caribbean Sea. One group of islands lies about 50 mi. (80 km) off the coast of Venezuela. The other group lies about 500 mi. (800 km) to the northeast of the main islands and about 160 mi. (257 km) east of Puerto Rico. The islands have a combined coastline of about 226 mi. (364 km).

The southern islands, made up of Bonaire and Curaçao, are low-lying, rocky, and dry. The northern group consists of volcanic rock. They include Saba and St. Eustatius Islands and the southern part of St. Martin Island.

CLIMATE

The islands have a dry, tropical climate, with temperatures moderated by northeast trade winds. The average annual temperature is 82°F (28°C). The average annual rainfall ranges from 20 in. (50 cm) on the southern islands to 39.4 in. (100 cm) on the northern islands. The northern islands are subject to hurricanes from July to October.

ECONOMY

The major economic activity is crude oil refining and tourism. Most economic activity takes place on the island of Curaçao. Crude oil is imported from Venezuela to refineries on the island. Almost all food must be imported because the rocky soil is too poor for farming.

Agriculture - aloes, peanuts, sorghum, tropical fruit, and vegetables
Manufacturing - crude oil refining and shipbuilding
Exports - refined petroleum
Imports - crude oil and food

LIFE-STYLE

Compared to other Caribbean countries, Netherlands Antilles enjoys a rather high standard of living. About nine-tenths of the population lives on the islands of Bonaire and Curaçao. The capital city of Willemstad reflects its Dutch influence in its pastel-painted houses and Dutch-styled architecture.

IT'S A FACT!

Willemstad - the center for banking, property investment, shipping, and warehousing for the southeast Caribbean area.

 DID YOU KNOW...

- The Spanish first occupied Curaçao in 1527, but the Dutch captured the Antilles area in 1634?
- Two of the oldest Jewish landmarks in the Western Hemisphere—a cemetery dating back to 1659 and a temple built in 1732—are located in the city of Willemstad?
- The island of Aruba was formerly part of the Netherlands Antilles?

NEW CALEDONIA
Overseas Territory of France

OFFICIAL NAME: Nouvelle-Caledonie (New Caledonia)
LOCATION: Coral Sea/South Pacific Ocean
AREA: 7,366 sq. mi. (19,079 sq. km)
POPULATION (Est. 1993): 165,000
CAPITAL/LARGEST CITY: Nouméa
GOVERNMENT: Overseas territory of France headed by a French official who is appointed by the government of France. A local congress shares governmental functions with the French official.
FLAG: Uses the flag of France.
ETHNIC GROUPS: Melanesian, European, others
LANGUAGE: French
MAJOR RELIGION: Christianity
BASIC MONETARY UNIT: CFP Franc

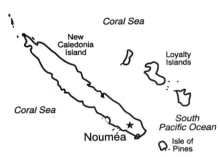

NEW CALEDONIA

GEOGRAPHY

New Caledonia is located in the South Pacific Ocean, about 1,100 nautical mi. (2,000 km) northeast of Sydney, Australia. The country consists of one main island, New Caledonia (also referred to as Grande Terre), and the lesser islands of Loyalty, Bélep, Pines, plus a few uninhabited islands. The islands have a combined coastline of about 1,400 mi. (2,254 km).

These islands are made up largely of coastal plains with mountains in the interior regions.

CLIMATE

The country enjoys a warm, tropical climate modified by southeast trade winds. The islands are subject to typhoons most frequently during the months of November to March.

ECONOMY

The basis of New Caledonia's economy is nickel mining. New Caledonia contains in excess of 25 percent of the world's known nickel resources and is one of the world's leading nickel producers.

Agriculture - bananas, coffee, copra, corn, cotton, manioc, pineapples, and tobacco
Industry - nickel mining and smelting
Mining - chromite, cobalt, and nickel
Exports - chrome, coffee, copra, and nickel
Imports - food, fuels, and machinery

LIFE-STYLE

New Caledonians live in two distinct societies: the Melanesian, which is black and poor, and whose people live in rural areas; and the European, which is white and financially well-off, and whose people live in urban areas.

 DID YOU KNOW...
- Under a plan agreed to in 1988, Melanesians and New Caledonians agreed to revisit a referendum on independence in 1998?
- *Caledonia* is Latin for "Scotland" and James Cook, a British navigator, called the island New Caledonia because it reminded him of Scotland?

NEW ZEALAND

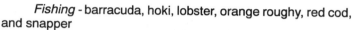

OFFICIAL NAME: New Zealand
LOCATION: Southwest Pacific Ocean
AREA: 103,883 sq. mi. (269,057 sq. km)
POPULATION (Est. 1995): 3,552,000
CAPITAL: Wellington
LARGEST CITIES: Auckland, Wellington, Christchurch
GOVERNMENT: Constitutional monarchy
FLAG: Blue field with the United Kingdom's flag in the upper hoist-side quadrant. Four white-trimmed red stars on the flag's outer half represent the constellation *Southern Cross*.
ETHNIC GROUPS: European, Maori
LANGUAGES: English, Maori
RELIGION: Christianity
BASIC MONETARY UNIT: New Zealand Dollar

GEOGRAPHY

New Zealand is an island country in the Southwest Pacific Ocean that belongs to a larger island group called *Polynesia*. New Zealand consists of two main islands—North Island and South Island—plus many smaller islands.

The North Island has three main land regions: 1) the Northern Peninsulas and Waikato Basin, 2) the Volcanic Region and Western Hill Country, and 3) the Eastern Hills. The South Island, likewise, has three main land regions: 1) the Southern Alps and High Country, 2) the Canterbury Plains, and 3) the Otago Plateaus and Basins.

The North Island covers 44,244 sq. mi. (114,592 sq. km). The northern part of the island contains forests, citrus orchards, hills, and sandy beaches. Much of the western half of the island is made up of volcanic rock from its active volcanoes. A mountain range runs through the southeastern region. The lowlands that run along the foot of the range are used for growing fruits and vegetables and raising livestock.

The South Island covers 58,965 sq. mi. (152,719 sq. km). This beautiful island is made up primarily of majestic mountains. Glaciers, forests and sparkling lakes can be found throughout this area.

CLIMATE

Overall, New Zealand has a mild, moist climate. Since it is south of the equator, its seasons are opposite those of the Northern Hemisphere. July is the coldest month, and January is the warmest. Temperatures range from 61°F (16°C) in July to 86°F (30°C) in January.

New Zealand's mountains largely control the distribution of rainfall. Westerly winds bring moisture from the ocean. On the west side of the mountains, an average of over 100 in. (250 cm) of rain falls annually. East of the mountains, average annual rainfall is less than 20 in. (51 cm). The country has around 400 earthquakes a year; about 100 are strong enough to be felt.

ECONOMY

New Zealanders have a standard of living that ranks among the world's highest. New Zealand's economy has depended heavily on farming and foreign trade, but manufacturing and tourism are becoming increasingly important.

Agriculture - apples, barley, cattle, kiwi fruit, milk, onions, potatoes, sheep, wheat, and wool

Fishing - barracuda, hoki, lobster, orange roughy, red cod, and snapper

Forestry - Douglas-fir and Radiata pine

Manufacturing - chemicals, dried milk products, iron and steel, machinery, motor vehicles, paper, processed foods (beef, butter, cheese, mutton, and lamb), textiles, and wood products

Exports - beef, butter, cheese, dried milk products, fish products, forest products, lamb, lobster tails, manufactured goods, and wool

Imports - iron and steel, machinery, motor vehicles, petroleum, scientific instruments, and telecommunication equipment

LIFE-STYLE

About four-fifths of all New Zealanders live in urban areas, though the country's cities generally are not crowded. Most people live in single-family homes and have a small garden. Some urban dwellers live in high-rise apartments. Virtually all homes have modern appliances.

In some rural areas, small settlements are linked by roads, but in rugged ranch country ranchers may be very isolated.

New Zealanders are among the best-fed people in the world. They eat more butter and meat per person than any other people. Lamb is a favorite meat. A special treat is *toheroa* soup, made from native green clams. Tea is the favorite drink.

Children ages six to 15 are required to attend school. Free education is offered to all students up to the age of 19. Children in remote areas may take correspondence classes.

New Zealanders love working and entertaining around their homes and gardens. They also love sports and outdoor activities. Camping, hiking, hunting, mountain climbing, and skiing are enjoyed along with cricket (similar to baseball), rugby (type of football), tennis, and swimming.

IT'S A FACT!

Lake Taupo - New Zealand's largest lake, is located on North Island and covers 234 sq. mi. (606 sq. km). It is a vacation area known for its trout fishing.

Mount Cook - the country's highest point, rises 12,349 ft. (3,764 m) above sea level. The Maoris gave this mountain the name *Aorangi*, meaning the "cloud piercer."

Mount Ruapehu - the highest point on North Island and an active volcano, rises 9,175 ft. (2,797 m) above sea level.

Sutherland Falls - the fifth highest waterfall in the world, plunges 1,904 ft. (580 m) down a mountain.

Waikato River - New Zealand's longest river, flows 264 mi. (425 km).

 DID YOU KNOW...

- In 1893, New Zealand became the first nation in the world to give women the right to vote?
- New Zealand is home to a flightless species of birds, which include the kakapo parrot, kiwi, takehe, and weka?
- The native kiwi is the only bird known to have nostrils in the tip of its bill?
- A common greeting among the Maori is the *hongi*— pressing noses together with eyes closed? This is accompanied by a low humming sound.
- In New Zealand, the trunk of the car is known as a *boot* and the hood is called a *bonnet*?
- *Kiwi* is used as a nickname for a New Zealander, and a white person is a *Pakeha*?
- The Maoris still create carefully detailed woodcarvings just as they did hundreds of years ago?
- *Wallabies* (small kangaroos) were introduced to New Zealand from Australia?

NICARAGUA

OFFICIAL NAME: Republica de Nicaragua (Republic of Nicaragua)
LOCATION: Central America
AREA: 50,200 sq. mi. (130,000 sq. km)
POPULATION (Est. 1995): 4,433,000
CAPITAL: Managua
LARGEST CITIES: Managua, Leon, Granada
GOVERNMENT: Republic governed by a president.
FLAG: Three horizontal stripes of blue, white, and blue. The coat of arms is centered on the white stripe.
ETHNIC GROUPS: Mestizo, Caucasian
LANGUAGE: Spanish
RELIGION: Roman Catholic
BASIC MONETARY UNIT: Gold Córdoba

GEOGRAPHY

Nicaragua is the largest country in Central America in area. It measures 293 mi. (472 km) from north to south and 297 mi. (478 km) from east to west at its greatest distances. The Pacific coastline covers 215 miles (346 km). The Caribbean coastline extends 297 mi. (478 km).

Nicaragua has three major land regions: 1) the Pacific Region, 2) the Central Highlands, and 3) the Caribbean Region.

The Pacific Region is a predominantly low, fertile area that extends from Honduras to Costa Rica. This region contains several volcanoes, some still active. Three-fifths of Nicaragua's people live here.

The Central Highlands is the highest region. The Caribbean Region is mainly a flat plain covered by rainforests.

CLIMATE

The country's climate is chiefly tropical. The Pacific Region's temperature averages 80°F (27°C) throughout the year. This area receives about 60 in. (150 cm) of rain per year.

Temperatures in the Central Highlands range from 60° to 70°F (16° to 21°C). Parts of the region receive over 100 in. (250 cm) of rain per year.

The average temperature of the Caribbean Region is 80°F (27°C). The annual average rainfall is 165 in. (419 cm).

ECONOMY

Nicaragua's leading economic activity is farming. The country's most valuable natural resource is the rich soil of the Pacific Region.

Agriculture - bananas, beans, beef cattle, coffee, corn, cotton, rice, and sugar cane

Manufacturing - food and beverage products, and clothing and textiles

Exports - bananas, coffee, cotton, sugar, and rice

Imports - chemicals, clothing, food, machinery, and petroleum

LIFE-STYLE

About a third of all Nicaraguans are poor farmers. Many in the Pacific Region are peasants who work on their own farms, on state farms, or on large private farms. In warm areas, these farm workers dwell in palm- or metal-roofed homes. In colder areas, farmers live in tile-roofed, adobe houses. The blacks and Indians of the Caribbean Region primarily live by farming small plots or by fishing, mining, or lumbering.

Nicaraguan children are required to attend school from ages six to 12. Before 1980, only half of the children, mostly in urban areas, actually attended. Since then, hundreds of rural schools have been built and the literacy rate has increased.

In Nicaragua, the extended family is the basis of society. Urban dwellers tend to be more modern in their thinking, while in rural families, the roles of men and women are more traditional.

Most people take a *siesta*, or afternoon rest, after eating the noon meal. Staples of the diet are beans, rice, and corn. Popular dishes include *nacatamales* (meat and vegetables with spices), *plátanos* (fried bananas), *baho* (meat, vegetables, and plantain), and *enchiladas*.

Dancing is a popular activity in Nicaragua. Baseball is the national sport. The people also enjoy soccer, boxing, softball, basketball, and volleyball. In rural areas, bullfights and cockfights are popular. Celebrations honoring local patron saints are annual main events in their respective regions and towns.

IT'S A FACT!

Lake Nicaragua - the country's largest lake, is the only freshwater lake in the world inhabited by sharks and sawfish.

Pico Mogotón - the country's highest point, rises 6,913 ft. (2,107 m) above sea level.

 DID YOU KNOW...

- The Nicaraguans elected a woman, Violeta Barrios de Chamorro, to the presidency in 1990?
- To show special respect, the titles "Don" and "Doña" are used with men's and women's first names?
- About 45 percent of Nicaragua's population is below the age of 15?
- In some rural areas, only mules or oxcarts can be used to get around?
- In 1972, the capital city of Managua was severely damaged by an earthquake? About 5,000 people were killed and most of the area was destroyed.
- During the 1980s, Nicaragua was involved in a war between the Sandinistas and Contras?

NIGER

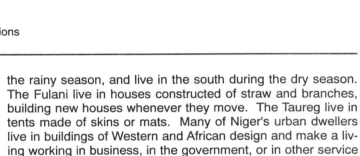

OFFICIAL NAME: Republic of Niger
LOCATION: West Africa
AREA: 489,200 sq. mi. (1,267,000 sq. km)
POPULATION (Est. 1992): 8,180,000
CAPITAL: Niamey
LARGEST CITIES: Niamey, Zinder, Maradi, Agadez (Agades), Tahoua
GOVERNMENT: Republic headed by a president.
FLAG: Three horizontal stripes of orange, white, and green. An orange circle, representing the sun, is centered on the white stripe.
ETHNIC GROUPS: Black (including Hausa, Djerma-Songhai, Kanuri, and Fulani), Tuareg, White, Asian
LANGUAGES: Hausa, Djerma-Songhai, French, Arabic
RELIGIONS: Islam, Christianity, Traditional African Religions
BASIC MONETARY UNIT: CFA Franc

GEOGRAPHY

At its greatest distances, Niger, a landlocked country, measures 825 mi. (1,328 km) from north to south and 1,100 mi. (1,770 km) from east to west. Niger's northern region is covered by part of the Sahara Desert and sandy plateaus. Its northwest-central region is home to the Aïr Mountains, and its southern region is savanna.

CLIMATE

Niger is often plagued by drought, but it has a rainy season which generally lasts from June to September. Temperatures in the Aïr Mountains may reach as high as 122°F (50°C); the mountains receive an average annual rainfall of less than 7 in. (17.5 cm). The surrounding desert region receives even less. Average annual temperatures in Niamey, the country's capital, range from 95°F to 100°F (35°C to 38°C), making its southern strip one of the hottest places in the world. Niger's heaviest rains fall in the south, with an average annual rainfall of 22 in. (55 cm) in the city of Zinder.

ECONOMY

Niger's economy is one of the poorest in the world; it has little arable land and few natural resources.

Agriculture - beans, cassava, cotton, hides and skins, livestock (camels, cattle, goats, and oxen), millet, peanuts, peas, rice, and sorghum

Manufacturing - brick, cement, chemicals, processed foods, and textiles

Mining - iron ore, natron, phosphate, salt, tin, tungsten, and uranium

Exports - cotton, hides, livestock, meat, onions, peanuts, peas, and uranium

Imports - cereals, chemical products, electronic equipment, food, machinery, petroleum products, pharmaceuticals, and vehicles and parts

LIFE-STYLE

About four-fifths of Niger's population is rural and many make a living by farming. Those near lakes or rivers make a living by fishing. The Hausa population mainly lives in crowded southern towns and villages constructed from sun-dried mud bricks. The Djerma-Songhai mainly live in the southwest and the Kanuri mainly live in the southeast. The Fulani and Tuareg are mainly nomads who raise livestock, live in the desert during the rainy season, and live in the south during the dry season. The Fulani live in houses constructed of straw and branches, building new houses whenever they move. The Taureg live in tents made of skins or mats. Many of Niger's urban dwellers live in buildings of Western and African design and make a living working in business, in the government, or in other service industries.

Staples of the diet include beans, macaroni, millet, rice, and sorghum often served in porridge form and usually eaten with sauces made from baobab leaves, okra, peanuts, and tomatoes. Goat is the most commonly eaten meat and popular dishes include *brochette* (similar to shish kebab), *hura* (fermented milk with millet and hot pepper), *kilshi* (spiced beef jerky), and *tuwo* (pounded millet with a sauce of okra or tomatoes).

Men usually dress in pants or knee-length shorts with loose shirts or robes. Women usually wear long, wraparound skirts with short shirts and sandals. Nomads generally wear long, loose robes as protection against the sun, and the Tuareg males may wear turbans with veils.

Education is mandatory at primary schools and is provided free of charge. Because there are few schools, however, only a small percent of children actually attend. Nomadic children are taught in "tent schools," which move with the people.

Niger has poor health conditions and limited rural medical facilities. Vaccinations have reduced deaths from measles and smallpox, but malaria and trachoma are widespread.

Popular recreational activities include basketball, camel racing, cycling, soccer, and wrestling. Popular arts include crafts, dance, gold and silver jewelry-making, leatherwork, pottery, and wood carvings. Traditional African music styles are popular.

IT'S A FACT!

Mount Gréboun - the country's highest point, rises 6,378 ft. (1,944 m) above sea level.

 DID YOU KNOW...

- Niger is named for the Niger River, which flows 350 mi. (563 km) through the country's southwest corner?
- Niger is one of the world's leading uranium producers and exporters?
- Niger has no railroads and few paved roads, and most Nigeriens travel by foot or on bus?

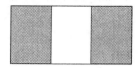

NIGERIA

OFFICIAL NAME: Federal Republic of Nigeria
LOCATION: Western Africa
AREA: 356,669 sq. mi. (923,768 sq. km)
POPULATION (Est. 1993): 119,473,000
CAPITAL: Abuja
LARGEST CITIES: Lagos, Ibadan, Ogbomosho, Kano
GOVERNMENT: In transition—governed by a president.
FLAG: Three vertical stripes of green, white, and green. Green represents agriculture and white represents unity and peace.
ETHNIC GROUPS: Black (Hausa, Yoruba, Ibo)
LANGUAGES: English, Hausa, Yoruba, Ibo
RELIGIONS: Islam, Christianity
BASIC MONETARY UNIT: Naira

GEOGRAPHY

Nigeria is the most populous country on the African continent and ranks as the world's tenth largest in population. At its greatest distances, Nigeria measures 650 mi. (1,046 km) from north to south and 800 mi. (1,287 km) from east to west. It has 478 mi. (769 km) of coastline.

Nigeria has ten land regions: 1) the Sokoto Plains, 2) the Chad Basin, 3) the Northern High Plains, 4) the Jos Plateau, 5) the Niger-Benue River Valley, 6) the Western Uplands, 7) the Eastern Highlands, 8) the Southwestern Plains, 9) the Southeastern Lowlands, and 10) the Niger Delta.

These regions display a multitude of landforms, including hot, rainy swamps; grassy plains; tropical forests; dry, sandy areas; rocky hills; and steep mountains.

CLIMATE

Most of the country has a tropical climate. The average temperature in the north is 85°F (29°C). In the south, the average temperature is 80°F (27°C). Coastal areas receive an average annual rainfall of approximately 150 in. (381 cm). Parts of northern Nigeria receive about 25 in. (64 cm) per year.

ECONOMY

Nigeria's developing economy is based on agriculture and mining.

Agriculture - beans, beef and hides, cacao, cassava, corn, cotton, millet, palm oil and palm kernels, peanuts, rice, rubber, and yams

Manufacturing - cement, chemicals, clothing, food products, and textiles

Mining - columbite, limestone, natural gas, petroleum, and tin

Exports - cacao beans, petroleum, rubber, timber, and tin

Imports - cement, chemical products, food products, machinery, manufactured goods, and textiles

LIFE-STYLE

About two-thirds of the Nigerian people live in rural areas and farm, fish, or herd for a living. Their homes are typically made of dried mud, grass, or wood with roofs of asbestos, corrugated metal, or thatch. These homes are situated in compounds (or clusters). A village usually contains several compounds and each compound houses a group of related families.

In Nigeria's cities, the wealthy live in modern apartments or houses. But overcrowding is a problem. The poor sometimes live in slums in mud huts along unpaved streets.

Many urban Nigerians wear Western-style clothing, but some city and most rural dwellers wear traditional clothing. Garments for both sexes include long, loose robes of white or bright materials. The men also may wear short jackets with shorts or trousers. Men often wear small, round caps while women wear scarves or turbans. In some rural areas, only a loincloth is worn.

Nigeria lacks a sufficient number of schools and teachers and children are not required to attend school. Only a third of Nigerians are literate.

Staples of the Nigerian diet are yams, corn, beans, and rice. Cassava roots and plantains are also eaten. Their food is often cooked in peanut or palm oil and seasoned with red peppers. In general, the people eat very little meat.

Nigerians enjoy sports, such as soccer, wrestling, polo, cricket, and swimming. In the cities, movies are popular. Traditional dance and song performances are well-attended in rural and urban settings.

IT'S A FACT!

Dimlang Peak - the country's highest point, rises 6,699 ft. (2,042 m) above sea level.

Kainji Dam - holds back the Niger River to form Kainji Lake and produces much of Nigeria's electric power.

Niger River - the third longest river in Africa, flows about 2,600 mi. (4,180 km) in western Africa.

 DID YOU KNOW...

- Nigeria has more than 250 ethnic groups?
- Nigerians prefer the term "ethnic group" over "tribe"?
- Dairy cattle are scarce in coastal regions because of the tsetse fly?
- Nigerian parents wink when they want their children to leave the room?
- Nigeria's history dates back to around 500 B.C. when the Nok civilization thrived?

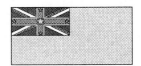

NIUE

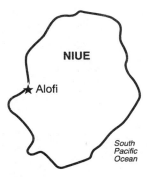

NIUE

★ Alofi

South Pacific Ocean

OFFICIAL NAME: Niue
LOCATION: South Pacific Ocean
AREA: 100 sq. mi. (259 sq. km)
POPULATION (Est. 1993): 1,977
CAPITAL/LARGEST CITY: Alofi
GOVERNMENT: Self-governing territory in free association with New Zealand. Niue is responsible for internal affairs, while New Zealand is responsible for external affairs.
FLAG: Yellow field with the United Kingdom's flag in the upper hoist-side quadrant. A blue circle centered on the UK's red cross features a large, yellow, five-pointed star. A small, yellow, five-pointed star lies at each end of the red cross.
ETHNIC GROUPS: Polynesian, European, Samoan, Tongan
LANGUAGES: Polynesian (closely related to Samoan and Tongan), English
RELIGIONS: Protestant (Ekalesia Nieue), Mormon, Roman Catholic, Jehovah's Witness, Seventh-Day Adventist
BASIC MONETARY UNIT: New Zealand Dollar

GEOGRAPHY

Niue, one of the world's largest coral islands, has about 40 mi. (64 km) of coastline along the South Pacific Ocean. Although the island has porous soil, three-fifths of the land is arable. About one-fifth of the land is covered by forest.

Niue has two levels. A central plateau, slightly depressed in the middle, rises to about 208 ft. (63 m) above sea level. The plateau slopes down to the second level, which is about 0.3 mi. (0.5 km) wide and rises to about 80-90 ft. (24-27 m) above sea level. The second level slopes down to coastal cliffs which lie about 30 ft. (9 m) above sea level. The island is surrounded by a reef, which has a break large enough to let through lighters (small boats that transport goods between ships and the mainland).

CLIMATE

Niue has a tropical climate that is subject to typhoons. The average monthly temperature ranges from 65° to 85° F (18° to 29°C). The average annual rainfall is 80 in. (203 cm). During the rainy season—December to April—temperatures and humidity levels are often highest. The island is periodically plagued by drought. Since Niue is primarily made up of coral, the soil does not catch and absorb precipitation. Therefore, the people of Niue construct the roofs of their houses to catch rain water.

ECONOMY

Niue's economy is based mainly on agriculture, but the island is heavily dependent on economic aid from New Zealand. There is some tourism, and the sale of postage stamps to foreign collectors is an important source of revenue.

Agriculture - cassava, coconuts, honey, limes, livestock (beef cattle, chickens, and pigs), passion fruit, pawpaw, sweet potatoes, taro, and yams

Manufacturing - coconut products and handicrafts

Exports - canned coconut cream, copra, footballs, handicrafts, honey, limes, passion fruit products, pawpaw, root crops, and stamps

Imports - chemicals, drugs, food, fuels, livestock, lubricants, machinery, and manufactured goods

LIFE-STYLE

Employed Niueans mainly work in agriculture, government, manufacturing and processing, or trade. However, there are few job opportunities, and many residents emigrate to New Zealand.

Niuean society follows an ancestral system. Though historically filled with traditional customs—like using the island's caves for burial—the only remaining custom is the wedding feast.

Education is free and children ages five to 14 are required to attend both elementary and secondary schools. Higher education is available in New Zealand.

Niue is noted for its plaited baskets and hats made from the pandanus (palmlike trees).

 DID YOU KNOW...
- Insects are rare on Niue?
- Niueans may not sell land to foreigners?

NORFOLK ISLAND
Territory of Australia

OFFICIAL NAME: Territory of Norfolk Island
LOCATION: South Pacific Ocean
AREA: 14 sq. mi. (36 sq. km)
POPULATION (Est. 1993): 2,665
CAPITAL: Kingston (administrative), Burnt Pine (commercial)
LARGEST SETTLEMENT: Kingston
GOVERNMENT: Australian territory.
FLAG: Three vertical stripes of green, white, and green with a large green Norfolk Island pine tree centered on the white stripe.
ETHNIC GROUP: Norfolk descendents of the British *Bounty* mutineers, Australian, New Zealander
LANGUAGES: English, Norfolk
RELIGION: Christianity
BASIC MONETARY UNIT: Australian Dollar

GEOGRAPHY

Norfolk Island, a fertile and beautiful island, lies in the South Pacific Ocean about 1,000 mi. (1,600 km) northeast of Sydney, Australia. The island is volcanic in origin, and the terrain is generally rugged. Most of the coast is bound by cliffs, some reaching more than 300 ft. (91.5 m) above sea level. The island's soil is fertile but easily eroded if stripped of vegetation cover. Norfolk Island pines, which once dominated the land, are still an important feature of the landscape. The territory's area includes the uninhabited islands of Nepean and Philip.

CLIMATE

In general, Norfolk Island has a warm climate. The average annual temperature is 60°F (15°C). The average annual rainfall often exceeds 50 in. (130 cm) annually. Norfolk Island is subject to typhoons, especially during the months of May through July.

ECONOMY

Tourism is the main source of income. Budgetary revenue is mostly gained from the sale of stamps, and from customs duty and liquor sales (a government monopoly).
Agriculture - bananas, citrus fruits, and vegetables
Exports - Norfolk Island pine seeds
Imports - consumer goods, food, and fuel

LIFE-STYLE

Many of the island's inhabitants are descendents of crew members from the British naval ship *Bounty*. (After crew members mutinied in 1789, they settled on Pitcairn Island. Along with a few newcomers, the descendents of the mutineers moved to Norfolk Island in 1856. Their population numbered 194.) Other inhabitants are descendents of settlers from Australia and New Zealand.

Many islanders are employed in various areas of the tourism industry, such as the operation of hotels and duty-free stores. Subsistence farming, livestock grazing, and fishing employ other islanders.

Education is free, and children ages six to 15 are required to attend school. Island schools offer education through the tenth grade. Higher education is available on the mainland.

IT'S A FACT!

Mount Bates - the island's highest point, rises 1,047 ft. (319 m) above sea level.

 DID YOU KNOW...
- Norfolk Island was used as a penal settlement by Australia from 1788 to 1814, and again from 1825 to 1856?
- About 20,000 or more tourists visit the island each year (sea and air services are regularly available)?
- A Norfolk Island pine tree grows to a height of about 200 ft. (60 m), and has trunk diameter of up to 10 ft. (3 m)?

NORTH KOREA

OFFICIAL NAME: Choson-minjujuui-inmin-konghwaguk (Democratic People's Republic of Korea)
LOCATION: Eastern Asia
AREA: 46,540 sq. mi. (120,538 sq. km)
POPULATION (Est. 1993): 23,051,000
CAPITAL: Pyongyang
LARGEST CITIES: Pyongyang, Chongjin, Nampo
GOVERNMENT: Communist state headed by a president.
FLAG: Three horizontal stripes of blue, red, and blue divided by two white bands. A red star—representing Communism—in a white circle is on the red stripe.
ETHNIC GROUP: Korean
LANGUAGE: Korean
RELIGIONS: Buddhism, Confucianism
BASIC MONETARY UNIT: North Korean Won

GEOGRAPHY

North Korea is the northern half of a peninsula that extends south of China. It measures 370 mi. (595 km) from north to south and 320 mi. (515 km) from east to west at its greatest distances. It has 665 mi. (1,070 km) of coastline on the Sea of Japan and the Yellow Sea. North Korea's area includes a few islands and three main land regions: 1) the Northwestern Plain, 2) the Northern Mountains, and 3) the Eastern Coastal Lowland.

CLIMATE

Seasonal winds, or monsoons, influence Korea's weather all year. During the summer, winds bring hot, humid weather. Cold, dry winds blow in cold weather in the winter. July temperatures average 70° to 80°F (21° to 27°C). January temperatures range from 35° to -5°F (20° to 21°C). North Korea receives an average of 30-60 in. (76-150 cm) of precipitation annually.

ECONOMY

North Korea's economy is dependent on industrial production. It lags behind South Korea in technology.
Agriculture - barley, corn, millet, potatoes, rice, and wheat
Fishing - pollock, sardines, shellfish, and squid
Manufacturing - cement, chemicals, iron and steel, machinery, metals, processed foods, and textiles
Mining - coal, iron ore, magnesium, phosphates, salt, and tungsten
Exports - cement, coal, iron ore, lead, machinery, minerals, rice, textiles, tungsten, and zinc
Imports - grain, machinery, petroleum, and transportation equipment

LIFE-STYLE

Although family life is important to North Koreans, the government has worked hard to break down extended family ties. The most important concept followed is *chuch'e*, or self-reliance. It influences every aspect of North Koreans' lives and leads them to believe they are better off than other nations.

Most of the country's urban dwellers work in factories and live in one- or two-room apartments. Rural dwellers also live in apartments and work on collective farms.

Rarely do Korean families have time to eat meals together. When they do, conversation during meals is limited. Spoons and chopsticks are the most common eating utensils. Staples of the diet are *kimchi* (a spicy, pickled cabbage) and rice. Other popular foods are barley, fish, fruits (such as apples, peaches, pears, and melons), and vegetables (such as beans, potatoes, and sweet potatoes). *Naengmyon*, a cold noodle dish, is popular. Tea is the traditional drink. Adults also drink *sake*, or rice wine.

The North Korean government encourages sports by providing many sports facilities. Soccer is the national sport. Table tennis is also popular. Attending movies, plays, and operas are frequent activities of those in urban areas. Family picnics and outings are common on Sundays.

All children are required to attend school for 11 years. This includes preschool and grades 1-10. Further education must be approved by the Communist Party. Schooling is paid for by the state.

IT'S A FACT!

Paektu Mountain - the country's highest point, rises 9,003 ft. (2,744 m) above sea level.
Yalu River - the country's longest river, flows 490 mi. (789 km) along the northern border to the Yellow Sea.

 DID YOU KNOW...
- All North Korean farmers work on collective farms that are operated by a large group of farmers?
- Slurping hot soups and noodles is considered acceptable behavior?
- Children always bow to adults as a form of greeting?
- The average monthly wage is equal to about U.S. $50?

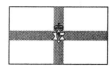

NORTHERN IRELAND
Division of the United Kingdom

OFFICIAL NAME: Northern Ireland
LOCATION: Western Europe
AREA: 5,461 sq. mi. (14,144 sq. km)
POPULATION (Est. 1994): 1,605,000
CAPITAL: Belfast
LARGEST CITIES: Belfast, Londonderry
GOVERNMENT: Constitutional monarchy governed by a cabinet of *ministers* (government officials), with the prime minister being the chief governing official.
FLAG: White field with a red cross. The coat of arms —featuring a crown, a white, six-pointed star, and a red hand—is centered on the cross.
ETHNIC GROUP: English, Scottish, Irish
LANGUAGES: English, Irish (form of Gaelic)
RELIGIONS: Protestant, Roman Catholic
BASIC MONETARY UNIT: Pound

GEOGRAPHY

Northern Ireland is the smallest of the four countries which make up the United Kingdom of Great Britain and Northern Ireland. It takes up the northeastern one-sixth of the island of Ireland, which it shares with the independent Republic of Ireland.

At its greatest distances, Northern Ireland measures 85 mi. (137 km) from north to south and 111 mi. (179 km) from east to west. It has 330 mi. (531 km) of coastline along the North Atlantic Ocean, the North Channel, and the Irish Sea.

The country consists of lower elevations in the center rising to higher elevations along the coast. There are three main *loughs* (pronounced *lahks*, they are lakes or large bays) within— Lough Erne and Upper Lough Erne in the southwest, and Lough Neagh in the center—and four along the coast—Lough Foyle in the northwest, Belfast and Strangford Loughs in the east, and Cartingford Lough in the southeast. Mountain ranges include the Sperrin Mountains in the northwest, the Antrim Mountains in the northeast, and the Mourne Mountains in the southeast.

CLIMATE

Northern Ireland experiences cold, windy winters and mild, wet summers. The average temperature ranges from 32°F (0°C) in the winter to 55°F (13°C) in the summer. The average rainfall ranges from 24 in. (60 cm) to over 39 in. (100 cm).

ECONOMY

Northern Ireland's economy is based mainly on its service industries.

Agriculture - apples, barley, butter, cheese, eggs, hay, livestock (cattle, chickens, hogs, and sheep), milk, mushrooms, pears, plums, potatoes, and turnips

Fishing - cod, herring, mackerel, salmon, shrimp, trout, and whiting

Manufacturing - aircraft, automobile parts, chemicals, china, computer chips, hand-cut crystal, Irish linen and other textiles, machinery, pottery, processed foods, ships, and videocassette recorders

Exports - clothing, finished fabrics (cotton, linen, and rayon), and textile-weaving machines

Imports - yarn (cotton, flax, and rayon), machinery, and unfinished cotton and woolen goods

LIFE-STYLE

The island of Ireland has been divided into two countries since 1920, when the British Parliament passed the Government of Ireland Act. Northern Ireland experiences continued disputes between its two religious groups. Protestants want the country to remain part of the United Kingdom, while Roman Catholics want the country to become part of the Republic of Ireland.

Northern Ireland's population is about 70 percent urban, with about one-fifth of the population centered in Belfast. The rural population mainly makes a living by farming.

Commonly eaten foods include beef, bread, dairy products, eggs, fish, potatoes, poultry, and vegetables. The most commonly consumed beverages are beer and tea.

Popular sports include *camogie* and *hurling* (somewhat similar to field hockey), *cricket* (played with a ball and bat), *football* (similar to the American game of soccer), *Gaelic football* (similar to soccer), handball, and *rugby* (a form of football). Leisure activities include boating, fishing, golfing, swimming, and socializing. *Pubs* (public houses where people drink, eat, and listen to music) are favorite places to socialize. Watching motion pictures and television are also popular. The country's most renowned cultural event is the international arts festival, which takes place in November and is hosted by the Queen's University of Belfast. It features art exhibits, dramatic productions, motion pictures, musical performances, and other events.

Children ages four to 16 are required to attend school.

IT'S A FACT!

Lough Neagh - the largest lake in both the United Kingdom and on the island of Ireland, has an area of 153 sq. mi. (396 sq. km).

Slieve Donard - the country's highest point, rises 2,796 ft. (852 m) above sea level.

 DID YOU KNOW...
- Northern Ireland is often referred to as *Ulster*, which was the name of one of Ireland's large provinces until 1920?

NORWAY

OFFICIAL NAME: Kongeriket Norge (Kingdom of Norway)
LOCATION: Northwestern Europe
AREA: 149,405 sq. mi. (386,958 sq. km)
POPULATION (Est. 1993): 4,274,000
CAPITAL: Oslo
LARGEST CITIES: Oslo, Bergen, Trondheim
GOVERNMENT: Constitutional monarchy.
FLAG: Red field with a white-trimmed blue cross shifted slightly to the hoist side.
ETHNIC GROUPS: Germanic, Lapps
LANGUAGE: Norwegian (Bokmål and Nynorsk)
RELIGION: Evangelical Lutheran
BASIC MONETARY UNIT: Norwegian Krone

GEOGRAPHY

Norway is a long, narrow country on the northwestern edge of Europe. It is known for the beauty of its rugged mountains and deeply indented coast. Norway's nickname is *Land of the Midnight Sun*, because it is located so far north that during a portion of the summer the sun shines for 24 hours. It measures 1,089 mi. (1,752 km) from northeast to southwest and 267 mi. (430 km) from northwest to southeast at its greatest distances. It has 1,647 mi. (2,650 km) of coastline on the Norwegian Sea, the North Atlantic Ocean, and the North Sea. Norway's average elevation is 1,500 ft. (457 m) above sea level. The country has three regions: 1) the Mountainous Plateau, 2) the Southeastern Lowlands, and 3) the Trondheim Lowlands. The Mountainous Plateau is the largest region. It consists largely of bare rock that was smoothed and rounded by ancient glaciers. Glaciers also formed many deep valleys and lakes. This region contains the Jostedal Glacier, the largest icefield in Europe outside Iceland. The two lowland regions consist chiefly of valleys. They are suitable for farming and are the most populated regions. The Southeastern Lowlands are also used for forestry.

The coast of Norway is characterized by many inlets, called fiords, and peninsulas. About 150,000 islands lie off the coast.

CLIMATE

The warm North Atlantic Current of the Gulf Stream keeps Norway milder than most areas so far north. The northwestern coast, in some areas, averages temperatures of 45°F (25°C) higher than the world average for that latitude. Nearly all the ports remain ice free. In the winter the inland regions are colder than the coast because the mountains keep the warm, west winds from reaching them. Snow covers the ground for at least three months. The inland valleys of the southeast have the warmest summers. The far north has periods of endless sun in summer and of darkness in winter.

ECONOMY

Norway has a well-developed economy.

Agriculture - barley, fruits and vegetables, hay, livestock, milk, oats, and potatoes
Fishing - capelin, cod, herring, and mackerel
Forestry - timber
Manufacturing - aluminum, chemicals, paper, processed foods, refined petroleum products, ships, and wood pulp
Mining - ilmenite, iron ore, lead, molybdenite, natural gas, petroleum, pyrites, and zinc

Exports - chemicals, fish, machinery, metals, natural gas, paper, petroleum, transportation equipment, and wood pulp
Imports - food, manufactured goods, and minerals

LIFE-STYLE

About three-fourths of all Norwegians reside in urban areas. Norwegian cities are smaller and have a slower pace than most European cities. The cities also are free of slums. Most Norwegians live in modern apartment buildings. Many also own cottages along the coast or in the mountains.

Most rural dwellers live in southeastern Norway or along the western coast. Many fish for a living. Farmers often have a second occupation to earn enough to support their families.

Almost all Norwegians are literate. Children ages seven to 16 are required to attend school.

Norwegian food specialties are smoked salmon, *lutefisk* (cabbage and mutton), and *smalahode* (sheep's head). Coffee is consumed throughout the day. Tea, milk, beer, and soft drinks are also popular.

Recreational activities include skiing (both Nordic and Alpine), fishing, ice-skating, soccer, swimming, hiking, and *Bandy*. Bandy is a form of ice hockey with 11-member teams. Many families participate in the cultural arts

IT'S A FACT!

Frogner Park - located in Oslo, features 150 works of sculpture by Gustav Vigeland.
Galdhøppigen - the country's and northern Europe's highest point, rises 8,100 ft. (2,469 m) above sea level.
Sogne Fiord - the longest inlet of the sea, extends 127 mi. (204 km) inland.

 DID YOU KNOW...
- Norway's total coastline, including its many fiords and peninsulas, covers 13,267 mi. (21,351 km), about half the distance around the world?
- During parts of winter, the *Aurora borealis*, or Northern lights, provide the only light in the far north?
- Norway generates more hydroelectric power per person than any other country?
- Norwegians have traveled using skis for thousands of years? Most Norwegians learn to ski before they start school.

OMAN

OFFICIAL NAME: Saltanat Uman (Sultanate of Oman)
LOCATION: Southeast Arabian Peninsula
AREA: 82,030 sq. mi. (212,457 sq. km)
POPULATION (Est. 1993): 1,677,000
CAPITAL: Muscat
LARGEST CITIES: Matrah, Muscat
GOVERNMENT: Absolute monarchy ruled by a sultan.
FLAG: Three horizontal stripes of white, red, and green edged by a vertical red stripe on the hoist side. The national emblem—featuring crossed swords and a dagger—lies in the upper hoist-side corner.
ETHNIC GROUP: Arab
LANGUAGE: Arabic
RELIGION: Islam (Ibadhi Muslim)
BASIC MONETARY UNIT: Omani Rial or Riyal

GEOGRAPHY

Oman is located in the southeast corner of the Arabian Peninsula. At its greatest distances, Oman measures 500 mi. (805 km) from north to south and 400 mi. (644 km) from east to west. It has about 1,060 mi. (1,700 km) of coastline along the Arabian Sea and the Gulf of Oman. The Musandam Peninsula in the north is a barren, mountainous region that is part of Oman although it is separated from it. The rest of Oman is divided into several distinct land regions. Al Batinah is a fertile, coastal plain along the Gulf of Oman. Date palms are grown here.

The Al Hajar mountain range separates Al Batinah from the flat, interior wasteland. Much of western Oman is covered by Rub al Khali (Empty Quarter), a desert.

The Dhofar region in the south contains tropical plants that grow along the coast. However, most of the coastal area is barren and rocky.

CLIMATE

Oman has one of the hottest climates in the world. During the summer, the temperature may climb to 130°F (54.4°C). Most of the country receives less than 6 in. (15 cm) of rain annually, though the Dhofar region may receive up to 25 in. (63.5 cm) of rain each year.

ECONOMY

Since 1964, most of Oman's income has come from petroleum. Before that time, Oman was a very poor country. Many of its people still struggle to earn a living, but economic improvements are being financed by oil exports.

Agriculture - alfalfa, bananas, coconuts, dates, limes, onions, pomegranates, tobacco, tomatoes, and wheat

Fishing - cod, sardines, and sharks

Mining - chromite, copper, natural gas, and petroleum

Exports - dates, fish, limes, nuts, processed copper, reexports, and refined oil products

Imports - food, livestock, lubricants, machinery, manufactured goods, and oil-drilling and transportation equipment

LIFE-STYLE

Approximately 89 percent of Omanis live in rural areas. Rural Omanis who live along the coast usually fish or work on date palm plantations to earn a living. Farmers grow dates, fruit, and grain in the interior.

In the urban areas, people live in whitewashed houses with enclosed courtyards. They often work as merchants, laborers, government officials, or sailors. Nomads still roam the desert with livestock herds (camels, goats, horses, or sheep). Newer rural homes in Oman are constructed of concrete blocks. In coastal villages, older houses are made of wood and palm thatch. Homes in interior villages have flat roofs, with mud and stone walls. Stone fortresses from the Middle Ages can still be found in many of the villages.

Most Omani men wear white robes and turbans for protection from the sun. Most Omani women wear long, black outer robes over colorful inner clothes. Some women wear black masks that cover most of the face. Most of the women follow the traditional roles of caring for children and the home.

The country's illiteracy rate is high. But since the 1970s, the government has set up adult literacy programs and built new schools for children.

IT'S A FACT!

Jabal Ash Sham - the country's highest point, rises 9,957 ft. (3,035 m) above sea level.

 DID YOU KNOW...

- The strategic Strait of Hormuz, through which much of the world's oil is shipped, lies at the northern tip of Oman?
- Wells and springs are the Omanis' major source of water? Many wells receive their water from ancient underground canals.
- The Dhofar region in southern Oman is famous for its frankincense trees?
- Many Omani men carry *khanjars* (ornamental knives) in brightly colored sashes?

PAKISTAN

OFFICIAL NAME: Islamic Republic of Pakistan
LOCATION: Southern Asia
AREA: 307,374 sq. mi. (796,095 sq. km)
POPULATION (Est. 1993): 133,490,000
CAPITAL: Islamabad
LARGEST CITIES: Karachi, Lahore, Faisalabad
GOVERNMENT: Republic governed by a president.
FLAG: Green field—which features a white star and crescent—overlapped by a vertical white stripe on the hoist side.
ETHNIC GROUPS: Punjabi, Sindhi, Pashtuns, Baluchi
OFFICIAL LANGUAGES: Urdu, English
MAJOR LANGUAGES: Punjabi, Sindhi
RELIGION: Islam
BASIC MONETARY UNIT: Pakistani Rupee

GEOGRAPHY

Pakistan has a diverse landscape that includes snow-capped mountains, plateaus, plains, and deserts. At its greatest distances, Pakistan measures 935 mi. (1,505 km) from north to south and 800 mi. (1,287 km) from east to west. It has 506 mi. (814 km) of coastline along the Arabian Sea.

The country can be divided into five main land regions: 1) the Northern and Western Highlands, 2) the Punjab Plain, 3) the Sind Plain, 4) the Baluchistan Plateau, and 5) the Thar Desert.

CLIMATE

Most of the country has a dry climate with hot summers and cool winters. The average annual rainfall is only 10 in. (25 cm). Most of this falls during the summer monsoon—July to September. Pakistan is subject to earthquakes.

ECONOMY

Pakistan's economy depends primarily on agriculture, which employs more than half of the work force. The country's most important natural resource is its rivers.

Agriculture - chickpeas, cotton, milk, rice, sugar cane, and wheat

Fishing - sardines, shark, and shrimp

Manufacturing - cement, cotton textiles and clothing, fertilizer, food products, and steel

Mining - natural gas, and petroleum

Exports - carpets, clothing, cotton, fish, leather goods, rice, and textiles

Imports - chemicals, electrical equipment, food products, iron and steel, machinery, petroleum products, and transportation equipment

LIFE-STYLE

Because Pakistan has a number of different culture groups, each with its own language, customs, and characteristics, it is difficult to find a common national bond. The Muslim religion seems to be the one major link that unites the various groups. Religious rituals are an important segment of Pakistanis' daily lives.

The majority of the Pakistani people are herders or farmers who live in rural villages. Recreation for them revolves around plays based on myths and legends from their particular cultures. People who reside in the urban areas are employed as craftsmen, factory workers, or shopkeepers. A favorite source of entertainment is motion pictures.

The *shalwar-qamiz*, loose trousers and a long overblouse, is worn by both men and women. Men wear solid, understated colors, sometimes adding a vest or coat for special occasions. Women, on the other hand, wear bright, bold colors and patterns. Women add a scarf, called a *dupatta*, around their heads.

Pakistanis are very hospitable and enjoy entertaining in their homes. A staple of the diet is wheat and other grains. Curry, ginger, onions, and peppers are frequent ingredients, so the food is generally hot and spicy. Yogurt and rice are important parts of most meals. The most common meats are beef, chicken, fish, and lamb, eaten by the poor majority only on special occasions. Fresh or dried fruit is used frequently as desserts.

IT'S A FACT!

K2 - the country's highest point, and the world's second highest point, rises 28,250 ft. (8,611 m) above sea level.

Khyber Pass - one of the most famous mountain passes in the world, links Pakistan with Afghanistan.

 DID YOU KNOW...

- Only about 25 percent of the people ages 15 years and over are literate?
- Children are not required by law to attend school?
- It is considered rude to use individual fingers when gesturing?
- In rural areas, transportation is provided by donkeys or horse-drawn carts?
- Life expectancy is about 56 years?
- Islamabad was built in the 1960s specifically to replace Karachi as the capital?

PANAMA

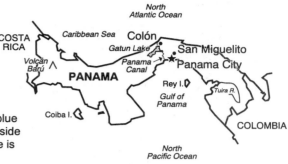

OFFICIAL NAME: República de Panamá (Republic of Panama)
LOCATION: Central America
AREA: 29,762 sq. mi. (77,082 sq. km)
POPULATION (Est. 1995): 2,659,000
CAPITAL: Panama City
LARGEST CITIES: Panama City, San Miguelito, Colón
GOVERNMENT: Republic governed by a president.
FLAG: Four quadrants: the upper hoist-side is white with a blue star, representing honesty and purity; the lower hoist-side is blue; the upper fly-side is red; and the lower fly-side is white with a red star, representing authority and law.
ETHNIC GROUPS: Mestizo, Mulatto, Black, White, Indian
LANGUAGES: Spanish, English
RELIGION: Roman Catholic
BASIC MONETARY UNIT: Balboa

GEOGRAPHY

The country of Panama is comprised of an isthmus that separates the Pacific and Atlantic Oceans. The Panama Canal cuts through this isthmus and joins the oceans. From east to west, Panama extends 410 mi. (660 km). From north to south it measures 130 mi. (209 km) at its widest point and only 30 miles (48 km) at its the narrowest. Its Pacific coastline stretches 746 mi. (1,201 km) while its Atlantic coastline is 397 mi. (639 km) in length. Panama's territory includes 800 islands, the largest of which are Coiba and Rey Islands.

There are three main land regions: 1) the Central Highland, 2) the Atlantic Lowland, and 3) the Pacific Lowland. The Central Highland is a mountainous region. The Atlantic Lowland and Pacific Lowland occupy narrow areas along the coasts.

CLIMATE

The country has a warm, tropical climate with little variation in temperature from season to season. The temperature averages 80°F (27°C) in the lowlands and 66°F (19°C) in the mountains. The Atlantic side of Panama receives about 150 in. (381 cm) of rain per year. The Pacific side receives about 68 in. (173 cm).

ECONOMY

The Panama Canal is the most significant factor in the country's economy. From the use of the canal, the Panamanian government receives $75 million a year. Agriculture provides the most jobs, though the majority of Panama's farmers produce only subsistence crops such as rice, corn, and beans.

Agriculture - bananas, beans, beef cattle, chickens and eggs, coffee, corn, milk, rice, and sugar cane

Fishing - anchoveta and shrimp

Manufacturing - beverages, cement, petroleum products, and processed foods

Exports - bananas, shrimp, and sugar

Imports - automobiles, chemicals, machinery, and petroleum

LIFE-STYLE

The area around the Panama Canal is a busy urban region. The rest of Panama consists mainly of rural areas with farms and small villages and towns. Many of Panama's whites are wealthy, others belong to the middle class. Most blacks are poor laborers. Many mestizos and mulattoes are part of the urban middle class, but the majority make up much of Panama's farm population. They struggle to feed their families.

Wealthy Panamanians live in large, luxury apartments or homes. The middle class have smaller apartments or homes. Poor urban dwellers live in shacks or ramshackle apartments. Most rural people live in small one- or two-room homes.

Western-style clothing is worn most of the time. On special occasions, women may wear a *pollera*, a white blouse and long skirt highly decorated with lace and embroidery or a white blouse and colorful skirt called a *montuna*. Men may wear a *camisilla* (long, white shirt) and trousers or a *montuno* (a white embroidered shirt) and short pants.

Staples of the Panamanian diet include kidney beans, rice, plantains, corn, and chicken. A favorite dish is *guacho* (rice cooked with beans). Tortillas and omelets also are popular.

About 90 percent of the country's adults are literate. Children are required to attend school from ages seven to 15, or until they complete 6th grade.

Many Panamanians play musical instruments for enjoyment. Baseball is the most popular sport, with boxing, basketball, and soccer also enjoyed by many. Going to movies, cockfights, and horse races are other popular pastimes.

IT'S A FACT!

Gatun Lake - the country's largest lake, forms part of the canal route and has an area of 163 sq. mi. (201 sq. km).

Tuira River - flows 125 mi. (201 km) in eastern Panama. It is the only one of Panama's 500 rivers that is navigable for long distances.

Volcán Barú - the country's highest point, rises 11,401 ft. (3,475 m) above sea level.

 DID YOU KNOW...
- Panama gains control of the Panama Canal from the United States on December 31, 1999?
- Panama is called the *Crossroads to the World* because thousands of ships use the canal yearly? The canal saves ships the long trip of going around the southern end of South America.

PAPUA NEW GUINEA

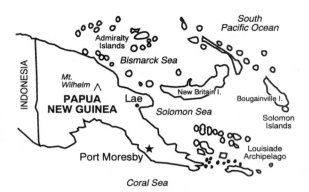

OFFICIAL NAME: Papua New Guinea
LOCATION: Pacific Ocean, north of Australia
AREA: 178,704 sq. mi. (462,840 sq. km)
POPULATION (Est. 1993): 4,144,000
CAPITAL: Port Moresby
LARGEST CITIES: Port Moresby, Lae
GOVERNMENT: Constitutional monarchy.
FLAG: Black triangle in the lower, hoist-side corner features five, five-pointed stars representing the constellation *Southern Cross*. A red triangle in the upper, fly-side corner features a yellow bird of paradise.
ETHNIC GROUPS: Papuan, Melanesian
LANGUAGES: Pidgin English, Police Motu, others
RELIGIONS: Christianity, Indigenous Beliefs
BASIC MONETARY UNIT: Kina

GEOGRAPHY

Papua New Guinea covers the eastern half of the island of New Guinea and includes a chain of tropical islands extending to the east and north for more than 1,000 mi. (1,609 km).

The largest islands—New Guinea, New Britain, and Bougainville—have many mountain ranges. Tropical forests cover 80 percent of the islands. The coastal land is mostly swamps. Many of the small islands are the tops of underwater mountains.

CLIMATE

Papua New Guinea's climate is hot and humid. The average annual temperature ranges from about 80°F (27°C) in the lowlands to about 68°F (20°C) in the highlands. The average annual rainfall is about 80 in. (203 cm).

ECONOMY

The economy of Papua New Guinea is centered on agriculture.

Agriculture - cocoa, coconuts, coffee, rubber, tea, and timber

Manufacturing - coconut oil and plywood

Mining - copper, gold, and silver

Exports - copper, cocoa, coffee, gold, and palm oil

Imports - food, fuels, chemicals, consumer goods, machinery, and manufactured goods

LIFE-STYLE

Papua New Guineans use head, eye, and eyebrow gestures when communicating. Raising the eyebrows shows agreement or acknowledgment. To show disgust, the people hiss and shake the head sideways. The most common greeting is the handshake.

Most people have a strong sense of belonging to a tribe or language group. They place great value on their families, ancestors, land, and their own physical abilities. Although they desire material things and personal wealth, it is rarely possible to hoard wealth because of the sense of obligation to share one's income and possessions with one's family and clan.

The extended family forms the basis of support for most people, although the majority live in nuclear family settings. Nuclear families tend to be quite large, with an average of six children. Extended families usually live near one another. Most families are patriarchal in structure, but there are some matriarchal societies in the country.

People usually eat two meals per day—breakfast and dinner; snacking takes place in between. The spoon is the most common eating utensil; otherwise hands are used. Although various dishes and bowls are commonly used throughout the country, in rural areas large leaves are still used for plates. The people sit on the ground or floor when eating. The staple food of the highlands is *kaukau* (sweet potato). The staple food on the coast and lowlands is *saksak* (a starchy extract from the sago palm). Taro is a staple throughout the country. Also enjoyed are wide varieties of fruits and vegetables. In some areas, bats, eels, and tree kangaroos are not uncommon food items.

The country's national pastime is sitting and talking. The most popular organized sport is rugby. Leisure time is also spent playing cards or making useful objects, such as bags and weapons.

IT'S A FACT!

Mount Wilhelm - the country's highest point, rises 14,793 ft. (4,509 m) above sea level.

 DID YOU KNOW...

• More than 700 languages are spoken in Papua New Guinea?
• Many houses in Port Moresby are built on stilts so they will be cooler?
• Some 70 species of non-poisonous snakes inhabit the country?
• Asking for second helpings implies the host has not provided an adequate amount of food?
• Staring at a person of the opposite sex is considered very offensive?
• Older men and women are often called "papa" and "mama" by all people?

PARAGUAY

BOLIVIA

PARAGUAY

BRAZIL

ARGENTINA

Asunción
San
Lorenzo
Lambaré

Itaipu
Dam

Paraguay R.

Paraná R.

OFFICIAL NAME: República del Paraguay (Republic of Paraguay)
LOCATION: Central South America
AREA: 157,048 sq. mi. (406,752 sq. km)
POPULATION (Est. 1995): 4,465,000
CAPITAL: Asunción
LARGEST CITIES: Asunción, San Lorenzo, Lambaré, Fernando de la Mora
GOVERNMENT: Republic governed by a president.
FLAG: Three horizontal stripes of red, white, and blue. This is the only flag with a different design on both sides: the coat of arms on the front and the Treasury seal on the back.
ETHNIC GROUP: Mestizo
LANGUAGES: Spanish, Guaraní
RELIGION: Roman Catholic
BASIC MONETARY UNIT: Guaraní

GEOGRAPHY

Paraguay, a landlocked country, measures 575 mi. (925 km) from north to south and 410 mi. (660 km) from east to west at its greatest distances. The Paraguay River flows from north to south and divides the country into two land regions: 1) the Chaco (Occidental Paraguay) and 2) Eastern Paraguay (Oriental Paraguay). The Chaco stretches west from the Paraguay River. It includes three-fifths of Paraguay's land but is mainly uninhabited. The region is covered largely with coarse grasses, scrub forests, and thorny shrubs. Eastern Paraguay lies between the Paraguay and Paraná Rivers and is home to more than 95 percent of the people. The eastern third is thickly forested, while the remainder is low, grassy plains and forested hills.

CLIMATE

Most of the country has a warm, humid climate. Temperatures in the capital city average 65°F (19°C) in July and 84°F (29°C) in January. About 50-65 in. (127-166 cm) of rain falls on the eastern region annually. The Chaco receives about 20-40 in. (51-102 cm) of rainfall yearly.

ECONOMY

Paraguay has a developing economy based chiefly on agriculture and forestry.

Agriculture - cassava, corn, cotton, livestock, rice, soybeans, sugar cane, tobacco, and wool

Forestry - cedar, coconut palm, holly, Quebracho, and wild citrus

Manufacturing - cement, leather goods, processed foods and beverages, textiles, and wood products

Exports - coffee, cotton, lumber, meat products, soybeans, tannin, tobacco, and vegetable oils

Imports - chemicals, fuels and lubricants, iron and steel, machinery, and transportation equipment

LIFE-STYLE

Paraguay's society is centered around the extended family. It is not uncommon to find three or four generations under the same roof. Approximately half of all Paraguayans live in rural areas. Most are farmers who grow food only for their families. Others work on cattle ranches, on large farms, in forestry, or in small factories. Rural dwellers usually live in one-room homes called *ranchos*. Ranchos typically have a dirt floor, reed, wood, or brick walls, a sloped, thatch roof, and no indoor plumbing. The kitchen is in an attached or separate shed.

City dwellers generally have a higher standard of living than rural dwellers. Urban people include unskilled laborers, craftworkers, factory and officer workers, shopkeepers, and professional people. City dwellers often live in small, pastel-colored houses of stucco or brick with red tile roofs. The poorest live in shacks.

Urban Paraguayans wear Western-style clothing. Rural women often wear a *rebozo* (shawl) and a simple dress or skirt and blouse. Men in rural areas usually wear *bombachas* (loose trousers), a shirt or jacket, a neckerchief, and a poncho. Most rural people go barefoot.

Paraguayans eat a lot of meat, especially beef. A favorite dish is *puchero* (a stew of beef and vegetables). Corn, cassava, and rice are important staples of their diet. A tea made of holly tree leaves, called *yerba maté*, is the favorite beverage.

More than 80 percent of Paraguayan adults are literate. The government provides free schooling through the university level. Children are required to attend school from ages seven to 14, but the law is not strictly enforced.

The people enjoy soccer, basketball, volleyball, horse racing, and swimming. Religious holidays are celebrated with festivals. Other activities include attending the theater, reading, and dancing. The national pastime is conversation.

IT'S A FACT!

The Itaipú Dam power plant - on the Paraná River, is one of the world's largest hydroelectric power projects.

 DID YOU KNOW...

- Paraguay's most famous handicraft is *ñandutí* (spider web) lace?
- American football and baseball are practically unknown in Paraguay?

 IF8201 Comprehensive World Reference Guide

PERU

OFFICIAL NAME:	República del Perú (Republic of Peru)
LOCATION:	Western South America
AREA:	496,225 sq. mi. (1,285,216 sq. km)
POPULATION (Est. 1995):	23,854,000
CAPITAL:	Lima
LARGEST CITIES:	Lima, Arequipa, Callao
GOVERNMENT:	Republic governed by a president.
FLAG:	Three vertical stripes of red, white, and red with the coat of arms centered on the white stripe.
ETHNIC GROUPS:	American Indian, Mestizo
LANGUAGES:	Spanish, Quechua
RELIGION:	Roman Catholic
BASIC MONETARY UNIT:	Sol

GEOGRAPHY

Peru is South America's third largest country. It measures 1,225 mi. (1,971 km) from north to south and 875 mi. (1,408 km) from east to west at its greatest distances. It has 1,448 mi. (2,330 km) of coastline along the Pacific Ocean.

Peru has great contrasts in landscape. Its three main land regions are: 1) the Pacific Coast, 2) the highlands, and 3) the selva. The coast is a narrow strip of land between the Peruvian Andes and the Pacific. Nearly all of this area is a dry, rugged desert. But about 50 rivers cross the region, providing irrigation and drinking water. The highlands include all areas of the Andes Mountains above 6,500 ft. (1,980 m). The selva is divided into two parts: high and low. The high selva covers the eastern foothills of the Andes. The low selva is almost completely covered by thick rainforests and jungles.

CLIMATE

Peru lies within the tropics, but a cold ocean current makes the coast cooler than is normal for this type of area. The average temperature from November through April is 73°F (23°C). From May through October, it averages 61°F (16°C). In the highest part of the Andes Mountains, the temperature never gets above freezing. The selva's average temperature is 80°F (27°C). The coast rarely receives more than 2 in. (5 cm) of rain per year. Most of the western highlands average 10 in. (25 cm) of precipitation yearly. The eastern highlands usually receive more than 40 in. (100 cm) of precipitation annually. Parts of the selva average 160 in. (400 cm) yearly, but the average for most of the area is 80 in. (200 cm).

ECONOMY

Instability within the government has caused many economic problems: rapid inflation, high unemployment, and low productivity. Farming is the principal occupation.

Agriculture - bananas, coffee, cotton, potatoes, and sugar cane
Fishing - anchovies and sardines
Manufacturing - fish meal, metals, sugar, and textiles
Mining - copper, iron ore, lead, petroleum, silver, and zinc
Exports - coffee, copper, cotton, fish meal, petroleum, silver, and sugar
Imports - dairy products, machinery, manufactured goods, meat, motor vehicles, and wheat

LIFE-STYLE

Until 1900, Peru had a strict class system based on ancestry. Since then, a middle class has evolved composed of whites and some mestizos. However, the small upper class is still composed chiefly of whites, and the majority of Peruvians still belong to the lower class. Most upper-class families speak Spanish, dress in Western clothing, and live in fashionable sections of Lima and other large cities. They seldom mix with people outside their class.

Mestizos wear Western-style clothing, speak Spanish, and have opportunities to advance, but most still belong to the lower class.

Most of Peru's Indians are poor and lack a formal education. They live in the highlands or along the coast. The majority are farmers. Some have only a thatched roof for shelter.

Housing ranges from high-rise apartments and modern housing to homes of cardboard, old metal, and other scraps.

About 25 percent of all adult Peruvians are illiterate, most of whom are rural Indians. Children ages six to 15 are required to attend school but a shortage of teachers and schools keeps many from attending.

The Peruvian diet includes fish, beans, rice, and tropical fruit. A popular dish on the coast is *cebiche* (raw fish seasoned with lemon and vinegar). Corn is a staple among Indians. Most food is purchased daily in small stores or open-air markets.

Music, dancing, and watching movies are popular in Peru. Basketball, volleyball, and bullfights are enjoyed by many, but soccer is the most popular sport.

IT'S A FACT!

Huascarán - an extinct volcano and the country's highest point, rises 22,205 ft. (6,768 m) above sea level.

Lake Titicaca - on the Bolivian border, is the country's largest and the world's highest navigable lake. The Peruvian part covers 1,914 sq. mi. (4,957 sq. km). It lies 12,507 ft. (3,812 m) above sea level.

 DID YOU KNOW...

- The first inhabitants of Peru were believed to be Indians who migrated from North America approximately 12,000 years ago?
- The highland Indians live at elevations up to 15,000 ft. (4,570 m) above sea level?
- Peru once had great Indian empires, which now lie in ruins? Chanchan, capital of the Chimu Indians, and Machu Picchu, a walled Inca city, are two such ruins.
- About 45 percent of Peruvians are Indians descended from the great Incas?

PHILIPPINES

PHILIPPINES

OFFICIAL NAME: Republic of the Philippines
LOCATION: Southwest Pacific Ocean
AREA: 115,831 sq. mi. (300,000 sq. km)
POPULATION (Est. 1995): 67,078,000
CAPITAL: Manila
LARGEST CITIES: Manila, Quezon City, Cebu City
GOVERNMENT: Republic governed by a president.
FLAG: Adopted in 1898. Two horizontal stripes of blue and red overlapped by a white triangle based on the hoist side. The triangle features a sun and stars.
ETHNIC GROUPS: Malays, Chinese
LANGUAGES: Filipino, English, other
RELIGION: Christianity
BASIC MONETARY UNIT: Philippine Peso

GEOGRAPHY

Philippines is an archipelago located in the southwest Pacific Ocean. The Philippines is made up of more than 7,000 islands, but only about 900 are inhabited. Eleven large islands make up most of the country. The islands have a combined coastline of about 10,900 mi. (17,500 km).

The Philippines can be divided into three main groups: 1) the northern group, consisting of Luzon and Mindoro; 2) the central group, made up of about 7,000 islands; and 3) the southern group, consisting of Mindanao and the Sulu Archipelago, a group of about 400 islands. Most of the Philippines were once covered by thick forests, but excessive lumbering has destroyed most of this resource.

The coasts of the islands have narrow strips of lowland. Wide inland plains are found on the islands of Luzon and Panay. Volcanic mountains, many of them active, cover much of the larger islands.

CLIMATE

The climate of the Philippines is generally tropical and humid. During the hot months, from March to May, the temperature may reach 100°F (38°C). During the rainy season, from June to February, the temperature may fall to 70°F (21°C). Rainfall averages 100 in. (250 cm) per year. An average of five typhoons hit the islands every year. Violent earthquakes frequently shake the islands.

ECONOMY

While manufacturing brings in the most money to the Philippines, almost half of the population works in agriculture, fishing, or forestry. Service industries also employ many people.

Agriculture - abacá, bananas, cassava, coconuts, corn, hogs, mangoes, pineapples, poultry, rice, sugar cane, and sweet potatoes

Fishing - milkfish, mother-of-pearl, scad, shrimp, sponges, and tuna

Forestry- ebony, kapok, and Philippine mahogany

Manufacturing - cement, chemicals, clothing, electronic equipment, food and beverages, petroleum products, textiles, and wood products

Mining - chromite, copper, gold, and nickel

Exports - electronic equipment, clothing, bananas, coconut products, copper, gold, lumber, pineapples, and sugar

Imports - chemicals, machinery, and petroleum

LIFE-STYLE

The majority of Filipinos have large families and maintain close relationships with all family members, no matter how distant the relationship. Men hold most positions of authority at home and at work, but many women now work in professional fields.

Children from ages seven to 12 are required to attend school through at least the sixth grade. About 90 percent of Philippine adults are literate. Around 30 percent of college-age Filipinos are enrolled in colleges.

Philippine food is a mixture of American, Chinese, Malay, and Spanish cuisine. Many dishes are highly spiced. Rice is the staple of the diet. The main source of protein in the diet is fish. A typical meal consists of rice, fish, vegetables, and tropical fruit. Popular dishes are *adobo* (a stew of chicken and pork in garlic, soy sauce, and vinegar) and *kare-kare* (a stew of meats and vegetables served in peanut sauce). *Halo-halo* is a favorite drink made from sweetened beans, milk, and fruits served in colorful layers with crushed ice.

Filipinos especially enjoy socializing with family and friends and watching movies during leisure time. Basketball is one of the more popular sports. Other activities include gambling, attending horse races or cockfights, and playing *mahjong*, a Chinese table game using tiles.

IT'S A FACT!

Mount Apo - the country's highest point, is located on Mindanao and rises 9,692 ft. (2,954 m) above sea level.

Philippine Trench - one of the deepest spots in the ocean, is located off the northeast coast of Mindanao and lies 34,578 ft. (10,539 m) below the surface of the Pacific Ocean.

 DID YOU KNOW...
- The voting age in the Philippines is 15?
- Public transportation is dominated by buses and *jeepneys*, decorated taxis which are shared by as many riders as can squeeze in?
- Farmers still grow crops on terraced mountain slopes that were built by Malay immigrants more than 2,000 years ago?

PITCAIRN ISLANDS GROUP
Dependency of the United Kingdom

OFFICIAL NAME: Pitcairn Islands
LOCATION: South Pacific Ocean
AREA: 10 sq. mi. (27 sq. km)
POPULATION (Est. 1993): 60
CHIEF SETTLEMENT: Adamstown
GOVERNMENT: British dependency headed by the British high commissioner to New Zealand.
FLAG: Blue field with the flag of the UK in the upper hoist-side quadrant. The Pitcairn Islander coat of arms (yellow, green, and light blue with a yellow anchor on a shield) is centered on the flag's outer half.
ETHNIC GROUPS: Mixture of Polynesian and European
LANGUAGES: English, Tahitian/English dialect
RELIGION: Seventh-Day Adventist
BASIC MONETARY UNIT: New Zealand Dollar

Oeno   Henderson

Adamstown   Ducie

Pitcairn   *South Pacific Ocean*

**PITCAIRN ISLANDS
GROUP**

GEOGRAPHY

The islands of Pitcairn, Henderson, Ducie, and Oeno are known collectively as the Pitcairn Islands Group. Only Pitcairn is inhabited. It has an area of 2 sq. mi. (5 sq. km). The islands are located in the South Pacific Ocean and lie south of the Tropic of Capricorn about 5,000 mi. (8,000 km) east of Australia. The island of Pitcairn was formed by a volcano. It is a rugged half crater that rises sharply to about 1,100 ft. (300 m). Its coastline is covered with rocky cliffs. The interior, though rugged, contains fertile soil.

CLIMATE

The islands have a subtropical climate. Average temperatures range from 75°F (24°C) in February to 66°F (19°C) in August. Annual average rainfall is 80 in. (200 cm). The islands are subject to typhoons particularly during the rainy season from November to March.

ECONOMY

Most of the island's cash income comes from selling postage stamps to collectors and carved curios to passengers of passing ships.

Agriculture - bananas, citrus fruits, coconuts, coffee, pumpkins, taro, sugar cane, sweet potatoes, watermelons, and yams
Exports - fruits and vegetables, and handicrafts
Imports - building materials, food, fuel, and machinery

LIFE-STYLE

Most of the population that lives on Pitcairn are descendants of H.M.S. *Bounty* mutineers and their Polynesian wives. The majority of the people make a living by farming or fishing. They also make and sell hand-carved wooden figures. Life in Pitcairn centers around the extended family and the church.

The people's traditional diet includes fish, and the fruits and vegetables grown on the island.

A 10-member Council composed of Pitcairn residents oversees local affairs.

Though children attend primary school on the island, older students often go to New Zealand to study. Many of these students never return.

 DID YOU KNOW...

- Adamstown, on the north coast of Pitcairn, is one of the few places on the rocky coast where island-made longboats can land?
- In 1990, over one quarter of Pitcairn's population was over the age of 65?
- In 1990, 42 of the 54 people who lived on the island were descendents of the mutineers from the British navy ship, H.M.S. *Bounty*?
- The English navigator Philip Carteret, named the island after Robert Pitcairn, the crew member who first sighted the island?
- In 1856, many of Pitcairn's people were moved to Norfolk Island because the population had reached 192 and there was not enough land to grow a sufficient amount of food for that many people?

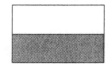

POLAND

OFFICIAL NAME: Rzeczpospolita Polska
(Republic of Poland)
LOCATION: Central Europe
AREA: 120,725 sq. mi. (312,677 sq. km)
POPULATION (Est. 1993): 38,816,000
CAPITAL: Warsaw
LARGEST CITIES: Warsaw, Łódź, Kraków
GOVERNMENT: Democracy governed by a prime minister.
FLAG: Two horizontal stripes of white and red.
ETHNIC GROUP: Polish
LANGUAGE: Polish
RELIGION: Roman Catholic
BASIC MONETARY UNIT: Zloty

GEOGRAPHY

Poland, a large, central European country, measures 395 mi. (636 km) from north to south and 430 mi. (692 km) from east to west at its greatest distances. It has 277 mi. (446 km) of coastline along the Baltic Sea.

There are seven major land regions in Poland: 1) the Coastal Lowlands, 2) the Baltic Lakes Region, 3) the Central Plains, 4) the Polish Uplands, 5) the Carpathian Forelands, 6) the Sudetes Mountains, and 7) the Western Carpathian Mountains. Most of Poland is covered by flat plains and gently rolling hills. The plains contain most of the land suitable for cultivation. The Sudetes and the Western Carpathian Mountains form part of the border in the south. Poland has thousands of small, scenic lakes in the northern part of the country (the Baltic Lakes Region).

CLIMATE

Poland's climate varies from region to region. The coastal regions have milder weather than the inland regions. The mountainous areas are cooler than the lowlands. Temperatures throughout the country average 26°F (-3°C) in January. The average July temperature is 73°F (23°C). Precipitation is common throughout the year and averages 24 in. (61 cm).

ECONOMY

Poland's economy has undergone a major upheaval since its change in government in 1990. The new democratic government set up a market economy that has resulted in rising prices and higher unemployment. With the help of other nations and rigid budget controls, Poland should be able to utilize its skilled labor and natural resources as a free market.

Agriculture - barley, hogs, potatoes, rye, sugar beets, and wheat

Manufacturing - chemicals, food products, iron and steel, machinery, ships, and textiles

Mining - coal, copper, silver, and sulfur

Exports - chemicals, coal, food products, machinery, metals, ships, and sulfur

Imports - chemicals, cotton, food products, iron ore, machinery, petroleum, and wool

LIFE-STYLE

Before World War II, Poland was largely agricultural. After the war, it grew into an industrial nation. People began moving from rural to urban areas. About 61 percent of the population now live in urban areas.

Most Polish families in urban areas live in simple, two- or three-room homes. In rural areas, families live in small wooden or brick cottages. Most Poles wear Western-style clothing, reserving folk costumes for special occasions.

The Polish people enjoy meaty stews, hearty beet or cabbage soup, and mushrooms. Pork is the favorite meat. Common dishes include *pierogi* (dumplings with cream cheese and potatoes), *uszka* (a kind of ravioli), *bigos* (sausages, mushrooms, cabbage), poppy seed desserts, and cheesecake.

About 98 percent of Poles aged 15 and older are literate. Most students attend free, government-operated schools, but a growing number are attending private schools. Children are required to attend school from ages seven to 15. After elementary school, students may attend four-year secondary or vocational schools.

Popular sports in Poland are soccer, track and field events, cycling, table tennis, skiing, basketball, and volleyball. Bridge is a very popular card game in Poland. Camping and hiking are also popular activities. Poland has produced many exceptional writers, musicians, and artists, among those the composer Frédéric Chopin.

IT'S A FACT!

Jagiellonian University - formerly the University of Kraków, was founded in 1364. It is Poland's oldest university.

Rysy Peak - the country's highest point, rises 8,199 ft. (2,499 m) above sea level.

Vistula River - the country's longest river, flows 675 mi. (1,086 km) from the Western Carpathians to the Baltic Sea.

 DID YOU KNOW...

- The name *Polane*, for which Poland is named, comes from a Slavic word that means "plain" or "field"?
- About 80 percent of Polish farms are privately owned and the average size is approximately 12 acres (5 hectares)?
- A Christmas Eve tradition practiced in some areas of Poland involves placing straw under the tablecloth during the evening meal? Family members then pull straws to determine fortunes.
- Poles sometimes entertain at *kawiarnas*, cafes which offer a variety of French pastries and Polish specialties?

PORTUGAL

OFFICIAL NAME: República Portuguesa (Portuguese Republic)
LOCATION: Western Europe
AREA: 34,340 sq. mi. (88,941 sq. km)
POPULATION (Est. 1993): 10,372,000
CAPITAL: Lisbon
LARGEST CITIES: Lisbon, Porto
GOVERNMENT: Parliamentary republic governed by a president.
FLAG: Two vertical stripes of green and red—representing hope and the blood of the country's heroes. The coat of arms—which features castles and shields—is centered on the colors' dividing line.
ETHNIC GROUPS: Mediterranean, small African minority
LANGUAGE: Portuguese
RELIGION: Roman Catholic
BASIC MONETARY UNIT: Portuguese Escudo

GEOGRAPHY

Portugal, the westernmost country of continental Europe, shares the Iberian Peninsula with Spain. At its greatest distances, Portugal measures 350 mi. (563 km) from north to south and 125 mi. (201 km) from east to west. It has 458 mi. (737 km) of coastline along the Atlantic Ocean.

Portugal has four main land regions: 1) the Coastal Plains, 2) the Northern Tablelands, 3) the Central Range, and 4) the Southern Tablelands. The Coastal Plains are flatlands lying along and near the southern and western coasts. The Northern Tablelands, Central Range, and Southern Tablelands are all extensions of a huge plateau called the *Meseta* that covers much of Spain. These regions are mostly plains broken by mountain ranges

CLIMATE

Portugal has a mild climate with lots of sunshine. In July, temperatures average about 70°F (21°C). The temperature average in January is 50°F (10°C). Average annual precipitation in the north is 55 in. (140 cm), while the south receives an average of 20 in. (51 cm) per year.

ECONOMY

Portugal has one of the poorest economies in Europe, but the last 30 years have seen definite growth. Portuguese wines are world-famous.

Agriculture - beef cattle, chickens, corn, grapes, hogs, milk, olives, potatoes, and tomatoes

Fishing - sardines and tuna

Manufacturing - cement, ceramics, cork products, electrical machinery, fertilizer, food products, paper products, shoes, and textiles

Mining - building stone, coal, copper, decorative marble, and wolframite

Exports - clothing and textiles, cork, paper, and wine

Imports - chemicals, grains, iron and steel, petroleum and petroleum products, textile yarn and fiber, and transportation equipment

LIFE-STYLE

Staples of the diet include meat, fish, rice, and potatoes. A popular dish throughout the country is *bife com ovo a cavalo* (steak and fried potatoes with an egg on top). Wine is served with meals to all members of the family. A strong espresso coffee, called *bica*, is served after the meal.

About two-thirds of Portugal's population live in rural areas. Many people in rural Portugal live along the coast in small fishing villages or on farms. Cities contain modern buildings mixed with structures built as far back as the 1500s.

Recreation for the Portuguese may include soccer, a bullfight, or folk songs. Families picnic, take walks, and go to the beach or park. Outdoor cafés are also frequented.

Portuguese children are required to attend school between the ages of six and 14. However, many leave school earlier to work.

IT'S A FACT!

Estrela - the country's highest point, rises 6,539 ft. (1,993 m) above sea level.

Fátima - Portuguese town where the Virgin Mary was reportedly sighted in 1917 by children tending sheep.

Tagus River - divides the country almost in half. The weather, population, and politics vary widely between the areas north of and south of the river.

 DID YOU KNOW...

- During bullfights in Portugal, it is illegal to kill the bull?
- Some Portuguese winemakers still crush the grapes with their bare feet?
- Stretching at the table is considered impolite because it indicates boredom?

PUERTO RICO
Dependency of the United States

OFFICIAL NAME: Commonwealth of Puerto Rico
LOCATION: Atlantic Ocean/Caribbean Sea
AREA: 3,515 sq. mi. (9,103 sq. km)
POPULATION (Est. 1993): 3,797,082
CAPITAL: San Juan
LARGEST CITIES: San Juan, Bayamón, Carolina, Mayagüez, Ponce
GOVERNMENT: Commonwealth governed by an elected governor.
FLAG: Designed in 1895 and adopted in 1952. Features five horizontal stripes—three red separated by two white—and a blue triangle on the hoist side with a five-pointed, white star in its center.
ETHNIC GROUPS: Black, Spanish, Portuguese, Italian, French
LANGUAGES: Spanish, English
RELIGION: Christianity
BASIC MONETARY UNIT: United States Dollar

PUERTO RICO

GEOGRAPHY

Puerto Rico is located about 1,000 mi. (1,600 km) southeast of Florida in the United States. Its total area includes Puerto Rico, Culebra, Mona, and Vieques Islands, as well as 56 sq. mi. (145 sq. km) of inland water. Puerto Rico measures 39 mi. (63 km) from east to west and 111 mi. (179 km) from east to west at its greatest distances. It has 311 mi. (501 km) of coastline along the North Atlantic Ocean and the Caribbean Sea.

Puerto Rico has four main land regions: 1) the Coastal Lowlands, 2) the Coastal Valley, 3) the Foothills, and 4) the Central Mountains. The island has many beaches and harbors.

CLIMATE

Puerto Rico has a mildly tropical climate. The average temperature ranges from 73°F (23°C) in January to 80°F (27°C) in July. The average annual rainfall ranges from 37 in. (94 cm) along the southern coast to 70 in. (180 cm) in the north. The tropical rainforest on El Yunque Mountain may get 200 in. (510 cm) of rain annually. Hurricanes can be a threat from June to November. Snow and frost are nonexistent.

ECONOMY

Service industries provide almost 60 percent of Puerto Rico's gross domestic product, and employ most Puerto Rican workers. Manufacturing is Puerto Rico's single most valuable industry. Many of the country's 2,000 factories were set up under the government's *Operation Bootstrap* program. Pleasant weather year-round attracts many tourists.

Agriculture - avocados, bananas, beef cattle, coconuts, coffee, milk, oranges, pineapples, plantains, poultry and eggs, and sugar cane

Fishing - fish, lobster, and shellfish

Manufacturing - clothing, electrical and non-electrical machinery and equipment, medicines, processed foods, and scientific instruments

Exports - clothing, machinery, medicines, petroleum products, rum, scientific instruments, and sugar

Imports - crude petroleum and food products

LIFE-STYLE

Puerto Rico's population is about two-thirds urban. The average population density is 1,004 persons per sq. mi. (387 persons per sq. km). Farmland covers more than half of the island's total land area. Most of the present population is of Spanish descent. This heritage is reflected in the customs and language of the people. Puerto Rico's ties with the United States are also evident. Its large cities have freeways, shopping centers, and housing projects much like those in the United States.

Popular Puerto Rican dishes are *arroz con pollo* (rice and chicken), *paella* (a spicy stew of rice, chicken, seafood, and vegetables), and plantain. Tropical fruit—such as bananas, pineapples, avocados, coconuts, and oranges—is often included in meals.

Puerto Rico has many public schools. About 90 percent of Puerto Rico's people are literate. English is taught as well as Spanish.

The most popular sport is baseball. Among men, cockfighting is a favorite. A love for art and music is encouraged in Puerto Rican homes. Almost everyone can play a musical instrument. The island offers a variety of water sports.

Puerto Rico has well-developed transportation.

IT'S A FACT!

Cerro de Punta - the country's highest point, rises 4,389 ft. (1,338 m) above sea level.

El Morro Fortress - built by the Spanish between 1539 and 1787 to guard the Bay of San Juan.

Hacienda Buena Vista - located in the city of Ponce, is a restored coffee and grain mill from the 1800s.

Rio Camuy Cave Park - located near the city of Arecibo, is home to limestone caves that were carved thousands of years ago by one of the world's largest underground rivers.

 DID YOU KNOW...
- *Puerto Rico* is Spanish for "rich port"?
- Puerto Rico is home to very few snakes, none of which are poisonous?
- El Yunque, "the anvil," is a mountain with a rainforest on its slopes; the only rainforest in the U.S. Forest Service?
- The Arawak Indians were Puerto Rico's first inhabitants; no full-blooded Indians now exist in the country?
- Puerto Rico is the only part of present-day United States where Columbus landed?

QATAR

OFFICIAL NAME: Dawlat al-Qatar (The State of Qatar)
LOCATION: Southwestern Asia
AREA: 4,247 sq. mi. (11,000 sq. km)
POPULATION (Est. 1993): 407,000
CAPITAL/LARGEST CITY: Doha
GOVERNMENT: Traditional monarchy governed by an *emir* (prince).
FLAG: White and maroon colors that meet in a zigzag pattern near the hoist side.
ETHNIC GROUPS: Arab
LANGUAGES: Arabic, English
RELIGION: Islam
BASIC MONETARY UNIT: Qatar Riyal

GEOGRAPHY

Qatar lies on a peninsula that juts from eastern Arabia into the Persian Gulf. At its greatest distances, Qatar measures 115 mi. (185 km) from north to south and 55 mi. (89 km) from east to west. It has 235 mi. (378 km) of coastline.

Most of Qatar is a low-lying, stony desert. Barren salt flats lie in the south. Qatar also has many small islands.

CLIMATE

The country has a dry, very hot climate. Temperatures in the summer often exceed 120°F (49°C). Winter temperatures are somewhat cooler.

Qatar averages only 4 in. (10 cm) of rainfall yearly. Sandstorms and dust storms are common.

ECONOMY

Since the 1950s, Qatar's economy has been based on the exporting of petroleum and petroleum products. Prior to that, Qatar's citizens herded camels, fished, and pearled to make a living.

Agriculture - fish, fruit, and vegetables

Manufacturing - cement, fertilizers, oil production and refining, petrochemicals, and steel

Mining - crude oil

Exports - fertilizers and petroleum products

Imports - animal and vegetable oil, chemicals, foodstuffs, machinery and equipment, manufactured goods, and meat

LIFE-STYLE

Almost 90 percent of the people live in urban areas. Most live in modern houses or apartments. Seventy percent work in industry, services, and commerce; 20 percent work for the government; and ten percent are employed in farming and fishing.

Less than one-third of all Qataris are native to Qatar. The other two-thirds are foreign workers with temporary-resident status who came to work in the petroleum industries.

A few Qataris wear Western-style clothing, but most prefer traditional Arab garments.

Children ages six to 16 are required to attend school. About half of the people can read and write. The country has special schools that teach adults to read and write.

The government provides free education, health care, and housing for the poor.

IT'S A FACT!

Tuwayyir al Hamir - the country's highest point, rises 338 ft. (103 m) above sea level.

DID YOU KNOW...

- Qatar ranks as one of the richest nations in the world in terms of average income per person?
- Qatar has little natural water, so it must distill water from the sea for drinking?
- Since Qatar's growing season lasts only from January to March, most food must be imported?

RÉUNION
Overseas Department of France

OFFICIAL NAME: Réunion
LOCATION: Indian Ocean
AREA: 970 sq. mi. (2,512 sq. km)
POPULATION (Est. 1993): 515,814
CAPITAL: Saint-Denis
IMPORTANT CITIES: Saint-Denis, Saint-Louis, Saint-Pierre
GOVERNMENT: Department of France governed by a prefect.
FLAG: Uses the flag of France.
ETHNIC GROUP: French Creole
LANGUAGES: French, Creole dialect (mix of French and African Bantu languages)
RELIGION: Roman Catholic
BASIC MONETARY UNIT: French Franc

GEOGRAPHY

Réunion is an oval-shaped, volcanic island in the Indian Ocean about 400 mi. (640 km) east of Madagascar. Although politically an overseas department of France, geographically the island is part of the Mascarene Islands, which also include Mauritius and Rodrigues. Most of Réunion consists of rugged mountains and high plateaus surrounded by a narrow coastal plain that contains fertile lowlands. Several swift streams flow from the interior and sometimes overflow and destroy crops.

CLIMATE

The coastal areas of Réunion have a tropical climate, while the inland mountainous region is more moderate. The eastern side of the island receives much more rain than the western side. The island has two seasons: cool and dry from May to November and hot and rainy from November to April. Hurricanes are apt to strike the coastal areas.

ECONOMY

The economy of the island is based on agriculture. High unemployment is a major problem. The government has been working to develop the tourist industry to reduce this problem.

Agriculture - coffee, corn, manioc, perfume plants, sugar cane, tea, tobacco, and vanilla

Manufacturing - perfume, rum distilling, and sugar cane processing

Exports - molasses, perfume, rum, and sugar

Imports - beverages, food, manufactured goods, petroleum products, raw materials, and transportation equipment

LIFE-STYLE

The majority of Réunion's people are farmers. Much of the cultivated land holds sugar cane plantations.

The people are descendants of Africans, Malays, Chinese, Indians, and French settlers.

There is an extreme gap between the living standards of the wealthy and the poor of the island.

IT'S A FACT!

Piton de la Fournaise (Furnace Peak) - is a still-active volcano.

Piton des Neiges (Snowy Peak) - the country's highest point, rises more than 10,000 ft. (3,070 m) above sea level.

DID YOU KNOW...

- Until 1848, the name of the island was *Bourbon*?
- Réunion was uninhabited when the Portuguese explorer, Pedro Mascarenhas, discovered it in the early 16th century?

ROMANIA

OFFICIAL NAME: Republica Românâ (Republic of Romania)
LOCATION: Southeastern Europe
AREA: 91,699 sq. mi. (237,500 sq. km)
POPULATION (Est. 1993): 23,595,000
CAPITAL: Bucharest
LARGEST CITIES: Bucharest, Constanta, Iasi, Timisoara
GOVERNMENT: Republic governed by a president.
FLAG: Three vertical stripes of blue, yellow, and red representing Romania's national colors.
ETHNIC GROUPS: Romanian, Hungarian, German
LANGUAGES: Romanian, Hungarian, German
RELIGIONS: Eastern Orthodox, Roman Catholic
BASIC MONETARY UNIT: Leu

GEOGRAPHY

Romania measures 320 mi. (515 km) from north to south and 450 mi. (724 km) from east to west at its greatest distances. It has 130 mi. (209 km) of coastline along the Black Sea.

Romania's six major land regions are: 1) Transylvania, 2) Bukovina, 2) Moldavia, 3) Walachia, 5) Banat, and 6) Dobruja. The country's landscape includes a group of mountain ranges that curve through the northern and central part of Romania. The mountains surround a flatland called the Transylvanian Plateau. In turn, the mountains are surrounded by plains on the east, west, and south. Romania has many rivers and lakes.

CLIMATE

Romania has hot, sunny summers and cold, cloudy winters. In general, the plains are warmer than the mountains. The average temperature ranges from 30°F (-1°C) in January to 70°F (21°C) in July. In some mountain areas, the average yearly precipitation is 40 in. (100 cm), while the plains may receive less than 20 in. (50 cm) annually.

ECONOMY

Romania has many natural resources, including fertile soil, mineral deposits, and large forests. Despite this natural wealth, it has always been one of Europe's least developed nations, due in part to an overdependence on agriculture. After the 1989 revolution, the government began to take steps to create a free-enterprise economy.

Agriculture - corn, grapes, milk, potatoes, sugar beets, sunflower seeds, wheat, and wool

Manufacturing - cement, clothing and shoes, iron and steel, machinery, petroleum products, processed foods, and wood products

Mining - coal, natural gas, and petroleum

Exports - cement, chemicals, clothing and shoes, fuels, industrial machinery, lumber, and processed foods

Imports - chemicals, coal, cotton, fuels, industrial machinery, and iron ore

LIFE-STYLE

Romanians have one of the lowest standards of living in Eastern Europe. About half of the people live in rural areas. Most workers make enough money to pay for their families' needs plus have a little left for recreation. But few Romanians can afford luxury items, such as cars and TVs.

Most rural dwellers live in simple, two- or three-room cottages decorated with hand-crafted rugs, plates, and so on.

Romania's cities feature buildings hundreds of years old alongside modern structures. Due to population growth, cities suffer from a housing shortage. Most people live in crowded apartments.

Favorite dishes in Romania include *mititei* (grilled meatballs), *patricieni* (grilled sausage), and *mamaliga* (cornmeal mush served like mashed potatoes). Wine or beer are popular drinks with meals. *Tzuica*, a plum brandy, is also popular.

Children are required to attend school from ages six to 16. After eight years of elementary school, students take tests to determine what they will study in secondary school. About half are assigned to vocational courses; most of the others take courses in advanced technical skills, teaching, or the arts.

Soccer is the most important spectator sport in the country. City dwellers enjoy dining at restaurants and attending concert halls where Romanian folk music is played. They also visit Romanian folk art exhibits. Festivals are an important social event in rural Romania. The mountains and the Black Sea coast are popular vacation areas. Mountain activities include skiing, hiking, and climbing.

IT'S A FACT!

Danube River - the country's longest and most important river, flows out of Yugoslavia for a distance of 900 mi. (1,400 km) in Romania.

Mount Moldoveanu - the country's highest point, rises 8,343 ft. (2,543 m) above sea level.

 DID YOU KNOW...

- The Romanians are the only Eastern Europeans who trace their ancestry and language back to the Romans?
- The best-known Romanian paintings appear on the outside walls of churches? These medieval works were done to remind the peasants of their faith.

RUSSIA

OFFICIAL NAME: Russian Federation
LOCATION: Northeastern Europe and Northern Asia
AREA: 6,592,850 sq. mi. (17,075,400 sq. km)
POPULATION (Est. 1993): 151,436,000
CAPITAL: Moscow
LARGEST CITIES: Moscow, St. Petersburg
GOVERNMENT: Federation in transition.

FLAG: Three horizontal stripes of white, blue, and red.
ETHNIC GROUPS: Russian, others
LANGUAGE: Russian
RELIGION: Russian Orthodox
BASIC MONETARY UNIT: Ruble

GEOGRAPHY

Russia is the largest country in area. It covers large portions of two continents—Europe and Asia. At its greatest distances, Russia measures 2,800 mi. (4,500 km) from north to south and 6,000 mi. (9,650 km) from east to west.

Russia boasts many large rivers and about 200,000 lakes. The country is divided into five main land regions: 1) the European Plain, which is flat to gently rolling, 2) the Ural Mountains, which form a boundary between the Asian and European sections of Russia and are rich in copper, iron, and other metals, 3) the West Siberian Plain, which is the world's largest level region, 4) the Central Siberian Plateau, with thick pine forests covering much of the land, and 5) the East Siberian Uplands, a wilderness area of mountains and plateaus that is rich in mineral deposits, but subject to a harsh climate making it difficult to utilize these resources. This region's Kamchatka Peninsula holds about 25 active volcanoes.

CLIMATE

Russia is known for its long and harsh winters. Because the northernmost portion of Russia is covered with snow almost three-fourths of the year, half of its farmland has permafrost beneath the surface. Coastal waters, lakes, and rivers are also frozen much of the year.

Even though northeastern Siberia is one of the coldest places in the world, it can have extremely high temperatures. In January, temperatures average below -50°F (-46°C). Records indicate temperatures have reached as low as -90°F (-68°C). In July, temperatures average 60°F (16°C), but may climb as high as 100°F (38°C).

Light to moderate precipitation occurs in the country. It varies from heavier precipitation in the European Plain, parts of the East Siberian Uplands, and mountainous areas along the southern border to very little precipitation in the interior regions.

ECONOMY

At the present time, Russia's economy is weak. The change from a Communist state to a federation has wreaked havoc with the economy. Prices are high and a shortage of goods is a continuing problem. The country is trying to establish a free market economy, but few people have had experience with a capitalist approach and so the change is a painful process.

Agriculture - barley, cattle, flax, fruits, hogs, oats, potatoes, rye, sheep, sugar beets, sunflowers, and wheat

Fishing - cod, haddock, herring, and salmon

Manufacturing - chemicals, construction materials, electrical equipment, iron and steel, lumber, machinery, and paper

Mining - coal, iron ore, manganese, natural gas, nickel, petroleum, and platinum-group metals

Exports - chemicals, machinery, minerals, paper products, petroleum, and wood products

Imports - consumer goods, food and beverages, industrial equipment, and machinery

LIFE-STYLE

Life under first the czars and then the Communists has caused older generations of Russians to be pessimistic about the future. Personal initiative and the desire to work independently were suppressed by the Communist government. With the fall of Communism and the breakup of the Soviet Union, greater political, legal, economic, and religious freedoms have been evolving. Younger generations are adapting quickly to the values of compromise, personal creativity, and risk-taking.

In the cities, housing is difficult to obtain, so more than one generation may live under one roof. Urban apartments usually consist of one room, a kitchen, and a bathroom. Oftentimes kitchen and bath facilities are shared among apartments. Rural homes are larger, but they lack modern conveniences such as running water.

Food shortages are common in Russian cities, so shoppers go from store to store and wait in long lines to get what they need. The same holds true for manufactured goods. In rural areas, while food is more plentiful, it lacks variety. Fortunately, people are now allowed to own their own farms rather than work the collective farms run by the government.

Russians prefer Western clothing, but high costs, scarcity, and cold weather tend to limit the variety available.

The Russian diet tends to be quite heavy, consisting of bread, meat, and potatoes. Frying is a common method of food preparation. Some favorite Russian dishes that are also popular in other parts of the world are *borscht* (beet soup), *piroshki* (stuffed dumplings), and *beef stroganoff* (strips of beef sautéed with onions and mushrooms in a sour cream sauce). Tea is a favorite beverage.

The people of Russia have little leisure time due to the long hours they must work to make ends meet. The favorite sport is soccer, but Russians enjoy many sports, particularly winter sports.

Russian people spend considerable amounts of time visiting museums, compared to people of other countries. These include historical, art, and scientific museums.

Most Russians take their vacations in the summer. They visit resort areas along the Volga River, the Black Sea, and the Baltic Sea. Many people who are nature lovers enjoy visiting the countryside.

Russia has always valued education and considered it a necessity for social advancement. Educators are working to change the curriculum to prepare students for the country's changing economy. Law requires that students attend school for eleven years; the most frequently taught foreign language is English.

IT'S A FACT!

Lake Baikal - the world's deepest lake, is located in Siberia and has a depth of 5,315 ft. (1,620 m) at its deepest point.

Lake Ladoga - the largest lake in Europe, is located near St. Petersburg and covers 6,835 sq. mi. (17,703 sq. km).

Lena River - the country's longest river, is located in Siberia and measures 2,734 mi. (4,400 m) long.

Mount Elbrus - the country's highest point, rises 18,510 ft. (5,642 m) above sea level.

 DID YOU KNOW...

- *Caviar*, the eggs of the sturgeon, is a famous Russian delicacy?
- A train trip from Moscow in the west to Vladivostok in the east passes through eight time zones and takes seven days to complete?
- Today, Russians rely on a network of friends and acquaintances to help supply food, clothing, and other hard-to-find goods?
- Because of the underdeveloped communications system in Russia, it can take years to complete telephone installations in a new apartment complex?
- Moscow's subway system, the Metro, is noted for its many beautiful subway stations?
- One of the world's largest art collections is housed in the Hermitage Museum in St. Petersburg?
- St. Basil's Cathedral, a Byzantine-style cathedral with onion-shaped domes, is one of the most widely recognized buildings in the world?
- The 1800s were a time of great productivity for Russian artists? Among them were the authors Anton Chekhov, Fyodor Dostoevsky, and Leo Tolstoy, who all wrote literary masterpieces, and the musical composer Peter Ilich Tchaikovsky.

RWANDA

OFFICIAL NAME: Republic of Rwanda
FORMERLY: Ruanda, the northern half of what was once Ruanda-Urundi
LOCATION: East-central Africa
AREA: 10,169 sq. mi. (26,338 sq. km)
POPULATION (Est. 1992): 7,735,000
CAPITAL/LARGEST CITY: Kigali
GOVERNMENT: Republic headed by a president.
FLAG: Three vertical stripes of red, yellow, and green with a black, uppercase letter "R" centered on the yellow stripe.
ETHNIC GROUPS: Hutu (Bahutu), Tutsi (Watusi), Pygmy, European
LANGUAGES: French, Kinyarwanda
RELIGIONS: Roman Catholic, Traditional African Religions
BASIC MONETARY UNIT: Rwandan Franc

GEOGRAPHY

At its greatest distances, Rwanda, a landlocked country, measures 110 mi. (177 km) from north to south and 145 mi. (233 km) from east to west. The country lies just south of the equator on a series of plateaus. The landscape ranges from volcanic mountains and winding valleys in the west to high plateaus which slope gently to marshy plains in the east. The northwest border is dominated by the Virunga Mountains; the western border is formed by Lake Kivu and the Rusizi River; the eastern border is formed by the Kagera River; and part of the southern border is formed by the Akanyaru River.

CLIMATE

Although Rwanda is located close to the equator, it maintains a cool and pleasant climate due to its high plateaus. Western Rwanda has an average annual temperature of 73°F (23°C) and receives about 30 in. (76 cm) of rain per year. The western mountain areas have an average annual temperature of 63°F (17°C) and receive about 58 in. (147 cm) of rain per year, with more rain falling in the Virunga Mountains. The plateaus have an average annual temperature of 68°F (20°C) and receive about 47 in. (119 cm) of rain per year.

ECONOMY

Rwanda is one of Africa's poorest countries. It has very little industry and a high population density.

Agriculture - bananas, beans, cassava, cattle, coffee, pyrethrum (insecticide), sorghum, sweet potatoes, and tea

Manufacturing - agricultural processing, cement, cigarettes, furniture, plastic goods, shoes, soap, and textiles

Mining - cassiterite (tin ore), gold, tin, tungsten, and wolframite

Exports - coffee, tea, pyrethrum, tin, and wolframite

Imports - capital goods, cement, construction material, food, machines and equipment, petroleum products, steel, and textiles

LIFE-STYLE

Most Rwandans belong to the Hutu ethnic group who make a living by raising crops or cattle, or growing coffee. Some Hutu work in urban areas or neighboring countries. The Tutsi population mainly hold jobs in business or government agencies. The Pygmies were once hunters, but many now live and work in urban areas. The Europeans mainly make a living raising tea and pyrethrum, mining, or serving as Christian missionaries.

Public education is free, and children ages seven to 14 are required to attend school. However, there is a shortage of classroom facilities, and not all children receive an education.

Rwanda has poor health conditions, and many Rwandans suffer from intestinal diseases, malaria, parasitic diseases, respiratory diseases, and venereal diseases.

Rwandans have a traditional culture based on ceremonies (related to birth, marriage, death, harvest, and hunting), oral literature (folk tales, myths, poetry, and proverbs), songs, and other arts (including basketry, dancing, and weaving).

IT'S A FACT!

Karisimbi - the country's highest point, is located in the Virunga Mountains and rises 14,787 ft. (4,507 km) above sea level.

Lake Kivu - Africa's highest lake, is located 4,829 ft. (1,472 m) above sea level.

 DID YOU KNOW...

- Rwanda's population averages 761 people per sq. mi. (294 people per sq. km), making it one of Africa's most crowded countries?
- Rwandans of the Batutsi ethnic group average over 6'6" in height?
- Rwanda averages only one doctor per 22,000 people?

SAINT HELENA
Dependent Territory of the United Kingdom

OFFICIAL NAME: Saint Helena
LOCATION: South Atlantic Ocean
AREA: 47 sq. mi. (122 sq. km)
POPULATION (Est. 1993): 6,720
CAPITAL: Jamestown
GOVERNMENT: Dependent territory of the United Kingdom governed by an executive council and a 12-member elected Legislative Council.
FLAG: Blue field with the flag of the United Kingdom in the upper, hoist-side quadrant. The Saint Helenian shield —which features a rocky coastline and a three-masted ship—is centered on the flag's outer half.
ETHNIC GROUPS: African, East Indian, European
LANGUAGE: English
RELIGIONS: Anglican, Baptist, Seventh-Day Adventist, Roman Catholic
BASIC MONETARY UNIT: Saint Helenian Pound

South Atlantic Ocean

★Jamestown

SAINT HELENA

GEOGRAPHY

Saint Helena lies about 1,200 mi. (1,930 km) off mainland Africa's southwest coast and has 37 mi. (60 km) of coastline along the South Atlantic Ocean. It is mainly rough, mountainous land scattered with small plains and plateaus. Less than one-third of the land is arable.

It has two dependencies: Ascension Island and the Tristan da Cunha island group. Ascension Island lies about 700 mi. (1,100 km) northwest of Saint Helena and has an area of about 34 sq. mi. (88 sq. km). Its population is approximately 1,500, and it is used as a breeding ground for sea turtles and sooty terns. The Tristan da Cunha island group consists of about six islands—the largest of which include Gough, Inaccessible, Nightingale, and Tristan da Cunha Islands—located about 1,500 mi. (2,414 km) south-southwest of Saint Helena. Tristan da Cunha Island has an area of about 40 sq. mi. (104 sq. km).

CLIMATE

Saint Helena has a mild tropical and marine climate, which is tempered by southeast trade winds.

ECONOMY

Saint Helena's economy is based primarily on financial assistance from the United Kingdom. Some of the country's income is earned from fishing, handicraft sales, and livestock raising.

Agriculture - cattle, maize, New Zealand flax, potatoes, sheep, and vegetables

Fishing - crawfishing (on Tristan da Cunha Island), skipjack, and tuna

Manufacturing - crafts (including furniture, lacework, and fancy woodwork), fiber mats, and fish curing

Exports - fish and handicrafts

Imports - animal feed, beverages, building materials, food, fuel, machinery and parts, motor vehicles and parts, and tobacco

LIFE-STYLE

Saint Helena was discovered by the Portuguese in 1502 and has been a British dependency since 1673.

There are few jobs to be had on Saint Helena, leaving many Saint Helenians to seek employment overseas.

IT'S A FACT!

Diana's Peak - the country's highest point, is located on Saint Helena and rises 2,700 ft. (823 m) above sea level.

DID YOU KNOW...

- Saint Helena was Napolean Bonaparte's place of exile from 1815 until his death in 1821, and is also his place of burial?
- Saint Helena is home to at least 40 plant species which are not known to exist any other place in the world?
- Saint Helena was evacuated between 1961 and 1963 following a volcanic eruption?

SAINT KITTS & NEVIS

OFFICIAL NAME: Federation of Saint Kitts and Nevis
(Also known as Federation of Saint Christopher and Nevis)
LOCATION: Caribbean Sea
AREA: 101 sq. mi. (262 sq. km)
POPULATION (Est. 1993): 44,400
CAPITAL: Basseterre
LARGEST CITIES: Basseterre, Charlestown
GOVERNMENT: Constitutional monarchy.
FLAG: Triangles of green and red separated by a yellow-trimmed, diagonal black stripe. Two white stars are on the black stripe.
ETHNIC GROUP: Black African
LANGUAGE: English
RELIGION: Christianity (mainly Protestant)
BASIC MONETARY UNIT: East Caribbean Dollar

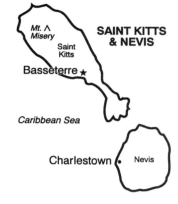

GEOGRAPHY

Saint Kitts and Nevis lies in the Caribbean Sea about 190 mi. (310 km) east of Puerto Rico.

Saint Kitts covers 65 sq. mi. (168 sq. km) and Nevis covers 36 sq. mi. (93 sq. km). The two islands are approximately 2 mi. (3.2 km) apart. They are actually the tops of two volcanic mountains that begin below the water. Each island has a narrow band of fertile plains along its coast.

CLIMATE

Saint Kitts and Nevis has a pleasant tropical climate that is cooled by northeast trade winds most of the year. The average rainfall is about 55 in. (140 cm) yearly. Temperatures average 78°F (25°C) annually. Both islands are subject to the destruction caused by hurricanes.

ECONOMY

The economy of these islands depends on sugar and tourism. Unemployment is frequently high, especially when sugar production and tourism are slow. Young people leave the island every year to look for jobs elsewhere.

Agriculture - cotton, fruit, sugar cane, and vegetables
Manufacturing - beverages, building construction, clothing, electronics, and sugar processing
Exports - beverages, clothing, electrical machinery, molasses, and sugar
Imports - building materials, chemical products, foodstuffs, fuel, machinery, and metal products

LIFE-STYLE

Almost two-thirds of the people live in rural villages and work on small farms or sugar plantations. Their houses are made of concrete, stone, or wood.

Lightweight cotton clothing—similar to that worn during the summer in the United States—is the common style of dress year round.

Both St. Kitts and Nevis have well-developed primary and secondary schools.

IT'S A FACT!

Mount Misery - the country's highest point, is located on Saint Kitts and rises 3,792 ft. (1,156 m) above sea level.

DID YOU KNOW...

- About 80 percent of the country's people live on Saint Kitts?
- Christopher Columbus sighted the islands on his second voyage to the New World in 1493?
- The first inhabitants of the islands were Arawak Carib Indians?
- Many of the beaches are made up of black volcanic sand?
- Saint Kitts and Nevis was controlled by Great Britain from 1713 to 1983, when it became an independent nation?

SAINT LUCIA

OFFICIAL NAME: Saint Lucia
LOCATION: Caribbean Sea
AREA: 240 sq. mi. (622 sq. km)
POPULATION (Est. 1993): 144,337
CAPITAL/LARGEST CITY: Castries
GOVERNMENT: Constitutional monarchy headed by a prime minister.
FLAG: Yellow isosceles triangle transposed over a white-edged, black arrowhead, centered on a blue field.
ETHNIC GROUPS: Black, mixed, East Indian, White
LANGUAGES: English, French patois
RELIGIONS: Roman Catholic, Protestant, Anglican
BASIC MONETARY UNIT: East Caribbean Dollar

GEOGRAPHY

Saint Lucia is the second largest of the Windward Islands and is located about 240 mi. (386 km) north of Venezuela. It has 98 mi. (158 km) of coastline along the Caribbean Sea.

Saint Lucia is a mountainous island covered by tropical vegetation. Broad, fertile valleys are the island's only flatland. The elevations are generally higher in the interior and lower near the coast.

CLIMATE

Saint Lucia has a tropical climate, with both a rainy season—May to August—and a dry season—January to April. The average annual temperature ranges from 70° to 95°F (21° to 35°C). The average annual rainfall is about 100 in. (254 cm). The island is subject to hurricanes and volcanic activity.

ECONOMY

Saint Lucia's economy is based primarily on agriculture. It is supplemented by tourism.

Agriculture - bananas, citrus fruit, cocoa, coconuts, root crops, and vegetables

Manufacturing - beverages, clothing, coconut processing, corrugated boxes, electrical parts, lime processing, paper products, and textiles

Exports - bananas, clothing, cocoa, coconuts and coconut oil, fruits, and vegetables

Imports - chemicals, food, fuels, livestock, manufactured goods, and machinery and transportation equipment

LIFE-STYLE

Saint Lucia's population is approximately 55 percent rural and 45 percent urban. Most Saint Lucians wear Western-style clothing and live in pastel-colored shelters constructed of wood.

IT'S A FACT!

Gros Piton and Petit Piton - twin peaks located in the southwest and surrounding a small bay, they are famous for their sugar loaf shapes.

Mount Gimie - the island's highest point, rises 3,145 ft. (959 m) above sea level.

 DID YOU KNOW...
- Saint Lucia was under British rule from 1814 to 1979, after which time it gained its independence?
- Originally made of wood, many of Castries's buildings were destroyed by fires in 1948 and 1951?
- About nine-tenths of Saint Lucia's population is descended from African slaves brought to the island by early British and French settlers?

SAINT-PIERRE & MIQUELON
Territorial Collectivity of France

SAINT-PIERRE
& MIQUELON

OFFICIAL NAME: Departement de Saint-Pierre et Miquelon
(Territorial Collectivity of Saint-Pierre and Miquelon)
LOCATION: North Atlantic Ocean
AREA: 93 sq. mi. (242 sq. km)
POPULATION (Est. 1993): 6,652
CAPITAL/LARGEST CITY: Saint-Pierre (on Saint-Pierre Island)
GOVERNMENT: Territorial collectivity of France ruled by an administrator who
is assisted by a privy council (made up of department chiefs).
FLAG: Uses the flag of France.
ETHNIC GROUPS: Basques and Bretons (French fisherman)
LANGUAGE: French
RELIGION: Roman Catholic
BASIC MONETARY UNIT: French Franc

GEOGRAPHY

Saint-Pierre and Miquelon is an archipelago of eight islands located about 10 mi. (16 km) south of Newfoundland,
Canada. The islands have a combined coastline of 75 mi. (120
km) along the North Atlantic Ocean.

The two largest islands—Miquelon and Langlade—are
connected to each other by a narrow, sandy strip called the Isthmus of Langlade. They have a combined area of 83 sq. mi.
(216 sq. km). Miquelon is the northernmost island. It has a
rocky cape that extends 4 mi. (6.4 km) in the northwest, under
which is the Plain of Miquelon. The plain is an area of marshes,
peat bogs, and small lakes. Southern Miquelon has an area of
rugged, barren hills called the Mornes. Langlade's coast is lined
with cliffs, except in the north, and the entire island is drained by
a number of short rivers, the longest of which is Belle Rivière.

Saint-Pierre Island lies southeast of Langlade and is separated from it by a channel, La Baie, that is about 3 mi. (4.8 km)
wide. Saint-Pierre has rugged hills in the northwest and rocky
lowland in the southeast, with peat bogs, ponds, and small lakes
in both areas.

Of the country's islets, only one—Île aux Marins—is
inhabited. It lies to the east of Saint-Pierre and has an area of
123 acres (50 hectares).

CLIMATE

Saint-Pierre and Miquelon has a cold, wet climate with
much fog and mist. It is generally windy during spring and autumn. The average annual temperature ranges from about 14°F
(-10°C) in the winter to about 68°F (20°C) in the summer. The
average annual rainfall is 59 in. (150 cm).

ECONOMY

Saint-Pierre and Miquelon's economy is based primarily
on fishing and servicing fishing fleets. It is supplemented by
tourism in the summer.
Agriculture - cattle, fish, pigs, sheep, and vegetables
Manufacturing - fish processing
Exports - fish and fish products, and fox and mink pelts
Imports - building materials, clothing, electrical equipment,
fuel, machinery, and meat

LIFE-STYLE

Almost 90 percent of Saint-Pierre and Miquelon's population lives on Saint-Pierre Island.

Originally occupied by immigrant seafarers from western
France in early 17th century, the country was alternately controlled by England and France until 1814, when final possession was taken by France under the Treaty of Paris. The country was granted self-government by France in 1956.

IT'S A FACT!

Morne de la Grande Montagne - the archipelago's highest
point, is located in the Mornes on Miquelon Island and rises 787
ft. (240 m) above sea level.

 DID YOU KNOW...
- There are no television stations and only four radio sta-
tions in Saint-Pierre and Miquelon?
- Saint-Pierre and Miquelon was first discovered in 1520
by Portuguese explorer José Alvarez Faguendez?
- The country's total population has changed very little
since 1902?
- The islands of Saint-Pierre and Miquelon are the only
remaining part of the French colonial empire in North
America?

SAINT VINCENT & THE GRENADINES

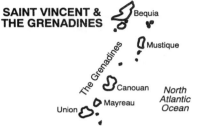

OFFICIAL NAME:	Saint Vincent and the Grenadines
LOCATION:	West Indies
AREA:	150 sq. mi. (388 sq. km)
POPULATION (Est. 1993):	119,000
CAPITAL/LARGEST CITY:	Kingstown
GOVERNMENT:	Constitutional monarchy headed by a prime minister.
FLAG:	Three horizontal stripes of blue, gold, and green. Three green diamonds appear on the gold stripe.
ETHNIC GROUP:	Black African
LANGUAGES:	English, French
RELIGIONS:	Anglican, Methodist, Roman Catholic
BASIC MONETARY UNIT:	East Caribbean Dollar

GEOGRAPHY

Saint Vincent and the Grenadines is one of the smallest island countries. It is located in the Caribbean Sea, about 200 mi. (320 km) north of Venezuela. The country consists of Saint Vincent and about 100 small islands of the Grenadine chain. Saint Vincent and the Grenadines is a rugged mountainous country formed by volcanic activity. Tropical vegetation covers much of the country.

CLIMATE

The country has a pleasant tropical climate. Temperatures range from 65° to 90°F (18° to 32°C). Annual rainfall ranges from 60 in. (150 cm) on southeastern Saint Vincent to 150 in. (381 cm) in the central mountains. The country's rainy season lasts from May to November.

ECONOMY

The country's economy is based largely on agriculture, though tourism is gaining in importance. Bananas are the chief crop.

Agriculture - arrowroot, bananas, coconuts, spices, and sweet potatoes

Manufacturing - food processing

Exports - arrowroot, bananas, coconuts, and spices

Imports - chemicals and fertilizers, foodstuffs, machinery and equipment, and minerals and fuels

LIFE-STYLE

Over 80 percent of the people live in rural areas. Many live in houses made of wood or concrete with tile roofs.

Staples of the diet are fish, rice, bananas, and a special dish of baked breadfruit and fried fish.

Most people work on farms and live in small villages, catching fish and growing food such as coconut palms, carrots, sweet potatoes, cassava, and groundnuts for their own use.

Primary education is free but not compulsory. Attendance is low.

IT'S A FACT!

The Botanic Garden - located in the capital city of Kingston, dates from 1765 and is the oldest such garden in the Americas. It contains a breadfruit tree grown from a plant brought from Tahiti by British sea captain William Bligh (1754-1817).

Mount Soufrière - the country's highest point and an active volcano, is located on Saint Vincent and rises 4,048 ft. (1,234 m) above sea level.

DID YOU KNOW...

- Most of the people of Saint Vincent and the Grenadines are descendants of black African slaves brought to the country by the French and English?
- There is one telephone for every six people in the country?

SAN MARINO

OFFICIAL NAME: La Serenissima Repubblica di San Marino (The Most Serene Republic of San Marino)
LOCATION: Europe
AREA: 24 sq. mi. (61 sq. km)
POPULATION (Est. 1995): 23,000
CAPITAL/LARGEST CITY: San Marino
GOVERNMENT: Republic headed by two members, officials called *captains-regent*, of the 60-member Grand and General Council.
FLAG: A blue and a white horizontal stripe. The state flag has a coat of arms in the center, but the national flag does not.
ETHNIC GROUPS: Sanmarinese, Italian
LANGUAGE: Italian
RELIGION: Roman Catholic
BASIC MONETARY UNIT: Italian Lira

GEOGRAPHY

San Marino is a tiny country located on the top and surrounding slopes of Mount Titano in the Apennines. Italy completely surrounds it.

CLIMATE

The country has a mild summer climate, but winters are cold. Temperatures average around 75°F (24°C) in the summer to below freezing in the winter. Rainfall averages 35 in. (89 cm) annually.

ECONOMY

San Marino's economy is primarily based on its income from tourism. Tourists flock to San Marino by auto, bus, and helicopter to view its beautiful mountaintop capital city featuring medieval and other ancient architecture. Farming and construction materials play an important role in the economy as well. In addition, the country receives an annual payment from Italy for certain privileges, such as the right to supply all tobacco and salt to San Marino and to tax all the goods for San Marino that are shipped through Italian ports. The sale of postage stamps is yet another source of income.

Agriculture - barley, cattle, grapes, fruits and vegetables, sheep, and wheat

Manufacturing - building stone, leather products, stamps, tiles, textiles, and varnish

Exports - building stone, ceramics, silk and woolen textiles, tin, and wine

Imports - manufactured goods

LIFE-STYLE

The people of San Marino are proud of their independence. The majority (90 percent) of the population live in urban areas. Many work in the tourist industry, in stone quarries, or make leather or cheese. San Marinese farmers raise cattle and sheep and grow grapes and wheat.

Children ages six to 14 are required to attend school. Almost everyone can read and write.

Most homes have a telephone, a radio, and a television. A popular recreational activity is attending movies.

IT'S A FACT!

Church of St. Francis - built in the 14th century, is in the city of San Marino.

Medieval Towers - located on each of Mount Titano's three peaks, were built during the Middle Ages.

Mount Titano - the country's highest point, rises 2,478 ft. (755 m) above sea level.

 DID YOU KNOW...

- San Marino is the oldest republic in the world?
- San Marino is known throughout the world for its beautiful postage stamps?
- Twice a year, the heads of all of San Marino's families meet, as they have for centuries, to discuss public issues?
- According to tradition, San Marino was founded in the A.D. 300s by a Christian stonecutter named Marinus? He and his followers settled on Mount Titano and used it as a refuge from religious persecution by the Romans.
- When offered additional land by Napoleon I in 1797, the San Marinese refused because they believed the country's small size and poverty protected it from larger countries?
- One story has it that the country was once saved from invasion because the invading army could not locate it in the thick fog surrounding the mountain?
- San Marino remained neutral during World War II? Hundreds of thousands of refugees from throughout Europe were given temporary homes during that time.
- San Marino, the capital city, is surrounded by a stone wall?

SÃO TOMÉ & PRÍNCIPE

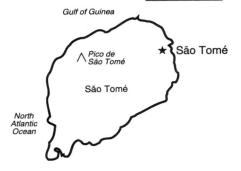

SÃO TOMÉ & PRÍNCIPE

OFFICIAL NAME: República Democrática de São Tomé e Príncipe
(Democratic Republic of São Tomé and Príncipe)
LOCATION: Gulf of Guinea
AREA: 372 sq. mi. (964 sq. km)
POPULATION (Est. 1995): 133,000
CAPITAL: São Tomé
LARGEST CITY: São Tomé, Santo Antonio
GOVERNMENT: Republic governed by a president.
FLAG: Three horizontal stripes of green, yellow, and green. A red triangle is based on the hoist side and the yellow stripe features two black stars. Green, yellow, red, and the black stars represent forests and the sea, soil, the struggle for freedom, and the two main islands, accordingly.
ETHNIC GROUPS: Portuguese-African mixture (Creoles), African
LANGUAGE: Portuguese
RELIGION: Roman Catholic
BASIC MONETARY UNIT: Dobra

GEOGRAPHY

São Tomé and Príncipe is made up of two main islands and several small islands, all located in the Gulf of Guinea. São Tomé, the largest island, has an area of 330 sq. mi. (855 sq. km). Príncipe has an area of 42 sq. mi. (109 sq. km). The islands lie about 180 mi. (290 km) west of mainland Africa.

The islands are part of a range of extinct volcanoes. The western sides of the main islands rise sharply from the sea. Mountains of basalt rock rise toward the center. From the center, the land slopes downward to the fertile east coasts. Rivers and streams are abundant.

CLIMATE

São Tomé and Príncipe islands lie slightly north of the equator. They have two seasons: a hot, humid season that lasts from September to May, and a hot, dry season from June to August. Temperatures average from 65° to 77°F (18° to 25°C). Average yearly rainfall is 16 in. (41 cm).

ECONOMY

The economy is based on agriculture, though fishing is important.

Agriculture - bananas, cacao, coconuts, coffee, copra, and livestock

Manufacturing - lime, soap, and vegetable oils

Exports - cacao, coconuts, coffee, copra, and palm oil

Imports - clothing, food, fuel, and manufactured goods

LIFE-STYLE

Almost 95 percent of the country's people live on the island of São Tomé. About three-fifths of the total population are farmers. They grow bananas, yams, and cassava for food.

Most of the land on the islands is owned by large European agricultural companies or absentee landlords. Laborers from Mozambique and Angola are employed on these plantations, which primarily produce cacao.

The native people of the islands, called Creoles, own small farms or businesses, or work on fishing crews or as laborers.

By law, children are required to complete elementary school, but many do not. The literacy rate is about 57 percent.

IT'S A FACT!

Pico de São Tomé - the country's highest point, is located on São Tomé and rises 6,640 ft. (2,024 m) above sea level.

Pico do Príncipe - Príncipe's highest point, rises 3,107 ft. (947 m) above sea level.

 DID YOU KNOW...

• São Tomé and Príncipe were a province of Portugal until 1975?

• During the 1500s, São Tomé Island became a center of the African slave trade? Slaves from the mainland of Africa were sent to the island and then shipped to the Americas.

SAUDI ARABIA

OFFICIAL NAME: Al-Mamlaka Al-Arabiyya Al-Saudiyya (Kingdom of Saudi Arabia)
LOCATION: Middle East
AREA: 830,000 sq. mi. (2,149,690 sq. km)
POPULATION (Est. 1993): 15,826,000
CAPITAL: Riyadh
LARGEST CITIES: Riyadh, Jidda, Mecca
GOVERNMENT: Monarchy with a king as executive.
FLAG: Field of green—the traditional color of Islam—with an Arabic message in white script above a white saber. The message reads: "There is no God but God; Muhammad is the Messenger of God."
ETHNIC GROUP: Arab
LANGUAGE: Arabic
RELIGION: Islam
BASIC MONETARY UNIT: Saudi Arabian Riyal

GEOGRAPHY

Saudi Arabia, the largest country on the Arabian Peninsula, is the world's 12th largest country. It is a country of dry and barren land with no rivers or other bodies of water. The country measures 1,145 mi. (1,843 km) from north to south and 1,290 mi. (2,076 km) from east to west at its greatest distances. The east coast measures 1,174 mi. (1,889 km) along the Persian Gulf, and the west coast measures 341 mi. (549 km) along the Red Sea.

Saudi Arabia has five land regions: 1) Western Highlands, 2) Central Plateau, 3) Northern Deserts, 4) Rub al Khali, and 5) Eastern Lowlands.

CLIMATE

Most of the country is hot year-round. The coastal regions are hot and humid with temperatures averaging over 90°F (32°C) in the summer. In the desert regions and the Central Plateau, temperatures in the summer may reach 120°F (49°C). However, in some parts of the country, winter temperatures may occasionally dip below freezing.

Asir, located along the southwestern coast, is the only part of Saudi Arabia that receives much rainfall. Due to summer monsoons, Asir receives an average rainfall of 12-20 in. (30-51 cm) per year. The remainder of Saudi Arabia receives less than 4 in. (10 cm) annually. The *shamal*, a northwesterly wind, causes sandstorms in eastern Saudi Arabia.

ECONOMY

The country has a rapidly developing economy. Underneath the dry and barren ground lies the world's largest oil deposits. Saudi Arabia exports more oil than any other country.

Agriculture - chickens and eggs, dates, melons, milk, tomatoes, and wheat

Fishing - shrimp

Manufacturing - cement, fertilizer, food products, petrochemicals, and steel

Mining - petroleum

Exports - petroleum and shrimp

Imports - food products, machinery, military equipment, and transportation equipment

LIFE-STYLE

The life-style of the Saudi people is tied directly to their religion, Islam. For them the Islamic teachings are not just a set of beliefs, but a way of life. Each year, several thousand Muslims travel to Mecca on a religious pilgrimage. Part of the tradition is to walk around the Ka'abah (House of God) seven times.

Three-fourths of all Saudis live in urban areas. The majority of Saudi Arabia's rural population lives on farms or oases. A farm village usually consists of a cluster of one- or two-room houses of stone or sun-dried mud. The remainder of the people are Bedouins (nomads) who move through the deserts with their livestock. In cities, houses made of mud have been replaced in large part by modern apartments.

Traditional Arab clothing is common. Saudi men wear a *kaffiyeh* (headdress) held on by a *igal* (braided black cord). An ankle-length white shirt, or *thawb*, is worn over long trousers. Women in most places wear a veil over their faces and a black robe, or *aba*, that covers the whole body.

Staples of the diet are dates, lamb, rice, and dairy products. Tea and coffee are favorite beverages. *Kabsah*, made of rice and lamb, is a favorite dish. Muslims are not permitted to eat pork or drink alcoholic beverages.

About half of adult Saudis are literate. The government offers free schooling at all education levels but school is not mandatory. Boys and girls attend separate schools.

Only men are allowed to play or watch soccer, the national sport. Men also enjoy horse and camel races, hunting, and hawking. Lively conversations, storytelling, and reciting from the Koran are some favorite activities.

IT'S A FACT!

Jabal Sawda - the country's highest point, rises 10,279 ft. (3,133 m) above sea level.

Mecca and Medina - Islam's holiest cities.

Rub al Khali - the world's largest sand desert, covers 250,000 sq. mi. (647,500 sq. km) in southern Saudi Arabia.

 DID YOU KNOW...

- On many Saudi Arabian roads, you will see automobiles and camels traveling side by side?
- During *Ramadan*, the Islamic holy month, Muslims may not eat, drink, or smoke from sunrise to sunset?

SCOTLAND
Division of the United Kingdom

SCOTLAND

OFFICIAL NAME: Scotland
LOCATION: Northeastern Europe
AREA: 30,420 sq. mi. (78,789 sq. km)
POPULATION (Est. 1994): 5,059,000
CAPITAL: Edinburgh
LARGEST CITIES: Glasgow, Edinburgh, Aberdeen, Dundee
GOVERNMENT: Constitutional monarchy headed by the British monarch and governed by a prime minister.
FLAG: Called *St. Andrew's Cross*, has a blue field with a X-shaped, white cross. Though flown for hundreds of years, it has never been officially adopted.
ETHNIC GROUP: Scottish
LANGUAGES: English, Gaelic
RELIGIONS: Presbyterian, Baptist, Episcopalian, Methodist, Roman Catholic
BASIC MONETARY UNIT: Pound

GEOGRAPHY

Scotland is one of the countries that makes up the United Kingdom of Great Britain and Northern Ireland. It is located in the northern portion of the Island of Great Britain in the British Isles and accounts for about one-third of the island's area. At its greatest distances, Scotland measures 274 mi. (441 km) from north to south and 154 mi. (248 km) from east to west. It has about 2,300 mi. (3,700 km) of coastline along the North Atlantic Ocean, the North Sea, and the North Channel. Scotland's area includes the island groups of Hebrides, Orkney, and Shetland.

Scotland has three main land regions: 1) the Highlands, 2) the Central Lowlands, and 3) the Southern Uplands. The highland region is dominated by the Northwest Highlands and the Grampian Mountains, which are separated by *Glen Mor* (Great Glen), a deep valley. The Central Lowlands have the country's best farmland. The Southern Uplands are made up of hills and moors that rise to the Cheviot Hills along the country's English border. The Tay is the country's largest river, and has a greater water volume than all other rivers in the United Kingdom. The River Clyde, which allows ships to travel from the Atlantic up to the city of Glasgow, is the country's most important river.

CLIMATE

Scotland generally has a wet, temperate climate. The average summer temperature ranges from 60° to 70°F (15° to 21°C). Winter temperatures are usually above freezing.

ECONOMY

Scotland's economy is based mainly on the energy industries, light manufacturing, and service industries.
Agriculture - barley, cattle, milk, oats, potatoes, sheep, and wheat
Fishing - cod, haddock, lobster, mackerel, prawns, and salmon
Manufacturing - foods and beverages, electronic equipment, chemicals, industrial machinery, paper, and textiles
Mining - natural gas and petroleum
Exports - Scotch whiskey

LIFE-STYLE

Over 85 percent of Scotland's people live in urban areas and most reside in the Central Lowlands. About two percent of Scotland's people live on the islands of Orkney, Shetland, and the Hebrides. Rural and urban communities are quite similar. Small houses, *row houses* (connected houses of a similar design), and stone apartment buildings are common in both settings, though apartments are less common in rural areas. Most rural residents work in urban areas, and only about two percent of rural residents make a living by farming, fishing, and forestry.

Scottish dishes are simple. Commonly eaten foods include fish and chips, oatmeal, roast beef, roast lamb, salmon, and steak. Traditional foods are *haggis* (chopped sheep heart, liver, and lungs mixed with animal fat, onions, oatmeal, and seasonings and boiled in a bag made from a sheep's stomach) and *kippers* (smoked herring). Tea is a common beverage and a favorite alcoholic drink is Scotch whiskey.

Golf originated in Scotland in the 1500s and it is still a very popular game. The most popular team sport is *association football* (soccer). Favorite winter sports include *curling* (a game in which a heavy stone is slid across the ice toward a target) and skiing. Other popular recreational activities are fishing, hiking, mountain climbing, and shooting. The Highland Games, similar to track meets, attract many from spring through fall. *Pubs* (public houses) are a popular place to socialize.

Bagpipe music, the Highland fling, and the Scottish reel are all an important part of Scottish culture.

IT'S A FACT!

Ben Nevis - the country's highest point, rises 4,406 ft. (1,343 m) above sea level.

Glamis Castle - located near the city of Dundee, is featured prominently in William Shakespeare's *Macbeth*. The castle, dating from the 1400s, is a major tourist attraction.

Royal and Ancient Golf Club of St. Andrew's - one of a number of Scotland's golf courses, is world-famous.

 DID YOU KNOW...

- *Peter Pan*, *Treasure Island*, and *Ivanhoe* were all written by Scottish authors?
- The Scottish are responsible for developing the Ayrshire, Aberdeen-Angus, Galloway, and Highland cattle breeds? They also developed the collie, the Clydesdale horse, and the Shetland pony.

SENEGAL

OFFICIAL NAME: République du Sénégal (Republic of Senegal)
LOCATION: Northwest Africa
AREA: 75,955 sq. mi. (196,722 sq. km)
POPULATION (Est. 1993): 7,958,000
CAPITAL: Dakar
LARGEST CITIES: Dakar, Thiès, Kaolack
GOVERNMENT: Republic governed by a president.
FLAG: Three vertical stripes of green, yellow, and red. A five-pointed, green star is centered on the yellow stripe.
ETHNIC GROUPS: Black (mainly Wolof, Fulani or Fula, Serer, Toucouleur, Diola, and Mandingo)
LANGUAGES: Wolof, French
RELIGIONS: Islam, Christianity, Traditional African Religions
BASIC MONETARY UNIT: CFA Franc

GEOGRAPHY

Senegal has 310 mi. (499 km) of coastline along the North Atlantic Ocean and extends farther west than any other country of mainland Africa. The small country of Gambia partially divides Senegal's southern region, called the Casamance, from its larger northern section.

Senegal has sandy coastal beaches with high sand dunes rising along the northern coast. Inland, the land is largely gently rolling plains covered with reddish sand. The Casamance region is covered with forests. Foothills lie in the southeast, and the Ferlo Desert lies in the central region. The country has three main rivers: the Sénégal, the Gambia, and the Casamance.

CLIMATE

Senegal has a tropical climate with a rainy and a dry season. The average annual temperature ranges from 71°F (22°C) along the coast to 84°F (29°C) farther inland. The average annual rainfall ranges from 60-70 in. (150-180 cm) in the south to less than 20 in. (50 cm) in the north.

ECONOMY

Senegal has a developing economy with widespread poverty. Its income is generated mainly by its peanut industry and is supplemented by cotton and poultry.

Agriculture - cassava, corn, cotton, millet, peanuts, poultry, rice, sorghum, tomatoes, and other vegetables

Manufacturing - building materials, fish processing, flour milling, peanut processing (mainly peanut oil and oil cakes), and petroleum refining

Mining - phosphates

Exports - fish products, manufactures, peanuts, petroleum products, and phosphates

Imports - coal, food, electric equipment, machinery, and petroleum

LIFE-STYLE

Approximately 60 percent of Senegal's population is rural, with about three-fourths of the population making a living in agriculture. Most rural homes are mud huts with thatched roofs, usually clustered into related family groups and surrounded by a wall or fence. Members of a compound share meals and chores. Middle-class urban dwellers live in modern apartments or bungalows. Poor urban Senegalese live in shelters made of boards, mud, or sticks.

Male Senegalese usually wear wide-legged trousers and *boubous* (roomy cotton robes). Women dress in brightly colored boubous, turbans, and jewelry.

The staple of the Senegalese diet is a grain called millet. Most meals consist of a main dish of rice, millet, or corn over which a sauce—made of beans, fish, poultry, vegetables, or milk and sugar—is poured. Popular dishes include chicken stew, spicy fried fish, fish or meat with peanut sauce, *thiebou dien* (fish and rice), and *yassa* (rice and chicken covered with a sauce composed of sliced onions and spices). A traditional Wolof dish is *mbaxal-u-Saloum* (rice served with a sauce made of ground nuts, dried fish, meat, tomatoes, and spices).

Traditional wrestling is the national sport, but soccer is the most popular sport. Other popular sports include basketball, jogging, and track and field. In urban areas with electricity, leisure activities may include attending concerts, going to the disco, watching movies, and reading. In rural areas, entertainment is centered around visiting urban relatives after harvest, attending village and family celebrations, and dancing. Senegalese arts include carved wooden masks and traditional artistic dances.

Children are required to attend school for six years, although the law is not enforced. The University of Dakar is the country's sole university. Adult literacy is low, about ten percent.

The Senegalese suffer from severe health problems—especially in rural areas—caused by contaminated food and water. The country also has a severe shortage of physicians (about one doctor for every 16,000 people).

IT'S A FACT!

Fouta Djallon Mountain Range - located in the southeast, is home to the country's highest point, which rises 1,634 ft. (498 m) above sea level.

 DID YOU KNOW...

- Senegal was ruled by France from the late 1800s until 1960, when the country gained its independence?
- What is now Senegal has probably been inhabited by black Africans since prehistoric times?
- In Senegal, it is considered bad luck to ask specific questions about another person's children?

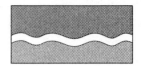

SEYCHELLES

Bird I.• •Denis I.
Silhouette I.• •Praslin I.
•La Digue I.
Indian Ocean
Amirante Islands • Mahé I.
•Desroches I.
•Platte I.

SEYCHELLES

•Alphonse I. Coetivy I.

Providence I.
Aldabra Islands St. Pierre I.• •Cerf I.
•Cosmoledo Group
•Farquhar Group

Victoria St. Anne I.
Morne Seychellois
Mahé I.

OFFICIAL NAME: Republic of Seychelles
LOCATION: Western Indian Ocean
AREA: 176 sq. mi. (455 sq. km)
POPULATION (Est. 1995): 74,000
CAPITAL/LARGEST CITY: Victoria (on Mahé Island)
GOVERNMENT: Republic governed by a president.
FLAG: Three wavy horizontal stripes of red, white, and green.
ETHNIC GROUPS: Mixed Asian, African, and French
LANGUAGES: English, French, Creole
RELIGION: Christianity
BASIC MONETARY UNIT: Rupee

GEOGRAPHY

Seychelles is an African country that consists of about 90 islands in the Indian Ocean. The islands cover an area of over 400,000 sq. mi. (1,035,995 sq. km) and are about 1,000 mi. (1,600 km) east of the African mainland.

Seychelles is made up of both granite and coral islands. The granite islands have central hilly areas and a narrow strip of coastline. Lush tropical gardens overlook white beaches and clear lagoons. The coral group is made up of ring-shaped islands (*atolls*) and low, flat islands with coral reefs.

CLIMATE

The country has a tropical oceanic climate. The average temperature ranges from 75° to 86°F (24° to 30°C). Average annual rainfall ranges from 52 in. (132 cm) on some of the coral islands to 92 in. (234 cm) on the main island of Mahé.

ECONOMY

The country's economy is based on tourism.

Agriculture - cinnamon, coconuts, patchouli oil, and vanilla beans

Manufacturing - cinnamon processing, construction, copra processing, food processing, and vanilla processing

Exports - cinnamon, copra, guano, patchouli oil, and vanilla

Imports - beverages, food, manufactured goods, petroleum products, rice, tobacco, and transportation equipment

LIFE-STYLE

Over 80 percent of the population live on the island of Mahé. The population is split almost evenly between rural and urban areas. About a third of the work force is employed by the government, 25 percent are employed in construction or tourism, and about 15 percent are farmers.

Almost all children between the ages of six and 15 attend school. Around 60 percent of the people can read and write.

IT'S A FACT!

Morne Seychellois - the country's highest point, rises 2,993 ft. (912 m) above sea level.

Victoria - the capital, is Seychelles's only town.

DID YOU KNOW...

- Cinnamon grows wild on the island of Mahé?
- The *coco de mer*, a double coconut that weighs as much as 50 pounds (23 kg), grows only in Seychelles?
- Giant tortoises live in Seychelles?
- One of the country's leading exports, patchouli oil, is used in making perfume?
- Between 1500 and 1750, the islands were used mainly as hiding places for pirates?
- There are no animals dangerous to man that inhabit the islands, but, sharks are prevalent in the sea around them?

SIERRA LEONE

OFFICIAL NAME: Republic of Sierra Leone
LOCATION: Western Africa
AREA: 27,699 sq. mi. (71,740 sq. km)
POPULATION (Est. 1993): 4,490,000
CAPITAL/LARGEST CITY: Freetown
GOVERNMENT: Military.
FLAG: Three horizontal stripes of green, white, and blue.
ETHNIC GROUPS: Temne, Mende, Creole
LANGUAGES: English, Tribal languages, Krio
RELIGIONS: Traditional African Religions, Islam, Christianity
BASIC MONETARY UNIT: Leone

GEOGRAPHY

Sierra Leone is a small country on the western coast of Africa, north of the equator. At its greatest distances, Sierra Leone measures 220 mi. (354 km) from north to south and 190 mi. (306 km) from east to west. It has 210 mi. (338 km) of coastline along the Atlantic Ocean.

Sierra Leone has three main land areas: 1) Sierra Leone mountains, 2) coastal swamps, and 3) the coastal plain. Most of the country's coastal region is covered by mangrove swamps. A coastal plain extends inland from the swamps and slopes up to an area of plateaus and mountains in the northeast. Sandy soil or gravel covers more than half of the country.

CLIMATE

The country has a rainy, tropical climate. In the south, a dry season occurs in January and February; in the north, it lasts from December through March. The average temperature ranges from 77° to 81°F (25° to 27°C). On the coast, the average rainfall is 144 in. (366 cm) yearly. Only a narrow strip in the north receives less than 80 in. (200 cm) of rain annually, and has a greater range in temperatures.

ECONOMY

Sierra Leone is a poor country. Most of the people are engaged in subsistence agriculture. Crop yields are kept low as a result of the poor soil, the dry season, and the traditional farming methods that do little to keep the soil fertile. Farmers move to a new site when the soil's richness is depleted. Many mine diamonds during the dry season. Women often have businesses selling goods in the marketplace.

Agriculture - cacao, cassava, coffee, ginger, oranges, palm kernels, peanuts, piassava, and rice

Manufacturing - beverages, cigarettes, footwear, and textiles

Mining - chrome ore, diamonds, iron ore, and rutile

Exports - bauxite, cacao, coffee, diamonds, ginger, kola nuts, palm kernels, and piassava

Imports - capital and consumer goods, food products, and petroleum

LIFE-STYLE

The extended family is the basic unit of society. Three to five generations may live in a family compound. Most families have at least nine children, but, on the average, only six survive to maturity. The people of the villages often live in concrete block houses. In the rural areas, many of the poor live in mud houses with thatched or corrugated iron roofs.

Most of the men and boys of Sierra Leone wear Western-style clothing. Women wear *lappas* (two yards of ankle-length cloth tied around the waist) and a Western or African blouse. A fabric that matches the brightly colored *lappas* covers the women's heads.

Rice is the staple of the diet. Traditional meals—a bed of rice with a sauce in the center—are usually served on a large platter. The *plassas* (sauce) is made of pounded cassava leaves, palm oil, and chili peppers. Other important food items are groundnuts, sweet potatoes, beans, fish, chicken, goat, small bush animals, and tropical fruits. People do not drink while eating, so after the meal, a cup of water is passed around to drink and wash the face and hands.

Sierra Leone has a literacy rate of only about 20 percent. Children are not required by law to attend elementary schools and about 15 percent go on to high school.

Government-provided health services are minimal. The people generally use a combination of traditional and Western medicines, the latter of which are often misused. Chronic illnesses and diseases such as malaria, anemia, tuberculosis, leprosy, and others are prevalent.

Soccer is the only popular organized sport. School children enjoy an event called a *paw paw* race, where students run while carrying smaller students on their backs. In urban areas, movies, reggae music, and disco dances are popular. Traditional music, dance, and theater are popular throughout the country.

Buses and pickup trucks outfitted with rows of seats provide transportation in rural areas. Taxis and buses provide transportation in cities. The country has one railroad line. Most of its roads are unpaved but in good condition, despite the heavy rains. However, only about one percent of the people own a car.

IT'S A FACT!

Loma Mansa - the country's highest point, rises 6,390 ft. (1,948 m) above sea level.

 DID YOU KNOW...

- Freetown, the capital city, was founded in 1787 as a settlement for freed slaves?
- Sierra Leoneans practice "fostering," a custom where a child is loaned to a childless woman? The woman raises the child as one who will care for her in her old age.
- Malnutrition is widespread among children because they receive the smallest portions of protein-rich foods?

SINGAPORE

OFFICIAL NAME: Republic of Singapore
LOCATION: Southeast Asia
AREA: 239 sq. mi. (618 sq. km)
POPULATION (Est. 1993): 2,811,000
CAPITAL/LARGEST CITY: Singapore
GOVERNMENT: Republic governed by a president.
FLAG: Two horizontal stripes of red (representing equality and brotherhood) and white (representing purity and virtue). A white crescent and five white five-pointed stars (representing democracy, peace, progress, justice, and equality) are on the hoist side of the red stripe.
ETHNIC GROUPS: Chinese, Malay, Indian, European
LANGUAGES: Chinese, English, Malay, Tamil
RELIGIONS: Buddhism, Taoism, Islam, Christianity
BASIC MONETARY UNIT: Singapore Dollar

GEOGRAPHY

Singapore is a small island country in Southeast Asia. It lies near the southern tip of the Malay Peninsula near the meeting point of the South China Sea and the Indian Ocean.

The country includes one large island and 50 smaller islands. The large island of Singapore covers 221 sq. mi. (572 sq. km) and the smaller islands have a combined total of 18 sq. mi. (46 sq. km). Rainforests cover most of the central part of the main island. Mangrove swamps lie on the northern coast.

CLIMATE

Singapore has a hot, moist climate. The temperature averages about 80°F (27°C). There are no distinct rainy or dry seasons. It is humid and rainy throughout the year. The main island receives an average of 95 in. (241 cm) of rain yearly.

ECONOMY

Singapore has a highly developed economy based on manufacturing and on the import and export of goods. Singapore is also a major financial center. After Japan, its people have the highest standard of living in East Asia. Only a small minority of the people work in agriculture.

Agriculture - eggs, pork, and poultry

Manufacturing - chemicals, clothing and textiles, electronic and transportation equipment, lumber, machinery, metals, paper, petroleum products, processed food, rubber, and ships

Exports - computer equipment, refined petroleum, rubber and rubber products, and telecommunications equipment

Imports - aircraft, chemicals, crude petroleum, food products, and raw materials

LIFE-STYLE

Singapore is sometimes called "Instant Asia" because of the great diversity of cultures. Three of the major Asian cultures—Chinese, Malay, and Indian—are found there.

About 90 percent of the country's people live in the city of Singapore, the busiest port in Southeast Asia.

The majority of Singaporeans wear Western-style dress; however, some Malays and Indians prefer traditional dress.

Traditionally, families have been large, but due to limited space, the government launched a family-planning campaign. Today, the government encourages three children.

Rice and seafood are the staples of the diet. With such a diverse culture, a wide variety of foods is available in the country. Common fruits are pineapples, papayas, bananas, and mangoes. Chopsticks are the most common eating utensils, but Western-style utensils are easily found.

School is free and compulsory for children ages six to 16. Instruction is in English. After ten years of school, many children continue in preuniversity programs, or vocational schools. The country's literacy rate is about 88 percent.

The medical facilities and health services of Singapore are excellent. Good housing, sound hygienic practices, and modern sanitation all contribute to a high standard of health.

Soccer, badminton, basketball, tennis, and golf are popular sports. Water sports are also enjoyed by many people. Among older Chinese, the exercise *taijiquan* (shadow boxing) is popular. The people of Singapore have access to a wide variety of cultural events. Many Singaporeans also participate in martial arts, such as *tae kwon do*. The country's many cultures are reflected in its art, music, and theater.

Public transportation is well-developed in Singapore. Many people also own cars. The country's communication system is modern as well as extensive.

IT'S A FACT!

Botanical Gardens - located in the city of Singapore, houses large collections of tropical and subtropical plants.

National Museum and Raffles Hotel - two buildings located in the city of Singapore that were built during the 1800s.

Timah Hill - the country's highest point, rises 581 ft. (177 m) above sea level.

 DID YOU KNOW...

- Singapore is often referred to as the cleanest city in Asia, in part because fines for littering are strictly enforced?
- In Singapore, it is against the law for couples to live together or have children without being married?
- Singapore is one of the world's most densely populated countries, with an average of 11,762 people per sq. mi. (4,549 per sq. km)?

SLOVAKIA

OFFICIAL NAME: Slovenská Republika (Slovak Republic)
FORMERLY: Part of Czechoslovakia
LOCATION: Central Europe
AREA: 18,933 sq. mi. (49,035 sq. km)
POPULATION (Est. 1995): 5,353,000
CAPITAL: Bratislava
LARGEST CITIES: Bratislava, Košice, Trnava, Nitra
GOVERNMENT: Parliamentary democracy headed by a president.
FLAG: Three horizontal bands of white, blue, and red. The national coat of arms is on the hoist side.
ETHNIC GROUPS: Slovak, Hungarian, Ukrainian, Gypsy, Czech, Russian, German, Polish
LANGUAGE: Slovak, Czech, Polish, German, Hungarian, Romany
RELIGIONS: Roman Catholic, Protestant, Orthodox, Judaism
BASIC MONETARY UNIT: Koruna

GEOGRAPHY

At its greatest distances, Slovakia, a landlocked country, measures 130 mi. (209 km) from north to south and 260 mi. (418 km) from east to west. Most of Slovakia is covered with part of the western branch of the Carpathian Mountains. The southwest is home to the Danubian Lowlands, which contain fertile farmland.

CLIMATE

Slovakia has a continental climate with warm, humid summers and cold, dry winters. The temperature ranges from a low of 14°F (-10°C) in January to a high of 68°F (20°C) in July. The average precipitation is 24-40 in. (60-100 cm) per year. Snow remains on the country's mountains for about 130 days out of the year.

ECONOMY

Slovakia's economy was once based mainly on agriculture. The country became industrialized under Communist rule, and today, service industries and manufacturing form the base of Slovakia's economy.

Agriculture - barley, corn, fruit, livestock, potatoes, sugar beets, tobacco, wheat, and wine grapes

Forestry - timber

Manufacturing - armaments, ceramics, chemical products, petroleum products, and steel

Mining - coal, copper, iron, lead, manganese, and zinc

Exports - chemical products, petroleum products, steel, and weapons

Imports - crude oil, electronic products, and natural gas

LIFE-STYLE

The standard of living in Slovakia is higher than in most formerly Communist European countries. Most families own an automobile, a television, a washing machine, and a refrigerator. More than half of Slovakia's population is urban. Many live in high-rise apartments constructed during the Communist period. Many families have a cottage in the country for weekends. Most rural families reside in single-family houses.

Staples of the diet include dairy products (such as butter, cheese, and milk), fresh-baked bread, soup, and seasonal fruits and vegetables (such as apples, cabbage, carrots, grapes, plums, and potatoes). Popular foods include *rezeň* (breaded steak) and potatoes, and other meats served with dumplings, pasta and sauce, potatoes, or rice. Some sweet dishes, such as prune dumplings, are served as main courses. One popular dish is *bryndzové halušky* (noodles with sheep's cheese). Popular desserts include *koláč* (nut or poppy seed rolls) and *torte* (cake).

Popular sports include ice hockey, skiing, soccer, and tennis. Popular recreational activities include attending art exhibits, cultural events, and local festivals, camping, going to the movies, hiking, and swimming. Slovaks especially love to sing.

Education is free at public institutions; children are required to attend for ten years, beginning at age six. Almost all adults can read and write.

IT'S A FACT!

Gerlachovský Štít - the country's highest point, rises 8,711 ft. (2,655 m) above sea level.

 DID YOU KNOW...

- Slavic tribes lived in what is now known as Slovakia as early as the A.D. 400s?
- The Slovaks and the Czechs were united, forming the country of Czechoslovakia, from 1918 to 1993?
- Bratislava was Hungary's capital from 1536 to 1683?

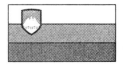

SLOVENIA

OFFICIAL NAME: Republika Slovenija (Republic of Slovenia)
FORMERLY: Part of Yugoslavia
LOCATION: Central Europe
AREA: 7,819 sq. mi. (20,251 sq. km)
POPULATION (Est. 1995): 2,012,000
CAPITAL: Ljubljana
LARGEST CITIES: Ljubljana, Maribor
GOVERNMENT: Republic governed by a president.
FLAG: Three horizontal stripes of white, blue, and red, with the national shield on the white and blue stripes in the upper hoist-side corner.
ETHNIC GROUPS: Slovene, Croat, Serb
LANGUAGES: Slovenian, Serbo-Croatian
RELIGION: Roman Catholic
BASIC MONETARY UNIT: Tolar

GEOGRAPHY

Slovenia is an Alpine country in central Europe between Austria and Croatia. At its greatest distances, Slovenia measures 100 mi. (160 km) from north to south and 155 mi. (250 km) from east to west. It has 20 mi. (32 km) of coastline along the Adriatic Sea.

Slovenia is a rather mountainous region with thick forests making up about half of the land. Hilly plains spread across the central and eastern parts of the country. The *Karst*, a limestone region of caves and underground channels, is also found in the central part of the country.

CLIMATE

The country's climate varies greatly by region. The mountains have extremely cold winters with heavy snow followed by heavy rains in the early summer.

The coastline has a mild climate with temperatures rarely getting below freezing. Summers are hot and dry. Northeastern Slovenia has temperatures as high as 100°F (38°C) in the summer and often below freezing in the winter.

ECONOMY

When Slovenia was part of Yugoslavia its economy was the strongest of the six republics. But its economy began to lag under Communism during the 1980s. After 1990, when non-Communists came to power, the country began to introduce a free enterprise system.

Approximately 46 percent of Slovenia's workers hold manufacturing jobs and another 46 percent are employed in the service industries. Only about eight percent have jobs in agriculture.

Agriculture - apples, cattle, cherries, corn, hogs, pears, plums, potatoes, sheep, sugar beets, and wheat

Manufacturing - automobiles, chemicals, metal goods, and textiles

Mining - coal, lead, and mercury

Exports - chemicals, consumer goods, machinery and transport equipment, and other manufactured goods

Imports - automobiles, chemicals, machinery and transport equipment, manufactured goods, natural gas, and oil

LIFE-STYLE

Almost 90 percent of the people of Slovenia are Slovenes. The country's ethnic homogeneity allowed its secession from Yugoslavia to be peaceful, unlike its sister republics.

About half of the population live in rural areas. Rural families often live in single-family houses with steep roofs. City dwellers frequently live in high-rise apartment buildings.

Favorite meats include veal and pork. A well-known Slovenian dish is *Ljubljana veal cutlet* (breaded slices of veal served with a cheese sauce). The country produces some excellent wines.

Virtually all adults in Slovenia are literate. Eight years of elementary and four years of secondary schooling are required.

Winter sports are an important part of Slovenian life. Excellent ski slopes are found throughout the mountains. Festivals also are an important part of life in Slovenia. Every February, the town of Ptuj holds a *Kurenti* festival, which dates from the pre-Christian era. At this festival, people dress up in animal masks and furs and perform rituals designed to drive away the "evil spirits" of winter.

Slovenians are proud of their high standard of living, their industries, and their cultural achievements. Many fine writers have emerged from Slovenia. Before independence, Slovenia was the most westernized part of Yugoslavia.

IT'S A FACT!

Mount Triglav - the country's highest point, rises 9,393 ft. (2,863 m) above sea level.

Postojna Cave - known for its stalactites, is the home of *Proteus anguinus*, an eyeless, transparent, fishlike creature.

 DID YOU KNOW...
- The caves of Postojna are the largest caverns in Europe?
- The city of Ljubljana dates to Roman times?
- The famous Lippizaner horses are taught to perform intricate, almost balletlike steps, to the sounds of Viennese waltzes? These horses originated in Lipica.
- The Slovenian language is written in the Roman alphabet rather than in the Cyrillic system of writing used for most Slavic languages?

SOLOMON ISLANDS

OFFICIAL NAME: Solomon Islands
LOCATION: Southwestern Pacific Ocean
AREA: 10,639 sq. mi. (27,556 sq. km)
POPULATION (Est. 1995): 378,000
CAPITAL/LARGEST CITY: Honiara (on Guadalcanal Island)
GOVERNMENT: Parliamentary democracy headed by a prime minister.
FLAG: Two large triangles of blue (top) and green separated by a narrow diagonal yellow band. The blue triangle features five white stars.
ETHNIC GROUP: Melanesian
LANGUAGES: English, Solomon Island pidgin, many local languages
RELIGION: Christianity
BASIC MONETARY UNIT: Solomon Islands Dollar

Map of Solomon Islands showing: Ontong Java Atoll, Choiseul I., Santa Isabel I., South Pacific Ocean, New Georgia Group, Malaita I., Santa Cruz Islands, Honiara, Gaudalcanal I., San Cristobal I., Nendo I., Solomon Sea, Bellona I., Rennell I., Utupua I., Vanikolo I., Indispensable Reefs, SOLOMON ISLANDS

GEOGRAPHY

Solomon Islands is an island nation in the southwestern Pacific Ocean. It is comprised of eight main volcanic islands and several small outlying islands and atolls. The main islands are rugged, mountainous, and covered by tropical plants, cascading waterfalls, and beaches of white and black sand. Each island has a central spine of mountains. The land drops sharply to the sea on one side and gently to a narrow coastal strip on the other.

The islands lie about 1,000 mi. (1,610 km) northeast of Australia and are spread over 230,000 sq. mi. (600,000 sq. km) of ocean. The size of the islands range from 40 to 120 mi. (140 to 190 km) long to 20 to 30 mi. (32 to 48 km) wide.

CLIMATE

The country has a hot and humid climate throughout the year. Temperatures range from 70° to 90°F (21° to 32°C). The annual rainfall averages 60-200 in. (150-500 cm).

ECONOMY

The Solomons have a developing economy based on agriculture, fishing, and lumbering. Tourism is growing.

Agriculture - cacao, coconuts, copra, and palm oil
Fishing - skipjack tuna
Manufacturing - batteries, boats, clothing, fiberglass, fish canning and freezing, lumbering, soft drinks, and tobacco
Exports - cocoa, copra, fish, logs and timber, and palm oil
• *Imports* - food, gasoline, machinery, and manufactured goods

LIFE-STYLE

Nearly nine out of ten people live in small villages near the coast in huts with thatched roofs. Most homes are built on stilts to keep them cool. Land ownership is the main source of an islander's status and is passed on by the mother or father, depending on local custom.

The main foods are chicken, fish, pork, coconuts, sweet potatoes, *taro* (a tropical plant with one or more edible rootlike stems), and tropical fruits.

Education is not required by law, although the majority of the children attend school.

High population growth is a problem for the country, which results in high unemployment.

IT'S A FACT!

Mount Makarakomburu - the islands' highest point and an active volcano, is located on Guadalcanal Island and rises 8,028 ft. (2,447 m) above sea level.

Tinakula Island - an uninhabited island that has the country's most active volcano.

 DID YOU KNOW...

• The islands were named after the fabled Isles of Solomon, thought to be the site of the biblical King Solomon's riches?
• The tropical forests are home to more than 140 species of birds, 70 species of reptiles, and beautiful butterflies and moths?
• Guadalcanal and other islands in the Solomons were the scene of terrible fighting between Allied and Japanese forces during World War II?
• There are over 230 varieties of wild orchids and other tropical flowers on the Solomon Islands?

SOMALIA

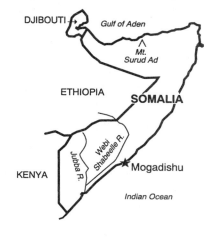

OFFICIAL NAME: Somali Democratic Republic
FORMERLY: Somali Republic
LOCATION: Eastern Africa
AREA: 246,201 sq. mi. (637,657 sq. km)
POPULATION (Est. 1992): 7,917,000
CAPITAL/LARGEST CITY: Mogadishu
GOVERNMENT: In transition.
FLAG: Design based on the United Nation's flag: a light blue field with a white star in the center.
ETHNIC GROUPS: Somali, Arab, Indian, Italian, Pakistanis
LANGUAGES: Somali, Arabic, English, Italian
RELIGION: Islam (mainly Sunni Muslim)
BASIC MONETARY UNIT: Somali Shilling

GEOGRAPHY

Somalia is the easternmost country of mainland Africa. At its greatest distances, Somalia measures 950 mi. (1,529 km) from north to south and 730 mi. (1,175 km) from east to west. It has 1,800 mi. (2,408 km) of coastline along the Gulf of Aden and the Indian Ocean.

Somalia consists mainly of dry, grassy plains. A northern coastal plain is backed by a mountain ridge that stretches behind it. The central and southern areas are flat. Two major rivers—the Jubba and the Webi Shabeelle—provide water for irrigation in the south.

CLIMATE

Somalia has two seasons when rain falls—March to May and September to December—but, it often suffers from droughts. Average temperatures range from 85° to 105°F (29° to 41°C) in northern Somalia and from 65° to 105°F (18° to 41°C) in southern Somalia. The average annual rainfall is only about 11 in. (28 cm). Yearly rainfall rarely totals over 20 in. (51 cm) even in the south, the wettest region. Some northern areas only receive 2-3 in. (5-8 cm) of rain yearly.

ECONOMY

Somalia is a developing country that has limited resources and is not self-sufficient in food. Although the land contains gypsum, iron ore, and uranium, they are not currently being mined.
Agriculture - bananas, camels, cattle, citrus fruits, corn, cotton, goats, grains, hides and skins, sheep, sorghum, and sugar cane
Manufacturing - cotton milling, leather goods, petroleum refining, processed fish and meat, sugar refining, and textiles
Exports - bananas, camels, goats, hides and skins, and sheep
Imports - construction materials, food, petroleum, and textiles

LIFE-STYLE

Although almost the entire Somali population shares the same culture, language, and religion, the people are grouped by clans. Many Somalis have fierce loyalty to their clan only, which often results in fighting between groups. The four largest clans, which are mainly nomadic, are collectively known as the Samaal. The nomads live in small, collapsible huts with arched wooded braces covered with grass mats and animal skins. Their diet mainly consists of milk, supplemented by rice and other grains, and mutton. Two other clans, mostly farmers who live along Somalia's southern rivers, are collectively known as the

Sab (or Saab). Most urban areas have housing shortages.

Most Somalis wear traditional clothing, which consists of brightly colored garments similar to togas. *Lungis* (kilt-like garments) are often worn by men. Some urban Somalis wear Western-style clothing.

Recreational activities include wrestling and other sports. The Somali culture is rich in oral literature based on subjects such as astronomy and astrology. Other leisure activities include folk dancing, leatherwork (including the making of saddles and dagger sheaths), reciting poetry and singing (popular topics include death, love, war, and such prized possessions as camels or horses).

Education is offered at the primary and secondary levels, but education is not required and less than 20 percent of Somali children attend school. About 40 percent of the adults are literate.

Somalia has few doctors and limited access to medical supplies. The major health problems include maternal and infant mortality and common diseases include tuberculosis and leprosy. Thousands have died since the early 1990s as a result of drought and civil war.

IT'S A FACT!

Mount Surud Ad - the country's highest point, rises 7,900 ft. (2,408 m) above sea level.

 DID YOU KNOW...
- Prior to gaining its independence in 1960, northern Somalia was ruled by Great Britain and southern Somalia was ruled by Italy?
- Prior to 1970, Somali women had few political and economic rights, but now they are free to work outside the home?
- The Somali language did not take on written form until 1970?

SOUTH AFRICA

OFFICIAL NAME: Republiek van Suid-Afrika (Republic of South Africa)
LOCATION: Southern Africa
AREA: 471,445 sq. mi. (1,221,037 sq. km)
POPULATION (Est. 1993): 42,823,000
CAPITAL: Cape Town (legislative), Pretoria (administrative), Bloemfontein (judicial)
LARGEST CITIES: Durban, Cape Town, Johannesburg
GOVERNMENT: Republic governed by a president.
FLAG: A green Y, based on the fly side, divides the flag into black (hoist side), red (top), and blue sections. The red and blue sections are trimmed in white. The black section is trimmed in gold.
ETHNIC GROUPS: Black, White, Coloreds, Asian
LANGUAGES: Afrikaans, English, Nguni, Sotho
RELIGIONS: Christianity, Hinduism, Islam
BASIC MONETARY UNIT: Rand

GEOGRAPHY

South Africa encompasses the southern tip of Africa. It measures 875 mi. (1,408 km) from north to south and 1,010 mi. (1,625 km) from east to west at its greatest distances. It has 1,650 mi. (2,655 km) of coastline on the Indian Ocean and the South Atlantic Ocean.

Walvis Bay in Namibia is also part of South Africa. It has an area of 434 sq. mi. (1,124 sq. km). Within the borders of South Africa is the small independent country of Lesotho.

The country's landscape varies greatly. There are plateaus, mountains, and deep valleys. South Africa has five major land regions: 1) the Plateau, 2) the Coastal Strip, 3) the Cape Mountains Region, 4) the Kalahari Desert, and 5) the Namib Desert.

CLIMATE

Most of South Africa has a mild, sunny climate. Due to its location south of the equator, its seasons are opposite those in the Northern Hemisphere. Differences in elevation, wind systems, and ocean currents affect the climate in varying manners throughout the country. The Cape Mountains Region has warm, dry summers and cool, wet winters. The Coastal Strip has hot, humid summers and dry, sunny winters.

Only one-fourth of the country receives over 25 in. (64 cm) of rain annually. Parts of the east coast may get over 40 in. (100 cm) yearly. The desert areas receive little, if any, rainfall.

ECONOMY

For its first 200 years, South Africa's economy depended mainly on agriculture. The discovery of gold and diamonds in the late 1800s quickly made mining the basis of the economy. Today, the country is the richest and most highly developed country in Africa. Oil is the only useful mineral the country lacks.

Agriculture - beef cattle, corn, citrus fruits, milk, potatoes, sugar cane, tobacco, wheat, and wool

Manufacturing - chemicals, clothing, iron and steel, machinery, metal products, motor vehicles, processed foods and beverages, and textiles

Mining - coal, copper, diamonds, gold, iron ore, limestone, platinum, and uranium

Exports - corn, diamonds, fruit, gold, metals and minerals, sugar, and wool

Imports - chemicals, machinery and transportation equipment, manufactured goods, and petroleum

LIFE-STYLE

South Africa's wealth is distributed unevenly. White people, a small minority, own most of the wealth while black people, the majority, own very little. Black and Colored (mixed black, white, and Asian) people have long been dominated by the white minority due to the country's past policy of *apartheid* (racial separation). Though now officially outlawed, the practices of apartheid still affect many aspects of life in South Africa. Most public schools and housing remain segregated. Moreover, legal restrictions once determined the jobs a person could hold. Though those restrictions were repealed, whites still hold the majority of the high-paying jobs.

Afrikaners (whites who speak Afrikaans) live in cities and largely control the country's government and farming. English-speaking whites largely control the businesses and industries.

Over three-fourths of all Coloreds live in cities, mainly in Cape Province. Colored people have worked for whites for many generations. In the cities, they typically work as servants, factory workers, or craftworkers. In the country, many work in orchards or vineyards.

Over 90 percent of the Asians (most of Indian descent) live in cities. Many of the women still wear the traditional *sari* (long cloth draped around body), but most men and young people wear Western styles. Most are poor and grow vegetables or work in factories. A few are prosperous lawyers, doctors, and so on.

Blacks make up about 74 percent of the population and are further divided into ten separate nations. These nations have been assigned reserves, or homelands. Each homeland has a government that handles local matters. Agriculture is the major occupation in the homelands. Today most black men periodically leave the homelands to work in white areas. They work in mines and factories and then move back home again.

Almost all white adults are literate, while only 85 percent of Asian adults, 75 percent of Colored adults, and 50 percent of black adults are literate.

The South African diet is dictated more by economic status than race. Staples of the diet include potatoes and rice. Beef, mutton, green vegetables, and pumpkins are part of most meals. Whites eat local specialties, such as *boerewors* (an Afrikaner sausage dish), and *curry* (an Indian dish of eggs, fish, meat, or vegetables cooked in a very spicy sauce). The traditional food of blacks is *mealies* (corn served as porridge). A popular snack is *biltong* (a jerkylike food made from various kinds of meat).

South Africa's national sport is Rugby football. Cricket, soccer, surfing, swimming, sailing, and boating are also enjoyed by many.

IT'S A FACT!

Champagne Castle - the country's highest point, rises 11,072 ft. (3,375 m) above sea level.

Kruger National Park - a world-famous game reserve, is South Africa's most popular tourist attraction.

The Orange River - the country's longest river, flows 1,300 mi. (2,100 km) from Lesotho into the Atlantic Ocean.

Witwatersrand - area around Johannesburg, is the world's largest gold field, covering 1,000 sq. mi. (2,600 sq. km).

 DID YOU KNOW...
- Small bands of hunters still roam the Namib and Kalahari Deserts, living on the plants and animals they find?

SOUTH KOREA

OFFICIAL NAME: Taehan-minguk (Republic of Korea)
LOCATION: Eastern Asia
AREA: 38,230 sq. mi. (99,016 sq. km)
POPULATION (Est. 1993): 43,894,000
CAPITAL: Seoul
LARGEST CITIES: Seoul, Pusan, Taegu
GOVERNMENT: Republic governed by a president.
FLAG: White field with a red and blue yin-yang symbol in the center which represents the universal balance between opposites. Each corner features a different black trigram from the ancient *I Ching*.
ETHNIC GROUP: Korean
LANGUAGE: Korean
RELIGIONS: Christianity, Buddhism
BASIC MONETARY UNIT: South Korean Won

GEOGRAPHY

South Korea lies on the southern half of a peninsula that extends south from northeastern China. South Korea measures 300 mi. (480 km) from north to south and 185 mi. (298 km) from east to west at its greatest distances. It has 819 mi. (1,318 km) of coastline on the Sea of Japan and the Yellow Sea.

South Korea's area includes many islands, the largest of which is Cheju Island, located about 50 mi. (80 km) south of the peninsula. Cheju has an area of 700 sq. mi. (1,800 sq. km).

South Korea has three main land regions: 1) the Central Mountains, 2) the Southern Plain, and 3) the Southwestern Plain.

CLIMATE

South Korea is affected by seasonal winds called monsoons. Summer weather varies little throughout the peninsula. July temperatures average 70° to 80°F (21° to 27°C). The average January temperature in South Korea is about 35°F (2°C). Most of the area receives about 30-50 in. (76-130 cm) of precipitation annually. Usually one or two typhoons hit the peninsula each year in the summer.

ECONOMY

South Korea has one of the fastest-growing economies in the world, largely due to its industrial expansion since 1953.

Agriculture - apples, barley, Chinese cabbage, melons, onions, potatoes, rice, soybeans, and sweet potatoes

Fishing - filefish, oysters, and pollock

Manufacturing - automobiles, chemicals, clothing, computer equipment, electrical appliances, iron and steel, machinery, plywood, processed foods, rubber tires, ships, shoes, televisions, and textiles

Mining - coal and tungsten

Exports - automobiles, clothing, electrical equipment, electronics, fish, ships, shoes, steel, and textiles

Imports - chemicals, crude oil and other industrial raw materials, and machinery

LIFE-STYLE

Most South Korean homes have two or three stories. They are constructed of brick or concrete blocks and have tile or slate roofs. Many of these homes have *ondol* (floors of thick stone) and are covered with mats. Traditionally, air passages beneath the floors carry warm air that heats the homes. Many homes now have pipes that carry heated water under the floors; others are heated by electric coils. Some city-dwellers live in modern homes or high-rise apartments.

Korean food is usually spicy. Staples of the diet are *kimchi* (a spicy mixture of pickled cabbage and other vegetables) and rice. Chicken and beef are the most common meats. A favorite delicacy is *pulkogi*, which are strips of marinated and barbecued beef.

South Koreans enjoy baseball, boxing, golf, soccer, table tennis, tennis, and wrestling. Judo and tae kwon do, types of martial arts, are very popular. In the cities and towns, the people enjoy reading and attending movies, plays, and concerts.

Children are required by law to complete elementary school. It is free, but if additional schooling is desired, the parents must pay tuition. Even so, 80 percent of the children continue their education.

The principles of Confucius are an important part of daily life. These may be found in South Koreans' many rituals of courtesy and formal behavior.

IT'S A FACT!

Halla-san - the country's highest point, is located on Cheju Island and rises 6,398 ft. (1,950 m) above sea level.

Naktong River - the country's longest river, flows 325 mi. (523 km) into the Korea Strait.

 DID YOU KNOW...

• Detailed genealogies, dating back many centuries, are kept by many families?
• South Korean women retain their maiden names when they marry?
• The average work week is 50 hours?
• Koreans often respond with laughter when embarrassed?

SPAIN

OFFICIAL NAME: España (Kingdom of Spain)
LOCATION: Western Europe
AREA: 194,885 sq. mi. (504,750 sq. km)
POPULATION (Est. 1993): 39,624,000
CAPITAL: Madrid
LARGEST CITIES: Madrid, Barcelona, Valencia, Seville
GOVERNMENT: Parliamentary monarchy.
FLAG: Three horizontal stripes of red, yellow, and red. The coat of arms is located slightly to the hoist side on the yellow stripe.
ETHNIC GROUPS: Spanish
LANGUAGES: Castilian Spanish, Catalan, Galician, Basque
RELIGION: Roman Catholic
BASIC MONETARY UNIT: Peseta

GEOGRAPHY

Spain is a sunny country in Western Europe well-known for its splendid castles and colorful bullfights. It measures 547 mi. (880 km) from north to south and 646 mi. (1,040 km) from east to west at its greatest distances. It has 2,345 mi. (3,774 km) of coastline on the Bay of Biscay, the Mediterranean Sea, the Strait of Gibraltar, and the North Atlantic Ocean.

Spain occupies most of the Iberian Peninsula. The country's area includes mainland Spain, the Balearic Islands in the Mediterranean Sea, and the Canary Islands in the Atlantic Ocean. Spain is separated from Africa by the Strait of Gibraltar. Its northeastern border is formed by the Pyrenees Mountains, which separate it from France.

Most of the country is a high, dry plateau called the *Meseta*. Throughout the plateau, hills and mountains rise above the plains. Other major land regions include: 1) the Northern Mountains, 2) the Ebro Basin, 3) the Coastal Plains, 4) the Guadalquivir Basin, 5) and the island provinces.

CLIMATE

The Meseta and other inland regions have dry, sunny weather for most of the year. They have hot summers and cold winters. Summers are hot and winters cold. Droughts are common throughout the year. During July, the temperature often rises above 80°F (27°C). In January, the temperature falls below 30°F (-1°C). The southern and eastern coastal regions have a more Mediterranean climate with dry summers and mild winters. In the winter, short, heavy rainstorms are common. January's average temperature rarely falls below 40°F (4°C). July's temperature usually reaches 80°F (27°C). The Northern Mountains region has mild, wet weather year-round and receives Spain's heaviest precipitation. The average January temperature is rarely below 40°F (4°C). In July, the temperature usually stays below 70°F (21°C).

ECONOMY

Prior to the 1950s, Spain was one of the most underdeveloped countries in Europe. Most of the people were poor farmers. Today, more Spaniards work in manufacturing and construction than on farms. Over 50 percent of the people work in service areas and over 30 percent are employed in industry. Tourism is important to Spain's economy. About 40 million tourists visit Spain each year.

Agriculture - barley, milk, olives, oranges, potatoes, sheep, tomatoes, wheat, and wine

Fishing - mussels, sardines, and squid

Manufacturing - automobiles, cement, chemical products, iron and steel, machinery, ships, shoes, and textiles

Exports - automobiles, chemicals, citrus fruits, iron and steel, machinery, olives and olive oil, textiles, and wine

Imports - chemicals, corn, machinery, petroleum, and soybeans

LIFE-STYLE

Approximately 90 percent of all Spaniards live in cities. Almost all live in modern apartment buildings and wear the latest Western-style clothing. Many families own TVs and automobiles. Despite this, they still observe some old customs, such as a three-hour lunch break (which sometimes includes a siesta) and a *paseo* (walk) before their evening meal, which is often not eaten until 10 or 11 P.M. Their dwellings are typically whitewashed houses made of clay or stone with tile roofs. Since the soil is so poor, many farmers raise sheep or other livestock rather than crops.

The number of people in rural areas has greatly diminished since the 1960s. Most farmers live in small towns and villages. Every morning and evening they walk or ride in donkey carts down the dirt roads to the fields and then back to their homes.

Family life is very important to the Spanish. The father is the head of the home. Today, about one-fourth of the women work outside of the home. Men sometimes have two jobs. Close contact with the extended family is frequent.

Typical foods in the Spanish diet include fresh vegetables, meat, eggs, chicken, and fish. Almost all foods are cooked in olive oil. One popular dish is *paella* (shrimp, lobster, chicken, ham, and vegetables, combined with saffron-flavored rice). Other dishes may include squid, crab, sardines, and fried baby eels. The most popular summer dish is *gazpacho* (cold soup made of strained tomatoes, olive oil, and spices). Adults normally drink wine with meals. *Sangría* (a drink which includes wine, soda water, fruit juice, and fruit) is also popular.

Soccer is the most popular sport in Spain. Bullfighting is Spain's most unusual and best-known sport. Almost all cities have at least one bull ring. The best matadors are considered national heroes. Local festivals and other celebrations are enjoyed throughout the year. Folk singing and dancing are popular and vary according to region.

About 97 percent of Spain's adult population is literate. Children are required to attend school from ages six to 13. Many quit school at age 14 or go to school at night and work during the day to supplement the family income.

Spain abounds with a variety of historic and beautiful architecture. Structures built by the ancient Romans, aqueducts and bridges, are still used. Ruins of other Roman structures also can be seen throughout Spain. The country boasts about 1,400 castles and palaces, including fortified palaces called *alcazars* that were built by the Moors. The Alhambra in Granada is the most famous.

Spain was also home to many famous artists. El Greco, Francisco Goya, Pablo Picasso, and Salvador Dali are just a few.

Spaniards love to be outdoors and will spend hours visiting at sidewalk cafes or village squares. Most people take a three- or four-week vacation in July or August.

IT'S A FACT!
Caves of Altamira - feature paintings by cavemen of bison, deer, and other wild animals that date as far back as 20000 B.C.

Pico de Teide - the country's highest point, is located on Tenerife in the Canary Islands and rises 12,198 ft. (3,718 m) above sea level.

The Prado - located in the capital city of Madrid, houses one of the world's finest art collections. It features works by such great painters as Goya and Diego Velásquez.

The Tagus River - the country's longest river, measures 626 mi. (1,007 km) long.

 DID YOU KNOW...
- During the festival of San Fermin in Pamplona, the people run the bulls through the streets to the bull ring?
- Spanish dances, such as the bolero, fandango, and flamenco, are famous worldwide?
- The Spanish see it as a duty to correct "errors" in others so that others may learn and avoid embarrassment?
- The walled city of Ávila, built from 1090 to 1099, is recognized as one of the world's best walled cities?

SRI LANKA

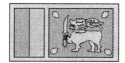

OFFICIAL NAME: Sri Lanka Prajathanthrika Samajavadi Janarajaya (Democratic Socialist Republic of Sri Lanka)
FORMERLY: Ceylon
LOCATION: Indian Ocean
AREA: 25,332 sq. mi. (65,610 sq. km)
POPULATION (Est. 1993): 17,876,000
CAPITAL: Colombo
LARGEST CITIES: Colombo, Kandy, Jaffna, Galle
GOVERNMENT: Republic governed by a president.
FLAG: Yellow field with two vertical stripes of green and orange on the hoist side. A dark red rectangle on the fly side features a yellow bo leaf in each corner and a yellow lion holding a sword.
ETHNIC GROUPS: Sinhalese, Tamil, Moor, Burgher, Malay, Veddah
LANGUAGES: Sinhala, Tamil
RELIGIONS: Buddhism, Hinduism, Islam, Christianity
BASIC MONETARY UNIT: Sri Lankan Rupee

GEOGRAPHY

Sri Lanka is an island country that lies about 20 mi. (32 km) off India's southeast coast. The island is linked to India by Adam's Bridge, a series of coral islands in the Palk Strait.

Southwestern Sri Lanka is almost totally covered by a tropical rainforest, while the north is almost totally covered by a plain. South-central Sri Lanka features mountains surrounded by plains on the south, east, and west.

CLIMATE

Sri Lanka has a tropical climate that is plagued by a northeastern monsoon between December and March, and by a southwestern monsoon between June and October. The average temperature ranges from 60°F (16°C) in the mountain region to 80°F (27°C) in the low coastal areas. The average annual rainfall ranges from about 50 in. (130 cm) in the northeast to about 200 in. (510 cm) in parts of the southwest. The country is occasionally hit by cyclones and tornados.

ECONOMY

Sri Lanka's developing economy is based mainly on agriculture.

Agriculture - coconuts, eggs, grains, hides, oil seeds, meat, milk, pulses, rice, roots, rubber, spices, sugar cane, and tea

Manufacturing - cement, clothing and textiles, coconut processing, refined petroleum, rubber products, tobacco processing, and tea processing

Exports - agricultural products, clothing and textiles, coconuts, gems and jewelry, graphite, marine products, petroleum products, rubber, and tea

Imports - food and beverages, machinery and equipment, petroleum and petroleum products, and textiles

LIFE-STYLE

Approximately four-fifths of Sri Lanka's population lives in rural areas. About half of all Sri Lankans make a living in agriculture. Shelters for poor, rural families are usually constructed of mud walls and thatched roofs. Housing for the middle and upper classes is usually more substantial. These houses are often surrounded by a walled compound.

Many urban male Sri Lankans wear Western-style clothing, while those in rural areas usually wear a shirt and a *sarong* (garment wrapped around the waist to form a long skirt). Sri Lankan women wear a *sari* (straight piece of cloth draped around the body as a long dress), or a blouse or jacket with a *redde* (similar to a sarong).

Rice is the staple of the diet and it is usually served with curry dishes (stewlike dishes made of eggs, fish, meat, or vegetables) that range from mild to very spicy. Sri Lankans usually eat very little meat, but do consume large amounts of beans, peas, and nuts. Tea is the most popular beverage.

The most popular sports include badminton, cricket, fishing, horse racing, rugby, soccer, swimming, and tennis. Table games, including bridge and chess, are also popular. Sri Lankans enjoy watching movies and attending both live and puppet theater. Elephant racing is popular during New Year's festivities. Dance is an important art form, and Sri Lankan craftworkers specialize in jewelry, pottery, wood masks, and woven baskets and mats.

Education is free from kindergarten to the university level, and children ages five to 14 are required to attend school. About 87 percent of the population age 15 and older is literate.

Because of inadequate health and sanitation facilities, Sri Lankans suffer from diseases such as malaria.

Most Sri Lankans travel by bus and less than one percent of the population owns a vehicle.

IT'S A FACT!

Pidurutalagala - the country's highest point, rises 8,281 ft. (2,524 m) above sea level.

 DID YOU KNOW...

- Sri Lanka gained its independence in 1948 after nearly 450 years under European rule?
- Sri Lanka is renowned for its tea?
- In 1972, the country changed its name to Sri Lanka, meaning "resplendent island"?
- Thousands of people have died and thousands of Tamils have fled to India as a result of fighting between the Sinhalese and Tamils, which began in 1983, over who would control the government?

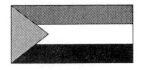

THE SUDAN

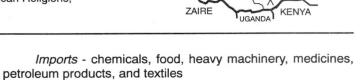

OFFICIAL NAME: Jumhuriyat as-Sudan (Republic of The Sudan)
LOCATION: Northeastern Africa
AREA: 967,500 sq. mi. (2,505,813 sq. km)
POPULATION (Est. 1992): 26,672,000
CAPITAL: Khartoum
LARGEST CITIES: Omdurman, Khartoum, Khartoum North, Port Sudan, Wad Madani, El Obeid (Ul Ubaid), Juba
GOVERNMENT: Headed by a 15-member Revolutionary Command Council (RCC).
FLAG: Three horizontal stripes of red, white, and black with a green triangle—representing Islam—based on the hoist side.
ETHNIC GROUPS: Arab, Nubian, Beja, Fur, Black (Dinka, Nuer, Shilluk, Azande)
LANGUAGES: Arabic, English, Dinka, along with over 100 different languages
RELIGIONS: Islam (mainly Sunni Muslim), Traditional African Religions, Christianity
BASIC MONETARY UNIT: Sudanese Pound

GEOGRAPHY

In terms of area, The Sudan is Africa's largest country. At its greatest distances, Sudan measures 1,275 mi. (2,050 km) from north to south and 1,150 mi. (1,850 km) from east to west at its greatest distances. It has 400 mi. (644 km) of coastline along the Red Sea.

Sudan has three main regions: 1) Northern Sudan, 2) Central Sudan, and 3) Southern Sudan. Northern Sudan is primarily desert; it is covered by the Nubian Desert in the northeast and parts of the Libyan and Sahara Deserts in the northwest.

Central Sudan is mainly a grass-covered plain. The Blue Nile River flows out of Ethiopia and meets the White Nile River in the city of Khartoum. Together they form the Nile River, which flows north into Egypt. Between the two branches of the Nile lies El Gezira (Al Jazirah), Sudan's most fertile area.

Southern Sudan consists of a swampland, the Sudd, caused by flooding of the Nile River's branches. The area is covered with junglelike vegetation and includes mountain ranges near its southeast borders.

CLIMATE

Sudan's climate ranges from arid in the north to tropical in the south. Northern Sudan's average high temperature ranges from 110° to 125°F (43° to 52°C) in summer, with an average low temperature of 60°F (16°C) in winter. Rainfall rarely exceeds 4 in. (10 cm) per year.

Central Sudan has an average temperature of 74°F (23°C) in January and 89°F (32°C) in July. Rainfall averages 4-32 in. (10-81 cm) per year. Southern Sudan has the lowest temperatures in the country and an average annual rainfall of 32-55 in. (81-140 cm) per year.

ECONOMY

Sudan's economy is based mainly on agriculture. Major industries and irrigated farmland are governmentally controlled.

Agriculture - camels, cattle, cotton, goats, gum arabic, millet, peanuts, sesame, sheep, sorghum, and sugar cane

Manufacturing - cement, edible oils, fertilizer, food products, petroleum refining, shoes, soap distilling, sugar, and textiles

Mining - chromium, gold, and gypsum

Exports - cotton, gum arabic, livestock, peanuts, sesame, and sorghum

Imports - chemicals, food, heavy machinery, medicines, petroleum products, and textiles

LIFE-STYLE

Sudan's population is approximately four-fifths rural and one-fifth urban. Most rural dwellers farm by traditional means or raise livestock. Many of the residents live in thatch-roofed huts or flat-roofed houses constructed of sun-dried brick. Other rural Sudanese are nomads. Employed urban Sudanese work largely in offices, shops, or factories. The residents live in apartment buildings or small, modern houses. Many of the poor and unemployed urban Sudanese live in tents or homes similar to those found in rural areas.

Sudanese wear both modern and traditional clothing. Generally, when a Sudanese woman wears a modern outfit, she also wears a *taub* (traditional outer garment which covers the entire body). Most men wear a *jallabiyah* (long robe) with a *taqiyah* (small skullcap) or an *imamah* (white turban). Sandals are commonly worn. Rural Sudanese often wear very little clothing due to the heat.

The Sudanese commonly eat *ful*, or *fool* (broad beans cooked in oil), and rarely eat meat. Beverages include coffee, *karkadai* (national drink made from the hibiscus plant), and tea.

Popular leisure activities include playing soccer, and visiting with family, friends, and neighbors. The Sudanese arts include traditional African and Islamic handicrafts.

Education is free and though nine years of attendance are required, the law is rarely enforced. Sudan has few health facilities and a shortage of medical personnel. Famine and malnutrition are health problems, and commonly suffered diseases include cholera, gastrointestinal infections, malaria, venereal disease, whooping cough, and yellow fever.

IT'S A FACT!

Mount Kinyeti - the country's highest point, rises 10,456 ft. (3,187 m) above sea level.

 DID YOU KNOW...

• It has been found that people lived near the Nile River in what is now Sudan as early as the 7000s B.C.?

SURINAME

North Atlantic Ocean

Paramaribo ★

Corantijn R.

Blommestein Lake

SURINAME

FRENCH GUIANA

Mt. Juliana Top ∧

Suriname R.

Marowijne R.

GUYANA

Corantijn R.

BRAZIL

OFFICIAL NAME: Republiek Suriname (Republic of Suriname)
FORMERLY: Dutch Guiana
LOCATION: Northeastern South America
AREA: 63,037 sq. mi. (163,265 sq. km)
POPULATION (Est. 1993): 447,000
CAPITAL/LARGEST CITY: Paramaribo
GOVERNMENT: Republic headed by a president.
FLAG: Five horizontal stripes of green, white, red, white, and green. A five-pointed, yellow star is centered on the red stripe.
ETHNIC GROUPS: Hindustani, Creole, Indonesian, Black, American Indian, Chinese, European
LANGUAGES: Sranan Tongo (also called Taki-Taki; a combination of Dutch, English, and several African languages), Dutch, English
RELIGIONS: Hinduism, Islam, Roman Catholic, Protestant, others
BASIC MONETARY UNIT: Surinamese Guilder, Gulden, or Florin

GEOGRAPHY

Suriname, also spelled *Surinam*, is the smallest independent South American country in both area and population. At its greatest distances, Suriname measures 285 mi. (459 km) from north to south and 280 mi. (451 km) from east to west. It has 226 mi. (364 km) of coastline along the North Atlantic Ocean.

Suriname has a narrow coastal area that is mainly swampland which has been drained for agricultural purposes. This area extends about 10-50 mi. (16-80 km) inland, where the land turns into a sandy plain. Further inland, behind the plain, is the mountainous rainforest region, which accounts for about 80 percent of the country's area. The southwest border has a high savanna.

Suriname has seven major rivers, the most important of which include the Marowijne, the Corantijn, and the Suriname.

CLIMATE

Suriname has a tropical climate with two rainy seasons: May to July and November to January. The average annual temperature is 81°F (27°C). The average annual rainfall ranges from 76 in. (193 cm) in the west to 95 in. (241 cm) in the city of Paramaribo.

ECONOMY

Suriname's economy is based mainly on mining and metal processing, and is supplemented by agriculture.

Agriculture - bananas, beef, chicken, coconuts, palm kernels, peanuts, plantains, rice, and sugar cane

Fishing - fish and shrimp

Forestry - hardwoods

Manufacturing - alumina and aluminum production, food processing, and lumbering

Mining - bauxite

Exports - alumina and aluminum, bananas, raw bauxite, rice, and shrimp and fish

Imports - capital equipment, consumer goods, cotton, food, and petroleum

LIFE-STYLE

Most Surinamers live in the flat coastal area, with nearly half of the population living in the city of Paramaribo.

Each of the country's ethnic groups has preserved its own culture, religion, and language. Some Hindustanis farm small pieces of land, and others work in industry. The Creoles mainly work in business or government. Many Indonesians are tenant farmers, renting their land from large landowners. Black residents are mainly descendents of black Africans who escaped slavery during the 1600s and 1700s. Called *Bush Negroes*, they live mainly in the rainforests and follow African tribal customs.

Children ages seven to 12 are required to attend elementary school. Some continue on to high school. About 65 percent of Suriname's people can read and write. The country has one university, which is located near Paramaribo.

The country's main means of transportation is based on its extensive river system. The country only has about 800 mi. (1,300 km) of main roads and limited railroad services.

IT'S A FACT!

Mount Juliana Top - the country's highest point, rises 4,200 ft. (1,280 m) above sea level.

 DID YOU KNOW...

- Suriname was ruled by the Netherlands most of the time between 1667 and 1975, when the country gained its independence?
- The area now known as Suriname was sighted by Christopher Columbus in 1498?
- The first permanent settlement in what is now known as Suriname was built by British explorers in 1651?
- The Dutch took over Suriname in 1667, and in exchange, gave Britain the land which is now known as the state of New York in the United States?

SWAZILAND

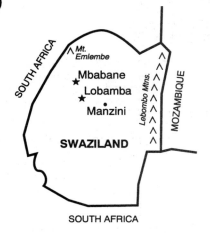

SOUTH AFRICA

OFFICIAL NAME: Kingdom of Swaziland
LOCATION: Southern Africa
AREA: 6,704 sq. mi. (17,363 sq. km)
POPULATION (Est. 1993): 872,000
CAPITAL: Mbabane (administrative), Lobamba (royal/traditional)
LARGEST CITIES: Mbabane, Manzini
GOVERNMENT: Monarchy ruled by a king.
FLAG: Five horizontal stripes. Top and bottom stripes are blue (for peace). Center stripe is red (for past battles) with a black and white shield, spears, and staff. Between the blue and red stripes are thin yellow stripes (for natural resources).
ETHNIC GROUP: African
LANGUAGES: siSwati, English
RELIGIONS: Christianity, Traditional African Religions
BASIC MONETARY UNIT: Lilangeni

GEOGRAPHY

Swaziland is a landlocked country in southern Africa. The Republic of South Africa surrounds it on three sides and Mozambique borders it on the east. It is only 120 mi. (193 km) from north to south and 90 mi. (140 km) from east to west at its greatest distances.

The country is divided geographically into four regions: 1) the mountainous high veld, 2) the middle veld, 3) the low veld, and 4) the Lebombo Mountains. Timber plantations are found throughout the high veld, rich soil is prevalent in the middle veld, and cattle ranching is extensive in the low veld.

CLIMATE

Swaziland's climate varies from subtropical to near temperate. In the mountains, temperatures average 60°F (16°C) and about 45-75 in. (114-191 cm) of rain falls annually. Temperatures average 66°F (19°C) in the middle veld. This region receives 30-45 in. (76-114 cm) of rain yearly. Temperatures average 72°F (22°C) in the low veld. Rainfall averages only 20 in. (51 cm) yearly.

ECONOMY

Swaziland has a varied economy with rich agricultural and mineral resources. Its exports outnumber its imports.

Agriculture - citrus fruit, corn, cotton, livestock, pineapple, rice, sugar cane, and tobacco

Manufacturing - cement, fertilizer, food products, and wood products

Mining - asbestos, coal, gold, iron ore, kaolin, and tin

Exports - asbestos, fruit, iron ore, sugar, and wood pulp

Imports - chemicals, foodstuffs, fuels, machinery and vehicles, and manufactured goods

LIFE-STYLE

Most Swazis farm and raise livestock and live in the old traditional way. They have a polygamous society. Men may have more than one wife. The typical family includes a man, his wives, his unmarried children, and married sons and their families. Each family lives in a homestead. For centuries, homesteads were comprised of circular huts built around a cattle pen. Now, wealthy Swazi live in modern houses. In rural areas, each wife has her own living quarters and a garden plot.

In urban areas, some people work in shops, offices, and factories.

Traditional Swazi clothing is constructed of leather, bright cloth, or skins of animals. Beaded ornaments are also worn. Most Swazi now wear Western-style clothes.

Only about 75 percent of children ages five to 14 attend school. Most of the schools are run by churches with financial help from the government. About 60 percent of adults can read and write in English or siSwati.

The people prize their cattle and respect those who have large herds. Cattle are rarely killed for food, but they may be sold for money or sacrificed at religious ceremonies.

IT'S A FACT!

Mount Emlembe - the country's highest point, rises 6,109 ft. (1,862 m) above sea level.

DID YOU KNOW...

• Most of the mines, processing plants, and profitable farms in Swaziland are owned by Europeans of South African origin?

• When a Swazi man marries, his family presents cattle to his wife's family to legalize her status as his wife?

SWEDEN

OFFICIAL NAME: Konungariket Sverige
(Kingdom of Sweden)
LOCATION: Northern Europe
AREA: 173,732 sq. mi. (449,964 sq. km)
POPULATION (Est. 1993): 8,528,000
CAPITAL: Stockholm
LARGEST CITIES: Stockholm, Göteborg, Malmö
GOVERNMENT: Constitutional monarchy.
FLAG: Blue field with a yellow cross
that is shifted slightly to the hoist side.
ETHNIC GROUPS: Swedish, Finnish, Lapps
LANGUAGE: Swedish
RELIGION: Lutheran
BASIC MONETARY UNIT: Swedish Krona

GEOGRAPHY

Sweden occupies the eastern half of the Scandinavian Peninsula and is one of the largest European countries in terms of area. Sweden measures 977 mi. (1,572 km) from north to south and 310 mi. (499 km) from east to west at its greatest distances. It has 4,700 mi. (7,564 km) of coastline on the Gulf of Bothnia, the Baltic Sea, Skagerrak, and Kattegat.

Spruce and pine forests cover over half of the country. The country also has beautiful lakes, snow-capped mountains, and fast-moving rivers. Most of the country is flat, with mountains found primarily in the northwest. The coast is made up of sandy beaches in the south and rocky cliffs in parts of the west and north.

Off the coast of Sweden are many groups of small islands. The two largest are Gotland and Öland Islands, both of which are located in the Baltic Sea.

The country has four main land regions: 1) the Mountain Range, 2) the Inner Northland, 3) the Swedish Lowland, and 4) the South Swedish Highland. The Mountain Range is part of the Kölen Mountains, which runs through Sweden's northern border with Norway. Hundreds of small glaciers cover the treeless higher slopes of the snow-capped range. The Inner Northland is a vast, thinly populated, hilly region covered by great forests and containing many rivers. The Swedish Lowland is the most populated and most fertile region. It includes the central and southern plains of Sweden. More than 40 percent of the plains are covered by farmland. The South Swedish Highland is a rocky upland with poor soils. It is mostly covered by forests.

CLIMATE

The difference between the climate in the northern and southern parts of Sweden is great. Warm southwesterly winds from the Atlantic Ocean provide southern Sweden with warm summers and mild winters. Northern Sweden also has warm summers but cold winters. The mountains block the warm Atlantic winds, keeping them from affecting the climate in the north.

In the south, the average January temperature is 32°F (0°C). In the far north, the average is 10°F (-12°C). During July, temperatures average 59° to 63°F (15° to 17°C) in the south and 54° to 57°F (12° to 14°C) in the north. Rainfall is greater in the mountains and the highlands than on the plains. The south is only snow-covered in January and February, but the north has snow from mid-October through mid-April.

ECONOMY

Sweden is a highly industrialized nation. Its economy changed from one based on agriculture into one of advanced technology largely because of its vast natural resources of timber, iron ore, and water power. Economic development also occurred because of the close cooperation among government, employer groups, and labor unions.

Swedes have one of the highest standards of living in the world. They spend more money on vacations than any other people in Europe. Almost one-fifth of the people own country homes where they spend weekends and holidays.

Agriculture - barley, beef cattle, hogs, milk and other dairy products, oats, potatoes, rye, sugar beets, and wheat

Forestry - birch, pine, and spruce

Manufacturing - agricultural machinery, aircraft, automobiles, ball bearings, diesel motors, electrical equipment, explosives, fertilizers, furniture, glass, matches, paper and cardboard, plastics, plywood, precision tools, prefabricated houses, ships, steel, steelware, telephones, textiles, and wood pulp

Mining - copper, gold, iron ore, lead, and zinc

Exports - automobiles, chemicals, electrical machinery, iron and steel products, lumber, paper products, safety matches, telephones, transportation equipment, and wood products

Imports - electrical machinery, farm products, food products, petroleum, raw materials for the chemical industry, and transportation equipment

LIFE-STYLE

About 84 percent of Swedes live in urban areas. Sweden's cities combine traditional and modern architecture. Many cities have castles and churches dating from the Middle Ages. Highways and public transportation systems link suburbs and cities.

Rural dwellers maintain a standard of living similar to that of urban dwellers since the government guarantees high prices for agricultural products and because many rural people work in industry or services in nearby towns. Moreover, many in rural areas work part-time on farms and part-time in factories.

The Lapps, a small indigenous group of people, live in the far north. Many Lapps are lumberjacks or miners and live in small towns or villages. However, some men still have the traditional job of caring for herds of reindeer, while wandering over the land.

Common Swedish foods include potatoes, cheeses, seafoods, fresh vegetables, and fruit. Breakfast foods include *fil* (a type of yogurt), *knäckebröd* (crisp bread), and strong coffee. The best known type of Swedish meal, the *smörgåsbord*, is reserved for special occasions. During this meal, Swedes often eat foods in a particular order. First, they eat cold fish dishes, such as eel, herring, or shrimp. Next, they eat cold meats, such as pâte, smoked reindeer, or ham with a vegetable salad. Thirdly, they eat small hot dishes, such as omelets, meatballs, or herring cooked in bread crumbs. Desserts may include cheese, fresh fruit, fruit salad, or a pastry. Like other Scandinavians, Swedes drink large quantities of coffee.

Children attend school free from ages seven to 16. Kindergarten is optional. The government also provides health care that is largely free and pays pensions to widows, orphans, and the old. In addition, the government provides health insurance and financial aid for housing.

Swedish people are athletic and love the outdoors. Popular sports are soccer, skiing, golf, swimming, tennis, ice skating, and ice hockey. Every year in March, a cross-country ski race (the Vasa Race) covering 55 mi. (89 km) is held in the province of Dalarna. Thousands of Swedes compete in this race. Other popular activities include hiking, hunting, fishing, bird watching, camping, sailing, and orienteering (using a map and a compass to cross an area).

IT'S A FACT!

Göta Canal - links lakes and rivers from Göteborg to Stockholm, a distance of over 350 mi. (560 km).

Lake Vänern - the country's largest lake and one of the largest lakes in Europe, covers 2,156 sq. mi. (5,584 sq. km).

Mount Kebnekaise - the country's highest point, rises 6,926 ft. (2,111 m) above sea level.

 DID YOU KNOW...

- Safety matches were invented in Sweden in 1844?
- Volvo and SAAB are Sweden's leading car-makers?
- Swedish workers enjoy one of the shortest workweeks in the world: less than 35 hours?
- Swedish workers receive at least four or five weeks of vacation per year?
- At the birth of a child, Swedish parents share a total of 12 months of leave to care for the baby?
- Singing in choirs is the most popular hobby in Sweden?
- The northern seventh of Sweden lies in a region called the "Land of the Midnight Sun" inside the Arctic Circle? During periods of the summer, the sun shines there 24 hours a day.
- The Skansen, a popular park located in the capital city of Stockholm, has an open-air museum that exhibits old Swedish homes?
- The University of Uppsala, founded in 1477, is Sweden's oldest university?
- Swedes celebrate St. Lucia Day, the Festival of Light, which takes place on December 13? Young girls wearing white dresses and a crown of evergreen boughs wake up their parents with a customary song. They then serve their parents coffee and buns.

SWITZERLAND

OFFICIAL NAME: Schweiz (German), Suisse (French), Svizzera (Italian) (Swiss Confederation)
LOCATION: Europe
AREA: 15,943 sq. mi. (41,293 sq. km)
POPULATION (Est. 1993): 6,653,000
CAPITAL: Bern
LARGEST CITIES: Zurich, Basel, Geneva, Bern, Lausanne
GOVERNMENT: Federal republic governed by Federal Council.
FLAG: Red field with a white cross—representing Christianity—in the center.
ETHNIC GROUP: Mixed Europeans
LANGUAGES: German, French, Italian
RELIGION: Christianity
BASIC MONETARY UNIT: Swiss Franc, Franken, or Franco

GEOGRAPHY

Switzerland is sometimes called the "roof of Europe" because of its location in the Alps. It is a landlocked country that measures 138 mi. (222 km) from north to south and 213 mi. (343 km) from east to west at its greatest distances. The country's area includes 523 sq. mi. (1,355 sq. km) of inland water.

The three main land regions are: 1) the Jura Mountains, 2) the Swiss Plateau, and 3) the Swiss Alps. The two mountain ranges, the Alps and the Jura, cover almost 65 percent of the country. But the plateau between them is where four-fifths of the people live.

A series of parallel ridges separated by narrow valleys make up the Jura Mountains region. This area is home to Switzerland's profitable watchmaking industry.

The Swiss Plateau is hilly with rolling plains. It lies 1,200-2,200 ft. (366-671 m) above sea level. This region contains Switzerland's richest farmland and most of its large cities.

The Swiss Alps cover 60 percent of Switzerland and are part of the largest mountain system in Europe. Much of the region is forested.

CLIMATE

Due to the wide range in altitude, the climate varies greatly within the country. Air from the Atlantic often produces thick fog on the plateau. Some areas are covered by fog for as many as 120 days of the year. On the central plateau and in the mountain valleys, January temperatures range from 29° to 33°F (-2° to 1°C). During the summer, the plateau is warm and sunny with July temperatures averaging 65° to 70°F (18° to 21°C). The southernmost part of the country often has hot summers. About 40-45 in. (100-114 cm) of precipitation fall annually on the central plateau. In some mountain regions, yearly precipitation totals more than 100 in. (250 cm).

The *foehn* (a warm, dry, southerly wind) sometimes blows down the valleys of the Swiss Alps and causes rapid changes in temperature and air pressure. It also can cause mountain snows to melt earlier than usual and avalanches to occur.

ECONOMY

Despite limited natural resources, Switzerland is a thriving industrial nation. It has one of the highest standards of living in the world. Inflation and unemployment are both extremely low. It is one of the few nations in the world that is virtually free of poverty. Tourism and banking are major industries. Switzerland is the banking and financial capital of the world. More than 11 million tourists visit Switzerland each year. Raising dairy cattle is the leading agricultural activity.

Agriculture - dairy products, fruit, potatoes, sugar beets, and wheat

Manufacturing - chemicals, drugs, electrical equipment, machine tools, paper, precision instruments, processed foods, textiles, and watches

Exports - cheeses, chocolate, electrical equipment, machine tools, precision instruments, silk, textiles, and watches

Imports - food and food products, and raw materials

LIFE-STYLE

About 700 years ago, the people of what is now Switzerland united and developed a policy of neutrality. This along with their location kept them out of the bitter fighting in World Wars I and II. Although they joined together for defense, people from different regions within Switzerland kept their own ways of life. Today, the people still cling to differences in language, customs, and traditions.

Switzerland has picturesque villages nestled in the Swiss Alps and cities (such as Bern) with charming downtown areas boasting fountains and old buildings with arcades that shelter the sidewalks.

About two-fifths of the Swiss people live in rural areas. In Swiss society, the nuclear family is the most important unit. Families tend to be small with only one or two children. Many women work outside the home, though they did not receive the right to vote in national elections until 1971. Swiss farms average only 8 acres (3 hectares).

Children are required to attend school but the age limits vary. Most children attend school from ages six to 14 and receive instruction in the local national language. Students who plan on pursuing a university education may go to one of three types of high schools that specialize in Greek and Latin, modern languages, or mathematics and science. Other students go to trade or technical schools while serving an apprenticeship. University students pay no tuition.

With so many different groups of people, the diet is quite diverse. Breakfast usually includes fresh breads, cheeses, and coffee. Meat, potatoes or pasta, and a salad are usually eaten for the main meal.

The people of Switzerland enjoy bicycling, bobsledding, camping, climbing, gymnastics, hiking, skiing, soccer, swimming, target shooting, and wrestling. They also enjoy taking walks and watching movies. Another Swiss favorite, a game called *hornussen*, has been played for hundreds of years. In this game, a batter hits a wooden disk with a 8-ft.- (2.4-m-) long wooden club. Players use wooden rackets to catch the disk. Almost every village and town has a singing group that performs in local festivals and in regional and national singing competitions. Also popular are folk dancing by Swiss wearing colorful national costumes.

Famous Swiss books include two children's classics: *Heidi* and *The Swiss Family Robinson.*

Switzerland does not maintain a regular armed forces, although it has a militia (citizens' army). All men at the age of 20 are required to begin a series of military training periods. They can be called into service until age 50. Men unable to serve must pay a special tax.

IT'S A FACT

Dufourspitze of Monte Rosa - the country's highest point, rises 15,203 ft. (4,634 m) above sea level.

Giessbach Falls - the country's highest waterfall, is located in the Bernese Alps and falls 1,982 ft. (604 m).

St. Gotthard Road Tunnel - the longest highway tunnel in the world at 10.14 mi. (16.32 km) long.

The University of Basel - the country's oldest university, was founded in 1460.

 DID YOU KNOW...
- The Latin name for Switzerland, *Helvetia*, appears on Swiss coins and postage stamps?
- Switzerland has a higher percentage of foreign-born residents than any other European country?

SYRIA

OFFICIAL NAME: Al-Jumhuria Al-Arabia Al-Suria (The Syrian Arab Republic)
FORMERLY: United Arab Republic (with Egypt)
LOCATION: Middle East
AREA: 71,498 sq. mi. (185,180 sq. km)
POPULATION (Est. 1993): 13,608,000
CAPITAL: Damascus
LARGEST CITIES: Damascus, Aleppo, Homs, Latakia, Hama
GOVERNMENT: Republic governed by a president.
FLAG: Adopted in 1980. Three horizontal stripes of red, white, and black with two five-pointed green stars on the white stripe.
ETHNIC GROUPS: Arab, Armenian, Kurd
LANGUAGES: Arabic, Armenian, Kurdish
RELIGIONS: Islam (Sunni, Alawite, and Shiite Muslims), Christianity
BASIC MONETARY UNIT: Syrian Pound

GEOGRAPHY

Syria is located at the western end of the *Fertile Crescent* (an area of rich farmland extending between the Euphrates and Tigris Rivers, from the Mediterranean Sea to the Persian Gulf). At its greatest distances, Syria measures 465 mi. (748 km) from north to south and 515 mi. (829 km) from east to west. It has 94 mi. (151 km) of coastline along the Mediterranean Sea.

Syria has three main land regions: 1) the coast, 2) the mountains, and 3) the valleys and plains. Much of the coastal region is cultivated, and few parts of it need to be irrigated. The mountain region includes Jabal an Nusayriyah just east of the coast and the Anti-Lebanon Mountains and Jabal ad Duruz in the southeast. The valleys and plains are generally found along the country's rivers. The southeast features the Syrian Desert.

CLIMATE

Syria's climate varies by region. The coast is usually mild and humid, and the average annual temperature ranges from about 48°F (9°C) in January to about 81°F (27°C) in July. The average annual rainfall is 40 in. (100 cm).

The average annual temperature in the mountains ranges from about 41°F (5°C) in January to about 72°F (22°C) in July. The mountains' west side has an average annual rainfall of up to 40 in. (100 cm), while the east side generally remains dry.

The average annual temperature in the valleys and plains ranges from about 41°F (5°C) in January to about 88°F (31°C) in July. This region receives very little rainfall.

ECONOMY

Syria has a developing economy that is mainly governmentally controlled, though a majority of farms, industries, and small businesses are privately owned.

Agriculture - barley, chickpeas, cotton, grapes, lentils, livestock (cattle, goats, and sheep), milk, olives, sugar beets, tobacco, tomatoes, and wheat

Manufacturing - beverages, cement, fertilizer, glass, petroleum products, oil refining, processed foods, sugar, textiles, and tobacco

Mining - gypsum, limestone, natural gas, petroleum, and phosphates

Exports - food products, petroleum, phosphates, raw cotton, tobacco, woolens, and other textiles

Imports - beverages, food, fuels, grains, machinery, metals, motor vehicles, petroleum products, and textiles

LIFE-STYLE

Most Syrians live in the western area. The rural population, which accounts for about half the people, mainly lives by traditional means in small villages. They make a living by farming, and their shelters are constructed of stone or sun-dried mud bricks. A few, called *Bedouins*, are nomads who live in tents and move with their grazing herds. The urban population mainly lives in cities or towns. Most Syrians wear Western-style clothing. Traditional clothing, worn mainly by rural Syrians, consists of billowy trousers for men and long, lightweight dresses with short sleeves for women. Syrians may also wear a large cloth head covering.

Wheat is the staple of the Syrian diet. Most Syrians also eat cheese, fresh fruit, and vegetables. Lamb dishes are popular. A commonly served restaurant item is *mezza* (table full of appetizers), which consists of bread, chickpea and eggplant pastes, olives, pickles, and raw or grilled meat dishes mixed with spices and wheat. Commonly consumed beverages include beer, strong black coffee, milk, tea, and *arak* (strong liquor made from dates).

Popular sports include basketball and soccer. Along the coast, water sports are popular. Leisure activities include socializing, and watching movies and television at home. Syrian craftworkers have been famous for their beautiful glassware, metalwork, and textiles, which date back thousands of years.

Public education is free. Children ages six to 11 are required to attend school, though many do not attend because of a shortage of classrooms and teachers. Education at private religious and private secular schools is also available.

IT'S A FACT!

Mount Hermon - the country's highest point, rises 9,232 ft. (2,814 m) above sea level.

 DID YOU KNOW...

- As early as 2000 B.C., the Syrian cities of Aleppo and Damascus were centers of world trade?
- All eligible Syrian males may be drafted for 30 months of military service?
- Damascus—believed by historians to have been founded about 3000 B.C.—is one of the world's oldest cities?
- *Damask* (a firm, lustrous fabric woven from any fiber) was introduced to Europe by way of Damascus?

TAIWAN

OFFICIAL NAME: T'ai-wan (Taiwan) or Republic of China
LOCATION: South China Sea
AREA: 13,892 sq. mi. (35,980 sq. km)
POPULATION (Est. 1993): 21,116,000
CAPITAL: Taipei
LARGEST CITIES: Taipei, Kaohsiung, Taichung, Tainan, Chilung
GOVERNMENT: Multiparty democratic regime governed by a president.
FLAG: Adopted in 1928. Red field with a blue canton in the upper hoist-side corner. The canton features a white sun with twelve rays. Red, white, and blue represent liberty and sacrifice, fraternity, and honesty, accordingly.
ETHNIC GROUPS: Taiwanese (mainly of Chinese ancestry), Chinese, Aborigines, others (those related to Filipinos and Indonesians)
LANGUAGES: Northern Chinese (Mandarin, or putonghua) and other Chinese dialects, Taiwanese, Hakka
RELIGIONS: Local Traditional Religion (combination of Buddhism, Taoism, and Confucianism), Buddhism, Christianity
BASIC MONETARY UNIT: New Taiwan Dollar

GEOGRAPHY

Taiwan is located about 90 mi. (140 km) off mainland China's southeast coast. Its area includes the nearby Pescadores Islands. Matsu and Quemoy (Chinmen) island groups, near mainland China, are also considered part of Taiwan. At its greatest distances, Taiwan measures 235 mi. (378 km) from north to south and 90 mi. (145 km) from east to west. It has 555 mi. (893 km) of coastline along the East and South China Seas, the Philippine Sea, the Taiwan Strait, and the Pescadores Channel.

Taiwan has a thickly forested mountain region, the Chungyang Range, which runs from north to south and covers about half the country's area.

CLIMATE

Taiwan has a subtropical climate, with hot, humid summers and a rainy season which generally lasts from June to August. The average annual temperature ranges from about 80°F (27°C) in the summer to 65°F (18°C) in the winter. The average annual rainfall is 100 in. (250 cm). The island is subject to earthquakes, and typhoons occur almost yearly.

ECONOMY

Taiwan has few natural resources, save for the forests in the mountain region. It is heavily dependent on foreign trade and manufacturing.

Agriculture - fruits, livestock, peanuts, rice, sugar cane, sweet potatoes, tea, and vegetables

Fishing - carp, eels, shrimp, snapper, tuna, and others

Forestry - cedar, hemlock, and oak

Manufacturing - calculators, cement, chemicals, clothing and textiles, forest products (including bamboo, camphor, paper, and plywood), furniture, iron and steel, petroleum refining, plastic goods, processed foods, radios, shipbuilding, shoes, sporting goods, sugar, television sets, and toys

Mining - coal, copper, gold, limestone, natural gas, petroleum, salt, and sulfur

Exports - calculators, clothing and textiles, food, footwear, plastic goods, radios, televisions, toys, and wood products

Imports - chemicals, crude oil, food, and machinery

LIFE-STYLE

Most of Taiwan's 25 percent rural population makes a living by farming, with modern methods gradually replacing traditional means. The average farm size is 2-3 acres (0.8-1.2 hectares). Farmhouses are mainly constructed of brick with tin roofs.

Most urban Taiwanese wear Western-style clothing. Shoes are usually removed before entering a Taiwanese home, with slippers being worn inside. Cone-shaped straw hats are worn by farmers and other Taiwanese who work in the hot sun.

Rice is eaten with almost every meal, and chopsticks and a soup spoon serve as the primary eating utensils. Commonly eaten foods include bread, chicken, noodles, pork, seafood, soup, fruits, and vegetables. The most common cooking method is stir-frying. Tea is the most popular beverage.

Popular sports include badminton, baseball, basketball, ping pong, soccer, tennis, and volleyball. Popular leisure activities include hiking, listening to music, picnicking, and watching movies. The elderly enjoy shadow boxing as a form of exercise and relaxation.

Education is free, and children are required to attend six years of elementary school and three years of high school.

IT'S A FACT!

Yü Shan (Mount Morrison) - the country's highest point, rises 13,113 ft. (3,997 m) above sea level.

 DID YOU KNOW...
- All young Taiwanese males are required to serve two years in the military?
- The Pescadores Islands were discovered in 1367 during a Chinese expedition and were given their name, meaning "fishermen's islands," by Portuguese sailors?
- Taiwan averages one automobile per every 30 people?
- The island now known as Taiwan, meaning "terraced bay," was named *Ilha Formosa*, meaning "beautiful island," by Portuguese sailors in 1590?
- Japan gained control of Taiwan in 1895 as a result of the first Chinese-Japanese war, and China regained control after World War II ended in 1945?

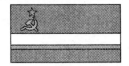

TAJIKISTAN

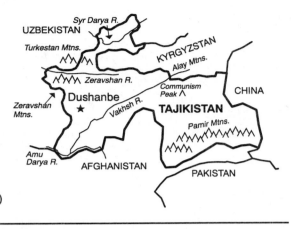

OFFICIAL NAME: Jumhurii Tojikiston (Republic of Tajikistan)
LOCATION: Central Asia
AREA: 55,251 sq. mi. (143,100 sq. km)
POPULATION (Est. 1993): 5,252,000
CAPITAL/LARGEST CITY: Dushanbe
GOVERNMENT: Republic headed by a president.
FLAG: Four horizontal stripes of reddish-orange, white, green, and reddish-orange. A five-pointed, yellow star with a reddish-orange center rests above a yellow hammer and sickle, all of which are in the upper hoist-side corner.
ETHNIC GROUPS: Tajik, Uzbek, Russian
LANGUAGE: Tajik
RELIGION: Islam (including Sunni, Shiite, and Ismaili Khoja Muslims)
BASIC MONETARY UNIT: Russian Ruble

GEOGRAPHY

At its greatest distances, Tajikistan, a landlocked country, measures 300 mi. (485 km) from north to south and 425 mi. (685 km) from east to west. Its land is about 90 percent mountainous, over half of which lies at elevations over 10,000 ft. (3,050 m) above sea level. The Pamir Mountains lie in the southeast, and the Alay and Tian Shan mountain ranges cover much of the rest of the country. Portions of the Turkestan and Zeravshan Mountains are located in the northeast. Earthquakes are common in the region.

Tajikistan's main agricultural regions lie in the north and the southwest. There are two main rivers—the Amu Darya and the Syr Darya—and a few lesser rivers—the Vakhsh, and the Zeravshan.

CLIMATE

Tajikistan's climate ranges from summers that are long, hot, and dry in the valleys to winters that are long and cold in the highlands. Most of the country's highest mountain peaks remain snow-covered year-round.

Temperatures in the valleys range from 36°F (2°C) in January to 86°F (30°C) in July. Temperatures in the highlands range from -4°F (-20°C) in January to 72°F (22°C) in July. Some eastern parts of the Pamir Mountains experience temperatures that may drop to as low as -58°F (-50°C). The country's average rainfall is usually less than 8 in. (20 cm) per year.

ECONOMY

Tajikistan's economy is based on agriculture, manufacturing, and mining, with agriculture being the most valuable.

Agriculture - cotton, fruit, grain, livestock (such as cattle, chickens, horses, Karakul sheep, pigs, and yaks), and vegetables

Manufacturing - aluminum, cement, food processing, freezers and refrigerators, hydroelectric power generation, textiles, vegetable oil, and wine

Mining - antimony, coal, fluorite, lead, molybdenum, natural gas, petroleum, salt, tungsten, uranium, and zinc

Exports - aluminum, cotton, fruits, textiles, and vegetable oil

Imports - chemicals, food, machinery and transport equipment, and textiles

LIFE-STYLE

Tajikistan's population is about two-thirds rural and one-third urban with most of the population living along oases and rivers. The rural population resides in villages comprised of sun-dried earthen dwellings surrounded by earthen walls. Families are generally extended and large in size. Because of marriage patterns, it is not uncommon for all villagers to be related. Urban dwellers live in multistory apartment buildings and single-story houses.

Tajiks wear both modern and traditional clothing. Traditional clothing for men includes loose cotton trousers and a dark or multicolored robe. Traditional clothing for women includes colorful, embroidered silk dresses. Both sexes may wear embroidered skullcaps.

Tajiks eat traditional foods, including *pilaf* (a rice dish) and *shashlik* (beef or lamb broiled on skewers). The most commonly consumed beverage is green tea.

Children ages six to 17 are required to attend school.

IT'S A FACT!

Communism Peak - the country's highest point, rises 24,590 ft. (7,495 m) above sea level.

Fedchenko Glacier - one of the world's longest glaciers, is located in the Pamir Mountains and extends 48 mi. (77 km).

 DID YOU KNOW...

- Tajikistan declared its independence from the U.S.S.R. in 1991, after more than 60 years under Soviet rule?
- Roads in the Pamir Mountain are closed for over half the year because of heavy snowfall?
- The area now known as Tajikistan has been inhabited for thousands of years, with its earliest inhabitants—the Persians of the Achaemenid Empire—dating back to the 500s B.C.?
- The language, Tajik, is very similar to Farsi, the language spoken in Iran?

TANZANIA

OFFICIAL NAME: Jamhuri ya Mwungano wa Tanzania
(United Republic of Tanzania)
FORMERLY: Tanganyika and Zanzibar (merged in 1964)
LOCATION: Eastern Africa
AREA: 364,900 sq. mi. (945,087 sq. km)
POPULATION (Est. 1993): 30,517,000
CAPITAL/LARGEST CITY: Dar es Salaam
GOVERNMENT: Republic governed by a president.
FLAG: Green triangle in the upper hoist side and blue triangle in the lower fly side, separated by a gold-trimmed, black diagonal stripe. The colors represent agriculture, the Indian Ocean, mineral resources, and the nation's people, accordingly.
ETHNIC GROUP: Black (120 ethnic groups)
LANGUAGES: Swahili, English
RELIGIONS: Islam, Christianity, Traditional African Religions
BASIC MONETARY UNIT: Tanzanian Shilling

GEOGRAPHY

Tanzania is composed of mainland Tanganyika and the islands of Mafia, Pemba, and Zanzibar. The country's main land regions are: 1) the coastal lowlands and islands, 2) the plateaus, and 3) the highlands. The Great Rift Valley, which runs north and south through eastern Africa, has branches in central Tanzania and along the western border. The Great Rift Valley is a series of cracks in the earth that form deep, steep-sided valleys.

CLIMATE

The equatorial climate of Tanzania's coast is tempered by inland areas where temperatures are mild. Annual temperatures average 85°F (29°C) along the coast and on the islands. Rainfall averages 31-55 in. (80-140 cm) in this region. The average daytime temperature on the plateaus is 84°F (29°C). This region receives less than 20 in. (50 cm) of rain annually. In the highlands, the temperature averages around 75°F (24°C). These areas often receive more than 40 in. (100 cm) of rainfall a year.

ECONOMY

Tanzania is one of the world's poorest countries. Its economy is based on agriculture. About 80 percent of the people farm for a living and a few raise livestock. Most farming is still done by hand with hoes and long-bladed knives. Many farmers grow only enough food to feed their families. Large, government-operated farms produce many of the export crops. Many urban dwellers work for government or in service industries.

Agriculture - bananas, beef, cashews, cassava, cloves, coconuts, coffee, corn, cotton, milk, millet, rice, sisal, sorghum, sugar cane, tea, tobacco, and wheat

Manufacturing - fertilizer, food products, and textiles

Exports - cashews, cloves, coconuts, coffee, cotton, diamonds, sisal, sugar cane, tea, tobacco

Imports - chemicals, construction materials, food, machinery, manufactured goods, petroleum and petroleum products, and transportation equipment

LIFE-STYLE

Most Tanzanian families are large and may include the father's brothers and their families. Urban families tend to be smaller. Under Tanzanian law, women and men have equal rights, but in practice, women have lesser rights. In rural areas, women frequently do more farm work than men. Most rural homes are made of wooden frames plastered with mud. In the city, homes may be made of baked clay bricks or cement blocks.

Traditional clothing includes colorful, wrap-style garments for women (the *kanga*) and the *kikoi* wrap for men. Muslim men often wear a long white robe called the *kanzu*. Western-style shirts and pants for men are becoming increasingly popular.

Staples of the Tanzanians' diet include grains, fruits, and vegetables. Goat, chicken, lamb, and fish are important parts of the diet. A popular communal meal is *ugali*, a porridge made from cornmeal, millet, sorghum, or cassava. Bananas, also important, may be roasted, fried, or made into a paste and mixed with meat and gravy. Rice is usually cooked with a variety of spices. A popular snack is *kitumbua* (fried bread).

About 80 percent of Tanzania's adult population are literate. This is among the highest literacy rates in Africa. Law requires seven years of elementary school, but only about half of the children go to elementary school. Many are needed to work at home.

Soccer, boxing, and track and field are popular sports. The most common artistic expressions involve traditional dance and music. Few of Tanzania's roads are paved or sufficiently maintained. Less than one percent of the people own automobiles.

IT'S A FACT!

Lake Tanganyika - the longest freshwater lake in the world, stretches 420 mi. (680 km).

Lake Victoria - Africa's largest lake, lies partly in Tanzania and covers 26,828 sq. mi. (69,484 sq. km) along Tanzania's western border.

Mount Kilimanjaro - the country and continent's highest point, rises 19,340 ft. (5,895 m) above sea level.

Selous Game Reserve - the largest animal reserve in the world, covers 21,000 sq. mi. (54,000 sq. km). It is home to about 50,000 elephants, one of the largest populations in Africa.

 DID YOU KNOW...
- Tanzania is known for its world-class runners?
- Serengeti National Park, in northern Tanzania, is known for its lions and huge herds of antelopes and zebras?

THAILAND

OFFICIAL NAME: Muang Thai (Kingdom of Thailand)
FORMERLY: Siam (until 1939)
LOCATION: Southeast Asia
AREA: 198,115 sq. mi. (513,115 sq. km)
POPULATION (Est. 1993): 57,989,000
CAPITAL: Bangkok
LARGEST CITIES: Bangkok, Chiang Mai
GOVERNMENT: Constitutional monarchy.
FLAG: Five horizontal stripes of red, white, blue, white, and red. Red, white, and blue represent the nation, purity, and the monarchy, accordingly.
ETHNIC GROUPS: Thai, Chinese
LANGUAGES: Thai, Chinese, Malay
RELIGIONS: Buddhism, Islam
BASIC MONETARY UNIT: Baht

GEOGRAPHY

Thailand measures 1,100 mi. (1,770 km) from north to south and 480 mi. (772 km) from east to west at its greatest distances. It has 1,635 mi. (2,631 km) of coastline.

Thailand has four main land regions: 1) the Northern Mountains, 2) the Khorat Plateau, 3) the Central Plain, and 4) the Southern Peninsula. Forests of evergreen and teak trees are found on the Northern Mountains. Many streams flow south from the mountains. Rice is grown in the valleys and the region has rich mineral deposits. The Khorat Plateau in northeastern Thailand covers 30 percent of the country's area. This region is the most heavily populated in Thailand. The Central Plain is located between the foothills of the Northern Mountains and the Gulf of Thailand. Farmers grow more rice here than in any other part of the country. The Southern Peninsula forms part of the Malay Peninsula. It is composed primarily of jungle with some mountains. Rubber trees grow here in abundance.

CLIMATE

Thailand has a tropical climate. Most of the country has three distinct seasons: spring, summer, and winter. Average temperatures for the city of Bangkok are 62°F (17°C) in January and 98°F (37°C) in May. In the north, temperatures average 32°F (0°C) in January and 90°F (32°C) in May. Thailand's monsoon season runs from July to December. The southern region receives an average of 100 in. (254 cm) rain yearly. Bangkok's yearly average is 55 in. (140 cm).

ECONOMY

Thailand has a developing economy. Over 75 percent of its people are farmers. Many others are employed in fishing, lumbering, and mining. Only seven percent work in manufacturing.

Agriculture - cassava, corn, cotton, rice, rubber, sugar cane, and tobacco

Fishing - anchovies, mackerel, and shellfish

Manufacturing - automobiles, cement, drugs, electronic equipment, food products, paper, plywood, and textiles

Mining - bauxite, iron ore, lead, manganese, natural gas, precious stones, tin, and tungsten

Exports - corn, rice, rubber, sugar, tapioca products, tin, and tobacco

Imports - chemicals, fuels, and machinery

LIFE-STYLE

Most Thai live in villages ranging in size from a few hundred to a few thousand people. Households usually contain members of several generations. The oldest male is the family's patriarch. Two or three children is the norm. Women here have more freedom than women in most Asian countries.

Villagers' houses are often of wood or thatch and are situated along rivers and canals. As protection against flooding, houses are built on stilts. In urban areas, many people live in small wooden or stucco homes.

Most city dwellers wear Western-style clothing. Villagers wear a colorful cotton or silk garment called a *panung*.

The staple food is rice, which is usually served with *curries* (spicy stews) and salads of meat, fish, and vegetables. The most common drink is water. The country has a large variety of tropical fruit available year-round. Specific communities in Thailand are famous for their specialty dishes.

More than 85 percent of the Thai aged 15 and older are literate. Children are required to attend school for six years. Only about 15 percent of the population have graduated from high school since most are privately owned and charge tuition.

The country's most popular sports are soccer, table tennis, badminton, volleyball, and *Thai-style boxing*, which involves both hands and feet. Favorite leisure activities include kite flying, movies, and television. Gambling is also popular, particularly betting on fish fights between male Siamese fightingfish. *Mak ruk*, a type of chess, and card games are also enjoyed.

IT'S A FACT!

Inthanon Mountain - the country's highest point, rises 8,514 ft. (2,595 m) above sea level.

The Temple of the Emerald Buddha - a beautiful temple in Bangkok guarded by giant statues.

 DID YOU KNOW...

- In rural areas, pedicabs (small, three-wheeled vehicle similar to a bicycle with a cab in back) are still common?
- Thailand is the only nation in Southeast Asia that has never been ruled by a Western power?
- The Chao Phraya River is the country's main transportation route?
- Bangkok's canals are known as the "floating market"?

 IF8201 Comprehensive World Reference Guide

TOGO

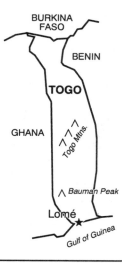

OFFICIAL NAME: République Togolaise (Republic of Togo)
LOCATION: Western Africa
AREA: 21,925 sq. mi. (56,785 sq. km)
POPULATION (Est. 1993): 3,879,000
CAPITAL/LARGEST CITY: Lomé
GOVERNMENT: Republic governed by a president and aided by a prime minister.
FLAG: Five horizontal stripes, three green and two yellow. A red square in the upper hoist-side corner features a five-pointed white star. Green, yellow, white, and red symbolize hope and agriculture, faith, purity, and charity and fidelity.
ETHNIC GROUPS: Ewe, Mina, Kabye (largest of 37 tribes)
LANGUAGES: Ewe, French, other African languages
RELIGIONS: Traditional African Religions, Christianity, Islam
BASIC MONETARY UNIT: CFA Franc

GEOGRAPHY

Togo is a long, narrow country located in western Africa. At its greatest distances, Togo measures 365 mi. (587 km) from north to south and 40 mi. (64 km) from east to west. It has 90 mi. (145 km) of coastline along the Gulf of Guinea.

The Togo Mountains divide the country into two main land regions. East and south of the mountains, the land graduates from a sloping plateau to a low, sandy coastal plain. North of the mountains, the land descends through rolling grasslands.

CLIMATE

Togo's climate is hot and humid. The temperature averages 81 F (27°C) year round. The north receives an average of 40 in. (100 cm) of rain annually. The south receives an average of 70 in. (180 cm) yearly. The south has rainy seasons from March to July and September to November. The north's rainy season lasts from April to October.

ECONOMY

Togo's economy is based on agriculture, though there is little adequate land.

Agriculture - cacao, cassava, coffee, corn, cotton, millet, palm kernels and oil, peanuts, sorghum, and yams

Manufacturing - cement, petroleum refining, textiles

Mining - phosphates

Exports - cacao, coffee, cotton, copra, palm products, peanuts, and phosphates

Imports - cloth, consumer goods, food, iron and steel products, machinery and transportation equipment, meat, and tobacco

LIFE-STYLE

Almost all of the people of Togo are black Africans. Most are rural dwellers and work on family-owned farms. Others work as sharecroppers. There is a difference in language, dress, and way of life between those in the north and south. This is partly due to the location of the mountains, which separate the areas.

Many southerners wear a *toga* (full-length, loose-fitting colorful garment) and live in traditional *compounds* (groups of huts inside walls). They speak the Ewe language. In relation to other groups, the Ewe of the south are better educated and more prosperous. Today, increasing numbers wear Western-style clothing and work for the government or own small businesses.

The northern Togolese live in villages consisting of adobe houses with cone-shaped thatched roofs. Traditional dress worn is a white cotton smock. Many different languages are spoken in the north.

Approximately 70 percent of the children of Togo attend primary school. Only a small minority (about 20 percent) attend secondary school.

IT'S A FACT

Bauman Peak - the country's highest point, rises 3,235 ft. (986 m) above sea level.

 DID YOU KNOW...

- In Ewe, the most commonly used language in Togo, the word *togo* means "behind the sea"?
- Between the 1600s and 1800s, Togo became known as the "Coast of Slaves"?
- Kpémé, which lies about 20 mi. (32 km) outside the city of Lomé, has one of the richest phosphate mines in the world?

TONGA

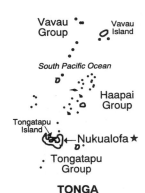

TONGA

OFFICIAL NAME: Kingdom of Tonga
LOCATION: South Pacific Ocean
AREA: 288 sq. mi. (747 sq. km)
POPULATION (Est. 1995): 99,000
CAPITAL/LARGEST CITY: Nukualofa (on Tongatapu Island)
GOVERNMENT: Hereditary constitutional monarchy.
FLAG: Adopted in 1866. Red background with a red cross centered on a white rectangle in the upper hoist corner.
ETHNIC GROUPS: Polynesian
LANGUAGES: Tongan, English
RELIGION: Christianity
BASIC MONETARY UNIT: Pa'anga

GEOGRAPHY

Tonga consists of about 150 islands in the South Pacific Ocean. They are located about 3,000 mi. (4,800 km) southwest of Honolulu, Hawaii.

Tonga has three main island groups: Haapai, Tongatapu, and Vavau. Most of the islands are coral reefs, but a chain of volcanic islands lies west of the coral islands. Some of the volcanoes are active. Only 36 of the islands are inhabited. Fertile clay soil covers most of Tonga, with strips of sandy soil along the coasts. About 14 percent of the land is covered with forests. The islands' vegetation is luxuriant.

CLIMATE

Tonga has a warm, wet, semitropical climate. Temperatures average 78°F (26°C) throughout the year. Average rainfall ranges from 70 in. (180 cm) on Tongatapu to 100 in. (250 cm) on some northern islands. Most rains fall from December through March. The islands are subject to cyclones from October to April.

ECONOMY

With Tonga's fertile soil and warm climate, agriculture is the most important part of the country's economy.

Agriculture - bananas, copra, sweet potatoes, tapioca, and vanilla beans

Fishing - shark and tuna

Exports - coconut oil products, copra, fruit, and vegetables

Imports - flour, meat, petroleum, sugar, textiles, and tobacco

LIFE-STYLE

Two-thirds of all Tongans live on the largest island, Tongatapu. Most Tongans live in small villages. Most of the islands have no running water and a number have no electricity. Almost all the people are Christians and follow the constitutional law which prohibits work or recreation on Sunday.

About three-fourths of all workers are farmers. The government owns all the land, and every male over 16 is allowed to rent a plot. Other people work in small-scale manufacturing, fishing, mining, or in tourism concerns.

Children ages six to 14 are required to attend school, and the literacy rate is extremely high. The government operates 60 percent of the schools, while the churches run the other 40 percent. Though Tonga's official language is Tongan, the children also learn English.

A typical meal consists of yams, taro leaves, sweet potatoes, cassava, fish, or pork. A popular dish, called *Lu pulu*, is cooked taro leaves with coconut cream and corned beef. Tropical fruits are also eaten frequently.

Rugby is the national sport. Cricket, volleyball, basketball, and tennis are also enjoyed by many. Popular recreational activities in larger villages include movies and dances.

IT'S A FACT!

Kao - an extinct volcano, is the country's highest point. Located in the Haapai group, it rises 3,380 ft. (1,030 m) above sea level.

 DID YOU KNOW...

- Captain James Cook, who first visited the islands in 1773, named them the *Friendly Islands* because of the way he was treated by the natives?
- The main source of government revenue is import duties?
- Tonga was a British protected state until 1990, when it became independent?

TRINIDAD & TOBAGO

OFFICIAL NAME: Republic of Trinidad and Tobago
LOCATION: Caribbean Sea
AREA: 1,981 sq. mi. (5,130 sq. km)
POPULATION (Est. 1993): 1,336,000
CAPITAL/LARGEST CITY: Port-of-Spain
GOVERNMENT: Parliamentary democracy governed by a president.
FLAG: Red background with a white-edged, diagonal black stripe running from the upper hoist-side to the lower fly-side.
ETHNIC GROUPS: Black African, East Indian, Mixed European/Black
LANGUAGE: English
RELIGIONS: Christianity, Hinduism, Islam
BASIC MONETARY UNIT: Trinidad and Tobago Dollar

GEOGRAPHY

The country consists of two islands in the West Indies. It is located in the Caribbean Sea, near the northeastern coast of South America. The larger island, Trinidad, accounts for about 95 percent of the land area and people. Tropical forests and flatlands cover most of Trinidad. A mountain range runs east and west across the northern part and hills are found in the central and southern sections. The smaller island, Tobago, has a central mountain ridge and beautiful beaches. The islands have a combined coastline of 292 mi. (470 km) along the Caribbean Sea and the North Atlantic Ocean.

CLIMATE

Trinidad and Tobago's climate is generally hot and humid. The average annual temperature is 78°F (26°C). Rainfall ranges from 50 in. (127 cm) on southwestern Trinidad to over 100 in. (254 cm) in the mountains of Tobago.

ECONOMY

Oil production and refining are the basis of the economy. Other major industries are tourism and agriculture.

Agriculture - bananas, citrus fruits, cocoa, coffee, and sugar cane

Manufacturing - cement, chemicals, cotton textiles, food processing, petroleum, and rum

Mining - asphalt and oil

Exports - ammonia, chemicals, citrus fruits, cocoa, coffee, fertilizers, minerals, petroleum and petroleum products, steel products, and sugar

Imports - capital goods, consumer goods, crude oil, and raw materials

LIFE-STYLE

Black Africans, about 43 percent of the population, and East Indians, about 40 percent of the population, have traditionally lived in different ways. Africans tend to live in towns or at the oil fields. They make up most of the labor force in the oil industry and much of the nation's civil service. East Indians live largely among themselves on small farms, in villages, or on the large sugar estates. Many own their own land. Other East Indians are businessmen or professionals.

The people of Trinidad and Tobago are lovers of music. For them, music is more than entertainment, it is almost a way of life. Trinidad is the home of a form of folk music called *calypso* and of the dance called the *limbo*. Trinidad's other contri-

bution to the music world is the steel band, which originated in the 1940s. The annual Carnival is an important time of celebration that includes colorful costumes, music, and dancing.

Children are required by law to attend school for eight years. About 95 percent of the people are literate.

IT'S A FACT!

Little Tobago Islet - home to a sanctuary for birds of paradise.

Mount Aripo - the country's highest point, rises 3,085 ft. (940 m) above sea level.

Pitch Lake - located on Trinidad, is the world's chief source of natural asphalt.

DID YOU KNOW...

- Christopher Columbus, who discovered the island in 1498, named the island Trinidad after the so-called Three Sisters, or Trinity Hills, in the southeastern part of the island?
- One of the country's unusual exports is Angostura bitters, a flavoring agent made in Port-of-Spain from ingredients said to be known only by four men?
- Steel bands use instruments called *pans*, which are made from discarded oil drums?
- After being a British possession since 1802, Trinidad and Tobago won independence in 1962?

TUNISIA

OFFICIAL NAME: Al Jumhuriyah at Tunisiyah
(Republic of Tunisia)
LOCATION: Northern Africa
AREA: 63,170 sq. mi. (163,610 sq. km)
POPULATION (Est. 1993): 8,701,000
CAPITAL/LARGEST CITY: Tunis
GOVERNMENT: Republic headed by a president.
FLAG: White circle centered on a red field with a red crescent and a red, five-pointed star—symbols of Islam—within the circle.
ETHNIC GROUPS: Arab, European, Jewish, Berber
LANGUAGES: Arabic, French
RELIGIONS: Islam, Christianity, Judaism
BASIC MONETARY UNIT: Tunisian Dinar

GEOGRAPHY

At its greatest distances, Tunisia measures 485 mi. (781 km) from north to south and 235 mi. (378 km) from east to west. It has 639 mi. (1,028 km) of coastline along the Mediterranean Sea, the Gulf of Tunis, the Gulf of Hammamat, and the Gulf of Gabes.

Tunisia's landforms range from mountains in the north to desert in the south. Parts of two mountain ranges—the Atlas and the Tabassah Mountains—make up northwestern Tunisia. The area between the two ranges is made up of hills and grasslands. South of the Tabassah Mountains is a plateau, which is covered with grass. In the far south is part of the Sahara Desert, which is home to great salt lakes and date palm oases. A fertile plain makes up Tunisia's northeastern coast.

CLIMATE

Tunisia's climate is Mediterranean in the north—hot, dry summers and warm, wet winters—and desert in the south. Coastal temperatures average 79°F (26°C) in the summer and 52°F (11°C) in the winter. Desert temperatures average 89°F (32°C) in the summer and 53°F (12°C) in the winter. The northern region receives most of its rain during the winter, but experiences droughts every three to four years. The southern region receives very little rain.

ECONOMY

Tunisia's economy is based largely on its phosphate and petroleum resources. Agriculture, light industry, and services also contribute.

Agriculture - almonds, barley, beef, citrus fruit, dates, grapes, olives and olive oil, poultry, sugar beets, and wheat
Forestry - oak and pine
Manufacturing - beverages, consumer goods, food processing, footwear, and textiles
Mining - petroleum, phosphates, iron, lead, lignite, and zinc
Exports - chemicals, petroleum, phosphates, and processed foods
Imports - consumer goods, food, and industrial goods and equipment

LIFE-STYLE

Slightly more than half of Tunisia's people live in urban areas. The majority of the cities are divided into both old and new sections, with old sections characterized by narrow streets and covered markets and new sections characterized by European-style buildings and tree-lined avenues. Urban Tunisians often wear Western-style clothing. Rural Tunisians live mainly on farms or in villages in homes constructed of stone or concrete, though some still live in mud huts or tents, as they did in the past. Most rural Tunisians wear traditional Arab clothing consisting of a long, loose gown or a long, coatlike garment with long sleeves and a skullcap or turban.

Staples of the diet include chicken, fish, lamb, olives, onions, peppers, potatoes, and tomatoes. In the summer, *hindi* (cactus fruit) is eaten. Popular dishes include *breek* (thin, fried dough stuffed with an egg, cooked vegetables, and tuna), *couscous* (steamed semolina with spices topped with meat and vegetables), and *tajine* (crustless quiche with meat and vegetables).

Leisure activities include attending art festivals, listening to music, watching movies, going to the beach, visiting with friends and relatives, and playing *shkubbah* (a card game). Popular sports include beach volleyball and soccer.

Education is free but not required. Almost all Tunisian children attend primary school and about one-third of the children attend secondary school. Further education is available at the University of Tunis and professional schools.

IT'S A FACT!

Mount Chambi - the country's highest point, rises 5,066 ft. (1,544 m) above sea level.

 DID YOU KNOW...

• Of all of Tunisia's rivers, only one—the Majardah River—does not dry up in the summer?
• Tunisia's northernmost tip is just 85 mi. (137 km) from Sicily?
• During World War II, Tunisia served as a major battleground, due to its relation to France?
• About one-fifth of the Tunisian government's budget is for education?
• *Hindi* (cactus fruit) is called the "sultan of all fruits"?

TURKEY

OFFICIAL NAME: Türkiye Cumhuriyeti (Republic of Turkey)
LOCATION: Southeastern Europe/Western Asia
AREA: 300,948 sq. mi. (779,452 sq. km)
POPULATION (Est. 1993): 59,200,000
CAPITAL: Ankara
LARGEST CITIES: Istanbul, Ankara, Izmir (Smyrna), Adana
GOVERNMENT: Republic governed by a president.
FLAG: Red field featuring a white crescent and a white star.
ETHNIC GROUPS: Turk, Kurd, Arab, Caucasian, Greek, Armenian
LANGUAGES: Turkish, Kurdish, Arabic, Greek, other
RELIGION: Islam (mostly Sunni Muslim)
BASIC MONETARY UNIT: Turkish Lira

GEOGRAPHY

About three percent of Turkey's area is located in *Thrace*, which is southern Europe's easternmost tip. Thrace is separated from the rest of Turkey—which is called *Anatolia* or *Asia Minor*—by the Bosporus, the Dardanelles, and the Sea of Marmara, bodies of water referred to collectively as the Straits. At its greatest distances, Turkey measures 465 mi. (748 km) from north to south and 1,015 mi. (1,633 km) from east to west. It has 2,211 mi. (3,558 km) of coastline along the Black Sea, the Aegean Sea, the Gulf of Antalya, the Gulf of Iskenderun, and the Mediterranean Sea.

Turkey has eight main land regions: 1) the Northern Plains, 2) the Western Valleys, 3) the Southern Plains, 4) the Western Plateau, 5) the Eastern Plateau, 6) the Northern Mountains, 7) the Southern Mountains, and 8) the Mesopotamian Lowlands.

CLIMATE

Turkey's climate varies. The coastal areas have hot, dry summers and mild, rainy winters. Summer temperatures range from 72°F (22°C) along the Black Sea to over 90°F (32°C) along the Aegean Sea. The average rainfall ranges from 20-30 in. (51-76 cm) along the Aegean and Mediterranean Seas, to over 100 in. (254 cm) along the Black Sea. Northeastern Turkey has mild summers and very cold winters. At times, the temperature may fall to -40°F (-40°C). Southeastern Turkey and Anatolia's interior experience windy, hot, extremely dry summers, and cold, snowy winters.

ECONOMY

Turkey has a developing economy based mainly on agriculture and manufacturing.

Agriculture - barley, corn, cotton, fruits, livestock, nuts, potatoes, sugar beets, tobacco, vegetables, and wheat

Manufacturing - clothing and textiles, cotton products, fertilizers, iron and steel, machinery, metal products, motor vehicles, processed foods and beverages, and paper products

Mining - bauxite, boron, chromite, coking coal, copper, iron ore, *meerschaum* (soft, white mineral used to make jewelry and tobacco pipes), and petroleum

Exports - clothing and textiles, cotton, food, fruits, fuels, manufactured goods, nuts, and tobacco

Imports - chemicals, food, machinery, manufactured goods, iron and steel, motor vehicles, petroleum, and raw materials

LIFE-STYLE

Turkey's population is approximately two-fifths rural, with many residents moving to urban areas in search of jobs. Turks near the Black Sea live in thatch-roofed shelters constructed of timber from nearby forests. In Thrace and northeastern Anatolia, old, wooden shelters are being replaced with one-story houses constructed of concrete blocks. Villagers in central Anatolia live in flat-roofed shelters of sun-dried brick. Many in southern and western Anatolia live in stone shelters. Wealthy, urban Turks live in concrete-block shelters or suburban apartment complexes. Middle-class, urban Turks live in two- or three-story concrete or wooden shelters.

Most Turks wear Western-style clothing. Some rural Turks wear traditional clothing of baggy trousers and a loose-fitting cloak for men, and pantaloons and a simple blouse for women.

Staples of the diet include cracked-wheat bread and yogurt. The Turks also eat a lot of lamb, rice, and eggplant. Popular Turkish dishes include *pilaf* (rice with almonds, meat, pine nuts, and raisins) and *shish kebab* (pieces of lamb, tomatoes, peppers, and onions cooked on a skewer). Popular desserts include *baklava* (thin layers of chopped nuts, honey, and pastry) and *muhallebi* (milk pudding). Commonly consumed beverages include tea, thick coffee with sugar, and *raki* (liquor made from raisins).

Popular sports include archery, horseback riding, soccer, and *greased wrestling* (Turkish form of wrestling for which contestants wear tight leather trousers and cover their bodies with olive oil). Turks attend concerts, movies, operas, and stage plays for leisure. Many men play the ancient dice game of backgammon in coffee houses.

Children must attend a five-year primary school, either until they graduate or reach the age of 15. Attendance at a three-year middle school is optional.

IT'S A FACT!

Hagia Sophia - a great-domed cathedral built in the A.D. 500s, it is a classic example of Byzantine architecture.

Istanbul University - founded in 1453, it is the country's oldest and largest university.

Mosque of Suleiman I - located in Istanbul, it was designed by Koca Sinan—who is considered Turkey's greatest architect—and is one of the world's most beautiful mosques.

Mount Ararat - the country's highest point, rises 17,011 ft. (5,185 m) above sea level.

 DID YOU KNOW...

- Archaeologists have found evidence that an advanced civilization lived in what is now Turkey prior to 6000 B.C.?

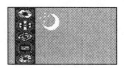

TURKMENISTAN

OFFICIAL NAME: Tiurkmenostan Respublikasy (Republic of Turkmenistan)
FORMERLY: Turkmen Soviet Socialist Republic, or Turkmenia
LOCATION: West-central Asia
AREA: 188,456 sq. mi. (488,100 sq. km)
POPULATION (Est. 1993): 3,631,000
CAPITAL: Ashkhabad
LARGEST CITIES: Ashkhabad, Mary, Tedzhen, Chardzhou
GOVERNMENT: Republic governed by a president.
FLAG: Green field with a vertical, maroon stripe near the hoist side. The stripe features five different carpet guls—in black, white, maroon, and orange—associated with five different tribes. A white crescent and five white, five-pointed stars are located to the right of the vertical stripe.
ETHNIC GROUPS: Turkmen, Russian, Uzbek
LANGUAGES: Turkmen, Russian
RELIGIONS: Islam (mainly Sunni and Shiite), Russian Orthodox
BASIC MONETARY UNIT: Russian Ruble

GEOGRAPHY

Turkmenistan measures 525 mi. (845 km) from north to south and 750 mi. (1,205 km) from east to west at its greatest distances. It has a 1,098-mi. (1,768-km) border along the Caspian Sea, but no maritime claims to it.

The Karakum (Black Sand) Desert, which is mostly uninhabited, covers over 80 percent of Turkmenistan and is one of the world's largest deserts. The Kopet-Dag Mountains stretch along the south and southwest. Several rivers flow from the mountains, including the Amu Darya, the country's major river.

CLIMATE

Turkmenistan's climate consists of long, hot, dry summers and very cold winters. Average summer temperatures in the desert range from about 95° to 122°F (35° to 50°C). Average winter temperatures may drop below -29°F (-34°C). The average annual rainfall is 3-12 in. (8-30 cm).

ECONOMY

Agriculture accounts for about 50 percent of the country's economic production. Crops can be grown only by using irrigation, and cotton is planted on over half of the farmland.

Agriculture - camels, cotton, grains, grapes, horses, Persian lamb, pigs, potatoes, sheep, and wool

Manufacturing - cement, glass, petrochemicals, and textiles (including cotton, silk, and wool)

Mining - bromine, building materials (limestone and sand), copper, gold, iodine, lead, mercury, natural gas, petroleum, salt, sodium sulfate, and zinc

Exports - butter, carpets, chemicals, cotton, fish, natural gas, oil, rugs, textiles, and wine

Imports - light manufactures, plastics and rubber, textiles, and transportation equipment

LIFE-STYLE

Turkmenistan's population is about 52 percent rural, and most Turkmens live in oases or along rivers. City dwellers live in red brick or limestone apartments. Some rural dwellers still live in *yurts* (traditional tentlike structures made of felt-covered wooden frames). Traditionally, Turkmens were nomads and horsemen warriors. They are known for their strong tribal loyalties. Tribal organizations still play an important role in society.

Social life in Turkmenistan is centered around the family. In rural areas, many members of an extended family live under one roof. A Muslim style of marriage in which a man may have up to four wives is sometimes still practiced. Many Turkmens marry only within their own tribe.

Western-style and traditional clothing are both worn. Traditional clothing for men consists of white shirts, dark trousers, and red robes, sometimes topped off with a *tilpek* (a shaggy, sheepskin hat). Women generally wear a long, loose dresses trimmed with embroidery.

Milk products are an important part of the Turkmen diet, and traditional dishes include *chishlik* (meat roasted on a skewer), *chorba* (a peppery meat soup), and *palov* (a rice dish). Turkmens drink green tea after meals.

Children ages six to 17 are required to attend school. Almost all Turkmen adults are literate.

Turkmens are known for weaving beautiful woolen carpets with geometric patterns. They also make and sell embroidery, handmade fabrics, leathercraft, and jewelry.

The country's highway and railroad systems are limited, linking only major urban areas. However, Ashkhabad features an airport that handles all flights.

IT'S A FACT!

Kara Bogaz Gol - the country's lowest point of elevation, is located 102 ft. (31 m) below sea level.

Karakum Canal - the world's largest irrigation project.

Kugitangtau Mountain Range - home to the country's highest point, rises 10,292 ft. (3,137 m) above sea level.

 DID YOU KNOW...
- Much of Ashkhabad was destroyed by an earthquake in 1948?

TURKS & CAICOS ISLANDS
Dependent Territory of the United Kingdom

TURKS & CAICOS ISLANDS

OFFICIAL NAME: Turks and Caicos Islands
LOCATION: North Atlantic Ocean
AREA: 166 sq. mi. (430 sq. km)
POPULATION (Est. 1995): 13,000
CAPITAL: Grand Turk (or Cockburn Town)
LARGEST TOWNS: Grand Turk, Cockburn Harbour
GOVERNMENT: British sovereign is represented by a governor, who presides over a council.
FLAG: Blue field with the flag of the United Kingdom in the upper hoist-side quadrant. The yellow colonial shield—featuring a conch shell, lobster, and cactus—is centered on the flag's outer half.
ETHNIC GROUPS: African, Mixed
LANGUAGE: English
RELIGIONS: Baptist, Methodist, Anglican
BASIC MONETARY UNIT: United States Dollar

GEOGRAPHY

The Turks and Caicos Islands lie at the southeasternmost extension of the Bahamian chain about 90 mi. (145 km) north of the Dominican Republic. The two island groups consist of about 30 islands and cays—eight of which are inhabited—separated by the 22-mi.- (35-km-) wide Turks Islands Passage. The Turks island group lies east of the passage. Its principal islands are Grand Turk and Salt Cay. The main islands in the Caicos island group are North Caicos, South Caicos, East Caicos, West Caicos, Grand or Middle Caicos, and Providenciales. Most of the islands in both groups are low-lying, and made up of coraline limestone. The islands also have some mangrove swamps, and marshes cover much of the islands. The islands have a combined coastline of about 242 mi. (389 km).

CLIMATE

The Turks and Caicos Islands have a tropical climate tempered by southeast trade winds. The average temperature ranges from 75° to 90°F (24° to 32°C) throughout the year. The average rainfall is 21 in. (53.3 cm). Hurricanes are common.

ECONOMY

The islands' economy is based on fishing and tourism. Subsistence farming exists—mainly beans, cassava, and corn—but most food must be imported.

Fishing - conch and lobster
Exports - conch, crayfish, and lobster
Imports - clothing, construction materials, drinks, foodstuffs, manufactures, and tobacco

LIFE-STYLE

Most islanders are employed in the fishing and tourism industries. Due to poor soil and limited water, farmers raise only enough to feed their families.

Education is free, and children are required to attend primary school. The overall literacy rate is very high.

DID YOU KNOW...

- The Turks and Caicos Islands were dependencies of Jamaica until 1959?
- Up until 1964, the islands' economy was based on salt production?
- Europeans discovered the islands in the early 1500s?
- Turks Island received its name from the Turk's head cactus, whose flowers look like a Turkish fez?

TUVALU

OFFICIAL NAME: Tuvalu
FORMERLY: Ellice Islands
LOCATION: South Pacific Ocean
AREA: 10 sq. mi. (26 sq. km)
POPULATION (Est. 1993): 9,000
CAPITAL/LARGEST CITY: Funafuti (on Funafuti)
GOVERNMENT: Parliamentary democracy governed by a prime minister.
FLAG: Light blue field with the United Kingdom's flag in the upper hoist-side quadrant. Nine yellow stars, representing the country's nine islands, are arranged on the flag's outer half.
ETHNIC GROUP: Polynesian
LANGUAGES: Tuvaluan, English
RELIGION: Christianity
BASIC MONETARY UNIT: Australian Dollar

Nanumea
Niutao
Nanumanga
South Pacific Ocean
Nui
Vaitupu
Nukufetau
TUVALU
Funafuti
Funafuti
Nukulaelae
Niulakita

GEOGRAPHY

Tuvalu is a tiny island country in the South Pacific Ocean that lies about 2,000 mi. (3,200 km) northeast of Australia. It is the fourth smallest country in the world. Its nine islands form a chain that extends about 360 mi. (580 km). The nine islands are, from north to south, Nanumea, Niutao, Nanumanga, Nui, Vaitupu, Nukufetau, Funafuti, Nukulaelae, and Niulakita. All but Niulakita are inhabited. Some of the islands are coral atolls that encircle large lagoons. Others are coral-reefs with small lagoons or small landlocked lakes. The soil is porous and of poor quality. The principal trees are coconut palms and pandanus palms.

CLIMATE

Tuvalu has a hot, humid tropical climate. Temperatures average 80°F (27°C) to 86°F (30°C) throughout the year. The average annual rainfall for the northern islands is 100 in. (250 cm) and for the southern islands, 125 in. (320 cm). The rain occurs mostly as heavy showers. Occasionally, severe droughts occur.

ECONOMY

Tuvalu is one of the least developed countries in the world. Subsistence farming and fishing are the main economic activities. Government revenues come from the sale of stamps and coins, worker remittances, and foreign aid.

Agriculture - bananas, coconuts, pandanus fruit, papaws, pulaka, and taro

Manufacturing - woven goods (bags, baskets, fans, and hats)

Exports - bêche-de-mer, copra, and handicrafts

Imports - animals, food, machinery, manufactured goods, and mineral fuels

LIFE-STYLE

Tuvaluans enjoy dancing and singing. At night, many gather at the local community hall (*maneapa*) for conversation, singing, and social dancing. Most people live in villages built around a church and a *maneapa*. The majority of Tuvaluans live in traditional thatched-roof houses with walls of woven mats. The houses on Funafuti are prefabricated, sturdier houses, which replaced houses destroyed by a 1972 hurricane.

About four-fifths of the country's labor force make their living in subsistence agriculture and fishing. Many raise their own chickens and pigs. The rest work in business, services, or government service. About 10 percent of the population is employed abroad or on ships.

Funafuti has a modern hospital and the other islands each have a dispensary. Telegraph and telephone service is available on the eight populated islands.

Staples of the diet are bananas, coconuts, fish, and taro. Pigs and chickens are eaten at special feasts. The drinking-water supply is sometimes limited because of the very porous soil. Often coconut milk is consumed instead of water.

Most Tuvaluans wear light, bright-colored cotton clothing. Each of the eight inhabited islands has at least one elementary school. Primary education is free.

 DID YOU KNOW...

- Although Tuvalu's name means "cluster of eight" or "eight standing together," the country actually includes nine islands?
- Tuvalu's islands were formed over thousands of years by tiny sea animals called coral polyps whose external skeletons fused onto those of dead polyps?
- Tuvalu has the second smallest national population in the world after that of Vatican City?
- In 1863, Peruvian "blackbirders" (slave traders), kidnapped 500 Tuvaluans to work in guano mines on islands off the coast of Peru? None of the people returned home.
- Tuvalu was ruled by Great Britain from the 1890s to 1978, when it became independent?
- Tuvalu's atolls are all less than 13 ft. (4 m) above sea level, a fact that makes Tuvaluan's worry about the possibility of the ocean levels rising as a result of the "greenhouse effect"?

UGANDA

OFFICIAL NAME: Republic of Uganda
FORMERLY: Uganda Protectorate
LOCATION: East-central Africa
AREA: 91,074 sq. mi. (235,880 sq. km)
POPULATION (Est. 1993): 20,099,000
CAPITAL/LARGEST CITY: Kampala
GOVERNMENT: Republic headed by a president.
FLAG: Six horizontal stripes of black, yellow, red, black, yellow, and red. A white circle with a red-crested crane facing the hoist side is in the center. Black, yellow, and red represent Africa, sunshine, and brotherhood, accordingly.
ETHNIC GROUP: Black (over 20 ethnic groups)
LANGUAGES: English, various African languages (over 20)
RELIGIONS: Christianity, Traditional African Religions, Islam
BASIC MONETARY UNIT: Ugandan Shilling

GEOGRAPHY

Uganda consists primarily of a plateau that lies about 4,000 ft. (1,200 m) above sea level. The north is mainly savanna, parts of the northeast are semidesert, the south has thick forests, while the east and west have highland areas. Behind the western highlands lies the Great Rift Valley, which is home to Lakes Albert, Edward, and George. Part of Lake Victoria, the world's second largest freshwater lake, lies in southeastern Uganda. Together, Uganda's lakes account for more than one-sixth of the country's area.

CLIMATE

Uganda generally has a rainy, tropical climate with two dry seasons: December to February and June to August. Although the equator runs through southern Uganda, high elevations account for mild temperatures. The average daily temperature ranges from 60° to 85°F (16° to 29°C). Average rainfall throughout the country is over 40 in. (100 cm) per year.

ECONOMY

Uganda's economy is based primarily on agriculture. Although the land has rich mineral deposits, only copper is mined on a large scale.

Agriculture - bananas, beans, cassava, coffee, corn, cotton, millet, sugar cane, sweet potatoes, tea, and tobacco
Manufacturing - brewing, cement, cotton textiles, refined sugar, and tobacco
Mining - copper
Exports - coffee, cotton, sugar cane, and tea
Imports - cotton piece goods, food, machinery, metals, petroleum products, and transportation equipment

LIFE-STYLE

Uganda's population is about 90 percent rural. Of the more than 20 ethnic groups, the largest and wealthiest is the Ganda (or Baganda). They reside in central and southern Uganda. Most Ganda make a living by farming, with much of the work being done by the women. Houses with corrugated iron roofs and walls of cement, cinder block, or mud shelter the Ganda.

Three other ethnic groups make a living by farming, but some northern groups, such as the northeastern Karamojong, make a living as herders. Karamojong males are noted for matting and elaborately patterning their hair with colored clay.

IT'S A FACT!

Margherita Peak - located on Uganda's border with Zaire, rises 16,762 ft. (5,109 m) above sea level. It is also considered Zaire's highest point.

Mount Elgon - located near Uganda's eastern border, rises 14,178 ft. (4,321 m) above sea level.

Owen Falls Dam - located near the city of Jinja, is the country's, and one of Africa's, largest hydroelectric power stations.

 DID YOU KNOW...
- Uganda has no single language understood by everyone?
- Uganda won its independence in 1962 after nearly 70 years under Great Britain's rule?
- Up until 1967, the Ganda (or Baganda), along with three other ethnic groups, had their own *Kabaka* (king); they also had their own *Lukiko* (parliament)?
- The White Nile headwaters drain Uganda?
- Wild animals freely roam Uganda's national parks?

UKRAINE

OFFICIAL NAME: Ukrayina (Ukraine)
FORMERLY: Ukrainian Soviet Socialist Republic
LOCATION: Southeastern Europe
AREA: 233,090 sq. mi. (603,700 sq. km)
POPULATION (Est. 1993): 53,125,000
CAPITAL: Kiev
LARGEST CITIES: Kiev, Kharkov, Donetsk
GOVERNMENT: Republic governed by a president.
FLAG: Two horizontal stripes of blue and yellow.
ETHNIC GROUPS: Ukrainian, Russian
LANGUAGE: Ukrainian
RELIGIONS: Christianity (including Orthodox Christian, Ukrainian Catholic, and Protestant), Judaism
BASIC MONETARY UNIT: Karbovanet

GEOGRAPHY

Ukraine is the second largest European country in area, second only to Russia. The country measures 550 mi. (885 km) from north to south and 830 mi. (1,335 km) from east to west at its greatest distances. It has 1,800 mi. (2,900 km) of coastline. Ukraine has six main land regions: 1) the Dnepr-Pripyat Lowland, 2) the Northern Ukrainian Upland, 3) the Central Plateau, 4) the Eastern Carpathian Mountains, 5) the Coastal Plain, and 6) the Crimean Mountains. About a fourth of the Dnepr-Lowland, in northern Ukraine, is covered by forests. The Northern Ukrainian Upland is a low plateau in northeastern Ukraine. The Central Plateau, which stretches from eastern to western Ukraine, contains the most productive farmland. The Eastern Carpathian Mountains occupy western Ukraine. The Coastal Plain lies along the coasts of the Black Sea and the Sea of Azov and includes most of the Crimean Peninsula. The Crimean Mountains rise in the southern part of the Crimean Peninsula.

CLIMATE

Most of Ukraine has cold winters and warm summers. Eastern temperatures average 19°F (-7°C) in January and 68°F (20°C) in July. Western temperatures average 25°F (-4°C) in January and 64°F (18°C) in July. Annual precipitation ranges from 30 in. (76 cm) in the north to about 9 in. (23 cm) in the south.

ECONOMY

Ukraine's economy is built around industry and agriculture. About two-fifths of the people work in industry and one-fifth work in agriculture. Ukraine's fertile steppes have made it one of the world's leading farming regions.

Agriculture - barley, beef and dairy cattle, corn, hogs, potatoes, sugar beets, sunflowers, tobacco, and wheat

Manufacturing - chemical fertilizers, clothing, iron and steel, machinery, military equipment, processed foods, refrigerators, shoes, television sets, transportation equipment, and washing machines

Mining - coal, iron ore, manganese, natural gas, and salt

Exports - coal, construction equipment, fish, food products, iron ore, machinery, manufactured goods, sugar beets, wheat, and wine

Imports - cocoa, coffee, consumer goods, footwear, natural gas, nonferrous metals, oil, rubber, tea, and wood products

LIFE-STYLE

Almost two-thirds of the Ukrainian people live in urban areas. High-rise apartment buildings are the most common type of housing. Pollution, high unemployment, and a growing crime rate are problems faced by city dwellers.

About one-third of Ukrainians live in rural areas. Most of the rural population works on farms or in the lumber industry. The standard of living is generally lower in rural areas than in cities. Small homes are common.

Only on special occasions do Ukrainians wear traditional clothing. These peasant costumes include white blouses and shirts decorated with colorful embroidery.

The Ukrainian diet includes chicken, fish, pork, potatoes, *kasha* (cooked buckwheat mush), sour rye bread, and sweetened breads. Popular beverages include tea, coffee, cocoa, and a soured milk drink. Traditional dishes include *varenyky* (boiled dumplings filled with potatoes, sauerkraut, cheese, plums, or blueberries), *borsch* (soup made of beets, cabbage, and meat), and *holubtsi* (stuffed cabbage rolls filled with rice, buckwheat, and meat).

Children are required to attend school from ages seven to 18. After ninth grade, students may enroll in trade or technical schools or continue pursuing the general academic program.

Soccer is the most popular team sport in Ukraine. Other popular sports and activities include volleyball, track and field, basketball, ice hockey, skating, swimming, chess, and camping.

Ukrainians enjoy music and many perform in choruses and folk dance groups. Ukrainians are renowned for their folk arts and crafts.

IT'S A FACT!

Mount Goverla - the country's highest point, rises 6,762 ft. (2,061 m) above sea level.

St. Sophia Cathedral - begun in the 11th century and finished in the 19th century, is Kiev's most famous church.

The Monastery of the Caves - located in Kiev, was the first and most important monastery of the Russian Orthodox Church.

 DID YOU KNOW...
- Ukraine is called the "breadbasket" of Europe?
- Ukrainian Easter eggs (*pysanky*), decorated with intricate and colorful designs, are world famous?

UNITED ARAB EMIRATES

OFFICIAL NAME: Ittihād al-Imārāt al-'Arabīyah (United Arab Emirates)
LOCATION: Southwestern Asia
AREA: 32,278 sq. mi. (83,600 sq. km)
POPULATION (Est. 1993): 1,698,000
CAPITAL: Abu Dhabi
LARGEST CITIES: Dubayy, Abu Dhabi
GOVERNMENT: Federation of emirates governed by a president.
FLAG: Three horizontal stripes of green, white, and black edged by a vertical red stripe on the hoist side.
ETHNIC GROUPS: Arab, Iranian, Pakistani, Asian Indian
LANGUAGES: Arabic, Persian, English, Hindi, Urdu
RELIGION: Islam
BASIC MONETARY UNIT: Emirian Dirham

GEOGRAPHY

The United Arab Emirates is a federation of seven Arab states in southwestern Asia. The states are located along the eastern coast of the Arabian Peninsula, at the south end of the Persian Gulf. They are Abu Dhabi, Dubayy, Ash Shariqah, Ajman, Umm al Qaywayn, Ras al Khaymah, and Al Fujayrah in succession from west to east. Swamps and salt marshes lie on the northern coast. A desert covers most of the inland area and hills and mountains are found in the eastern part.

CLIMATE

The country has a hot, dry climate. Temperatures range from 60° F (16°C) in winter to an average of more than 90°F (32°C) during the summer. The average annual rainfall is less than 5 in. (13 cm).

ECONOMY

The economy depends largely on the production and export of petroleum.
Agriculture - dates, melons, and tomatoes
Fishing - fish and shrimp
Mining - petroleum and natural gas
Manufacturing - crude oil
Exports - dates, fish, natural gas, and petroleum
Imports - building supplies, clothing, consumer goods, food, and machinery

LIFE-STYLE

Most of the United Arab Emirates population are Arabs. Many others are guest workers from other countries.

Around three-fourths of the people live in urban areas. Most city-dwellers live in modern houses or apartment buildings. In rural areas and on the outskirts of many cities, people live in small, thatched huts.

A few people wear Western-style clothing, but most prefer traditional Arab clothing, which consists of loose-fitting garments that cover most of the body and head. This type of clothing shields them from the sun.

Education is free and children ages six to 12 are required to attend school. Around 50 percent of the people are literate.

The government provides free hospital treatment and medical care.

IT'S A FACT!

Jabil Yibir - the country's highest point, rises 5,010 ft. (1,527 m) above sea level.

 DID YOU KNOW...

* Each emirate is ruled by an *emir* (prince) who controls his state's internal political and economic affairs?
* The government of United Arab Emirates emphasizes education for women and encourages women to enter the work force?
* Life expectancy (68 for males and 72 for females) is among the highest in the Arab countries?
* The name of each capital city is the same as the name of the emirate it is in?

UNITED KINGDOM
(Great Britain)

OFFICIAL NAME: United Kingdom of Great Britain and Northern Ireland

LOCATION: Northwestern Europe

AREA: 94,267 sq. mi. (244,154 sq. km)

POPULATION (Est. 1993): 57,757,000

CAPITAL: London

LARGEST CITIES: London, Birmingham, Leeds, Glasgow

GOVERNMENT: Constitutional monarchy

FLAG: Known as the *British Union Flag* or *Union Jack*. Large red cross in the middle, with red and white stripes and blue triangles around it.

ETHNIC GROUPS: English, Scottish, Irish, Welsh

LANGUAGES: English, Welsh, Scottish and Irish Gaelic

RELIGIONS: Church of England, Church of Scotland, Roman Catholic

BASIC MONETARY UNIT: Pound

GEOGRAPHY

Great Britain is an island country that includes four countries united under one government: England, Northern Ireland, Scotland, and Wales. Great Britain encompasses most of an island group called the British Isles. The British Isles includes numerous small islands and two large islands of Great Britain and Ireland. England, Scotland, and Wales are on the island of Great Britain. Northern Ireland is on the northeastern part of the island of Ireland. Only 20 mi. (32 km) of water separate Great Britain from mainland Europe at the closest point.

Great Britain is divided into eight main land regions: 1) the Scottish Highlands, 2) the Central Lowlands, 3) the Southern Uplands, 4) the Pennines, 5) Wales, 6) the Southwest Peninsula, 7) the English Lowlands, and 8) Northern Ireland.

The northern half of Scotland is covered by the Scottish Highlands, a region of mountains, plateaus, and deep valleys. This rugged, windswept region has poor soil and few people. South of this region lies the Central Lowlands, largely a gently rolling plain that holds Scotland's richest coal deposits, best farmland, and most of its people. The Southern Uplands, an area of rolling hills, lies south of the Central Lowlands. This region's Cheviot Hills form the border between England and Scotland. The Pennines are rounded uplands that reach about halfway down England's length. Wales is southwest of the Pennines. It is covered, in large part, by the Cambrian Mountains. A plateau cut by river valleys lies in Southern Wales. The Southwest Peninsula, south of Wales, is a plateau with a surface broken by large granite masses. South of the Pennines lie the English Lowlands. The lowlands are predominantly vast, gently rolling plains with a few low hills. Most of Great Britain's people, industries, and farmable land are found in this region. Northern Ireland's landscape consists of small mountains, deep valleys, and rich farmland.

CLIMATE

The country has a mild climate despite its location in the far north. The climate is influenced by the Gulf Stream, a warm ocean current that flows past the British Isles. The steady southwest winds bring warm temperatures in the winter and cooling breezes in the summer. The temperature in the winter rarely drops below 10°F (-12°C). Summer temperatures rarely reach 90°F (32°C).

Great Britain has rain throughout the year. It is rare for any part of the country to be dry longer than three weeks. Some areas of the highlands in western Great Britain receive as much as 150-200 in. (381-510 cm) of rain annually. In southeastern England, the average yearly rainfall reaches only 20 in. (51 cm).

ECONOMY

Great Britain is one of the world's leading manufacturing and trading nations. It is known for its production of automobiles, ships, steel, and textiles. Since its farms produce only two-thirds of the food its people need, the United Kingdom must import the rest. The country has few natural resources and must import many of the raw materials used in manufacturing.

Agriculture - barley, beef cattle, milk, pigs, potatoes, poultry and eggs, sheep, sugar beets, and wheat

Fishing - cod, haddock, and mackerel

Manufacturing - chemicals, clothing, electrical goods, foods and beverages, glass and glassware, machinery, metal goods, motor vehicles, pharmaceuticals, printing and publishing, ships, steel, and textiles

Mining - clays, coal, natural gas, and petroleum

Exports - aerospace equipment, chemicals, heavy machinery, medicines, motors, petroleum, and transportation equipment

Imports - coffee, tea, electrical appliances, fruits and vegetables, metal ores, office machines, paper, vehicles, and yarns and fibers

LIFE-STYLE

Approximately 90 percent of the United Kingdom's population dwell in urban areas. Today many of the country's once-thriving cities are in decline due to rising crime, inadequate housing, and rising unemployment. Many of the cities' people are leaving for the suburbs and rural areas.

Rural areas once were devoted solely to farming. But now many people live in rural areas while working in the city. Full-time farmers are often outnumbered by retired persons, commuters, and tourist-industry workers.

British meals are usually simple and might include roast beef, mutton, or pork with potatoes and other vegetables. Poultry, frozen vegetables, and fresh fruit increasingly are being eaten, as is fast food, often called *takeaway*. A favorite is still the traditional Sunday meal of roast beef and Yorkshire pudding. The favorite hot beverage is tea with milk and sugar.

Most British children must attend school from ages five to 16. Children in Northern Ireland begin school at age four. Most schools are free. Usually, children attend elementary school until they are 11 and then go on to high school. Oxford and Cambridge are Britain's most honored and oldest universities.

The British government provides many services, such as free medical care for expectant mothers. Moreover, many of its citizens live in government-owned, low-rent dwellings.

The most popular British sport is soccer, also called football. Golf, archery, bowls (similar to bowling), hockey, horseback riding, horse racing, rugby football, sailing, and tennis are other favorite sports. Cricket has a history in England that dates back hundreds of years. Almost all British schools, universities, towns, and villages have cricket teams. The British people enjoy the outdoors. They often spend vacations walking or mountain climbing, or taking bicycle or automobile trips. A popular recreational activity is gardening. About half of the country's families boast a garden. Socializing in pubs (taverns) is enjoyed by many.

IT'S A FACT!

Ben Nevis - the highest point in the British Isles, rises 4,406 ft. (1,343 m) above sea level and is located in the Scottish Highlands.

Lough Neagh - the largest lake in the British Isles, measures 18 mi. (29 km) long by 11 mi. (18 km) wide and is located in Northern Ireland.

The Pennines - stretch from the Scottish border halfway down the length of England. They are often referred to as the "backbone of England."

White Cliffs of Dover - white, chalk hills near the city of Dover. On a clear day, the people of Calais, France, can see the cliffs.

 DID YOU KNOW...

- Most of Great Britain's coastline is so broken by bays and inlets that there is no point on the island located more than 75 mi. (121 km) from the sea?
- Great Britain's longest rivers are the Severn and the Thames?
- The "pea soup" fogs of London—made famous in motion pictures—now seldom occur? They were the result of pollution rather than precipitation, and antipollution laws have cleaned up the air.
- Since 1066, no foreign enemy has crossed the English Channel and invaded Great Britain?
- The British drive on the left side of the road, and the car's steering wheel is on the right side of the car?
- Speaker's Corner, in London's Hyde Park, is an open-air auditorium where anyone may make a speech?
- Curling is a popular winter sport in Scotland? Players slide stones across the ice toward the center of a target.
- Great Britain has an average of 613 people per sq. mi. (237 people per sq. km)?
- Great Britain was responsible for beginning the Industrial Revolution and once was the largest and most powerful empire in history?

UNITED STATES OF AMERICA

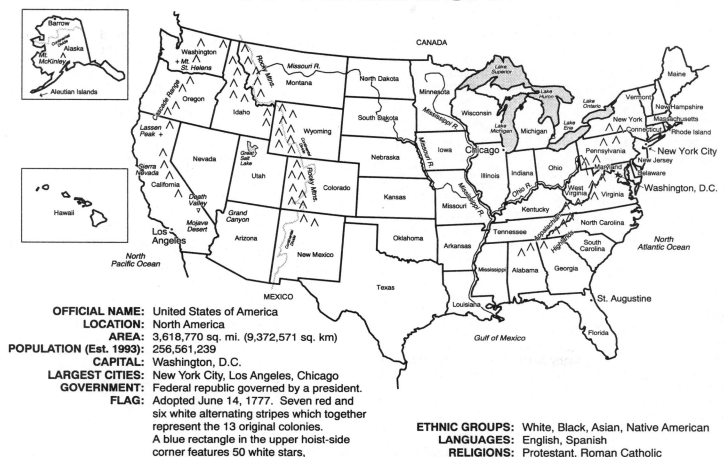

OFFICIAL NAME: United States of America
LOCATION: North America
AREA: 3,618,770 sq. mi. (9,372,571 sq. km)
POPULATION (Est. 1993): 256,561,239
CAPITAL: Washington, D.C.
LARGEST CITIES: New York City, Los Angeles, Chicago
GOVERNMENT: Federal republic governed by a president.
FLAG: Adopted June 14, 1777. Seven red and six white alternating stripes which together represent the 13 original colonies. A blue rectangle in the upper hoist-side corner features 50 white stars, representing the 50 states.

ETHNIC GROUPS: White, Black, Asian, Native American
LANGUAGES: English, Spanish
RELIGIONS: Protestant, Roman Catholic
BASIC MONETARY UNIT: United States Dollar

GEOGRAPHY

The United States is the fourth-largest country in the world in area. It covers the midsection of North America, stretching from the Atlantic Ocean to the Pacific Ocean. It also includes Alaska, located in the northwest corner of the continent, and Hawaii, located in the Pacific Ocean southwest of the contiguous United States. At their greatest distances, the 48 contiguous states stretch 1,598 mi. (2,572 km) from north to south and 2,807 mi. (4,517 km) from east to west. Alaska measures 1,200 mi. (1,930 km.) from north to south and 2,200 mi. (3,540 km) from east to west at its greatest distances. From northwest to southeast, Hawaii stretches 1,610 mi. (2,591 km). The United States coastline, including Alaska and Hawaii, covers 12,383 mi. (19,929 km).

The United States—excluding Alaska and Hawaii—has seven major land regions: 1) the Appalachian Highlands, 2) the Coastal Lowlands, 3) the Interior Plains, 4) the Ozark-Ouachita Highlands, 5) the Rocky Mountains, 6) the Western Plateaus, Basins, and Ranges, and 7) the Pacific Ranges and Lowlands.

The Appalachian Highlands stretch from the northern tip of Maine to Alabama. Within this region are many mountain ranges.

The Coastal Lowlands begin in southeastern Maine and stretch along the eastern and southern United States into eastern Texas. Forests of hickory, oak, pine, and other trees are found throughout the region.

The Interior Plains occupy a large part of the country that stretches from the Appalachian Highlands to the Rocky Mountains. During the Ice Age, much of the area was covered by glaciers. Today, much of the northern part of the region is covered by forests. Farther south, the glaciers deposited rich soil. The western part, referred to as the Great Plains, is made up of grasslands and large areas of rich soil. Within the Interior Plains region is found the largest group of freshwater lakes in the world: the Great Lakes.

Between the Interior Plains and Coastal Lowlands is an area called the Ozark-Ouachita Highlands. These highlands cover southern Missouri, northwestern Arkansas, and eastern Oklahoma. The landscape includes forested hills, artificial lakes, and many underground caves and springs.

The Rocky Mountains form the largest mountain system in North America. They extend from northern Alaska, through Canada and the western United States, as far as northern New Mexico. The *Continental Divide*, an imaginary line that separates streams flowing toward the Pacific Ocean from those flowing toward the Atlantic Ocean, cuts through in the Rocky Mountains.

West of the Rocky Mountains are the Western Plateaus, Basins, and Ranges. This region stretches from the state of Washington south to the Mexican border. It is the driest part of the United States. The northernmost part of the region is occupied by the Columbia Plateau. To the south lies the Colorado Plateau. The Basin and Range part of the region is a large area of mountains and desert between the two plateaus. Death Valley and the Great Salt Lake are both found in this area.

Stretching across western Washington and Oregon and most of California are the Pacific Ranges and Lowlands. This region's eastern boundary is formed by the Cascade Mountains in the north and the Sierra Nevada in the south. Two active volcanoes—Lassen Peak in California and Mount St. Helens in Washington—are found in the Cascade Mountains.

Alaska is the largest of the 50 states. It has beautiful mountains and huge areas of unspoiled wilderness. Hawaii is a string of islands in the North Pacific Ocean. The islands were created by volcanoes built up from the floor of the ocean.

The United States is also divided into seven regions based on similarities in economy, traditions, history, geography, and climate. The regions from northeast to west are: 1) New England, 2) the Middle Atlantic States, 3) the Southern States, 4) the Midwestern States, 5) the Rocky Mountain States, 6) the Southwestern States, and 7) the Pacific Coast States.

The New England Region is known for its many historical sites, many fine fishing harbors, and beautiful scenery. The Middle Atlantic States Region has many large harbor cities which accounts for this region being a major international trade center. The Southern States Region's economy is mainly based on agriculture and the tourist trade. The fertile soil in the Midwest has allowed this region to produce large quantities of corn, wheat, and other crops. The Rocky Mountain States Region is named for the majestic Rocky Mountains which slice down through its center. The Southwestern States Region has huge ranches and wide-open land. Mountains, thick forests, and miles of shoreline dominate the Pacific Coast States Region.

CLIMATE

Since the United States covers such a vast amount of land and has such a variety of landscapes, the climate varies greatly from place to place. Average annual temperatures range from 9°F (-13°C) in Barrow, Alaska, to 78.2°F (25.7°C) in Death Valley, California.

Precipitation is also quite varied from region to region. For example, Death Valley averages less than 2 in. (5 cm) per year, while Mount Waialeale in Hawaii averages 460 in. (1,170 cm) annually.

Most parts of the country experience seasonal changes in temperature and moderate precipitation. The Midwest, the Middle Atlantic States, and New England have warm summers and cold, snowy winters. The Southern states experience long, hot summers and mild winters. Along the Pacific coast the climate is mild year-round. In the West, the mountain areas are cooler and wetter than the surrounding plains and plateaus. Some parts of the West and Southwest experience a desert climate.

ECONOMY

The economy of the United States is based on a free enterprise system. It ranks first in the world in economic production.

Service industries employ about 76 percent of the nation's work force, including 15 percent who work for the government. About 17 percent are employed in manufacturing. The rest work in construction, agriculture, and mining.

Agriculture - beef cattle, chickens, cotton, corn, eggs, hogs, milk, soybeans, and wheat

Fishing - crab, salmon, and shrimp

Manufacturing - airplanes and their parts, clothing, computers and computer parts, fabricated metal products, gasoline and other refined petroleum products, industrial chemicals, industrial machinery, motor vehicles and parts, paper, pharmaceuticals, plastics, printed materials, processed foods, and steel

Mining - coal, natural gas, and petroleum

Exports - agricultural products, automobiles, capital goods, consumer goods, and industrial supplies and raw materials

Imports - beverages, consumer goods, crude oil and refined petroleum products, industrial raw materials, and machinery

LIFE-STYLE

The United States is often referred to as a "nation of immigrants." With the exception of Native Americans, which comprise one percent of the population, all other Americans or their ancestors came to this land from other parts of the world. Today whites, which also include Hispanics, make up about 80 percent of the population. Blacks total about 12 percent, Asians comprise three percent, Native Americans make up one percent, and the remaining four percent are other nationalities. Nine percent of today's population are Hispanics who are primarily of Mexican, Puerto Rican, or Cuban descent.

While Americans have many things in common, this country is not a true "melting pot," where people from many cultures have come together to form one unified culture. In most ways, United States society is an example of *cultural pluralism*, in which large numbers of people have retained some features of their own cultures passed down by their ancestors.

About 75 percent of Americans live in urban areas. The wealthy live in luxurious houses, apartments or condominiums; the middle class reside in comfortable though less luxurious homes; and many of the poor live in substandard housing. The rural areas also have a variety of economic classes, however, there are fewer job opportunities than those available to urban dwellers. Most families live in single-family homes. Compared to most of the world, Americans enjoy a high standard of living.

Education is free and compulsory for children ages five to 16. More than 99 percent complete elementary school and 75 percent complete high school. Many of the large cities have substandard schools, which do not provide students with the necessary skills to obtain and hold jobs. Violence and crime are major problems in the United States.

Americans eat a wide variety of foods. A typical American evening meal includes meat and potatoes, plus a salad or vegetable. Americans enjoy beef, chicken, ham, and turkey. Fish and shellfish are also popular as main courses. Snacking between meals is popular with most Americans. Americans drink more soft drinks than any other beverage.

In the United States, the basis of society is the family unit, which has been changing form over time. Today, only one-fourth of families are traditional, with both parents in the home and one or two children. Over half of all American households today have no children. Non-traditional family structures, which include single parent households or unmarried couples with or without children, are becoming very common. Many American families today are very mobile, moving from region to region because of employment opportunities, education, or a change in personal living situation.

Americans spend their leisure time pursuing hobbies, participating in sports, attending sporting events, watching movies or television, or reading. Sports rank as the leading American pastime. Events such as plays, concerts, operas, and dance performances are well-attended by Americans. Many people take occasional trips to museums, beaches, parks, playgrounds, and zoos. About 60 percent of all Americans belong to an organized religious group.

The United States has a wealth of famous authors, architects, painters, composers, and musicians. Washington Irving and James Fenimore Cooper were among America's first well-known authors. Frank Lloyd Wright's "Fallingwater" house is indicative of his place in American architecture. Many forms of popular music, such as jazz, rock, and country, had their beginnings in the United States. Louis Armstrong, Elvis Presley, and Merle Haggard are only a small sampling of America's many great music performers.

IT'S A FACT!

Death Valley - the country's lowest point of elevation, is located in California and lies 282 ft. (86 m) below sea level.

Lake Superior - the deepest of the Great Lakes, is the world's largest freshwater lake. It covers an area of about 31,700 sq. mi. (82,100 sq. km).

Mississippi River - the country's second longest river, flows 2,340 mi. (3,766 km). It is the country's major inland waterway.

Missouri River - is the country's longest river. Its muddy waters flow 2,540 mi. (4,090 km).

Mount McKinley - the country's highest point, is located in Alaska and rises 20,320 ft. (6,194 m) above sea level.

St. Augustine - located in Florida, is the country's oldest permanent European settlement. It was founded in 1565 by a Spanish explorer.

Grand Canyon - one of America's most famous scenic wonders, is located in northwest Arizona. The Colorado River runs through the 277-mi.- (446-km-) long canyon. The red and brown rock walls are 1 mi. (1.6 km) deep.

Mt. Rushmore National Memorial - in South Dakota, is a huge memorial honoring four American Presidents: George Washington, Thomas Jefferson, Abraham Lincoln, and Theodore Roosevelt. George Washington's head is as tall as a five-story building.

Statue of Liberty - on Liberty Island in New York Harbor, is a famous American tourist attraction for people from all over the world. It was given to the United States by France in 1884 as a token of friendship and liberty.

Washington, D.C. - the capital of the United States, is also a famous tourist attraction. Many government buildings, such as the United States Capitol and the White House are located here. The popular Washington Monument, Lincoln Memorial, and Vietnam Veterans Memorial are also visited by many.

 DID YOU KNOW...
- A mnemonic device for remembering the names of the five Great Lakes—Huron, Ontario, Michigan, Erie, and Superior—is "HOMES"?
- The United States uses about 400 billion gallons (1,500 billion liters) of water daily?
- The United States has the largest number of private airline companies in the world?
- Bathers cannot sink in the Great Salt Lake, located in Utah, because the high amount of salt provides natural buoyancy?
- Descendents of almost all the world's ethnic groups reside in the United States, making the population more varied than that of any other country?
- The United States has the world's third-largest population?
- U.S. farms provide about one-third of the world's food exports?
- The U.S. has an average ratio of 75 automobiles for every 100 people?

URUGUAY

OFFICIAL NAME: Republica Oriental del Uruguay
(Oriental Republic of Uruguay)
LOCATION: Southeastern South America
AREA: 68,500 sq. mi. (177,414 sq. km)
POPULATION (Est. 1993): 3,148,000
CAPITAL: Montevideo
LARGEST CITIES: Montevideo, Salto
GOVERNMENT: Repubic governed by a president.
FLAG: Adopted in 1830. Nine horizontal stripes—five white divided by four blue—represent the nine departments into which Uruguay was originally divided. A white rectangle in the upper, hoist-side corner features a yellow sun. The sun has a human face—known as the *Sun of May*—and 16 rays.
ETHNIC GROUP: European (mainly Spanish and Italian)
LANGUAGE: Spanish (generally spoken with an Italian accent)
RELIGION: Roman Catholic
BASIC MONETARY UNIT: Uruguayan Peso

GEOGRAPHY

Uruguay is South America's next to the smallest country in area. At its greatest distances, Uruguay measures 330 mi. (530 km) from north to south and 280 mi. (450 km) from east to west. It has 410 mi. (660 km) of coastline along Río de la Plata and the South Atlantic Ocean.

Uruguay has two main land regions: 1) the coastal plains and 2) the interior lowlands. Although the coastal plains occupy only one-fifth of Uruguay's area, most of the population lives in this region. Huge, grass-covered plains, hills, and many rivers and streams make the interior lowlands ideal for raising live-stock. *Cuchilla Grande* (Big Knife), a long narrow chain of highlands, cuts across the interior from the north to the south. Sandy beaches cover the Atlantic shore, and large plantations and small farms cover much of the southwestern and western coastal plains. Río Negro is the country's largest river.

CLIMATE

Uruguay has a mild, humid climate. The average annual temperature in Montevideo ranges from 51°F (11°C) in July to 73°F (23°C) in January. Rain falls throughout the year, and the average annual rainfall is about 40 in. (102 cm).

ECONOMY

Uruguay has a developing economy based mainly on agriculture.

Agriculture - corn, livestock (cattle and sheep), potatoes, rice, sugar beets, sugar cane, and wheat

Fishing - anchovy, croaker, hake, and weakfish

Manufacturing - beer, cement, footwear, leather goods, meat packing and processing, petroleum refining, sugar, textiles, and tires

Mining - gravel, sand, and stone

Exports - beef, fish, hides, livestock, rice, vegetable products, and wool and woolen textiles

Imports - appliances, chemical products, fuel, machinery, metal goods, petroleum, and transportation equipment

LIFE-STYLE

About 85 percent of the people live in cities and towns. Most Uruguayans enjoy a comfortable standard of living with adequate housing and food. They also have access to good medical care. Most of the 15 percent who live in rural settings live in one-story adobe homes on small farms they rent or own. Others work as laborers on plantations or as *gauchos* (cowboys) on *estancias* (huge ranches). Families of migrant laborers and ranch workers live in shacks with mud floors and thatched roofs. Wealthy landowners may have country estates, as well as homes in the cities. The majority of Uruguayans wear Western-style dress. Gauchos may still be seen in the traditional costume of a flat, wide-brimmed hat, a blanketlike poncho, and baggy pants tucked into boots.

The Uruguayan diet includes a wide variety of fish, fruits meats (beef being a particular favorite), and vegetables. A favorite meal is *parrillada criolla*. One version consists of a mixture of barbecued *chorizos* (sausages), *riñones* (kidneys), and strips of beef. The national beverage is a tea called *yerba maté*. Traditionally, it is sipped from a gourd through a silver straw.

Fútbol (soccer) is the national sport, but basketball, volleyball, swimming, and other water sports are equally popular. Leisure activities include going to the beach, and watching movies and television. Gaucho rodeos attract many spectators.

Education is free, and children ages six to 15 are required to attend school.

IT'S A FACT!

Independence Plaza - located in the heart of Montevideo, features a statue of José Artigas, the country's national hero.

Mirador Nacional (Cerro de las Animas) - the country's highest point, rises 1,644 ft. (501 m) above sea level.

 DID YOU KNOW...
- About two-fifths of Uruguay's population lives in Montevideo?
- At age 18, all Uruguayan citizens are required to vote?

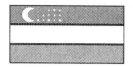

UZBEKISTAN

OFFICIAL NAME: Uzbekiston Respublikasi (Republic of Uzbekistan)
FORMERLY: Uzbek Soviet Socialist Republic (until 1991)
LOCATION: Central Asia
AREA: 172,742 sq. mi. (447,400 sq. km)
POPULATION (Est. 1993): 20,453,000
CAPITAL: Tashkent
LARGEST CITIES: Tashkent, Samarkand, Bukhara
GOVERNMENT: Republic governed by a president.
FLAG: Three horizontal stripes of blue, white, and green separated by narrow red stripes. A white crescent and 12 white stars are on the hoist side of the blue stripe.
ETHNIC GROUPS: Uzbek, Russian
LANGUAGES: Uzbek, Russian
RELIGIONS: Islam (Sunni Muslim), Eastern Orthodox
BASIC MONETARY UNIT: Ruble

GEOGRAPHY

Uzbekistan, a landlocked country, measures 575 mi. (925 km) from north to south and 900 mi. (1,450 km) from east to west at its greatest distances. It extends from the foothills of the Tian Shan and Pamir Mountains to just west of the Aral Sea. The country's border with Kazakhstan runs through the Aral Sea. About 80 percent of the country's land consists of plains and deserts.

CLIMATE

Uzbekistan's climate consists of long, dry, hot summers and extremely cold winters. The average annual summer temperature may reach 113°F (45°C) in the south, and the average annual winter temperature may drop to -35°F (-37°C) in the north. Over 70 percent of the country's precipitation falls in winter.

ECONOMY

Under Soviet rule, Uzbekistan was the third-largest producer of cotton in the world. Cotton is still its chief agricultural product. Most businesses are state-owned, but free enterprise is now encouraged.

Agriculture - cotton, eggs, grapes, livestock, milk, potatoes, and rice
Manufacturing - agricultural machinery, chemicals, food products, paper, and textiles
Mining - coal, copper, gold, natural gas, and petroleum
Exports - cotton and heavy machinery
Imports - foodstuffs and light manufactures

LIFE-STYLE

About 60 percent of the country's people live in rural areas and are farmers. Most rural homes are made of sun-dried earthen bricks and lack modern conveniences. Urban dwellers live in one-story houses or multilevel apartment buildings. Many homes are decorated with brightly colored rugs and folk art.

The people of Uzbekistan wear both Western-style and traditional clothing. Traditional dress for men includes a long robe and black boots. Women occasionally wear bright cotton or silk dresses and silk scarves. A traditional embroidered skullcap is worn with both styles of dress.

Most families are large, with as many as six children. In rural areas, extended family living is the rule. It is common for all people in a rural village to be related to one another.

Common foods in Uzbekistan include rice, vegetables, fruit, mutton, and a flat round bread called *nan*. A well-known Uzbek dish is *palav* or *pilaf*, which is mutton and rice. Tea is the most popular beverage.

Uzbekistan children attend elementary and general secondary schools. Many go on to trade schools, institutes, or universities.

Soccer is a popular sport in the country. Traditional Uzbek sports are wrestling, tightrope walking, and *ulag*. *Ulag* is a game played on horseback where riders try to grab a dead sheep and carry it across a goal. The people also enjoy wearing traditional costumes during holidays and festivals.

The people of Uzbekistan are well-known for their crafts, which include carpet-making, embroidery, glazed pottery, jewelry-making, metalwork, and woodcarving.

IT'S A FACT!

Sarykamysh Lake - a seasonal salt lake bed and the country's lowest point of elevation, is located 65 ft. (20 m) below sea level.

Twenty-Second Congress of the CPSU Peak - the country's highest point, rises 15,233 ft. (4,643 m) above sea level.

 DID YOU KNOW...

- The city of Samarkand was first mentioned in writing in 329 B.C. when it was conquered by Alexander the Great? The city was known for decades as the "precious pearl of the world."
- The silkworm has been cultivated in Uzbekistan since the fourth century A.D.?
- Today, the water in the Aral Sea is too salty and too toxic to sustain life?
- The ancient Silk Road that once connected Europe with China passed through the southern part of Uzbekistan's territory?
- The people of Uzbekistan have raised Karakul sheep for centuries? This animal is famous for the black, curly fur of its lambs.

VANUATU

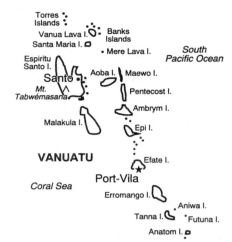

OFFICIAL NAME: Ripablik Blong Vanuatu (Republic of Vanuatu)
FORMERLY: New Hebrides
LOCATION: Southwestern Pacific Ocean
AREA: 4,700 sq. mi. (12,200 sq. km)
POPULATION (Est. 1993): 160,000
CAPITAL: Port-Vila (on Efate Island)
LARGEST CITY: Port-Vila, Santo (on Espiritu Santo Island)
GOVERNMENT: Republic governed by a prime minister.
FLAG: Black triangle based on the hoist side features a yellow boar's tusk encircling two crossed namele leaves. Two horizontal stripes of red and green are separated from each other and the black triangle by a black-edged yellow stripe in the shape of a horizontal Y.
ETHNIC GROUP: Melanesian
LANGUAGES: Bislama, French, English
RELIGIONS: Christianity, local religions
BASIC MONETARY UNIT: Vatu

GEOGRAPHY

Vanuatu is an island country composed of 80 islands. It is located in the southwest Pacific Ocean about 1,100 mi. (1,800 km) east of Australia. Vanuatu forms a Y-shaped chain that extends about 560 mi. (900 km) from north to south.

The islands were formed by volcanoes, several of which are still active. Most of the islands have narrow coastal plains and mountainous interiors. All of the islands have thick forests. The country's largest islands are Espiritu Santo, Malakula, Efate, Erromango, and Tanna.

CLIMATE

The northern islands are hot and rainy. The average year-round temperature is about 80°F (27°C). They receive about 120 in. (305 cm) of rainfall annually. Temperatures on the southern islands range from 67° to 88°F (19° to 31°C). They receive about 90 in. (230 cm) of rain yearly. During the months of January through April, the islands are subject to typhoons or tropical cyclones.

ECONOMY

The country's economy is based on agriculture and fishing. Tourism is also important. The country is heavily dependent on foreign aid.

Agriculture - cocao, coffee, copra, and livestock
Manufacturing - fish processing
Fishing - bonito and tuna
Exports - copra, fish, and meat
Imports - fuel, foodstuffs, manufactured goods, machinery and vehicles, and raw materials

LIFE-STYLE

Melanesians, who make up over 90 percent of Vanuatu's people, are the shortest peoples of the Pacific Islands. They have dark skin and most have black, wooly hair.

Over 100 languages are spoken on the islands, and many Vanuatuans can speak five or six languages. Bislama, a combination of English words and Melanesian grammar, is often used in Vanuatu.

Though education is not compulsory, most children attend primary school.

Three-fourths of the people live in rural villages, many of them in houses made of wood, bamboo, and palm leaves. Most are subsistence farmers, while some are employed on plantations or cattle ranches.

IT'S A FACT

Mount Tabwémasana - the country's highest point, is located on Espiritu Santo and rises 6,165 ft. (1,879 m) above sea level.

 DID YOU KNOW...

- The name Vanuatu means "our land"?
- In 1774, Captain James Cook named the islands New Hebrides after the Hebrides Islands of Scotland?
- Pigs are important in the traditional cultures of the people of Malakula and Espiritu Santo? Tribes and leaders try to acquire as many as possible.
- Great Britain and France jointly governed the islands from 1906 until 1980, when the islands became an independent nation?

VATICAN CITY

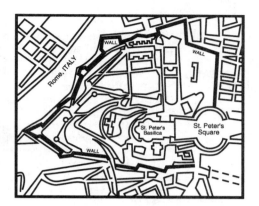

OFFICIAL NAME: Stato della Città del Vaticano (The State of Vatican City)
LOCATION: Rome, Italy
AREA: 109 acres (44 hectares)
POPULATION: 1,000
CAPITAL: Vatican City
GOVERNMENT: Papal state headed by the pope, who is absolute ruler. Administrative, internal, and foreign affairs are handled by a governor, the Pontifical Commission for the State of Vatican City, and the Cardinal Secretary of State, accordingly.
FLAG: Uses the pope's banner: two horizontal stripes of yellow and white with the pontifical arms centered on the white stripe.
ETHNIC GROUPS: Italian, European
LANGUAGES: Latin, Italian
RELIGION: Roman Catholic
BASIC MONETARY UNIT: Vatican Lira

GEOGRAPHY

Vatican City is the smallest independent country in the world and is located entirely within Rome, Italy. Vatican City rests atop Vatican Hill, which is west of the Tiber River, and is largely surrounded by high stone walls.

The country also owns/controls several buildings outside Vatican City proper: St. John Lateran, St. Paul's-outside-the-Walls, St. Mary Major, the Vatican observatory, and the pope's summer villa.

CLIMATE

Vatican City has a Mediterranean climate. The average temperature ranges from 45°F (7°C) in January to 77°F (25°C) in July. The average annual rainfall is 26 in. (65 cm).

ECONOMY

Vatican City's economy is based on banking and communications, pilgrimages, and tourism. The country also receives donations from Roman Catholic congregations throughout the world.

LIFE-STYLE

Vatican City is often referred to as *The Vatican*. Its government is often called *Vatican*.

Despite its small size, Vatican City is run much like a larger city. It has its own electrical services, freight railroad system, jail, telephone and telegraph services, and printing plant. The country also makes and issues its own coins, license plates, and postage stamps. The country's daily newspaper, *L´Osservatore Romano*, is among the most influential in the world. The country's news, along with messages from the pope, are broadcast in 30 different languages. Vatican City's police force is comprised of the St. Peter and Paul Association. Additional security is provided by the Central Office of Vigilance. The Vatican has a military corps, the Swiss Guard, whose sole purpose is to protect the Pope.

IT'S A FACT!

St. Peter's Basilica - the world's largest Christian church, is built over a tomb thought to be the final resting place of the first pope, Saint Peter.

Sistine Chapel - located in the Vatican Palace, displays some of the greatest works by artist Michelangelo.

Vatican Museums - located in Vatican Palace, house priceless statues, Egyptian and Etruscan antiquities, and works by such artists as Fra Angelico, Pinturiccio, Raphael, Titian, and Leonardo da Vinci.

Vatican Palace - a group of buildings containing over 1,000 rooms, including the pope's apartment, the Vatican Museums, the Vatican Archives, and the Vatican Library.

 DID YOU KNOW...

- Roman Catholicism is the world's largest branch of Christianity, and Vatican City serves as its center of government and spirituality?
- On file in the Vatican Archives is the original report of Galileo's trial, which took place in 1633?

VENEZUELA

OFFICIAL NAME: República de Venezuela (Republic of Venezuela)
LOCATION: Northern South America
AREA: 352,145 sq. mi. (912,050 sq. km)
POPULATION (Est. 1993): 21,165,000
CAPITAL: Caracas
LARGEST CITIES: Caracas, Maracaibo, Valencia
GOVERNMENT: Republic governed by a president.
FLAG: Three horizontal stripes of yellow, blue, and red. The coat of arms is in the upper hoist-side corner, and an arc of seven white stars is centered on the blue stripe.
ETHNIC GROUPS: Mestizo, Spanish, Italian, Black, American Indian
LANGUAGES: Spanish, tribal languages
RELIGION: Roman Catholic
BASIC MONETARY UNIT: Bolivar

GEOGRAPHY

Venezuela measures 790 mi. (1,271 km) from north to south and 925 mi. (1,489 km) from east to west at its greatest distances. It has 1,750 mi. (2,816 km) of coastline along the Caribbean Sea and the North Atlantic Ocean.

Venezuela has four main land regions: 1) the Maracaibo Basin, 2) the Andean Highlands, 3) the Llanos, and 4) the Guiana Highlands. Most of northern Venezuela is covered by mountain ranges. The central part is covered by large plains, called the *Llanos*. High plateaus and low mountains are found in the south.

CLIMATE

The country lies entirely within the tropics, but the climate varies by region. The average annual temperature ranges from 83°F (28°C) in the northern and central area to 67°F (19°C) in the Highlands. Average rainfall in the Períja Mountains and Guiana Highlands is about 120 in. (305 cm), while much of the Caribbean coast may receive as little as 16 in. (41 cm) yearly. The Llanos has an average annual rainfall of 40 in. (100 cm).

ECONOMY

Although Venezuelans have a high standard of living, the wealth is not evenly distributed. Extreme poverty and high unemployment are major problems in some parts of the country. Petroleum is Venezuela's most important natural resource. In fact, Venezuela is one of the world's leading producers and exporters of petroleum.

Agriculture - bananas, beef cattle, chickens, coffee, corn, eggs, milk, and oranges
Manufacturing - aluminum, petrochemicals, processed foods, refined petroleum, steel, and textiles
Mining - natural gas and petroleum
Exports - aluminum, petroleum, and petroleum products
Imports - chemicals, industrial machinery, and transportation equipment

LIFE-STYLE

Venezuela's population is about 90 percent urban. The middle class has grown since the 1940s when many rural people began to urbanize. Some families dwell in single-story, Spanish-style homes with a central courtyard. But in many cities these homes are quickly being replaced by high-rise apartments.

Due to scarce housing, many poor Venezuelans live in crowded squatter settlements on the cities' outskirts, often in tiny shacks called *ranchos*. Most of these people are unskilled laborers from rural areas. Since the 1960s, the government has sought to improve the living conditions of its poor and to encourage people to stay on farms.

Staples of the diet include black beans, plantains (a type of banana), and rice. These are normally eaten with some type of meat. *Arepa*, a round cornmeal cake, is the traditional bread. Venezuela's national dish is the *hallaca*, which is cornmeal dough filled with butter, meat, and cheese and cooked in wrappers made of a banana leaf. Coffee and hot chocolate are popular drinks.

About 85 percent of Venezuelans are literate. Children ages seven to 13 are required to attend school. Students can receive a free education from kindergarten through university graduate school.

Baseball and soccer are the most important spectator sports. People also attend bullfights. Leisure activities may include fishing, hunting, swimming, tennis, basketball, and golf. The people also enjoy music and dancing. The national folk dance of Venezuela is the *joropo*, a stamping dance performed to music of *cuatros* (four-stringed guitars), the harp, and maracas.

IT'S A FACT!

Angel Falls - the world's highest waterfall, is located in the Guiana Highlands and plunges 3,212 ft. (979 m).

The Orinoco River - the country's longest river, extends 1,284 mi. (2,066 km).

Pico Bolívar - the country's highest point, rises 16,411 ft. (5,002 m) above sea level.

 DID YOU KNOW...
- *Gúacharos* are large birds found only in northern South America, most of which live in the Cave of Guacharo near the town of Caripe?
- The largest known petroleum deposits in South America are found in the Maracaibo Basin?
- The expressway interchange in Caracas is called the *Araña*, which is the Spanish word for spider?
- Columbus discovered the area in 1498? It was later named Venezuela ("Little Venice") because the natives' houses on stilts reminded the early explorers of Venice.

VIETNAM

OFFICIAL NAME: Cong Hoa Chu Nghia Viet Nam
(Socialist Republic of Vietnam)
LOCATION: Southeast Asia
AREA: 128,066 sq. mi. (331,689 sq. km)
POPULATION (Est. 1993): 70,297,000
CAPITAL: Hanoi
LARGEST CITIES: Ho Chi Minh City, Hanoi, Haiphong
GOVERNMENT: Communist state led by a president.
FLAG: Red field with a yellow star—representing
Communism—in the center.
ETHNIC GROUPS: Chinese, Tay, Thai, Khmer
LANGUAGES: Vietnamese, minority group languages
RELIGIONS: Buddhism, Taoism, Christianity (mainly Roman Catholic)
BASIC MONETARY UNIT: New Dong

GEOGRAPHY

Vietnam stretches south from China forming a long, narrow *S*. It measures 1,030 mi. (1,657 km) from north to south and 380 mi. (612 km) from east to west at its greatest distances. In the central part of the country, its narrowest point is only 30 mi. (48 km) wide. It has 2,140 mi. (3,444 km) of coastline along the Gulf of Tonkin, the South China Sea, and the Gulf of Thailand.

The country has five major land regions: 1) the Northern Highlands, 2) the Red River Delta, 3) the Annamite Range, 4) the Coastal Lowlands, and 5) the Mekong Delta. Much of Vietnam is mountainous. The majority of its people live in the delta regions. The Mekong Delta is Vietnam's leading agricultural area.

CLIMATE

Vietnam has a tropical climate with monsoons (seasonal winds) affecting the weather throughout the year. There are only two seasons in most of the country: a wet, hot summer and a drier, cooler winter. Some parts of the northernmost part of the country, however, have four seasons. In northern Vietnam, the temperatures average 63°F (17°C) in January and 85°F (29°C) in June. This area receives approximately 72 in. (183 cm) of rain per year. In southern Vietnam, temperatures average 79°F (26°C) in December and 86°F (30°C) in April. This area receives approximately 80 in. (200 cm) of rain per year.

ECONOMY

Vietnam's economy, having suffered from war and political unrest, is still largely dependent on agriculture. It has a socialist economy with the government owning most means of production. About 70 percent of the country's workers are farmers.

Agriculture - cassava, coconuts, coffee, corn, cotton, jute, peanuts, rice, rubber, soybeans, sugar cane, sweet potatoes, tea, and tobacco

Fishing - lobster, shrimp, and squid

Manufacturing - bicycles, cement, farm tools, fertilizer, iron and steel, paper products, simple machines, and textiles

Mining - chromium, clays, coal, petroleum, phosphates, salt, and tin

Exports - coal, handcrafted bamboo and rattan products, peanuts, rice, rubber, and tea

Imports - food, machinery, medicines, military supplies, refined petroleum products, and vehicles

LIFE-STYLE

Most Vietnamese live in villages on the coastal plain and on deltas formed by rivers. They grow rice and a few other crops. Many on the coast make a living by fishing.

Vietnamese families are traditionally extended with parents, unmarried children, and married sons and their families sharing the same household. The people maintain strong family ties. Single-family homes are more prevalent in the cities.

In towns and cities, houses are usually built of wood, brick, and tile. Traditionally in the rural north, people built simple wood or bamboo homes with tile roofs. In the south, homes had walls and roofs made of palm leaves or straw. Today, metal sheets or plastic are used for roofs.

Most Vietnamese wear cotton clothing. In cities of the north, the majority of people wear black trousers with tightly buttoned dark-colored or white jackets. Sandals made of old automobile tires are common. In cities of the south, the same style of clothing is sometimes worn, but many, especially men, wear Western-style clothing. Women often still wear the traditional *aodai* (a long, coatlike garment) over trousers.

Rice is the main food in Vietnam. Other staples of the diet include fish, rice, and vegetables. Chopsticks and rice bowls are used for most meals. A fermented fish sauce, called *nuoc mam*, is the main seasoning used by the Vietnamese. Beverages are served after the meal, not during it.

Most Vietnamese can read and write, despite the Vietnam War and a poor economy. The Communist party controls the operation of all schools.

The people enjoy team sports, such as volleyball and soccer. Badminton, ping pong, swimming, and tennis are popular. It is not unusual to see people of all ages exercising in the early morning.

IT'S A FACT!

Fan Si Pan - the country's highest point, rises 10,312 ft. (3,143 m) above sea level.

 DID YOU KNOW...
- *Rickshaws*, or tricycles, are commonly used as taxis in Vietnam's cities?
- Less than one percent of the people own automobiles?
- Half of Vietnam's population is under the age of 20?

VIRGIN ISLANDS
Territory of the United States

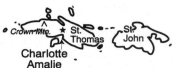

Atlantic Ocean

OFFICIAL NAME: The Virgin Islands of the United States
LOCATION: Between the Atlantic Ocean and Caribbean Sea
AREA: 132 sq. mi. (342 sq. km)
POPULATION (1990): 101,809
CAPITAL/LARGEST CITY: Charlotte Amalie
GOVERNMENT: Self-governing territory headed by a governor.
FLAG: White field that features a yellow eagle, holding an olive branch in its right talon and three arrows in its left talon. A shield is superimposed on the eagle, and the blue initials *V* and *I* are on either side of the eagle.
ETHNIC GROUPS: Black, White
LANGUAGE: English
RELIGIONS: Baptist, Roman Catholic, Episcopalian
BASIC MONETARY UNIT: United States Dollar

U.S. VIRGIN ISLANDS

Caribbean Sea

GEOGRAPHY

The U.S. Virgin Islands lie between the Atlantic Ocean and the Caribbean Sea about 40 mi. (64 km) east of Puerto Rico. They include three inhabited islands—St. Croix, St. John, and St. Thomas—and many surrounding islets. The islands have a general coastline of 117 mi. (188 km) along the Atlantic Ocean and the Caribbean Sea. This island group is the United States's most eastern possession. Ancient animal fossils and the makeup of the island's rocks indicate that the Virgin Islands were formed when volcanoes pushed them up from the depths of the ocean.

All of the U.S. Virgin Islands are rugged and hilly, except St. Croix. Despite the lack of natural freshwater resources, the islands have fertile soil.

CLIMATE

The U.S. Virgin Islands experience a year-round tropical climate that is tempered by trade winds. The average annual temperature ranges from 70° to 90°F (21° to 32°C). The rainy season lasts from about May to November. Rainfall varies by island and the average annual rainfall is 40-60 in. (100-150 cm). The islands are subject to drought, flooding, and earthquakes.

ECONOMY

The economy of the U.S. Virgin Islands is based mainly on tourism due to its beautiful beaches, perfect climate, and lovely scenery.

Agriculture - beef and dairy cattle, chickens, eggs, goats, hogs, and vegetables

Manufacturing - aluminum ore refining, concrete products, electronics, petroleum refining, rum production, scientific instruments, textiles, and watches

Exports - alumina, perfume, petroleum products, rum, and watch movements

Imports - building materials, consumer goods, crude oil, and food

LIFE-STYLE

U.S. Virgin Islanders are citizens of the United States. The majority of U.S. Virgin Islands' population live in rural areas, and more than half of all residents make a living in the tourism industry. Others work for the government, in manufacturing, or for the park service. Less than one percent of the islanders are employed in agriculture.

Children ages 4½ to 16 are required to attend school. The Virgin Islands' public school system provides education through high school.

Unlike motorists in the United States and every other U.S. possession, motorists in the U.S. Virgin Islands drive on the left side of the road.

IT'S A FACT!

Crown Mountain - the country's highest point, is located on St. Thomas and rises 1,556 ft. (474 m) above sea level.

The Whim Greathouse - located on St. Croix, the house and grounds of this historical landmark date back to the islands' sugar industry.

 DID YOU KNOW...

- The U.S. Virgin Islands suffered three deaths and about $500 million in damage as a result of 1989's Hurricane Hugo?
- The Virgin Islands were once used by Spaniards as a place to hide their treasure ships from pirates?
- Christopher Columbus arrived at the Virgin Islands in 1493, naming them in memory of St. Ursula and her 11,000 maidens?
- During World War II, the U.S. Virgin Islands served as an outpost to protect the Panama Canal?
- Spanish-speaking people refer to St. Croix as *Santa Cruz*, the name given to the island by Christopher Columbus?
- What is now known as the U.S. Virgin Islands was purchased by the United States in 1917 from Denmark for $25 million?
- The Virgin Islands of the United States are the westernmost of the Virgin Islands, the other half of which are called the British Virgin Islands?

WALES
Division of the United Kingdom

OFFICIAL NAME: Cymru (Wales)
LOCATION: Western Europe
AREA: 8,018 sq. mi. (20,766 sq. km)
POPULATION (Est. 1994): 2,941,000
CAPITAL/LARGEST CITY: Cardiff
GOVERNMENT: Constitutional monarchy headed by the British monarch and governed by a prime minister.
FLAG: Two horizontal stripes of white and green with a red dragon—the symbol of Wales for almost 2,000 years—in the center.
ETHNIC GROUP: Welsh
LANGUAGES: Welsh, English
RELIGION: Protestant (mainly Methodist, Anglican)
BASIC MONETARY UNIT: Pound

GEOGRAPHY

Wales is one of the four countries that make up the United Kingdom of Great Britain and Northern Ireland. Wales is a broad peninsula that occupies about one-tenth of the Island of Great Britain. At its greatest distances, Wales measures 137 mi. (220 km) from north to south and 116 mi. (187 km) from east to west. It has 614 mi. (988 km) of coastline along the Irish Sea, St. George's Channel, Cardigan Bay, and Bristol Channel. Wales's area includes the Isle of Anglesey located off the country's northwest coast.

About two-thirds of Wales's area is occupied by the Cambrian Mountains, mostly in the north. Plateaus with river valleys and coastal plains lie in central and southern Wales. The plateaus feature a variety of terrain: *bogs* (swamplands), forests, grassy plains, *moors* (open wastelands), and pastures. Cliffs are a prominent feature near the coast. The Severn and the Wye are the country's longest rivers.

CLIMATE

Wales has an Atlantic maritime climate that is influenced by the Gulf Stream. The average yearly rainfall is 55 in. (140 cm). Snowstorms in the mountains can be severe. The average temperature ranges from 40°F (4°C) in January to 61°F (16°C) in July and August.

ECONOMY

Wales's economy is based mainly on manufacturing and service industries.

Agriculture - barley, cabbage, cattle (beef and dairy), cauliflower, hay, oats, potatoes, and sheep

Manufacturing - aluminum, chemicals, electrical and electronic equipment, iron, motor vehicle and airplane parts, petroleum products, plastics, steel, synthetic fibers, and tin plate

Mining - coal, limestone, and slate

LIFE-STYLE

Over 75 percent of Wales's people are urban dwellers, with most residents living in the country's southern region. Urban areas feature large public housing developments, which is where many urban dwellers reside. Many of these housing facilities are dilapidated. *Row houses* (connected houses of a similar design) are the most common dwelling for Welsh residents of southern coal-mining towns. Wales's rural population lives largely in stone cottages on small farms and mainly raises livestock.

Welsh dishes are generally simple. A common meal is Welsh lamb with mint sauce. Other favorite dishes include *cawl* (a soup), *laver bread* (made from oatmeal and seaweed), and *Welsh rarebit* (toast covered with butter and melted cheese). Bread and butter is traditionally eaten with canned fruit. Preferred beverages include beer, fruit juice, lemonade, and water.

Popular team sports include cricket, *football* (similar to American soccer), and rugby football. Leisure activities include climbing, fishing, hiking, hunting, and other mountain sports.

Education is free, and children ages five to 16 are required to attend school. Welsh children learn the country's native tongue as either a first or second language.

Wales has a wealth of poets and singers. The traditions of Welsh music and literature date back more than 1,000 years to the days of the *bards* (poet-singers) of the Middle Ages.

IT'S A FACT!

Royal National Eisteddfod - the largest *eisteddfod*, a festival of poetry and music that is held throughout Wales. It is a tradition that dates from the Middle Ages.

The Severn - Britain's longest river, flows 220 mi. (354 km) through Wales and England.

Snowdon - the country's highest point, rises 3,561 ft. (1,085 m) above sea level.

 DID YOU KNOW...
- Prehistoric people lived in Wales's northeastern caves over 200,000 years ago?
- Wales united with England in 1536?
- During the Welsh feast of St. David, residents wear the traditional Welsh symbols of the leek and daffodil?
- The letters j, k, q, v, x, and z are not used in the Welsh language, which is one of the oldest in Europe?
- One of Wales's greatest literary achievements is considered to be the complete translation of the Bible into Welsh, a work that was published in 1588?

WALLIS & FUTUNA
Overseas Territory of France

Île Uvéa
Mata-Utu →★

OFFICIAL NAME: Territoire de Îles Wallis et Futuna
(Territory of the Wallis and Futuna Islands)
LOCATION: South Pacific Ocean
AREA: 106 sq. mi. (274 sq. km)
POPULATION (Est. 1993): 14,175
CAPITAL: Mata-Utu
LARGEST TOWNS: Ono, Vaitupu, Mata-Utu
GOVERNMENT: Self-governing French overseas territory headed by a French-appointed Superior Administrator.
FLAG: Uses the flag of France.
ETHNIC GROUP: Polynesian
LANGUAGES: Wallisian (indigenous Polynesian language), French
RELIGION: Roman Catholic
BASIC MONETARY UNIT: CFP Franc

WALLIS & FUTUNA
South Pacific Ocean

Île Futuna
Sain Chenal
Île Alofi

GEOGRAPHY

Wallis and Futuna consists of the islands of Île Uvéa (Wallis), Île Futuna, and Île Alofi, and 20 islets. Together, the islands have a coastline of about 80 mi. (129 km) along the South Pacific Ocean. Uvéa is located about 125 mi. (200 km) northeast of Futuna and Alofi. Futuna and Alofi—also known together as Îles de Horne (the Hoorn Islands)—are separated by the deep *Sain Chenal* (Sain Channel).

Uvéa has an area of about 24 sq. mi. (63 sq. km). Its eroded, volcanic landscape is dotted with craters that form small lakes. It has sandy beaches surrounded by an enclosing atoll reef and coral islets.

Futuna has an area of about 25 sq. mi. (64 sq. km) and Alofi has an area of about 11 sq. mi. (30 sq. km). Both islands have a rugged, forest-covered, volcanic landscape with hot springs and are ringed by reefs. Alofi is uninhabited.

CLIMATE

Wallis and Futuna has a tropical climate with a hot, rainy season—which lasts from November to April—and a cooler, dry season—which lasts from May to October. The average annual temperature ranges from about 77° to 82°F (25° to 28°C) but may reach as high as 91°F (33°C) during the rainy season. The average annual rainfall is 100 in. (254 cm). Rainfall captured in cisterns supply the islands with fresh water. Mild earthquakes occur periodically on Futuna and Alofi.

ECONOMY

Wallis and Futuna's developing economy is based mainly on coconuts. There is no manufacturing except handicrafts.

Agriculture - bananas, breadfruit, coconuts, livestock (mainly chickens and pigs, some cattle), tapioca, taro, and yams
Fishing - tuna
Forestry - tamanou
Exports - copra and *tapa* (paintings on wood)
Imports - clothing and textiles, food, fuel, and machinery and transport equipment

LIFE-STYLE

Wallis and Futuna was established as a French protectorate in the 1880s and became a French Overseas Territory in 1961. The majority of the country's islanders are employed in subsistence agriculture, business and trade, or public service.

Some have emigrated to nearby New Caledonia for work.

Most homes are built in the traditional manner. They are founded on earthen platforms faced with coral slabs, and are constructed with palm thatch roofs and plaited-reed screens and lattices.

Primary education is offered through Catholic mission schools, which are governmentally funded.

IT'S A FACT!

Mount Bougainville (or Kolofau) - the highest point on Alofi, rises 1,310 ft. (400 m) above sea level.

Mount Singavi (or Mount Puke) - the islands' highest point, is located on Futuna and rises 2,493 ft. (760 m) above sea level.

 DID YOU KNOW...
- Wallis and Futuna was settled by French missionaries in the mid-19th century?
- Uvéa is named for Captain Samuel Wallis of the H.M.S. *Dolphin,* who explored it in 1767?
- Futuna and Alofi were first sighted by Europeans in 1616 by Dutch navigator Jakob Le Maire and were named for the city of Hoorn in Holland?

WESTERN SAHARA

OFFICIAL NAME: Western Sahara
FORMERLY: Province of Spanish Sahara
LOCATION: Northwest Africa
AREA: 102,700 sq. mi. (266,000 sq. km)
POPULATION: 220,000
CAPITAL: none
PRINCIPAL TOWN: El Aaiún
GOVERNMENT: Morocco currently claims and administers the state of Western Sahara. It is yet to be determined whether Western Sahara will become part of Morocco or gain independent status.
ETHNIC GROUPS: Arab, Berber
LANGUAGES: Hassaniya Arabic, Moroccan Arabic
RELIGION: Islam
BASIC MONETARY UNIT: Moroccan Dirham

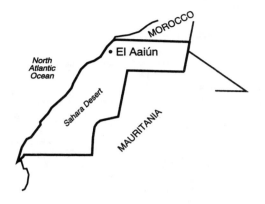

GEOGRAPHY

Western Sahara lies on the northwestern coast of Africa. Its land is completely covered by a portion of the Sahara Desert. Portions of the south and northeast have small mountains but most of the land is a combination of rocky and sandy flatland. Western Sahara has 689 mi. (1,110 km) of coastline along the Atlantic Ocean. The coastal region has the only vegetation: scarce amounts of grass and bushes. The country has very little water and land suitable for agriculture.

CLIMATE

Western Sahara's climate is hot, dry desert with very little rainfall. The mountainous areas are generally cooler and receive slightly more rain. Fog and dew are produced by cold, offshore air currents, and a hot, dry sirocco wind brings dust and sand during winter and spring months. Both factors often cause low visibility. The temperature is very hot during the day, often reaching over 90°F (32°C) in the summer, and gets cool at night.

ECONOMY

Western Sahara's economy is based mainly on fishing, nomadism, and phosphate mining. Subsistence farming produces very little food, thus most food must be imported.
Agriculture - barley, camels, goats, and sheep
Manufacturing - detergents and fertilizers
Mining - iron ore and phosphates
Exports - dried fish and phosphates
Imports - food and fuel

LIFE-STYLE

Western Sahara's population is largely nomadic. These Sahrawi nomads move with their herds of camels, goats, and sheep in search of food and water. Some coastal Sahrawis fish for a living. A few Sahrawis grow fruit and vegetables or barley, during nondrought years, in the scattered oases.

DID YOU KNOW...

- The word *sahara* stems from the Arabic word *sahrá*, meaning "desert"?
- Western Sahara has been ruled by either Spain or Morocco since 1509, and for a few years was divided between and ruled by Mauritania and Morocco?

WESTERN SAMOA

OFFICIAL NAME: The Independent State of Western Samoa
LOCATION: South Pacific Ocean
AREA: 1,093 sq. mi. (2,831 sq. km)
POPULATION (Est. 1993): 170,000
CAPITAL/LARGEST CITY: Apia
GOVERNMENT: Constitutional monarchy.
FLAG: Adopted in 1962. Red field with five white, five-pointed stars—representing the constellation *Southern Cross* —on a blue rectangle in the upper hoist-side quadrant.
ETHNIC GROUP: Samoan (Polynesian)
LANGUAGES: Samoan, English
RELIGION: Christianity
BASIC MONETARY UNIT: Tala

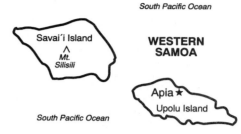

GEOGRAPHY

Western Samoa, an island country, is located about 1,700 mi. (2,740 km) northeast of New Zealand in the Pacific Ocean. The country consists of two main islands, Upolu and Savai'i, plus several smaller islands. The two main islands have a combined coastline of 230 mi. (370 km).

The islands of Western Samoa are mountainous and of volcanic origin. A volcano on Savai'i is still active. The islands are edged by coral reefs, and tropical rainforests can be found on the volcanic peaks located in the centers of the islands.

CLIMATE

Western Samoa enjoys a tropical climate with a cool, dry season (May to November) and a rainy season (December to April). Southeast trade winds keep the temperatures mild and the humidity bearable. The average annual temperature ranges from 75° to 85°F (24° to 29°C). The average rainfall ranges from 70 in. (180 cm) on the northwest coast to more than 150 in. (381 cm) in the southeast. Samoa experiences hurricanes from time to time.

ECONOMY

Western Samoa's economy is based largely on agriculture, but tourism is becoming a major growth industry.

Agriculture - bananas, cacao, coconuts, taro, and yams
Exports - cacao, coconut oil, and copra
Imports - food, manufactured goods, and petroleum products

LIFE-STYLE

Samoans live much as their ancestors did. They build their own houses, raise most of their own food, and make most of their clothing. They live in open-sided houses, called *fale*, that have thatched roofs supported by poles. Palm leaf blinds can be lowered for privacy or when it rains. Life centers around the extended family group called *aiga*. A *matai*, who serves as head of the family, is elected by the aiga.

Western Samoan clothing is very simple. Men wear a *lava-lava*, a piece of cloth wrapped around the waist. Women wear a longer *lava-lava* with a blouse-like garment called a *puletasi*.

Diet consists of boar, fish, poultry, and tropical fruits and vegetables. Because of the tropical climate, Samoans often prepare their foods over an open fire away from the main house.

Singing and dancing serves as both a popular recreational activity and a means of handing down history and tradition. Some Samoans enjoy a Samoan version of the English game, cricket.

Education is free, but it is not mandatory. A very high percentage of the people can read and write.

Western Samoans enjoy relatively good health. This is due in large part to good medical care that is provided free in government hospitals.

IT'S A FACT!

Mount Silisili - the country's highest point, is located on Savai'i and rises 6,095 ft. (1,858 m.) above sea level.

Vailima - located in Apia, is the former home of writer Robert Louis Stevenson and is now the official residence of the head of state.

 DID YOU KNOW...

- Some scholars believe Samoa is the "cradle of Polynesia," the origin of all Oceania's Polynesians?
- The famous writer Robert Louis Stevenson lived in Western Samoa and is buried near Apia?

YEMEN

OFFICIAL NAME: Al Jumhuriyah al Yamaniyah (Republic of Yemen)
FORMERLY: Yemen (Aden) and Yemen (Sana), or South/Southern Yemen and North/Northern Yemen (until 1990)
LOCATION: Southwestern Arabian Peninsula
AREA: 203,877 sq. mi. (528,038 sq. km)
POPULATION (Est. 1993): 13,013,000
CAPITAL: Sana
LARGEST CITIES: Sana, Aden
GOVERNMENT: Republic headed by a five-member ruling council that includes a president, a vice-president, and three other leaders.
FLAG: Three horizontal stripes of red, white, and black.
ETHNIC GROUP: Arab
LANGUAGE: Arabic
RELIGION: Islam
BASIC MONETARY UNIT: Yemeni Rial

GEOGRAPHY

Yemen has 1,020 mi. (1,642 km) of coastline along the Arabian Sea, the Gulf of Aden, and the Red Sea. The country's area includes the islands of Kamaran and Perim in the Red Sea and Socotra Island in the Indian Ocean.

Yemen is flat along its southern and western coasts. Bordering the coastal plain along the Red Sea are rocky hills that rise to steep cliffs. Broad valleys and plateaus surrounded by high mountains lie east of the cliffs. Beyond this, an area of desert extends into Saudi Arabia.

The plain along the southern coast is bordered by a hilly plateau, beyond which lies desert. This plain and plateau contain some fertile areas. Since the 1980s the country has strove to convert desert into farmland.

CLIMATE

Yemen's climate is mostly desert. It is hot and humid along the west coast, and extremely hot and dry in the eastern desert areas. The mountainous areas have a temperate climate. The average annual temperature along the west coast ranges from 68° to 130°F (20° to 54°C). Temperatures are cooler at higher elevations. The average annual rainfall is 5 in. (13 cm) in the city of Aden and 10-15 in. (25 to 38 cm) at higher elevations. Desert areas may go without rain for five years or longer.

ECONOMY

Yemen's economy is based primarily on farming, foreign aid, outside earnings, and the petroleum industry.

Agriculture - apricots, bananas, barley, cattle, citrus fruits, coffee, cotton, *durra* (a sorghum), grapes, *khat,* millet, papayas, pomegranates, poultry, sesame, sheep, vegetables, and wheat

Manufacturing - building materials, cement, cotton textiles, handicrafts, leather goods, petroleum refining, and processed foods

Mining - petroleum

Exports - coffee, cotton, crude oil, dried and salted fish, hides, and vegetables

Imports - cement, chemicals, flour, food, grain, machinery, manufactured consumer goods, petroleum, textiles, and sugar

LIFE-STYLE

Most Yemeni make a living by farming or herding. Many others are craftworkers—famous for their textiles, leatherwork, and iron work since ancient times. They make such things as brassware, inlaid *jambiyas* (daggers), jewelry, and wooden chests. Many of the goods used by the Yemeni are also made by hand: dyed and woven cloth, glassware, pottery, rope, and saddles. The Yemeni living in coastal regions make a living by fishing. Many young men leave the country to find work.

Dwellings range from modern houses and apartment buildings in cities to three- or four-story mud-brick houses in towns. Many residents near the Red Sea coast live in straw huts.

Some Yemeni—especially those in urban areas—wear Western-style clothing. Others wear traditional clothing, which consists of cotton breeches or a striped *futa* (kilt) for men, and long robes, black shawls, and veils for women. Men may also wear skull caps, turbans, or *tarbooshes* (tall, round hats).

Staples of the diet include bread, fish, lamb, rice, and vegetables. *Salta* (a spicy stew) is the national dish.

Most Yemeni men and some women chew khat, which releases a mildly intoxicating stimulant.

About one-sixth of the population age 15 and older are literate. Cities and larger towns have public schools. Children in rural areas are educated in Muslim religious schools.

Automobiles and trucks are the major means of transportation, yet many Yemeni still use camels, donkeys, and horses.

IT'S A FACT!

Mount Hadur Shuay - the country's highest point, rises 12,336 ft. (3,760 m) above sea level.

DID YOU KNOW...

- Sana is shaped like a figure 8, and its central district is surrounded by a high wall that has eight gates for entering and leaving?
- Yemen is famous for its Mocha coffee?
- Aden has served as an important port and trading center since ancient Roman times?

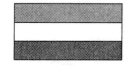

YUGOSLAVIA

OFFICIAL NAME: Federativna Republika Jugoslavija (Federal Republic of Yugoslavia)
LOCATION: Southeastern Europe
AREA: 39,499 sq. mi. (102,173 sq. km)
POPULATION (Est. 1993): 10,643,000
CAPITAL: Belgrade
LARGEST CITIES: Belgrade, Novi Sad, Nis, Subotica
GOVERNMENT: Republic governed by a president.
FLAG: Three horizontal stripes of blue, white, and red.
ETHNIC GROUPS: Serb, Montenegrin, Albanian, Hungarian, Slovak, Romanian
LANGUAGE: Serbo-Croatian
RELIGIONS: Serbian Orthodox Church, Ethnic Churches (such as Hungarian Evangelical Lutheran and Slovak Evangelical Christian)
BASIC MONETARY UNIT: Yugoslav New Dinar

GEOGRAPHY

Yugoslavia was formerly made up of six dependent republics. Between 1991 and 1992, four of these six republics—Bosnia-Herzegovina, Croatia, Macedonia, and Slovenia—became independent. Today, Yugoslavia is made up of the republics of Serbia and Montenegro.

At its greatest distances, Yugoslavia measures 305 mi. (490 km) from north to south and 235 mi. (380 km) from east to west. It has 124 mi. (199 km) of coastline along the Adriatic Sea.

Yugoslavia has three main land regions: 1) the Coastal Plain, 2) the Interior Highlands, and 3) the Pannonian Plains. The Coastal Plain is a narrow piece of land along the Adriatic Sea that has rocky cliffs and little fertile soil. The Interior Highlands are generally hilly or mountainous. Earthquakes often plague this region. The Pannonian Plains are located in the north. They are generally flat with a few low hills, and contain the country's richest soil. About one-half of the country is covered by farmland, and about one-fourth is covered by forests. The country's longest river is the Danube, which flows out of Hungary in the northwest, through Belgrade, and on to Bulgaria.

CLIMATE

Yugoslavia's climate varies by region. The Coastal Plain has mild winters and hot, sunny summers. The Interior Highlands have snowy, bitterly cold winters. Heavy rains fall in early summer, and temperatures range from cool in the mountains to warm in the valleys. The Pannonian Plains have cold winters and hot, dry summers. Spring and autumn bring heavy rainfall and frequent flooding.

ECONOMY

Yugoslavia's economy is based on its large variety of natural resources, including rich farmlands, forests, and mineral resources. In Montenegro, tourism is a good source of income.

Agriculture - cherries, corn, figs, grapes, livestock (cattle, hogs, and sheep), olives, peaches, pears, plums, potatoes, tobacco, and wheat

Manufacturing - aluminum, automobiles, cement, iron and steel, paper, plastics, textiles, and trucks

Mining - bauxite, coal, copper ore, lead, and zinc

Exports - chemicals, machinery, manufactured goods, metals, processed foods, shoes, textiles, tobacco, and wood products

Imports - chemicals, food, fuels, livestock, machinery, manufactured goods, and raw materials

LIFE-STYLE

Yugoslavia's population is approximately 50 percent urban, with most living in older apartment buildings or homes. More modern apartment buildings are available for those living in suburban areas. Rural residents mainly live in shelters made of brick, stone, or wood.

Serbians are known for their highly seasoned meats and spicy salads. Common beverages in Yugoslavia are plum brandy and thick, sweet Turkish coffee.

The most popular sports are soccer and basketball. During the winter, many people hike, hunt, or ski in the mountains. In the summer, they fish, swim, or enjoy other water sports in the Adriatic Sea.

Education is free, and children ages seven to 14 are required to attend school.

A good road system extends from Belgrade. Roads throughout the rest of the country are not as well developed.

IT'S A FACT!

The Iron Gate - a gorge located in the Carpathian Mountains, is considered one of Europe's greatest natural wonders.

Mount Daravica - the country's highest point, rises 8,714 ft. (2,656 m) above sea level.

 DID YOU KNOW...

- The name *Yugoslavia* means "Land of the South Slavs"?
- The 4th-century emperor Constantine I (the Great) was born in the city of Nis?
- About 10 mi. (16 km) inland from the Gulf of Kotor is the "wettest place in Europe," so named because it has an average annual rainfall of 180 in. (457 cm)?

ZAIRE

OFFICIAL NAME: République du Zaïre (Republic of Zaire)
FORMERLY: Congo
LOCATION: Central Africa
AREA: 905,568 sq. mi. (2,345,409 sq. km)
POPULATION (Est. 1992): 38,338,000
CAPITAL: Kinshasa
LARGEST CITIES: Kinshasa, Lubumbashi, Kananga, Mbuji-Mayi
GOVERNMENT: Republic governed by a president.
FLAG: Yellow circle centered on a light green field. The circle features a black arm holding a brown torch with a red flame.
ETHNIC GROUPS: Black (over 200 African ethnic groups), Pygmy, European
LANGUAGES: About 200 local languages (most of which belong to the Bantu language group) and four regional languages (including Kikongo, Lingala, Swahili, Tshiluba), French
RELIGIONS: Christianity (including Roman Catholic, Protestant, and Kimbanguists), Islam, Traditional African Religions
BASIC MONETARY UNIT: Zaire

GEOGRAPHY

At its greatest distances, Zaire measures 1,300 mi. (2,090 km) from north to south and 1,300 mi. (2,090 km) from east to west. It has 25 mi. (40 km) of coastline along the Atlantic Ocean.

Zaire can be divided into three regions: 1) a tropical rainforest, 2) savannas, and 3) a highland. Northern Zaire is mainly rainforest, with a small strip of savanna in the extreme north. A savanna also covers most of southern Zaire, which is dotted with trees and has some small forests in its valleys. The highland region forms the country's eastern and southeastern borders and consists of plateaus and mountains.

CLIMATE

The equator runs through the rainforest in northern Zaire. North of the equator, the rainy season usually lasts from April to October. South of the equator, the rainy season usually lasts from November to March.

Zaire's tropical region is hot and humid almost all year. Its average annual daytime temperature is 90°F (32°C) with an average annual rainfall of 80 in. (203 cm), much of which falls during heavy thunderstorms. The savanna regions have an average annual daytime temperature of 75°F (24°C) with an average annual rainfall of 37 in. (94 cm). The highland region has an average annual daytime temperature of 70°F (21°C) with an average annual rainfall of 48 in. (122 cm).

ECONOMY

Although presently a poor country, Zaire has a developing economy. It is one of the world's largest sources of copper and the world's leading producer of industrial diamonds.

Agriculture - bananas, cassava, cocoa, coffee, corn, cotton, peanuts, rice, and tea

Forestry - palm oil, rubber, and timber

Manufacturing - beer, cement, processed foods, soft drinks, steel, textiles, and tires

Mining - cadmium, cobalt, copper, gold, industrial diamonds, manganese, petroleum, silver, tin, and zinc

Exports - cobalt, coffee, copper, industrial diamonds, palm oil, and petroleum

Imports - food, fuels, manufactured goods, textiles, and transport equipment

LIFE-STYLE

Zaire's population is about three-fifths rural. Most rural Zairians live in villages and work as farmers. Their houses are constructed of mud bricks or dried mud and sticks with thatched roofs. Younger rural Zairians are moving to urban areas and looking for jobs in business, industry, or government, causing overcrowding and unemployment. Urban apartments and houses are mainly constructed of baked mud bricks or cinder blocks. Wealthier urban Zairians live in bungalows.

Male Zairians usually wear a shirt with short or long trousers while females usually wear a long, one-piece dress or a blouse with a long skirt.

Staples of the diet include bananas, beans, cassava, corn, fruits, peanuts, potatoes, rice, vegetables, and yams. Fish and meat are eaten only when affordable. The most popular beverage is beer.

Recreational activities include dancing, listening to Zairian jazz and drum music, socializing, and playing sports, the most popular of which is soccer. Their arts include mask, pottery, raffia weaving, and carved wooden statues.

Zaire has poor education and health programs. Children ages six to 12 are required to attend school, but the law is rarely enforced. Few physicians are available and diseases are widespread, the most common of which include AIDS, cholera, malaria, and yellow fever. Most Zairians suffer from malnutrition, due to a lack of protein in their diet.

IT'S A FACT!

Congo River - the world's fifth largest river, flows 2,900 mi. (4,667 km), is Zaire's most important waterway, and carries more water than all but the Amazon River.

Margherita Peak - the country's highest point, rises 16,762 ft. (5,109 m) above sea level. It is also considered Uganda's highest point.

DID YOU KNOW...

- Zaire is Africa's third largest country in area, following Sudan and Algeria?
- The *okapi* (related to the giraffe) makes its home in the forest and can be found only in Zaire?

ZAMBIA

OFFICIAL NAME: Republic of Zambia
FORMERLY: Northern Rhodesia
LOCATION: South-central Africa
AREA: 290,586 sq. mi. (752,614 sq. km)
POPULATION (Est. 1992): 9,093,000
CAPITAL: Lusaka
LARGEST CITIES: Lusaka, Kitwe, Ndola, Chingola
GOVERNMENT: Republic headed by a president.
FLAG: Green field with an orange eagle in the upper fly-side corner. Three vertical stripes of red, black, and orange —representing freedom, the people, and mineral wealth, accordingly—are under the eagle.
ETHNIC GROUPS: Over 70 different African ethnic groups
LANGUAGES: Bantu, eight major local languages, English
RELIGIONS: Christianity, Islam, Hinduism, Traditional African Religions
BASIC MONETARY UNIT: Zambian Kwacha

GEOGRAPHY

At its greatest distances, Zambia, a landlocked country, measures 700 mi. (1,127 km) from north to south and 900 mi. (1,448 km) from east to west.

Zambia lies on a plateau and is mainly bush and tree covered flatland. The Muchinga Mountains lie in the northeast. The Zambezi River—for which the country takes its name—lies in the west and flows southward, flooding a plain in the southwest.

CLIMATE

Zambia has a mild tropical climate as a result of its altitude. Temperatures during the winter season—May to August—range from 60° to 80°F (16° to 27°C). Midday temperatures during the summer season—September to November—range from 80° to 100°F (27° to 38°C). Zambia's rainy season, which lasts from November to April, is violent and often floods the rivers by March. The average annual rainfall ranges from about 50 in. (130 cm) in the north to about 20-30 in. (51-76 cm) in the south.

ECONOMY

Zambia is one of the world's largest producers of copper, with about four-fifths of its export income coming from copper and its products.

Agriculture - cassava, cattle, coffee, corn, cotton, eggs, goats, millet, peanuts, rice, sorghum, sugar cane, sunflowers, and tobacco

Fishing - perch and whitebait

Manufacturing - beverages, cement, chemicals, construction, copper products, fertilizers, flour, food, textiles, and wood products

Mining - coal, cobalt, copper, lead, and zinc

Exports - cobalt, copper, lead, tobacco, and zinc

Imports - food, fuels, machinery, manufactures, and transportation equipment

LIFE-STYLE

Zambia's population is almost equally rural and urban. In remote rural villages, life is much the same as it has been for hundreds of years. The people make a living by farming and live in circular, grass-roofed huts. With the development of mining, more rural Zambians are moving to mining towns. Modern clothing is commonly worn in Zambia, though rural women usually make their own clothing.

The staple of the diet is corn. A favorite dish is *nshima* (a dough or thick porridge made from cassava, corn, or millet), which is sometimes eaten with a relish of fish or meat stew and vegetables. Beer is the most common beverage.

Popular sports include basketball, golf, soccer, and tennis. Music is an important part of Zambian culture and other recreational activities include dancing, and *ifisela* (drama). Zambian art is mainly traditional and consists of basket weaving, painting, pottery, and wood carving.

Education is free, but children are required to bring their own paper to class. Most Zambian children attend elementary school, but only about one-fifth continue on to high school.

Zambian health conditions are poor due to poor living conditions, a shortage of medical personnel, and inadequate health care facilities. Commonly suffered diseases include diarrhea, malnutrition, and measles among children, and AIDS, malaria, parasitic infection, and pneumonia among adults.

IT'S A FACT!

Kariba Dam - located on the Zambezi River, is one of the world's largest hydroelectric projects and serves both Zambia and the neighboring country of Zimbabwe.

Victoria Falls - located on the Zambezi River in the south, is one of the world's most beautiful waterfalls.

 DID YOU KNOW...

- Between 1953 and 1963, Zambia (formerly Northern Rhodesia) was part of the Federation of Rhodesia and Nyasaland with Zimbabwe (formerly Southern Rhodesia) and Malawi (formerly Nyasaland)?
- Most Zambians do not know their age as they don't celebrate their birthdays?
- Zambia gained its independence in 1964?
- Most rural Zambians brew their own alcohol?

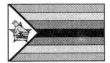

ZIMBABWE

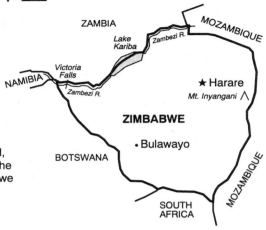

OFFICIAL NAME: Republic of Zimbabwe
FORMERLY: Rhodesia (until 1980)
LOCATION: Southern Africa
AREA: 150,804 sq. mi. (390,580 sq. km)
POPULATION (Est. 1993): 10,643,000
CAPITAL: Harare
LARGEST CITIES: Harare, Bulawayo
GOVERNMENT: Parliamentary democracy headed by a president.
FLAG: Seven horizontal stripes of green, yellow, red, black, red, yellow, and green with a black-edged white triangle on the hoist side. The triangle features a yellow Great Zimbabwe bird superimposed on a red star.
ETHNIC GROUP: Black (Shona, Ndebele, and other ethnic groups)
LANGUAGES: English, Shona
RELIGIONS: Traditional African Religions, Christianity
BASIC MONETARY UNIT: Zimbabwean Dollar

GEOGRAPHY

Zimbabwe, a landlocked country in Southern Africa, consists mainly of a high plateau. There are three main land regions: 1) the High Veld, 2) the Middle Veld, and 3) the Low Veld. The country's major cities are located in the High Veld (grasslands), a central plateau that crosses Zimbabwe from northeast to southwest. The Middle Veld falls on either side of the High Veld. The Low Veld includes sandy plains in the Zambezi and other river basins.

CLIMATE

Although the country is located in the tropics, its high altitude provides a mild climate. Summer lasts from October to April and is hot and wet. Winter is from May to September and is cool and dry.

The average temperature ranges from 54° to 85°F (12° to 29°C). The average annual rainfall ranges from 15 in. (38 cm) in the west to 50 in. (130 cm) in the east.

ECONOMY

Since 1965, Zimbabwe's economy has struggled due to civil war, economic sanctions, and most recently the worst drought in this century.

Agriculture - cattle, coffee, corn, cotton, sugar, tea, tobacco, and wheat

Manufacturing - chemicals, clothing and footwear, iron and steel, metal products, processed foods, and textiles

Mining - asbestos, chromite, coal, copper, gems, gold, and nickel

Exports - asbestos, chrome, coal, copper, corn, cotton, equipment, footwear, furniture, gold, nickel, sugar, tea, tin, and tobacco

Imports - food, machinery, petroleum products, and transport equipment

LIFE-STYLE

The majority of Zimbabweans (98 percent) are black, of which three-fourths live in rural areas. Most are farmers, raising only enough to feed their families. Many work on commercial farms owned by whites, while others work in towns and cities. Urban families often have running water and electricity, but some rural families still live in thatched-roof homes without modern conveniences.

The traditional extended family is still prevalent in rural areas, but nuclear families are becoming the rule in urban settings. Family ties are extremely strong and the elderly are considered a family treasure. Polygamy is still common in parts of the country. The father makes all final decisions and supports the entire family.

The staple food for most Zimbabweans is *sadza*, a stiff porridge made from maize or cornmeal. Vegetables and meat, when available, are also eaten. Fruit, such as mangoes, bananas, melons, guavas, and papayas are popular. Tea is a popular drink. In rural areas, parents and children eat separately.

The majority of Zimbabweans wear Western-style clothing. Most women wear cotton dresses. Traditional African dress is usually reserved for special occasions.

Almost three-fourths of the people of Zimbabwe are literate. The government is working to provide free, compulsory education for all.

Soccer is the most popular sport. Other sports enjoyed by many are tennis, boxing, rugby, cricket, polo, bowling, field hockey, squash, golf, and horse racing. The people also enjoy swimming in outdoor pools.

IT'S A FACT!

Mount Inyangani - the country's highest point, rises 8,514 ft. (2,595 m) above sea level.

Victoria Falls - located in northwestern Zimbabwe on the Zambezi River, is about 1 mi. (1.6 km) wide and falls from a height of 256-355 ft. (78-108 m). The falls create a mist and a constant roar, earning it the name *Mosi oa Tunya*, meaning "smoke that thunders," given by the locals.

 DID YOU KNOW...
- The word *Zimbabwe* means "house of stone" in the Shona language?
- Zimbabwe is a leading mineral producer?

Appendix A

CONTINENT MAPS

AFRICA

AFRICA IN BRIEF

AREA: 11,681,000 sq. mi. (30,253,000 sq. km)
GREATEST DISTANCES: 5,000 mi. (8,047 km) N–S; 4,700 mi. (7,564 km) E–W
COASTLINE: 22,921 mi. (36,888 km)
POPULATION (Est. 1995): 717,000,000
HIGHEST POINT: Mount Kilimanjaro in Tanzania - 19,340 ft. (5,895 m) above sea level
LOWEST POINT: Lake Assal in Djibouti - 509 ft. (155 m) below sea level
DESERTS: Kalahari, Namib, Sahara
LAKES: Chad, Nyasa (Malawi), Tanganyika, Turkana, Victoria
MOUNTAIN RANGES: Ahaggar, Atlas, Drakensberg, Tibesti
RIVERS: Congo, Limpopo, Niger, Nile, Orange, Zambezi

ANTARCTICA

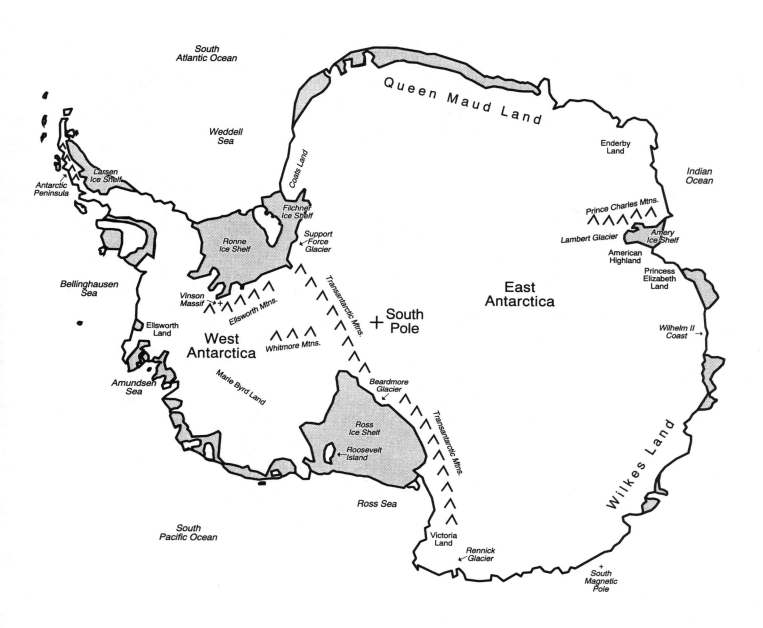

ANTARCTICA IN BRIEF

AREA:	5,400,000 sq. mi. (14,000,000 sq. km)
GREATEST DISTANCE:	3,450 mi. (5,550 km) from Antarctica Peninsula to Wilhelm II Coast
COASTLINE:	19,800 mi. (31,900 km)
HIGHEST POINT:	Vinson Massif - 16,864 ft. (5,140 m) above sea level
LOWEST POINT:	Sea level
GLACIERS:	Beardmore, Lambert, Rennick, Support Force
ICE SHELVES:	Amery, Filchner, Larsen, Ronne, Ross
MOUNTAIN RANGES:	Antarctic Peninsula, Ellsworth, Prince Charles, Transantarctic, Whitmore

ASIA

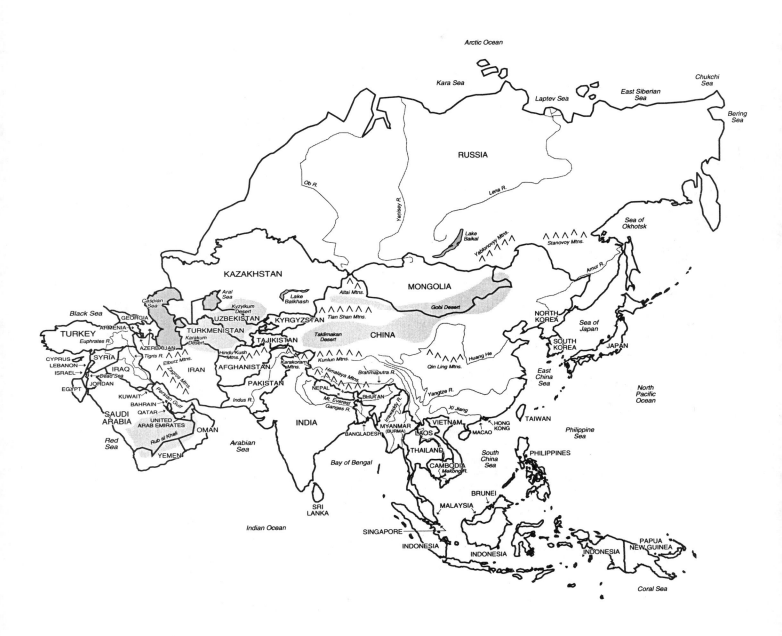

ASIA IN BRIEF

AREA: 16,992,000 sq. mi. (44,008,000 sq. km)
GREATEST DISTANCES: About 5,400 mi. (8,690 km) N–S; about 6,000 mi. (9,700 km) E–W
COASTLINE: 80,205 mi. (129,077 km)
POPULATION (Est. 1995): 3,506,000,000
HIGHEST POINT: Mount Everest, along China/Nepal border - 29,028 ft. (8,848 m) above sea level
LOWEST POINT: Shore of the Dead Sea, along Israel/Jordan - 1,310 ft. (399 m) below sea level
DESERTS: Gobi, Karakum, Kyzylkum, Rub al Khali, Taklimakan
LAKES: Baikal, Balkhash
MOUNTAIN RANGES: Altai, Elburz, Himalaya, Hindu Kush, Karakoram, Kunlun, Qin Ling, Stanovoy, Tian Shan, Yablonovyy, Zagros
RIVERS: Amur, Brahmaputra, Euphrates, Ganges, Huang He, Indus, Irrawaddy, Lena, Mekong, Ob, Tigris, Xi Jiang, Yangtze, Yenisey

AUSTRALIA

AUSTRALIA IN BRIEF

AREA: 2,978,147 sq. mi. (7,713,364 sq. km)
GREATEST DISTANCES: 1,950 mi. (3,138 km) N–S; 2,475 mi. (3,983 km) E–W (mainland)
COASTLINE: 17,366 mi. (27,948 km), including Tasmania and offshore islands
POPULATION (Est. 1995): 17,820,000
HIGHEST POINT: Mount Kosciusko - 7,310 ft. (2,228 m) above sea level
LOWEST POINT: Lake Eyre - 52 ft. (16 m) below sea level
DESERTS: Gibson, Great Sandy, Great Victoria
REEF: Great Barrier
RIVERS: Darling, Murray
MOUNTAINS: Australian Alps, Darling, Hamersley, MacDonnell, Musgrave, Snowy

EUROPE

EUROPE IN BRIEF

AREA: 4,033,000 sq. mi. (10,445,000 sq. km)
GREATEST DISTANCES: 3,000 mi. (4,800 km) N–S; 4,000 mi. (6,400 km) E–W
COASTLINE: 37,887 mi. (60,973 km)
POPULATION (Est. 1995): 709,000,000
HIGHEST POINT: Mount Elbrus in Russia - 18,510 ft. (5,642 m) above sea level
LOWEST POINT: Shore of the Caspian Sea - 92 ft. (28 m) below sea level
ISLANDS: Balearic Islands, British Isles, Corsica, Crete, Faeroe Islands, Iceland, Malta, Sardinia, Shetland Islands, Sicily
LAKES: Caspian Sea, Ladoga
MOUNTAIN RANGES: Alps, Apennines, Balkans, Carpathians, Caucasus, Pyrenees, Sierra Nevada
RIVERS: Danube, Don, Elbe, Rhine, Rhône, Seine, Thames, Volga

 IF8201 Comprehensive World Reference Guide

NORTH AMERICA

Bering Sea

Arctic Ocean

Greenland Sea

GREENLAND

U.S.A.

Yukon R.

Beaufort Sea

Queen Elizabeth Islands

Ellesmere I.

Alaska Mtns.

+ Mt. McKinley

Banks I.

Devon I.

Baffin Bay

Gulf of Alaska

Mackenzie R.

Great Bear Lake

Victoria I.

Baffin I.

North Pacific Ocean

Great Slave Lake

Southampton I.

Labrador Sea

Coast Mtns.

Rocky Mtns.

Lake Athabasca

Hudson Bay

Newfoundland Island (CANADA)

Vancouver Island (CANADA)

Fraser R.

CANADA

Nelson R.

Gulf of St. Lawrence

Columbia R.

Lake Winnipeg

St. Lawrence R.

Cascade Mtns.

Rocky Mtns.

Missouri R.

Lake Superior

Lake Huron

North Atlantic Ocean

Sierra Nevada Mtns.

Great Basin

Great Salt Lake

Great Salt Lake

Lake Michigan

Lake Ontario

Mississippi R.

Lake Erie

Death Valley

Colorado R.

UNITED STATES OF AMERICA

Missouri R.

Appalachian Highlands

Hawaiian Islands (U.S.A.)

Painted Desert

Mojave Desert

Arkansas R.

Ohio R.

Mississippi R.

Rio Grande

BAHAMAS

North Pacific Ocean

Sierra Madre Occidental

Sierra Madre Oriental

Gulf of Mexico

DOMINICAN REPUBLIC

MEXICO

CUBA

JAMAICA

HAITI

PUERTO RICO

BELIZE

HONDURAS

Caribbean Sea

NETHERLANDS ANTILLES

GUATEMALA

NICARAGUA

Lake Nicaragua

TRINIDAD & TOBAGO

EL SALVADOR

PANAMA

COSTA RICA

NORTH AMERICA IN BRIEF

AREA: 9,348,000 sq. mi.
(24,211,000 sq. km)
GREATEST DISTANCES: 5,400 mi. (8,900 km) N–S;
5,400 mi. (8,900 km) E–W (including islands)
COASTLINE: About 190,000 mi. (300,000 km)
POPULATION (Est. 1995): 453,000,000
HIGHEST POINT: Mount McKinley in United States of America - 20,320 ft. (6,194 m) above sea level
LOWEST POINT: Death Valley in United States of America - 282 ft. (86 m) below sea level
DESERTS: Great Basin, Mojave, Painted
ISLANDS: Cuba, Greenland, Hispaniola (Haiti and Dominican Republic), Jamaica, Newfoundland, Puerto Rico, Vancouver
LAKES: Athabasca, Erie, Great Bear, Great Salt, Great Slave, Huron, Michigan, Nicaragua, Ontario, Superior, Winnipeg
MOUNTAIN RANGES: Alaska, Appalachian, Cascade, Coast, Rocky, Sierra Madre, Sierra Nevada
RIVERS: Arkansas, Colorado, Columbia, Fraser, Mackenzie, Mississippi, Missouri, Nelson, Ohio, Rio Grande, St. Lawrence, Yukon

SOUTH AMERICA

Gulf of Venezuela

Caribbean Sea

Lake Maracaibo

VENEZUELA

Orinoco R.

North Atlantic Ocean

Gulf of Darién

North Pacific Ocean

Andes Mtns.

Magdalena R.

COLOMBIA

Angel Falls

Cuquenán Falls

GUYANA

SURINAME

FRENCH GUIANA

Marajó Island (BRAZIL)

Galapagos Islands (ECUADOR)

ECUADOR

Guiana Highlands

Amazon R.

Amazon R.

Gulf of Guayaquil

PERU

Andes Mtns.

Purus R.

Madeira R.

BRAZIL

Brazilian Highlands

São Francisco R.

Lake Titicaca

BOLIVIA

Lake Poopó

Paraguay R.

South Pacific Ocean

Atacama Desert

Pilcomayo R.

PARAGUAY

Alto Paraná R.

CHILE

Andes Mtns.

Paraná R.

Uruguay R.

South Atlantic Ocean

URUGUAY

Mirim Lake

+ Aconcagua

ARGENTINA

Patagonia

San Matías Gulf

Valdés Peninsula

San Jorge Gulf

FALKLAND ISLANDS

Tierra del Fuego (CHILE/ARGENTINA)

SOUTH AMERICA IN BRIEF

AREA: 6,885,000 sq. mi. (17,833,000 sq. km)
GREATEST DISTANCES: 4,750 mi. (7,645 km) N–S; 3,200 mi. (5,150 km) E–W
COASTLINE: 20,000 mi. (32,000 km)
POPULATION (Est. 1995): 318,000,000
HIGHEST POINT: Aconcagua in Argentina - 22,831 ft. (6,959 m) above sea level
LOWEST POINT: Valdés Peninsula in Argentina - 131 ft. (40 m) below sea level
DESERTS: Atacama, Patagonia

ISLANDS: Falkland Islands, Galapagos Islands, Marajó, Tierra del Fuego
LAKES: Maracaibo, Mirim, Poopó, Titicaca
MOUNTAIN RANGES: Andes, Brazilian Highlands, Guiana Highlands
RIVERS: Amazon, Madeira, Magdalena, Orinoco, Paraguay, Paraná, Pilcomayo, Purus, São Francisco, Uruguay
WATERFALLS: Angel, Cuquenán

Appendix B

BLANK MAP OUTLINES

AFRICA

ANTARCTICA

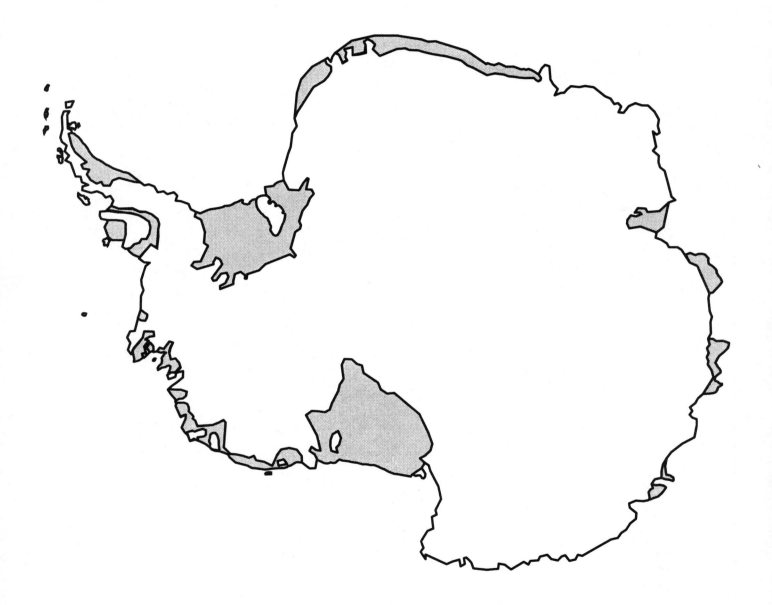

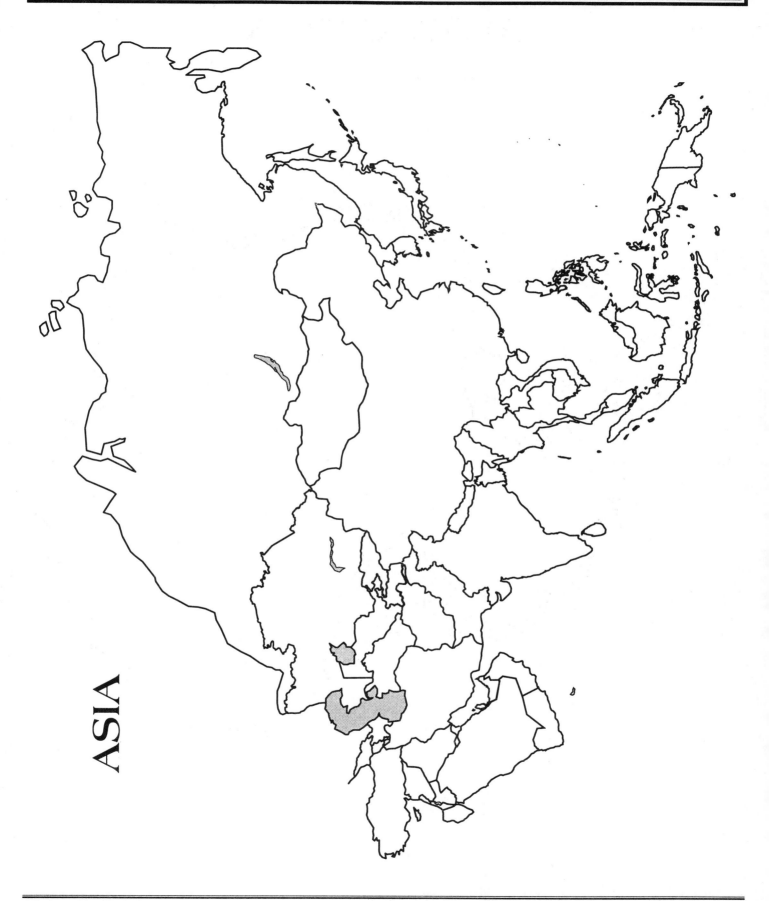

ASIA

AUSTRALIA

CANADA

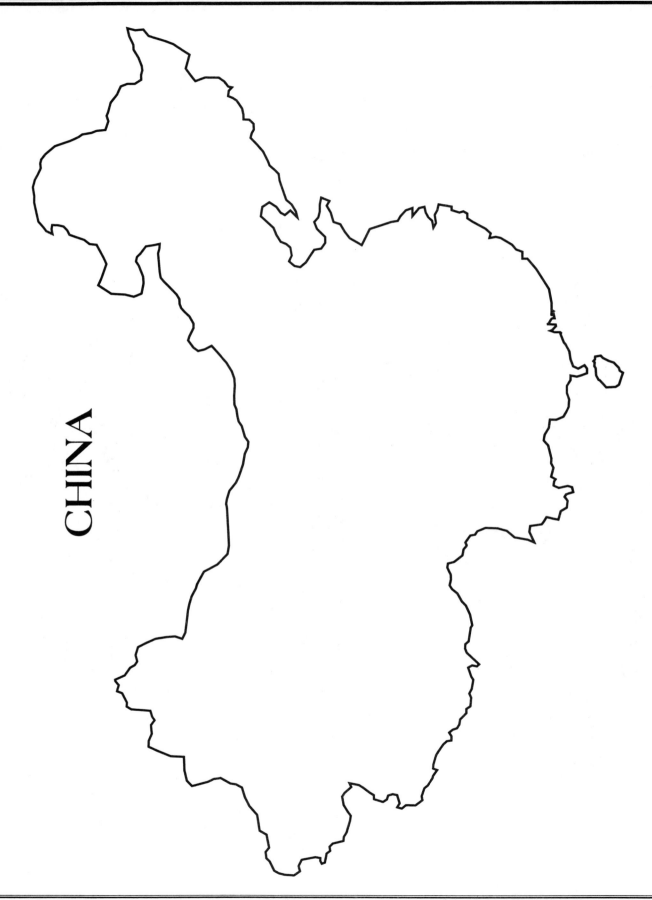

CHINA

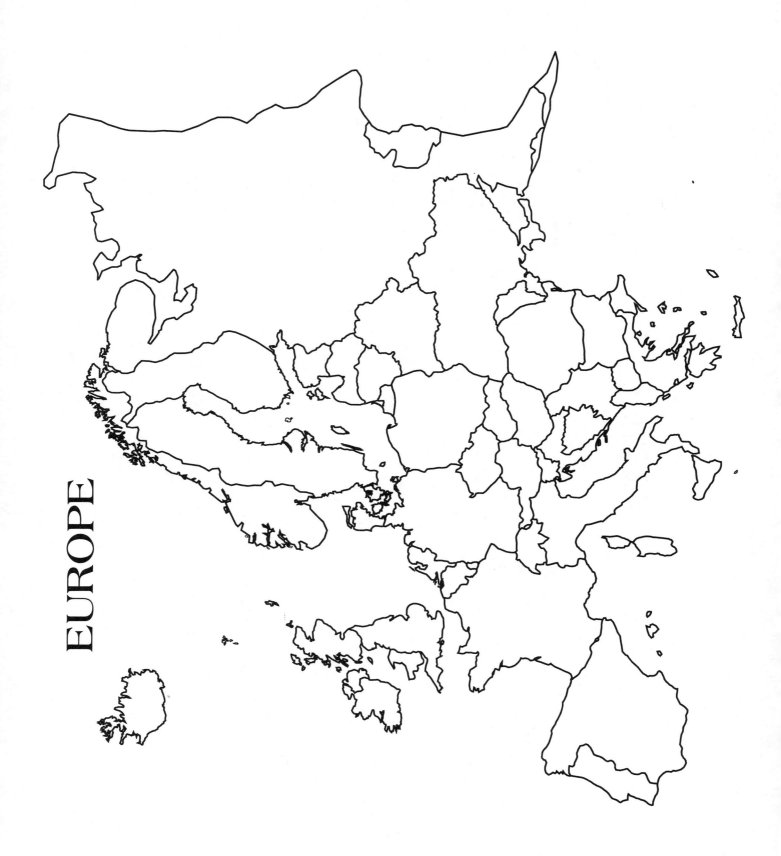

EUROPE

FRANCE

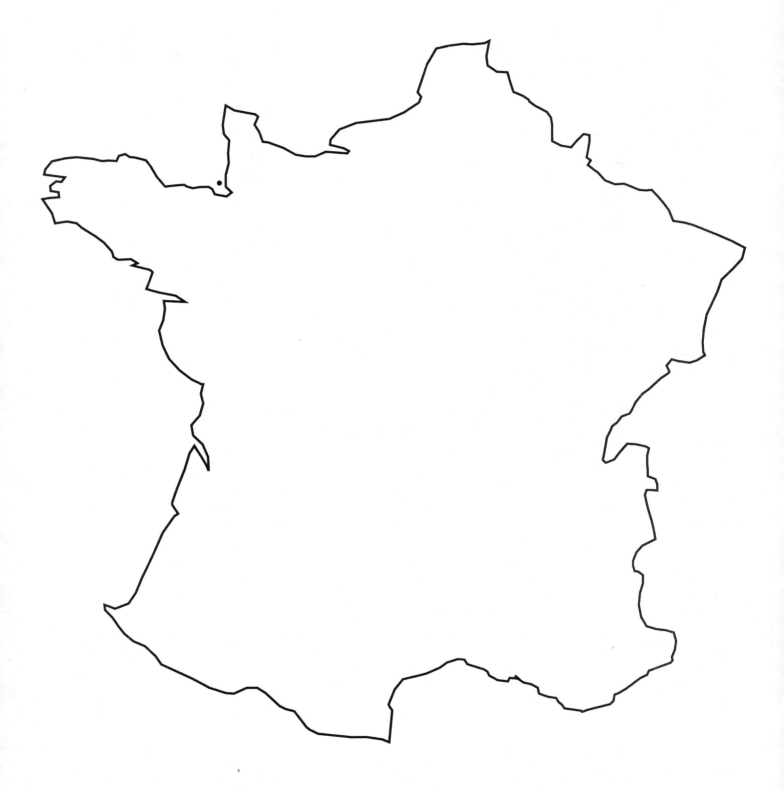

JAPAN

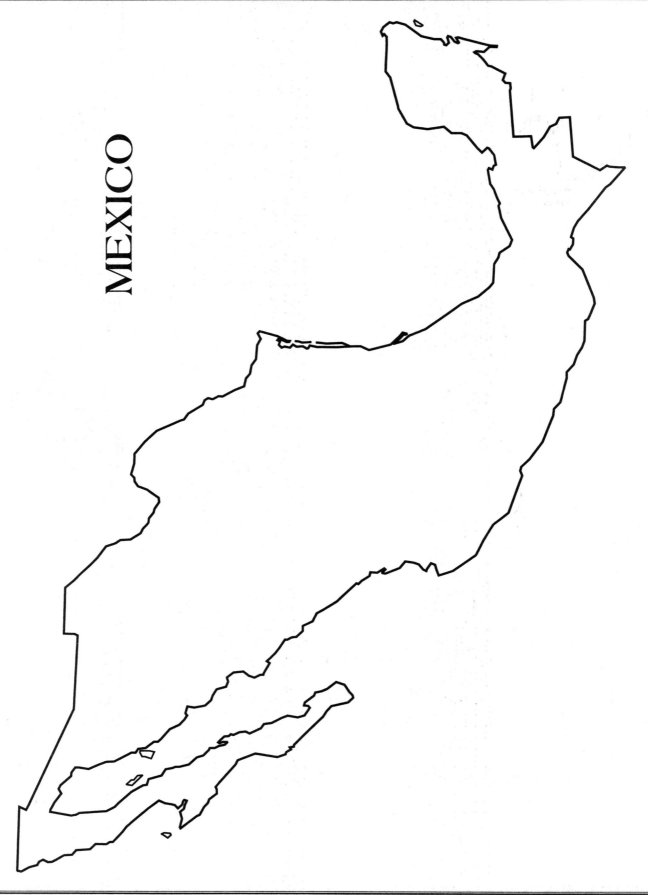

MEXICO

NORTH AMERICA

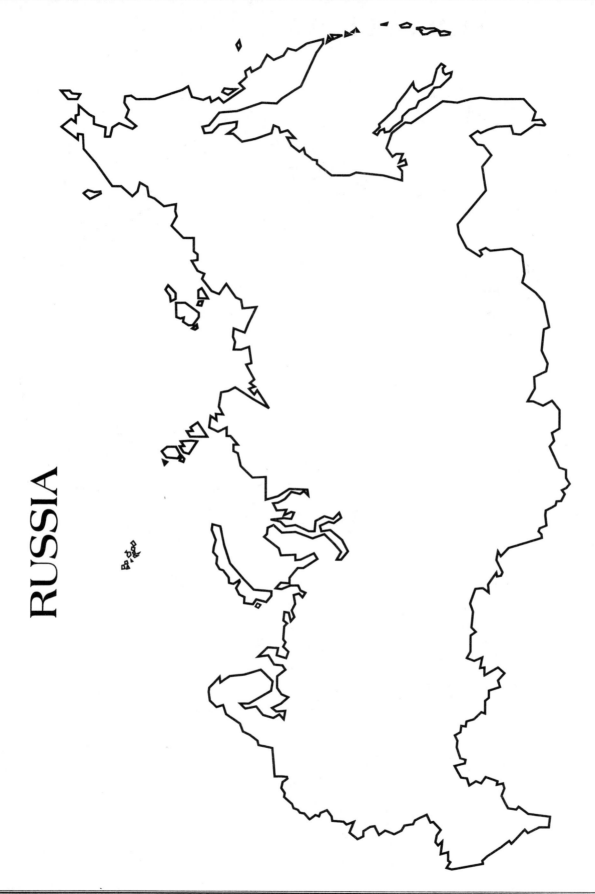

RUSSIA

SOUTH AMERICA

Appendix C

CURRENCY

CURRENCY

COUNTRY	BASIC UNIT	EQUIVALENT
Afghanistan	afghani	100 puls
Albania	lek	100 qidarka or 100 qintars
Algeria	dinar	100 centimes
American Samoa	dollar	100 cents
Andorra	franc peseta	100 centimes 100 céntimos
Angola	kwanza	100 kwei
Anguilla	dollar	100 cents
Antigua & Barbuda	dollar	100 cents
Argentina	peso	100 centavos
Armenia	ruble	n/a
Aruba	florin	100 cents
Australia	dollar	100 cents
Austria	schilling	100 groschen
Azerbaijan	manat	10 Russian rubles
Azores	n/a	n/a
Bahamas	dollar	100 cents
Bahrain	dinar	1,000 fils
Bangladesh	taka	100 paise
Barbados	dollar	100 cents
Belarus	ruble	n/a
Belgium	franc	100 centimes
Belize	dollar	100 cents
Benin	franc	100 centimes
Bermuda	dollar	100 cents
Bhutan	ngultrum	100 chetrum
Bolivia	peso	100 centavos
Bosnia-Herzegovina	dinar	100 paras
Botswana	pula	100 thebe
Brazil	real	n/a
British Virgin Islands	dollar	100 cents
Brunei	dollar	100 cents
Bulgaria	lev	100 stotinki
Burkina Faso	franc	100 centimes
Burundi	franc	100 centimes
Cambodia	riel	100 sen
Cameroon	franc	100 centimes
Canada	dollar	100 cents
Canary Islands	peseta	100 céntimos
Cape Verde	escudo	100 centavos
Cayman Islands	dollar	100 cents
Central African Republic	franc	100 centimes
Chad	franc	100 centimes
Channel Islands	pound	100 pence
Chile	peso	100 centavos
China	yuan	10 jiao
Colombia	peso	100 centavos

COUNTRY	BASIC UNIT	EQUIVALENT
Comoros	franc	100 centimes
Congo	franc	100 centimes
Cook Islands	dollar	100 cents
Costa Rica	colón	100 céntimos
Croatia	dinar	100 paras
Cuba	peso	100 centavos
Cyprus	pound lira	100 cents 100 kurus
Czech Republic	koruna	100 haleru
Denmark	krone	100 re
Djibouti	franc	100 centimes
Dominica	dollar	100 cents
Dominican Republic	peso	100 centavos
Easter Island	n/a	n/a
Ecuador	sucre	100 centavos
Egypt	pound	100 piasters
El Salvador	colón	100 centavos
England	pound	100 pence
Equatorial Guinea	franc	100 centimes
Eritrea	birr	100 cents
Estonia	kroon	n/a
Ethiopia	birr	100 cents
Faeroe Islands	krone	100 ore
Falkland Islands	pound	100 pence
Fiji	dollar	100 cents
Finland	markka	100 pennia
France	franc	100 centimes
French Guiana	franc	100 centimes
French Polynesia	franc	100 centimes
Gabon	franc	100 centimes
The Gambia	dalasi	100 bututs
Georgia	coupon (ruble also used)	n/a
Germany	Deutsche mark	100 pfennige
Ghana	cedi/new cedi	100 pesewas
Gibraltar	pound	100 pence
Greece	drachma	100 lepta
Greenland	krone	100 re
Grenada	dollar	100 cents
Guadeloupe	franc	100 centimes
Guam	dollar	100 cents
Guatemala	quetzal	100 centavos
Guinea	franc	100 centimes
Guinea-Bissau	peso	100 centavos
Guyana	dollar	100 cents
Haiti	gourde	100 centimes
Honduras	lempira	100 centavos
Hong Kong	dollar	100 cents

CURRENCY

COUNTRY	BASIC UNIT	EQUIVALENT
Hungary	forint	100 filler
Iceland	krona	100 aurar
India	rupee	100 paise
Indonesia	rupiah	n/a
Iran	rial	10 tomans
Iraq	dinar	1,000 fils
Ireland	pound	100 pence
Isle of Man	pound	100 pence
Israel	shekel	100 new agorot
Italy	lira	100 centesimi
Ivory Coast	franc	100 centimes
Jamaica	dollar	100 cents
Japan	yen	100 sen
Jordan	dinar	1,000 fils
Kazakhstan	ruble	n/a
Kenya	shilling	100 cents
Kiribati	dollar	100 cents
Kuwait	dinar	1,000 fils
Kyrgyzstan	som	n/a
Laos	new kip	100 at
Latvia	lat	n/a
Lebanon	pound	100 piasters
Lesotho	loti	100 lisente
Liberia	dollar	100 cents
Libya	dinar	1,000 dirhams
Liechtenstein	franc franken franco	100 centimes 100 rappen 100 centesimi
Lithuania	litas	n/a
Luxembourg	franc	100 centimes
Macao	pataca	100 avos
Macedonia	denar	n/a
Madagascar	franc	100 centimes
Madeira Islands	n/a	n/a
Malawi	kwacha	100 tambala
Malaysia	ringgit	100 sen
Maldives	rufiyaa	100 laaris
Mali	franc	100 centimes
Malta	lira	100 cents
Mariana Islands	dollar	100 cents
Marshall Islands	dollar	100 cents
Martinique	franc	100 centimes
Mauritania	ouguiya	5 khoums
Mauritius	rupee	100 cents
Mexico	peso	100 centavos
Micronesia	dollar	100 cents
Midway Island	dollar	100 cents
Moldova	leu	n/a

COUNTRY	BASIC UNIT	EQUIVALENT
Monaco	franc	100 centimes
Mongolia	tughrik	100 mongos
Montserrat	dollar	100 cents
Morocco	dirham	100 centimes
Mozambique	metical	100 centavos
Myanmar (Burma)	kyat	100 pyas
Namibia	rand	100 cents
Naura	dollar	100 cents
Nepal	rupee	100 paisa
Netherlands	guilder, gulden, or florin	100 cents
Netherlands Antilles	guilder, gulden, or florin	100 cents
New Caledonia	franc	100 centimes
New Zealand	dollar	100 cents
Nicaragua	gold córdoba	100 centavos
Niger	franc	100 centimes
Nigeria	naira	100 kobo
Niue	dollar	100 cents
Norfolk Island	dollar	100 cents
North Korea	won	100 chon
Northern Ireland	pound	100 pence
Norway	krone	100 re
Oman	rial or riyal	1,000 baiza
Pakistan	rupee	100 paisa
Panama	balboa	100 centesimos
Papua New Guinea	kina	100 toea
Paraguay	guaraní	100 centimos
Peru	sol	100 centavos
Philippines	peso	100 centavos
Pitcairn Islands Group	dollar	100 cents
Poland	zloty	100 groszy
Portugal	escudo	100 centavos
Puerto Rico	dollar	100 cents
Qatar	riyal	100 dirhams
Réunion	franc	100 centimes
Romania	leu	100 bani
Russia	ruble	100 kopeks
Rwanda	franc	100 centimes
Saint Helena	pound	100 pence
Saint Kitts & Nevis	dollar	100 cents
Saint Lucia	dollar	100 cents
Saint-Pierre & Miquelon	franc	100 centimes
Saint Vincent & the Grenadines	dollar	100 cents
San Marino	lira	100 centesimi
São Tomé & Príncipe	dobra	100 centimos
Saudi Arabia	riyal	100 halalas
Scotland	pound	100 pence
Senegal	franc	100 centimes

CURRENCY

COUNTRY	BASIC UNIT	EQUIVALENT	COUNTRY	BASIC UNIT	EQUIVALENT
Seychelles	rupee	100 cents	Turkey	lira	100 kurus
Sierra Leone	leone	100 cents	Turkmenistan	ruble	n/a
Singapore	dollar	100 cents	Turks & Caicos Islands	dollar	100 cents
Slovakia	koruna	100 haleru	Tuvalu	dollar	100 cents
Slovenia	tolar	n/a	Uganda	shilling	100 cents
Solomon Islands	dollar	100 cents	Ukraine	karbovanet	n/a
Somalia	shilling	100 centesimi	United Arab Emirates	dirham	100 fils
South Africa	rand	100 cents	United Kingdom (Great Britain)	pound	100 pence
South Korea	won	100 chon	United States of America	dollar	100 cents
Spain	peseta	100 céntimos	Uruguay	peso	100 centesimos
Sri Lanka	rupee	100 cents	Uzbekistan	ruble	n/a
The Sudan	pound	100 piasters	Vanuatu	vatu	100 centimes
Suriname	guilder, gulden, or florin	100 cents	Vatican City	lira	100 centesimi
Swaziland	lilangeni	100 cents	Venezuela	bolivar	100 céntimos
Sweden	krona	100 öre	Vietnam	new dong	100 xu
Switzerland	franc franken franco	100 centimes 100 rappen 100 centesimi	Virgin Islands	dollar	100 cents
			Wales	pound	100 pence
Syria	pound	100 piasters	Wallis & Futuna	franc	100 centimes
Taiwan	dollar	100 cents	Western Sahara	dirham	100 centimes
Tajikistan	ruble	n/a	Western Samoa	tala	100 sene
Tanzania	shilling	100 cents	Yemen	rial	n/a
Thailand	baht	100 satang	Yugoslavia	new dinar	100 paras
Togo	franc	100 centimes	Zaire	Zaire	100 makuta
Tonga	pa'anga	100 seniti	Zambia	kwacha	100 ngwee
Trinidad & Tobago	dollar	100 cents	Zimbabwe	dollar	100 cents
Tunisia	dinar	1,000 millimes			

INDEX

210

Franc 11, 29, 31, 42, 43, 45, 51, 52, 58, 59, 67, 77, 85, 87, 88, 89, 100, 103, 123, 139, 141, 144, 149, 153, 161, 173, 177, 196, 200, 204, 210, 229, 236, 260

France 9, 11, 29, 52, 53, 76, 85-86, 88, 92, 121, 141, 153, 161, 173, 196, 204, 210, 221, 229, 239, 248, 251, 254, 260, 275

Franceville 89
Franco 229
Franken 229
Franz Josef Land 198
Fraser River 276
Freeport 24
Freetown 212
French 9, 11, 15, 29, 31, 42, 43, 44, 45, 46, 51, 52, 58, 59, 67, 85, 86, 87, 88, 89, 100, 103, 106, 123, 133, 135, 141, 144, 149, 153, 154, 155, 157, 161, 173, 177, 192, 194, 196, 200, 203, 204, 205, 210, 211, 229, 236, 239, 254, 260, 265

French Alps 85
French Cameroun 45
French Equatorial Africa 51, 59, 89
French Guiana 37, 87, 225, 277
French Guinea 103
French Indochina 133
French patois 68, 99, 203
French Polynesia 88
French Revolution 86
French Riviera. See Riviera
French Somaliland 67
French Sudan 149
French West Africa 42
Friendly Islands 237
Frijoles 157
Fritten, Ham an Zalot 141
Frogner Park 183
Fuerteventura Island 48
Fufu 45, 94
Fujiyama 126
Ful 224
Fula 90, 210
Fulani 42, 45, 90, 103, 104, 149, 154, 177, 210
Funafuti 243
Funchal 145
Funchal Islands 145
Fungee 14
Fur 224
Furnace Peak 196
Futa 263
Fútbol 252
Futon 126
Futuna Island 254
Ga 94
Gabon 45, 59, 77, 89, 271
Gaborone 36
Gaelic 117, 182, 209, 247
Gaelic football 118
Gaizina 134

Galabiyaha 72
Galapagos Islands 71, 277
Galdhøppigen 183
Galician 221
Galilee 120
Galileo, Galilei 255
Galle 223
Galloway cattle 209
Gambia River 90, 210
Gambia, The 90, 210, 271
Gambier Islands 88
Ganda 244
Ganges Delta 26
Ganges River 26, 111, 112, 273
Garden of Eden 116
Garri 45
Gash River 78
Gatun Lake 186
Gaucho 16, 186, 252
Gauguin, Paul 88
Gaza Strip 120
Gazpacho 221
Geba River 104
Geisha 126
Gelati 91
Gelfille fish 120
Geneva 229
Genghis Khan 162
Genoese 160
George Cross 150
George Town 50
Georgetown 105
Georgia 249
Georgia, country of 17, 22, 91, 198, 240, 273, 275
Georgian 91
Georgian Military Highway 91
Ger 162
Gerlachovský Štít 214
German 15, 21, 53, 66, 92, 121, 132, 134, 139, 141, 167, 197, 214, 229
Germanic 139, 183, 229
Germany 21, 29, 65, 66, 85, 92-93, 141, 170, 192, 275
Geta 126
Geysir 110
Ghana 42, 94, 123, 236, 271
Gheg 8
Ghent 29
Giant Mountains 65
Gibanica 62
Gibraltar 95, 221
Gibraltar Harbor 95
Gibraltar-Azores Ridge 23
Gibson Desert 20, 274
Giessbach Falls 230
Gikuyu 129
Gilbert Islands 130
Gilbertese 130
Gio 137
Giza 72
Glamis Castle 209
Glasgow 209, 247
Glen Mor 209
Glima wrestling 110
Go fio 48
Gobi Desert 55, 162, 273

Godthåb 98
Golan Heights 120
Gold Coast 94
Gold Córdoba 176
Gold Museum 57
Golfe de la Gonâve 106
Gombey dancers 32
Gombo 51
Gomera Island 48
Good Land 141
Göta Canal 228
Göteborg 227, 228
Gothic 79
Gotland Island 227
Gough Island 201
Goulash 109
Gourde 106
Goya, Francisco 222
Goyaves River 100
Gozo Island 150
Graciosa Island 23
Grampian Mountains 209
Gran Canaria Island 48
Gran Chaco 15
Granada 176, 222
Grand Bahama Island 24
Grand Caicos Island 242
Grand Canyon 249, 251
Grand Cayman 50
Grand Etang 99
Grand Terre Island (New Caledonia) 173
Grand Theater of Monte Carlo 161
Grand Turk 242
Grand-Terre Island (Guadeloupe) 100
Grande Comore Island 58
Granite Plateau 21
Graz 21
Greased wrestling 240
Great Abaco Island 24
Great Artesian Basin 20
Great Australian Bight 19, 274
Great Bahama Bank 24
Great Barrier Reef 19, 20, 274
Great Basin 276
Great Bear Lake 276
Great Britain. See United Kingdom
Great Buddha 126
Great Dividing Range 20
Great Egghill 79
Great Escarpment 37
Great Exuma Island 24
Great Fire of London 76
Great Glen 209
Great Inagua Island 24
Great Lakes 46, 249, 251
Great Mosque of Samarra 116
Great Plains 249
Great Rift Valley 43, 80, 120, 127, 129, 146, 234, 244
Great Salt Lake 249, 250, 251, 276
Great Sandy Desert 19, 20, 274
Great Slave Lake 276

Great Sphinx 73
Great Thatch Island 39
Great Tobago Island 39
Great Victoria Desert 19, 20, 274
Great Wall of China 55, 56
Greater Buenos Aires 16
Greater Sunda Islands 113
Greco, El 97
Greece 8, 41, 96-97, 143, 240, 275
Greek 8, 20, 64, 96, 116, 229, 240
Greek Civil War 96
Greenland 98, 276
Greenland Sea 98, 110, 276
Greenlander 98
Greenlandic 98
Grenada 99
Grenadines 205
Griots 103
Gros Piton 203
Grossglockner 21
Gúacharos 256
Guadalajara 156
Guadalcanal Island 216
Guadalquivir Basin 221
Guadalquivir River 221
Guadalupe Day 157
Guadeloupe 100
Guajira Peninsula 57
Guam 101, 151
Guana Island 39
Guanches 48
Guangzhou 55
Guantánamo 63
Guaraní 188
Guatemala 30, 74, 102, 107, 156, 276
Guatemala City 102
Guaya beras 30
Guayaquil 71
Guernsey Island 53
Guiana Highlands 256, 277
Guilder 170, 172, 225
Guinea 103, 104, 123, 137, 149, 210, 212, 271
Guinea Highlands 103
Guinea-Bissau 103, 104, 210, 271
Gulden 170, 172, 225
Gulf of Aden 67, 217, 263
Gulf of Alaska 276
Gulf of Anadyr 198
Gulf of Antalya 240
Gulf of Aqaba 72, 120, 127
Gulf of Bahrain 25, 195
Gulf of Bothnia 84, 227, 275
Gulf of California 156
Gulf of Carpentaria 19, 274
Gulf of Darién 277
Gulf of Finland 79, 84, 198
Gulf of Gabes 239
Gulf of Guayaquil 277
Gulf of Guinea 31, 45, 77, 94, 123, 178, 207, 236
Gulf of Hammamat 239
Gulf of Iskenderun 240
Gulf of Kotor 264

Jabal ad Dukhan 25
Jabal ad Duruz 231
Jabal an Nusayriyah 231
Jabal Ash Sham 184
Jabal Katrinah 72
Jabal Ramm 127
Jabal Sawda 208
Jabil Yibir 246
Jaffna 223
Jagiellonian University 192
Jai alai 157
Jaipur 111, 112
Jakarta 113, 114
Jakobshavn 98
Jalalabad 7
Jallabiyah 224
Jamaica 50, 124, 242, 276
Jambiyas 263
Jambo 152
James Island 90
Jamestown 201
Japan 125-126, 148, 151, 213, 273
Japan Current 125
Japanese 20, 101, 125, 145, 159, 216, 232
Japanese Alps 125
Java 113, 114
Javanese 113
Jebel Toubkal 164
Jeepneys 190
Jefferson, Thomas 251
Jehovah's Witness.
　See Religion
Jellaba 164
Jerk 124
Jersey Island 53
Jerusalem 120
Jewish 120, 134, 172, 239
Jidda 208
Jinja 244
Johannesburg 218
Johnny Cakes 14
Jola 90
Jordan 116, 120, 127, 208, 231, 273
Jordanian 127
Joropo 256
Jos Plateau 178
Jost van Dyke Island 39
Jostedal Glacier 183
Joyce, James 118
Juba 224
Jubba River 217
Judaism. See Religion
Judd mat Gaardebounen 141
Judo 220
Jug-jug 27
Jumna River 111
Juozapines 140
Jura Mountains 85, 229
Jutland 66
K2 185
Ka'abah 208
Kabaka 244
Kabsah 208
Kabuki 126
Kabul 7

Kabye 236
Kachkéis 141
Kaffiyeh 127, 208
Kafka, Franz 65
Kagera River 200
Kainji Dam 178
Kainji Lake 178
Kains 113
Kalahari Desert 36, 167, 218, 219, 271
Kalenjin 129
Kamakura 126
Kamaran Island 263
Kamba 129
Kamchatka Peninsula 198
Kampala 244
Kananga 265
Kanchenjunga 112
Kandy 223
Kanga 234
Kano 178
Kansas 249
Kanto Mountains 125
Kanto Plain 125
Kanuri 177
Kanzu 234
Kao 237
Kaohsiung 232
Kaolack 210
Kapama 35
Kara Bogaz Gol 241
Kara Sea 198, 273
Karachi 185
Karagiye Depression 128
Karakoram Mountains 273
Karakum Canal 241
Karakum Desert 241, 273
Karamojong 244
Karbovanet 245
Kare-kare 190
Kariba Dam 266
Karisimbi 200
Karkadai 224
Karpas Peninsula 64
Karst 35, 215
Kasha 245
Käsknöpfle 139
Kathmandu 169
Kato 133
Kattegat 66, 227
Kaukau 187
Kaunas 140
Kava 83
Kawiarnas 192
Kazak 128
Kazak Soviet Socialist
　Republic 128
Kazakstan 55, 128, 132, 198, 241, 253, 273, 275
Ke*bab* 115
Kediet Ijill 154
Kempenland 29
Kendo 126
Kennedy, John F. 63
Kentucky 249
Kenya 80, 129, 217, 224, 234, 244, 271
Keshkumai 132

Key West 63
Kha 133
Khadag 162
Khamsin 72
Khanjars 184
Kharg Island 115
Kharkov 245
Khartoum 224
Khartoum North 224
Khat 67, 263
Khatchkars 17
Khmer 44, 257
Khorat Plateau 235
Khulna 26
Khuzistan Plain 115
Khyber Pass 185
Kibbutzim 120
Kidd, Captain William 144
Kiev 245
Kigali 200
Kii Mountains 125
Kikoi 234
Kikongo 59, 265
Kikuyu 129
Kilshi 177
Kimbanguists 265
Kimchi 181, 220
Kina 187
King Fahd Causeway 25
King George VI Falls 105
King Louis II 93
King Louis Phillippe 86
King Solomon 216
Kingston 124, 180
Kingstown 205
Kinshasa 265
Kinyarwanda 200
Kippers 209
Kirghiz 132
Kiribati 130
Kiritimati Atoll 130
Kirovakan 17
Kirundi 43
Kishinev 160
Kitakami Mountains 125
Kitami Mountains 125
Kitumbua 234
Kitwe 266
Kiwi 175
Klaipeda 140
Kl*ompen* 170, 171
Knäckebröd 228
Knickers 21
Knödel 21
Kodry Hills 160
Kohtla-Järve 79
Koláč 214
Kölen Mountains 227
Kolo 62
Kolofau 260
Kolumadulu Atoll 148
Komodo Dragon 114
Komodo Island 114
Komoé River 123
Kongo 12, 59
Kopet-Dag Mountains 241
Kopkar 128
Korcë 8

Korea Bay 181
Korea Strait 125, 220
Korea. See North Korea,
　South Korea
Korean 181, 220
Koro Sea 83
Koruna 65, 214
Košice 214
Kourou 87
Kowloon 108
Kowloon Peninsula 108
Kpelle 137
Kpémé 236
Krahn 137
Krakatau 114
Kraków 192
Krentebollen 170
Krio 212
Krkonose Mountains 65
Kroket 170
Krona 227
Krone 66, 81, 98, 183
Kroon 79
Kru 123, 137
Kruger National Park 218, 219
Kuala Belait 40
Kuala Lumpur 147
Kublai Khan 162
Kugitangtau Mountain Range 241
Kula Kangri 33
Kumasi 94
Kumayri 17
Kumiss 128, 132
Kumkum 112
Kunama 78
Kunene River 167
Kunlun Mountains 273
Kura River 22, 91
Kura Valley 91
Kurd 17, 115, 116, 231, 240
Kurdish 115, 116, 231, 240
Kurenti 215
Kuril Islands 198
Kutaisi 91
Kuwait 116, 131, 208, 273
Kuwait Bay 131
Kuwaiti 131
Kwacha 146, 266
Kwahu Plateau 94
Kwajalein Atoll 152
Kwando River 167
Kwanjin 152
Kwanza 12
Kwanza River 12
Kyat 166
Kyrenia Mountains 64
Kyrgyz 132
Kyrgyz Mountains 132
Kyrgyzstan 55, 128, 132, 233, 253, 273
Kyushu Island 125
Kyushu Mountains 125
Kyzylkum Desert 273
L'Osservatore Romano 255
La Baie 204
La Condamine 161
La Désirade 100

Malagasy 144
Malagasy Republic 144
Malaita Island 216
Malakula Island 254
Malawi 146, 165, 234, 266, 271
Malay 40, 147, 190, 196, 213, 223, 235
Malay Peninsula 147, 213, 235
Malaysia 40, 147, 213, 235, 273
Maldives 148
Malé 148
Malé Atoll 148
Malé Island 148
Mali 9, 42, 103, 123, 149, 154, 177, 210, 271
Malinke 103, 104
Malmö 227
Malosmadulu Atoll 148
Maloti Mountains 136
Malta 150, 275
Maltese 95, 150
Mamaliga 197
Mambo 63
Man in the Tiger's Skin, The 91
Mana 87
Managua 176
Manama 25
Manas 132
Manat 22
Manaus 37
Manchuria 55
Mandalay 166
Mandarin 40, 55, 232
Mande 42
Mandingo 90, 104, 123, 137, 149, 210
Mandinka 90
Mandjia 51
Maneapa 130
Mangaia 60
Manhattan Island 29
Manihiki Island 60
Manila 190
Manitoba 46
Manjaca 104
Manjako 104
Mano 137
Mansef 127
Manua Islands 10
Manuae 60
Manx 119
Manzini 226
Maori 60, 174, 175
Maputo 165
Mar del Plata 15
Marab River 78
Maracaibo 256
Maracaibo Basin 256
Maracas 69
Maradi 177
Marajó Island 277
Maravi 146
Margaret Island 109
Margherita Peak 244, 265
Mariachi 157
Mariana Islands 101, 151
Maribor 215
Marie Byrd Land 272

Marie-Galante 100
Marimba 102, 157
Marina Cay 39
Marinus 206
Marka 42
Markka 84
Maromokotro 144
Maroni River 87
Marowijne River 225
Marquesas Islands 88
Marseille 85
Marshall Islands 152
Marshall Plan 92
Marshallese 152
Martinique 153
Mary 241
Maryland 249
Mascarene Islands 196
Mascarenhas, Pedro 196
Maseru 136
Massachusetts 249
Mata-Utu 260
Matai 262
Matatus 129
Maté 16, 38
Matrah 184
Matsu Island Group 232
Maug Islands 151
Mauke Island 60
Mauritania 9, 149, 154, 210, 261, 271
Mauritius 155, 196
Maya Mountains 30
Mayaguana Island 24
Mayagüez 194
Mayan 30, 102, 107, 156, 157
Mayombé Escarpment 59
Mayotte Island 58
Mayreau 205
Mazar-e Sharif 7
Mbabane 226
Mbaxal-u-Saloum 210
Mbuji-Mayi 265
Mbundu 12
Mealie meal 136
Mealies 219
Mecca 208
Medan 113
Medellín 57
Medieval Towers 206
Medina 208
Mediterranean 193
Mediterranean Sea 9, 64, 72, 85, 86, 95, 96, 120, 121, 135, 138, 150, 161, 164, 221, 231, 239, 240, 271, 275
Meghna River 26
Mekong Basin 133
Mekong River 44, 133, 257, 273
Melanesian 83, 173, 187, 216, 254
Melbourne 19
Melville, Herman 88
Mende 212
Mendelssohn, Moses 92
Mendoza 15
Meo 133
Mere Lava Island 254

Merengue 69
Mesaoria Plain 64
Meseta 193, 221
Meseta Central 61
Meshed 115
Meshwi 154
Mesopotamia 15, 116
Mestizo 12, 15, 30, 34, 54, 57, 61, 71, 74, 104, 107, 156, 176, 186, 188, 189, 256
Methodist. See Religion
Metical 165
Meuse River 29
Mexican 250
Mexican Revolution 157
Mexico 30, 102, 156-157, 249, 276
Mexico City 156, 157
Mezza 231
Michelangelo 122, 255
Michener, James 88
Michigan 249
Micronesia 151, 152, 158
Micronesian 101, 130, 158
Middle Ages 139, 184, 206, 259
Middle Atlantic States 250
Middle Caicos 242
Middle Congo 59
Middle East 96, 115, 120, 127, 208, 231
Midway Island 159
Midwestern States 250
Mikuni Mountains 125
Miladummadulu Atoll 148
Milan 121
Mina 236
Mindanao Island 190
Mindelo 49
Mindoro Island 190
Minnesota 249
Minorca 221
Minsk 28
Minuit 29
Miquelon Island 204
Mirador Nacional 252
Mirim Lake 252
Miskolc 109
Mississippi 249
Mississippi River 249, 251, 276
Missouri 249
Missouri River 249, 251, 276
Mitiaro 60
Mititei 197
Mixtec 156
Moai 70
Môco 12
Moen Island 158
Mogadishu 217
Moheli Island 58
Mojave Desert 249, 276
Mojo picón 48
Moldavia 160, 197
Moldova 160, 197, 245, 275
Moldovan 160
Moluccas 113
Mombasa 129
Mona Island 194
Mona Lisa 86, 122

Monaco 85, 161, 168
Monaco Grand Prix 161
Monadh 119
Monastery of the Caves 245
Mondongo 107
Monégasque 161
Monet, Claude 86
Mongol 162
Mongolia 55, 162, 198, 273
Mongolian 162
Monroe, James 137
Monrovia 137
Mont Blanc 85, 86, 121, 122
Mont de la Lékéti 59
Mont Kartala 58
Mont Pelée 153
Mont-St.-Michel 85, 86
Montagua River 102
Montana 249
Monte Carlo 161
Monte Carlo Rally 161
Monte Cristo 74
Montenegrin 264
Montenegro 264
Monterrey 156
Monteverdi, Claudio 122
Montevideo 252
Montreal 46
Montserrat 163
Montuna 186
Montuno 186
Monument of Saddam's Qadissiya 116
Moor 149, 154, 223
Moore, George Augustus 118
Moors 259
Moraine 66
Morava River 65
Moravian 27, 65
Mormon. See Religion
Morne de la Grande Montagne 204
Morne Diablotin 68
Morne Seychellois 211
Mornes 204
Moro Naba 42
Morocco 9, 164, 261, 271
Moroni 58
Moscow 198, 199
Moselle River 141
Moshi-Dagomba 94
Mosi oa Tunya 267
Mosque 35, 42, 115, 155
Mosque of Suleiman I 240
Mosquitia 107
Mosquito Coast 107
Mossi 42
Mossi-Dagomba 94
Mostar 35
Mosul 116
Motorway 76
Moundou 52
Mount Adam 82
Mount Agel 161
Mount Apo 190
Mount Aragats 17
Mount Ararat 240
Mount Aripo 238

Mount Balaneshty 160
Mount Bates 180
Mount Bazar Dyuzi 22
Mount Bia 133
Mount Binga 165
Mount Bougainville 260
Mount Cameroon 45
Mount Chambi 239
Mount Cook 174
Mount Damavand 115
Mount Daravica 264
Mount Elbrus 199, 275
Mount Elgon 244
Mount Emlembe 226
Mount Etna 122
Mount Everest 56, 169, 273
Mount Fuji 126
Mount Gimie 203
Mount Goverla 245
Mount Gréboun 177
Mount Gunnbjørn 98
Mount Hadur Shuay 263
Mount Haltia 84
Mount Hekla 110
Mount Hermon 231
Mount Hillaby 27
Mount Iboundji 89
Mount Illimani 34
Mount Inyangani 267
Mount Jamanota 18
Mount Juliana Top 225
Mount Kebnekaise 228
Mount Kékes 109
Mount Kenya 129
Mount Keokradong 26
Mount Kilimanjaro 234, 271
Mount Kinabalu 147
Mount Kinyeti 224
Mount Korabit 8, 143
Mount Kosciusko 19, 20, 274
Mount Lamlam 101
Mount Logan 46, 47
Mount Maglić 35
Mount Makarakomburu 216
Mount McKinley 249, 251, 276
Mount Meron 120
Mount Misery 202
Mount Moldoveanu 197
Mount Morrison 232
Mount Nimba 103, 123
Mount Okso' Takpochao 151
Mount Olympus 64, 94, 96
Mount Pioa 10
Mount Puke 260
Mount Ruapehu 174
Mount Rushmore National
    Memorial 251
Mount Sage 39
Mount St. Catherine 99
Mount St. Helens 249, 250
Mount Sapitwa 146
Mount Shkhara 91
Mount Silisili 262
Mount Singavi 260
Mount Soira 78
Mount Soufrière 100, 205
Mount Surud Ad 217
Mount Tahat 9

Mount Tengri 128
Mount Titano 206
Mount Tomanivi 83
Mount Triglav 215
Mount Troglav 62
Mount Waialeale 250
Mount Wilhelm 187
Mountains of Connemara 117
Mountains of Kerry 117
Mountains of Mayo 117
Mourne Mountains 182
Mousaalli 67
Moussaka 41, 96
Mozambique 146, 165, 207,
    218, 226, 234, 266, 267, 271
Mozambique Channel 144, 165
Mozart, Wolfgang Amadeus 21
Muchinga Mountains 266
Muhallebi 240
Mulaka Atoll 148
Mulatto 13, 24, 27, 39, 57, 63,
    68, 100, 106, 186
Mullah 7
Munich 92, 93
Münster 92
Murray River 19, 274
Musaka 35
Musakhan 127
Musala Peak 41
Musandam Peninsula 184
Muscat 184
Musée d'Orsay 86
Musgrave Ranges 19, 274
Muslim (Islam). See Religion
Musseques 12
Mustique 205
Myanmar 26, 55, 111, 133, 166,
    235, 273
Mycenae 96, 97
Mykines 81
N'Djamena 52
Nacatamales 107, 176
Naengmyon 181
Nagoya 125
Naira 178
Nairobi 129
Nakhichevan Autonomous
    Republic 22
Naktong River 220
Nama 167
Namib Desert 167, 218, 219, 271
Namibe 12
Namibia 12, 36, 167, 218, 266,
    267, 271
Namorik Atoll 152
Nampo 181
Namu Atoll 152
Nan 253
Ñandutí 188
Nanumanga 243
Nanumea 243
Naples 121
Napoleon I 206
Narrows, The 39
Narva 79
Nassau 24
Nassau Island 60
National Archaelogical

Museum 97
National Mosque 147
National Museum (Singapore)
    213
National Museum of
    Anthropology, The 157
National Park of American
    Samoa 10
National Wildlife Preserve 159
Native American 249, 250
Nauru 168
Nauruan 168
Navan 117, 118
Nazi 93
Ndebele 267
Ndola 266
Nebraska 249
Negev Desert 120
Nelson River 276
Neman 140
Neman River 28
Nemunas 140
Nendo Island 216
Nepal 55, 56, 169, 273
Nepalese 33, 169
Nepali 169
Nepean Island 180
Neptune 27
Neretva River 35
Netball 14
Netherlands 18, 29, 92, 170-171,
    172, 225, 275
Netherlands Antilles 18, 172,
    276
Netherlands East Indies 113
Netzahualcóyotl 156
Neuschwanstein Castle 93
Neusiedler Lake 21
Nevada 249
Nevado del Ruiz 57
Nevado Sajama 34
Nevis Island 202
New Britain Island 187
New Brunswick 46
New Caledonia 88, 173, 260
New Cedi 94
New Delhi 111
New Dinar 264
New Dong 257
New England 250
New Georgia Group 216
New Guinea 113, 187
New Hampshire 249
New Hebrides 254
New Jersey 249
New Kip 133
New Kowloon 108
New Mexico 249
New Providence Island 24
New Siberian Islands 198
New South Wales 19
New Territories 108
New York 225, 249
New York City 249
New York Harbor 251
New Zealand 60, 83, 88,
    174-175, 179, 191, 262
New Zealander 180

Newfoundland 46, 204, 276
Newton, Sir Isaac 76
Ngalop 33
Ngonde 146
Ngoni 146
Ngultrum 33
Nguni 218
Niamey 177
Niari Valley 59
Nicaragua 61, 107, 176, 276
Nice 85
Nicosia 64
Niger 9, 31, 42, 45, 52, 138, 149,
    177, 178, 271
Niger River 177, 178, 271
Nigeria 31, 45, 52, 177, 178, 271
Nightingale Island 201
Nihon 126
Nilandu Atoll 148
Nile Basin 43
Nile River 72, 73, 224, 271
Nilgiri Hills 111
Nimba Mountains 137
Ninevah 116
Nippon 126
Nis 264
Nitra 214
Niue 179
Niulakita 243
Niutao 243
No 126
Nobel Prize 35
Nok 178
Nome de Deus de Macao 142
Norfolk Island 180, 191
Norman 117, 150
Norman Island 39
North Albanian Alps 8
North America 46, 54, 98, 124,
    189, 204, 249, 276
North Atlantic Current 66, 117,
    183
North Caicos Island 242
North Carolina 32, 249
North Channel 182, 209
North Dakota 249
North Island 174
North Korea 55, 181, 198, 220,
    273
North Sea 29, 66, 75, 76, 92,
    170, 183, 209, 247, 275
Northerly Range 69
Northern Ireland 75, 117, 182,
    209, 247, 248, 259, 275
Northern lights.
    See Aurora borealis
Northern Limestone Alps 21
Northern Mariana Islands.
    See Mariana Islands
Northern Rhodesia 266
Northern Territory 19
Northern Valira River 11
Northwest Highlands 209
Northwest Territories 46
Norway 84, 183, 198, 227, 275
Norwegian 81, 98, 183
Norwegian Sea 81, 183, 275
Nossa Senhora da Conceição

Polder 29, 170
Police Motu 187
Polish 28, 134, 140, 192, 214
Pollera 186
Polo, Marco 126
Polotsk 28
Polygamy 8
Polynesia 174
Polynesian 10, 60, 70, 88, 179, 191, 237, 243, 260, 262
Ponce 194
Poncho 16, 156
Ponta Delgada 23
Ponta do Pico 23
Pope 255
Port Louis 155
Port Moresby 187
Port of Monaco 161
Port Royal 124
Port Sudan 224
Port-au-Prince 106
Port-of-Spain 238
Port-Vila 254
Porto 193
Porto Santo Island 145
Pôrto Alegre 37
Porto-Novo 31
Portugal 23, 37, 49, 142, 145, 165, 193, 207, 221, 275
Portuguese 12, 14, 18, 37, 49, 94, 95, 104, 141, 142, 165, 193, 194, 196, 201, 204, 207, 232
Portuguese Guinea 104
Portuguese West Africa 12
Posadas 157
Postojna 215
Postojna Cave 215
Pound 53, 64, 72, 75, 82, 95, 117, 119, 135, 182, 201, 209, 224, 231, 247, 259
Pozole 157
Pozzuolana 49
Pra River 94
Prado 222
Prague 65
Praia 49
Praslin Island 211
Presbyterian. See Religion
Presley, Elvis 251
Pretoria 218
Prickly Pear Cays 13
Prince Albert 161
Prince Charles Mountains 272
Prince Edward Island 46
Princess Caroline Library 161
Princess Elizabeth Land 272
Princip, Gavrilo 35
Príncipe 207
Prins Alexander Polder 171
Pripyat Marshes 28
Protestant. See Religion
Proteus anguinus 215
Providence Island 211
Providenciales Island 242
Prut River 160
Ptuj 215
Pubs 76, 118, 182, 209, 248

Puccini, Giacomo 122
Puchero 16, 188
Puerto Rican 250
Puerto Rico 13, 39, 163, 172, 194, 202, 258, 276
Pukapuka 60
Pula 36
Puletasi 262
Pulkogi 220
Pulses 111
Puncak Jaya 114
Punjab Plain 185
Punjabi 185
Puppet 126
Pupusas 74
Purus River 277
Pusan 220
Pushtu 7
Pushtuns 7
Putonghua 55, 232
Pygmy 77, 89, 200, 265
Pygmy,Twa 43
Pyhä Falls 84
Pyongyang 181
Pyrenees Mountains 11, 85, 86, 221, 275
Pysanky 245
Qahwa 25
Qandahar 7
Qatar 195, 208, 246, 273
Qattara Depression 72, 73
Qin Ling Mountains 273
Qonduz 7
Quebec 46, 47
Quechua 34, 71, 189
Queen Charlotte Islands 46
Queen Elizabeth II 24
Queen Elizabeth Islands 276
Queen Maud Land 272
Queen's University of Belfast 182
Queensland 19
Quemoy Island Group 232
Quetico Provincial Park 47
Quetschentaart 141
Quetzal 102
Quezon City 190
Quinoa 34
Quito 71
Qurnat as Sawda 135
Rabat 164
Raffles Hotel 213
Railway Trail, The 32
Rakahanga 60
Raki 240
Ralik chain 152
Ramses II 73
Ramsey 119
Ramsey Bay 119
Ranchos 188, 256
Rand 167, 218
Rangoon 166
Rapa Nui 70
Rapanui 70
Raphael 255
Rarotonga 60
Ras al Khaymah 246
Ras Dashen 80

Rastafarian. See Religion
Rat Point 148
Ratak chain 152
Razdan River 17
Real 37
Rebozo 188
Recife 37
Red River 257
Red Sea 72, 73, 78, 208, 224, 263, 271, 273
Red Volta River 42
Redde 223
Redonda Island 14
Reggae 124
Religion. Anglican 13, 14, 24, 27, 50, 53, 82, 99, 124, 167, 201, 203, 205, 242, 259
Religion. Animism 49, 59, 104, 133, 165
Religion. Bali-Hinduism 113
Religion. Baptist 24, 50, 124, 201, 209, 242, 258
Religion. Buddhism 33, 40, 44, 55, 108, 125, 126, 133, 142, 147, 162, 166, 181, 213, 220, 223, 232, 235, 257
Religion. Catholic, Belarusian 28
Religion. Catholic, Ukrainian 245
Religion. Christian Congregationalist 10
Religion. Christianity 8, 14, 17, 19, 22, 31, 32, 36, 40, 42, 45, 46, 51, 52, 54, 59, 60, 63, 75, 77, 78, 79, 82, 83, 85, 88, 89, 92, 94, 102, 103, 104, 105, 108, 113, 123, 127, 131, 135, 136, 137, 140, 143, 144, 146, 151, 152, 155, 158, 160, 163, 165, 168, 172, 173, 174, 177, 178, 180, 187, 190, 194, 202, 210, 211, 212, 213, 216, 218, 220, 223, 224, 226, 229, 231, 232, 234, 236, 237, 238, 239, 243, 244, 245, 254, 255, 257, 262, 265, 266, 267
Religion. Church of God 50
Religion. Confucianism 55, 181, 232
Religion. Congregational 50
Religion. Coptic Christianity 78
Religion. Dutch Reformed 167, 170
Religion. Episcopalian 209, 258
Religion. Evangelical Christian 264
Religion. Hinduism 26, 33, 83, 105, 108, 111, 131, 147, 153, 155, 169, 223, 225, 238, 218, 266
Religion. Islam 7, 8, 9, 22, 25, 26, 31, 33, 35, 40, 41, 42, 44, 45, 51, 52, 58, 59, 67, 72, 78, 80, 83, 90, 91, 94, 103, 104, 105, 108, 111, 113, 115, 116, 120, 123, 127, 128, 131, 132, 135, 137, 138, 143, 144, 146,

147, 148, 149, 154, 155, 164, 165, 177, 178, 184, 185, 195, 208, 210, 212, 213, 217, 218, 223, 224, 225, 231, 233, 234, 235, 236, 238, 239, 240, 241, 244, 246, 253, 261, 263, 265, 266
Religion. Jehovah's Witness 179
Religion. Judaism 108, 120, 214, 239, 245
Religion. Lutheran 79, 134, 167, 227
Religion. Lutheran, Evangelical 66, 81, 98, 84, 110, 183, 264
Religion. Methodist 13, 24, 27, 205, 209, 242, 259
Religion. Mormon 179
Religion. Muslim 40, 113, 263
Religion. Muslim, Alawite 231
Religion. Muslim, Bosnian 35
Religion. Muslim, Ibadhi 184
Religion. Muslim, Ismaili Khoja 233
Religion. Muslim, Shi'a 25
Religion. Muslim, Shiite 231, 233, 241
Religion. Muslim, Sunni 9, 25, 58, 67, 127, 138, 148, 217, 224, 231, 233, 240, 241, 253
Religion. Muslim, Sunnite 64
Religion. Orthodox 65, 214
Religion. Orthodox Christianity 80, 128, 245
Religion. Orthodox Church, Russian 245
Religion. Orthodox, Bulgarian 41
Religion. Orthodox, Eastern 22, 28, 64, 79, 143, 160, 197, 253
Religion. Orthodox, Georgian 91
Religion. Orthodox, Greek 8, 96
Religion. Orthodox, Russian 22, 91, 134, 198, 241
Religion. Orthodox, Serbian 35, 62, 264
Religion. Presbyterian 50, 209
Religion. Protestant 10, 12, 18, 30, 35, 39, 43, 65, 68, 95, 106, 109, 129, 130, 152, 158, 179, 182, 202, 203, 214, 225, 245, 249, 259, 265
Religion. Rastafarian 124
Religion. Roman Catholic 8, 10, 11, 12, 14, 15, 18, 21, 24, 27, 29, 30, 34, 35, 37, 43, 48, 49, 50, 57, 58, 61, 62, 65, 68, 69, 70, 71, 74, 87, 95, 99, 100, 101, 106, 107, 109, 117, 118, 121, 124, 129, 130, 134, 139, 141, 150, 151, 153, 156, 158, 161, 165, 167, 170, 176, 179, 182, 186, 188, 189, 192, 193, 196, 197, 200, 201, 203, 204, 205, 206, 207, 209, 214, 215, 221, 225, 247, 249, 252,

255, 256, 257, 258, 260, 265

Santo 254
Santo Antão 49
Santo Antonio 207
Santo Domingo 69
São Francisco River 37, 277
São Jorge Island 23
São Miguel Island 23
São Nicolau 49
São Paulo 37
São Tiago 49
São Tomé & Príncipe 207, 271
São Tomé 207
São Vicente 49
Sara 51, 52
Sarajevo 35
Sarakole 154
Sarawak 147
Sardinia 64, 121, 275
Sarh 52
Sari 26, 112, 155, 218, 223
Sarigan Island 151
Sark Island 53
Sarkas 64
Sarmi 41
Sarong 40, 44, 113, 147, 223
Sarong soet 44
Sarykamysh Lake 253
Sashimi 126
Saskatchewan 46
Sassandra River 123
Sataraš 143
Satay 147
Saudi Arabia 25, 72, 116, 127,
    131, 184, 195, 208, 246, 263,
    273
Sauerbraten 92
Sauerkraut 92
Sava River 35, 62
Savai'i Island 262
Scaffell Pike 75, 76
Scandinavian 66, 81, 228
Scandinavian Peninsula 227
Schelde River 29, 170
Schilling 21
Schubert, Franz Peter 21
Schweitzer, Albert 89
Scotland 75, 119, 173, 209,
    247, 248, 254, 275
Scottish 182, 209, 247
Scottish Sea 209
Scrub Island 13
Sea of Azov 198, 245, 275
Sea of Crete 96
Sea of Galilee 120, 127
Sea of Japan 55, 125, 181,
    198, 220, 273
Sea of Marmara 240
Sea of Okhotsk 125, 198, 273
Seal Island 13
Sechura Desert 189
Seine River 275
Selametan 113
Selous Game Reserve 234
Selva 37
Selvagens Island Group 145
Sena 146
Senegal 49, 90, 103, 104, 149,
    154, 210, 271

Sénégal River 154, 210
Senufo 42
Seoul 220
Sepaktakraw 147
Serahuli 90
Serb 35, 62, 215, 264
Serbia 264
Serbian 62
Serbo-Croatian 35, 62, 215, 264
Serengeti National Park 234
Serer 210
Seria 40
Serpent Mounds Provincial
    Park 47
Serpent's Mouth 238
Sertão 37
Sesotho 136
Setswana 36
Seven Enchanted Cities 38
Seventh-Day Adventist.
    See Religion
Severn River 75, 247, 248, 259
Seville 14, 221
Seychelles 211
Sha Tin 108
Shakespeare, William 76, 209
Shalom 120
Shalwar-qamiz 185
Sham Chun River 108
Shaman 169
Shamma 80
Shandong Peninsula 55
Shanghai 55
Sharchop 33
Shashe River 36
Shashlik 91, 233
Shaw, George Bernard 118
Shekel 120
Shenyang 55
Shepherd's pie 76
Sherbro Island 212
Sherpas 169
Shetland Islands 81, 209, 275
Shetland pony 209
Shikoku Island 125
Shikoku Mountains 125
Shilling 129, 217, 234, 244
Shilluk 224
Shinto. See Religion
Shire River 146
Shish kebab 240
Shkodër 8
Shkubbah 239
Shkumbin River 8
Shona 267
Shopska 41
Shurpa 132
Shu´ra 26
Shwe Dagon Pagoda 166
Siam 235
Šiauliai 140
Siberia 160, 199
Sichuan Basin 55
Sicilian 150
Sicily 64, 121, 150, 239, 275
Sierra de Bahoruco 69
Sierra de los Órganos 63
Sierra de Neiba 69

Sierra Leone 103, 137, 212, 271
Sierra Leone Mountains 212
Sierra Madre 74
Sierra Madre Occidental 276
Sierra Madre Oriental 276
Sierra Maestra Mountains 63
Sierra Nevada 249, 250, 275,
    276
Siesta 176
Silhouette Island 211
Silk Road 132, 253
Sinai Peninsula 72
Sinan, Koco 240
Sind Plain 185
Sindhi 185
Singapore 147, 213
Singapore Strait 213
Sinhalese 148, 223
Siqueiros, David 157
Sistine Chapel 122, 255
siSwati 226
Sitrah Island 25
Skagerrak 66, 227
Skansen, The 228
Skopje 143
Skúvoy 81
Skyr 110
Slavic 62, 192, 215
Slieve Donard 182
Šljivovica 143
Slovak 65, 214, 264
Slovakia 21, 65, 109, 192, 214,
    245, 275
Slovene 121, 215
Slovenia 21, 62, 109, 121, 215,
    264, 275
Slovenian 215
Smalahode 183
Smörgåsbord 228
Smørrebrød 66
Smyrna 240
Snaefell 119
Snap Point 24
Sněžka 65
Snowdon 259
Snowy Mountains 19, 274
Snowy Mountains Scheme 20
Snowy Peak 196
Society Islands 88
Socotra Island 263
Sofia 41
Sogne Fiord 183
Sokoto Plains 178
Sol 189
Soldeu 11
Solomon Islands 187, 216
Solomon Sea 187, 216
Solway Firth 75, 76
Som 132
Somali 67, 80, 217
Somali Republic 217
Somalia 67, 80, 129, 217, 263,
    271
Sombrero 156
Sombrero Island 13
Somerset Island 32
Songhai 149
Sotho 218

Souse 14
South Africa 36, 136, 165, 167,
    218-219, 226, 267, 271
South America 15, 16, 34, 37,
    54, 57, 71, 87, 99, 105, 186,
    188, 189, 225, 238, 252, 256,
    277
South Australia 19
South Caicos Island 242
South Carolina 249
South Dakota 249, 251
South Island 174
South Korea 181, 220, 273
South Magnetic Pole 272
South Malé Atoll 14
South Pole 272
South West Africa 167
Southampton Island 276
Southern Alps 174
Southern Cross 19, 174, 187,
    262
Southern Limestone Alps 21
Southern Rhodesia 266
Southern States 250
Southwestern States 250
Souvlaki 96
Soviet Socialist Republic of
    Moldova 160
Soviet Union 17, 22, 28, 79, 91,
    92, 132, 140, 199, 233, 253
Soyombo 162
Spain 11, 14, 18, 48, 63, 85, 95,
    101, 193, 163, 164, 221-222,
    275
Spaniards 221, 222, 258
Spanish 11, 15, 16, 18, 30, 34,
    48, 54, 57, 61, 63, 69, 70, 71,
    74, 77, 95, 102, 107, 124, 150,
    156, 172, 176, 186, 188, 189,
    190, 194, 221, 222, 249, 251,
    252, 256
Spanish Sahara 261
Speaker's Corner 248
Sperrin Mountains 182
Spice Islands 114
Split 62
Squash 76
Sranan Tongo 225
Sri Lanka 111, 148, 223, 273
Stalin, Joseph 91
Stanley 82
Stanley Pool Region 59
Stanovoy Mountains 273
State Academic Theatre of
    Opera and Ballet 17
State of Chuuk 158
State of Kosrae 158
State of Pohnpei 158
State of Truk 158
State of Yap 158
Stations 20
Statue of Liberty 251
Steak and kidney pie 76
Steppes 128
Stevenson, Robert Louis 88,
    262
Stockholm 227, 228
Stone Age 150, 154